Industrial Relations
Text and Case Studies

Fourth Edition

G D GREEN

Dean of Faculty, Boston College

PITMAN
PUBLISHING

To all those who have taught me much about relationships, especially my family.

PITMAN PUBLISHING
128 Long Acre, London WC2E 9AN

A Division of Longman Group UK Limited

© G D Green, 1991, 1994

First published in Great Britain 1991
Fourth edition 1994

British Library Cataloguing in Publication Data
A CIP catalogue record for this book can be obtained from the British Library.

ISBN 0-273-60285-3

Typeset by Avocet Typesetters, Bicester, Oxon

Printed and bound in Great Britain by Clays Ltd, St Ives plc

Contents

Preface   v
Acknowledgements   vi
Abbreviations   vii

1 **Introduction**   1
   1.1 Defining industrial relations   1
   1.2 Growth of industrial relations   2
   1.3 Perspectives   3
   1.4 Structure of the book   8

2 **Trade unions**   10
   2.1 Purpose and functions   10
   2.2 Size and growth   15
   2.3 Organisation   27
   2.4 The TUC   31
   2.5 International bodies   35

3 **Employers**   37
   3.1 Organisations and their
        management   37
   3.2 Management in practice   43
   3.3 Associations   48
   3.4 The Confederation of British
        Industries   52

4 **The State**   55
   4.1 The role of the State   55
   4.2 State intervention   57
   4.3 The Advisory, Conciliation
        and Arbitration Service   64
   4.4 Political aspects   67

5 **Local organisation**   73
   5.1 Shop stewards   73
   5.2 Committees and branches   80

6 **Collective bargaining**   85
   6.1 What is collective bargaining?   85
   6.2 Negotiations   94
   6.3 Conflict and sanctions   97
   6.4 Resolving failures to agree   102

7 **Collective agreements**   106
   7.1 Agreements   106
   7.2 Procedural agreements   112
   7.3 Types of agreement   114
   7.4 Substantive agreements   120
   7.5 Example agreements   125

8 **Historical aspects**   130
   8.1 Origins and growth   130
   8.2 Legal developments   142

9 **The legal system**   152
   9.1 The law and the judiciary   152
   9.2 The administration of justice   155

10 **Industrial relations law**   159
   10.1 The status of trade unions
         and employers' associations   159
   10.2 Trade union immunities   160
   10.3 Employment protection   166
   10.4 Discrimination in
         employment   170
   10.5 Rights of a trade union
         member   176

11 **Codes of practice**   179
   11.1 Code of Practice on
         Industrial Relations   179

11.2   Code of Practice on
       Disciplinary Practice and
       Procedures in Employment   183
11.3   Code of Practice on the
       Disclosure of Information
       to Trade Unions for
       Collective Bargaining
       Purposes   185
11.4   Code of Practice on Time
       Off for Trade Union
       Duties and Activities   187
11.5   Code of Practice on Closed
       Shop Agreements and
       Arrangements   189
11.6   Code of Practice on
       Picketing   192
11.7   Code of Practice for the
       Elimination of Racial
       Discrimination and the
       Promotion of Equality
       of Opportunity in
       Employment   195
11.8   Code of Practice, Equal
       Opportunity Policies,
       Procedures and Practices
       in Employment   196
11.9   Code of Practice on Trade
       Union Ballots on Industrial
       Action   198

12   The terms and conditions of
     employment   201
12.1   The contract of employment   201
12.2   Sources of terms   205
12.3   Pay   210

13   Dismissal   213
13.1   What is dismissal?   213
13.2   Reasons for dismissal   214
13.3   Acting reasonably   216
13.4   Remedies   216
13.5   Procedure   218

14   Redundancy   222
14.1   Defining redundancy   222
14.2   Redundancy payments   222
14.3   Handling redundancies   224
14.4   Redundancy arrangements   227

15   Industrial relations issues   230
15.1   Strikes and lockouts   230
15.2   Picketing   240
15.3   The closed shop   242
15.4   Flexibility   247
15.5   Equal opportunities   251

16   Industrial democracy   255
16.1   The concept of industrial
       democracy   255
16.2   Schemes for participation   258

17   Future developments   270
17.1   Occupational structure   270
17.2   The European dimension   275

Assignments   284
Case Studies   293
Answers to multiple-choice questions 360
Answers to mini-questions   361
Answers to assignments   366
Glossary   367
Index   371

Preface

The objective of this book is to provide an introductory text on industrial relations that covers all the major topics of the subject. The aim is to give an across-the-board coverage that enables the reader to grasp the essential features of the subject. The coverage is comprehensive so as to satisfy the requirements of BTEC for a variety of their unit specifications at National, Higher National and Continuing Education levels and for supervisory management courses such as NEBSM, ISM, the Institute of Management and others. It will serve as an introductory text for those coming to the subject for the first time, for example on degree courses and for professional courses such as the IPM, ITD, and for NVQ management certificate and diploma courses. The book aims to give sufficient material to enable the reader to understand the many aspects of the subject. Having imparted this basic knowledge the book should help to improve industrial relations skills and be an aid to understanding the often complex industrial relations issues of our working lives.

The approach used in the book is a blend of fundamental ideas and principles and practical illustrations. An attempt has been made to achieve a balance between the academic, conceptual treatment of the subject and a practical approach. While some industrial relations topics are surrounded by controversy, like picketing and the closed shop, the text aims to give a neutral, unbiased approach and to include the more undisputed facts and figures. However, this is not to try to exclude debate in these areas, and some of the student exercises and case studies are designed to stimulate informed debate.

The subject of industrial relations is also a practical subject. The book aims to improve skills in industrial relations. By giving examples in the text, by including case studies and through setting student exercises, the book should help the student to improve these skills. This may be no substitute for the 'real thing', but skills taught and improved upon, and mistakes made, in the classroom or seminar, can avoid costlier errors at the workplace. As such, the case studies and some of the exercises can be used as training exercises.

The book is designed to be used as a course textbook. At the end of each chapter there are student exercises. Depending on the subject matter of the chapter, various modes of assessment have been used, including multiple-choice questions to test factual knowledge, mini-questions to test basic knowledge, and exercises requiring essay answers, to test understanding. On page 284 there are a series of longer assignments. Answers are given wherever possible to aid home study or for distance learners to carry out some self-assessment.

A selection of fifteen case studies has been included at the end of this book. These are designed to enable students to apply what they have learned from the text to novel situations, to gain further insight into the subject and to practise essential skills. A short Lecturer's Guide providing learning points from the cases is available from the Publishers.

One point needs noting here which relates to the legal position. Frequently changes are made.

If it is important to know the current position the reader should refer to a reference book that is updated regularly (most libraries have one) or, for specific points, ask the advice of a body such as ACAS. This point is particularly true for monetary figures (for awards or payments) as these are regularly updated.

Finally, I should like to thank all those who helped in the preparation of this book, those colleagues who kindly gave their advice, and the publisher's reviewer, who gave many hints and suggestions on how to improve the book for this edition. Last, but not least, my thanks to my wife, Shirley, for her constant encouragement, gentle persuasion to keep going and help in typing the manuscript. Any errors, omissions or faults are entirely my responsibility. I trust the reader will find the book informative, educational and above all an enjoyable introduction to a fascinating subject.

Acknowledgements

I wish to thank various organisations for their help in writing this book. Thanks are due first to those giving permission to reproduce material from their publications: HMSO for the figures relating to the number of unions, size of unions, incidence of striking, tribunal case statistics and closed shop statistics, extracted from *British Labour Statistics, Annual Abstract of Statistics* and *Employment Gazette*, and for the use of the ACAS Codes of Practice; the Department of Employment for the use of the Codes of Practice on the closed shop and picketing, all much used in Chapter 11; the Equal Opportunities Commission and the Commission for Racial Equality for extracts of their Codes of Practice; and the TGWU for extracts from their Rule Book.

I also wish to record my appreciation of those bodies that gave freely of their advice and assistance, particularly with publications. A large number of unions were particularly helpful, as were ACAS, the TUC and the CBI. Without their help the book would be much poorer. My thanks to them all.

Abbreviations

ABS	Association of Broadcasting Staff
ACAS	Advisory, Conciliation and Arbitration Service
AEU	Amalgamated Engineering Union
APEX	Association of Professional, Executive, Clerical and Computer Staff (now merged with GMBATU to become GMB)
ASLEF	Associated Society of Locomotive Engineers and Firemen
ASE	Amalgamated Society of Engineers
ASTMS	Association of Scientific, Technical and Managerial Staffs (now MSF)
BIFU	Banking, Insurance and Finance Union
CAC	Central Arbitration Committee
CBI	Confederation of British Industries
CO	Certification Officer
CPSA	Civil and Public Servants Association
CRE	Commission for Racial Equality
CSEU	Confederation of Shipbuilding and Engineering Unions
CSU	Civil Service Union
CWU	Communications Workers' Union (now UCW)
DATA	Draughtmen's and Allied Technicians' Association
EAT	Employment Appeals Tribunal
ECA	Electrical Contractors' Association
EEC	European Economic Community

EEF	Engineering Employers' Federation
EETPU	Electrical, Electronic, Telecommunication and Plumbing Union
EOC	Equal Opportunities Commission
EPA	Employment Protection Act 1975
EPA	Equal Pay Act 1970
EP(C)A	Employment Protection (Consolidation) Act 1978
ETA	Entertainment Trade Alliance
ETUC	European Trade Union Confederation
foc	father of the chapel
GMB	General, Municipal and Boilermakers
GMBATU	General, Municipal, Boilermakers and Allied Trade Union (now GMB)
GNCTU	Grand National Consolidated Trade Union
GPMU	Graphical, Paper and Media Union
HASAW	Health and Safety at Work, etc., Act 1974
HSC	Health and Safety Commission
ICFTU	International Confederation of Free Trade Unions
ILO	International Labour Office
ILO	International Labour Organisation
ILP	Independent Labour Party
IRA	Industrial Relations Act 1971
ISTC	Iron and Steel Trades Confederation

IWC	Institute of Workers' Control	NUPE	National Union of Public Employees
JIC	joint industrial council	NUR	National Union of Railwaymen
JSSC	Joint Shop Stewards' Committee	NUS	National Union of Seamen
LACSAB	Local Authority Conditions of Service Advisory Board	POEU	Post Office Engineering Union
LRC	Labour Representatives' Committee	RRA	Race Relations Act
		SCPS	Society of Civil and Public Servants
MSC	Manpower Services Commission (latterly Training Commission)	SDA	Sex Discrimination Act
MSF	Manufacturing, Science and Finance	SJIC	statutory joint industrial council
		sosr	some other substantial reason
NATTKE	National Association of Theatrical, TV and Kine Employees	SRSCR	Safety Representatives and Safety Committees' Regulations 1978
NALGO	National and Local Government Officers' Association	TC	Training Commission (now Department of Employment)
NEC	National Executive Council	TGWU	Transport and General Workers' Union
NCU	National Communications Union	TSSA	Transport Salaried Staffs' Association
NFU	National Farmers' Union	TUC	Trades Union Congress
NGA	National Graphical Association (1982)	TULRA	Trade Union and Labour Relations Act 1974
NUAAW	National Union of Agricultural and Allied Workers (now part of TGWU)	uma	union membership agreements
		UCW	Union of Communication Workers
NUCPS	National Union of Civil and Public Servants	USDAW	Union of Shop, Distributive and Allied Workers
NUJ	National Union of Journalists	UCATT	Union of Construction, Allied Trades and Technicians
NUM	National Union of Mineworkers		

1

Introduction

1.1 Defining industrial relations

One of the management subjects that has achieved public prominence on a regular basis over a long period of time is the subject of industrial relations. Probably one of the reasons for this is that it has a popular appeal, very often making the headlines. Strikes, redundancies, the actions of unions and representations from employers' associations have been regular features of news broadcasts and newspaper articles. The subject is also interlinked with politics and necessarily enters the headlines for this reason. Some of the less savoury aspects of our industrial relations, such as striking, picketing and the closed shop, are given a lot of media attention. Other subjects could be given more prominence but are less attractive. For example, every year far more days are lost through accidents at work than are lost through strikes (not counting the number of fatal accidents) but industrial accidents make the news only when they constitute a disaster. The subject also has more popular appeal because all workpeople are affected by some aspect of industrial relations, one way or another, for most of their working lives.

The subject of industrial relations is not easily defined. It broadly deals with the relationships encountered by workpeople in their working lives (as opposed to their private lives). The subject is very broad based, drawing on subject matter from economics, law, sociology, psychology, organisational theory and many others. The levels covered by the subject range from individual relationships in the office or on the factory floor to national and international bodies. The subject has grown complex in some areas, for example in wage determination and the use of complicated economic models and equations. The legal side of industrial relations is now quite complex and ever changing. Indeed the specialism of industrial relations has given rise to sub-specialisms in some areas. The subject has evolved to cover all the various factors that affect people at work. Often, and all too simplistically, industrial relations is thought to be all about trade unions. While they are an important part, they are not the only part. The subject includes:

- **Institutions**   Trade unions, union federations, employers' associations, the TUC, the CBI, trade councils, tribunals, courts, ACAS, wage councils, joint industrial councils, government ministries, works councils, and other organisations which have an input into industrial relations activity, for example colleges, universities and independent bodies such as the Industrial Society.
- **Characters**   Shop stewards, convenors, full-time officials of unions and employers' associations, personnel officers, directors, conciliators, arbitrators, tribunal chairpersons, judges, ministers of state and others.
- **Procedures**   Bargaining, negotiating, settling disputes, settling grievances, handling discipline, handling redundancies, forming closed shops, achieving union recognition, policy making, rule changes, tribunal hearings, calling strikes, avoiding industrial action and referrals to conciliation or arbitration.

- **Topics** Pay, hours, conditions of work, content of work, contracts of employment, termination of employment, industrial policy, government policy, political decision making, internationalism, union membership or non-membership, political affiliation, union duties and activities, maternity benefits, discrimination, discipline, picketing, strikes and lock-outs plus a number of other recent additions like safety, employee participation and technological change.

1.2 Growth of industrial relations

Industrial relations has grown into a subject in its own right. This is evidenced in several ways. Colleges and universities have recognised it as such and the subject can be studied, in its own right, from BTEC levels through to first degree and master's degree levels. Organisations have evolved separate departments dealing with industrial relations. Personnel departments often employ people who deal only with agreements, interpretation of agreements, negotiations, resolving conflicts and so on. The subject has also developed its own language. A full list of words used in the special context of industrial relations is provided at the end of this book. Words like leap-frogging, wild cat strike, lay-off, closed shop, picketing, branches, convenors and agreements are all part of the language of industrial relations. This is indicative of a topic becoming a subject in its own right.

Another reason for the growth of industrial relations as a topic is the increasing amount of law relating to the employer/employee relationship. Particularly since the mid-1960s there has been a great expansion of legislation. The 1971 Industrial Relations Act attempted to provide a comprehensive legal framework for industrial relations. Almost every area of the employer/employee relationship was governed by some legal rule. The 1971 Act failed for a variety of reasons, mainly because the unions, nationally, did not cooperate in its operation. Many organisations and people believe that it is folly to try to create such a legal framework at all, but

that it is better to leave organisations to develop industrial relations to fulfil the needs of each organisation as they see fit. There still remains a large quantity of industrial law governing trade union immunities, contracts of employment, dismissal, redundancy, the closed shop, striking, picketing, discrimination, employee rights plus many others. As there is an obligation to comply with the law, industrial relations had to grow if only for the reason that there was so much law applicable in that area.

Industrial relations at the workplace is important for many reasons. If relations between workforce and management are good then the enterprise has a good chance of being successful. The opposite is also true that where relations are poor the enterprise is far less likely to succeed. What produces good industrial relations is a question without a complete answer. It depends on correct attitudes like trust, confidence and honesty, good personal relationships between the people involved, sensible, workable agreements and, above all, a willingness to work together. There are many examples of the effects of a total breakdown of relations between workforce and management. The miners' strike in 1973 led ultimately to a three-day working week, black-outs and eventually a General Election. Not all strikes are so wide ranging in their effect but all have an adverse economic effect on the enterprise. If strikes were avoided the economy would obviously benefit. However, strikes are only a manifestation of the state of industrial relations. Some firms enjoy good relations but suffer the odd strike. Others suffer from poor relations but this does not spill over into strikes. Industrial relations is more complex and important than mere strike avoidance. It is about setting up the correct working climate in which the enterprise can be best assured of a successful future. By working towards good industrial relations, in all contexts, the objective is to motivate employees at all levels, towards achieving a productive, successful enterprise.

The growth of industrial relations at the workplace and nationally has been due to many factors. Organisations themselves have changed from the small family concerns of the eighteenth century to the huge multinational corporations of today. The economy now has a large public sector element comprised of the civil service, local government and nationalised industries. By reason of size alone, the relationships between employer and employee are complex. Large organisations are more difficult to manage and demand a greater attention to relations than the small firm, where relations are more simple and straightforward. Other reasons for the growth of industrial relations derive from the sociological and political changes in the last 150-odd years of an industrialised society. Concepts of master and servant are a thing of the past. The spread of democracy and consensus politics has led to changes in the power structure of organisations. The 'bosses' no longer determine what and how work should be done and that it happens merely because they say so. In many organisations now almost all the elements of the employer/employee relationship are discussed or negotiated. The very emergence and growth of trade unionism is based on the shift of power within the workplace. The situation exists now where the next stage of development in industrial relations is the extension of industrial democracy. There employees will have power-sharing rights with regard to decision making within the organisation. The management prerogative to make decisions unilaterally will be finished.

As industrial relations grows, so it assumes greater importance. As an area of management concern it has become increasingly important to ensure that industrial relations is managed correctly. If this area is neglected, or managed badly, the enterprise will struggle. For this reason industrial relations has come of age as a subject in its own right and has been recognised as an important management function. This function occurs not only in the specialist personnel area but at all management levels. Supervisors and line managers have to acquire an adequate knowledge and possess the basic skills of industrial relations to be able to carry out their tasks efficiently. A brilliant engineer who is unable to meet the industrial relations' demands of running a workshop is no use as a production

manager. Industrial relations also has assumed greater importance as a business and management studies subject. Its wider acceptance as a subject, and one that a greater number of people are studying, must inevitably help to improve the performance of an enterprise. Educational and training needs are being satisfied in many ways. Business and technician educational awards can include a study of the subject. Supervisory and management courses have placed much emphasis on the subject. Specialist courses are run by colleges, polytechnics and universities, including the Open University. The trade unions have put much emphasis on the training of officials through their own colleges or those sponsored by the TUC. There are even legislative rights for this training.

1.3 Perspectives

Industrial relations can be viewed from many different angles. These range from the political, sociological and economic to the legal, psychological and organisational. No one perspective gives a perfect view but each adds to our understanding of the subject. Additionally, industrial relations is not susceptible to any fundamental, objective enquiry (such as a science is) because it is an eclectic system made up of people and organisations holding many differing views. Even among employers (as a class) and trade unions there is a wide and often diverse set of views. In turn, these lead to a range of manifestations as we observe industrial relations in practice. Essentially, industrial relations is pragmatic in that, at the end of the day, the system works and problems are solved. A major factor in the pragmatism of industrial relations is evidenced in the element of compromise which exists, for example, in negotiations whereby both sides move to meet each other and agree on a workable solution. Sometimes this does not work when the two sides remain rigidly entrenched in their own positions and refuse to move sufficiently to promote a settlement. In the 1984/5 miners' strike British Coal refused adamantly to move on the issue of the closure of uneconomic pits based on a capitalist view of efficiency and profitability, while the NUM refused to accept British Coal's proposals based on a socialist view of maintaining employment and communities.

There are several different perspectives and analyses which all seek to give greater understanding of industrial relations. Some are based on a set of principles or ideologies, others are more pragmatic and reflect actual experience. The list includes:

- **unitary perspective** and a more recent variant, the neo-unitarist perspective
- **conflict theory**, including the Marxists and pluralist perspectives
- **systems approach** and the contrasting social action perspective

The unitary perspective starts from the position that organisations, and all those who work in an organisation, have a single, common aim. This precludes any conflict between groups within it. The conflict theory takes an entirely different perspective, admits to the existence of conflict between groups and perceives that industrial relations is the means of regulating and resolving conflict. The systems approach is more descriptive which takes a total view of the system and its components. The social action theory views industrial relations from the individual's viewpoint and motivation.

There are a number of variations on all these themes. Generally a viewpoint, perspective or theory is put forward and this is then modified in the light of experience, criticism and changing circumstances.

1.3.1   Unitary theory

This view of industrial relations is an organisational philosophy based on the premise that everyone in an organisation shares a common purpose and all are committed to these objectives. This automatically excludes the existence of conflict in any form and certainly any institutional recognition of it. This contrasts with the conflict theory discussed in the next section.

The basic assumption made is that all employees are dedicated to the aims of the organisation and they all identify with its method of operation. The relationship is seen as a partnership between the suppliers of capital, management and employees. The aims of the organisation are a shared set of objectives such as efficient production, profits, increased market share and good working conditions. Many firms look on the management of the enterprise as a team effort. In this situation there cannot be two sides. To admit unions into the situation would be admitting an opposition party to management. The traditional roles of a union, to represent employees and to maintain and improve the terms and conditions of its members, have no place in an organisation based on the unitary perspective.

Unitarist organisations can be authoritarian, whereby management has the declared and exclusive right to manage the enterprise as it wishes. Trade unions are seen as an intrusion and as a challenge to management's right to manage. Other unitarist organisations are more paternalistic and look after their employees by establishing good employer/employee relationships and by being committed to the welfare of their employees. Again unions have no role to play. Their representational role is not required.

A frequent criticism of this viewpoint is the refusal to accept the existence of conflict. Conflict is seen as a fact of life in most organisations and it is only reasonable to admit to its existence and to deal with it openly. Others state that conflict necessarily exists as a reflection of the conflict that exists in society. The counter argument is that conflict need not exist. When conflict does arise it is the result of the system not working properly, not that the system itself is flawed. Conflict may arise because of:

- poor leadership given by management
- a breakdown in communication about aims or methods
- a failure to grasp the communality of interest
- resistance of employees

The philosophical base of some firms is grounded in the unitary perspective. It is the predominant philosophy of some American firms such as Kodak and IBM, including their British operations. A number of British firms are also run on similar lines. The unitary view can also be held by managers in organisations although the whole organisation is not based on this perspective. With the unitary viewpoint being based on managerial prerogative many managers will naturally incline to this view to legitimise their position and authority. Neo-unitarism is a recent variant on the unitarist's perspective which grew in the 1980s. This view is a market orientated philosophy where the whole organisation is dedicated to success in its marketplace, with a commitment to customer satisfaction and high standards of quality. Another managerial development which underpins the neo-unitarists' perspective is that of human relations management (HRM) (*see* Section 3.2.1). This development is based on looking at organisational change and achievement through developing the full potential of employees. It hinges on an organisational culture that seeks to develop everyone to their full potential and hence secure full and enthusiastic commitment to the aims of the organisation. It focuses strongly on the individual through training, career development plans, opportunities for promotion and performance related pay. This runs counter to the idea of collective bargaining which tends towards determining the terms and conditions of employment of employees on a group basis.

The potential to develop these new strategies in the 1980s was helped very much by the other changes which took place at the same time. For example, there were the changes in national politics, with a strong swing towards the right. A further important political change was the attachment to the dogma that the market is preeminent and that market forces should be left to determine everything. This challenged the prevalent thinking of the postwar years where the institutions and processes of industrial relations controlled certain aspects of the labour market. Formerly governments helped to regulate some elements of the labour market, e.g., through Wage Council Regulations, incomes

policies and employment protection laws (*see* Section 4.2). This runs counter to allowing market forces to determine the terms and conditions of employment. Periods of high unemployment always tend to increase the relative power of the employer, and this occurred in the 1980s. Unions already weakened by political events (*see* Section 8.1.5) saw their membership fall dramatically and legislation curbed their activities as never before. Also the changes in occupational structure (*see* Section 17.1) allowed management to redesign organisations on the lines it preferred rather than having to accommodate strong union views or traditional systems. This preference, in many cases, was an adherence to the unitarist's perspective.

The neo-unitarist's viewpoint is almost identical to the traditional unitarist's viewpoint, but the means employed to achieve these ends and the environment in which they could achieve their objectives was different. The means employed embraced new techniques in securing employee commitment to the organisation's objectives. The personnel function was pivotal to this, right through from recruitment, selection, induction, career progression, training and remuneration. The environment was much more market orientated, where the customer was put first and customer satisfaction paramount.

The unitary theory is often seen as representing an ideal world where there is an absence of conflict. It does not admit to the competition for scarce resources between groups nor the conflict which arises from this. It is essentially a managerial view of industrial relations (or employee relations as a preferred term) which seeks to secure the cooperation and commitment of employees.

1.3.2 Conflict theory

This is based on the premise that conflict exists in society and in organisations and it is essential to recognise this and to have a framework that deals with it. In organisations, conflict arises because of the differing values and interests of management and employees. This prevalent viewpoint, developed in various ways over the last century, has moulded industrial relations in the United Kingdom. Unions emerged to represent the views of workers, which were different from those of the owning group. The whole basis of collective bargaining is that employers and employees have to resolve their differences and various institutions emerged to serve this purpose (*see* Chapter 6). In order to resolve difficult problems, which could not be resolved between the parties themselves, there emerged various institutions and processes to resolve conflict externally. (This is examined in Section 6.4.) The basis for these various facets of industrial relations is the recognition of conflict. There are a number of variations of conflict theory.

(a) The oldest, and possibly better known, is the Marxist view. Marx had little to say directly about industrial relations in the form we know it, but his general theory applies. His theory was that society is made up of two conflicting classes, the capitalists who own the means of production and the workers who offer their labour to the capitalists. The expression used to describe this situation is dialectic materialism. The capitalists are the powerful ruling group (bourgeoisie) and the labourers the weaker ruled group (proletariat). This class war should lead to a socialist revolution which should then be followed by a classless, communist society. Marxists see no difference between the conflict in society generally and that which exists in organisations. Hence the class conflict in industry is a reflection of conflict in society as a whole and the outcome will be the same, a revolution. The institutions in a capitalist society grow out of this power base and do not represent a permanent solution to the conflict. Trade unions exist to enable the workers to gain a power base on which they can secure improved terms and conditions from the capitalists. Unions offer a protection against the owners and managers, hence the need for collectivism which is more powerful than individualism. Trade unions are not necessarily seen as the basis for the revolution but may contribute to the wider class struggle in society. They are one and the same thing. The Marxists' perspective is criticised because it fails to recognise the changes that have taken place in society since Marx's seminal works were written over 100 years ago. The distribution of power and property has changed and is more widely spread than in previous times. There is much more social mobility today and the simple division between the classes as described by Marx no longer exists.

(b) The second variant of conflict theory is the pluralist viewpoint. Again this accepts the existence of conflict in society and organisations. Society has to accept that there are a range of groups, each with their own beliefs, values and interests. It is essential to enable compromise to be reached to accommodate these often disparate groups. This involves negotiation and concession. The workplace reflects this situation. Organisations comprise a number of groups that have a variety of beliefs and interests. These are to be held in balance by management. Pluralists accept that conflict exists and that the institutions and processes of industrial relations seek to resolve this by reaching a workable compromise acceptable to all the groups involved. Hence collective bargaining has a central role as a process in resolving conflict and achieving agreement. Trade unions are important and are to be accepted for their representational role and regulatory function. Each group within this framework can retain its own identity with some control mechanism operating to keep a balance between the various groups. The overriding consideration for management is to ensure that harmony exists, as far as possible, and to ensure that compromises and agreements work. There are 'hard' and 'soft' variants of pluralism. The former is conflict based and seeks to resolve the conflict by collective bargaining. The latter is based on a problem solving approach, which involves joint consultation.

Criticism of pluralism comes from those of a Marxist persuasion who see collective bargaining as a manifestation of a class conflict that will only be resolved by a socialist revolution. The current system, it is argued, cannot sustain itself because of the class conflict it represents. Others criticise pluralism because there is an assumption that the interest groups have roughly the same amount of power, and this is held not to be so as the managerial groups inherently have more power. Pluralism also assumes that everyone in the system accepts a pluralist view and is prepared to compromise to reach agreement. Again in practice this may not always be so.

Essentially the pluralist perspective is widely accepted because it reflects reality. It comes closest to providing an analytical framework for the industrial relations system in the UK. Many managers and trade unionists are pragmatists and find that the current system of industrial relations works for them. This implies a dynamic situation as change inevitably takes place over time and managers and unions adjust their positions accordingly.

1.3.3 Systems model

A different approach to providing a framework for understanding industrial relations is the systems approach. This was developed by an American J. Dunlop in the late 1950s. Figure 1.1 illustrates the system. It aimed to give the tools of analysis to interpret and gain an understanding of industrial relations.

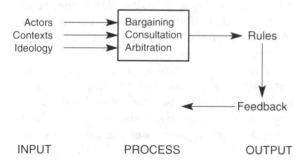

Fig 1.1 Industrial relations system

Dunlop identified three main factors in a system of industrial relations:

- **The actors** These are the people and organisations involved in the system. This includes the hierarchy of managers and their representatives, a hierarchy of employees and their representatives and thirdly the specialised industrial relations agencies which operate within the system. These can be governmental or not. In Britain this includes such agencies as ACAS and others who provide a service to the system, for example conciliators.
- **The contexts** These are the main elements of the environment within which the system operates. These include the technological aspects, the budgetary and market constraints and the locus of power in society. Dunlop regarded technology as being particularly important. This seems rather prophetic for someone writing in the 1950s! The situation in the 1990s is that technology is now one of the prime movers of change in organisations. This subject is dealt with in Sections 15.4 and 17.1. Many of the profound changes in occupational and industrial structure have been, and remain, due to the effects of technology. This has in turn affected the contexts within which our system of industrial relations operates.

The budgetary and market constraints can be both national, sectoral and organisational. Clearly all organisations have to work within an economic framework at several levels, and this affects the system of industrial relations. The system for public sector employees is different from that of a multinational organisation because different budgetary and market factors bear on the system. The final contextual factor is the locus of power in society. This relates to the distribution of power outside the system of industrial relations. The nature of the national political system has a direct bearing on the system of industrial relations.

- **The ideology of the system** This is the set of beliefs held by the participants that allow them to operate the system. This is the body of common ideas that defines the role and place of each actor and the ideas which each actor holds towards the place and function of others in the system. Individuals within the system may well have differing views but there has to be sufficient common ground for everyone to establish a working relationship.

This work was influential, particularly in

America. There are a number of criticisms of this analysis. One is that it is static and does not provide an analysis of the processes of industrial relations. It is also difficult to analyse change using this model. Any systems analysis tends to give a static picture and does not attempt to provide answers only to provide a picture of the situation.

Social action theory provides an opposite viewpoint to industrial relations from the systems approach outlined above. This theory makes its approach from the individual responses of the actors in the system. Max Weber originally developed these ideas. The theory seeks to analyse why the actors in the system take certain lines of action, and to understand the actors' own definitions of the situation they are in. This contrasts with the systems approach which states that behaviour is a result of the structure and processes of the system. Social action arises out of the expectations, norms, values, experiences and goals of the individuals working in the system. This approach seeks to understand particular actions in industrial relations but falls short of providing a framework for the system. Put simply, the systems theory is a top down approach, whilst the social action theory is a bottom up approach. Both have a contribution to make in understanding industrial relations. A suggested compromise approach would be to show the interactive nature of social structure and social behaviour. In practice, the actors in the system are influenced by the system and in turn they influence the system.

1.4 Structure of the book

The approach of this book is, as far as is possible, factual and unbiased. The aim is to produce a broad guide to the subject and to balance the various elements within the subject. The book includes a study of the institutions involved, the processes, background (historical and legal), industrial law and industrial relations issues. There is an overlap in some areas, so cross-referencing is fairly extensive. The more debatable, less factual areas, particularly the

political arguments, have been kept to a minimum. It is necessary to grasp the essential features and basic facts before going on to debate some of the other issues. The book may lose out on some interesting material to ensure the content does not become biased one way or another. The aim is to give a balanced, comprehensive treatment of the subject, without undue emphasis on any particular area. As far as possible the subject matter is treated in a practical manner rather than taking a particularly academic or analytical line. Students wishing to delve deeper into a specific aspect, or to study a particular line of thinking, will find many books available. Suggestions for further reading are given at the end of each chapter. Examples are given from a cross-section of industries and sectors of the economy rather than being specific to one industry or sector.

The layout of the book was designed to look at the subject in an orderly way, trying to link one chapter to the next. Partitioning the book was avoided as this tends to compartmentalise the subject when each area of the subject is often linked or reliant on another. Each chapter is broken down into sections and subsections and divides the subject matter into manageable chunks rather than allowing one topic to merge into the next with no indication of the change.

Chapters 2–5 look primarily at the institutions: the trade unions, employers and their associations, the State and local union organisations. Industrial relations has evolved many different organisations and institutions to act as the machinery or vehicle for the conduct of industrial relations at all levels. Trade unions and employers are obvious choices to begin with, being the main parties in institutionalised relations. The State has always played a role and has recently, particularly in the legislative field, enlarged this role. The courts, as a part of the State, have always had a role to play. At a local workplace level there is a distinctive organisation centred on the shop steward and the branch. This has been separated from the chapter on trade unions firstly to keep the chapters to a reasonable length and secondly because local organisations tend to be separate anyway (for good or for bad).

Chapters 6–9 are background topics. First the process central to industrial relations, that of collective bargaining, is examined. It is so fundamental and important that it requires separate treatment. Second the historical development of the unions, certain legal developments and the political aspects of the trade unions are discussed. Third the basis of the English legal system is explained. As much of industrial relations is covered or touched on by statutory or common law it is felt necessary to explain briefly the fundamentals of our legal system, which will be helpful to those not familiar with it. Those who are familiar with it can skip this chapter.

Chapters 10–16 deal with specific industrial relations topics. In Chapter 10, several topics, ranging from immunities to discrimination, are put together under industrial relations law. Chapter 11 gives the main points of the nine Codes of Practice that relate to industrial relations with comments. Chapters 12–14 deal with three important topics, those of the contract of employment and the two related issues of dismissal and redundancy. For every person at work, the contract of employment is the basis of the relationship between employer and employee. Dismissal and redundancy are ways in which the contract can be terminated. As statutory law has virtually created these two

aspects and they have acquired their own peculiar and complex rules, they are dealt with separately.

Five issues are covered in Chapter 15: striking, picketing, the closed shop, flexibility and equal opportunities. These topics are dealt with as factually as possible, giving data wherever possible. There is a subsection in each section on the law relating to each issue. The penultimate chapter looks to the likely developments of our industrial relations system and various schemes for greater employee participation and industrial democracy. The final chapter gazes into the future and looks at a number of topics which are shaping the nature of industrial relations in the years ahead.

Further reading

R Bean, *Comparative Industrial Relations*, Routledge, 1985, 0-415-04940-7
J T Dunlop, *Industrial Relations Systems*, Harvard Business School Press, 1993, 0-87584-334-4
R Hyman, *Industrial Relations: a Marxist introduction*, Macmillan, 1982, 0-333-18667-2
M Salamon, *Industrial Relations Theory and Practice*, Prentice Hall, 1992, 0-13-457433-8
H Gospel, *British Industrial Relations*, Routledge, 1993, 0-415-08453-9

2

Trade unions

2.1 Purpose and functions

2.1.1 Trade unions defined

The classic definition of a trade union was given by Sidney and Beatrice Webb in 1896 as 'a continuous association of wage earners for the purpose of maintaining or improving the condition of their working lives'. This was based on their researches into trade union history and has been accepted ever since. The form of association is various: in the Webbs' time many of the trade union organisations were small and local, representing a specific skill: nowadays there are still some small unions plus all sizes through to the large, national trade unions of today. The definition implies a permanent association rather than one which is created for a particular purpose and disbanded at a later date. Many early eighteenth-century organisations lacked this permanence. The term 'wage earners' would today be extended to include salary earners. The object of such associations is to maintain and improve the members' conditions. This may be narrowly concerned with wages and hours of work or be extended to include the much wider issues relating to work and employment. Trade unions have become pressure groups on issues such as nationalisation, the welfare state, economic policy and other issues which they see as affecting their members. Apart from this, trade unions have sought to achieve these wider aims by their involvement in politics.

Another definition is given in the Trade Union and Labour Relations (Consolidation) Act 1992 which states that a trade union is 'an organisation (whether permanent or temporary) consisting wholly or mainly of workers of one or more descriptions whose principal purpose includes the regulation of relations between workers of that description and employers or employers' associations'. This definition is a drier, legal wording but is of importance in relation to the process of being registered as a trade union (particularly for tax purposes) with the Certification Officer. Under this definition a group of workers who combine for even a brief period (and then disband), for example to secure something from the employer, are, for the period they are in combination, accorded the status of a trade union in law. As we shall see in Chapter 10 this is very important, otherwise they could be open to legal action for their activities. A trade union need not have the vestiges of the large, permanent organisations we are more familiar with in order to be a trade union. However, to be of use to its members in the long term a trade union becomes characterised in certain ways.

The characteristics which define a trade union are many and may include:

- a statement that the organisation is a trade union (in a similar way that a company has to make a statement in order to become a plc)
- registration with the Certification Officer as a trade union which accords it a special legal status
- independence from the employer, which may be evidenced by a Certificate of Independence from the Certification Officer

- affiliation to the TUC, Labour party or joining a confederation of unions
- its principal aim being that of maintaining and improving the conditions of its members
- the possible use of sanctions to further its aims, i.e., taking industrial action

Not all unions will include every one of these characteristics, although many of the large trade unions do. Some staff associations have the characteristics of a trade union and perform the same function for their members as a trade union. Staff associations are more common in the service sector (insurance, building societies and banks) and among more senior staff in private organisations. Often they perform a trade union function at the encouragement of the employer to prevent an external trade union from gaining bargaining rights for the group. Notably the Association of Scientific, Technical and Managerial Staffs (now the Manufacturing Science and Finance) grew rapidly by taking over many staff associations. However, not all staff associations should be considered as a trade union as often they have only an advisory or social role. Nevertheless, their organisation needs to be examined to see if they exhibit some of the characteristics of a trade union.

Some unions are not affiliated to the TUC. Of the registered unions, in 1992, only 73 were affiliated to the TUC, although they represented 86% of trade union membership. Other unions are not affiliated to the Labour party while others are not certified as independent. Further, some unions refuse to take industrial action in pursuance of their objectives such as the Royal College of Nursing and the Professional Association of Teachers. Hence there are a range of organisations that can be considered to be a trade union, and no single set of characteristics can define an organisation as a trade union.

2.1.2 General aims

Trade unions have as their overall aim that of protecting and advancing the interests of their members. Unions are essentially organisations of a number of workpeople who collectively aim to ensure they keep what they already have and to improve on this. Trade unions (in the form we know them today) developed from the 1850s onwards. At first the organisations were very local and based outside the workplace. They tended to be weaker than now, but the essential ingredients were there. Workpeople joined together in some sort of organisation to further their interests. The issues have changed over the years (some have not, like pay and hours), organisations have become larger and more complex and a framework of industrial relations has developed. However, the basic purposes of trade unions have not altered. Workpeople join unions and collectively, through representatives, aim to ensure that the issues relating to their employment are protected and improved upon.

The ability of trade unions to achieve their primary purpose is based on the important factor that individuals within a group or organisation have a common set of goals and these can be best achieved by collective organisation. While the individuals in a group hold a variety of views, which sometimes may be in conflict, the group has a cohesiveness which leads to permanency, based on the common interest of improving their conditions at work. This common interest may often lead to conflict with other groups of employees or with employers, and in order to defend itself the group will have allegiance to the organisation (trade union) that it believes can best serve its interests.

This aspect of collective organisation is the basis of trade unionism, in which the union articulates the views of the membership to the various other groups or organisations with which it has to do business. This has led to a variety of aims within the trade union movement. Craft workers seek to maintain their status as skilled workers and this may mean defending themselves against other groups of workers (unskilled) and against the employer. This may involve them in seeking to maintain (as one of their prime objectives) the pay differentials traditionally accorded to those workers with a specialist skill that has required specific training. During periods of technological change when traditional skills may be displaced by machinery, the group seeks to defend its livelihood. General workers are interested in improving general levels of pay for everyone, not just a section of the workforce. Those given staff status in an organisation (white collar workers) seek to maintain their status with such conditions as a shorter working week, longer holidays and fringe benefits.

In addition to the workplace interests of the group, unions have developed wider aims that would help improve the lives of the group. This has meant that the unions have become a pressure group within society, and this has led them necessarily to become political, though not necessarily party political. The trade union movement has long been identified with the Labour party (indeed the Labour party grew out of the trade union movement) but trade unions seek to act politically by using their representational powers. Trade unions try to influence government policy regardless of which party is in power. The issues unions have campaigned for have included law reform, health and safety, the welfare state, economic policy and even foreign policy. The aim of this is to provide a better working life for their members.

While there is no definitive list of the aims of the trade union movement, the TUC, in its evidence to the Donovan Commission in 1965, gave the following aims of a trade union:

- to improve the terms of employment
- to improve the physical environment at work
- to achieve full employment and national prosperity
- to achieve security of employment and income
- to improve social security
- to achieve fair shares in national income and wealth
- to achieve industrial democracy
- to achieve a voice in government
- to improve public and social services
- to achieve public control and planning of industry.

Clearly such a range of objectives seeks to improve the condition of the members of unions. The means of achieving these aims requires a variety of activities. Some can be pursued within the workplace while others require action at national level.

2.1.3 Specific functions

Every union has a number of specific functions that it needs to carry out to fulfil the needs of its members. These vary from union to union and change over time. Some aspects of a trade union's function can now be considered residual. In the nineteenth century a union's friendly society benefits were very important and would possibly have been the union's number one function. Now, with the welfare state and social security, a union's function in this area is minimal. Other aspects of a union's function have increased, especially the numbers of issues negotiated by a union. Annual negotiations have widened from pay and hours to include holidays, sick pay, pensions, promotions, paid leave, health and safety, and many others. In some employment situations there are hardly any features of work that are not covered by union/management negotiated agreements.

One of the best places to find the specific aims of a union is the *Rule Book*. All unions have a Rule Book and most start off with a list of the aims of the union. There are often a large number of objectives appearing. For example the TGWU lists 11, AEU 19, EETPU 5, NALGO 16, USDAW 14. Below is an abbreviated list of aims appearing in the TGWU Rule Book:

The principal objects of the union are the regulation of the relations between workmen and employers and between workmen and workmen and also the provision of benefit to members.

The objects further include:

- **the organisation of all members and other persons qualified for membership**
- **the settling and negotiating of differences and disputes between the members of the union and employers and other trade unions and persons by collective bargaining or agreement, withdrawal of labour or otherwise**

- to promote the welfare of members
- the provision of benefits to members as follows
  - assistance when out of employment, in sickness, old age, trade disputes, funeral expenses
  - legal expenses
  - grants and endowments for the education of trade unionists
- furtherance of political objectives
- the extension of cooperative production and distribution
- the establishment of printing or publishing publications furthering the interests of the union
- participation in the work of any body having as its objectives the interests of labour and trade unionism
- the furthering of any action or purpose that will further the interests of labour and trade unionism
- the provision of opportunities for social intercourse and promotion of sports and social events among members

As can be seen, some aims are of less importance now, e.g., the provision of benefits to members, and others are of more importance now. The TGWU was formed in 1922 and has changed with the times. Rule Books are amended frequently (usually at the Annual Conference) to accommodate these changes.

The traditional functions of trade unions can be summarised under six headings:

- **Collective bargaining** This is a central function of a trade union, to determine the wages, hours and other conditions of employment of its members. (This is dealt with in Chapters 6 and 7.)
- **Safeguarding jobs** Keeping members in their jobs and protecting these jobs is a prime function. The skilled person's craft union sets up regulations regarding the training for a skill and the protection of the skill through demarcation (i.e., defining who does what job). This function can become the primary function of the union, particularly in times when the group of workers is under threat from, say, technological changes. The skill of a job may be taken over by a machine, e.g.,

a computer-controlled machining centre will carry out the work of skilled, trained engineers and reduce the labour requirements to that of a machine minder who needs no skill training. In such cases the engineering union will seek to maintain the jobs of its members even though this militates against the advantages (to the firm) of the investment in the new machinery. Some agreements reached have compromised by moving the person with the job, i.e., if a machine takes over the job previously carried out by a person, that person moves on to the new machine. This is a formula for overstaffing, at least temporarily until labour is reduced by natural wastage or by relocating the displaced, skilled workers. In times of redundancy, unions try to fight job loss or at least minimise the effects of job loss. Very often there are agreements on redundancy procedure and, additionally, unions have to be consulted on redundancies by law (see Section 14.3.1).

- **Cooperation with employers** Much of the function of unionism in the workplace involves cooperation with employers. Some trade unionists argue (especially those with strong political views) that this function dilutes or compromises the trade union movement as a force for change. Cooperation is considered to be accepting the status quo and, perhaps, even upholding the present system which, from a trade union viewpoint, should be changed. This definition of cooperation is sometimes applied to trade union leaders who make agreements at national level to resolve a dispute to be greeted by cries of 'sell out' by local officials and union members. The miners felt this to be the case after the General Strike in 1926 failed to support fully the miners, who eventually lost their claim of 'not a penny off the wage, not a minute on the day'. However, other trade unions argue that they should cooperate because if they can help the organisation to become successful this will in turn be of direct benefit to their members. Where they see things that should be changed, to the benefit of their members, they are prepared to fight within the system.

Very often there are joint committees covering many topics, for example health and safety, production, complaints, works councils. At national level this cooperation is seen in the joint representation of employers and unions on bodies such as the Training Commission, Industrial Training Boards (which are being phased out from 1990 onwards), the Health and Safety Commission, the National Economic Development Council, and many others.

- **Political activities**   Unions have long played the role of pressure group, particularly for the reform of legislation. A Parliamentary Group was set up in 1870 and the first union-sponsored MP was elected in 1873. The formation of the Labour party in 1900 saw an important step forward and in the next ten years the unions affiliated to this new political party. Today the unions are of great importance in the Labour party. They provide the bulk of the funds and they hold the bulk of the votes at Labour's Annual Conference. *See* Chapter 4 for more detail on this.

- **Provision of social services**   Some unions still provide financial assistance for sickness, unemployment, retirement and death but generally these are small and of little importance now. Unions provide strike pay (for official strikes) but this can be small if funds are low. Some unions have convalescent and retirement homes. Legal services are also provided which, in the age of increasing legislation, are of importance.

- **Provision of friendly services**   The union once provided facilities for leisure in clubrooms. These also acted as labour exchanges to give information on the jobs available. In most instances this latter function has been superseded by open advertising, job centres and employment agencies, but still exists in the national newspaper printing industry whereby the chapel is the supplier of labour. Should a newspaper wish to employ someone, this is done through the union chapel.

The following paragraphs from the Amalgamated Engineering Union give an illustration of the range of services provided by a typical large union.

Contributions The level of contributions varies, depending on which section the member is in, but in 1987 the rates varied from 82p per week to 52p per week. With the extra benefits of superannuation, sick and unemployment benefit an extra 31p per week was payable.

Benefits About one quarter of income is returned as benefits to members, which is a high proportion. In 1985 £3.78m was paid out. This included £1.66m in superannuation, £92,000 in benevolent grants, £166,000 in death benefit, £508,000 in dispute benefit and £1.77m in legal defence of members. The latter led to 9,300 settlements amounting to £21.20m. Dispute benefit was £18 per week (where paid), funeral benefit £50 and death benefit £100.

In 1986 the union introduced a financial service for its members to include advice on mortgages, savings, investments, etc.

Education In 1985 expenditure totalled £100,000 with the main thrust being for steward's and secretary's education.

Political fund At the end of 1985 the political fund stood at £746,000, from an annual levy of £1 per member per year. Of this, one-third is given to districts for local political work. The union sponsors 15 MPs.

The Electrical Electronic Telecommunication and Plumbing Union has a similar range of benefits for its members. These include:

- retirement grant of between £60 and £80
- funeral benefit of between £60 and £80
- disablement grant paid to those who are incapacitated as a result of an accident at work (the grant varies, depending on the degree of disability, ranging from £400 to £1,000)
- fatal accident grant of between £1,400 and £2,000

Accident benefit is paid if a member is incapacitated from working. This is paid at a daily rate of between 75p and £1.00. There is a technical training service at the union's own training centre and education grants are also available for certain courses, usually as non-cash benefits.

Further, a legal service provides free legal advice. In 1988 it processed or helped in over 5,000 cases and recovered £5.0m for its members. An employment law advisory and representational service is available, including representation at Industrial Tribunals.

The union operates its own hotel and leisure service, as well as providing a range of personal, insurance, financial and motorists' services to its members through other agencies, often at a discount.

2.2 Size and growth

2.2.1 Number of unions

The number of unions in the country has gone through a spectacular cycle. For our purposes the growth of unions started in the 1850s. The environment then was quite different from that existing today. Communications were poor; there were no mass communication networks; factories were locally owned; there were few national or multinational companies. Generally, the people were poorly educated with only a few having the ability to read and write. The law had forbidden unions to form and there was much resistance to them. In spite of these factors the unions emerged. First came the craft unions of the better trained, skilled worker, followed by the general unions for the unskilled. Unions tended to be very localised, restricted to a town or area, and were specific to a trade or industry. Some amalgamations did occur, such as the Amalgamated Society of Engineers, which was a combination of millwrights, smiths, machinists and patternmakers, but generally the trend was for numerous, local unions. Through a series of legal reforms (*see* Chapter 8), unions became more widely accepted and grew in number. By 1893 there were 1,279 separate unions with a total membership of 1,559,000. As a result of

amalgamations and new unions forming, the number fluctuated around the 1,200–1,300 mark for many years. It peaked at 1,384 in 1920, and fell slowly from then on. There were still 1,004 unions in 1940. It has to be noted that the vast majority of these unions never affiliated to the TUC (which had started in 1868). The TUC had 179 unions affiliated to it in 1893, representing 1.1 million trade unionists. The number of affiliated unions rose to 266 in 1918 (representing 5,284,000 members). This number then fell, but less rapidly than that of the unions in total. Gradually the number of unions has fallen to below 400 and in 1992 stood at around 302. The number of unions affiliated to the TUC in 1992 was 73, representing 8,192,664 members. Figure 2.1 shows the general trend of the number of unions.

As changes took place in the economy and society, so these caused changes in trade unionism. As communications networks grew, a centralised national leadership became easier. A union could have its headquarters in London and communicate with its members elseswhere. As companies became national, there was the need to coordinate trade union effort on a national scale rather than just locally. Politics became more important, especially after the creation of the Labour party. Also the unions found that there was great strength in numbers so that if their efforts were coordinated they could be effective. This is especially true of the general unions who have less direct power through skills. By reducing the number of unions, i.e., going from many small unions to fewer, large unions, this would strengthen the trade union's hands. Also the individual unions had a natural desire to grow and there have been many take-over battles. This is often to the advantage of the smaller union when merging with a larger one. The power of the larger organisation is of benefit to the members so that losing the identity of the smaller union is of little consequence. An example of this occurred when the National Union of Agriculture and Allied Workers became part of the TGWU. Traditionally the agricultural workers have had little power because of their dispersed population

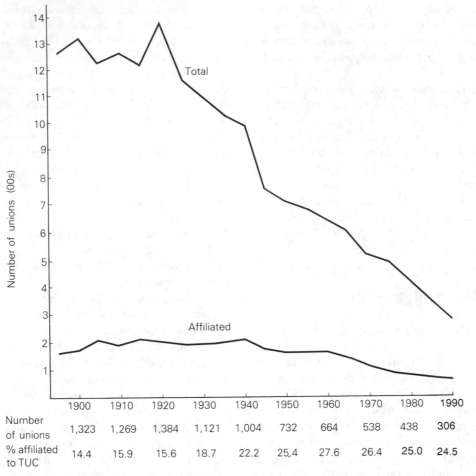

	1900	1910	1920	1930	1940	1950	1960	1970	1980	1990
Number of unions	1,323	1,269	1,384	1,121	1,004	732	664	538	438	306
% affiliated to TUC	14.4	15.9	15.6	18.7	22.2	25.4	27.6	26.4	25.0	24.5

Fig 2.1 Number of trade unions 1895–1990

and low numbers locally. Combined with the TGWU they feel that they can move towards equalising the power of their members with respect to the more powerful employers' organisation, the National Farmers' Union (NFU).

Another factor in the reduction of the number of unions is the natural desire of organisations to grow. Many small unions have been taken over by larger unions, frequently amicably but sometimes after a take-over battle. Craft unions, often seeing their membership falling due to technological change, have devised strategies to expand their membership. In some instances this has taken the form of amalgamating with other craft unions, e.g., the EETPU which was formed out of an electricians' union and a plumbing union. An alternative strategy has been to create various categories of membership, e.g., the AEU has a skilled section, a non-skilled section and a staff section. The law facilitates the process of unions merging through the Trade Union (Amalgamations, etc.) Act 1964 in which the procedures to be adopted are laid down. This can take the form of a merger or a complete take-over of one union by another.

Competition remains between unions for members and there are few inter-union policies for recruitment although frequently there are understandings based on custom and practice. The TUC has a procedure called the Bridlington Agreement to help minimise the friction that may be caused by such competition for members. If a person wishes to join a union other than the one recognised by the employer as representing that group, or wishes to change to another trade union, then the application for membership must be referred to the other union. Normally 'poaching' is not allowed and any attempts by one union to oust another in a workplace would be against the Bridlington Agreement and the union could be subject to disciplinary action by the Disputes Committee of the TUC.

2.2.2 Number of members

The number of trade union members has risen from the early days of trade unionism to stand at 9.81m in 1990 with a peak of over 13 million in 1980. However, the rise has not been steady but more a series of fluctuations. In the nineteenth century, trade union membership could often be a hindrance to employment, so in times of slump trade union membership dropped. Also in times of recession, out-of-work members fell behind with their subscriptions and finally no longer counted as members. This is less true of the craft unions as a union card is necessary to get a job. Another factor has been the legal developments that have occurred. As a hurdle was cleared, membership rose. This was particularly the case in the early twentieth century. There was a heavy fall due to the depression in the 1920s and a greater fall after the 1926 General Strike. Recovery only occurred in 1933 and then only gradually. Membership stood at 9,810,019 in 1990. Figure 2.2 shows

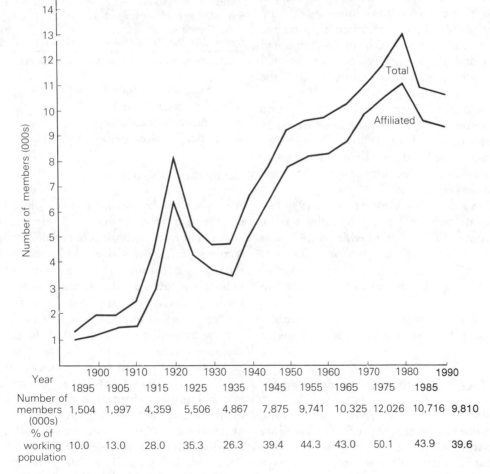

Year	1895	1900	1905	1910	1915	1920	1925	1930	1935	1940	1945	1950	1955	1960	1965	1970	1975	1980	1985	1990
Number of members (000s)	1,504		1,997		4,359		5,506		4,867		7,875		9,741		10,325		12,026		10,716	9,810
% of working population	10.0		13.0		28.0		35.3		26.3		39.4		44.3		43.0		50.1		43.9	39.6

Fig 2.2 Membership of trade unions 1895–1990

the pattern of growth of trade union membership.

The proportion of the working population that is in union membership has risen from about 10% in 1895 to about 43% in 1980. In 1993 there were about 24.7 million people in employment of whom around 3 million were self-employed. Of the remaining 21.7 million, some, such as members of the police and armed forces, could not become trade union members and others were not likely to, e.g., top management grades. About 17 million had their terms and conditions of employment determined by collective bargaining and of these about 9 million belong to a trade union, of which almost 90% are in TUC affiliated unions.

The number of people in membership of a trade union is dependent on a number of factors, with no single factor predominating. Those affecting trade union membership include organisational factors such as occupational structure and size of organisation, and external factors such as economic conditions and the political environment.

The statistics given in the Certification Officer's Annual Report showed there were 306 trade unions listed in 1990. There is no compulsion to be listed but a union cannot apply for a certificate of independence (*see* Section 2.3.4) unless it is listed.

The 306 unions that made returns in 1990 had an aggregate membership of 9.81 million and a total income of £561.8m, of which 82.4% was raised from members' subscriptions. Out of a total of £555m expenditure, £365m (65.8%) was distributed in the form of benefits to members.

Table 2.1 shows the income and membership figures for the top ten trade unions in 1991.

2.2.3 Factors affecting union membership

The number of trade unions and union membership has fluctuated over time. There are many factors which bear on the level of trade union membership. This section identifies a number of the major factors. These are:

Table 2.1 Membership and income of top 10 trade unions 1991

	Membership (000s)	Income (£000s)
Transport and General Workers' Union	1,126	61,394
GMB	863	54,867
National and Local Government Officers' Association	760	68,299
Amalgamated Engineering Union	623	24,545
Manufacturing and Finance Union	604	23,487
National Union of Public Employees	551	29,599
Electrical, Electronic, Telecommunication and Plumbing Union	357	15,170
Union of Shop, Distributive and Allied Workers	341	14,331
Royal College of Nursing of the United Kingdom	293	10,133
National Union of Teachers	214	9,651

Source: Certification Officer's Annual Report

- occupational structure
- size of organisation
- economic conditions
- political environment

Occupational structure

A number of changes have taken place in the employment structure in the UK. First there has been a shift from both the primary and secondary sections (i.e., extractive industries such as mining, agriculture and the manufacturing industries) towards the tertiary sector (i.e., banking, insurance, personal services, public service and distribution). The size of the shift may be gauged from the fact that the first two categories accounted for 51% of the working population in 1961, whereas the latter accounted for 57% in 1981. This trend continues as manufacturing industries become less labour intensive due to technological factors such as automation, and economic factors such as the recession and lack of competitiveness.

The effect of this is a fall in trade union membership, especially with the decline of industries traditionally having high levels of union membership, e.g., shipbuilding, railways, mining and the docks. Additionally, the tertiary sector tends to have a low trade union membership with much of the work being part-time and predominantly staffed by females. There has traditionally been a lower proportion of women than men who join a union. Also part-time workers do not tend to join a union, although this group has been targeted for recruitment drives by trade unions.

A second change in employment structure has been the shift in the types of jobs in which people are employed. In addition to the changes mentioned in the previous paragraphs, there have been changes caused by technology. The mechanisation and automation of processes have shifted the job structure of organisations away from labour (due to mechanisation) and skilled labour (due to automation) to clerical and professional grades. (This topic is developed more fully in Section 17.1.)

Size of organisation

As trade has expanded and transport and communications systems have grown, organisations have grown in size both as a result of their own expansion through increased trade and by acquisition and merger. The trend is for fewer organisations to account for a greater proportion of economic activity. This has led to the concentration of activity on fewer sites which employ large numbers of people. There is a strong positive correlation between the size of establishment and trade union membership. In larger firms there is also the tendency for more senior people to be unionised. This is probably due to the feeling of insecurity and remoteness from the people who make decisions affecting their working lives and the impersonal nature of a large organisation. This movement towards larger organisations is also reflected in the public sector with local authorities, health authorities, water, gas and electricity boards and the nationalised industries. In the case of these latter organisations, in many instances, the employers often encourage trade union membership.

Alongside this continuing development throughout the latter years of the 1980s there was an increase in the number of new jobs created through the growth of small firms. These have been strongly encouraged by government policy. People setting up their own businesses (and the few people they employ), do not tend to join a union. The growth of new firms has been strongest in the service sector, which again tends to have a low level of unionisation.

Economic conditions

Changes in economic conditions have an effect on trade union membership, but it is an effect which is difficult to measure. In times of inflation, research has shown that membership tends to expand, probably due to employees perceiving union membership and collective bargaining as a means of protecting their living standards. During periods of recession, when unemployment rises, membership falls, particularly among general workers who, when unemployed, allow their membership to lapse. Skilled workers tend to maintain their membership as this may be necessary for them to obtain another job.

Political environment

The attitude of governments towards trade unions has a direct effect on trade union membership. When government policy encourages trade union growth then membership flourishes. This is illustrated by the encouragement during the period 1974–9 when the Labour government enacted much pro-union legislation. This was part of the Social Contract in which the unions, through the TUC, agreed a wages policy in return for legislation favourable to trade unions. The result was the Trade Union and Labour Relations Acts 1974 and 1976 and the Employment Protection Acts 1975 and 1978, much of which was designed to enable trade unionism to expand. Over the years 1974–8 trade union membership grew at between 2 and 3.5% per year.

The Conservatives, during and after their successful 1979 election campaign, made it no secret that they believed that the trade unions had too much power and that this must be curbed. Ideologically the right wing of the Conservative party, led by Mrs Thatcher, was against trade unions in principle. They were, and still are, seen as a restriction on the operation of free market forces in the labour market. The government made clear its intention to restrict union power by passing a series of Acts to achieve this aim. This it has done; looking at the sections on immunities (10.2.2.) and also on the closed shop (Section 15.3) demonstrates this point. One aspect of industrial relations that the government was intent on eliminating was the closed shop. The practice was seen as unfair and unjust. The other obvious point is that the trade unions are socialist by conviction and were (and still are) opposed to many of the policies of the Conservative government.

The background to the 1979 election was that of the 'winter of discontent' when labour relations nationally were at a low ebb, especially in the public sector, and where the relationship between the Labour party, under James Callaghan, and the unions was at breaking point. The disputes and strikes of the time led to public opinion riding high against the unions.

Such legal changes were intended to curb trade union power and were effective in achieving this. The list of Acts passed and the measures they introduced are too many and complex to explore here. The law that gave trade unions immunity from being sued for calling a strike has been altered to narrow the protecton given to a very narrow band. There are requirements for a ballot in many situations, including calling a strike. The closed shop has been acted against legally. Employment protection measures, that are seen as restrictions on businesses, have been relaxed. The power of the Wage Councils was curbed and they were finally abolished in 1993. The pace of this change has not let up and more changes are on their way. Tables 2.2 and 2.3 show the recent changes in trade union membership and the size structure of trade unions.

The legislation of the 1980s was intended to curb union power and particularly to redistribute power from the union leaders (often referred to

Table 2.2 Trade union membership, 1977–90

Year	Number of unions	Number of members (000s)	% change
1977	481	12,846	+3.7
1978	462	13,112	+2.1
1979	453	13,289	+1.3
1980	438	12,947	−2.6
1981	414	12,106	−6.5
1982	408	11,593	−4.2
1983	394	11,337	−2.2
1984	371	11,086	−2.2
1985	370	10,821	−2.4
1986	335	10,539	−2.6
1987	330	10,475	−0.6
1988	314	10,238	−2.3
1989	309	10,158	−0.8
1990	306	9,810	−3.4

Source: Annual Abstract of Statistics

Table 2.3 Size structure of trade unions, 1990

Number of members	Number of unions	% of unions	% of total membership of unions
0–1,000	131	45.8	0.4
1,000–10,000	85	29.7	2.7
10,000–50,000	40	14.0	11.4
50,000–250,000	21	7.3	27.3
over 250,000	9	3.1	58.2

Source: Annual Abstract of Statistics

as 'barons' in the 1970s) to the supposedly moderate members. In many instances this policy backfired as the members did not act as predicted nor as hoped for. For example, the changes in legislation regarding political funds was supposed to reduce union involvement in politics, especially through their financial links to the Labour party. In virtually every instance the ballots were in favour of political funds. The requirement to elect leaders has, if anything, strengthened the position of union leaders. They are now elected to office and this gives them even greater legitimacy. Leaders such as Arthur Scargill have seen their position confirmed, if not enhanced, as a result of legislation that was designed to see them voted out of office! Overall the effect of the legislation was to repress union activity particularly by making some trade union activities unlawful or making trade unionists cautious because of the threat of court action.

2.2.4 Recruitment

The last section discussed the factors which affect levels of trade union membership. Unions are in the business of retaining members and admitting new members. During the decade of the 1970s union membership numbers rose and peaked in 1979. Also union density (*see* next section) rose. There were a number of reasons for this:

- There was a movement for blue and white collar workers, who previously tended not to be in a union, to join a union. This led to the growth of unions such as ASTMS (now MFU). With organisations growing larger (*see* last section) staff in these jobs looked to a union for representation and protection. There were only 16% of nonmanual workers in a union in 1965 and the figure is currently about 32%.
- Women workers have always been less unionised than men. The proportion of men to women in unions changed from 81:19 in 1945 to 66:34 in 1987. This is partially because there are more women at work now and also because unions deliberately targeted this group for recruitment, not least in pursuit of equal opportunities. Previously some unions did not admit women. For example the AEU did not allow women members until 1943!
- A further major factor in the growth of union membership during the 1970s was the rapid growth of the closed shop (*see* Section 15.3). The number of closed shops grew during this period in spite of the fact that the industries where the closed shop was traditionally very strong went into decline, e.g., the railways, mining and shipbuilding.

Clearly the political environment from 1974 onwards was very favourable to the unions. The Labour government passed legislation favourable to trade unions as part of the Social Contract set up between Harold Wilson (the then Labour Prime Minister) and prominent national trade union leaders such as Hugh Scanlon (AUEW), Jack Jones (TGWU) and David Basnett (GMBU). Unions were involved in government in a major way during this period, and this helped recruitment.

The pattern of trade union recruitment in this era was for unions to recruit within the groups of employees that were legitimately within the scope of that union. Whilst there was often an overlap between unions, the engineers recruited engineers, the teachers' union teachers, etc. Any disagreements were formally regulated by the Bridlington Agreement (*see* Section 2.2.1) and unions not operating this agreement could be expelled from the TUC.

During the 1980s the situation completely reversed. Many of the factors that caused an expansion in the 1970s reversed to cause a huge fall in the 1980s. This caused trade unions to rethink their recruitment policies and to develop strategies for survival. Some unions suffered greater decline than others and the pattern was not even. For example, the banking union BIFU retained its membership whilst ASTMS (after 1988 MFU) and APEX (now part of GMB) both saw a decline in membership although they all recruit people in similar occupations. The decline in union density in some industrial sectors is given in Table 2.4.

Table 2.4 Decline in union density in the 1980s

Sector	Union density 1984	Union density 1988
Non-manufacturing	58	49
Manufacturing	58	47
Energy	88	71
Transport	85	62
Public administration	78	59
Chemicals	58	41
Electrical engineering	51	32

Source: Labour Force Survey 1989. Dept. of Employment

To combat this loss of business unions adopted a number of strategies.

Mergers were commonplace and unions which were one time rivals found it in their mutual interests to join together. This has also led to a fundamental change in trade union structure in the UK (*see* next section). The list below shows some of the mergers:

Union	joining with	to form
ASTMS	TASS	MFU
GMB	APEX	GMB
CSU	SCPS	NUCPS
NGA	SOGAT	GPMU
POEU	CPSA	NCU
NATTKE	ABS	ETA

(*See* Abbreviations on page vii.)

The average size of union increased from 25,500 members to 28,500 between 1975 and 1987.

During the 1980s unions also had to work hard to retain recognition with firms and to gain recognition in new firms. Derecognition did not take place to any great extent and unions retained their recognition. The Workplace Industrial Relations Survey (1980–4) showed this to be the case. There were some extreme campaigns, particularly in America, for union recognition to be cancelled in firms as part of a wider anti-union campaign. This had little effect in the UK. One area where there was extensive derecognition was in the national newspaper industry where both the traditional print unions (NGA and SOGAT) and the journalists' union (NUJ) were derecognised by several newspapers.

However, unions have found it much more difficult to gain recognition with new firms on green field sites. One strategy employed by organisations locating on green field sites was to allow single-union recognition on management's terms. This led to single union agreements and to no-strike clause agreements (*see* Section 7.1.3). This caused a great deal of strife in the trade union movement and led to the Electricians' union being expelled from the TUC for acting contrary to TUC policy, which was not to accept single-union deals. Noticeably, several other unions now accept single-union deals, which is a triumph of pragmatism over principle. In some instances, notably in the national newspaper industry, companies relocated and only accepted unionism on the basis of a single-union agreement. Where new firms, locating on green field sites have suggested they would recognise a single union (to represent all employees), there have been so-called 'beauty contests' where unions wishing to gain recognition have presented themselves to the organisation's management. The prize for the best presentation won the single-union deal. Some unions distanced themselves from this process as it was felt to be degrading and not good trade unionism. It also went against previous practice, where unions, by and large, stuck to their own areas of interest and did not trespass onto the natural recruiting ground of other unions. The TUC developed a Code of Practice for regulating single-union deals in an attempt to defuse a potentially divisive situation.

Trade union policy has changed towards being more competitive in attracting new members. This has included emphasising the benefits of trade union membership, such as pension schemes, financial packages, mortgages, insurance and legal help. This policy is not always helpful to the trade union movement as a whole, as often unions are competing against each other in sectors where union membership is already quite high. The term 'market share' unionism has been adopted to describe how unions are competing to maintain their total membership in a declining membership base. Clearly in this situation there must be losers. The reason for this line of policy is due to the traditional union organisation failing to adapt to the new situation.

The TUC carried out surveys to identify target industries and groups for recruitment. The private service sector is seen as a market with potential for trade union recruitment. It is a different market characterised by part-time work, female employees, small establishments and self-employment. Unions need to appeal to employers by demonstrating the benefits of union recognition and to employees who seek representation and various forms of benefit. The two are interlinked, as a union without members will not gain recognition and members in a nonrecognised union are unlikely to maintain their membership.

Table 2.5 below shows trade union density in a range of industrial sectors and shows the decline in employment in sectors with traditionally high union density and the growth in employment in sectors with traditionally low union density.

Table 2.5 Union density for certain industrial sectors

Sector	Employment (000s) 1976–86	% Union density
Decline		
Engineering	493	55
Vehicle equipment	322	81
Metal and mineral products	299	68
Transport	123	85
Energy and water	61	88
Increase		
Banking, finance and insurance	709	43
Business services	383	21
Hotel and catering	211	21
Wholesale and distribution	162	32

A survey carried out in 1990 by Mason and Burns (reported in the *Industrial Relations Journal*) found that unions put specific recruitment policies as the priority and only pursued a merger, by policy, as a priority in a small number of cases: they also put seeking recognition as an important means of expanding recruitment. The report also identified that organisationally unions were slow to adapt to needs of marketing themselves and rarely had an official dedicated to this task, nor were funds made available in the budget for marketing. The prevailing philosophy was that it was everyone's job throughout the union structure.

The situation in the early 1990s is that the rate of decline has slowed down and membership numbers remain static. A further factor to take into account is that the system is dynamic. Unions are constantly losing and gaining members. Many unions are reaching the point of equilibrium. For example, the TGWU membership peaked at around 2 million in 1979 (as the largest single union). By 1991 membership had fallen to 1.1 million. However, in that year the union recruited 245,000 new members. Hence the pattern of membership has changed fundamentally, with large numbers leaving from traditional recruiting grounds to be replaced, in more modest numbers, from pastures new.

2.2.5 Union density

Union density is a measure of the proportion of the population who are trade union members. As with all statistical measures, it is necessary to define the terms used, i.e. trade union membership and population. The number of trade union members, should, on the face of it, be an easy statistic to quote. However, trade union membership numbers are often swollen by members who retain their membership into retirement and should not be counted. Some people who are categorised as economically inactive (i.e. are not in work and not registered as seeking work) may also retain union membership, especially where union membership is required to obtain a job some time in the future. There is also the question of staff association membership. The position of these is not always clear. Some are social clubs, others have a representational function whilst others do act as a trade union. Section 2.1 discussed this in detail.

The number of union members and trade unions is given in the Certification Officer's Annual Report. There is no compulsion to be listed but a union cannot apply for a Certificate of Independence (*see* Section 2.3.4) unless it is listed. In practice, the majority of unions are listed and these account for the vast majority of union membership but even this source is not 100% comprehensive.

It is also necessary to define 'population'. This can be taken as civil employment plus those who are unemployed. Another definition excludes the unemployed. A further definition includes the self-employed. Given these difficulties in defining the terms used, the figures for trade union density vary. This also gives rise to problems in interpreting comparative statistics, e.g., comparisons with other countries. To be a true comparison all countries should use exactly the same definitions, but this is a difficult task.

However, it is possible to give an indication of trade union density and to compare the trend over time (provided the definitions do not change over the period of comparison).

Union density has risen from about 10% in 1895 to about 43% in 1991, peaking at over

50% in 1979. In 1993 there were 24.7 million people in civilian employment of whom 3 million were self-employed. Some of this group cannot become union members, e.g., the police, and others are never likely to become members, e.g., top management.

Table 2.6 gives categorised figures for trade union density in Great Britain.

Table 2.6 Union density in Great Britain, 1989

Category	Number (000s)	Density %
Full-time	17,051	43
Part-time	4,995	22
Male (all)	11,862	44
full-time	11,315	45
part-time	546	12
Female (all)	10,187	33
full-time	5,736	40
part-time	4,449	23
Non-manual	12,357	35
Manual	9,659	43
Manufacturing	5,434	41
Non-manufacturing	16,584	37
Self-employed	3,425	9
All employees	22,049	39
All in employment	25,962	34

Source: Labour Force Survey

The Department of Employment carries out a Labour Force Survey which collects statistics of this nature on a sample basis. These figures are reported in the *Employment Gazette*. This gives an up-to-date picture but suffers from the fact that it is based on a sample of those in work. All sampling is subject to error and the results should be used with care. One study, using the Labour Force Survey results proposed an adjusted trade union membership figure of 9.4 million for 1987 compared to the figure of 10.5 million based on trade union returns.

The results of the survey give an insight into the spread of trade union membership among the various categories of employed people in Great Britain. Figures for Northern Ireland show a higher level of union density, with an overall figure of 49%.

Size of workplace is also significant. Workplaces with less than 6 people have a union density of 11%, those employing between 6 and 24 a density of 23%. This is for size of workplace (i.e. location) not size of firm.

The survey results give figures for union density in certain occupational categories. Table 2.7 gives the figures for certain occupations.

Table 2.7 Union density for certain occupations, 1989

Occupation	Males Employees	Density	Females Employees	Density
Non-manual	5,547	37	6,810	34
Managerial	3,953	37	2,547	49
Clerical	760	45	3,224	28
Other	834	29	1,040	28
Manual	6,286	50	3,373	31
Craft	2,749	52	381	38
General	140	56	16	n/a
Other	3,397	48	2,975	30
All employees	11,862	44	10,187	33

Union density is also a function of age and length of service. The union density among 16–19 year olds is 16%, rising steadily to 51% for the age band 35–39 years old, with a slight rise to 54% for those in the age band 50–59. For those employees with less than three months' service with their current employer, the union density is 16%, rising steadily with increased length of service. For those with over 20 years' service the union density figure is 64%.

Table 2.8 shows some international comparisons of trade union density.

Table 2.8 International comparisons of trade union density

Country	Union density (1985)
Austria	61
Australia	57
Belgium	84
Canada	37
Denmark	98
Finland	85
France	28
Ireland	51
Italy	45
Japan	29
Netherlands	37
Norway	61
Sweden	95
Switzerland	35
UK	52
USA	18

Source: J Kelly, Trade Unions and Socialist Politics, p. 269

The same source also notes that in the period 1979 to 1985 trade union density increased in several countries, with the greatest increase noted in Denmark, which had a 12% increase, followed by Belgium at 7%. The greatest decline in the same period was 7% in the USA followed by 6% in the UK, Netherlands and Italy.

These figures give a valuable insight into union membership and support the comments made in Section 2.2.3.

2.2.6 Types of union

For a century, up until the 1980s, there was a fairly distinct pattern to the structure of trade unions in the UK. From the emergence of the first unions there existed a categorisation of trade unions based on a union representing a specific group of employees. The categories identified were never rigid and none existed in a pure form. The exercise of categorising unions is useful as it helps understand some of the historical and current industrial relations issues. Whilst this analysis is not as pertinent in the 1990s, it still provides a useful framework.

Traditionally the four main types of union are:

● craft
● general
● industrial
● staff

Craft unions

Craft unions sought to recruit those who had a skill or trade, usually acquired by training or apprenticeship. These unions exhibited several features. Often entrance to the union was restricted to those who had served their time as an apprentice, the terms of which were often governed by the union. This system was used to restrict entry to a trade and was used to maintain wage levels by restricting the supply of labour. The bargaining power of these unions was through their members being in key positions and where the withdrawal of labour would be especially damaging. Also if skilled workers left a firm they would be hard to replace. Craft

unions tended to organise outside the workplace in order to maintain a degree of independence from the employer and to enhance labour mobility between firms. For a description of the historical development of trade unions, *see* Section 8.1.

Craft unions developed a system of strictly recruiting in one trade only, e.g., engineers into the AUEW, electricians into the EETPU, printers into the NGA. This pattern started to break down as unions amalgamated, particularly when a trade went into decline and the union found it hard to survive alone.

With this as the basis of trade union organisation, restrictive practices grew, whereby only certain jobs could be done by members of a particular union. This led to inflexibility and inefficiency, with each union out to protect its own interests. It also gave rise to a number of inter-union disputes which were difficult to resolve. An example of a restrictive practice would be when, for a simple repair task, a fitter might be called in to remove nuts and bolts, an electrician to disconnect the wiring and an instrument engineer to mend a faulty instrument when with some training one person could do the whole job.

Craft unions found that employers were particularly diligent in breaking down these practices in the 1980s (supported by the political climate and the favourable legislation). The pattern now is that the craft unions have amalgamated to the extent that the strict categorisation described above no longer exists. For example, the engineers (AEU) and electricians (EEPTU), long-time rivals, have now joined together. However, the pattern of behaviour and attitudes established over a long time will take some considerable time to disappear.

General unions

The general unions emerged later than the craft unions to fill the gap left by the craft unions. A person without a skill had no union to join, as the craft unions restricted entry. After a series of successful strikes in the late 1880s the general unions grew. They recruited widely and had no restrictions on membership. Their strength derived from numbers whereby a complete withdrawal of labour would help secure their demands. In times of recession employers had the greater power as they could easily recruit at lower wages and any strike threat was not serious. Many employers found that with a combination of general unions and craft unions, they had to conclude agreements with several unions, often having to balance the demands of one union with those of another. This led to a complex system of industrial relations for very many firms, as they tried to compromise between the conflicting demands of the various sectional interests and reach separate agreements with all the unions. Recent developments have tried to minimise these problems, such as single-table bargaining and single-union agreements (*see* Sections 6.1.3 and 7.1.3).

Examples of such general unions are the Transport and General Workers' Union (TGWU) and the Union of Shop, Distributive and Allied Workers (USDAW).

Industrial unions

Industrial unions seek to have in their membership all the workers in a particular industry. This idea has not had a strong following in the UK though it has in other countries, such as Germany (ironically advised by the British to do so after the war). There are, however, a few examples in the UK, one being the National Union of Mineworkers which recruited all underground miners until the rival union, the Union of Democratic Mineworkers was set up during the 1984 dispute. There was another union in the mining industry for the shotfirers and winders, the National Association of Colliery Overmen, Deputies and Shotfirers (NACODS) and another for colliery management, the British Association of Colliery Management. Two other examples of industrial unions, the National Union of Railwaymen and the National Union of Seamen, amalgamated to become the Railway, Maritime and Transport Union.

There are many arguments in favour of industrial unions. These include:

- fewer inter-union disputes
- simpler collective bargaining
- demarcation less of a problem
- a single voice presented to management

In 1924 the TUC passed a resolution, which was never acted upon, calling on unions to work towards a minimum number of unions by reorganising on an industrial basis. The well-established craft and general unions opposed this and hence the policy never operated.

Staff unions

Staff unions emerged later, in the second half of this century, to recruit from the nonmanual occupations including clerks, secretaries, supervisors, managers, technicians, etc. As the economy has become more of a service economy, a greater proportion of the working population is in these occupations (*see* Section 17.1). The public sector has also expanded, which employs many people in these occupations. These unions have less well-defined characteristics but their bargaining tends to be more sophisticated, e.g., they look to maintain 'staff' conditions such as improved pensions, better conditions of work, and longer holidays.

Examples of staff unions are Manufacturing, Science and Finance (MFU) and APEX (Association of Professional, Executive, Clerical and Computer Staff (now in the AEU).

Position today

With the changes that have taken place in the last two decades, the pattern of trade unionism in the UK has become blurred. The classification noted above is still recognisable but is not as dominant a factor in the UK system of industrial relations. The 1980s caused unions to retrench and rethink, and in doing so many have changed their policies, if only to survive. Many craft unions now cover several craft areas, general unions include some groups of skilled workers and staff unions have amalgamated with other non-staff unions.

2.3 Organisation

2.3.1 Local and national level

There is quite a diversity of organisation among trade unions. The general picture is that the members of a union in a department select (usually by election) a shop steward, or in the print industry a father or mother of the chapel. In a workplace with many shop stewards a senior steward or convenor is appointed. In some unions, usually the general unions, this will form the branch. In the craft unions the members join a branch nearby. At branch level there is a committee having at least a chairperson, secretary and treasurer. Above branch level there is district level. The district committee has representatives of stewards from branches within the district. The next level can be regional, whereby the country is split into, say, eight regions. Again there would be a committee at this level on which delegates from district level would sit. Finally there is national level. Every union has a National Executive which has the task of implementing union policy as laid down by the Annual Conference. The Executive Council consists of delegates from the regions plus the national full-time officers. Figure 2.3 is a diagram of the TGWU organisation, Figure 2.4 is a diagram of the AEU organisation and Figure 2.5 is a diagram of the EETPU organisation.

So far as the vast majority of union members are concerned, the branch is the main contact with the union. The shop steward is the person who deals with most matters. The involvement of full-time officials is minimal at local level as there are only a few officials to many thousand members. The AEU had 221 full-time officials for about 1 million members in 1986. It also has 28,000 shop stewards. Only when a situation gets critical are the full-time officials called in. In some unions the district full-time officer helps in negotiating the annual wage agreement. Often the disputes procedure involves the full-time official at the higher stages, e.g., local conference. Until then the shop steward or convenor acts to represent the workpeople.

2.3.2 Democracy and organisaton

An important aspect of union organisation is the influence of democracy at all levels. The decision making process, either procedural, e.g., rules and standing orders, or substantive, e.g., policy, negotiations and resolving disputes, is often conducted democratically. The appointment of officials is often by vote, especially for the shop steward.

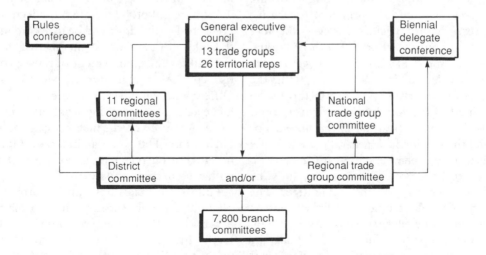

Fig 2.3 Transport and General Workers' Union organisation

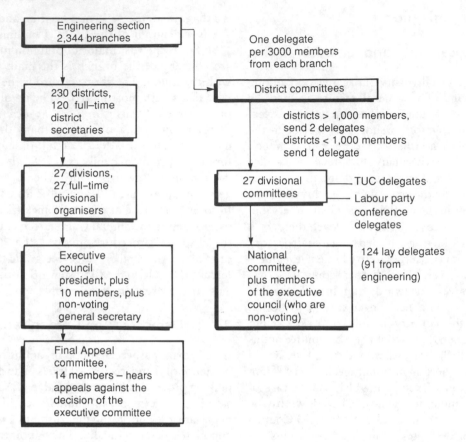

Fig 2.4 Structure of the Amalgamated Engineering Union

The Trade Union Act 1984 makes specific requirements relating to the election of voting members of a union's principal executive committee. The Act specifies that every member of such a committee (often called the National Executive Committee) who has the power to vote has to be elected in accordance with the provisions of the Act. This applies to those who are members of the committee by virtue of their holding some other position in the union. For example, the president or general secretary of a union is usually a member of the NEC *ex officio*. For them to have voting powers they must be elected as members of the committee. The provisions of the Act require that all the members of the union (of the relevant class of membership) are entitled to vote. This could be all the members or just the members of a particular section of the union. Voting has to be by secret ballot which is fairly and accurately counted. The method of voting can be by postal ballot or workplace ballot. The system of election is not prescribed so that it should be in accordance with the rules of the union. A member of the union can call for the enforcement of these provisions by reporting the matter to the Certification Officer who will investigate the matter and can make a declaration stating what the union ought to do. Alternatively the member can apply to the High Court. The court can make an enforcement order requiring the union to comply with the Act within a specified time period.

Full-time officials have an important role to play but can only act according to the policies approved by the various committees at whatever level. Invariably these committees have a majority of lay members elected on to the committee from local or district levels. These

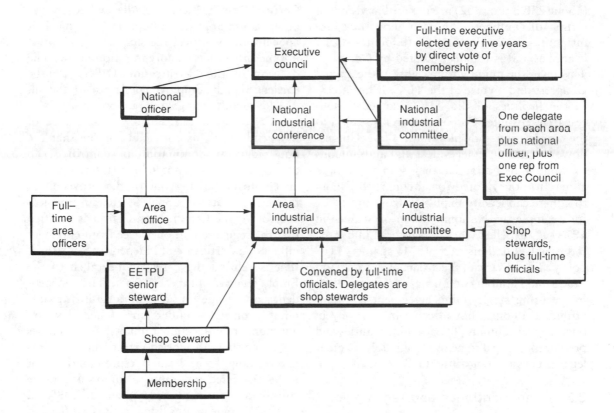

Fig 2.5 Industrial structure of the Electrical, Electronic, Telecommunication and Plumbing Union (EETPU)

delegates have a remit from their own members to support or oppose a particular issue. Through this the union, and its officers, are controlled by a democratic process.

A very important item of a union's organisation is the Rule Book, and the standing orders for conference and committees. The Rule Book contains the framework within which officials and members must operate. All aspects of the union are covered: objects, constitution, conference, councils, committees, voting, officers, financial, auditing, subscriptions, benefits, political fund, discipline, appeals and industrial action. The Rule Book can be altered only by a rules conference on which elected members sit. The rules themselves demand a level of democracy and participation by members hardly seen in any other organisation. The election of officers, voting on action, voting on agreements, voting on motions and policy are

some of the areas of democratic involvement of members in the union's activities.

Another important feature of a union is the annual or biennial conference. Here all manner of issues are debated of both internal and external interest. It is the policy laid down by conference that the national executive must adhere to. The various levels of the union, local, district and regional, send their delegates to the conference often with a mandate to vote a particular way on the various issues. This ensures, through democratic channels, that the branch membership's voices can be heard.

2.3.3 Affiliation

This is a process whereby a union joins the TUC. All the large unions are now affiliated and the TUC represents 90% of trade union members. As seen in section 2.2, a majority of unions (about 230 out of 302) are not affiliated, but in terms of numbers of members they are insignificant. A union can ask to join the TUC; it applies and is usually accepted by Congress. This gives the union voting rights at the annual Congress and a voice in the TUC. It has access to the facilities of the TUC, like education, research, Disputes Committee, and is subject to the constitution and rules of the TUC. Unions, however, remain independent and autonomous to conduct their affairs as they wish but have to adhere to policy voted for at congress. Failure to adhere can lead to expulsion from the TUC, for example the National Union of Seamen in 1972 was expelled when it registered under the Industrial Relations Act 1971 against TUC policy. The Electrical, Electronic, Telecommunication and Plumbing union was expelled in 1989 for securing single union agreements. A non-affiliated union is not affected in any way in operating as a union. The legal immunities and privileges attached to being a union rely on other legal processes, not affiliation.

2.3.4   Independence and registration

Unions, in order to have their funds protected against paying tax, have to go through a process of registration as trade unions. This was previously done by applying to the Registrar of Friendly Societies. Much of the problem with the Industrial Relations Act 1971 was that the Act required trade unions to submit their Rule Books for approval. The TUC made it policy that unions were not to register under the Act as they objected to this scrutiny of Rule Books. This had the effect of invalidating large parts of the Act. Now unions register under the Trade Union and Labour Relations Act 1974, by applying to the Certification Officer.

The Certification Officer is an employee of ACAS. A trade union is registered with the officer either because it was listed as a union prior to the 1971 Act or because it was registered under the 1971 Act. Applications can be made by a new trade union to become registered. It has to supply a copy of the Rule Book (but not for scrutiny) and some administrative details. The Certification Officer decides whether the organisation appears to be a trade union. If it appears so, the officer registers it as a union. If not the officer lets the organisation know. The decision of the Certification Officer can be challenged in the Employment Appeals Tribunal.

Additionally, a registered union can apply to the Certification Officer for a Certificate of Independence. This is issued to unions that 'are not under the domination or control of an employer . . . and is not liable to interference by an employer (arising out of the provision of financial or material supply) . . . tending towards control'. If the Certification Officer is satisfied that the registered union is free from employer influence a Certificate of Independence is issued. If it is refused the case can be taken to the Employment Appeals Tribunal. The independence of a trade union is important in that a number of rights under employment law are given only to independent unions. This includes rights for time off work for trade union duties and training, to be a safety representative, not to be dismissed for joining a union and to be consulted about redundancy plans. In 1990, 92 of the 287 trade unions listed by the Certification Officer did not have a Certificate of Independence.

2.3.5   Confederations

In some circumstances unions have seen it to be in their mutual interest to act jointly. This has occurred in many industries where a number of unions exist within the same industry. In order to negotiate an agreement with employers the unions join together, for the purposes of negotiating national agreements, into a separate organisation. This does not mean the unions have a common policy or that it is a movement towards one big union. It is a stable organisation that exists to fulfil a common purpose, i.e., to secure a national agreement with the employers. In their turn the employers form a federation (*see* Chapter 3).

Confederations date back to the 1890s and some still remain. There are around 40 federations today. Three of the largest confederations are listed in Table 2.9. Each one has its own organisation. The CSEU has full-time officials and a 33-person executive of delegates voted from the unions and the Confederation's district committees. The Confederation covers every manual and staff grade in the shipbuilding and engineering industry, from labourer to manager. There is an industry committee structure covering shipbuilding, aerospace, railways, foundries, power, manufacturing and public sector. The regional structure is based on 50 area committees covering the UK, including Northern Ireland. There was a very complex national agreement negotiated every year that covered the terms and conditions for this wide range of personnel in the various industries. However, in 1989 the Engineering Employers' Association decided to pull out of the national agreements' negotiations on pay and working time, mainly as a result of a failure to agree on a reduction in the working week, which had been contentious for several years. The procedural agreements will be maintained, as will the substantive agreements on matters other than pay and the working week. Negotiations on these last two will be conducted at local level where the EEF will be involved if the firms so wish.

Table 2.9 Largest federations

	Unions	Members (million)
Confederation of Shipbuilding and Engineering Unions	23	2
National Federation of Building Trades	19	0.5
Printing and Kindred Trades Federation	17	0.3

2.3.6 Trades councils

There are about 400 trades councils in England and Wales. They act as local agents for the TUC. They are composed of representatives of local trade unions and coordinate local trade union activity. Trades councils are registered with the TUC but do not have the right to send voting delegates to Congress; only individual trade unions do this. Trades councils have a longer history than the TUC, as it was the Manchester and Salford Trades Council that convened the first TUC in 1868. They now operate under rules approved by Congress. Some are more active than others. They do not have any great funds and are restricted in their political activities as their funds, and those of the contributing unions, must comply with the Trade Union Act 1913 (*see* Chapter 4). In England and Wales there is a regional council level and a national joint council at TUC level.

2.4 The TUC

2.4.1 The role of the TUC

The letters TUC stand for Trades Union Congress which is an Annual Conference (held in September) where delegates from all affiliated unions meet. The issues discussed range widely from internal TUC/union affairs to the economy and other political issues. The TUC acts as an organisation which all unions can join to formulate collective policy which can then be the voice of the trade union movement as a whole. The TUC originated in 1868, being a local affair where 34 delegates met under the auspices of the local trades council. The idea was to form some central national organisation for the trade unions to formulate common policy. The TUC moved to Birmingham in 1869, in which year a Parliamentary Committee was set up, to look after member interests in legislation in the House of Commons. After a one-year gap the TUC moved to London, where the headquarters are now situated. The 1871 TUC had delegates representing 289,000 members from 49 unions. The number of affiliated unions grew (*see* Section 2.2.1).

The role of Congress is to:

- consider the report of the General Council submitted to Congress
- debate and take decisions on the motions put before congress. These become the policy of the TUC which the General Council has to implement
- elect the General Council

A full list of the objectives of the TUC is given in the TUC Rule Book. Increasingly the TUC has been recognised as the spokesbody of the trade union movement on matters affecting members, e.g., health and safety, welfare, education, job security, social security and other matters. It acts as a pressure group to influence government policy. The TUC is not attached to any political party. It has no direct link with the Labour party. Individual unions can, and do, affiliate to the Labour party and set up political funds to help the party. In 1980, 61 of the 113 affiliated unions were also affiliated to the Labour party, hence there is an indirect link but TUC policy does not become Labour party policy or vice versa. In 1971 a Labour Party Liaison Committee was set up to provide a forum to exchange views on a number of topics, initially legislation, now widened. In practice the Labour party and the TUC are close together on policy but not always so. In 1978 the Labour government wanted a pay policy (5% limit) but the TUC would not accept it.

The TUC's role within the trade union movement is only advisory and it has no powers of its own, it cannot intervene directly in disputes (but *see* Rules 11 and 12 in Section 2.5.4), nor does it do any negotiating at company or national level. The individual unions remain autonomous to do what they decide within their own organisation. The only power the TUC has is for Congress itself to expel a member union. If TUC policy, or the recommendations of one of its committees, is not acted upon or is ignored, a motion can be carried to expel the union. Generally the unions act in the interests of solidarity and voluntarily accept TUC policy.

The important role of the TUC is to be the spokesbody of the trade union movement. The TUC gains much political power from being able to speak on behalf of the eight million or so trade union members who are affiliated to it. Governments have responded to this by involving the TUC in discussions on government policy through the normal processes of consultation. This is carried out informally or through TUC representatives being on various committees, commissions, public bodies and quangos. The TUC also acts as a pressure group by formulating its own policies on a range of issues such as economic policy, the welfare state and legislation and acts as a lobby in its own right. It often coordinates action on the trade union movement's response to government action. This occurred, for example, in the opposition to the 1969 Labour government's White Paper entitled *In Place of Strife*, which ultimately led to the withdrawal of the Paper after the TUC had given a 'solemn undertaking' to carry out some internal reforms of the trade unions. More recently the TUC has campaigned against the legislation of the Conservative government where it has been TUC policy to oppose totally the changes and not to cooperate in any way. This has led to some internal problems with unions who have used the 1980 Employment Act's provisions to claim government money for postal ballots. This is viewed as cooperation and could lead to disciplinary action against such unions.

The ability of the TUC as a body to influence events depends on the nature of the government. The Conservative administration from 1979 onwards has allowed the TUC only the minimum of influence, whereas the Labour administration of 1974–9 saw the TUC maximise its influence with agreements between itself and the government. Currently the membership of the TUC is falling, due to the effects of unemployment and government legislation, hence its political power diminishes accordingly.

2.4.2   Congress

Each affiliated union is entitled to send one delegate per 5,000 members. In practice the very large unions send only a proportion of delegates. Congress would, under this rule, become too big (about 1,800 compared to the present 1,000 delegates) to accommodate. Also the smaller unions would be swamped. If voting is on a show of hands then the smaller unions get a proportionately greater voice, as they send a full delegation. Delegates from each union vote in line with their own union's policy.

Congress discusses the General Council's Annual Report. This is sent out five weeks before Congress for the unions to read and consider. It also contains the agenda. Each union can propose two amendments to this. The motions to be debated are submitted by member unions seven weeks before Congress but after having been passed at their own annual conference. Often motions on the same issue are put together as a composite motion. The actual business of conference is arranged by a general purposes committee of members of Congress who are not members of Council.

Voting at Congress is initially by a show of hands or voice. If the chairperson thinks there is an overwhelming majority one way or the other then they say so. If the split is even, the chairperson or a delegate, can call for a card vote. This is then a formal vote where each union has one 'card' for each 1,000 members, or part of 1,000. The cards are counted and the greater number voting one way carries or defeats the motion. This gives the unions a vote in relation to their size. Now the top six unions can carry Congress if they all vote the same way. These are, in order of size, the TGWU, GMB, NALGO, AEU, MSF and NUPE. However, the 13 smallest unions, below 1,000 members, still have a card to vote with. Congress also votes in the new General Council including a chairperson and vice-chairperson.

The motions passed at Congress form the basis of TUC policy. It is the duty of the General Council to pursue this policy and for the member unions to conform to it. The resolutions of Congress are a fundamental part of the trade union movement as these represent the views and intentions of the trade union movement on a whole range of issues. While Congress's policy is not binding on any government or political party it is of importance to the Labour party as any resolutions that are passed at Congress, if they are included in the agenda at the Labour party conference, are likely to be carried by the block votes of the trade unions. Nevertheless, TUC policy is not automatically Labour government policy nor is it reflected in the Labour party's manifesto.

While there is no legal compulsion for member unions to follow TUC policy, it is custom for unions to adhere to that policy. Conflicts can arise within individual unions when their own

conferences have voted for a certain policy which is opposite to the policy of Congress. If the matter cannot be resolved (and frequently it is, by negotiation), Congress can expel a union that acts against TUC policy.

In 1993 there were 72 trade unions affiliated to the TUC, with a total membership of 7.8 million. The number of unions affiliated continues to fall, mainly due to mergers and amalgamations of unions. The number of members has fallen in line with the national fall in trade union membership. Affiliation fees, in 1993, were £1.33 per member per year.

2.4.3 General Council

In 1992 this consisted of 53 members elected at Congress plus the General Secretary and the Assistant General Secretary of the TUC. These members, while full-time trade union officials, are responsible and accountable to Congress, not to their individual unions. Council was instituted in 1921 and was split into 18 trade groups plus a women's section. The trade groups represented the cross-section of affiliated unions.

The present composition of the Council is based on the following formula:

Section	Total seats	for unions sized (000s)
A	6	1,200–1,449
	5	900–1,199
	4	650– 899
	3	400– 649
	2	200– 399
		unions >200,000 members and with 100,000 women members must nominate 1 woman
B	1	100– 199
		(not including any section D seats)
C	8	<100
D	4	women's seats for unions <200,000 members

Council implements the policy of Congress and acts during the year on developments as they arise. Council meets once a month. It acts as an executive body to carry out policy voted for at Congress, within the rules and standing orders.

A large amount of Council's work is delegated to subcommittees which report back to the full General Council for its approval or otherwise. Currently there are nine committees – Finance and General Purposes, Economic, Education and Training, Employment Policy and Organisation, International, Social Insurance and Industrial Welfare, Equal Rights and European Strategy and Trade Union Education. In addition to this the General Council has membership of many outside committees like the National Economic Development Council (Neddy) and sits with employers' representatives on 'quangos'. These include the Advisory, Conciliation and Arbitration Service (ACAS) and the Health and Safety Commission (HSC). This enables the unions' voices to be heard at the highest level. The unions no longer rely on lobbying MPs as their only way of getting their voices heard.

The TUC has a permanent staff of 220 and headquarters at Congress House, London. The nine departments fall roughly into line with the subcommittees listed in the last paragraph. There is also a small staff in the regional education offices.

There are other functions carried out by the TUC. Several industrial committees have been set up to coordinate the activities of the various unions in different industries. They compare and contrast details covering a wide range of topics. Currently there are committees for steel, construction, local government, health, energy, nuclear energy, transport, hotels, catering and tourism, printing, textiles and clothing, distribution, food, drink and tobacco and financial services. The committees are supported by the TUC but they are not accountable to the General Council in the same way as the standing committees.

2.4.4 Rules

There are three rules of the TUC that are of interest to relations between the TUC and member unions and also to industrial relations generally.

- Rule 11 requires affiliated unions to keep the TUC informed of disputes between unions

and employers and between union and union. The general policy is one of nonintervention. If, however, other workpeople are likely to be involved, then the General Council can arrange for consultations. It can then give its opinion and advice. If the union or unions concerned refuse the assistance or advice then they can be suspended or finally expelled from the TUC under Rule 13.

- Rule 12 requires the General Council to use its influence to promote a settlement in disputes between two or more unions. No union should allow a stoppage of work under such a dispute until it has informed the TUC. The General Secretary can refer the matter to the Disputes Committee. If the union or unions fail to carry out the decision of the committee it can be suspended or finally expelled from the TUC.

- Rule 13 enables the General Council to investigate the conduct of a union if it believes the activities of the organisation are detrimental to the interests of the trade union movement, or the principles or policy of Congress. If, upon investigation, this is found to be true, then the union can be suspended by the General Council or finally expelled from the TUC. Only Congress can expel a union and there is a right of appeal and possible readmission.

Some unions have been expelled under these rules. The National Union of Seamen was expelled in 1928 for supporting a nonpolitical union. In 1961 the Electrical Trade Union was expelled for ballot-rigging. In 1972 the National Union of Seamen and the National Union of Bank Employees were expelled for acting contrary to TUC policy on the Industrial Relations Act 1971. The TGWU was temporarily expelled for not acting upon the decision of the Disputes Committee. In 1988 the EETPU was expelled from the TUC by Congress for refusing to accept the General Council's directives to accept two Disputes Committee awards. The EETPU has been a 'moderate' union since the ballot-rigging incident, after which communists were debarred from office.

The EETPU was prepared to enter into single-union agreements, particuarly with the newspaper proprietors after they had moved operations from Fleet Street. This brought the union into dispute with the print unions, who traditionally organise a major part of that industry. The EETPU was one of the first TUC affiliated unions which applied for, and used, government money for ballots although many other unions followed suit. A rival, TUC-affiliated union, the Electrical and Plumbing Industries Union, was formed after this incident to recruit disaffected EETPU members.

2.5   International bodies

The TUC is affiliated to three international trade union organisations:

- **The International Confederation of Free Trade Unions**   This was founded in London in 1949. In 1989 it had a membership of 88m from 142 organisations in 97 countries. There is a biennial Congress and an executive board of 30 to implement policy and to look after more immediate business. The ICFTU encourages the growth of free trade unions (i.e., those free of government interference). Member organisations contribute to funds, which are mainly used for educational purposes in developing countries.
- **European Trade Union Confederation**   This was formed in 1973 with all the major European (not necessarily EEC) countries affiliating through their national bodies. In 1989 there were 36 organisations representing 44m trade unionists from 21 countries. The idea is to provide a trade union organisation that monitors economic matters in Europe. The EC has, in its constitution, to consult with unions and this body makes for a coordinated approach. There are committees within the EC on which unions have representatives (one-third of the seats) and the ETUC is a useful body in which to formulate policy.

- **International Labour Organisation**   This was part of the now defunct League of Nations, started in 1919. The ILO remained intact and is now part of the Economic and Social Council of the United Nations. Its aim is to promote social justice by establishing humane conditions of work. It does this through international standards, information and assistance. The ILO conference meets annually with delegates from the trade unions (TUC), employers (CBI) and government. Conventions can be passed which, if ratified by a country's parliament, become obligatory for the member states to bring their practices and laws into line with. Recommendations and Resolutions of Conference are not subject to ratification and are only advisory. The ILO publishes standards which are used, for example threshold limit values for inhaled substances and standard values for works study engineers.
- **Trade Union Advisory Committee**   This is an organisation of national trade unions which seeks to influence the Organisation of Economic Cooperation and Development (OECD). The OECD is an international organisation of the developed industrialised countries of the world.

Multiple-choice questions

2.1   The number of unions in the country now is about:
   (a)   1,000
   (b)   500
   (c)   300
   (d)   150

2.2   The largest number of unions ever was about:
   (a)   2,000
   (b)   1,800
   (c)   1,400
   (d)   500

2.3   The percentage of unions affiliated to the TUC is about:
   (a)   95%
   (b)   75%
   (c)   50%
   (d)   25%

2.4 The number of trade union members now is about:
   (a) 18 million
   (b) 15 million
   (c) 10 million ⟲
   (d) 8 million

2.5 The TUC represents about what percentage of the working population?
   (a) 90%
   (b) 60%
   (c) 45%
   (d) 33% ⟲

2.6 What percentage of the working population is in a union?
   (a) 90%
   (b) 65%
   (c) 40% ⟲
   (d) 30%

2.7 What percentage of trade union membership is in nonmanual occupations?
   (a) 30% ⟲
   (b) 25%
   (c) 15%
   (d) 10%

2.8 What percentage of trade union membership are women?
   (a) 45%
   (b) 35%
   (c) 25% ⟲
   (d) 15%

2.9 Put the following types of union in order of emergence:
   3 (a) Industrial
   1 (b) Craft
   4 (c) White collar
   2 (d) General

2.10 Put the following unions in order of size:
   4 (a) NUM
   1 (b) UNISON
   3 (c) AEU
   2 (d) TGWU

Mini-questions

2.1 State the fundamental objective of all trade unions.
2.2 List three other objectives of a trade union.
2.3 State three of the main functions of a union.
2.4 State two areas of potential recruitment for trade unions.
2.5 Sketch a graph of the pattern of trade union membership this century.
2.6 Explain what a craft union is and give three examples.
2.7 Explain what a general union is and give three examples.
2.8 Explain what an industrial union is and give three examples.
2.9 Explain what a staff union is and give three examples.
2.10 Define the term affiliation.
2.11 Differentiate between registration and independence.
2.12 Describe what a confederation is.
2.13 State what the letters TUC stand for.
2.14 Describe what a card vote is.
2.15 State what the Disputes Committee of the TUC deals with.

Further reading

TUC, *Organising for the 1990s*
N Millward and M Stevens, *British Workplace Industrial Relations*, Dartmouth, 1992, 1-85521-321-4
B Sherman, *The State of the Unions*, Wiley, 1986, 0-471-91146-1
K Hawkins, *Trade Unions*
W E J McCarthy, *Trade Unions*, Penguin, 1987, 0-14-022641-9
K Coates and T Topham, *Trade Unions in Britain*, Fontana, 1988, 0-00-686121-0
H Pelling, *A History of British Trade Unionism*, Penguin, 1988, 0-14-013640-1

3

Employers

3.1 Organisations and their management

3.1.1 Organisations – diversity and development

The previous chapter dealt with trade unions generally, their aims, functions and organisation. This chapter is an attempt to do the same for what is often termed 'the other side' of industrial relations, that is management or the employer. While unions are identifiable and have a certain commonality about them, the term management or employer is not so easily defined. One reason for this diversity is that while the management function exists in all organisations, the organisations themselves can be so different. In our economy there are several forms of organisation: sole trader, partnership, private company, public company, multinational corporation, nationalised industries, government departments, local authority, public authority, cooperatives, worker cooperatives and industrial partnership. All these, if they are of any size, have an identifiable management structure. The exact nature, the aims and functions of the management side of the organisation will be somewhat different in all of them. Table 3.1 shows the characteristics of the common forms of business.

One of the reasons why it is difficult to define management is that over time there have been many changes. The Industrial Revolution saw the emergence of a new class of entrepreneur. The first factories were owner occupied and managed by the same person. The owner was the manager and employer. Gradually there emerged the family firm where ownership was still with the few and the functions of management were carried out by the owners. Also partnerships flourished, which are again characterised by the owners managing.

This situation was reflected in the industrial relations of the time. The trade unions had not emerged and were not of any consequence until the last quarter of the nineteenth century. Owners were in a powerful position. They could hire and fire as they pleased and the workers had to take the terms and conditions offered, with little negotiation. The social order of the day very much influenced this as well. Owners were in a newly emerged middle class with authority over those they employed by virtue of their social status. The law confirmed this attitude and talked of the relationship between owner and worker as that of master and servant. The contract of employment was (and still is often) called a contract of service. The ordinary laws of contract applied to the contract of employment and few changes were made until the late nineteenth century (*see* Chapter 8). In fact until 1875 a striking worker could be liable to criminal prosecution. Industrial relations in this atmosphere were not likely to flourish and the function, as we know it today, did not exist then.

Not until the legal changes in the mid-nineteenth century did limited companies emerge and not until 1907 were private companies allowed to exist. From the turn of the century onwards, companies became the important form of business. This change from individual or

Table 3.1 Types of business

Business		Liability	Stability	Legal	Identity	Capital	Formalities	Management
Sole trader	Simple	Fully liable to extent of personal wealth	Business ends with personal involvement	No legal requirements (except name)	The owner(s) is/are the business	Provided by the trader/ partner	Register name (if need be)	By the owner
Partnership		Includes all partners (except limited)		A few legal requirements	No separate identity		Can draw up a deed to formalise relations	By the partners
Private company		Liability limited to extent of investment	Business is perpetual, until dissolved by a process of law	Must conform to a large number of legal rules	Company is a separate legal body	Provided by shareholders	Created by a process of law, under the Companies Act	Management divorced from ownership
Public company								Owners are involved through the AGM
Nationalised industries	↓ Complex	Answerable to a minister and to Parliament	Perpetual, at will of Parliament	Rules specified by Act of Parliament	Separate legal body	Provided by state	Created by Act of Parliament	An independent management answerable to a minister

family ownership and management to a company has many implications. One is that there is a separation of ownership and management (except with small private companies). This saw the emergence of a new phenomenon, that of a paid, professional manager, who is someone employed by the business to manage its affairs. The employer for both worker and management is the company. This means that the company is managed by a section of its employees. This gave rise to the identification of a group labelled as management. It is this group that the other employees deal with and with whom the unions, as they became widespread, carried out their function. Modern industrial relations' practice is based on the dealings of the unions, and their representatives, with the group identified as management. The management are not the owners, which contrasts with the previous position. A second important aspect of this change was the identity of the company as a separate legal entity. An employee was now employed by a fictitious body called *the company*. The contract of employment was not with the individual owner (as had been the case) but with a corporate body, the company. Obviously any questions arising from the contract of employment have to be dealt with by a real person, i.e., a manager. Any legal responsibilities arising are answerable by real people, again the managers or directors.

The present-day position is still one of change. The trend in the postwar years is a movement towards very large organisations. Increasingly a greater percentage of our manufacturing capacity is controlled by fewer companies. It is estimated that soon 60% of manufacturing capacity will be owned by the 200 largest companies. Another factor in this trend is the growth of multinational companies, whereby a company's ultimate ownership is in the hands of a foreign organisation. For example, the UK car industry, with the main exceptions of the Rover Group and Rolls-Royce, is foreign owned. The movement towards large organisations is seen in the public sector. The National Health Service employs 1.022 million and the civil service 553,900, including defence.

The most common form of organisation is the company. A company can be limited by shares or limited by guarantee and be public or private. The majority of people in Britain work for a company of one sort or another. There are about 15,000 public companies and about 500,000 private companies in the UK. A company is a separate legal entity set up by a process of law and has a separate legal personality. The company is the 'person' that employs the employees and it is the company with whom all the contracts are made. However the company created by a process of law (under the Companies Act 1985) cannot act on its own. It has to employ real people actually to do the tasks required for it to function. This is the role of management. It is the management that operates and carries out the functions regarded as managing. To this end each company has a management structure.

The management structure varies from company to company, but traditionally follows a hierarchical pattern. At the top is a board of directors. This is elected by the shareholders to look after their interests. By law the board has to act in the best interests of the shareholders. The board is responsible for setting policy and making major decisions. The board consists of directors who may be executive or nonexecutive. The nonexecutive directors do not participate in the day-to-day running of the company. The executive directors have responsibilities for the main operational areas, e.g., production, sales, finance, personnel, engineering, marketing, etc. Below the board are the executives, managers and supervisors of the company who have their responsibilities for the management of the company. These tend to go down in steps from the executive responsible for the function, to the managers responsible for a department in that function down to the supervisor of each section in that department. In this way the function of management is broken up into separately identifiable roles. For example a despatch supervisor is responsible to a production manager who is in turn responsible to a factory manager who reports to the production director. *See* Fig. 3.1 for a typical organisation chart.

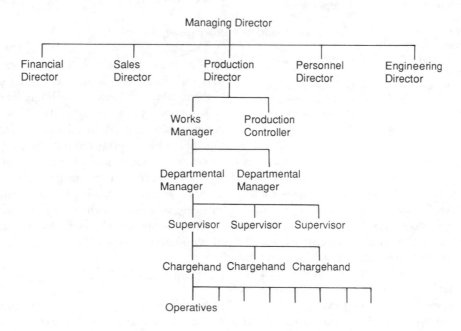

Fig 3.1 Typical management structure

3.1.2 Role of management

A basic feature of all formal organisations (as opposed to social groups) is that they have specific objectives. The prime reason for the existence of an organisation is to achieve these objectives. The precise objectives for an organisation will vary depending on the type of organisation. In the private sector the prime objective is to make profit. In the public sector it is to provide an adequate service. Charities have similar service objectives while other organisations such as clubs, societies and institutions exist to achieve some formal objectives. Trade unions (as we have already noted in Chapter 2) have their own objectives. Table 3.2 compares some typical objectives for a private sector company and for a public sector service organisation.

Table 3.2 Typical organisational objectives

Company	Hospital
	Provide:
1 Maximise profit potential.	1 A health service to the community.
2 Survival of the organisation.	2 Facilities for surgery and after care.
3 Plan for future expansion.	3 Emergency service.
4 Secure a greater % of the available market.	4 Expert medical advice.
5 Satisfy customer requirements.	5 Health care advice.
6 Utilise resources efficiently.	6 Diagnostic service and medical treatment.
7 Take care of employees/community.	7 Work within budgetary constraints.

Arising out of the existence of organisational objectives is the fundamental role of management, that is to achieve the objectives of the organisation. Whatever the type of organisation a managerial role has to be performed by someone or by a body/committee that is primarily responsible for the achievement of objectives. The manner in which this is accomplished varies, and some of this variety has been mentioned in the context of industrial relations in Section 1.3. Attached to this role are the concepts of authority, responsibility and accountability. These bear some examination as they have some relevance to industrial relations.

Authority

This is the legitimate power to get things done. Within an organisation action is required to achieve objectives and this is accomplished by people being given authority and by them, in turn, using this authority. This may derive from either position, personality or expertise. In most organisations the source of authority is a mixture of these. Traditionally, authority is derived from position within the organisation, whereby someone holding a certain office is vested with a certain amount of authority by virtue of the position held. The chief executive has the greatest authority with the junior positions possessing least authority. Increasingly it is the case that authority is accepted not merely because of the position held by a person but also by their ability to motivate or lead the people subordinate to them. This touches on the human relations aspects which will be mentioned later. In some instances authority derives from technical expertise, for example a functional specialist who gives advice to others.

Responsibility

It is a well-founded rule of management that arising naturally out of authority is responsibility, and that these should be co-equal. If someone is given authority to accomplish certain tasks (in order to achieve objectives) then that person is responsible for ensuring that the tasks are completed satisfactorily. Authority can be delegated from a senior manager to a junior manager but responsibility cannot be delegated. The delegator is still ultimately responsible to the superior for the tasks to be performed, regardless of who carries them out.

Accountability

Directly arising out of responsibility is the concept of managers being accountable to their superiors for their actions. In the traditional (and commonest) form of organisation, accountability moves up the organisation from subordinate to superior and finally resides with the chief executive/chairperson/managing director. In companies, ultimate accountability is to the shareholders as the shareholders delegate the running of the organisation to the managers it appoints. In the public sector this accountability may be to a board of governors, a district council, county council, secretary of state or Parliament.

Recently there have been proposals to amend company law so that the directors' accountability is not only to shareholders but also to employees, to customers and to the community. Firms now have to make a statement in their annual reports on health and safety and include paragraphs on employment policies, the industrial relations situation and other wider issues. The Employment Act 1982 states that the directors' report should contain statements on the action that has been taken to maintain and develop arrangements relating to providing employees with information, consulting employees prior to taking decisions, involvement of employees in the company's performance (e.g., through share schemes) and the steps taken to create an awareness of the factors affecting company performance. This is all evidence of the move to widen the accountability of companies. In the public sector, such legal constraints do not exist and public bodies, particularly elected bodies, have evolved such policies as a response to their accountability to the public who elected them.

These concepts bear on the industrial relations system because the manager in practice is primarily charged with achieving organisational objectives and is given authority to do so but finds that conflicts arise which need to be resolved. Employees have a loyalty not only to the firm (and its system of authority), but to their family, their work colleagues and their trade union.

Trade unions are viewed as being a countervailing authority to the authority of the organisation. In some instances trade unions are a challenge to the ultimate authority of management and are seen as a check on the managerial process. Indeed it was for this purpose that trade unions were originally formed. Individuals within the firm were powerless to challenge the authority of the owner/manager. Any individual who did so ran the risk of being dismissed. However, collectively union members were able to provide a check on any perceived management excesses and through the threat of strike action were able to counteract any moves to dismiss workers. Members, whilst having a loyalty to the firm, often choose to be loyal to the authority of the union. One of the principles of good trade unionism is solidarity within the movement and the strength of this cannot be underestimated. Any challenge to this solidarity (say from management) will often strengthen the resolve of the group. Hence the authority of management cannot be envisaged as the only system of authority in an organisation. The ideal of management authority implies that management has the right to manage. This may not always be accepted by everyone. Often industrial conflicts are seen as a challenge to managerial authority and the dispute becomes a power struggle to decide 'who manages'. Interestingly the EEF's joint dispute procedure with the CSEU has in its preamble a statement that 'the union recognizes management's right to manage'.

Other conflicts arise in organisations such as the clash between organisational objectives and the personal objectives of employees. The objective of a company to maximise profit can conflict with the employee's objective of maximising earnings. The industrial relations system is clearly required to deal with this situation. The objective of the efficient use of resources can lead to proposals to reduce the labour force (say by investing in efficient and labour saving machinery) which clashes with the employees' objective of retaining their jobs. The industrial relations system deals with this by negotiations in which both parties seek an acceptable solution. Negotiation implies the acceptance of compromise and in doing so both sides may have to amend their specific objectives. As a result of negotiating an agreement, for example on introducing new technology, the organisation may have to give certain guarantees on jobs which, in the absence of a trade union's negotiating power, it would not have given. Nevertheless, the compromise reached then assures continuity of operation which is to the advantage of both sides.

3.1.3 Functions of management

In order to achieve the objectives of the organisation, those who are designated managers have to perform certain tasks. The following functions of management are fundamental to all organisations. The nature and extent of each function will depend on the type of organisation and the manner in which each function is performed will depend on the style of management.

Planning

Planning is the function of making decisions about the organisation's future activities, i.e., it is directed to the achievement of objectives. It can be long-term strategic planning (looking decades ahead) through to short-term operational planning (looking at tomorrow's work). Part of the planning function is to determine how objectives are going to be achieved. A firm may wish, for example, to increase its market share by $x\%$ or to increase productivity by $y\%$. These need to be translated into operational plans. At this level there may well be implications for the industrial relations system within the firm. At the detailed level of planning, one aspect of the operation that must be planned is the level of staffing. In order to raise productivity there may be plans to introduce automated machinery or plans to redefine jobs to make them more flexible. Necessarily this will have implications for industrial relations within the firm. Such plans will eventually have to be accepted (although reluctantly) by the workforce. The implementation of the plan will need careful consideration of this aspect. The plan may include a reduction in the level of staffing and if this is not handled properly the plan may be jeopardised.

Coordination

The function of coordination is that every department works together towards achieving organisational objectives. This function is important in larger organisations, but with the trend towards much larger organisations this function assumes even greater importance. One of the activities that needs to be part of the function of coordination is the personnel aspect of a plan. As plans are drawn up at a detailed level and implemented, the aspects of staffing levels, recruitment, wage levels, bonus schemes, job evaluation, job descriptions and possibly redundancy should all be examined where necessary. This will involve coordination between the various departments within the organisation. Where formal procedures exist these should become part of the plan with the timings coordinated. If a procedure requires prior consultation then the procedure should be instigated. If prior approval is needed from a consultative body, then this should be sought in good time.

Control

The function of control is checking that activities are going according to plan and, if necessary, making adjustments (either to activities or plans). Once plans have been made, it is imperative that activities are supervised to ensure that the objectives of the plan are achieved. Planning always includes a degree of uncertainty and if what has been planned does not happen, adjustments have to be made. This adjustment can be to the operations or to the plans themselves. For example, commercial plans include presumptions about economic factors (rates of inflation, growth, exchange rates, etc.). As these vary from those presumed, the plans may need adjusting. Operational plans on what products to make over a period of time need controlling in the light of machine breakdowns, raw material availability and labour resources. The ability of a department to react to such situations has implications in industrial relations. If a machine breaks down, and if there are very strong lines of demarcation between the process operators' jobs and the maintenance staff jobs, then the machine must await the attendance of the maintenance staff. The job may simply be tightening a nut but time will be wasted awaiting the simple repair. Where a firm has greater freedom the operator may be able to carry out the repair. In other situations a supervisor may require operators to move from one job to another. Again this may or may not be a workable solution depending on the degree of flexibility allowed by the system. Increasingly firms are negotiating (or imposing) changes in working practices so that supervisors and managers have greater flexibility in making adjustments to plans as operations proceed.

Communication

Communication is transmitting and receiving information, and this underpins all organisational functions. Management needs to make known its policies, aims, plans and instructions to its employees, and there needs to be a system of feedback from employees to management. The bulk of communication is oral and this can be within a formal framework (e.g., committees) or informally (e.g., *ad hoc* meetings, phone calls). The effectiveness of the first three functions, already described, depends on effective communication. The best laid plans will not become reality if they are not communicated to those who will implement them. It is important in industrial relations that communications are effective. The manner in which each function is performed depends on the style of management. Whether employees are told about plans for the future, whether they are consulted or whether they are involved in the decisions is a question of managerial style. As we shall see later in Chapter 16, industrial democracy raises these questions. It also raises questions relating to the role of management. In some organisations the style is closed and employees are told very little. While management may see this as enabling them to remain fully in control, the employees are likely to be suspicious and probably reactionary as a result of being kept in

the dark. Other organisations have a more open style whereby employees are kept informed. This may include a formal system of communication through a works council, consultative committees or briefing groups. This style induces trust and, whilst problems may exist, there is a mechanism for resolving them. Some topics are within the ambit of formal negotiations procedures, so such topics are referred to the negotiating machinery.

3.2 Management in practice

3.2.1 Developments in management thought

Over the past century or so there is a history of developments to provide a set of management principles and to gain an understanding of the management of organisations. Needless to say there has been a gradual evolution of thinking on what constitutes good management. Also there is no single set of principles which applies universally; there are some guidelines on which good management should be based. As we saw in the last section and will state again in the next section, the style of management utilised is dependent both on the firm's situation and environment. A small firm, operating locally, producing high-tech components, owned by its founder who is the Managing Director will be managed quite differently from the branch of a large multinational, with a stock market quotation producing fast-moving consumer goods.

This section aims to provide a brief sketch of the history of management thought. The book list at the end of the chapter provides suggestions for further reading.

Scientific management

One of the first attempts to provide a framework for the management of organisations was developed at around the turn of the century. The name synonymous with scientific management is that of F W Taylor. He worked in a number of engineering firms and a steel works and developed his ideas at a practical level as he sought to improve the efficiency of the firms he worked for. He applied scientific principles (often simple ones) to practical situations to improve efficiency. This led to the practice of planning work by determining the best method to be used by the workforce. This function, he stated was a management task (quite a new idea for the time!). It was also management's job to select and train the best person for the job and to provide a monetary incentive for greater effort. He also suggested that the role of the generalist supervisor should be split into eight specialist roles, with each person acquiring specialist knowledge and skills. These specialisms included time and cost clerk, disciplinarian, speed boss and inspector.

Whilst these ideas seem to be simple and obvious now, they were revolutionary in their day and influenced management practice for many years to come.

The application of Taylor's ideas has influenced the system of industrial relations. The idea that management had a right to manage, e.g., determine the way in which work was done and to set piece work rates as incentives, was a development that caused some problems in the UK engineering industry. Hence the Engineering Employers' Federation agreement of 1922 stated that 'the Employers have the right to manage their establishments'. The settlement of a dispute in 1898 also contained a similar term. Partially this derives from management applying the principles of scientific management to their workplaces and determining how work should be done. This was resisted by the trained tradespeople who thought this an infringement of their right to determine their own methods of work.

Other contemporaries of Taylor's developed his ideas, such as the Gilbreths (a husband and wife team) and Henry Gantt. The Gilbreths developed work study and method study. They also created a system of working on their building sites which involved specifying the methods to be used and these rules had to be adhered to. Again, scientific principles were applied to the various jobs that were carried out, a best method was developed and laid down, which employees had to use. They also evolved the basis for method study which was adopted worldwide. Their contribution is laid down in posterity, as the symbols used in motion study are called therbligs (Gilbreth written backwards!).

Human relations

The name synonymous with the pioneering development of management thinking on the topic of human relations is that of Elton Mayo. His Hawthorne experiments are renowned as being the starting point in understanding the importance of human relations in organisations. He also contributed much more than this. Some of his initial work (around 1915) was done on the fatigue of repetitive work. He concluded that workers did not slow down merely because of internal biological conditions but because of external factors such as boredom induced by repetition. The Hawthorne experiments were conducted 1928–33. These studies demonstrated the complexities of working life. The attempt to improve physical working conditions to find an optimal set of conditions (based on the principles of scientific management) proved that a major factor was the effect of human relationships within the workplace, e.g., between workers as a group and with supervisors. The work also investigated the role of work groups and teams and the attitude of employees. These ideas were further developed in the postwar years by a number of well-known people. Chris Argyris looked at human behaviour in the workplace. He attempted to draw on various aspects of psychology and sociology. For example he examined the conflict between systems and individuals. This has a direct bearing on industrial relations, e.g., the conflict theory supports the idea that conflict inherently exists in organisations (see Section 1.3). Further work looked at the development of personality and how this fitted in with the world of work. He postulated that there were basic incongruities between the characteristics of a mature personality and formal organisation and these could manifest themselves in various ways, e.g., leaving, apathy, loss of interest, tension, aggression and lower standards. The means to overcome these problems again has a direct bearing on industrial relations policy. One important factor in overcoming this conflict is to set up good communications between management and worker. This affects policy relating to consultation procedures and industrial democracy (*see* Section 16.1). Genuine participation is seen as a major factor in overcoming the problem of conflict.

Douglas McGregor's famous Theory X and Theory Y provides a description of two possible states. Theory X is a traditional view that workers are naturally lazy, disinclined to work, hence they must be coerced into working and that the average human wishes to be directed and controlled. Theory Y is an opposite view that states that workers are willing to work under the correct conditions. People can exercise self-control, will accept responsibility and have an innate capacity for creativity, which is underutilised. This latter set of ideas moves towards an organisation that is more unitarist with everyone committed to the goals of the organisation. This does not mean that such a state exists naturally but an organisation can be developed along these lines to bring the best out of their employees. Industrial relations policy can influence this very directly. A very formal collective bargaining system presupposes the existence of conflicting objectives and seeks to resolve these by negotiation. A more cooperative system moves towards a unitary approach. This does not exclude trade unions but it does redefine their role.

Other writers to mention are Rensis Likert and Frederick Herzberg (and there are many others). They have all contributed to the development of management thought.

Human relations management

A more recent development during the 1980s was the emergence of the human relations management philosophy. There is no precise definition of HRM but it is essentially a business-orientated approach to the management of people. Whilst HRM has made an impact, it is by no means universal and several writers argue that it is only appropriate for certain organisations. HRM has certain key characteristics:

- strategy is orientated to fulfilling market needs
- the approach is individualist not collectivist
- matches human resources to business strategy
- based on securing employee commitment to organisational goals
- employees must be flexible to meet changing circumstances

The approach covers all the traditional personnel management activities and more. It requires a reappraisal of recruitment, selection, induction, training, promotion, payment systems, appraisal, development and so on to meet organisational aims. This contrasts with the more traditional approach of personnel management as that of a welfare agency within the firm.

There is a stress on valuing employees as the means of turning the inanimate factors of production into wealth. Being supportive should make employees more productive, satisfied and adaptable. There is also a high rewards culture based on success. In turn management expects a high level of commitment from their employees.

Flexibility is also required to enable firms to adapt to changing market conditions. Employees have a flexible job description and must willingly move within the organisation or accept major change to their jobs as market needs dictate.

Allied to HRM is quality management. Many organisations are paying attention to this, often by seeking third party approval such as the British Standard 5750 or the equivalent ISO 9000 Standard. Another similar philosophy to HRM has evolved regarding quality, that of Total Quality Management. Again TQM seeks the full commitment of employees to quality. It is market-led and it devolves the management of the function to line managers, with the specialists having a more strategic role.

HRM has had a very direct impact on industrial relations. The approach is essentially unitarist (*see* Section 1.3) although it acquires the tag neo-unitarist to differentiate it from the older, traditional form of unitarism which was more paternalistic. The unitarist's approach does not accept the need for trade unions in their traditional role, i.e., as representatives of a group nor as the institution for resolving conflict (as no conflict exists). Also trade unions can be seen as an alternative source of authority for employees and in HRM there is only one source of authority – management.

HRM also focuses on the individual, rather than the group. Again this contrasts with the principles of collective bargaining, where the terms and conditions of employment for a group are decided collectively. Collective bargaining can also be seen to be reactionary and a force against change. For example, when change is required quickly, it should not be necessary to renegotiate collective agreements before any change is made. There should be instant adaptation without necessarily any form of recompense as change is part of the job.

HRM policies can effectively be pursued without the need for a trade union. Also by developing good management practices there is little need for a trade union to defend employees against bad management.

However, trade unions do operate in firms practising HRM but their role is completely different. In the USA there is evidence that the introduction of HRM policies was used to derecognise trade unions. There is no evidence of this in the UK. As management implemented the likes of HRM policies so some trade unions adapted their policies and redefined their role. In Section 7.1.3 single-union agreements are examined and these often are based on a completely different approach to trade unionism. The trade union movement adopted the term 'new unionism' to describe the strategic changes they made to adapt to the new situation facing them. Trade union involvement in these situations is seen as wholly supportive of management and the objectives of the organisation. It seeks to act as an agent for change and collaboration rather than the traditional role of defending the interests of members against the demands of management.

3.2.2   Management of industrial relations

One result of the growth of the industrial relations function in organisations is the need for the various aspects of this function to be managed in the same way that the other areas of a firm's operations are managed. Just as a firm should have a policy with regard to production, sales, marketing and finance, then it should have a policy with regard to industrial relations. As we have already noted, the primary role of management is to achieve objectives and the statement of these objectives is enshrined in a policy. The policy of a firm may not be explicit, in that it has not been formalised in a document. As a minimum every organisation has a policy, even if it is only an implicit one, that is a reflection of what it is currently doing. However, more frequently organisations develop policies which not merely reflect current activities but attempt to make statements with regard to its future operations, i.e., pointing to where it aims to go and what it hopes to achieve. Also these policies tend to be written down, especially in larger organisations. The need for, and usefulness of, a written policy is summarised in the list below:

- It gives certainty to what is to be achieved. Everyone can see the objects of the organisation.
- It achieves a consistency which is very difficult to achieve with verbal statements transmitted among management.
- Accuracy can be achieved by carefully choosing the form of words which reflects the intentions of management.
- It is a useful reference document for managers who may need to know what they should do in certain circumstances.
- It can be changed as a result of negotiations or a change in circumstances. A written document is easier to change than custom and practice or any prejudice that may exist.

There have been calls both by the Commission on Industrial Relations (now no longer in existence) and in the Donovan Commission Report (1968) for firms to develop specific industrial relations policies. With the growth of larger and larger organisations the need is even greater. The purpose of having such a policy includes the points listed above in terms of certainty, consistency and accuracy and they provide a frame of reference within which managers can work. Additionally, because industrial relations can affect the performance of an organisation, industrial relations policies should be laid down within the framework of other policies in such areas as production, sales and finance. The policies on each aspect of an organisation's operations interact and affect each other. A rise in sales affects production and finance. A policy to diversify into other markets must have implications in industrial relations. The first requirement is that an industrial relations policy must be part of the overall business plan and be an integral part of it, not merely an adjunct to it.

The statement of policy is meaningless unless there is a means laid down for achieving those objectives. If the policy is the strategy then tactics also need to be stated. This translates the aims into operational plans and raises many practical questions. These will include looking at the environment within which the organisation is operating. Relevant factors may be economic such as the rate of inflation and unemployment levels, market factors such as the state of the order book on current wages increases, technological factors such as product changes and changes in the methods of manufacturing, and financial factors such as profits and cash available. These factors will affect the possible targets of any negotiation, for instance during wage negotiations. The environment also determines the relative power of the parties in an organisation. When labour is in short supply the unions have greater power not merely in wage demands but also for other demands they may make. The reverse is true in times of high unemployment. A further important part of this stage is to assess the likely reaction of trade unions and employees to a certain line of action. This is a difficult exercise because it involves trying to predict human behaviour, which is notoriously difficult. A range of tactics may have to be evaluated and the one which is likely to receive least resistance would possibly be the one to choose. Choosing a tactic which will predictably receive a hostile reception is running the risk of failing to meet the other business objectives.

The third part of a comprehensive policy is to monitor what is actually happening and to control the performance leading to the achievement of objectives. Clearly, if the targets laid down for, say, wage increases are exceeded, then this will affect the other parts of the business's policy. This will have to be fed back to the financial policy and the implications worked out. This is a control function which needs to be performed carefully to ensure that objectives are achieved or, if necessary, to amend the objectives. It is pointless carrying on trying to achieve objectives that are clearly no longer realistic.

A practical policy statement would contain statements on the following:

- **The recognition of trade unions within the organisation** Often this means (because of the structure of trade unionism in the UK) deciding which trade union has the right to represent which group or class of employees. This is often called the 'sphere of influence' of the trade union. Where unions already exist this can be complicated by some groups being represented by more than one union. It may have to be a long-term aim to have one union represent one group, but in the short term to have some intermediate structure continue with all new employees joining the recognised union for that group. Alternatively, a phasing out period can be stated during which members will transfer or be represented by the steward of the recognised union.
- **The role of the trade union within the organisation** This may involve stating the role and function of the trade union

representatives and recognising such representatives after their election to office. Some organisations accord such status officially by accepting the credentials of the nominated representative. There may also be a statement of the circumstances under which such credentials may be withdrawn, i.e., the firm no longer recognises that representative. This may have to occur in extreme circumstances but can cause problems. The representatives of the union will be accorded certain rights (now backed by legislation – *see* Section 5.1.5) and certain functions (often prescribed in procedural agreements).

- **The role and extent of collective bargaining** This statement will clarify the topics that are the legitimate concern of the bargaining arrangements. In some firms the topics may be limited to pay, hours, holidays and the like. In other firms the topics may extend to pensions, health and safety, disciplinary rules and so on. Also, the structure of the bargaining arrangements needs stating. Some firms have a joint approach to bargaining where all the unions are involved jointly with management. In other firms there may be separate arrangements for separate groups. The composition and procedural rules of the committees carrying out the bargaining are further details for consideration.
- **Management's approach to pay, conditions of service and productivity** These are the guidelines that management will use in its approach to settling levels of pay and maintaining and improving conditions of service. This may be linked to productivity whereby pay increases or improvements in conditions are financed by improvements in efficiency.
- **The use of consultative bodies and procedures** This statement sets down the consultative process within the organisation apart from the collective bargaining arrangements. There may be forums within which management and employees (or trade union representatives) exchange information and views on a range of topics such as productivity, improvements (e.g., suggestion schemes), health and safety, or more generally a works council

system for a broader exchange. In some firms the consultative process may be extended to joint decision making bodies, which will include an element of industrial democracy.
- **Use of procedural agreements** These agreements state the manner in which various topics are to be dealt with. Such agreements may be used for discipline, disputes, grievances, redundancy, technological change and the closed shop. This will formalise not only the way in which the topics are dealt with but will include the personnel involved, any time limits and the records needed (*see* Chapter 7).
- **Membership and role of an employers' association** If the firm is a member of an employers' association, this will possibly affect the organisation. Where national agreements exist, membership will bind the organisation to observe such agreements. It will also imply that the firm will observe the policy of the association by acting in concert with other members.
- **Management's approach to personnel matters** Any industrial relations policy necessarily impinges on the wider personnel function. Topics that may be affected are recruitment, selection, training, appraisal, development, promotion, retirement and dismissal.

The specific policy for an organisation will have to be made within its environment, both internal and external. An independent, private sector organisation will have quite a different policy from a public sector organisation. Each is quite legitimate but suited to its own circumstances. Nevertheless, any policy should be kept constantly under review if it is to remain a useful, workable policy. One that is merely drawn up and left unaltered is likely to become outdated and useless.

3.3 Associations

3.3.1 Origins and types

As a parallel to the emergence of trade unions in the mid-eighteenth century, the employers formed their own associations. There is a history of some employers' associations prior to this time. They were used in some trades, like printing, to control certain aspects of the trade. They were local and unstable and eventually were banned by the Combination Acts 1799. The first employers' associations (in the modern sense) were more national and stable in character and were formed to combat the spread of unionism.

The growth period for employers' associations occurred in the 1880s and 1890s. This was largely as a result of the spread of general unionism. After several successful strikes in the late 1880s trade unions grew rapidly. It was at this time that the general unions emerged, and with them a much wider trade union membership. Trade union organisation at this time was still fairly local but mainly outside the factory. Shop stewards and union organisation inside the factory was not a feature of the nineteenth-century industrial relations system. The union structure was developing nationally, with the formation of national executives and national union leadership. Alongside this developed a system of employers' associations that formed to counter both the local and national trade union movement.

The purpose of the first employers' associations that emerged was to oppose trade unionism and to join together in the common fight to destroy the newly formed unions. Employers became increasingly aware that they could not combat unionism single-handed but by forming an association they might. As unions became permanent in character, employers realised the value of coordinated, uniform policy. They could help each other if necessary if one firm was picked out for action by a union. There is evidence that firms combined to agree a common policy on not admitting trade union members to their workplaces. This was operated by all prospective employees being required to sign a pledge ('the document') not to join a union. When strikes took place, employers naturally helped each other in resisting claims because should one employer give in to a claim, the other employers would find it increasingly difficult to resist any claims by their employees.

In 1852 the engineering employers in London

and Lancashire locked out their employees after their tradesmen had refused to accept an increase in the number of unskilled workers. The concerted action worked and the men had to return to work on the basis that they would not be members of a union. In 1853 cotton workers in Cheshire and Lancashire went on strike for higher pay. Initially, in Stockport, the employers acceded to the demand. In Preston they did not and a long strike ensued, with the employers acting in concert. The employers brought in labour from Ireland. This led to even greater problems but eventually the strike collapsed after seven months, largely because the employers had acted together to resist the wage claim.

The initial objective of employers' associations was to resist unionism because it was seen as an interference in the owners' right to manage the firm the way they wished. Such an attitude prevailed, not merely against unions, but against governments and any other outside agency. Management's right to manage was a freedom to be defended against anyone that challenged it.

Gradually this fundamental opposition to trade unionism weakened as it became apparent that unions were no longer transient organisations but were permanent. By the 1880s employers were ready to give tacit recognition to the unions by entering into negotiations with them. Such negotiations, prior to the First World War, took place at district level with employers' associations. It was only later that unions were recognised fully in the workplace for the purposes of collective bargaining. The employers found this system of collective bargaining to their benefit as it prevented the unions from using a system of 'leap-frogging' their pay claims. If pay claims could be sorted out locally once a year it prevented a number of successive claims being made, each one higher than its predecessor. Another feature of the joint negotiations between employers' associations and trade unions at this time was the emergence of joint procedures to resolve disputes. This again proved useful to both sides as any dispute that could not be resolved at plant level could be taken up to district or even national level to seek a solution to the problem.

There are far more employers' associations

than unions today; they number about 1,850 compared with the 306 unions (in 1990). This is only an approximate figure as there is no compulsion to be listed with the Certification Officer. Of this total only a proportion are of importance to industrial relations. There are three types of employers' associations:

- those that deal with industrial relations and collective bargaining. These are formed to act as a bargaining unit in order to negotiate agreements with the parallel union organisation. They also act to give their members help and advice on industrial relations matters. In addition, they operate joint procedures on disputes with the unions.
- those that deal only with trade and commercial matters. These are concerned with topics of common interest like the local trades' association that brings all the local shopkeepers together. They join together to discuss matters of joint interest and agree on action to their mutual benefit.
- those that deal with both matters of trade and industrial relations.

It is the first and third types that are of importance to industrial relations.

Not all employers see it as being in their interests to join an employers' association. Ford have never joined one; wishing to remain autonomous and believing they can stand on their own, they can see no advantage in federating. Esso were once in an association but withdrew to negotiate the Fawley Productivity Agreements, which they felt they could only do outside the national agreements' structure.

3.3.2 Organisations and activities

There are a variety of organisations among employers' associations. They can be classified as follows:

- a single national association which individual organisations join. The Association of Metropolitan Authorities falls into this category. All of the 35 metropolitan districts join to negotiate terms and conditions for the employees of their authority.
- a national federation which local associations join. The Engineering Employers' Federation is an example of this. Fourteen regional associations join the Federation that covers the 5,000 establishments that employ about two million people. The regional associations have their own staff and management board and they carry out a range of industrial relations functions locally.
- a national association that has local branches throughout the country. The Electrical Contractors' Association operates like this, with 70 branches representing 3,000 member firms, which cover about 80% of the firms in this field. The ECA negotiates with the EETPU a standard wage which applies across the UK.

The industrial relations activities of employers' associations are varied. Many national associations or federations are involved in concluding national agreements with the corresponding union or union confederation. The National Farmers' Union negotiates annually with the National Union of Agricultural and Allied Workers (now part of the TGWU) to conclude an agreement on pay, hours and other conditions that will apply in agriculture the following year. The agreements themselves vary in nature. In the public sector they invariably lay down the set rate for the job. Other agreements lay down minimum rates that provide a basis for local plant level negotiations. This happens in the engineering industry where the national agreements are then negotiated that often improve on the national agreement. A third type of agreement lies between the two whereby the national agreements lay down minimum rates for the individual establishment, with no workplace bargaining. In the footwear industry there is a national agreement on time study, setting out a detailed incentive scheme. These types of national agreements are examined again in Section 7.1.2.

A further important function of an employers' association is the setting up and operating of disputes procedures. These procedures are agreed at national level and apply in each federated firm.

A disputes procedure starts at shop floor level, but if the matter remains unresolved it can go to works conference, local conference and eventually to a national conference. For many years the Engineering Employers' Federation operated the York Memorandum that was concluded in a central (national) conference at York. Often disputes were resolved before getting that far. These procedures do allow for a dispute to be taken beyond company level that might otherwise stick at company level and result in industrial action. Some national procedures allow for a process of arbitration to resolve any disputes that the procedure has failed to resolve.

The agreements reached between employers' associations and unions can be classified into three groups:

- comprehensive agreements where virtually all the terms and conditions of the workers covered are determined in the agreement. There is little room for local variation. This occurred with the teachers where their pay and conditions were set by the Burnham Committees. A Pay Review body now operates and there are no negotiations. Local authority workers who come under the Administrative, Professional, Technical and Clerical conditions of service have a very comprehensive national agreement with little local variation.
- minimum agreements which determine the lowest wages and terms for the workers covered. It is for local agreements to improve on these terms, if necessary. Over the years this has caused wage drift as local agreements have constantly added to the national minimum and cumulatively the gap has widened. This occurs in the engineering, chemicals and rubber manufacturing industries.
- there are agreements which lay down certain terms and conditions as fixed at national level and leave other terms to be negotiated at local level. These types of national agreement are examined again in Section 7.1.2.

A similar procedure exists in the paper and board industry, where there are three distinct levels, ranging from internal to local/district and then finally to national level, with the British Paper and Board Industry Federation maintaining the procedural agreement.

Other activities include giving advice and assistance. Associations have officials who disseminate information to members and go to firms to give advice on specific problems. Some run courses on a variety of topics and provide specialists' service on topics like recruitment, training, works study and so on. Legal advice, and sometimes representation, is given especially as more and more industrial relations topics are covered by legislation, which can lead to tribunal cases. Some associations provide a statistical service to member firms on a range of topics like earnings and human resources.

The advisory services of employers' associations can be of both a general nature, by keeping member firms up to date with developments, and problem solving to help member firms overcome industrial relations problems. The range of advice that is given can cover interpretation of agreements, payment systems, job evaluation and other related topics. Employers' associations have a representational role to play for their members. They are involved with government departments and agencies, the EC and independent organisations which have an impact on the industry represented as well as voicing their opinions through the CBI. A prime example of such an employers' association is the National Farmers' Union which represents farmers at all levels. Employers' associations also provide nominations for bodies such as Industrial Tribunals and the National Economic Development Council.

An example of a comprehensive set of national agreements negotiated between an employers' association and trade union is seen in the electrical contracting industry. The Joint Industry Board (JIB) is made up of the Electrical Contractors' Association and the Electrical, Electronic, Telecommunication and Plumbing Union (now amalgamated with the AEU). The agreement suits both parties in a labour intensive industry where firms need to control labour costs in what are often long-term contracts. The JIB also regulates aspects of training and safety in the industry.

The objectives of the Engineering Employers' Federation in their new constitution are:

- to promote and further the interests of federated firms, and to protect and defend those interests
- to represent the interests of federated firms in the human resource, economic and legal fields locally, nationally and internationally
- to provide information, advice and assistance to federated firms on all matters related to the management of human resources
- to regulate relations between federated firms, their employees and trade unions
- to do all such things as are in the opinion of the federation incidental or conducive to the attainment of the objects above

These objectives are broader than the previous ones and notably do not make direct reference to 'making and maintaining agreements' which the previous ones did.

The EEF is run by a Management Board and there is a 92-member General Council which meets once a year. There are several sub-committees covering the topics of commercial and economic policy, finance, health and safety, manpower and training policy and membership. The EEF had an income of £2.14m in 1989. It represents firms in employment sectors ranging from foundries to boilermakers, machine tool manufacturers, electronic capital goods and shipbuilding and motor vehicles. These firms employed a total of 2.1 million people and accounted for an aggregate turnover of £120 billion.

The Annual Report of the Certification Officer states that there were 128 employers' associations listed at the end of 1990, with a further 147 making a return to the CO's office but who were not listed. There were a total of 285,740 firms in membership of these listed associations. In 1990 the gross income of employers' associations was £150.8m, with £83m of this income from members.

The list below gives some statistics for some of the larger employers' associations:

Income and membership 1990

	Income (£m)	Membership
National Farmers' Union	16.591	108,770
Federation of Master Builders	2.837	20,905
Retail Motor Industry Federation	4.865	13,033
Freight Transport Association	9.359	13,423
National Pharmaceutical Association	1.976	6,961
Engineering Employers' Association	4.603	15,523
British Printing Industries Federation	5.183	3,377

Source: Annual Report of the Certification Officer.

3.4   The Confederation of British Industries

Just as the employers' associations emerged parallel to trade union organisations, so some overall national body for employers was likely to emerge, parallel to the TUC. Surprisingly, the advent of one single body acting for the employers of the UK did not occur until 1965. A variety of organisations were formed at the time the employers' associations were being formed, but all were short-lived. In 1916 the Federation of British Industry was formed and survived. Shortly after this the National Association of British Manufacturers was formed to represent small businesses. A third organisation emerged, called the British Employers' Confederation, after some internal disagreements in the FBI, to deal with labour and employment issues. Eventually in 1963 a plan was devised to bring the three bodies together. Governments found it difficult to talk to more than one organisation representing employers, and the employers increasingly found it necessary to speak with one voice on various subjects. In 1965 the Confederation of British Industries was formed by Royal Charter out of 12,600 firms, the nationalised industries and 250 employers' associations. Some members of the NABM did form a separate group for small businesses called the Smaller Businesses' Association.

The objectives of the CBI are set out in its Royal Charter:

- to provide for British industry the means for formulating, making known and influencing general policy in regard to industrial, economic, fiscal, commercial, labour, social, legal and technical questions, and to act as a national point of reference to those seeking industry's views
- to develop the contribution of British industry to the national economy
- to encourage the efficiency and competitive power of British industry, and to provide advice, information and services to British industry to that end.

The CBI now represents not only manufacturing industries but also commercial organisations, public sector corporations plus about 150 employers' associations. Nevertheless, some gaps remain with some large firms, many small firms and employers' associations preferring to remain outside membership along with all the local authorities (who have separate national associations in the Association of County Councils and the Association of Metropolitan Authorities). This contrasts with the TUC where all the unions of any size are now affiliated to it (enabling the TUC to speak on behalf of 95% of union members). However, the present position of the CBI acting as a single spokesbody for British employers is an improvement on the previous, fragmented position.

The role of the CBI has developed in recent years as governments have increasingly intervened in industrial relations. This intervention has occurred particularly in the field of pay and prices policies. Where governments (of both parties) have imposed some kind of restraint on pay and/or prices, the detail of the policy has been worked out in conjunction with the CBI and the TUC. Statutory incomes policies have affected not only pay increases but dividend restraint and profit limits on firms. The CBI has acted to coordinate employers' actions in seeking to implement such policies and also to act representationally to government departments responsible for the policy (such as the Prices and Income Board of the mid-60s). The CBI sought to develop its own price restraint policies in

1971–2, which would have had the effect of a binding policy on member firms.

The other field of government intervention in industrial relations has been the legislative field. Again the CBI has developed its policies and reactions to legislative proposals and seeks to convey these to the government. Governments often issue a Green Paper (discussion document) or a White Paper (proposal document) prior to formulating legislation. The CBI would clearly be involved in giving a detailed reply to such documents to represent the view of employers on the issues raised.

Other areas of government policy are clearly the subject of discussion and policy formulation within the CBI. These include economic policy affecting interest rates, exchange rates and inflation, fiscal policy affecting employers' national insurance contributions and taxation, and wider issues such as social security and nationalisation (or, in the early 1980s, de-nationalisation). The CBI formulates and promulgates its policy on behalf of its members on such a wide range of issues.

The CBI, in seeking to represent a broad spectrum of employer organisations from small businesses through to multinational corporations and in a wide range of sectors, has a difficult task in attempting to find a policy that is broadly acceptable to all its members. In doing so it often takes a middle line and seeks to modify any extreme views of member organisations. This may be acceptable in enabling the CBI to act as a spokesbody but it also has to act in a way which will maintain internal cohesion and loyalty.

The CBI has, since 1977, had an Annual Conference. This provides a larger forum for its members to discuss policy issues and for it to promulgate its policies. However, such policies are not voted upon nor does it become binding in quite the way TUC policy is binding on its member unions. The CBI is a much looser affiliate organisation and is not bound by stringent rules.

It is worth noting that, like the TUC, the CBI does not directly negotiate as a body with trade unions. It leaves the individual firms to do that. In fact the CBI does not get involved in disputes at all (unlike the TUC which can sometimes; *see* Section 2.5.4). The CBI, again like the TUC, is not attached to any political party although some of its member firms do contribute to political party funds, notably to the Conservative party. There is however, a strong correlation between CBI policy and Conservative party policy. In the main the two agree on many matters both on industrial relations and on economic policy. While there is no direct, formal link between the two organisations, and certainly CBI policy does not become Conservative party policy, the views of the CBI are of great import to the party and its views are sought and representations are made on a wide range of issues. Sometimes the CBI, through its President, may occasionally criticise the Conservative party or government and, while this is not unknown, it is usually done circumspectly so as not to attract too much attention from the media on a CBI/party split. There is a much greater divergence of opinion between the CBI and the Labour party on many issues. The two maintain contact when there is a Labour administration if only for the CBI to perform its representational function on behalf of British employers. Its influence in such circumstances is much reduced.

The CBI is run by a Council. This consists of 400 members from the constituent organisations. Detailed policy formation is carried out by 26 Standing Committees which cover employment, policy, industrial relations and manpower, safety, health and welfare, companies, economic policy, education and training, overseas, Europe, and taxation. There is a permanent staff headed by a Director-General. The organisation is split into Directorates covering economics, education, overseas, social affairs, administration, information, company affairs, regional and small firms. There is a regional structure involving 12 regions, each of which has its own Council.

The CBI also acts as a source of nominees for the various tripartite bodies like the National Economic Development Council and the employers' appointments on quangos like the Training Agency and the Health and Safety Commission and it provides a panel of employer representatives for industrial tribunals.

Mini-questions

3.1 List five forms of organisation.
3.2 State the two common forms of company.
3.3 Draw a typical line organisation chart.
3.4 Briefly describe the main functions of management in any organisation.
3.5 State the overall responsibility of a board of directors.
3.6 Describe what an employers' association is.
3.7 Explain two of the functions of an employers' association.
3.8 Describe two types of employers' association structure.
3.9 State what the letters CBI stand for.
3.10 State two of the aims of the CBI.

Exercises

3.1 Describe the legal status of a company. How has the emergence of the company affected organisations and in particular the conduct of industrial relations?
3.2 Describe the different functions of a national agreement in various sectors of employment.
3.3 Explain the role of employers' associations in industrial relations. Evaluate their usefulness in the functions they perform.

Further reading

A Flanders, *Management and Unions*, Faber, 1975, 0-571-10711-7

P F Drucker, *The Practice of Management*, Butterworth-Heinemann, 1989, 0-434-90389-2

C Argyris, *Integrating the Individual and the Organisation*, Wiley, 1964, 0-471-03315-4

ACAS, *Employment Policies*

N Millward and M Stevens, *Workplace Industrial Relations*, Dartmouth, 1992, 1-85521-321-4

D Torrington and L Hall, *Personnel Management*, Prentice Hall, 1991, 0-13-658667-8

K Hawkins, *The Management of Industrial Relations*, Penguin, 1978, 0-14-0220917

J A C Brown, *The Social Psychology of Industry*, Penguin, 1988, 0-14-009109-2

4

The State

4.1 The role of the State

So far we have considered the two main parties in industrial relations, the unions and the employers. The bulk of everyday industrial relations is conducted by these two parties. A third party that is involved in industrial relations is the State. The State is involved at several different levels. By necessity it has to be involved because the framework of law is created and maintained by the State. Increasingly so since the mid-1960s the industrial relations system has been drawn into the legal framework. Already it can be seen, and it will become clearer later, that most industrial relations topics have a legal element. Also certain areas of industrial relations involve a political element. This leads in practical terms to the involvement of politics in industrial relations and for some sections of our industrial relations system to be involved in politics, as we saw in Chapter 2. A further involvement of the State has emerged over the years, in the area of economics. Incomes are an important factor in the economic system and industrial relations is involved in setting levels of pay and pay settlements. Some governments have found it necessary, in order to control the economy, to lay down an incomes policy of one sort or another.

Before examining, in detail, the various roles the State plays in industrial relations, it is worth explaining what is meant by the 'State'. Conventional constitutional analysis splits the role of the State into three separate and distinct functions:

- **The legislature** This has the function of making and creating law. In this country our legislature is the Houses of Parliament, comprised of the House of Commons and the House of Lords. They have the sovereign right to make whatever laws they wish, subject only to their own procedures. Royal assent is also necessary, but this is never withheld. There is now a source of law that is superior to Parliament, that is EC law. Under the Treaty of Rome all member countries have to adopt community law into their own.

- **The executive** This has the function of administering and operating the law. In England this is the government. The government, headed by the Prime Minister, is usually formed by the party that secures a majority of MPs at a general election, but coalition governments are possible. A government minister introduces legislation (in the form of a bill) into Parliament and, after it becomes law, is required to ensure that the provisions of the law are put into operation. The government is split into ministries such as education, employment, industry, Home Office, treasury, etc. Most industrial relations law is within the portfolio of the Secretary of State for Employment.

- **The judiciary** This has the function of enforcing the law. In this country this is the courts of law. The courts system is used to enforce criminal and civil law. If the law is broken, then the accused person or party is taken to court. The judges have an important role to play. This is examined in greater detail in Section 9.1.

Each of the functions of the State has a role in industrial relations.

The legislature

On many occasions legislation has been passed by the Houses of Parliament affecting employment and industrial relations. Today there are upwards of 50 Acts of Parliament affecting employment. These range from health and safety to employee rights to trade unions.

As will be seen later in Section 10.2, trade unions would be unable to operate without the intervention of the legislature. If the common law (the law expounded by the courts themselves) had been left unaltered the trade union functions taken for granted today, especially striking, would have remained illegal. The Houses of Parliament saw fit at various times to amend the common law to allow unions to operate as they desired. In more recent times there have been attempts to create a legal framework for the industrial relations system. This necessarily involves the legislature. The 1971 Industrial Relations Act was a major attempt. This largely failed but was followed by the Trade Union and Labour Relations Act 1974, its amendment Act 1976, the Employment Protection Act 1975, the Employment Protection (Consolidation) Act 1978, the Employment Acts 1980, 1982, 1988, 1989 and 1990 and the Trade Union Act 1984.

A major part of the employee/employer relationship is now governed by law, much of this in the form of employee rights in employment. Chapters 10 and 12 to 15 examine these in detail. The content of the law is a matter for Parliament itself. Often this is a matter of politics where a party will, in its election manifesto, declare what it intends to do and then translates this into a bill which, when it finally becomes an Act, the government will implement.

The executive

The Houses of Parliament, having passed an Act,

give the executive a role in industrial relations. The executive has to implement the law and provide the administrative structure within which the law can take effect. An example of this is seen in Section 4.3 with the composition and role of ACAS.

Various bodies have been set up under Acts of Parliament to deal with industrial relations. Their existence is derived from an Act. For example, ACAS was set up under the Employment Protection Act 1975. Funds are made available by the State, under the Act, through the Secretary of State for Employment. The composition of ACAS is determined by law and it is accountable to a Secretary of State. All these features need implementing and this is administered by the executive, mainly through the civil service.

Another example is the use of tribunals (*see* Section 9.2). Various Acts have referred matters to tribunals for them to decide cases brought under various parts of industrial relations law. The constitution of tribunals and the rules under which they operate are determined under different Acts of Parliament, as are questions of funds and expenses.

The judiciary

The courts of law enforce the various Acts of Parliament. As and when cases come before the courts under the various Acts (or under common law) the courts have a duty to decide the case. The majority of civil cases arising under employment Acts are referred to tribunals. They are not full courts in several senses (*see* Section 9.2) but serve the same function.

An important aspect of the work of the judiciary is the interpretation of law. Parliament's intentions are laid down in an Act but the exact meaning of the words in a particular situation is a matter for the courts to decide. This important role is discussed in more detail in Section 9.1.4.

The courts have become involved in industrial relations in recent times as a result of the welter of legislation passed in the 1980s. In several disputes the courts have heard applications for interlocutory injunctions (*see* Section 10.2.3) on application from employers to restrain unions from taking industrial action. The courts issue an order if, legally, there appears to be a case to hear. The union or personnel against whom the order is issued must obey it. If they do not, they are in contempt of court and that inevitably leads to heavy fines or imprisonment. The courts have also issued orders leading to the sequestration of union funds. This occurs where an injunction has been issued and ignored. The union's funds and property are then put into the hands of a sequestrator who manages the union and its funds. This effectively prevents the union from functioning normally. Again such orders are issued under the power invested in the courts under an Act of Parliament.

4.2 State intervention

One of the fundamentally important features of our industrial relations system is the principle of free collective bargaining. This is generally taken to mean 'free from government interference'. The parties to an agreement are free to make whatever bargain they like, with no outside governmental interference. Governments, of all parties, have generally taken the line that, unless there is an extra special reason, they will not intervene or interfere with the functioning of collective bargaining. This is clearly the case as most agreements, especially at local level, are the result of free, unhindered negotiation leading to an agreement.

Apart from the intervening role of the State from a constitutional point of view, outlined above, the State (mainly through the government) has intervened in various ways in industrial relations. There are two main areas of intervention: wage determination and the settlement of disputes.

4.2.1 Wage determination

Wage determination is of great importance to governments as the levels of wages and earnings are an important factor in the national economy. Governments have imposed pay policies at certain times to try to achieve control over this factor in the economy. This aspect is dealt with in Section 4.2.2. However the history of government intervention in wage determination goes back into the late nineteenth century. As the result of a series of economically damaging strikes, the Government in the early 1890s was concerned that a formula be found to prevent similar strikes in the future. Collective bargaining was not as advanced as it is today; employers were still reluctant to accept the role of the trade unions and some groups did not possess the power to achieve higher wage settlements.

Parliament recognised this problem and for certain industries set up trade boards in 1909. These boards fixed minimum rates of wages for the industry. The employer was to pay this wage as a minimum and an inspectorate was set up to enforce these provisions. The Trade Board Act 1918 enabled the Minister of Labour to set up other boards as was seen fit where there was no adequate machinery for the regulation of wages in that trade. By 1937 there were 50 boards, plus the agricultural wages board. These trade boards became wages councils.

Wages councils operated until 1993 and covered about three million employees in some 40 councils. Their coverage was extended to piecework rates, overtime rates, holidays and holiday pay. It was the intention that these wages councils would lead to free collective bargaining in these trades. Wages councils made their own wage regulation orders, so that government interference was kept to a minimum. Wages councils covered trades like licensed residential establishments, retail drapery, outfitters and footwear, retail food, road haulage and many others. The Employment Protection Act 1975 extended the role of the councils, and created statutory joint industrial councils. These were similar to wages councils but their terms of reference extended to all the terms and conditions of the workers concerned. Again the intention was that these would provide a basis for permanent collective bargaining machinery in the industry concerned.

A further form of intervention in wage determination was through the use of fair wages resolutions. These were not a direct form of intervention in wage determination but affected the terms and conditions of those employed by firms engaged on work funded by public money. The contracts the resolutions applied to were originally central government contracts but latterly extended to local authority contracts and other contracts where public money was used. The fair wages resolutions were made by the House of Commons and had no direct legal effect except that they became a part of the contract between the government (or other public body) and its contractor. The most recent fair wages resolution was passed in 1946. The system was abolished in 1983.

To tender for a public contract (say to build a motorway or a hospital) the firm had to show that it observed the established rates of pay and hours for that trade. The contractor had to show in particular:

- the rates of pay, hours of work and conditions of labour were no less favourable than those recognised in the industry or area
- these were observed for at least the preceding three months
- these terms applied to all employees
- that employees were free to join an independent trade union
- that any subcontractors employed observed the terms of the resolution

In addition, government contracts included a term requiring the firm to conform to the provisions of the Race Relations Act 1968.

The Employment Protection Act 1975 created the right for workers to claim the terms and conditions generally observed in a particular locality or trade. The process, under Schedule 11, was instituted by a union claiming a certain level of wages (or other terms) based on what was paid or observed elsewhere. ACAS looked at the claim initially and tried for a conciliated settlement. If this failed the matter could be referred to the Central Arbitration Committee (CAC). The findings of the CAC were binding and could be imposed by the CAC on the employer. Schedule 11 was repealed by the Employment Act 1980.

4.2.2 Incomes policies

An important factor in the management of the economy is the level of incomes received. The question of controlling wage levels and settlements to ensure a controlled economy has been debated by both Labour and Conservatve governments over many years. Some politicians believe in free market forces, saying that excessively high wage settlements will lead to higher unemployment. This then takes the demand out of the labour market which then leads to lower wage settlements. Others believe in a planned economy whereby incomes and prices are matched as closely as possible and standards of living are thereby maintained. Another more practical approach is to try to achieve a social contract between government, employers and employees. This is a bargain where it is agreed that for a limitation on wage increases there are nonmonetary benefits given in the form of changes in legislation, measures to encourage trade union membership and greater participation of the trade union movement in government business.

Any massive intervention of a government by operating an incomes policy obviously meets with resistance. A fundamental feature of our industrial relations system is the freedom to bargain collectively, with no restraints, except those imposed by the parties. Any incomes policy will interfere with this process as the parties are not allowed to come to their own conclusions. This fetters the stronger groups particularly, who are not able to use their 'muscle' to gain higher levels of wages. It also raises problems with groups who believe themselves to be 'special cases' and should be allowed to settle outside of the policy. Many attempts have been made, since the Second World War, to operate an incomes policy. Some have been short-term affairs, others long-term attempts at a permanent incomes policy. So far there has been no permanent form of incomes policy.

Prior to the Second World War, governments of all persuasions had allowed the economy largely to control itself with little intervention. This policy of *laissez-faire* had operated right through the Industrial Revolution until the 1940s. This attitude had pervaded industrial relations in that employers and unions defended the system of free collective bargaining with no government intervention. Apart from government intervention in wages (*see* previous section) and legislation, the system was largely a self-regulatory one. During the 1930s, in an attempt to solve the problem of economic cycles with booms and depressions which brought periods of prosperity followed by unemployment and falling living standards, new ideas in economic thinking were developed. The most influential person in developing these new ideas was J M Keynes. He believed that the State should regulate demand in the economy, if necessary financing it by deficit budgeting and borrowing, which would lead to full employment. Full employment is one of the prime objectives of economic policy along with low inflation and improved standards of living. The Labour party in particular and the trade union movement espoused these ideas because such policies promised to lead to full employment. Such policies necessarily involved greater planning of the economy and higher levels of government intervention, which had an impact on the industrial relations system.

With the implementation of greater interventionist economic policies came other problems. With the advent of full employment (at around the accepted 'base' figure of 97%) being sustained over relatively long periods during the postwar boom, high wage rises became a problem. Full employment means that, overall, labour is in relatively short supply and if demand for labour is high then the outcome is that wages rise comparatively quickly. Certainly this proved to be the case in the 1950s and 60s, with aggregate high levels of employment and resultant high wage settlements. However, for some sectors of the economy this was not true nor did it apply in some regions that were affected by the decline of an industry. Hence aggregate levels can mask some local problems. It had been argued, particularly by Beveridge, that in the interests of a stable economy unions would show restraint in their wage demands (although they had the power to make such demands) and help control wage levels in the economy. In the event wage levels increased which led to inflationary pressures in the economy. Higher wage levels also have the effect of an increase in the labour cost of products and services (which leads to pressures for increasing prices, i.e., inflation) and a reduction in competitiveness.

Eventually it was apparent that it was necessary to control the level of wages and wage rises. By the mid-50s the UK was suffering a balance of payments deficit and a reduction in the UK's proportion of world trade. In the postwar period the increase in earnings was always higher than the rate of inflation (sometimes by as much as 5%) and unemployment never exceeded 3% in the 1960s. Such wage rises are only acceptable, in their effect on competitiveness, if increases in productivity are achieved to pay for the increased wage costs, i.e., there are improvements in efficiency effected by improved methods, technological developments or changes in working practices. Further, such wage rises will only be noninflationary if output matches the increases in wages, i.e. increased output (supply) can match increased demand caused by people having more money to spend. If it does not, then the tendency is for imports to increase to satisfy demand. This is one factor in the balance of payments deficit (higher imports) added to the problem of lower competitiveness (lower exports).

The link between levels of employment and wage rises was recognised in the Phillip's curve effect which demonstrated an inverse relationship between unemployment and wages. An OECD (Organisation for Economic Cooperation and Development) report in 1961 recognised the direct link between higher wages and higher inflation. From all this it was seen that in order to control all these factors an incomes policy was an important arm of economic policy.

The problem is, however, to devise a policy that is both acceptable and workable. Incomes policies can be categorised as equity-based or efficiency-based:

- **Equity**-based policies aim to treat everyone equally. Such policies are usually simply stated as £x per week limit on wage increases. If everyone is to be treated equally there is pressure for everyone to comply or run the risk of being criticised. Pay negotiations become relatively simple. With a flat rate increase the skilled and higher paid groups have their differentials reduced which can lead to resentment. Special cases for preferential treatment are difficult to deal with.

- **Efficiency**-based policies aim to improve productivity and pay increases are to be paid for by increased efficiency. This favours the manufacturing sector where it is easy to identify the areas of work that can be improved, which can then finance increased pay. The problems are greater in the public and service sectors where the potential for increased productivity is more difficult to identify. Such policies have a sounder economic basis but are inherently more difficult to apply. Negotiations become complex in identifying the factors that can lead to increased productivity and the way in which such improvements are going to be measured.

Below is a list of the postwar wages/incomes/prices policies:

1948–9	Wage freeze – pay increases actually 2% per year.
1961	Pay 'pause' for public sector.
1962–4	Pay guidelines 2–2.5% per year.
1964	Declaration of Intent – link pay to productivity.
1965	Pay 'norm' – Prices and Incomes Board introduced.
1966	Pay and prices freezes, with legal sanctions.
1967	Nil norm, with exceptions.
1968	Wages and dividend 'ceiling'.
1971	$n-1$% policy in public sector. PIB abolished.

1972	6-month wage and price freeze – statutory.
1973	£1 + 4% per week; Price Commission and Pay Board set up.
1973	£2.25 per week; 7% max. + threshold agreements.
1974	Policy of restraint + Social Contract. Pay Board abolished.
1975	£6 per week max.
1976	5% limit; £2.50 per week min.; £4 per week max.
1977	10% guideline.
1993	1½% max. increase for all public sector workers.

All the policies achieved a modicum of success but none were wholly successful. As any incomes policy is perceived as an interference in free collective bargaining, most of the parties to the process object to such restraint. Trade unions are usually the most vocal opponents as any government imposed pay constraint will strengthen the hand of management in wage negotiations. Added to this, any policy brings its own problems with regard to particular groups being favoured or disadvantaged, special cases arising or the penalties imposed for non-compliance. The following list states some of the main problems encountered:

- Settlement dates for wages vary from group to group. Any policy implemented on a specific date will catch some group, due to settle, unable to pursue its claim or finding difficulty in doing so. Groups who are trapped will have a legitimate ground for complaint and they will feel disadvantaged. Pay negotiations take into consideration the 'going rate'. If that rate is higher than the stated policy, negotiators will find it difficult to resist such claims.

- Employees funded directly or indirectly by government are directly affected by an incomes policy. They are also the groups who find it difficult to identify productivity improvements in order to finance pay increases. Some policies have affected these groups only (in 1961 and 1993).

- As much final wage bargaining occurs at plant

or local level, there are difficulties in monitoring the strict implementation of the policy. Often firms will settle higher than the stated level rather than run the risk of a strike. This is true of firms whose businesses are going well at the time. Firms doing less well are less concerned about the effect of a strike. Also locally negotiated bonus schemes can increase wage levels and add to differentials between groups.

- While policies may operate in the short term and restrain wage increases, when the period of the policy ends or further agreement is not possible, there is then a period of 'catching up'. Most groups can identify reasons why they are a special case and put in a claim to make up the ground lost during the operation of the incomes policy.

- The final problem, and probably the most important to solve, is the one of consent. A policy which is wholeheartedly supported by all parties – employers, unions and employees – is likely to succeed, such as the 1948 pay freeze. Conversely, a policy that fails to gain support is likely to fail. Frequently incomes policies are designed and implemented during periods of crisis, such as the balance of payments crises of the 1960s and the high levels of inflation in the 1970s. This may be in spite of the avowed government's policy not to have such a policy.

By seeking the cooperation of all the parties concerned, and through negotiation, many policies have been introduced with varying degrees of support. Added to this, governments have introduced monitoring bodies such as the Pay and Incomes Board (1965) and the Pay Board (1973). These bodies were the watchdogs for ensuring that the policy was applied correctly and, in some instances, for determining what, if any, pay or price rises could be made. Further, some policies have had a statutory backing that made it an offence for a firm to exceed the levels stated. Such statutory-backed policies tend to receive a less than warm welcome and governments may use them without other bodies supporting them. The Labour government did this in 1966 with little support for the use of legal sanctions.

A further step was taken in 1975 to secure consent for an incomes policy with the Labour government negotiating a Social Contract with the TUC. In exchange for an incomes policy (£6 per week limit) the government promised to introduce a number of legal reforms which would have to be abandoned in the absence of a pay policy. This Social Contract policy worked well for a time but eventually support dwindled to the pay guidelines in 1977 and with no agreement at all in 1978. The lack of agreement in 1978 led to the 1978/9 'winter of discontent', which was characterised by a number of serious pay disputes, particularly in the public sector, with the firemen and refuse collectors.

The Conservative government of 1979 onwards had used monetary policies and the operation of market forces to adjust pay levels. However, the stringent monetary policies applied to the public sector have had the effect of keeping wage rises down by making a maximum sum of money available to a service (and local government) with annual adjustments less than the rate of inflation. In 1992 the Conservative government introduced a 1.5% maximum pay increase for all employees in the public sector, in an attempt to control public expenditure. After a gap of thirteen years a pay policy has been utilised to control wages. So far Britain has developed no long-term pay policy, and it appears that such policies are only workable as an emergency, short-term measure.

4.2.3 Law making and enforcement

Constitutionally the role of Parliament is to make laws; it is for the government to implement them and for the judiciary to enforce them. However, in the UK there is considerable overlap between the first two State functions. In most matters the government introduces legislation into Parliament, in the form of a bill, and the various stages are proceeded through in both Houses. Prior to introducing a bill the government can issue a White Paper. This is a nonlegislative document stating what legislation the government proposes to introduce on a particular issue. Comments are invited and from the discussion generated a bill is drafted. Two such documents – *In Place of Strife* and *A Fair Deal at Work* – are discussed in Section 8.1.4, both of which were to be the basis for legislation subsequently. The lawmaking power of the government is also expanded with the use of secondary legislation in the form of Statutory Instruments. This aspect, and that of the court-made case law, is discussed in greater detail in Chapter 9.

The role of enforcing the law lies with the judges and the courts system. Again Chapter 9 deals with this in some detail, particularly with the use of industrial tribunals for enforcing employment law. The judiciary is independent of both Parliament and government, except that the Lord Chancellor has a position in all three areas. In theory the judiciary are nonpolitical and their role is to interpret and apply the law. Needless to say, because judges have to try politically sensitive cases, they are branded as being of one or other political persuasion. In some instances judges have openly stated their bias in favour or against a particular cause and some eighteenth-century judges made no secret of their dislike of trade unions. Nevertheless, judges are never put under the direction of a government or minister and must remain outside normal political activity. Their role in industrial relations can be crucial because, no matter what Parliament intended, the final arbiter of what an Act of Parliament means in practice is the judge and his or her interpretation of the Act. This can effectively settle an issue one way or the other and can have a great effect on the outcome of a dispute. During the 1984 miners' strike various legal actions were taken out against the NUM, and its leaders, which led to the sequestration of the union's funds, which hampered their action in the dispute.

The State has intervened over many centuries in matters related to industrial relations. In the Elizabethan age magistrates set fair wages and prices for journeymen in a number of skilled trades represented by the Craft Guilds. This power was given to them by Statute to ensure just and equitable treatment in these matters. During the eighteenth century, as the Industrial Revolution gained momentum, the pervading philosophy became the capitalist, economic ideals based on market forces and self-determination. This led to the development of the *laissez-faire* attitudes which precluded state intervention. It was for master and servant, subject to economic forces, to decide all matters relating to the employment relationship. Any interference by government legislation would be resisted. The courts also adopted the same *laissez-faire* attitudes to the developing laws, for example, in the law of contract where the rule is that it is for the parties to determine the terms of a contract and the courts have no interventionist role. Such a philosophy still holds today, with some modification of the excesses such a policy can produce. This 'hands off' policy by government carried on throughout the nineteenth century and it is the main reason why we still have no fully developed legal framework for our industrial relations system in the UK.

If the policy of nonintervention were taken to extremes it would lead to a number of injustices and excesses. It became apparent, for instance, early in the nineteenth century that some employers were employing children to work very long hours. Parliament saw it right to intervene to curb this practice and passed the Health and Morals of Apprentices Act 1802. Several Acts were to follow this one, particularly in the field of health and safety. Such legislation was not wholly accepted by employers as it was seen as an interference in running their businesses as they wished. Later in the century various groups, including the genesis of the trade union movement, campaigned and lobbied to have the law altered to allow greater freedom for trade unions to operate. Parliament again decided to intervene and acted accordingly by altering the law to aid the development of trade unionism. This development is discussed in Section 8.2 and Chapter 10. The pattern is still one of piecemeal development with no thought for developing a comprehensive legal framework. This has led to the law prescribing which acts are unlawful rather than a statement of positive rights, i.e., what unions, employers and employees can lawfully do. For example, there is no positive right to strike laid down by law but the law has been amended to allow strike action in some circumstances to be free from legal action. There have been numerous cases on whether a particular strike comes within the ambit of the law or not, the most notable being the Taff Valley Railway Case in 1902 (*see* page 145).

The areas of legislative intervention by the State are listed below:

- trade union law: status of unions; recognition; immunities; right to join or not; closed shop
- disputes: striking and its limitations; resolution of disputes; picketing
- wage determination: wages councils; equal pay
- contract of employment: terms of employment; termination; dismissal; redundancy; periods of notice; maternity benefits
- discrimination: not to be treated less favourably on grounds of sex or race
- health and safety: hours of work

4.2.4 Settlement of disputes

In the majority of cases where disputes arise the situation is left to the two parties concerned to find a solution. Often a disputes procedure exists which is designed to facilitate the resolution of disputes. This was also noted in the last chapter where some employers' associations have a national procedure, with the unions concerned, for resolving disputes. However, situations arise that require the intervention of a third party to provide a solution. This may be due to the lack of procedures available to deal with the dispute, or because the procedures have been abandoned or the parties have got themselves entrenched. Whatever the cause, the situation needs a third party to help. This need has given rise to the processes of conciliation, arbitration and mediation. These are described in Section 6.4.

A number of disputes procedures are designed so that, in the event of the two parties finally

failing to agree, the matter can be submitted to arbitration. This is a private arbitration that the parties have previously agreed will be used. Apart from the domestic procedures, the State has been involved in these processes. Today ACAS provides a conciliation service and can set up arbitration.

The first direct intervention by the State to provide a means of settling disputes by a third party was through the Conciliation Act 1896. This provided that conciliation could be set up at the request of either side in a dispute or that arbitration could be set up at the request of both sides. The Secretary of State appointed the people to carry out this service. The Board of Trade also had powers to set up an enquiry into an industrial dispute. A full-time conciliator was appointed in 1907 and this proved to be very useful in settling disputes. An Industrial Committee was set up during 1917 to serve the same purpose during the First World War, but it proved a short-lived idea. Partly as a result of the Whitley Committee Reports' recommendations, the Industrial Courts Act in 1919 set up a system of voluntary arbitration. The reference could only be made if both parties agreed and if domestic procedures had been exhausted. An arbitrator could be appointed by the Secretary of State or the Industrial Court could act as a board of arbitration. Under neither Act were there any legal sanctions; the process remained entirely voluntary. The success of the procedure can be gauged by the fact that there were 1,323 conciliated settlements in 1919.

During both World Wars the State introduced compulsory arbitration through the Munitions of War Act 1915 and the Conditions of Employment and National Arbitration Order in 1940. These laws forbade striking and lockouts, in view of the war effort, and imposed binding arbitration. The 1915 Act was repealed in 1918 but the 1940 Order was not repealed until 1951. Even then this Order was replaced by another Order that set up the Industrial Disputes Tribunal for compulsory, unilateral arbitration. This Order was not repealed until 1958, by which time 1,270 awards had been made. The tribunal awards were legally binding. The 1896 and 1919 Acts remained in force until 1971 when the Industrial Relations Act repealed them. This Act introduced alternative machinery for resolving disputes through Department of Employment conciliators, the forerunner of the Advisory, Conciliation and Arbitration Service.

As a result of the Industrial Relations Act 1971, and also the advent of government pay policy, the role of a government conciliation and arbitration service was questioned. The outcome was that the Advisory, Conciliation and Arbitration Service (ACAS) was set up in 1974. Virtually all previous State machinery for settling disputes now lies with ACAS. The one area of ACAS's work that involves a compulsory process of intervention is in cases of individual employment rights. When a person applies to an industrial tribunal, as the result of an alleged infringement of their statutory employment rights, the matter is referred to a conciliation officer of ACAS. Such matters include unfair dismissal, sex and racial discrimination, maternity rights, redundancy and other issues. Once referred to an ACAS officer they will attempt to reach a settlement prior to the case being heard. While the process of referral is compulsory, the officer cannot impose a conciliated settlement. If a settlement is not reached, or either side refuses conciliation, the case is sent to an industrial tribunal for a hearing. All forms of arbitration service offered by ACAS are now entirely voluntary.

4.3 The Advisory, Conciliation and Arbitration Service

4.3.1 Background and organisation

As we saw in Section 4.2.4, the State has played a part in industrial relations by providing facilities external to domestic procedures for the settlement of disputes. In addition governments have provided an advisory service to firms in the area of industrial relations and personnel policies. The aim of these services is to improve industrial relations through encouraging better policies, practices and procedures. In 1945 the Ministry of Labour established a Personnel Management Advisory Service to this end. As industrial relations continued to become more important and the function of the personnel department grew, the government provided advice on these matters. In the late 1960s this was renamed the Manpower and Productivity Service (of the Department of Employment) to reflect the greater emphasis on manufacturing productivity. This service was contracted to a manpower and industrial relations service in 1971.

In the early 1970s a problem arose with this service due to the introduction of incomes policies (*see* Section 4.2.2). As the service was part of the Department of Employment it was bound by government policy. The single question most frequently referred to the service was on pay and conditions of service. The service was bound to give advice on pay policy as laid down by government policy on incomes. Any attempt to give independent advice was not possible. It emerged at this time that there was a need to provide an impartial, independent advisory service, that was not duty-bound to follow any specific government policy. Such a service could give advice in line with government policy but did not necessarily need to. In May 1974 the incoming Labour government proposed to set up such an independent service. ACAS commenced operations in September 1974, and the legislative provisions for the service were passed in the Employment Protection Act 1975.

ACAS is now an independent body that provides the advisory service mentioned above, and also performs the functions formerly carried out under the Conciliation Act 1896 and some of the functions under the Industrial Courts Act 1919. Its current functions are examined in the next section. ACAS is headed by a council of 10. Three members are drawn from an employers' association (the CBI), three from the trade unions (the TUC) and there are three independent members. These are all part-time appointments. There is a full-time chairperson of the Council. The chairperson has to prepare and submit an Annual Report to the Secretary of State for Employment. The Council lays down policy for the service which the full-time officers have to implement. Currently about 820 staff are employed by ACAS. These work in the head office or in one of the nine regional offices.

4.3.2 Functions

As the title ACAS suggests, its functions are split into three main areas: advice, conciliation and arbitration.

Advice

The service provides free advice on any matter of industrial relations and employment policies ranging from collective bargaining to disputes, discipline, human resource planning, recruitment, payment systems and job evaluation. This is set out in Section 4 of the Employment Protection Act 1975. It may also publish material for advice on these topics. Currently a range of booklets is available, with a wider range available from the Department of Employment. These useful booklets are available free from the Department and cover the whole range of employee rights. The mode of advice given can range from an over-the-phone answer to a visit to a diagnostic survey and report. The Annual Report of ACAS gives details of the proportion of time spent on these functions and the topics dealt with. These tend to vary as new provisions, laws, codes or documents raise the demand for advice in that area. In 1989 the ACAS information service dealt with over 11,000 enquiries and the advisory service dealt with 350,000 enquiries. The advisory service staff made over 7,200 advisory visits and 1,144 in-depth exercises were carried out on a range of topics, the main topics being disciplinary and grievance procedures.

Conciliation

Section 6.4 describes the process of conciliation. ACAS provides a collective conciliation service which it has to provide by law (under the Employment Protection Act 1975). Where a dispute exists, or looks likely to occur, either side can request the help of ACAS, or the officers of ACAS can take the initiative. ACAS officers can act as conciliators to try to settle a dispute. The initial step is to encourage the parties to exhaust their own procedures first. The conciliator can then proceed to meet both sides, hear their arguments, state the facts as they see them, etc. An attempt can then be made to promote a settlement by suggesting the basis on which they can get together again and find a solution. Pure conciliation does not consist of suggesting a solution but this can be done if it is felt it will help. In 1991 ACAS completed 1,226 cases of collective conciliation. In 86% of cases a settlement or progress towards a settlement was made. The dominant topic (40%) was pay and terms and conditions. There was a notable trend towards joint requests for conciliation; this occurred in 586 cases out of the 1,226, with unions making 452 applications and employers 112.

Individual conciliation is a form of conciliation that is often prescribed by law in cases of individual claims against an employer. Under unfair dismissal law, redundancy law and discrimination (race and sex) laws, before the case can come before a tribunal, an attempt has to be made at reaching a conciliated settlement. An ACAS officer has to do this if requested by either side or if it is considered there is a reasonable prospect of success. An important proviso is that the enquiry carried out by a conciliation officer is not admissible as evidence at a future tribunal case. In 1991 the service dealt with nearly 60,600 cases of individual conciliation. The number of discrimination cases rose to 6,200. There were 39,200 unfair dismissal complaints received, making up 65% of the total case-load. Of these, 89% were so-called 'non-IT1' cases, i.e., unfair dismissal cases that were not being taken to an industrial tribunal. The outcome of these applications was that 40% were settled, 29% withdrawn and 32% were referred to a tribunal for a hearing.

Arbitration

Section 6.4 describes the process of arbitration. This can be provided by the service under the

Employment Protection Act 1975. Where a dispute exists, or looks likely to occur, either side can request arbitration. Where both sides consent the matter can be referred to arbitration. ACAS officers cannot act as arbitrators, but they can appoint one or several people for that purpose. Alternatively the matter can be referred to the Central Arbitration Committee. The initial step is to encourage the parties to exhaust their own procedures first. If the service thinks conciliation could settle the dispute this should be tried. There are also some industry-wide arbitration tribunals which ACAS is responsible for, like those for the railways, Post Office, and the police. In 1991, 157 cases were referred to arbitration or mediation, with 122 being dealt with by a single arbitrator and eight by a board of arbitrators. 35% were cases relating to dismissal and 22% relating to grading.

ACAS has a few other functions. Mediation (*see* Section 6.4) is possible but is rare. The service can carry out enquiries into industrial relations generally, or on specific issues, and issue reports. This it does from time to time, but only a few times per year. Another important function of ACAS is to issue Codes of Practice. It has statutory authority to do this under the Employment Protection Act 1975. It has issued three Codes, one on disciplinary procedures, one on time off for trade union duties and one on disclosure of information for the purposes of collective bargaining. Codes have to be issued in draft form to allow for comments. The final form is sent to the Secretary of State for Employment who then has to lay it before Parliament for approval by both Houses. Codes are not law but can be used in evidence at a tribunal to show the law has not been complied with. Under the 1975 Act two issues were frequently referred to ACAS. These were claims under Schedule 11 (*see* Section 4.2.1) for a wages parity claim and claims under Section 11 for trade union recognition. Both these sections have been repealed by the Employment Act 1980, so no longer feature as a function of ACAS.

4.3.3 Central Arbitration Committee

As we saw in Section 4.2.4, the State has had the power to intervene in disputes for some time. The Industrial Courts set up in 1919 have existed for this purpose. They were renamed in 1971 the Industrial Arbitration Board and finally, in 1976, renamed the Central Arbitration Committee. It is now formally part of ACAS. References pass to it through ACAS. Usually if arbitration is to take place it is carried out by a single arbitrator, though less commonly by a board. In 1990 only eight references were made to the CAC. The bulk of the work of the CAC was under Schedule 11 references for pay parity. In 1978 there were 535 such claims. Since 1980, when the Employment Act came into force, no such claims can be made under Schedule 11.

The CAC is comprised of a chairperson and at least two others, usually including one employer's representative and one employee's representative. The committee listens to the evidence given to it (or reads the written submissions) and makes a decision. The practice has been to give a decision quickly but not to publish any reasoned decision or report. The committee tries to reach a unanimous decision but if there is not full agreement, the majority decision is taken or the chairperson can act as umpire and overrule the other two.

4.3.4 Commissioner for the Rights of Trade Union Members

The Employment Act 1988 (now contained in the Trade Union and Labour Relations (Consolidation) Act 1992) created this post. The Commissioner's function is to assist union members who are taking legal action against their union. There is a right, for example, for a trade union member to apply to a court to prevent their union from going ahead with proposed industrial action because the requirements of the law relating to holding a ballot before industrial action have not been complied with. The assistance includes bearing the applicant's legal costs. The decision to support will depend on the complexity of the case or whether it involves a matter of principle or is of public interest.

In the Green Paper issued in March 1989

entitled *Removing Barriers to Employment* the government suggested that the Commissioner's powers could be extended to appear with the assisted person in court and to give assistance in relation to cases regarding the breach of union rules.

In the first year of operation, the Commissioner reported that there were 324 enquiries, of which 70 fell within the officer's powers. About one-third of the enquiries related to union disciplinary action. Eventually only five cases were taken up and resolved.

4.4 Political aspects

4.4.1 Involvement in politics

It can be seen from the chapter so far that many of the changes needed to advance the cause of trade unionism have had to be fought for. Often these changes have been legal changes and this requires political involvement as Parliament has the power to make or repeal laws. Political movements involving the working classes are known to have existed throughout the period that unions emerged and grew. Early unions were not known to be very political, although they doubtless contributed to the causes of the time. The Chartism movement in the 1830s was characteristic in that it sought changes to the constitution, mainly aimed at greater representation for the working classes. The trade unions of the day did not identify very strongly with the movement.

Not until the 'new model unions' emerged in the 1850s was political awareness evidenced. A strong feature of the 'new' unions was the importance attached to representations to governments and moves to have MPs represent trade union views in Parliament. A major step towards this was the setting up of the TUC Parliamentary Committee in 1871. Soon after its formation there were several trade union-sponsored MPs elected for the first time in 1874. This enabled a union's views to be put to Parliament and for MPs to make representations to ministers on behalf of the unions. This drew

the unions into the political arena and it quickly paid dividends. The Acts of 1875 were partly due to union influence on the subject. By the 1890s there were calls for a separate body or party for Labour MPs. An Independent Labour Party was formed in 1893 which had little success at the polls but whose members had influence in the trade union movement. In 1900 the TUC formed a Labour Representation Committee which put up candidates for election as MPs. In 1906 54 Labour or Liberal/Labour MPs were elected. The LRC changed its name to the Labour Party in that year.

There are a number of reasons why the Labour party emerged from within the trade union movement. The trade union movement had, up to that time, supported a number of MPs by way of sponsorship and had an alignment with the Liberal party. The craft union leaders had been politically active, particularly for legal reform, but were not, in the main, socialist. This was more a characteristic of the leaders of the general unions who embraced the ideals of Engels and Marx and saw the trade union movement as a means of changing society. Within the political system there was no party which enshrined the new principles of socialism although there were a number of societies which trade unionists joined, such as the Social-Democratic Federation and later, in 1893, the Independent Labour Party.

Two further factors influencing the emergence of the Labour party was the widening of the franchise to all male voters. This brought greater numbers of working class, trade union members into the electorate and hence there was a need for a party with which these new voters could identify. A second factor was that there was firm evidence that the trade union movement had benefited from political action within and without Parliament that had effected changes in the law. Such legislative changes had enabled trade unions to operate with greater freedom and the spread of unionism was partially due to changes in the law. With a greater number of MPs dedicated to the cause of trade unionism and the possibility of such a party forming a government, there was potential for even more change. This came to fruition in 1924 with the formation of the first Labour government under Ramsay Macdonald. His Cabinet of 20 contained seven trade unionists but the minority government only lasted a year. Ironically this was a period of great industrial unrest which culminated in the General Strike of 1926.

Currently there are several formal links between the Labour party and the trade union movement:

- The vast majority of trade unions are affiliated to the Labour party. This gives them a direct input into formulating party policy. This is formulated at the Annual Conference at which the trade unions use their votes to influence policy decisions.
- The National Executive Committee of the Labour party has a trade union section, reflecting the influence of the affiliated trade unions. The NEC and its subcommittees are very influential in formulating policy for ratification at Conference. Trade union leaders are able to become involved in this process.
- Through the process of affiliation, the trade unions provide the bulk of Labour party funds. This is collected by means of a political levy (see below) on trade union members.
- Many trade unions still sponsor MPs by providing funds for their election (the amount being limited by law) in return for the MP campaigning on their behalf in Parliament. However, MPs cannot be mandated by their sponsoring union, i.e., the union cannot dictate how an MP must vote on an issue. This would be a breach of privilege.
- There is a Labour Party Liaison Committee which acts as a link between the TUC and the Labour party. Originally this was set up to coordinate opposition to the Conservative government's 1971 Industrial Relations Act but it has now been established as a permanent body dealing with wider issues.

While there are these very strong and permanent links between the trade unions and the Labour party there have been, and still are, a number of problem areas. In 1969 the Labour government, under Harold Wilson, published a White Paper entitled *In Place of Strife* which proposed a number of reforms to the industrial relations system. These proposals were given a hostile reception by the trade union movement and relations were strained. Eventually the proposals were withdrawn when the TUC gave a 'solemn undertaking' to carry out some internal reforms within the trade union movement. In any case the 1971 General Election intervened and a Conservative government was elected. A further area of contention has been pay policies (see Section 4.2.2) which the trade union movement has always opposed in principle (as being an interference in free collective bargaining) but has reluctantly accepted as an emergency measure or in exchange for some benefit to the unions.

During the 1970s the Labour government entered into a number of 'solemn agreements' and 'social compacts' with the TUC. The basis of these agreements was that, in return for favourable employment and trade union legislation, the government would receive the support of the trade union movement for its economic policies, including an incomes policy. This worked for about three years but latterly broke down and led to the 1978/79 'winter of discontent'.

During the 1979 general election campaign it was claimed that the Labour party was in the hands of the trade union barons and that the trade unions had become too influential. Public opinion certainly was against the extent of the power of the unions and that there was a need to curb these excesses. Indeed, relations between the Labour party and the trade union movement were severely strained at the time.

The involvement of the trade unions and the TUC in government diminished rapidly when the Conservatives took office in 1979. The extensive consultation processes that the TUC and the major trade union national officials had grown used to came to a sudden end. Also their influence fell, as the incoming government's policies were diametrically opposed to those of the trade union movement (see also Section 2.2.2). Successive Acts of Parliament in the

1980s have weakened the trade unions (by design) and their objections have been met largely with rebuttal. The TUC are still consulted on certain matters (as are many organisations) and they respond to policy consultative documents, such as Green and White papers. However, their influence is minimal. During this period the Labour party has undertaken a major review of its policies, not least because it has lost four general elections in a row. There has been a purge of left-wing extremists from the party, notably the Militant Tendency. This small group was influential in the party and in some trade unions. Whilst Neil Kinnock was leader of the Labour party, there was a shift of policy towards the centre of the political spectrum, including policies on trade union law and industrial relations. The party has said it will review the current legislative position but is not going to repeal all the trade union legislation of the Conservative administration. A further distancing of the Labour party from the trade unions is the internal electoral reform in the Labour party that will lead to the block vote influence at the Labour party's Annual Conference being reduced. The move is towards a 'one member, one vote' system which will give the individual members of the party and its MPs a greater voice in formulating policy at the expense of unions. As part of the Labour party's policy review it has issued a five-point plan for industrial relations. The points are:

- basic legal rights for all workers, including a minimum weekly wage
- the UK will become a signatory to the EC Social Charter
- a new court will be set up to deal with industrial disputes
- the right to take sympathetic industrial action will be restored, i.e., secondary action
- enhanced union representative rights, including the legal right to trade union recognition

The Conservative party has no formal links with the trade union movement and only loose formal links with employers' organisations. Philosophically the Conservative party is much more aligned to the CBI and the employers' associations. Inevitably a Conservative government consults with and listens to these organisations in formulating and implementing policy. The CBI, NFU and Institute of Directors, for example, are given a sympathetic hearing and are influential with a Conservative administration, with the TUC and trade unions having far less influence. However, this does not prevent the normal processes of consultation and the TUC has always claimed that it will consult and cooperate with any government.

The 1980s

The political environment was the single major factor which produced such profound changes to industrial relations in the UK during the 1980s. The Conservative party which took office in 1979, under the leadership of Margaret Thatcher, was on its own admission radical, right-wing and determined to bring about change in all aspects of national life. These objectives were met in full as the party remained in power, with Margaret Thatcher as Prime Minister, for the whole of the decade.

The unions were left out in the cold so far as the machinery of government was concerned. National trade union leaders had become used to being near to the centre of power through very close contact with the preceding Labour government. In the full glare of publicity, trade union leaders were often seen entering 10 Downing St. When the Conservatives took over this stopped abruptly. Unions were also involved in government agencies through the many quangos (quasi-autonomous nongovernmental organisations) that existed at the time. The incoming government dismantled these very rapidly and substituted direct Whitehall and ministerial decision making. The National Economic Development Councils (which were part of the economic decision making machinery) on which trade union leaders sat, were sidelined and became powerless. Ideas such as central economic planning were anathema to the government.

Ministers made no secret of the fact that they

were fundamentally opposed to trade unionism both philosophically and in practice. They set about a programme of legislation which reduced trade union power dramatically. Sir Keith Joseph, one of the major influences, stated that he believed that the British working person would have been better off had trade unions never existed. They were an undue interference in the labour market and they were a negative influence in the workplace. The prevailing philosophy of this government was that market forces should determine everything which dominated policy for the decade. Where markets did not exist, they were created, e.g., in the power generation industry. Where markets did exist, such as in the labour market, market forces were made to operate unhindered. Trade unions and employment legislation were seen as hindrances to the operation of a free market and their influence had to decrease.

Initially legislation was introduced to curb the excesses of trade union power demonstrated so vividly in the late 1970s, with large-scale strikes, demonstrations and all too often violent picketing. The government claimed a mandate from the electorate to do this and pursued the policy vigorously. The closed shop was targeted as being particularly objectionable. Legislation, commencing in 1980, did not prohibit its existence but the rules to set one up or sustain one were very onerous (*see* Section 15.3). This involved ballots requiring an 80% vote in favour. Contrasted to the 40% vote majority to return a government, these rules were very strict. Picketing was also tackled but this proved more difficult as the law is more complex (*see* Section 15.2.2). There were also claims that restricting or banning picketing was an infringement of human rights, i.e., the freedom to meet. The Code of Practice issued in 1980 recommended that the maximum numbers on a picket line should be six. Given the mass picketing of the 1970s, this was met with contempt from the unions. These changes did not stop the mass picketing by the miners in 1984, although the authorities did take very firm action against the miners.

The rules relating to political funds held by trade unions were altered, although they did not revert to making contracting in a requirement (i.e., where union members have to elect that they wish to allow some of their union dues to go to the union's political fund). Such a move would devastate the Labour party, which receives the bulk of its funds from trade unions.

The pace of legislative reform during the 1980s did not let up as Mrs Thatcher was twice reelected Prime Minister. Indeed in the 1990s the Conservative government under John Major is keeping up the reforms, for example by passing legislation to scrap Wage Councils.

The effect of the legislation (and other factors, such as the economy) has caused trade union membership to slump (*see* Section 2.2.2). The unions are no longer the force they were, even allowing for the drop in union membership. They are now well outside the machinery of government and with little influence. This is also true of their power base within the Labour party. The Labour party does not now have a policy of reversing all the Tory trade union legislation.

Another major area to feel the impact of the Conservative government's philosophy of allowing free market forces to work is the EC. This has led to some severe difficulties both in the UK and in Europe. The European Community's programme was seen by Mrs Thatcher's government as an interference. Mainly on the economic front, this eventually led to Mrs Thatcher's downfall, in 1990. An area of direct relevance to industrial relations is the EC Social Charter (*see* Section 17.2.1). This was promoted by the European Commission as a framework to develop economic and social union amongst member states. The UK government alone among all the EC member states opposed the idea in principle (both the Thatcher and Major administrations). The Maastricht Treaty had to be redrafted to allow the UK to opt out of the Social Chapter. The only area where the UK government does accept EC Directives, is in the area of safety. By not accepting the Social Charter the UK will not develop its systems in the way the other EC states will (*see* detail in Section 17.2.1).

4.4.2 Political funds and political action

During the early years of their existence, trade unions had used some of their funds to help political causes and their leaders had participated in politics. The Labour Representation Committee, which emerged from the TUC in 1900, was supported financially by the unions. Such financial support was to increase in the next few years, culminating in 40 candidates being fielded by the Labour Representation Committee in the 1906 General Election and a further 15 supported by the Parliamentary Committee of the TUC. This resulted in 54 Labour or Lib-Lab MPs being elected in 1906. Such political action was thought to be legal but was struck a body blow by the Osborne case in 1909. (The details of this case appear in Section 8.2.2.) In essence the Law Lords decided that the raising of money by trade unions for political purposes was *ultra vires* ('outside their powers') and thus not legal. The situation was altered by the 1913 Trade Union Act. This Act allowed trade unions to use their funds for political purposes but with some conditions and restrictions. These were that the unions had to keep such money in a separate political fund. Such a fund could only be set up after a ballot of the union members had approved the matter. Additionally, a union had to allow any member who wished to do so to contract out of paying into such a fund. The Trade Disputes and Trade Union Act 1927 reversed this latter provision and made it a contracting in situation whereby union members could contribute if they so wished. This Act was repealed in 1945 to restore the 1913 position of contracting out, the position today. A change from contracting out to contracting in has a devastating effect on the finances of the Labour party.

The requirements to have ballots to set up a political fund was amended by the Trade Union Act 1984. This Act (now contained in the Trade Union and Labour Relations (Consolidation) Act 1992) requires a union to hold a ballot of its members to create and maintain a political fund at least every ten years. Such a ballot must be either postal or at the place of work (with employers required to make facilities available).

Any ballot which does not authorise the union to have a political fund prevents that union from having such a fund or spending money for political purposes. It cannot transfer money from another fund to a political fund (although it can transfer funds the other way). The political objectives of a union can include:

- contributing to a political party
- providing services or property for a political party
- contributing to the candidature of a person as an MP, MEP or councillor and the maintenance of such an elected person
- the holding of a conference by or on behalf of a political party
- the production, publication or distribution of literature, documents, film, etc., for political campaigning

Government funds were available to assist unions in holding ballots to create or maintain a political fund but were withdrawn in 1993. The union had to comply with some detailed requirements to be eligible for such funds. The method of balloting must be postal and the ballot must be conducted under independent scrutiny. Workplace ballots are not acceptable for this particular purpose. The Certification Officer administered this system and decided whether a union was eligible for funds.

If a union does not fulfil these, or any other legislative requirements on political funds, then a member of the union can take their union to court. Additionally, they can be financially assisted in their court action by the Commissioner for the Rights of Trade Union Members (*see* Section 4.3.4).

Many unions were opposed to the requirement to hold a ballot and also to the government making funds available to pay for a ballot. There was much heated debate between unions. Some availed themselves of the money for ballots, others refused to as a matter of principle. The TUC were very much involved and, had the TUC passed a resolution stating it was TUC policy not to use these funds, several unions would have been expelled from the TUC. However the way in which the legislation was drafted, to compel a vote, forced the unions to comply, otherwise they could not continue to collect a political levy or raise money for political purposes. The hope was that many unions would find their members voting not to have a political fund. In the event, all the major unions had large majorities in favour of a political fund and levy. For example, the AEU balloted its members in 1985 and 238,604 voted in favour out of 283,000 members. The AEU levy in 1985 was £1 per member per year giving an income of £745,777. The union sponsors 15 Labour MPs as part of its political activities. The position on a member paying levy is that of contracting out, i.e., the assumption is that all members pay the levy unless they explicitly ask not to.

Industrial action taken by trade unions is normally aimed at securing the resolution of a dispute in the favour of the union's claim. However, the aims of such action can become political if the object of the action is to persuade the government to change its mind on a particular issue. The line between the two forms of action can be a fine one, particularly when the employees involved are the government's own employees, e.g., civil servants or those funded by the government in some way such as local government employees, NHS employees or those in the nationalised industries. Such political action was defined as 'any attempt to coerce the government either directly or by inflicting hardship on the community' in the 1927 Trade Disputes and Trade Union Act which made such industrial action illegal. This Act was repealed in 1945. The current definition of a trade dispute and its interpretation is considered in Section 10.2.2.

The statistics given in the Certification Officer's Annual Report for 1990 show that 54 unions had a political fund and the total income to these funds was £15.64m with an expenditure of £12.71m. Of these 6.11m members made contributions to their union's political fund, with 1.21m members having 'contracted out' of

paying the political levy. The table below gives the statistics for the five largest unions (except NALGO which does not have such a fund):

Union	No. of members contributing (000s)	No. of members exempt (000s)	Income £000s	Fund £000s
TGWU	1,091.2	23.2	3,466	4,739
AEU	360.6	229.1	851.4	114.2
GMB	742.2	57.9	2,305	2,686
MSF	296.6	356.4	517	342
NUPE	557.5	21.5	1,870	943

Source: Certification Officer's Annual Report, 1990

Mini-questions

4.1 Explain briefly the role of (a) the legislature, (b) the executive, (c) the judiciary.

4.2 Discuss the role of the legislature in industrial relations.

4.3 Discuss the role of the executive in industrial relations.

4.4 Give three examples of when ACAS performs individual conciliation.

4.5 What is the CAC?

Exercises

4.1 Discuss how incomes policies can be considered to be an intervention in collective bargaining. What difficulties might be caused at local and national level?

4.2 Describe the role and function of ACAS. Explain if you think it is of importance that this service is independent of the government and if so, why. What difficulties might ensue if it is not?

4.3 What was the impact of the Employment Act 1980 on the functions of ACAS? Assess how these changes may affect industrial relations.

Further reading

S Kessler and F Bayliss, *Contemporary British Industrial Relations*, Macmillan, 1992, 0-333-56815

5
Local organisation

5.1 Shop stewards

5.1.1 What is a shop steward?

In industrial relations one of the most important, but least understood, characters is the shop steward. Most people have heard of shop stewards and have an image of what they are like. Others have met several at work and base their judgements on that. However, in terms of an overall understanding of the shop steward's role, function, power, responsibilities and importance there is a lack of material. The framework within which a shop steward operates is essentially a local one, usually in a department or section. The role has emerged as one of kingpin in shop floor and local industrial relations who has a strong influence on national industrial relations. As we shall see in the next section, the emergence of the shop steward as one of the most important people in the industrial relations system is a relatively recent development and one which was not the result of deliberate policy.

The public image of the shop steward is sometimes one of a militant, usually very left-wing, disruptive, vocal person whose sole aim in life is to protect the union's members at all costs, even if it causes the firm to go bust! It is doubtful if this is true at all and is hardly the description of the 'average' shop steward. In the main the shop steward is the person to whom union members go for information, to raise queries and to take their problems. The steward takes up any outstanding problems with management according to some procedure.

Sometimes the steward has to collect union dues and ensure that members are paid up and acts as a recruitment agent for the union. The vast bulk of local union activity centres around the shop steward. The implementation of agreements falls to the steward to ensure that the members are receiving what they are due under the agreements. Any difficulties are raised by the members to the steward who tries to resolve the issue. Problems on pay, bonuses, premiums, benefits, holidays, overtime, work allocation, discipline, grievances, safety and others are all within the province of the shop steward. The steward needs to know about these topics and be able to argue the members' case to management. This role is further extended by collective bargaining (*see* Chapter 6) when they are often involved in the negotiating process.

Shop stewards exist in all areas of unionised labour. The name given to them varies. In the printing industry the shop steward is known as the father/mother of the chapel; by designers, the corresponding member; in the steel industry, the works' representative; and in staff unions, the staff representative. More often than not, the shop steward represents a well-defined group of workers, either a department, a section or a shift. The steward usually acts only for that group and only for the particular union. Shop stewards are ordinary employees of the firm and have a designated job within the group or department they represent, carrying on that job until some union business arises that needs their attention, when in most cases they seek permission to attend to that business. Often this is an informal chat and a word with the supervisor and the matter is dealt with. In other instances it may be a meeting with a manager or a committee meeting. Generally the shop steward is appointed through elections by the group he or she represents. Most stewards are elected unopposed. In a few instances there are no candidates and the group has no elected representative. This can cause problems as both management and the group have no person to refer to as a representative of the group. Usually the union Rule Book stipulates a term of office (one, two or three years) after which the steward can stand down or seek reelection. A steward, when appointed, receives credentials from the union office and usually will officially inform management of the appointment. The average constituency of a shop steward is between 50 and 60, but this varies enormously. The number of stewards in the country is not known, but is probably about 300,000. A survey carried out in 1980 found that, in establishments which recognised trade unions, 75% had shop stewards and 50% had convenors, 10% of which were full-time. In establishments employing more than 2,000 people 66% had a full-time convenor. (*See* Section 5.2.1).

The essential function of the shop steward is to act as the representative of the union members. The steward is the spokesperson for the group on most matters relating to the group. Personal matters may be dealt with by the individual but group matters are the concern of the steward. The steward is recognised by management as the group representative and should management want to pass information to, or ask the opinion of the group, this can be done through the steward. The reverse situation operates whereby the steward reports back to the members from management and keeps them informed. This two-way communications process is of great importance to shop floor industrial relations. The group needs to have its views, opinions and grievances taken to management and management wants its view, opinions and decisions transmitted to the group. This role of the steward is not an easy one. Making representations on matters can involve the steward trying to assess the consensus of opinion on a matter and, regardless of personal views, pass it on to management. It can involve arguing a case the group wants to be taken up but which the steward does not support. If there is a major disagreement the steward might resign but normally would carry out the task as mandated. In reverse, the steward has to pass on information from management as factually and as objectively as possible without biasing it towards personal opinion.

A second essential function of a steward is to act as the union's representative to the members. The steward should encourage membership and recruitment to the union, ensure dues are paid, ensure that the Rule Book is observed, encourage attendance at branch meetings and pass on union information. So far as the members are concerned, the shop steward is their point of contact with the union. The majority of members have little to do with the union except their contact with the steward. An often criticised feature of our system of trade unionism is low level of branch attendance. Few (10% or less) attend so the steward's role in encouraging good trade unionism among members is an important one.

5.1.2 Background

The universal existence of the steward is a recent development since the Second World War, and the extent of the steward's functions has expanded considerably since this time. Stewards have existed since the 'new' unions emerged in the 1860s. Initially the unions were not recognised by the employers of the time. This obviously restricted the role of the steward to a non-bargaining agent of the union. Factory organisation of unions was not strong due to employers' resistance. A change occurred in the First World War in certain industries. In order to increase production for the war effort, certain changes in work practices were needed. In engineering this included the introduction of 'dilutees'. These were unskilled or semiskilled workpeople carrying out skilled people's jobs. The unions were reluctant to allow this, fearing the practice would continue after the war and dilute the skilled person's status. Eventually the Treasury agreements were signed in which the unions allowed dilution, subject to certain conditions. However, the implementation of these agreements at local level required careful monitoring. This was where the shop stewards found a role and established themselves as shop floor representatives. Under wartime measures, striking was made illegal but this law was severely challenged. On the Clyde the shipbuilders' shop stewards had formed their own committee which became very powerful. Against the advice of their full-time officials the stewards called a strike. It was very successful, with about 8,000 to 10,000 workers out. With the impossibility of gaoling so many the measure was dropped. It did prove that the shop stewards could usurp a lot of power.

The economic decline following the war reduced the power of the unions, and the local power of the shop stewards especially. Union membership dropped, especially after the 1926 General Strike and did not recover until the late 1930s. During the Second World War a similar situation arose with the production workers engaged in the war effort. Special agreements were made and the person on the scene, the shop steward, emerged as the supervisor of the agreements. After the war, the shop steward continued to act as a local union representative. Increasingly employers recognised shop stewards and allowed them to engage in the functions we now recognise.

The growth of the number of stewards and the extent of their functions are due to several factors:

- Greater numbers of agreements at local level. Increasingly employers are negotiating agreements at local level as opposed to national level. This involves the steward in negotiations and implementation. The agreements are formulated, negotiated, agreed and signed by the stewards. A recent survey found that 80% of establishments that recognised a manual trade union had procedures for discipline, dismissal and grievances. This necessarily expands their role. The implementation and interpretation

of these agreements is a function for all the stewards in the firm and is ongoing, so giving them a day-to-day function.

- The growth of the personnel function in organisations gave recognition to shop stewards. If a separate department is set up to deal with personnel matters, including industrial relations, then the managers in that department have to deal with union people at plant level. This naturally is the shop steward. The development of personnel policies on human resource planning, recruitment, promotion, pay structure, bonuses and so on has widened the scope of bargaining and so the scope of the shop steward's functions.

- Since the 1960s Parliament has passed many Acts relating to employment, starting with the Contracts of Employment Act 1963. Much of this legislation gave rights in employment (*see* Chapters 10–15) and trade union rights on recognition, joining unions, taking part in union activities, no discrimination for joining a union and facilities and training. This enhanced the power of the steward and extended the role once more into areas that could be claimed as of statutory right.

- As organisations grew, the distance between the shop floor and top management grew, so there was a need for someone at shop floor level to deal with local matters with local management. This is the change that was noted in Section 3.1.1. As the management of organisations became divorced from ownership, so the reluctance to recognise the shop steward diminished, though not altogether. It was also convention for management to have an on-site union representative rather than having to use the union's full-time officials. Also management prefers to deal with shop stewards as they have a greater knowledge of local agreements and arrangements.

5.1.3 Functions and duties

The shop steward has a wide range of functions to perform in order to fulfil the role described so far. As far as actually being instructed what to do, there is no official source of instruction apart from being required to adhere to union policy. Union Rule Books on the whole tend not to have reflected the changes noted in Section 5.1.2. Rule Books were written when shop stewards were less numerous, so they specify very little regarding the shop steward. They often mention the mode of appointment, term of office and the restriction of not sanctioning industrial action on their own. Apart from that there is no detail on the function of the steward. Many unions have a shop stewards' handbook. These give greater detail about the shop stewards' functions to help new stewards find out what they should do. The subsections below list the main functions of a steward.

Collecting dues

This function is now on the decline as most firms operate the check-off system whereby union dues are, by agreement, deducted from wages or salary at source by the employer. A survey in the 1980s suggested that 75% of establishments had a check-off system in operation with the figure nearly 100% in the nationalised corporations and public corporations. The function was of importance not merely to collect money but it also became a regular (weekly) contact between member and steward. Some unions allocated this task to a collecting steward. For carrying out this duty the steward was given a commission on the subscriptions of about 5 or 10%.

Checking cards

This function is connected to the one above. The check-off system has largely diminished this function also. The member's union card was signed by the steward when payment was made. Any arrears had to be paid and, if they were not, eventually the members could be expelled from the union. Some unions, such as the AEU, had a system of checking cards at the branch meeting. This was an attempt to ensure attendance at branch meetings. Nonattendance at such a meeting (say every fortnight) led to a fine being imposed, per the Rule Book.

Recruiting members

An important function of the steward, from the union's point of view, is trying to achieve as high a membership as possible in the group represented. All unions have a 100% union membership policy. This is not the same as a closed shop as membership is not linked to obtaining and keeping a job (*see* Section 14.3.1). Where there is a closed shop, in practice or by agreement, the steward has to ensure that the new entrant is, or will apply to become a member of the union. In a pre-entry closed shop the function is less important, as a prerequisite to obtaining the job is a union card. In a post-entry closed shop the function is very important. If this function is not diligently carried out, the closed shop may become difficult to enforce at a later date.

Complaints

The steward is the first person a member comes to, after their immediate supervisor, regarding a complaint. The steward then has the function of investigating the complaint and, if substantiated, pursuing it to a satisfactory conclusion. The range of topics can vary considerably from wages, bonuses, holidays, sick benefit, safety, welfare, working practices, overtime allocation and many others. Often these are the subjects of an agreement which then has to be referred to. Much of the day-to-day work of the steward is relating to complaints raised by the members. If there is a disciplinary complaint against a union member, the steward is called to accompany that person if they wish. This should be a feature of the disciplinary procedure.

Disputes

Where collectively the members have a disagreement with management over an issue, the matter is pursued as a dispute. Frequently a disputes procedure exists and this is followed. Initially this will involve the steward seeing the member of management specified in the first stage of the procedure. If there is a failure to agree, maybe after several attempts at finding a solution, the matter is taken to the next stage. This may then be put in the hands of the convenor (or senior steward) or even a district officer. Disputes arise quite often when the annual negotiations are taking place where the members feel entitled to some claim the management will not yield on. Disputes may also arise where the group as a whole is affected or the group acts in sympathy with one member who has an outstanding grievance or complaint.

Negotiating

Increasingly stewards are involved in negotiations at plant level, the stewards of one or several unions acting collectively to present a claim to management. Usually a small number of the stewards are selected to act as negotiators. Where there are several unions in an organisation, the negotiations may be conducted by a joint shop stewards' committee (JSSC) (*see* Section 5.2.1). Annual agreements and procedures are negotiated by stewards, who finally sign the negotiated settlements.

Communications

The steward has a very important role in acting as a communicator between the members and management and vice versa. The steward also acts as communicator from the union to the members. Often management, if it wishes to consult with employees, will consult the steward. If a policy decision is to be announced, this may be done through the steward. The results of negotiations or procedures are conveyed to the members through the steward.

5.1.4 Power and responsibility

Shop stewards have varying degrees of power derived from several sources. The degree of power possessed by the individual steward depends on a variety of factors. One factor is the degree of commitment of the person to the job. Some prefer to act as a strong leader, others prefer to carry out their duties as and when demanded by members. The position of the shop steward is so loosely defined that stewards can do as little or as much as they please. Most stewards carry on quietly doing a responsible job for the people they represent, while others take a more active role as leader. Another factor is the industry the steward is in. Some industries have a tradition of strong shop floor organisation and hence strong stewards. In the print industry the father or mother of the chapel is in a very strong position and acts as a supervisor to the members, with little being done without their approval. The newspaper industry has a reputation for lightning strikes which reflects the powerful position of the steward (foc or moc). A third factor that causes variation in the amount of power a steward possesses is the nature of the agreements in the firm. If the agreements are wholly locally negotiated, this tends to give the shop steward power in the area of implementation and interpretation. Where agreements are national, the steward's freedom to manoeuvre is restricted.

There are several sources of shop steward power. The following subsections list the main ones in order of importance:

The work group

The steward, being a representative appointed by the group, has to act broadly in line with what the group desires. If a steward is too weak or too strong the group is likely to reject them and their actions, this being manifest eventually by the steward not being reappointed. This does not always happen as a work group sometimes gives its steward a free hand and control may be difficult. However, if issues need raising with management then the steward must take the matter up with them. If the group is particularly strong the steward will reflect this. In times when industrial relations are at a low ebb the stewards have to use their authority, both towards management and their members. How the steward acts is crucial in controlling a situation. Sometimes they restrain the members from extreme action, at other times they persuade them that a certain line of action must be taken. So far as most trade union members are concerned the steward is the union. The expectation that the union can do something for them gives the steward the power and authority to take certain action.

Collective bargaining

The gradual broadening of the scope of collective bargaining (*see* Chapter 6) has given the steward increasingly more power. The greater the number of issues negotiated between union and management, the greater is the steward's authority to act on many issues. The list in Section 6.1.2 shows the wide variety of topics that can be dealt with in negotiations. Agreements and procedures often specify the steward as the person to deal with an issue. This is a direct source of power.

Branch organisation

Each group of workers is attached to a branch of the union (*see* Section 5.2). Branches hold regular meetings and are the local policy making body of the union. Ostensibly the branch would give the steward a certain amount of power as they seek to implement the policy of the branch. In practice branch meetings are poorly attended and often do not provide a power base for the steward. The branches of some unions are formed at plant level so the steward and the members are more closely associated with the branch. Where the branch is outside the place of work there is less enthusiasm for attending meetings. Branch officials are stewards attached to the branch but the number of stewards involved is proportionally low.

Trade union structure

The hierarchy of trade union officials is a source of power to the steward. The policies developed by the union are implemented at the workplace through the steward. This is of importance in times of industry-wide disputes, where the national executive has called for industrial action. The action taken at local level is organised by the stewards. When industrial

relations are normal the steward tends to be autonomous. Stewards may act as a body at plant level but tend to have little contact with the full-time officials. The internal government of a union is laid down in the Rule Book. This frequently involves the steward in being a delegate at district and national level and to national conference. This is the democratic structure of the unions whereby the voice of the shop floor can be transmitted up through the trade union structure by the stewards.

Union Rule Book

As was noted in Section 5.1.3, the Rule Book gives very little guidance on the authority and responsibilities of the steward. Most do not specify what they can or cannot do. Usually there is a rule stating that industrial action cannot be sanctioned by the steward alone. The authorisation of industrial action lies with either a full-time official or the national executive committee. This is more important now as the Trade Union Act 1984 altered the law on immunities (*see* Section 10.2.2). Obviously stewards are required to observe the rules of their union and keep to the procedures specified. Some unions have a rule protecting the steward against discriminatory dismissal. This can take the form of a union enquiry if a steward is dismissed to ensure there has been no victimisation.

Having had a look at the power (or authority) of the steward it is important to note the responsibilities of the steward. It is a rule of any organisation that where there is authority there should be a corresponding level of responsibility. So far as shop stewards are concerned they are responsible to their members, the union and arguably (though not all would agree) to the organisation they work for. Their prime responsibility is to the members that appointed them. The steward is their representative and has been entrusted with protecting them and, where possible, improving wages and conditions, taking their grievances and problems to management, ensuring they receive union, company and State benefits and being responsible for keeping members informed. Stewards see this as their overriding responsibility and if there is conflict they will back their members, even if it is against the union. The steward's responsibilities to the union are to ensure that the shop floor organisation is maintained and strengthened. This is achieved through encouraging membership, collecting dues (if this is still done), attending meetings and educating members. The steward also has a responsibility to keep the branch and union officials informed of developments by being involved in the branch. A third area of responsibility that exists, though it is not always accepted, is the responsibility of the steward to the employer. Some would argue that the steward is appointed by the work group to represent them and that is their sole responsibility. Others argue that the steward has a responsibility to the firm to ensure its continued existence and prosperity which, in the end, will benefit the members.

5.1.5 Training and facilities

With the ever-widening range of functions a steward is required to carry out, the need for training and facilities becomes more relevant. If stewards are to negotiate meaningfully with management on a wide range of issues, some of them complex, they must possess enough knowledge to deal with them intelligently. As businesses and organisations are becoming more complex, this adds to the need for training. The areas of knowledge extend from payment systems to job evaluation, work study, employment legislation, health and safety, benefits, pensions, finance and others. Additionally they need to be acquainted with the company, its procedures, products and technology. This all places a heavy requirement on the steward.

In response to this demand for training the unions, the TUC and colleges have set up courses. The TUC has an education department which has developed several courses for shop stewards and safety representatives which are run in colleges and university extramural departments. Also the TUC has a publications

department with booklets on a range of topics. Some of the larger unions have their own colleges to which a steward can go for training. Other unions have home-study packs which introduce the steward to the union, trade unionism and management subjects. Also the Workers' Education Association sets up and runs courses at local centres and has a range of publications.

As a steward is an employee, and is required to do a job of work, this may preclude being absent on training courses, unless they accept a loss of pay. The Employment Protection Act 1975 introduced a provision for reasonable paid time off work to be given to a trade union officer (steward) during working hours to undergo training in aspects of industrial relations that are relevant to their duties. Supporting this statutory right is a Code of Practice on 'Time Off Work for Trade Union Duties and Activities'. This gives further details and guidance on how this section of the Act can be implemented (*see* Section 11.4).

Alongside the provision for training is the provision of facilities. There are no legal rights here but the TUC has suggested that facilities include the following:

- the provision of a list of new entrants
- facilities to explain to new entrants the union situation and the agreements in operation
- facilities to collect dues and inspect cards
- a room, or at least a desk, storage facilities and ready access to office facilities
- use of a notice board
- use of a room for consulting members and for committee meetings
- sufficient time off, with pay, to perform these duties

In respect of the latter, the Employment Protection Act 1975 made provision to give the steward reasonable time off work, with pay, to carry out those duties concerned with industrial relations between the employer and any associated employer and their employees. The Employment Act 1989 restricted the purpose for which paid time off work was taken to those duties concerned with negotiations with the direct employer. The Code of Practice referred to above has been revised and gives further details on this. In the event of an employer not complying with the provisions of the law, the steward can make a complaint to a tribunal. The tribunal, if it finds for the steward, can make an order that the steward be paid for such reasonable time off as is necessary to carry out duties or acquire training.

5.2 Committees and branches

5.2.1 Organisation within the firm

Wherever there are trade union members in the firm, there will be a shop steward. Sometimes in large organisations the local trade union organisation can be complex. Even medium-sized firms may have six or more unions in their collective bargaining structure. The shop floor will have at least one union (depending on the levels of skill), the staff another (say MSF), the maintenance department another (AEU), the transport drivers would likely be in the TGWU and maybe there would also be a union for the ancillary staff. In sites employing 1,000 and more, there may be over 20 unions. In order to provide a coherent and coordinated approach to industrial relations these various unions and their stewards need to have a structure within which to operate efficiently. There is no general pattern to this, as each firm has developed its own system to deal with its unique situation, but there are some common features that are frequently encountered.

To coordinate the actions of a large number of stewards there has developed the office of senior steward or convenor. This office is held by the shop floor union, as it has the largest number of members. The convenor is a steward in the sense that he or she is still an employee, but generally the position is nominal and the convenor is engaged most of the time on union business. Where convenors exist they act as a focal point for union business in the firm. They will be recognised by management and are often mentioned in procedural agreements, such as a disputes procedure, where the convenor is involved in the second stage after a steward. Sometimes facilities are provided for the

convenor such as an office, telephone, access to typing and so on. In negotiations, the convenor will be the chief negotiator and will lead the union side in joint negotiations with management. As such the convenor will be the signatory to any agreements made. Union rules either do not mention the convenor or merely say that one can be elected from among the stewards of that union in the firm. As local union business is focused on the convenor they can become very strong and influential. If they have the backing of the stewards and the members, the convenor can hold out against the full-time officials of the union. This has created conflict where the full-time officials, say at national level, have reached agreement with the employers, but this is not accepted at local level by the convenor or stewards.

Another device that has been used to coordinate the stewards in a firm is a Joint Shop Stewards' Committee (JSSC). This is used extensively in federated engineering companies where the Confederation of Shipbuilding and Engineering Unions recommends the use of these at local level. It is on these JSSCs that the regional and national committees of the CSEU are built. A JSSC is a committee representing all the unions in the firm. Not all the stewards sit on the committee as this might be impractical (with shift working) and be numerically cumbersome. Usually a formula for representation is worked out so that a reasonably sized committee is formed on which all the unions have a seat or are represented by another steward. The committee deals with all business that is of common interest. Where national agreements exist covering all the unions in the industry (e.g., in engineering) there is a large amount of common ground. The JSSC is useful for deciding a joint approach to management, formulating claims and coordinating activities. This is of advantage to the unions as it gives them solidarity. It is of advantage to management as there is the one set of negotiations rather than several. This is especially true where the annual wage negotiations are concerned. Usually for negotiations the JSSC will appoint from its number several stewards to act as negotiators.

A development, in the 1980s, to overcome the problem associated with having several unions recognised in one firm, was the growth of single-union agreements. This was a management-led development that was not welcomed by a large section of the trade union movement. A single-union agreement is an agreement between an employer and one union such that the sole bargaining rights for all employees is vested in the one union. No other union is recognised for any category of employee so all employees wishing to join a union join the one recognised trade union. Hence the agreement eliminates many of the problems that are inherent in a multi-union plant where potential rivalry exists over which union represents whom, differentials between groups, restrictive working practices and recognition disputes. The benefits to management are manifest and the union gaining the agreement also stands to benefit in terms of membership and power. Such agreements tend to be comprehensive agreements whereby the firm distributes the full agreement to a number of unions. It then enters into discussion with several unions with a view to inviting one of these to be the single union. The terms in the agreement have, for instance, included flexible working practices clauses, a simple grading structure for employees and a so-called no strike clause. The latter is not strictly true as employees could strike at any time (by ignoring the agreement) but a clause exists which specifies that industrial action will not be taken until procedure has been exhausted.

Instituting single-union agreements is relatively simple for a new firm starting up but is far more difficult for existing firms. The problem is how to introduce a new single union agreement within the existing framework of procedures and agreements. The resistance from the current unions to such a change would be very high. It would require the scrapping of the existing agreements and starting afresh. With a new firm such constraints do not exist. This has been especially true of Japanese companies setting up operations in the UK. A notable single-union agreement has been made between Nissan and the EETPU for the new car plant in Washington New Town. Proposals to follow this example have come from British companies who have difficult industrial relations. For instance several firms in the newspaper printing industry moved their operations from the traditional sites in Fleet Street to new premises in London's dockland and entered into single-union agreements. This occurred in early 1986 when the Times Newspaper Group transferred its print facility from Fleet Street to Wapping. The employers took on new staff and the EETPU became the trade union recognised by the employer (not the traditional print unions, the NGA and SOGAT). Such proposals are partially political in order to break the monopoly of the traditional print unions in Fleet Street. This explains why the trade union movement has been opposed to these agreements as it is perceived as an erosion of traditional trade union power (*see also* Section 7.1.3).

5.2.2 Safety representatives

The Safety Representatives and Safety Committees Regulations 1977 introduced the legal right for a trade union to become directly involved in the management of health and safety in the workplace. The Regulations provide that an independent trade union has the right to appoint a Safety Representative (where the union is recognised by the employer). The original draft Regulations allowed for 'the election by employees' of a Safety Representative. This is not the case now, i.e., only an independent recognised union has the legal right to appoint or, indeed, insist on having a Safety Representative.

The Health and Safety at Work Act 1974 makes it a legal duty for the employer to 'consult with Safety Representatives with a view to the making and maintenance of arrangements which enable him and his employees to cooperate effectively in promoting and developing measures to ensure the health and safety at work of the employees and checking the effectiveness of such measures'. An interesting concept is introduced here – a legal duty to cooperate!

Alongside the Regulations comes a Code of Practice and a set of Guidance Notes issued by the Health and Safety Commission. The Safety Representative is appointed (there is no requirement to be elected) and the union should inform management of the appointment. The person appointed should, if possible, have worked for the firm for two years. The functions of the Safety Representative are:

- to investigate potential hazards and dangerous occurrences
- to investigate complaints by an employee
- to make representations to the employer on each of the above and general matters of health, safety or welfare
- to carry out inspections of the workplace
- to represent the employees in consultations with Health and Safety Executive Inspectors
- to receive information from Inspectors
- to attend safety committee meetings

The Safety Representative has no legal liability for these duties, i.e., if anything goes wrong, blame cannot be attached to a Safety Representative for what they have done or not done.

The Code suggests that the Representative:

- take reasonable steps to keep informed of legal requirements, the hazards of the workplace and the employer's safety policy
- encourage cooperation between the employer and employee in promoting health and safety
- bring to the employer's notice, usually in writing, any unsafe or unhealthy condition or practice or unsatisfactory arrangement for welfare

The Regulations state that the employer should allow the Safety Representative paid time off work to receive training for their function. If this is not granted, or it is not with pay, the member can complain to an Industrial Tribunal. A separate Code of Practice has been issued on 'Time off for the Training of Safety Representatives'. The Code states that the Representative, as soon as possible after appointment, should be allowed paid time off to attend basic training facilities approved by the TUC or the member's union. Up-dating training should also be given. The training should include:

- the legal requirements for health and safety
- the nature and extent of workplace hazards and the measures necessary to eliminate or minimise them
- the health and safety policy of employers and the organisation and arrangements for fulfilling these policies

The trade union is responsible for appointing the Safety Representative and, when training has been arranged, the union should inform management of the course and its syllabus. The usual interpretation of this training is the TUC ten-day course, which is run at many institutions.

Under the Regulations, the Safety Representative can inspect the workplace by giving the employer notice of their intention to do so. This can be performed once every three months or where there has been a major change or after a reportable accident. The employer's representative can be present at the inspection. The Safety Representative can inspect or take copies of relevant documents which the employer is legally required to keep, except records relating to an individual. There are exceptions to this, e.g., on the grounds of national security or commercial sensitivity. The Code of Practice recommends that the employer should provide the Safety Representative with information:

- on the plans and performance of the undertaking, insofar as they affect health and safety
- of a technical nature
- which the employer keeps about accidents, dangerous occurrences and industrial diseases
- specifically relating to matters of health and safety including the results of any measurements taken

Finally the employer has to set up a safety committee if requested to do so by two or more Safety Representatives. The employer must consult with all the Representatives and post a notice stating the composition of the committee. The composition and constitution of the committee are for agreement between the parties. The Code gives no extra information on this topic although the Guidance Notes do give many helpful suggestions. The Guidance Notes issued give further practical suggestions on implementing the Regulations and Code. The Notes do not have any legal significance, in the way that the Code of Practice does. The topics covered include the criteria for deciding the number of Safety Representatives, the functions of Safety Representatives, inspections and the membership, objectives, function and conduct of a safety committee.

It can be seen from this comprehensive set of rules that the role of the union-appointed Safety Representative has been made central to the operation of health and safety management in an organisation. The law sets up a right to have representatives, it confers rights on these representatives, including direct involvement, and gives a right to have a committee to discuss relevant topics. There is no parallel in any other area of a firm's operations where this occurs. Indeed, the UK is behind its EC partners in providing a legal framework and on the practices of consultation and involvement of employees in an organisation. Health and safety are seen as key issues where employee involvement is crucial, not only to the success of the aim of improving health and safety but also to involving workpeople in a topic that directly affects them. The basis of this is that if employees are involved in the management of health and safety in the workplace they will be committed to achieving its objectives.

5.2.3 External associations

While the steward is the focus of attention of activity on the shop floor, the steward is also the link pin to other outside bodies and the union hierarchy. The immediate point of contact for a steward is the branch. Every member and steward is attached to a branch of the union. This is the basic unit of the union. In large unions there are several thousand. All unions have branches, the print unions call them chapels and the miners' union lodges. The branch is where the members go to participate in their union's affairs, to exchange information and help formulate policy. It also has an important function regarding the payment of union dues, but this has diminished since the check-off system

became popular. However, the branch still retains the responsibility for collecting the dues from the employees, keeping proper accounts and passing the money on to headquarters. Stewards are required to attend all branch meetings but seldom do. Some unions have a rule that a member is only eligible to become a steward if they have attended a minimum of 50% of branch meetings in the preceding year.

Branches are formed in a variety of ways. Some are based on trade groups where all the members from a particular trade are allocated to a branch set up for that trade. Other branches are composite in character where members from different industries are attached to the branch. This happens where there are insufficient members to form a trade branch. A third type of branch occurs in large firms where there are sufficient members in the firm to form their own branch.

Each branch has its own officers. These consist of a chairperson, secretary and treasurer as a minimum plus others such as vice-chairperson, collector, education secretary and publicity officer. There is a branch committee which runs the branch. All these offices are honorary and held by members of that branch. Usually the functions of the branch and its officers are set out in the union Rule Book and sometimes a branch constitution is given as well.

It is from the branch that delegates are sent to the other committees of the union such as regional committees, trade committees and the national executive council, plus delegates to the annual or biennial conference. It is these delegates who provide the input from the shop floor level to regional and national levels and this contact is a very important factor in the democracy of a union. Also branches develop policy and submit motions to conferences that may become the national policy of the union.

Association with other bodies is also determined at the branch. Representatives are sent to the local trade councils and Labour party with whom the unions have a strong connection. The role of the trades councils was described in Section 2.4.4 and the relationship to the Labour party is described in Section 4.4.

Mini-questions

5.1   List the five main functions of a shop steward.

5.2   State the four main sources of power for a shop steward.

5.3   Explain briefly the representative function of the shop steward.

5.4   Describe three factors that have enlarged the job of the shop steward in recent times.

5.5   State the responsibilities of the shop stewards to their union.

5.6   State the responsibilities of the shop stewards to their members.

5.7   List the facilities a shop steward might need.

5.8   List five training requirements for a shop steward.

5.9   State what a convenor is.

5.10 List four functions of a safety representative.

Exercises

5.1   Discuss how democratic trade unions are and the ways and means used to achieve democracy in a trade union.

5.2   In what ways can a shop steward be considered to be one of the most important characters in our industrial relations system?

5.3   From a manager's point of view, explain why you would, or would not, prefer your workforce to be represented through a shop steward.

5.4   Discuss the importance of the branch to the trade union member and the union itself. What reasons might there be for the lack of enthusiasm for branch activities and attendance?

5.5   Debate the motion 'single union agreements are good for British industrial relations'.

5.6   Draw up a model constitution for a health and safety committee, including its composition and a typical agenda.

Further reading

N Millward and M Stevens, *British Workplace Industrial Relations*, Dartmouth, 1992, 1-85521-321-4

E Baston and I Boraston, *Shop Stewards in Action*

Case study

(8) The mushrooming problem, page 331.

6

Collective bargaining

6.1 What is collective bargaining?

6.1.1 The basis of collective bargaining

The single most important aspect of our industrial relations system is that it is based, for the most part, on the function known as collective bargaining. Fundamentally this consists of an employer, or group of employers, negotiating the terms and conditions of employment of their employees with the representatives of one or several worker organisations and reaching agreement on these issues. While this process can involve different levels, units and issues, the basis is the same, in that various aspects of a worker's contract of employment are determined not individually but collectively. It is estimated that out of a working population of around 24.7 million (in 1992), about 16 million workers come under this system. Also collective bargaining deals with the procedural aspects of industrial relations, that is the relationship between the parties, the bargaining units, the people involved and the procedures to be used in particular situations.

Most employees will be unable to negotiate their own contract of employment. Very often the features of this, to a greater or lesser extent, are laid down in negotiated agreements. Jobs are offered on standard terms and conditions which are accepted or refused as they stand. Neither side at an interview can haggle over these predetermined terms. Frequently the rate of pay, hours, holidays and the like are pre-set and cannot be altered to suit individuals. This is almost universally true for junior positions and

even at management levels. Occasionally individuals might negotiate their own terms and conditions for a completely new job or a job at the executive grade. Most jobs are advertised at a fixed rate or scale, only a few state that the salary is open to negotiation. Once employed in an organisation the changes that necessarily take place from time to time are determined collectively, through some negotiating machinery, not with each individual separately. The rest of this chapter will explore the issues raised in bargaining, the processes used and the units involved.

Collective bargaining gradually emerged over time for a variety of reasons. From the workers' point of view collective bargaining enables the numerical strength of the workforce to be used to their advantage. Employers have the power to run their businesses as they see fit. This has always been the presumption in Britain, especially at English law, and governments also take this line unless there is a good reason to interfere. The employers' power to run their businesses as they will (often called management prerogative) obviously gives them a great deal of strength. The unions emerged to combat this strength by combining individuals, who were separately weak, into a more powerful collective organisation. Employers having to negotiate with employees collectively was seen, certainly by the unions, as achieving a better balance of power. Should the employer not concede a point (say on a wage increase) sanctions could be taken not only by the individual, but by the whole group. Such a disruption is more persuasive if the business is to continue. From the employers' point of view it enables them to negotiate with large numbers of their employees at one time rather than one by one. It also promotes fairness and equality between employees. From both sides it enables the conditions of service to be worked out on a regular, systematic basis. As we shall see, an important aspect of collective bargaining has been the emergence of national agreements. These regularise the position of employees in the industry as a whole. This has many advantages to both sides.

Historical developments

The process of collective bargaining grew slowly from the first signs, in the 1890s, of its emergence as a permanent process. The first evidence of such bargaining was restricted mainly to two categories of employment. The first was the skilled occupations in such industries as shipbuilding, engineering and the print industry. The second was the industries in which piece work predominated such as coal, iron and steel, cotton, textile and the boot and shoe industries. This also reflected the level of unionisation during this period, which was not as high (in terms of the proportion of the working population) as it is today.

The next major step forward in the spread of collective bargaining came during the First World War. Trade unionism was strengthened by the reorganisation that took place as a result of the war efforts (*see* Section 8.1.3). The nationalisation of the coal industry and the railways during the war extended the process into these industries. The Munitions of War Act 1915 introduced arbitration at a national level which inevitably brought the two sides of industry together to solve problems. During this period a very influential factor was the outcome of the Whitley Committee Reports (1916–18). These reports recommended the creation of permanent organisations for the purposes of collective bargaining which became known as joint industrial councils (*see* Section 8.1.4). Trade union membership rose a great deal during this period which aided the extension of collective bargaining.

The postwar years did not see a great expansion of the collective bargaining system and in some areas it declined. The economic conditions that prevailed, and the repercussions of the General Strike of 1926, took their toll so that conditions for further expansion of the system did not exist. Trade union membership fell during this period. The next period of development occurred during the Second World War when, for the same reasons as in the First World War, the system of collective bargaining expanded. This was sustained after the war because the economy recovered and there was a boom in the 1950s and 1960s.

Prerequisites

Two conditions are prerequisite to the establishment of collective bargaining. These are the freedom to associate and the recognition of trade unions by employers. To a lesser degree the existence of employers' associations is required. As we shall see in Chapter 8, the law prohibited the existence of either type of organisation up until 1824. After the repeal of the Combination Acts in 1824 there was a series of changes in the law that enabled trade unions and employers' associations both to exist and to operate. The freedom to associate was established by the mid-nineteenth century but the aims of a union were questioned in a series of court cases. The changes in the law were gradual and it was not until 1906 that legislation was passed that provided the conditions that enabled trade unions to operate free from the threat of legal action.

Once the freedom to associate was established the next stage towards collective bargaining was the recognition of trade unions by employers. Clearly, without recognition at some level collective bargaining cannot function. The process of recognition was also gradual and started with the growth of the 'new' unions in the 1850s. The initial reaction of employers was to resist trade unionism. Indeed, the purpose for which the first employers' associations were formed was to put up a common front in the resistance to unionism. The resistance was an ideological one as unions were seen as an interference with the employers' freedom to run their businesses as they wished to. The law supported this by declaring that unions were acting in restraint of trade by seeking to influence the terms and conditions which employers offered to their employees. Gradually employers started to acknowledge the existence of trade unions, especially when forced to through industrial action organised by the trade unions. From this, tentative steps were taken towards recognition and finally, in the 1890s, in the industries indicated above, collective bargaining grew.

The recognition of trade unions was, until 1975, a purely voluntary matter between employer and trade union. Some employers had the terms and conditions on which they had to employ people imposed on them by law, for example, by a wages council order. However, this did not necessarily involve the individual employer in recognising a union. Direct recognition at employer level was purely voluntary. Frequently pressure was put on an employer to recognise a union by the union using its industrial power. This involved using the strike as a weapon. A union seeking recognition recruited members within the firm, and when the level of membership was sufficiently high, if a formal claim for recognition was refused, the union could call its members out on strike to force the employer's hand.

The Employment Protection Act 1975 introduced a complex procedure whereby an employer could have trade union recognition imposed on it. Under this Act a union could refer a rejected recognition claim to ACAS, who would try to conciliate. If this did not result in recognition, ACAS could conduct an enquiry and make recommendations. Again, if the recommendations were not accepted the claim could be referred to the Central Arbitration Committee. If the CAC upheld the claim the recommendations would be unilaterally imposed on the employer. The process was complex, but the threat of such a procedure led many employers to recognise a trade union where otherwise they would not have. This was not always the case as was illustrated in the Grunwick dispute in 1977 when the recognition dispute at a photographic processing plant became a bitter struggle involving a strike and mass picketing. Eventually, the union claim was rejected because ACAS had not ascertained the views of the whole of the workforce on the matter of recognition. In fact, it could not because the employer refused permission for their employees to be approached!

This procedure was repealed by the Employment Act 1980. The current position is that recognition is purely voluntary with no legislative backing for claims for recognition. Although much of the legislative programme during the 1980s was pro-employer and anti-union, there is little evidence of union derecognition by employers.

The government issued a Green Paper in 1991 entitled *Industrial Relations in the 1990s* which raised the possibility of a requirement for trade union recognition, by an employer, to be subject to support by ballot. The subsequent White Paper did not make any such legislative proposals but it does indicate that this topic will be on some future agenda.

The extent of collective bargaining is wider than trade union membership figures indicate. The number of employees affected by collective bargaining, i.e., those whose terms and conditions of employment are contained in a collective agreement, is far in excess of the number of trade union members. The reason for this is that in most places of work where unions are recognised, levels of trade union membership are not 100%. Nevertheless, the terms and conditions of employment of all employees (union and non-union) are determined by collective bargaining. This fact is used by trade unions to argue for 100% membership or for a closed shop, as those who are not members (so-called 'free riders') are benefiting from the union's negotiating activities. It is possible that with the operation of national agreements an individual employer may not recognise a union but because their employees are covered by the agreement, collective bargaining affects them. For example, this is the case at the General Communications Headquarters (GCHQ) where, after a government decision, unions were banned from this civil service establishment, but civil service conditions of service still apply to the employees.

Reasons for collective bargaining

Collective bargaining can be considered to operate for several different reasons. These can be classified as political, economic and governmental:

- **Political** This is the viewpoint that collective bargaining is a balance of power between the naturally stronger employer and the individually weaker employee. By joining together, usually as a union, employees can speak and take action collectively. Also employers (especially small ones) can join a larger employers' association and derive benefits by having the backing of such an organisation and its agreements.
- **Economic** This is the viewpoint that collective bargaining is a process whereby the price of labour (wages, hours and other terms) is determined. An important aspect of employer/employee relations is the price of labour. Employers seek to pay what they can afford and employees seek to be paid sufficient to maintain and improve their standard of living. The process finds a compromise solution between these factors.
- **Governmental** This is the viewpoint that collective bargaining is the framework of rules and procedures within which industrial relations are conducted. The relations between employers and employees are determined by the framework set up by this process. It involves the unions participating in the management of an organisation and it allows the employer to take into account the employee's view as made known by the unions.

These categories are not mutually exclusive and exist to some extent in all the forms of collective bargaining.

Another aspect of collective bargaining of importance is the idea that the process is free from outside interference. Free collective bargaining allows the parties to come to whatever conclusions they wish, as a result of their own negotiations, with no outside body restraining the process. This aspect was noted in Section 4.2, where State intervention, in the form of a pay or incomes policy, severely restricts the freedom of the parties to bargain. Such policies have either been persuasive or, in some instances, mandatory. In either case negotiators have had to accept some restraint imposed on them from an outside agency (government) which restricts the freedom to make whatever bargain the two sides agree on. Even where the incomes policy has not been backed by statutory sanctions, there is pressure to work within the stated limits. This strengthens management's hand in keeping claims towards a lower limit. Firms can decide to ignore the policy in such instances but this runs the risk of being seen by the public to be ignoring government policy. With policies having a statutory backing the pressure to conform is even greater, especially on management. The penalties contained in some incomes policies could affect the firm's commercial operations, for example, in not being able to pass on increased labour costs in the form of price increases where the agreed wage increase exceeds the income policy limit.

6.1.2 The content of collective bargaining

The process of employer and employee representatives negotiating issues jointly has grown considerably. Some of the agreements reached in negotiations are highly complex documents and leave few areas, relating to the individual's contract of employment, untouched. The first attempts at collective bargaining were restricted in their scope to areas like pay and hours. All the other terms and conditions were determined unilaterally by the employer. Gradually the scope of negotiations grew to include other areas like holidays, holiday pay, bonuses, safety and so on. As trade unions became established, especially at national level, so it was possible for the scope of the negotiations to be extended.

The terms and conditions in the contract of employment that the majority of employees work under today are largely determined by collective bargaining. Chapter 12 examines this in greater detail. Below is a list (not exhaustive) of items that are potentially the subject of negotiation in a collective bargaining situation:

- **Pay** salary, salary scales, basic rates, grading, lay-off pay, guarantee pay, method of pay, interval of pay
- **Premiums** for overtime, shifts, week-end and holiday work, call-in pay
- **Bonuses** piecework scheme, piecework payment, measured day work, group bonuses, commission, profit sharing
- **Allowances** working conditions, abnormal work, travel, tools
- **Hours** basic working week, normal working week, guaranteed hours, shift working and patterns, start and finish times, flexitime, breaks, overtime requirements, on-call duty
- **Holidays** basic entitlement, service entitlement, qualifying days, holiday pay
- **Safety** protective clothing, safe working practices, injury benefits
- **Welfare** medical checks, canteen facilities, changing rooms
- **Pensions** contributions, benefits, insurance, early retirement
- **Notice** by employer to employee and vice versa, pay arrangements, length of notice, leaving early, pay in lieu
- **Redundancy** procedure for consultation and selection, payments, redeployment, training
- **Job description** job title, main functions and responsibilities
- **Staffing** levels, flexibility, mobility, cover
- **Training** entitlement, further education, craft training, payment of fees, block releases
- **Equal opportunities** in recruitment, appointments, training, promotion, transfer, equal pay, maternity benefits, and job evaluation

In the various employment sectors there may well be others not listed above.

In addition to the individual terms and conditions of employment there are issues of a collective nature that are the subject of union/management agreements. Subjects like the closed shop and any union membership agreement (*see* Section 15.3) are now often the subject of an agreement. Redundancies are often dealt with according to a set procedure laid down in an agreement.

Finally, collective bargaining also has a very important role (referred to as the governmental role in Section 6.1.1) in determining the rules and procedures to be used in industrial relations. Such procedural agreements cover discipline, grievances, disputes, staffing levels, making claims, negotiations, rule changes and other constitutional arrangements. This framework is very important in ensuring that matters are dealt with efficiently and fairly.

6.1.3 Bargaining units

The process of collective bargaining is carried out at all levels, from small work groups in a private firm to national agreements relating to hundreds of thousands of workers. National negotiations take place for a large proportion of employees. These negotiations are carried out, usually by an employers' federation and a union confederation, whereby each side has an agreed number on the negotiating panel to represent the various interests involved. This process was noted in Sections 2.4 and 3.3. These bargaining units are very large and the content of the agreements varies. Sometimes the national agreement is comprehensive, as is often the case for public sector workers like firemen and council workers. In other cases it deals only with the basic issues or minimum rates and leaves the details to be worked out at local level. Bargaining at local level depends on the nature and existence of national agreements. If the national agreements are comprehensive there is little scope for individual employment unit bargaining, while conversely where there is no national agreement, or it is only of a basic kind, there is much scope for local bargaining.

A further feature of the bargaining unit is the number of unions involved. Even in a small organisation the number of unions could exceed six, and in a large organisation it can be upward of 20. Separate negotiation with each union is not desirable. For the employer it is time-consuming and often leads to 'leap-frogging', where the latest claim has to be above the last settlement. For the unions it can lead to a fragmented approach and a disunity among the various unions. To overcome this multi-union problem a joint approach to negotiations is sometimes used. The unions at plant level or company level agree to form a joint committee in which the claim is formulated and the negotiations discussed. From this committee delegates are sent as negotiators. This has not always worked well as the various factions in such a body may disagree. Traditional craft unions seek to maintain differentials whereas the general unions seek flat rate increases. Sometimes this leads to claims for separate negotiating rights which, if refused, can lead to a dispute which is difficult to resolve. Multi-union national agreements are also conducted in this way whereby the delegates on the negotiating panel are drawn from several unions.

In the 1980s, a move to overcome the problems associated with multi-union, plant bargaining was the introduction of single-union agreements. These were mentioned in Section 5.2.1. Established firms may have some difficulty in introducing a single-union agreement but new firms have less difficulty. One tactic being employed is to move the firm's operations to a new site and to make employment at the new site conditional on a single-union agreement, i.e., all employees may join the one union only. This tactic was employed by parts of the newspaper industry in 1986 when moving their Fleet Street operations to new sites.

Firms who are setting up on green field sites clearly are not constrained by previous practice and can set up the system that best suits them. In many cases their purpose has been not to abandon trade unions and collective bargaining but to insist that the systems and procedures are on management terms. Frequently this has meant a union entering into a single-union agreement, often after competing with other unions to be recognised as the union with sole bargaining rights.

During the 1980s the major changes that took place in the UK system of industrial relations led to a significant shift from national bargaining to local bargaining. The list of industries abandoning national agreements includes road passenger transport, newspaper journalists, retailing, engineering and independent television. The pattern in the industries which were denationalised in the 1980s varies. Some have maintained national agreements, e.g., gas, others have decentralised, e.g., water. There are several reasons for the move to local bargaining. In the first instance, firms themselves are often decentralised which makes local management more responsible for the success of local operations, with local establishments being set up as profit centres. This means that local managers should have some say in pay determination. A further reason is that when national agreements operate the power base of national trade union leaders is seen by some as too great. To remove bargaining to local level effectively sidelines the national officials. However, some companies still operate national level bargaining because they have a concern that local union officials may be even worse to deal with!

Bargaining within an organisation can take place at various levels. Some firms have company-wide agreements (that apply to all sites and plants) while others have plant or site agreements. The choice is partly related to the type of organisation. Ford is a centralised organisation and has company-wide agreements. General Electric Company is a decentralised organisation and has plant agreements. Both forms can lead to problems where a company has several plants around the country. Levels of earnings vary geographically and with company-wide agreements there is parity country-wide. Then the plants located in the more expensive areas, like the South East, complain that they need extra, i.e., a differential, over and above employees in the North East. This leads to pressure for plant-level bargaining. Plant-level bargaining can allow wage drift to occur but then the employees in the lower paid plants start to pressurise for a company-wide agreement to achieve parity.

Other forms of pay determination

The determination of the pay and conditions of employment is a vital area of industrial relations.

The most common cause of strikes is pay and clearly everyone concerned has a strong interest in the outcome of pay bargaining. For some sectors pay bargaining has been replaced by some other form of pay determination. This became a significant feature in the public sector during the 1980s. The major objective of the Conservative government's economic policy was to control inflation, after the record levels of inflation in the 1970s. In order to achieve this objective one important plank in this policy was to control public expenditure (plus the fact that the government wanted to reduce public expenditure for other reasons, such as enabling tax cuts). Inevitably the government had to tackle the thorny question of pay in the public sector, as this accounted for a high percentage of the budget, typically around 80%. For several groups of employees (including those employed by local authorities) pay bargaining was substituted by some other form of pay determination. The three main forms are pay review bodies, the use of pay formulae and pay comparability.

Pay review bodies

Pay review bodies are set up by the government as independent bodies who have a remit to examine the pay and conditions of that sector and to make recommendations to the minister concerned. The remit to the pay review body can be whatever the minister wishes; it can be open-ended or it can be constrained, e.g., by budgetary considerations, cash limits or a percentage limit. The review body listens to evidence from the employers and the unions concerned and then makes a report. The minister can also accept the report in part or in full or reject it. Most reports are accepted but modified in some way. For a number of groups who have a strong claim that they are underpaid (e.g., the nurses) the review bodies' recommendations have been phased in over a period. This costs the government less in cash terms in the year of the award but the group eventually gets the pay rise. In fact, between 1984 and 1991, pay review body recommendations were fully accepted only once.

Almost half a million employees are now covered by five pay review bodies.

Pay formulae

This system links the pay of the groups concerned to a national average pay level. In essence this means that the jobs of the group are held as equivalent to a comparable set of workers. In the case of the fire service this is to the upper quartile of male manual weekly earnings. The government's statistical service provides the data using an earnings survey. A similar system operates for the police force. Other conditions of service are negotiated.

Pay comparability

This system is a hybrid arrangement used for civil servants where their pay (except for the senior staff, who have a review body) is negotiated annually but the settlement has to be pegged to the middle range of private sector pay awards. Again data is collected and used as a basis for settlement in negotiations with the Treasury.

In addition to the decline of collective bargaining for public sector employees there is a move, by the government, towards individual contracts, with many more jobs including a performance related pay element. This has always been difficult to set up in the service sector as the targets are more difficult to specify. However it is not impossible and there are several examples where this has been implemented especially with senior posts. The Citizens Charter has helped this process by setting performance targets for various public services. These can then be interpreted for the various jobs within the organisation and an element of pay is then linked to achieving these targets.

The number of workers in the public sector has fallen as a result of the wide-scale programme of privatisation in the 1980s (continuing into the 1990s). In some cases this has meant the scrapping of national agreements and local agreements being substituted, e.g., the Water Boards although some national agreements still exist, e.g., with British Gas.

It is usual practice that an agreement will contain a clause specifying the group or section of employees to whom the agreement applies. This may be specified by grade, by job title, by department or by location, depending on the nature of the industrial relations system. Agreements can be comprehensive and cover all employees in one agreement, as is often the case in national agreements. Alternatively agreements are made separately for different groups or grades of employee. This is the case with a local agreement in a multi-union environment where there is no mechanism for a comprehensive agreement to cover all employees.

Single table bargaining

This is where there is a single set of negotiations covering the terms and conditions for all employees, or at least all those in a particular category, e.g., manual workers. Where there are several unions covering a group of workers, separate negotiations are time-consuming and often divisive. This is not an entirely new idea and is a step forward from single settlement date arrangements whereby all negotiations are concluded on a set date (rather than being spread throughout the year). The move to single table bargaining will aid the process of flexibility as the negotiators can examine occupational distinctions and make the necessary amendments.

6.1.4 Productivity bargaining

A development in collective bargaining has been the advent of productivity bargaining. The basis of traditional bargaining has been the relative strength of the two sides. Negotiations refer to current wage levels, national agreements, profits, labour markets, inflation and so on. The process of negotiation is one of claim and counter claim with eventually a compromise solution being found. It is sometimes referred to as 'zero sum' bargaining where each side receives and gives something that in total adds up to zero. Productivity bargaining is an attempt to reform this process, where neither side really gains anything, to a situation where both sides do gain

something. The basis of a productivity agreement is that the employees agree to make changes that lead to more efficient and economic working. This improved efficiency will lead to the workers gaining an increase in income and the firm an increase in profits. The nature of negotiations is changed by this process as there is not a constant trade-off of one concession against another gain.

In practice productivity bargaining is an attempt to improve productivity (measured as output per unit of an input like labour) by changing the way in which the work is done. These changes can include the following:

- **Flexibility** By employees agreeing to move from machine to machine or section to section at request, as work levels dictate. It is the practice in some firms for workers to keep to one machine or section and if there is no work they are idle. Clearly this is inefficient and as workloads vary one section may have too much or too little work. By introducing flexibility workers can be moved around as demand dictates, and efficiency can be raised. (*See* Section 15.4 for a discussion on this topic.)
- **Nature of work** By eliminating the practices of 'demarcation' where no one could do the work defined as that of another group of workers. This was prevalent among craft and maintenance workers where each branch of the crafts had an exclusive right to perform their particular kind of work. Such practice led to inefficiency and disagreement. A fitter had prescribed duties as would the electrician, the plumber, the bricklayer, the instrument mechanic and so on. Production operatives could not do the work of any craftsperson (not even to tighten up a loose screw!). The fitter would be needed to take a fitment off a machine and an electrician to disconnect the wiring. By agreeing to carry out a limited range of each other's work and allowing production operatives to carry out simple maintenance tasks, much time could be saved and perhaps staffing levels reduced.
- **Overtime** Actual hours of work frequently exceed the basic working week. In this way

wages are increased, although often official union policy is to minimise overtime, as overtime can be used to keep staffing levels down. Management allows some overtime to achieve flexibility on labour hours but gradually, in some establishments, overtime has become structured and permanent. This adds greatly to costs as overtime usually attracts premium rates. By reorganising the hours of work output can be maintained but costs lowered.

- **Staffing** Custom and practice in the craft and maintenance trades has been for the craftsperson to have a mate. This has led to overstaffing where this extra labour can no longer be justified. Where new machinery has been introduced some agreements have been made where the 'operator moves with the job'. This means that the person that carried out a particular task moves to the new situation. If one machine requiring one operative carries out the work previously done by several operatives, all those people move to the new machine. This overstaffing is inefficient and can be reduced by redeployment, retraining or voluntary redundancy.

Following an agreement to make such changes the cost benefits accruing to the firm are then shared with the employees. These may take several forms:

- increased pay related to the cost savings or increased output
- hours of work reduced, longer holidays
- single, lump sum payment to buy out a previous practice
- fringe benefits such as improved sick pay schemes and pension arrangements
- enhanced redundancy payments
- increased job satisfaction due to job rotation or job enlargement

An early example of a productivity agreement was the Esso agreement at their Fawley refinery made in 1965. This agreement was concerned with the improvement of productivity at a new refinery. The basis of the agreement was the amalgamation of the process and maintenance functions under a single supervisory structure. Under the new working practices craft grade personnel worked on the plant as process operators. Conversely, operators were trained to carry out 'operating maintenance' such as making and breaking pipe joints on valves (a routine operation in a chemical plant), pressure testing lines, removing and replacing pumps and other work previously carried out only by maintenance personnel.

In the latter part of the 1970s, bargaining was aimed at maintaining living standards in the face of inflation. Productivity bargaining cannot guarantee a fixed increase at a point in time because, by its nature, it pays out from results obtained in the future. With inflation falling to low levels, the emphasis may well change to productivity bargaining again whereby gains over and above the rate of inflation can be gained in the workers' income with parallel benefits to the organisation. Some occupations are difficult to evaluate in such an agreement, like nursing or teaching, but contributions can still be made to organisational efficiency. Other jobs, especially in the manufacturing sector, are more easily subject to productivity agreements. Overall the alternative approach to collective bargaining by this method of productivity bargaining and agreements may be the start of the next stage of the ever-evolving industrial relations system.

The introduction of productivity bargaining has changed the process of collective bargaining. Traditionally, pay bargaining, based on 'zero sum' bargaining, seeks to distribute an amount of money available for pay increases. It tends to be based on the conflict model whereby each side seeks to achieve its own, separate, different objectives. Productivity bargaining is based on integrative (or cooperative) bargaining whereby each side has a vested interest in the same proposals. By increasing flexibility, for example, both the firm and the employees benefit directly. The negotiations also require greater openness with the need for greater amounts of information on which to base the decisions and on which to monitor the actual benefits. Productivity bargaining also involves a move towards the joint control of working practices with neither side in a dictatorial position.

The style of bargaining is affected by the type of negotiations and agreements being sought. In distributive bargaining the two sides are wishing to get the best deal out of the other side. This competition leads to suspicion and lack of openness. With integrative bargaining the sides need to have much more trust in each other as the approach is one of joint problem solving.

In the 1980s a trend emerged towards multi-skilling and flexibility. These are examined in Section 15.4.

6.2   Negotiations

The basis of collective bargaining in practice is the process whereby the various demands of the different groups involved are resolved in a workable agreement on a subject (or range of them). This may involve, at the simplest level, a manager and an employee. Alternatively, it may involve several groups, for example a team of managers meeting the representatives of the several unions recognised at a firm. At national level negotiations will involve many different employees, represented by the employers' association, and several unions, represented by a confederation.

Negotiation can be defined as *the process of discussing a matter with a view to reaching agreement*. This process is fundamental to collective bargaining and without it agreements could not be made. The unilateral imposition of a set of conditions by one side does not constitute a collective agreement, although these imposed conditions may become part of the terms and conditions of employment. A declaration by the management that employees will be employed on management's terms alone is not a collective bargain. Also, working practices introduced by employees without management agreement are outside collective bargaining. In both instances there may be resistance from the other side to accept the changes, especially if it is normal to negotiate changes and not impose them unilaterally. This

has happened in many firms many times. Companies have not been unknown to declare redundancies without prior notification or prior negotiation (although this would now be in violation of the legal requirements: *see* Section 14.3). On the other hand, unions have introduced working practices without agreement with management. In both cases problems occur leading to dissatisfaction often spilling over into a dispute. An example of this occurred in 1992 when British Coal declared several thousand miners redundant without any prior notice or consultation. This was against both the agreements with the unions and British Coal and the legal requirements in such cases. There was a major political row about this involving both the minister (Michael Heseltine) and the Prime Minister (John Major). The unions took the case to court and won.

The context in which negotiations take place are determined by three main factors:

- **The institutional factors**   This includes the level or stage at which they are occurring within the procedures, the type of claim (e.g., of interest or of right – *see* Section 6.3), the balance of power between the sides and the degree of formality (large group negotiations are always longer and more difficult).
- **The behavioural factors**   The size of the groups negotiating, the personalities, the interests represented and the level of negotiating skills.
- **The ideologies**   When people meet formally they bring their beliefs, prejudices and values to the negotiations. If these dominate they will affect the negotiating process. Typically (or more likely mythically) the militant, left-wing trade union representative is wanting to do down the capitalists, whilst the macho-management, trade union bashing, free market executives will want their own way despite any talking that goes on!

Having established that negotiations are aimed at reaching agreement between parties (and for these to form the basis of collective bargaining) the following section examines the process of negotiating. It is impossible to state a precise formula for negotiating, as the exact nature of any negotiation depends on the people involved and the circumstances under which it takes place. However, the steps in a typical negotiation procedure can be stated, including some generally accepted rules of good practice.

Initially, negotiation can be envisaged as the two parties stating their relevant positions and, as the process takes place, moving towards a more central position where agreement is possible. Traditionally, the initial positions of the two parties are set where settlement is not possible. Demands are set high or low, depending which side you are on, with each side making adjustments with a view to finding the middle ground of settlement. This can be illustrated as a continuum as in Fig. 6.1. The limits set in this

bargaining or interpersonal behaviour. The method is based on a pragmatic approach which enables everyone to acquire the necessary skills of negotiation.

The model uses an eight-step plan:

prepare	argue	signal	propose
package	bargain	close	agree

1 Preparing

An essential first step for all negotiators is to prepare fully. To go into negotiations unprepared is to run a high risk of failure. Preparation consists of deciding what the objectives are and how to achieve these. Objectives should be set (*see* later) and priorities listed. Each

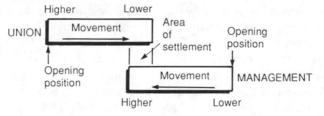

Fig 6.1 The negotiating process

example could clearly lead to an agreement. Alternatively, if the limits of each side do not overlap, no agreement is possible. In this case the outcome will be either an adjustment of the limits or a dispute. A simple illustration of this is frequently seen in wage negotiations. The union claim will be set high initially, to which the management will reply low. Eventually the unions will move down while management move up.

The process of negotiation can be seen as a number of interlinked steps that move towards agreement being reached. A number of steps can be identified. One useful, practical model is supplied by G Kennedy, J Benson and J McMillan in their book *Managing Negotiations*. This model is a very practical one based on involvement and observations in many real negotiations. It does not analyse the psychological basis of negotiations, such as transactional analysis, need theory, manipulative

side will wish to settle as close to their ideal as possible. To assume that all objectives are equally important is to head towards deadlock. Another important aspect of preparation is gathering intelligence on 'the other side'. (Often 'the other side' is called 'the opponent' in negotiations). In industrial relations it is commonplace for the level of formal activity to rise just before a set of important negotiations commences. This is posturing but can give some leads on the thinking of the other side. Employee opinion should be sounded out, as this is vital information. What is their mood? What are their concerns? What do they want? Objectives should be set and prioritised. 'Managing negotiations' suggests three levels of priority:

  L – like to achieve
  I   – intend to achieve
  M – must achieve

These can be related to the simple model in Fig. 6.1. The 'like' objectives may have to be dropped in course of negotiations. The 'intend' ones are what you would expect to achieve. The 'must' ones are those at the limit and are the fallback position. The roles of the team of negotiators also need to be decided in advance. Three main roles need to be identified:

A leader who will conduct the negotiations

A summariser who will ask questions and summarise progress to date

An observer who does not speak during the negotiations but observes what is going on and particularly looks for signals.

2 Arguing

This initial phase in the actual negotiation meetings is to exchange information. The communications should be reasonable and constructive. Whilst conflict exists (that's why the negotiations are taking place!) it is necessary not to manifest this in disruptive argument. The overall objective is to settle not fall out. The communication should be two-way although there are plenty of times when one side should just listen and remain silent. The information given should indicate objectives, commitment and intentions.

When one side is stating its case or making an opening statement the other side should remain silent. Listening skills are more important but more difficult than talking. Avoid any attack/defence cycle or blaming. You may well feel this, but don't let it show. Constructive behaviour consists of listening more than talking and encouraging the other side to talk.

As discussions continue it is important to use open questions, not closed questions laden with prejudice. Objectivity is also important. Summaries from time to time can help keep the negotiations on the right lines. Questions of clarification are important as all too often the recipient of information has misread the communicator's true meaning. Discussions can break down as a result of misunderstanding and a question of clarification can obviate this. If assumptions are made, check that they are valid.

When one side has made its opening statement, the other side will need to respond.

The response can include a detailed set of alternatives, which further discussion can work on. Amendments can be suggested to move towards a settlement. The items can be ranked to give an order of priority. An explanation should be given on items which are opposed.

3 Signalling

During the arguing phase the sides are weighing each other up and looking for the way ahead to a solution. Signals are the means by which one side indicates to the other that it is willing to move on an item to help arrive at agreement. These movements are seen as concessions, i.e., one side gives something the other wants. It is then for the other side to respond in like manner and ask for a concession from the other side. Obvious signals are 'we can discuss that point'. More subtle ones include 'we can't agree to that in its present form'. This calls for a modification to the present proposal. 'We would find it extremely difficult' might mean that movement is possible. This is where the excellence of listening skills is tested. It may only be one word like 'might'. Qualified or non-absolute statements are signals.

Once a signal has been received it needs treating carefully. To take an initial statement as an indication of final agreement could lead to the talks collapsing because one side is overenthusiastic. After no movement at all the relief of some indication of movement should not lead to every concession being given to secure agreement. Concessions should be traded carefully, one at a time, small concessions first. If, after signalling possible movement, there is no response from the opposition, it may be useful to call for a specific response or to call for an adjournment. A signal may need some exploration. What do you mean by . . . ? Have you got a suggestion?

4 Proposing

All negotiations must contain proposals. Merely stating a grievance does not lead to settlement but proposing a remedy does. Initial proposals are often modified into secondary proposals as the result of argument. Conditional proposals are often used, which helps in trading concessions. 'I will do this if you will do that.' Proposals are tentative, which allows a way forward for both sides. To be specific and rigid does not leave any room for movement. Initially the concessions should be small. If a large concession is made, the other side may well be rubbing its hands with glee at achieving more than it had expected. Presenting an either/or proposal is useful as it gives the other side some choice.

Proposals should be itemised first and then explained. Don't mix proposals with explanations. The other side should sit and listen to the proposals and should not reject them out of hand immediately. Clarification should be sought to ensure the proposal is fully understood.

5 Packaging

This stage moves the negotiations towards final agreement. It brings together all that has been said so far. Packaging is not used in the sense of presenting a package at the start of the negotiations and saying 'this is what is on offer, take it or leave it'. Such tactics are employed but they can lead to problems as they do not necessarily address the needs of the other side. Sometimes packaging is used as an opening gambit.

The package must be of interest to the other side. It requires creative thinking on what can be put into the package and still leave the proposer within limits. Variables can be traded, for example, the percentage wage rise or the associated percentage rise in productivity. Look at the how, when, how much, price variables. It is important to refer back to the objectives set at the preparation stage and to check the L I Ms.

6 Bargaining

This part of the process involves gaining something for the loss of something. This is often called zero sum bargaining. The key word at this stage is IF. If you agree to X, I will agree to Y. Keep the two points tied together. If you say 'I'll agree to this, will you agree to that?' that means the opponents have got something for nothing! Another trap to avoid is constructing a statement that allows for an answer of no. Do not ask 'Will you agree?' Put the conditions first 'If you agree to . . .' then put the concession 'I will . . .'. When items have been put together as a package, do not allow items to be teased out and dealt with separately.

7 Closing

The key question towards the end of a negotiation is how to close and when. The purpose of closing is to reach agreement. The closing package must meet all the needs of the opponents. To try to close too early might cause the opposition to react angrily or to try for another concession.

One tactic to indicate a close is to grant a final, and possibly large, concession. However, to remain credible only one final offer can be used. To go further and negotiate again may lead towards a second final offer. Another tactic is to summarise everything that has transpired, especially the concessions. An adjournment may be used to consider a reply. An ultimatum can be used but the danger is it can backfire. A close is necessary when one side has reached the limits of its concessions. Again the sides need to refer to their objectives.

8 Agreement

The final act is to agree on what has been agreed on. This may require a written text and some explanations and definitions. There may be some final stumbling blocks as each side's recollection of a point may be different, especially when it is seen in writing.

6.3 Conflict and sanctions

The word conflict does not mean quarrel or feud but is a description of the state between two parties when the rights or interests of either party are threatened. The distinction between conflicts of rights and of interest is discussed at the end of Section 6.3. The existence of conflict does not mean that the relationship between the parties has broken down. Quite the reverse, in most situations it is healthy to recognise that conflict exists and to do something about it. Negotiations allow the underlying relationship between employer and employee or management and union to continue. In fact, it is the need to continue the relationship (i.e., to employ or be employed) that forces agreement, eventually.

The idea of conflict in industrial relations has already been discussed in Chapter 1. Apart from the unitary perspective there is a general acceptance of the existence of conflict, for whatever reason. The system of collective bargaining exists to institutionalise and resolve these conflicts and to produce a workable solution. Simplistically, the procedural agreements in collective bargaining provide the means for resolving the issues relating to the terms and conditions of employment subsisting in an organisation which are enshrined in substantive agreements. This may occur as a very loose, informal structure in a small firm or as a strict, formal structure in very large organisations or sectors. Within the framework of collective bargaining sanctions exist which can be used by either side.

Sanctions are used either before, during or after attempts to find solutions to the very many problems that arise within organisations. They exist to provide both sides with the means of demonstrating strength of feeling on a matter over and above verbal persuasion. The use of sanctions prior to negotiations commencing is a tactic employed to demonstrate the strength of feeling on an issue and to force an improved opening offer. Using sanctions (or the threat of them) during negotiations is to try to force an improved offer and to lay down a challenge to the other side. Sanctions used when negotiations have finished show a final failure to agree and the unacceptability of the final proposals. It has to be recognised that sanctions, and the threat of them, are often used tactically to try to force the issue, to extract a better offer or to provide a rapid solution. This may not always work. If

a union threatens a strike, management may believe that the workforce would not obey such a call and then call the union's bluff. Alternatively, management may not be too worried about sanctions being taken, especially if trade is not very good.

Another aspect of the conflict that exists in an organisation is that it may not necessarily show itself through the taking of sanctions. A rather naive view of strikes is that they are a direct measure of discontent or conflict. The level of strikes in a firm or in the economy depends on a number of factors, only one of which is conflict. Other more appropriate measures of conflict and its negative effect on employees is the level of absenteeism, lateness, labour turnover and productivity. A firm may suffer high levels of absenteeism, lateness and labour turnover and never suffer a strike, but there may be a great deal of conflict within. The converse may also be true of a firm which normally has a low level of conflict but suffers an uncharacteristic dispute in which sanctions are taken.

The existence of sanctions and their use within collective bargaining can be explained in several ways.

(a) Collective bargaining is the means of institutionalising conflict and as such tries to contain the conflict within the bounds of acceptable conduct, as expressed in the procedural rules. The conflict deriving from the sometimes opposing objectives of an organisation and its employees needs to be contained to prevent any extreme behaviour. If conflict is not dealt with it will inevitably manifest itself, sometimes in an ugly form such as the use of violence. The processes of collective bargaining already described seek to deal with the problem and find solutions acceptable to both sides. Having said this, occasionally the conflict cannot be contained by the system, particularly when an acceptable solution is not forthcoming, and this will precipitate one or other side to take sanctions.

(b) The means of resolving conflict involves a negotiating process in which the sides seek to persuade each other of their case. Arguments for and against are made and gradually each side is persuaded to come closer to a solution. The strength of conviction for a particular case is usually demonstrated by the use of verbal and written communications skills plus some specialist tactical skills. A further means of persuasion is to use sanctions. In essence, taking sanctions is a means of sending a strong message to the other side on the strength of feeling on a particular issue. Frequently neither side resorts to sanctions, or even the threat of them. The humorous view of negotiations being a matter of threat and counter-threat is merely a joke! In addition, the use of sanctions can reflect, not merely a strength of feeling on the one issue under discussion, but also the release of feelings pent up over a period. If the opinion is that one or other side has been abusing or ignoring the system in recent times, one set of negotiations could be the scenario for a demonstration of the frustration that has been building up.

(c) Sanctions are used to demonstrate the seriousness of a claim. Apart from sending a clear message to the other side they should also have the effect of including greater resolve to find a negotiated solution. If a situation is misjudged and a matter is not dealt with as quickly as one side would like or it is not given the attention it should receive, the use of sanctions can cause a jolt to the system and get things moving. Some agreements require a period of notice before sanctions are taken. This is a useful procedural rule as it has the effect of inducing greater resolve without either side having to suffer the effects of sanctions.

There are several types of sanction that can be taken. All forms seek to cause maximum inconvenience to the other side and minimum inconvenience to the side applying the sanction. The common perception of an industrial sanction is the strike, but it is not the only form of sanction that can be taken by a workforce, nor is it necessarily the best form of action. In a strike situation each party withstands the costs of the sanction while incurring costs. If a union takes strike action its members lose pay, the union pays out strike money and the firm loses profits. Hopefully this leads to a reappraisal of the situation and talks start again in order to end sanctions and find a solution. Sometimes strikes become a war of attrition with both waiting to see who will give in first. Such power struggles are seen as determining the outcome of the negotiations. The side giving in loses its claim. The parallel employer's sanction to the strike is the lockout. The employer may decide that a situation can no longer continue and the enterprise will be closed until there can be a resumption of work on mutually acceptable terms. The use of lockouts still occurs but much less frequently than in the last century. Employers, and their associations, would often lock out their employees (especially if trade was bad) in order to resist a claim or to weaken any signs of trade unionism. On occasions where there is a stoppage of work there are arguments as to whether it is a lockout or a strike. This reflects the confusion that surrounds some disputes.

Whilst strikes are a common sanction, they are costly to both sides and can cause real hardship. By taking some form of limited sanction the objective of causing the other side to incur costs, with little or no cost to the side applying the sanction may be achieved. Such alternative sanctions open to the employer include:

- **Lay-offs**   Rather than close the whole enterprise down, numbers of employees are laid off, especially a group which is in dispute.
- **Dismissal**   A possible consequence of a group of workers going on strike is that the employer will consider them dismissed. Technically, employees on strike have dismissed themselves and an employer cannot sack them. However, to avoid any claims for unfair dismissal if an employer wishes to dismiss a group taking 'official' industrial action, everyone must be dismissed (to avoid discrimination). Additionally, should the employer wish to re-engage them, everyone must be re-engaged, not a select number. If the strike is 'unofficial' (*see* Section 10.2.2), the employer can dismiss any or all employees

taking action without the risk of a claim for unfair dismissal.

- **Withdrawal of overtime**   In some firms overtime is regularly worked. This boosts earnings and is looked on as a permanent feature of employment. The cancellation of overtime is a sanction that will cost little to the employer but makes an impression on the employee's pay packet. Economic circumstances will dictate if this is an appropriate sanction.

- **Closure**   Large firms with several establishments in various locations may rationalise operations when operations on a particular site become untenable due to industrial unrest. This sanction may fit in with the organisation's long-term plans and the unrest may merely bring the date forward. In some instances, operations may be shifted to alternative locations to avoid areas where there are uneconomic working practices. For example, firms moved haulage operations out of areas covered by the Docks Labour Scheme, particularly when containerisation was introduced.

- **Unofficial sanctions**   Certain other steps are sometimes taken by employers. While these are not good industrial relations practice they have been used as sanctions in a dispute. Such measures might include discriminating against individuals or groups in order to create ill feeling or demonstrate disgust. Such action might include the pedantic enforcement of rules, zealous attention to detail, constant criticism, rebukes and generally trying to make life miserable. In the extreme, an employee may consider the pressure too much, leave and claim constructive dismissal (*see* Section 13.2.4). Such action against a group tends to harden the resolve of the group in the face of the challenge and embitter relations even more. Sanctions of this nature cause long-term damage to relationships and any restoration of normal working will take a long time. Another form of unofficial sanction is to take similar action in the hope of precipitating a strike. In certain circumstances employers would not regret a strike taking place and will sometimes contrive to create a situation that will lead to strike action. Again such action is perceived as bad practice which sours relations and makes settlement very difficult. If the group believes the strike was prompted by the employer's action, a return to work precondition, before further negotiations, creates a very difficult situation.

Alternative sanctions open to the employee/ union include:

- **Overtime ban**   To refuse to work any overtime can cause considerable disruption to operations, particularly if the overtime is regular or structural and the additional output is needed. Such action is less costly to the employee but can be very costly to the employer. For example, where essential maintenance work is carried out at weekends, an overtime ban will effectively prevent normal work commencing at the start of the next week. In other instances the overtime may be structural, whereby the basic working week is, say, 40 hours and the normal working week is 42 hours. This occurs in continuous plant operations where four shifts cover the 168 hours of the week.

- **Work-to-rule**   This is a situation in which the employees perform the minimum required of them under their contracts of employment or observe the rules of the job to the extreme. Such action can be effective where the job is covered by detailed rules and employees can apply them fastidiously. For example, the railway drivers' union, ASLEF, carried out such action in one dispute so that it caused complete chaos on the railways. The safety checks that are normally carried out quickly or cursorily were carried out with great attention to detail. This prevented the trains from running normally, since much time was spent checking the trains and the simplest defect was reported with the driver refusing to drive until the matter was put right. Where clear rules do not exist the question arises 'what are the rules of the job?' Disputes then arise about the jobs themselves and make for a very messy situation.

- **Go-slow** This is a similar form of action to a work-to-rule in its disruptive effect but this sanction involves the job being carried out much more slowly than normal. Again, with no definition of normal speed of working it is difficult to know where the border line is between going slow and not doing the job at all. The latter clearly could lead to discipline and eventual dismissal. This form of action is very frustrating to management but of little cost to the employee.

- **Sit-ins** This is an occupation of the employer's premises by the workforce. It is an extreme sanction used occasionally in such circumstances as when an employer has declared that operations are being much reduced or finished at a particular location. Clearly such action frustrates the employer's ability to continue business. Initially the response may be to sit it out and wait for a peaceful repossession of the premises. Legal action can be resorted to but there are some practical difficulties of serving notices to quit. One novel solution at an occupied plant of a motor manufacturer in Manchester was to send in a helicopter to retrieve some vital equipment!

- **Boycott** This is a term used to indicate a refusal to work a certain machine or work on certain material. For example, if a new piece of equipment is installed but there is no agreement on staffing levels, the union may refuse to allow its members to work the machine. Another practice, common in the print industry, is that work will only be performed on material received from another union shop. Anything received from a non-union establishment (called an unrecognised office) should not be worked, i.e., boycotted. The NGA Rule Book contained a rule to that effect. Such practice is unlawful and a refusal to work could lead to the dismissal of the employees and legal action for loss of profit.

- **Ballot** A new and unexpected sanction emerged in the 1980s as a result of the need to hold a ballot before industrial action. This has led to the tactic of unions using the pre-strike ballot as a means of pressurising employers during negotiations. A very high proportion of ballots follow the union recommendation, so employers are reluctant to call the union's bluff and ignore this sanction. Of course, if a ballot goes against the strike, this severely weakens the union position. Where a ballot has voted in favour of action, the employer will be under much greater pressure to move towards settlement as the employees have shown the strength of feeling.

Disputes of right and interest

A final note in this section on sanctions relates to a categorisation of disputes (or conflicts) that is common in some sectors. This is to divide disputes into disputes of *right* and disputes of *interest*. A dispute of right is a dispute relating to a claim under a current agreement. The matter is one on which there is a negotiated right but the actual application or interpretation is under dispute. A dispute of interest is a dispute relating to a new term or condition which is not currently covered in the substantive agreements in existence. This is a claim for something new or different. The dividing line between the two is sometimes very grey and one side may claim something as of right but the other side may claim the matter is a new one of interest.

The subdivision can be important in deciding how to deal with the matter. A dispute of right, if it is clearly accepted by both sides as such, can be dealt with by a procedural agreement, e.g., a dispute or grievance procedure. Should there be a final failure to agree, the matter can be resolved by arbitration or a similar outside procedure. The arbiter can hear the claims or interpretations from both sides and decide, on balance, who has the better claim or suggest a compromise solution. Questions of application or interpretation can be dealt with in this way. A dispute of interest, on the other hand, can be dealt with as a matter of negotiation, either to make a new agreement or to incorporate a new clause into an existing agreement. This may well require the use of a separate procedural agreement and the claim may be resisted from the start or be rejected. A question of right cannot be rejected in the same way. A further problem arises if there is a final failure to agree. Arbitration is often not an appropriate means for resolving disputes of interest. A claim for something new or an improvement on what already exists is for the parties themselves to resolve. For example, pay claims are rarely the subject of arbitration in the private sector. Arbitration on such matters is more common in the public sector where, for example, British Rail have a scheme for arbitration which can help settle such matters.

The division is more important in other systems of collective bargaining. In the USA, where they have fixed-term agreements, the questions arising during the term of the agreement are disputes of right. These can, if necessary, be referred to arbitration to resolve the question arising. The negotiation of the term agreement itself is a question of interest and is not referred to arbitration. In the UK, because we do not have such a distinction between agreements and the system is more fluid, the distinction is less important.

6.4   Resolving failures to agree

The procedures used in collective bargaining are designed to resolve the many questions that arise in industrial relations, both with individuals and groups. Negotiators use their skill to try and ensure a settlement favourable to both sides. Inevitably there are bound to be occasions when a settlement is not reached, which could be for a number of reasons. Procedures often provide for the registration of a failure to agree at the various stages if no settlement is reached. If further stages are provided for in the agreement, then they can be used in a further attempt to reach a settlement. However, when the final stage has been reached and a failure to agree registered, the ensuing deadlock needs to be resolved. Even if the parties have embarked on a war of attrition and relations are at a low ebb, eventually a settlement must be contemplated. It is very rare for a dispute never to be resolved, indeed many disputes are settled without resort-

ing to sanctions, let alone involving a drawn out strike.

The problem of resolving disputes after domestic procedures have been exhausted has produced a variety of solutions. In some instances, where agreements exist between employers and unions at national level, then there may be an external procedure whereby the dispute or question raised is passed to representatives of the employer (or employers' association) and the union (or confederation) at a higher level, at local, regional or national level. Such external procedures are extensions of the normal domestic procedures and are often incorporated into them. Where such machinery exists, it is useful in resolving disputes. In other instances there may be no external procedure that can be used, particularly with local agreements between managements and unions within an establishment. In such cases some means has to be found of resolving the disputes should there be a final failure to agree.

The need to resolve disputes in these situations has led to the development of the processes of conciliation, arbitration and, to a limited extent, mediation. There is evidence of these processes (described below) existing as far back as 1830 with a Committee of Conciliation in the Potteries. There was a growth period in the 1860s and 1870s, notably the Board of Conciliation and Arbitration in the Nottingham hosiery industry set up by A J Mundella, a Nottingham industrialist. Other examples include arbitration in Wolverhampton for the building trades. These spread to other industries such as engineering, mining and shipbuilding and to the boot and shoe industry in 1890. By 1894 there were 64 conciliation and arbitration boards rising to 162 in 1905 and 325 in 1913. All these were in addition to the State system for arbitration, as described in Section 4.2.4, which grew during this time. The use of conciliation and arbitration was well established by the turn of the century and the processes are of great importance today in the resolution of disputes.

There are a number of variations on the theme of third party intervention in industrial disputes. The two of importance have already been mentioned, i.e., conciliation and arbitration. In addition there is the process of mediation which is used occasionally.

Conciliation

Conciliation is a procedure whereby a person (or persons) helps the parties to reach a mutually acceptable settlement. The conciliator does not impose a solution but works with and between each party to enable them to produce their own solution. Essentially the agreement is made between the two parties.

Conciliation can be used to resolve complaints by an individual. This is much used in disputes relating to statutory employment rights where it is now a compulsory stage in references to industrial tribunals. On application to an industrial tribunal for any alleged infringement of an individual's rights, ACAS are sent the documents initially. An ACAS officer contacts the parties and tries to promote a settlement between the parties. The parties can be seen separately or together, to promote a settlement by exchanging information, clarifying issues, clearing up misunderstandings and listening to both sides. Very importantly the ACAS officer must remain totally impartial and must not be seen to have an opinion on the merits of the case. That is for the parties themselves or for an industrial tribunal. Any information given to a conciliator is confidential and cannot be used at an industrial tribunal unless the party agrees. Conciliation can be attempted prior to any application to an industrial tribunal if a request is made. If an internal procedure exists the officer may suggest that it is used initially. Often such cases are resolved by conciliation and the industrial tribunal hearing becomes unnecessary (*see* statistics in Section 13.1). The powers for this function are contained in the relevant employment legislation.

Collective conciliation is a procedure that can be used to settle collective disputes. A request can be made by either side or jointly. Such assistance has to be given by ACAS, if requested, under the Employment Protection Act 1975, where the dispute is a trade dispute as defined by the Act (amended by the Employment Act 1982). As with individual conciliation, the conciliator has to be careful to be impartial, neutral and in no way take sides or give opinion. By acting as a go-between the person seeks to clarify the issues and find any common ground on which the sides can make a settlement. Conciliation is based on listening, questioning and timing and requires certain personal characteristics. Each act of conciliation is unique and the actions of a conciliator will vary to suit the circumstances. The pattern may include initial meetings with each side followed by a joint meeting, possibly with the conciliator chairing it. It may be that local procedures can be used, in other cases it is a matter of prompting negotiations.

Mediation

Mediation is a procedure whereby a person (or persons) helps the parties reach a mutually acceptable agreement by making recommendations for the sides to consider. This is a process part way between conciliation and arbitration. It is similar to conciliation in that it is the parties that make a final agreement and similar to arbitration in that the mediator attempts to find the solution. The procedure is similar to conciliation but at an appropriate stage the mediator is required to make proposals or recommendations for a solution. The preconditions to mediation are the same as those for arbitration. Mediation is not a common means of resolving industrial disputes and remains little used.

Arbitration

Arbitration is a procedure whereby a person (or persons) settles the dispute by making an independent decision for the parties in dispute. In this situation the arbitrator makes a decision which may or may not be binding on the parties. Arbitration is sometimes preferred as a method of resolving disputes as it shifts the responsibility for finding a solution on to a third party. This allows both parties to retain their credibility in the eyes of their own people. As arbitration requires a decision to be made by the arbitrator, ACAS officers do not carry out arbitration to avoid any accusations of bias. Others argue that arbitration is not a suitable method of resolving complex industrial relations problems by using the offices of those who do not understand the particular situation in an industry. Conciliation is to be preferred, enabling the parties to the dispute, who understand the complexities of the situation, to come to a solution.

Before arbitration commences, a number of issues need to be resolved. Prior agreement, in a procedural agreement, on these issues is of immense help as agreement on any matter in the midst of a dispute is difficult. The procedure laid down by ACAS includes:

- the prerequisite that both parties must agree to the reference to arbitration
- that any agreed procedures have been exhausted
- an agreement that both parties will accept the results of arbitration.

The agreement to go to arbitration will include detail on the form of arbitration (single arbitrator or a board) and the terms of reference of the arbitration.

It is possible, in other forms of private arbitration, that either party can refer the matter to arbitration or there may be an automatic reference to arbitration in the case of a final failure to agree. In some cases, procedures have a permanent form of arbitration available, such as in the British Rail procedures.

The initial step in arbitration is for the arbitrator to receive the facts of the case from both sides, called a statement of case. As the terms of reference will have been given, or agreed in advance, the arbitrator has to stay within their ambit. Attempts to broaden the issues or be side-tracked should be resisted. After this the arbitrator meets the parties together or separately, to obtain information and for a question and answer session to take place. After the arbitrator has sufficient information a report is written in which specific recommendations are made. Usually these are not supported by reasons for the decision. It is generally recommended that

the decision of the arbitrator is binding. This makes sense, as arbitration is likely to be the very last step and a breakdown at this stage will leave no other options open for a solution to be found. Sometimes binding arbitration cannot be agreed as one or other side is obviously concerned about an unacceptable solution but needs to keep up the momentum in seeking a solution. There can be prolonged discussions on whether the arbitration will be binding or not.

As has been noted in the previous section, it is usual that disputes of right are deemed the legitimate subject of arbitration but disputes of interest are not, as they require a final arbitration on matters of substance. As such, matters of substance should be negotiated between the parties. This is not wholly the case in British industrial relations and in some cases substantive issues, such as pay awards, are the topic of arbitration. This was certainly true of references to the Central Arbitration Committee under Schedule 11 of the Employment Protection Act 1975 (now repealed) for wage claims based on the 'general levels of terms and conditions' in a trade in a district.

Pendulum arbitration

A form of arbitration that has become popular recently has been the so-called 'pendulum arbitration'. Under this arrangement a disputed issue is referred to binding arbitration. The submissions to the arbitrator are made in the same manner as above, the important difference being that the arbitrator has to choose the statement of claim of one or the other side. The arbitrator cannot make any change to the statements or opt for the usual 'splitting the difference'. This procedure has the effect of moderating claims and tends to alter the style of negotiations in an organisation. Traditionally claims start high or low and move to the middle ground, but, under these conditions, any extreme claims sent to the arbitrator are likely to be rejected. This form of arbitration has become a feature of the collective agreements made by Japanese companies operating in the UK.

One of the reasons that this form of arbitration developed was that under the standard system of arbitration either side or both sides may hold something back in the negotiations. If the arbitrator 'splits the difference' (as they reputedly do) the sides do not lose as much if the negotiations do fail and the matter is referred to arbitration. If the arbitrator (under pendulum arbitration) has to choose one or the other side's position, then the sides will want to move to a reasonable position earlier, so any arbitration is more likely to go their way.

The other effect of pendulum arbitration is that the sides will be more willing to reach a conclusion in their own negotiations rather than run the risk of losing the decision at arbitration.

There are variations on pendulum, or final offer arbitration. Often negotiations are a complex set of interlinked issues, with the negotiators seeking to strike a balance between the various issues (conceding some items reluctantly in order to secure another more desirable item). Arbitrators may wish to disaggregate the issues and decide the claim on an issue by issue basis. This allows the arbitrator more discretion in coming to what they consider to be a balanced decision. Some systems allow the claim to be broken into its constituent parts. Others make a decision on the total packages presented.

Mini-questions
6.1 Describe the main characteristics of collective bargaining.
6.2 If you were a shop steward, explain the main advantages of collective bargaining.
6.3 If you were a manager, explain the main advantages of collective bargaining.
6.4 Describe the two main preconditions for collective bargaining.
6.5 Write an account explaining the different reasons why collective bargaining operates.
6.6 Explain what is meant by the term 'free collective bargaining'.
6.7 Describe the basis of productivity bargaining.
6.8 Briefly describe the main stages in negotiation.
6.9 List and briefly describe six sanctions that might be used in a dispute.
6.10 Differentiate between conciliation, mediation and arbitration.

6.11 Outline the advantages of pendulum arbitration.

Exercises
6.1 If you were applying for a job (or if you have done), discuss whether you would prefer to negotiate the details of the job (i.e., its terms and conditions) for yourself, or have them offered to you as part of a collective agreement.
6.2 Examine your own place of work, or one known to you, and suggest areas where productivity could be improved under a productivity agreement.
6.3 Assume the role of a union negotiator and write out a detailed wage claim.
6.4 Draw up an agreement for setting up arbitration to be used in a disputes procedure after there has been a final failure to agree. Ensure that it covers all the practical points required to set up arbitration. For the selected method, write some notes addressed to your colleagues and managers, explaining the reasons for your choice.
6.5 Prepare a report on 'the principles and practice of pendulum arbitration' for your Personnel Director.

Further reading

E Batstone, *The Reform of Workplace Industrial Relations*, Clarendon Press, 1988, 0-19-827282-0
ACAS *Collective Bargaining in Britain*
M Jackson, J Leopold and K Tuck, *Decentralisation of Collective Bargaining*, Macmillan, 1993, 0-333-57427-3
G Burrows, *No Strike Agreements and Pendulum Arbitration*
G Kennedy, J Benson and J McMillan, *Managing Negotiations*, Business Books, 1984, 0-09-158231-8

Case studies
(5) Going to arbitration, page 322.
(7) Negotiating a disciplinary procedure, page 328.
(81) The mushrooming problem, page 331.

7
Collective agreements

7.1 Agreements

7.1.1 Nature of agreements

The outcome of collective bargaining is an agreement. During negotiations the topics under consideration are discussed until eventually agreement is reached. These are then drafted into written form and finally signed by both sides. It has always been presumed, both at law and in practice, that collective agreements are not legally binding contracts. They are essentially documents binding in honour only. This means that in the event of either side not keeping to its side of the bargain there can be no legal proceedings by the injured party against the party breaking the agreement. While collective agreements show some of the characteristics of a contract, it is the intention of the parties not to be legally bound, but to be free to act as circumstances might dictate. Also collective agreements are not worded in legal language and they are difficult to apply strictly. It is possible for the parties to agree to let the collective agreement be legally binding. A clause to that effect would make the agreement into a contract, binding at law in the courts. Ford did attempt to do this (in line with American practice) but failed. In 1971 the Industrial Relations Act reversed this common law presumption, of the nonbinding nature of agreements, by saying that the presumption would be for agreements to be legally binding, unless the contrary was stated. Almost universally riders were added to agreements stating that they were not intended to be legally binding. This provision was repealed in 1974. The government's Green Paper *Industrial Relations in the 1990s*, issued in 1991, resurrected the idea of legally binding collective agreements. Again opt-out clauses would be allowed. There is little advantage to either employer or union to have agreements legally binding as both sides will, on occasion, wish to retain the flexibility the system affords now. Under the Trade Union and Labour Relations (Consolidation) Act 1992 an agreement is legally enforceable if it is in writing and if it states the parties intend it to be legally binding.

While the agreement itself is not binding on the parties, the terms and conditions contained in the agreement are binding on the individual contracts of employment of the employers covered by the agreement. Hence, if the agreement is to raise pay by £5 per week then, once the agreement is operable (say from the normal settlement date), the employer must pay the employees the £5 rise. Failure to do so could lead to a court claim for the money, apart from the inevitable industrial dispute. If the agreement states that in future employees have to work more flexibly or be mobile in moving from one department to another, any refusal could lead to disciplinary action and maybe even dismissal. An essential feature of a contract of employment is that certain of the terms change from time to time. An important source of these changes terms is the collective agreement. It is presumed that the negotiated terms are accepted by the individual employees through the union representatives acting on their behalf. In a group only part unionised, normally the nonunion employees are given the same terms as the union members. Occasionally this can lead to difficulties if the nonunion members refuse to be bound by the negotiated terms. In this case the employer, wishing to effect a change to the contract, has to obtain the individual employee's agreement. However, failure to accept reasonable changes to a contract can lead to a dismissal which would be fair.

A notable feature of the British system of collective bargaining is that the agreements made are not static, fixed term agreements but are of a continuing nature. Some other systems, particularly the Canadian and American systems, have fixed-term agreements whereby at the end of negotiations an agreement is made covering all aspects of the labour contract for a fixed period of time. During this period the terms in the agreement are binding and cannot be renegotiated. Hence when an agreement comes up for a renegotiation this can lead to problems. Periods of peace during this contract period are followed by storm, especially if the unions feel a lot of catching up has to be done. It is notable that the strike record of the two countries mentioned is somewhat worse than that of the UK.

The British system is much more open and flexible. Agreements on wages are often made annually, on some fixed date, but this does not preclude claims within that period, or for agreements to cover a period longer than one year. Where the agreement states a settlement date, this is usually adhered to so that, even if negotiations are protracted, the settlement is back-dated. Other agreements tend to be completely open and the terms of such agreements are negotiable at any time. To ensure orderliness within the system, agreements often contain a clause which states that either side may seek renegotiation of part or all of the agreement by giving a certain period of prior notice (usually a lengthy period, such as six months). This arrangement keeps the system very fluid and also gives it the ability to react to new or evolving situations without being constrained by a fixed-term agreement.

Collective agreements are frequently available as written documents which the employer and union officials have signed. As many of the terms and conditions of an individual's contract of employment are contained in these documents, the written particulars to be given to an employee can refer to these documents. Being written documents these agreements are subject to interpretation. If care is not taken in drafting the wording, false interpretations can be made (even though innocently). This can lead to problems where the employer has one interpretation and sticks to it and the unions have another. This often has to be resolved by taking the matter through a disputes or grievance procedure, to try to find an interpretation that is acceptable to both sides. These are disputes of right which were referred to earlier. Some agreements give interpretative notes to clarify the position and so leave no room for alternative interpretations. This is especially important in national agreements as it is not possible to refer the matter to the negotiators of the agreement. At local level it is easier as the interpretation is often carried out by those who negotiated the agreement. For local authority workers' national agreements there is a separate body, the Local Authorities Conditions of Service Advisory Board (LACSAB), to deal with the question of the interpretation and application of agreements.

It is often argued that all agreements should be formal and written. The Donovan Commission argued in favour of making agreements (particularly local agreements) formal rather than unwritten and informal. The Code of Practice on Industrial Relations (*see* Section 11.1) also makes this same point. The considerations in favour of formality are that the rules will be both known and seen by (or available to) everyone. This eliminates any disagreement on whether a subject is encompassed in an agreement. To rely on memory or recollection is dangerous and is likely to lead to a dispute. Communication is also made easier. When agreements have been made, these can be transmitted to all those affected. Verbal messages are notoriously inaccurate even when the sender is trying to be accurate and unbiased. A definitive document eliminates such problems. Finally, the preparation of a written document eradicates inconsistency and ambiguity. Often the most difficult and demanding step in negotiations is to agree on the form of words. Translating a verbal agreement into words requires precision to minimise problems of interpretation, and agreements often define the meaning of any words that need interpretation.

However, there are some disadvantages associated with having formal written agreements. The first is that flexibility and discretion are lost. A manager has to observe the agreement even if they would rather not in a particular circumstance (maybe for perfectly good reasons, such as helping someone with special difficulties or problems). If an agreement exists, the rules of industrial relations say it must be observed. Should a manager choose not to apply an agreement, for some reason, then others could claim exceptional treatment at some later date. This would clearly make a mockery of having an agreement. Secondly, formal agreements cannot anticipate every possible future situation and informality could help solve a novel problem whereas, with a formal agreement, the manager must follow the book. This can certainly constrain a manager in some situations.

Agreements can be classified into two categories, substantive and procedural, depending on the function of the agreement:

- **Substantive** These are agreements that set out the content of matters affecting employees. They contain references to the list in Section 6.1.2 (though perhaps not all of these). These are matters of right that individual employees can consider they are entitled to under that agreement.
- **Procedural** These are agreements that set out the rules and procedures to be used by the two sides. There can be procedures for disputes, grievances, discipline, recruitment, redundancies, consultation, technology and similar issues. Also they contain the rules for the conduct of negotiations, who the negotiators are, who is the chairperson, voting powers of the chairperson, time limits, references back, exclusion of industrial action before exhausting procedures, alterations and so on. These agreements are not legally binding and if the

procedures are not followed neither the unions nor the employer can be taken to court for not having done so.

The benefits of a procedural agreement include:

- Both sides are involved in making the agreement and then they are committed to it. An unwritten rule of industrial relations is that agreements must be adhered to both in spirit and in specifics.
- The agreement recognises the right for certain issues to be raised as part of an agreement. If there is a redundancy agreement then, should redundancies arise, the agreement will operate. This tends to take the heat out of a situation because if a matter arises it can be referred to the grievance or disputes procedure. This introduces some calm into the situation. Such agreements recognise the potential for conflict and provide a means for dealing with it.
- It is often important for issues to be dealt with consistently and with fairness. Where a procedure exists then each time a particular situation arises it can be dealt with in the same way, rather than arbitrarily.
- Control can be kept in a potentially difficult situation by records being made (as required by the procedure) and for those to be used in evidence at later stages if necessary. In the absence of written records much of the evidence may be hearsay or rumour. Such inaccurate records can be dispelled with an agreement in operation.

Often one single document or agreement will contain a mixture of both classifications. Sometimes they are kept entirely separate, or negotiated by a separate body.

7.1.2 Local and national agreements

It will probably be clear by now that a feature of our collective bargaining system is that collective agreements are made at various levels. This spectrum can be viewed as going from those made wholly at national level to those made wholly at local level. National agreements are ones which are negotiated between full-time national trade union officials and high-level representatives of the employers themselves or the full-time national officials of the employers' association. At the other end of the scale local agreements are negotiated between the shop stewards and local management (often below board level). Between these two extremes lie a number of variations. Some sectors have a national agreement for certain basic features of employment with regional/district agreements for the more detailed features. Others have national agreements that set down minimum terms of employment for a sector and these are modified by local agreements. A similar picture emerges with individual companies. Large organisations operating on many sites vary between having a company-wide agreement (no local bargaining), such as at Ford, through to purely local agreements at each establishment. Individual practice reflects the centralised or decentralised nature of the organisation concerned. Clearly there is no one pattern to the levels at which agreements are made in Britain. Furthermore, this 'mixed' system also changes over time. During the 1980s there was a significant shift from national to local bargaining to enable local mangement to have the freedom to manage its own affairs flexibly.

The first collective agreements known to exist were mainly on a local basis, with just a few examples of national agreements. The First World War saw the growth of national agreements. A reversal of this trend occurred after the Second World War back towards more local agreements. This move was probably due to low unemployment. When local employers have to compete for scarce labour, pressure is on them to offer more attractive terms. If employers are bound wholly by a national agreement, they can do nothing about offering such terms. By entering into local negotiations, they can improve them. The reasons for national agreements evolving include:

- They take wages out of price competition locally. Local competition between employers in the local labour market becomes irrelevant if wages are fixed at national level
- Administratively it is advantageous to have a few negotiators covering a large number of people. The time-consuming negotiations exercise does not have to be repeated many times.

In the public sector, comprehensive national agreements are almost universal. This includes the Civil Service, local authority workers and the nationalised industries (BSC, BR). Some slight variations exist, for example British Coal has local agreements for pit bonuses introduced after encountering problems with negotiating a national, output-related bonus scheme.

In the private sector, national agreements have been used with great effect but there have been problems. As suggested, one way to solve the problems of a formal, rigid, national agreement is to negotiate local variations. A prime example of this was, until 1989, seen in the engineering industry. The Engineering Employers' Federation negotiated with the Confederation of Shipbuilding and Engineering Unions a national agreement on the main terms and conditions of employment that applied in the companies federated to the EEF. Due to a disagreement over working hours, these national agreements are no longer used to negotiate matters of pay or working hours. These are for local negotiation. Increasingly, the practice has been for these national agreements to be used as a minimum on which to base local negotiations. This causes a drift from the terms of settlement in the national agreement at local level. This gap is ever likely to increase as negotiators at local level establish the custom of taking the improvements awarded at national level as the minimum locally, and if possible, to improve upon this. Cumulated over a number of years, this leads to an ever-widening gap.

The dual nature of the British industrial relations system of national and local agreements, was examined by the Donovan Commission in 1965. The report concluded that while the nature of the system was satisfactory, the manner in which local bargaining was taking place left much to be desired. The Commission favoured local bargaining for its ability to react to local conditions and for people on the spot to make the agreements that best suited them, but it was too informal and tended to undermine the national agreements. The system needed rationalising so that each level dealt with particular matters, i.e., national level with the regulatory process and local level the substantive issues.

The report recommended that at local level the bargaining process should become more formalised and systematic. This meant developing specific industrial relations' policies at employers' board level, having explicit procedural agreements and regularising matters which previously had been resolved informally. The situation that had developed was that the shop stewards' role had developed so that they made unwritten understandings, especially with supervisors, by settling grievances and disputes informally. There tended to be a lack of procedural agreements that determined the way in which negotiations, grievances and disputes would be handled. The Donovan Commission considered that this was bad industrial relations practice and recommended that agreements should be made to secure a comprehensive, formal system at local level. This recommendation is not that easy to achieve because resistance is likely to arise. Those with a vested interest in a particular system are not likely to give up their position of strength. A move from the informal to the formal may be difficult for some to accept. Also, when a practice has continued for some time this may be perceived as the accepted rule on the grounds of custom and practice. While custom and practice may not be enshrined in a formal agreement, it is very difficult to ignore or change.

Local bargaining

From the late 1980s onwards there has been a definite shift from national bargaining to local bargaining. There are a number of reasons for this:

- The shift from the primary and secondary sectors (*see* Section 17.1). The sectors with traditionally high union membership, such as mining, the railways, shipbuilding and steel making, had national agreements which have suffered decline over the 1980s.
- Privatisation of certain nationalised industries (with national agreements) has led to the break-up of the monoliths into smaller units where local bargaining can take place.
- Decentralisation of companies has caused a shift to local bargaining. Large firms are increasingly making individual units profit centres and this calls for flexibility and discretion at local level. Pay deals can be more closely matched to local conditions, profitability and productivity, giving local managers control over this aspect of their enterprise.
- The growth of small firms has led to local agreements, where the firm is not part of a conglomerate.
- The commercialisation of the public sector is leading to the introduction of local negotiations in a sector previously dominated by national negotiations. For example, the once rigid national agreements for teachers and lecturers now allow for more local bargaining. The NHS senior managers laid plans, in 1990, to move to local bargaining for the NHS and for the abandonment of the national agreements.

7.1.3 Single-union agreements

A notable item to appear on the industrial relations agenda in the 1980s was the topic of single-union deals. These are deals in which an employer recognises only one union for the purposes of collective bargaining and that union represents all categories of employee. This development was not without controversy and it led to a bitter and divisive struggle in the trade union movement. This was one of the reasons why the EETPU was expelled from the TUC.

The idea was introduced into the UK by Japanese firms setting up operations in the UK. They were prepared to recognise trade unions but wished to avoid the problems that had beset industrial relations in UK manufacturing firms.

One of the perceived causes of the problem was the large number of unions that individual UK firms had to deal with and the difficulties arising from this, for example demarcation between the crafts and production staff. They also used this as an opportunity to incorporate a number of novel features into the deal. Single-union agreements have also been used by employers wishing to loosen the stranglehold that some unions had in certain industries, notably the national newspaper industry. Several newspapers relocated on to new production sites and insisted on single-union agreements for the new operation.

Given the initial opposition to these deals several of the larger trade unions have entered into such deals. The EETPU (now part of the AEEU) has secured the largest number of deals, with the TGWU, the AEU (now the AEEU), USDAW, SOGAT and the NGA (the latter two are now the GPMU) all having signed such deals. The major argument against single-union agreements is that it is divisive; one union is set against another. Inevitably one union gains all the members, with all the other unions losing out. It is instructive that survey evidence shows that the level of trade union membership in firms with a single-union agreement is at least 70%, compared with an average of 40%.

These new deals often incorporated so-called 'no-strike' clauses. In fact, these are often binding arbitration clauses, frequently utilising pendulum arbitration. This means that procedures have to be followed through, without industrial action taking place and, in the event of a failure to agree, the parties go to arbitration, the findings of which are binding on both parties. In fact there is no legal binding agreement not to strike, nor does it prevent workers from taking industrial action, but it would be outside the agreed procedure (as is most industrial action in any case). Pendulum arbitration is a process whereby both sides present their case to an arbitrator and the arbitrator has to select one or other case (*see* Section 6.4).

The arbitrator cannot create a compromise solution. This has the effect of moderating both sides' claims in their statements to the arbitrator.

It was these alleged no-strike clauses in single-union deals that the trade unions were opposed to and which led to the TUC recommending that unions should not sign such deals. Disputes have occurred at firms with such deals and 90% of disputes are unofficial and outside agreed procedures in any case. The other components of a single-union agreement (although not in all such agreements) are:

- the achievement of single status for all employees, whereby all employees have the same hours of work, holiday entitlement, sick pay and pensions rights, etc.
- a measure of industrial democracy in which employees are involved in decision making
- increased flexibility which derives from the two points above and the fact that there is only a single union

Where single-union agreements have been made, firms respond positively to the benefits that are gained under such arrangements. It is likely that more firms will try to secure such agreements. The majority of single-union agreements made to date are on 'green field' sites where there are no existing arrangements. Clearly this is much easier to implement than on existing sites where several unions are recognised. There is now less union resistance, with the TUC having issued a Code of Practice and amended its own procedures to deal with the introduction of single-union agreements.

The content of single-union agreements reveals the new approach to industrial relations heralded by this development. The AEEU states that all its single-union agreements contain the following points:

- a single union for all employees from shop floor to senior management
- single status for all employees
- independent conciliation and arbitration facilities
- provision for the flexible use of labour and the necessary training to maximise flexibility and productivity

The AEEU has concluded agreements with some large organisations such as Nissan, Coca-

Cola, Komatsu and Toyota. Extracts from these agreements demonstrate the style and content of these agreements:

- to ensure the fullest use of plant, equipment, vehicles and manpower, there will be complete flexibility and mobility of employees . . .
- the objectives of this agreement are to maintain the prosperity of the company and its employees and to recognise that all employees, at whatever level, have a valued part to play in the success of the company
- Both parties have the common objective of ensuring the efficiency and prosperity of the company. The parties recognise the need to have well-trained and flexible employees.

Surveys of single-union agreements show that trade union membership levels are high where single-union agreements exist; an Industrial Relations Services Survey in 1989 found an average membership level of 75% in the firms surveyed. Only half the agreements included a pendulum arbitration clause and a few more had a binding arbitration clause. The employers' reasons for entering into these agreements were to provide for flexibility within the workforce and for stability in industrial relations.

7.2 Procedural agreements

7.2.1 Content

We have already seen that procedural agreements make up the framework that supports the system of collective bargaining. They lay down the rules and procedures to be observed in a particular situation. Such agreements tend to be permanent, with few changes made over time, as opposed to substantive agreements (*see* below) which are renegotiated regularly. It must be stated that any agreement can contain both procedural and substantive clauses. It is neither necessary, nor always practicable, that the two types of agreement are kept separate. For the purposes of simplicity, however, the two are discussed separately in this section.

The effectiveness of any agreement can be measured by the ability of the procedure to deal effectively with the issue concerned. The object is to find a mutually acceptable solution to a problem or issue without disruption to normal activity. In order for this to happen, the parties to the agreement must be willing to accept the use of procedure and be committed to it working. While the underlying presumption of all agreements is that they will be honoured, there is a great deal of difference between restrained reluctance and committed enthusiasm. If the parties to the agreement and those affected by it derive satisfaction from the outcome of using procedures, then the agreement will remain workable. The parties may have somewhat different objectives. Management may see the need for the orderly resolution of a problem, while the union and employees may be more interested in a quick solution to it. Provided both sides find satisfaction, however, such duplicity of purpose does not matter. Nevertheless, whatever the situation, commitment is necessary as frequently hard work is needed to find a solution. Without commitment either side might give up and the procedure fall into disrepute.

It is important for the long-term stability of the system that procedural agreements are observed. If either side continually ignores or does not show commitment to the procedures laid down, then it is likely that the other side will react in like manner when it suits them. If one side has evidence that the other side has been operating outside the spirit of the agreement it will cause problems and provoke accusations of lack of commitment. The alternative to using procedure is the blatant expression of industrial conflict evidenced by poor relations, low morale and motivation and possibly industrial action. It is usually assumed that both parties are committed to using procedure rather than resorting to sanctions.

Procedural agreements are comprised of clauses which set down the rules. The following list gives the factors and issues that are contained in a typical procedural agreement:

- **Preamble** This states the purpose of the agreement and the situations in which it is to be used. These clauses tend to be general statements that put the agreement into context. The parties to the agreement are usually named and the date of the agreement recorded.

- **Units** The groups, sections, plants, sites, etc., to which the agreement applies are stated. This may range from a single group at one site to a national agreement applicable to many thousands of employees across the country.

- **Subjects** The subjects, topics or items which can be brought up under the procedure are stated. This is important as everyone needs to be clear on exactly what can be referred to procedure. If they are not stated, disputes can arise as to whether the agreement applies in a particular situation. Such disputes revolve around whether the dispute is one of right (when the procedure will apply) or one of interest (when the procedure will not apply; *see* Section 6.3).

- **Stages** The levels at which the procedure will operate are clarified. Normally a statement is made that the issue is to be resolved as near as possible to the point of origin. Some state that an issue should be taken to the employee's supervisor or manager first, then the procedure is to be used if there is no satisfaction. Each subsequent stage may involve the next level of the management hierarchy with the more senior trade union officials involved at the later stages. Some agreements involve the use of 'outside' stages which utilise the facilities of an employers' association and the full-time trade union officials. The end stage may be at national level with national officials from both sides. The clauses on the various stages will usually state the people involved at each stage, i.e., supervisor, manager, director, steward, convenor, etc. The stages are linked to the next two features.

- **Time limits** The time limits within which each stage must start and finish are stated. This may be specific, such as x working days,

or may be more flexible, or be the subject of a negotiated exception, e.g., three working days, except where agreed otherwise. Time limits prevent stalling, which induces frustration, but rigid limits can prevent adequate investigation and preparation.

- **Appeals** In some procedures, for instance grievance and disciplinary procedures, usually there is a right of appeal to the next level of management against the decision at a particular stage.

- **Sanctions** Agreements can have a clause which specifically precludes the use of any sanctions by either side while the matter is still within procedure. Such clauses attempt to maintain commitment (the only way out is to agree) but can cause problems if sanctions are used. If employees strike, management may make a return to work a precondition of further negotiations, arguing that the procedure cannot be used if it is being broken. These clauses are not strictly 'no-strike' clauses as they do not prohibit strikes nor do they make them unlawful. Employees can still strike but it can exacerbate the problem rather than help solve it. It is very doubtful if any trade union would accept, in an agreement, a full 'no-strike' clause unless the rules of the union were to prohibit this, such as the Royal College of Nursing. Other sanctions clauses may stipulate that a certain period of notice is required before sanctions are taken. Indeed, legislative proposals in the government's White Paper *People, Jobs and Opportunity* reintroduced the idea of a statutory 7-day cooling-off period between a ballot approving industrial action and the action being taken. By giving notice, this may sharpen resolve to find a solution under the procedure before relations break down. A similar idea was proposed in the White Paper *In Place of Strife* in 1968. This suggested a 28-day 'cooling off' period within which workers could not strike. This would have had legislative backing had the proposals become law.

- **Records** It is normal that written records are made at the conclusion of each stage or meeting. This may be a record of what was said and the statements or claims made by one or both sides. If no agreement is made the record can show a 'failure to agree'. Often such a record will trigger off the next stage in procedure. It may state that there was agreement to meet again to pursue the matter under discussion or to break for further investigation or to gather further information. Records are important so that the process is formalised and memories are not relied upon. Written records are very important should the matter eventually involve high level officials, arbiters or legal proceedings.

- **Status quo**   A clause may be included which states that until agreement has been made under procedure, nothing shall change. These clauses are inserted at union insistence to prevent management from making changes that may be detrimental to employees' terms and conditions of employment. If management proposes to take action on some issue, e.g., to introduce new machinery or change methods of working, and there are no objections raised, the changes go ahead. However, if an employee or the union were to object, the matter would be referred to a negotiating or grievance procedure. Once referred, the proposed action cannot be implemented until the matter is resolved or the procedure has been exhausted. These clauses and the ones referred to below in the next paragraph are mutually exclusive.

- **Right to manage**   A clause stating that management has the right to manage. These clauses are inserted at management's insistence to maintain management's prerogative to do as it sees fit without reference to a negotiations procedure. Consultations may be included at a certain stage but this does not preclude management's right to implement any proposed changes.

- **Alteration and termination**   Clauses which allow for the amendment or abandonment of the agreement. The alteration of an agreement is usually negotiated by either side giving notice of a proposition for change. This is then negotiated and incorporated as an amendment, when agreement is reached. In extreme situations either side may wish to terminate the agreement. Often this requires advance notice of several months. Clearly abandonment at will or on very short notice would be recipe for chaos.

- **Information**   The basis of good negotiation is sound information. Generally management has access to more information and can maintain a superior position in negotiation because of this. Allowing unions access to or providing information is required by law as explained in a Code of Practice (*see* Section 11.3). A clause may specify the sort of information that will be supplied.

- **External procedure**   A clause is included stating what happens when the procedure is exhausted and there is a final failure to agree. This will normally involve reference to some form of conciliation, mediation or arbitration. Practice varies as to whether such a reference can be made by either party or if there is to be a joint reference by both parties. Similarly the decisions or recommendations made by the third party in some instances are binding, in others only advisory. Further detail may be needed on the selection of the person to carry out the function and the agreed terms of reference. Such matters can be referred to ACAS who can conciliate or supply an arbiter.

7.3   Types of agreement

7.3.1   Negotiating procedure

One of the fundamental requirements for a formal collective bargaining system is to have a joint negotiating procedure. The procedure can be used to negotiate substantive agreements or it can be used as the basis for the other procedural agreements described in this section. Indeed a negotiating procedure can be used as a disputes procedure and a grievance procedure and can easily be adapted for use in other circumstances. The procedure can contain clauses on:

- the stages in the agreement (*see* above) specifying who is involved at each stage and a time limit on when the meeting must take place plus a provision for adjournments
- the subjects which can be brought up under this procedure, specifying the exact nature of the items which will be referred to the negotiating procedure, e.g., wages, bonuses, premiums, holidays, working practices, etc.
- what happens if there is a final failure to agree, i.e., any references to arbitration or external procedure to secure a settlement

For example, *see* Section 7.5.1.

7.3.2 Disputes and grievance procedure

A second important agreement that is most beneficial in collective bargaining is a procedure for resolving the inevitable problems that arise from time to time. Wherever there are agreements there are bound to be problems of interpretation and practice plus the novel situations that are not clearly covered by the agreement. The need for a disputes or grievance procedure is essential if the problems that arise are not satisfactorily dealt with or if they are dealt with in an arbitrary or inconsistent manner. Often, if questions raised had been dealt with effectively and efficiently, many industrial disputes would not have occurred.

The difference between a dispute and a grievance is that a grievance is a question raised or applicable to an individual while a dispute is a question raised or applicable to a group. However, the two overlap considerably because a grievance can easily become a dispute when several people are involved in raising the same question or the issue becomes applicable to the group. Also a question raised as a dispute often becomes the subject of a negotiation, hence the comment made above that a negotiating procedure is sometimes used as a disputes procedure.

Grievances are frequently concerned with an individual's terms and conditions of employment and the employee raises a question of entitlement on wages, job grading, allowances, bonuses, holiday pay or entitlement or the many other terms enshrined in a contract of employment. The object of the procedure is to resolve the question quickly and as near the point of origin as possible. Such action prevents what may initially be a small matter mushrooming into a major dispute. Sometimes it is necessary to refer a question raised to a higher authority as the implications may be very wide, especially if the answer could affect many other employees.

The clauses that appear include the three specified in 7.2.1 on time limits, subject matter and external procedure. The preamble might contain clauses on the need for speedy resolution and the employees that the procedure applies to.

For example, *see* Section 7.5.2.

7.3.3 Disciplinary procedure

An inevitable consequence of employing people is that there must be rules within the organisation to regulate their behaviour. Arising from this there is a need to have a procedure to deal with those who offend the rules. With the advent of the legal aspects of discipline being set out in the laws of unfair dismissal and the corresponding Code of Practice (*see* Chapter 13 and Section 11.2), there is all the more need for a formal disciplinary procedure. Firms operating without a procedure will find problems defending any legal action for unfair dismissal. There is a great need for fairness and equality in the treatment of individuals being disciplined and a procedure can be designed to achieve this. So often it is the handling of the disciplinary action that is defective rather than there being no lawful reason for the action.

Discipline implies the application of rules. Specifying the rules can be an integral part of the procedure but often it is for management to set the rules and to apply them using the agreed procedure. Rules are often subdivided into acts of gross misconduct, for which the employee can be summarily dismissed, and misconduct for which an employee can be disciplined, e.g., given warnings. The rules must be communicated to the employees and it must be made clear what the consequences might, or would, be if the rule is broken. The wording of the rules needs meticulous attention. The possible interpretation of the word 'shall' is quite different from 'may be'. If it is the former, anyone committing that offence has to be dismissed (or whatever else is specified). If it is the latter, the person taking the disciplinary action has discretion whether to dismiss or to apply some lesser sanction.

A disciplinary procedure might contain the following:

- A preamble that explains to whom the agreement applies and the underlying philosophy of the disciplinary procedure, e.g., fairness of treatment.
- The right to be accompanied by a friend or union representative.
- The stages of the procedure, usually starting with a verbal warning, followed by a written warning, a final written warning and finally dismissal. The stages are triggered by subsequent offences within the period of the warning. Dismissal can occur directly, for an act of gross misconduct, or by the accumulation of warnings, i.e., working through the stages.
- Appeals are to be as of right against the decision at each stage in the procedure. It should be made clear how the appeal should be made, to whom and within a specified time period. Also there should be a statement as to whether the disciplinary action is suspended pending an appeal. This is important when people are dismissed. It may be appropriate to suspend (with or without pay) pending an appeal. A clause should state who shall hear the appeal and should normally be someone more senior who has not previously been involved.
- Penalties should be stated. These are normally the warnings themselves at the early stages of the procedure. Other forms of sanction, which should be specified, can include forfeiture of holiday entitlements, suspension with or without pay, demotion, withholding discretionary bonuses, dismissal followed by reengagement, or fines (the latter being rare now). Any dismissal should be stated as being with or without notice. This can be important to the dismissed person in monetary terms as a dismissal with notice entitles the employee to pay for the full period of notice.
- Time limits on the warnings are usually stated, whereby the various warnings are expunged after a stated period. Normally the second and third warnings remain active for longer periods than the first warning.
- Trade union representatives who are to be disciplined should have special provisions applied to them, not to give them preferential treatment but to ensure scrupulous treatment of the representative. If such disciplinary action is not treated very carefully then there could be accusations of victimisation or discrimination. The usual requirement is for a full-time union official to be contacted and involved from the start of the procedure. A shop steward's credentials will state that a trade union representative is to be treated as an ordinary employee and this includes disciplinary action.
- Records of disciplinary action are important if for no other reason than that, should the action lead to dismissal and an industrial tribunal case, evidence will be required of the disciplinary action taken. At each stage a record should be made of the reason for discipline, brief notes on any relevant matters raised and the possible consequences of any further acts of discipline. Notices of appeal should be required to be in writing to avoid any dispute regarding verbal messages.

For example, *see* Section 7.5.3.

7.3.4 Redundancy procedure

One reason for having procedural agreements is to provide a means of dealing with situations so that if they do occur the matter can be dealt with rather than spending time deciding on how to deal with it. In the heat of a moment of crisis it can be difficult to deal with questions of procedure in the detached manner with which they should. Everyone will want to deal with the substantive issues rather than the procedural.

The existence of a redundancy procedure is necessary for this reason. If the unfortunate circumstance arises where redundancies are declared, then a means of negotiating in that situation is needed, particularly as relations are likely to be strained.

The legal right to redundancy pay was introduced in 1965, being one of the first Acts on employment law. Subsequently the rules were added to in terms of consultations, offers of alternative employment and protective awards by the Employment Protection Act 1975, now consolidated into the Employment Protection (Consolidation) Act 1978. As there are certain legal rights in a redundancy situation the procedure will enshrine these as a minimum and may well exceed them.

A possible contradiction is raised in negotiating a redundancy procedure as it does presuppose that the trade union will contemplate a redundancy situation. As the objective of a trade union is to protect its members' terms and conditions of employment, this will not be realised if redundancies are made a subject of negotiation. The more pragmatic view is that unfortunately redundancies may have to be reluctantly accepted, if all else fails, to ensure the security of employment of the remaining employees.

A typical redundancy procedure might contain the following:

- A preamble stating the basic principles relating to employment policies in the organisation and the circumstances in which redundancies may have to be contemplated. There may be a recognition of legal rights in the situation and whether the procedure exceeds these.
- Consultations will take place, before any redundancies are declared, between union and management. These will normally examine how the number of redundancies can be minimised by seeking to find alternative solutions. The manner of consultation may have to be specified, including the participants and when such meetings will be called. There are certain legal requirements regarding this whereby if between 10 and 99 employees are involved, the period is 30 days and if 100 or more are involved, the period is 90 days. The alternatives to redundancy are natural wastage, freezes on recruitment, redeployment, retraining, cancelling overtime, cancelling subcontract working and early retirement. Redeployment is an alternative often pursued, especially in large firms. This may involve retraining and a trial period or taking the job of a volunteer for redundancy.

- Selection of personnel for redundancy is normally laid down as some priority rule. The first to be made redundant may be part-timers, then those over retirement age followed by volunteers and finally compulsory redundancies. Other procedures use the LIFO rule (last in, first out). Management may wish to retain the right to refuse to accept some applicants for voluntary redundancy, e.g., from key personnel. Any rule for selection must be fair and nondiscriminatory if for no other reason than there would be a risk of claims for unfair dismissal.
- Payment due to those made redundant must be the legal minimum or above. The calculation for this is explained in Section 14.2.1 but this may be supplemented by the employer. A new formula for payment entitlement may be given in the procedure. This clause would be a substantive clause and doubtless would need updating from time to time.
- Periods of notice to be given to those selected for redundancy need stating. Often redundancies apply from a particular date and do not vary as the periods of notice for individual employees do, which may vary with length of service. The period of notice may be worked out or the redundant employees given pay in lieu of notice. If employees are working out notice, they are entitled to paid time off work to seek a job. This may extend to the employer taking positive steps to find alternative work for employees, especially in the case of trainees or apprentices. Should an employee find

another job, the procedure should state whether, if the employee leaves early, they will still be entitled to redundancy pay.

7.3.5   Productivity agreement

The idea of productivity bargaining was discussed in Section 6.1.4. This section looks at the practicalities of a productivity agreement. Such bargaining requires a different approach to negotiations as the process is a cooperative, joint effort much more like problem solving than the traditional, distributive bargaining. Such productivity agreements provide for improvements in the terms and conditions of employment in return for a more effective use of resources giving a corresponding increase in productivity. A typical agreement might include:

- **Parties to agreement** Organisations involved; areas of company/categories of employee covered; specific exclusions
- **Purpose of agreement** Circumstances of agreement; reasons for the parties concluding an agreement
- **Principles** Those upon which the agreement will be based
- **Scope** Areas where the agreement is to operate and where changes will be made
- **Pay** Basic rates, incentives, merit pay; calculation of bonuses; waiting time; rectification work; multi-machine staffing; job grading; sick benefits; transfers; mobility; call out allowances
- **Work practices** Methods of working; measurement of work; production procedures; introduction of new machinery
- **Security of employment** Measures to avoid redundancy; periods of warning and notice; dismissal criteria; appeals; compensation; preferential reengagement rights; consultation
- **Communications** Chain of command; consultative systems; suggestion scheme; disputes procedure
- **Implementation** Interim conditions during introduction of new structure; interim payments; programme for implementation; provision for review and termination

- **Revision and termination** Procedure for amending agreement; phasing and period of agreement; notice for termination
- **Signature and agreement** That of the parties to the agreement.

7.3.6   Other types of agreement

Apart from the procedural agreements detailed above, many others can and do exist. Often they cover specific situations and tend to be specific to an organisation and its environment. It should be made clear that in many instances firms with a well-developed collective bargaining system may have one comprehensive agreement which incorporates many of the agreements that have been noted in this section. Additional agreements may be made in the light of new circumstances or as the collective bargaining system develops. The following subsections give some further types of procedural agreement that can exist.

Recognition agreement

This is a formal statement of which union is recognised by management as representing a group, section or grade of employee for the purposes of collective bargaining. This formalises who represents whom and minimises the possibility of a disagreement between unions on the matter. Certainly a union other than the one specified in the agreement which tries to recruit members in the stated group would be guilty of 'poaching' and this would be in contravention of the TUC's Bridlington Agreement. The agreement would specify the name of the employer, the relevant union or unions and who is to represent the stated categories of employee. The agreement would imply, or state specifically, that trade unions were free to recruit members, and that employees were free, or encouraged, to join a trade union. Clarity of definition is necessary to ensure that there is no ambiguity concerning the unions recognised or the groups which they are to represent. The facilities for the trade union representatives can be stated, including the arrangements for training and time off for their trade union duties, and the agreed rules on the unions holding meetings.

Accreditation of union officials

This is a statement of recognition, by the firm, that a person has been accorded the status of official trade union representative for a particular group, section or grade, in accordance with the recognition procedure. Normal practice is for a trade union to appoint its representative according to its own Rule Book and for the name of the appointed person to be forwarded to management for it to issue the credentials. Rarely would a firm refuse to recognise a duly elected official unless it had very good grounds for doing so. Trade unions strongly defend their right to run their own affairs without interference. The credentials will formally set out the rights and duties of the official. This will include a requirement to observe the agreements made between management and union and to act in good faith. Certain facilities may be made available to the official (room, telephone, information) and the rules stated regarding pay while on union duties.

For example, *see* Section 7.5.4.

Consultation agreement

This is a document setting out the arrangements for consultations within the organisation between management and employees. With the growth of greater employee involvement, through the widening of collective bargaining and moves towards industrial democracy, there is firm evidence that a greater number of firms have arrangements for consultations.

Care needs to be taken to clarify which issues are to be the subject of negotiation and those specified as being within the ambit of the consultative arrangements. There will be overlap, as a change which is discussed in a consultative forum may well be raised in a bargaining session. If management discusses a proposal to introduce new machinery, this will inevitably raise certain questions in the minds of the unions. In organisations where trade unions are very strong, they may resist a move to consultative procedures on the grounds that all matters are negotiable and that a separate consultative structure would undermine the union's authority. The agreement would specify the detailed arrangements for the consultative procedure including the composition of the body, the topics that can be raised, the purpose and power of the body, the frequency, calling, chairing and minuting of the meetings.

Union membership agreement

This is the formal agreement on the formation and maintenance of a closed shop within an organisation. During the mid-1970s the number of closed shops grew to cover about 23% of the working population. This figure fell during the 1980s, as a result of legislation and the economic climate, but nevertheless closed shops exist in many industries. The growth in the 1970s occurred in sectors with well-developed systems of collective bargaining and as a result many closed shop situations became the subject of a formal union/management agreement. Such agreements required management to recognise formally the existence of a closed shop, as in some organisations closed shops had existed but barely with the tacit approval of management. A closed shop would be claimed as custom and practice by the trade union concerned and if resisted it would be difficult to dismantle it.

A further factor that led to more formal closed shop agreements (latterly called union membership agreements) was the legislative aspect. The Trade Union and Labour Relations Act 1974 introduced the rules of unfair dismissal and raised the thorny problem of the position of a non-trade union member dismissed for not being a trade union member in a closed shop. Further legal developments have occurred since then, with the Employment Act 1980 introducing a further requirement that a closed shop can only be recognised at law if a ballot of employees indicates an 80% majority in favour of such an agreement. (*See* also Section 15.3.) The position, as a result of the Employment Act 1988, is that dismissal in this situation is automatically unfair.

A union membership agreement sets out the precise details of the arrangements between a specified union and group of employees. The legislative requirements will be embodied plus any other negotiated clauses. Questions which should be addressed include the problem of current, non-union members, possible grounds for not joining a union, the effect of expulsion from, or lapsed membership of, the union and the manner of recruiting new employees into the union.

Technology agreement

This is an agreement on the procedure to be followed when new equipment, machines, computers or other technological devices are being proposed for introduction into an organisation. This would involve a consultative stage or a negotiating stage, and will take the form of a procedure. In addition, a technology agreement would specify, in its preamble, the agreed policy on introducing new equipment, the effects on the workforce and the arrangements for discussions on the various issues arising. The issues will include job security, redeployment, job descriptions, regrading, health and safety, training and pay. One question to be addressed is whether management can go ahead with its plans if the procedure has not been worked through. Section 7.2.1 discussed 'status quo' and 'right to manage' clauses. Such clauses are important in a technology agreement. The former clause would restrict management's ability to introduce change without prior agreement. Modern agreements would contain a means of consulting employees but with a right to implement change. If there is a failure to agree, there needs to be provision for whether or not management can go ahead with the introduction. Technology agreements have been developed by the white collar unions particularly, such as GMB and MSF, as a result of the implementation of office technology.

Equal opportunities agreement

This is an agreement stating the organisation's formal position on giving all classes of employee an equal employment opportunity in recruitment, promotion and training. The agreement is rather a statement of policy which is to be applied in the firm's operations. (*See also* the Code of Practice, Section 11.8.)

Leave of absence agreement

This sets out the situations in which the firm will allow employees time off work for specified reasons, such as bereavement. It will allow a certain length of time off, with pay, for the death of defined close relatives, moving house, birth of a child, etc.

7.4   Substantive agreements

These agreements contain the terms and conditions of employment for the employees covered by the agreement. The agreements are of a continuing nature as opposed to the static nature of a procedural agreement. The content of a substantive agreement needs updating from time to time. As trade unions seek to improve the terms and conditions of employment of their members, they will seek to negotiate improved terms. In wage negotiations trade union officials will seek to improve levels of pay (basic, bonuses, premiums, etc.) and the other negotiable terms, e.g., holidays, sick pay, pensions, etc. This entails current agreements being updated. This fluidity is a notable feature of the British collective bargaining system where we do not have fixed-term agreements. There is some rigidity to the system, usually by way of annual agreements, to prevent the chaos of claims constantly being made. Procedural agreements tend to be fixed and often contain a clause to the effect that they can only be amended given a stated period of notice.

The content of a substantive agreement can range from a simple agreement on wages through to a comprehensive agreement on virtually all the terms and conditions of employment. Section 6.1.2 indicated a fairly comprehensive list of the topics which could be contained in one or more substantive agreements. As formal agreements between employers and trade unions (at local or national level) become permanent and develop, the content of such agreements will expand. Agreements purely on wages will expand to include holidays and hours, then sick pay and pensions and on to more detailed arrangements.

The process of expansion of the scope of substantive agreements may not be easy. As noted in Section 6.3, questions arising can be classified into conflicts of right and conflicts of interest. Employers will be willing to negotiate on the topics already contained in the agreements (which will be considered questions of right) but may be reluctant to expand the scope of the agreements to cover a wider number of issues of interest. An attempt to expand the scope of an agreement to include additional issues may be resisted by the employer and a conflict of interest will arise. Such a conflict may have to be resolved under a disputes procedure before there is agreement on the expanded range of topics to be included in the substantive agreement. Once a topic becomes the subject of negotiation it is then within the ambit of a substantive agreement and is likely to be renegotiated as the need arises.

Such an expansion of collective bargaining was anticipated in the system of wages councils, so that as the machinery expanded eventually more comprehensive agreements would be made. To this end statutory joint industrial councils were established to encourage the movement to comprehensive collective bargaining arrangements at employer level. Notably, the remit of wages councils was expanded from minimum wages to include piece-work, overtime rates, holidays and holiday pay. However, the Wages Act 1986 restricted the remit of wages councils to standard rates of pay and overtime rates of pay. The government announced, in 1992, its intention to scrap all wages councils.

Wage bargaining

Wage negotiations are the basis of collective bargaining. The primary feature of the employment relationship is that it is a pay-work bargain. The setting of the levels of pay and, in some instances the amount of work, is the central bargaining feature. The process is also assuming greater economic importance over time as a greater proportion of national income is created by wage earners. The results of pay negotiations are watched closely by economists and politicians as pay increases have an effect on many economic factors such as demand, inflation and product costs. For the individual firm or industry it is clearly of importance as pay awards affect unit costs, prices and competitiveness.

The concept of conflict discussed earlier has its origins in wage bargaining. The fundamental conflict in an organisation is that which arises beween the needs of the business for profit, competitiveness, efficiency, production and staying within budgets and the needs of the employees for maintaining and improving their wages and hence standard of living. It is for the purpose of resolving this conflict that collective bargaining exists. Negotiations seek to arrive at a settlement point which both sides feel they can accept and which satisfies (with some element of compromise) the needs of both sides.

The structure of collective bargaining affects wage agreements. Where there is a structure of strictly national agreements, pay awards are settled at national level with no local variation. Where there are national agreements with local variations, a phenomenon called wage drift occurs. This is the difference between the nationally negotiated wage rates and the actual level of earnings (excluding overtime). This is caused by workplace bargaining on bonuses, piece rates, shift premiums, working condition allowances and any other additional payments. Other causes of wage drift are the use of increments on pay scales (e.g., adding to them), regrading jobs under a job evaluation scheme or by combining grades, e.g., automatic progression. Wage drift is of importance as it accumulates over time and the gap between wage rates and earnings grows larger and larger. Eventually the nationally negotiated wage levels become meaningless in real terms. Wage drift is evidence of the strength of local bargaining where employers are prepared to pay the extra over and above the national rates to attract labour. This is a reflection of the demand and supply in local labour markets. This wage drift effect was noted by the Donovan Commission which commented that, while it was in favour of local bargaining, it found the current system created disorder in local industrial relations. There needed to be much more attention paid to orderly pay structures and to the negotiating process.

Wage negotiations are inherently difficult exercises. Apart from the need to reach a compromise between the conflicting demands of the organisation and its employees there are a number of factors that complicate the exercise.

- **Wage structure** Each group within an organisation has its own specific claims. In industry, shop floor workers are looking for an across-the-board, flat-rate increase in pay and they are often able to negotiate output-related bonuses and shift and overtime premiums. Craft workers are interested in maintaining pay relativities and look for percentage wage increases. There may also be pay structures for staff workers. They seek to maintain their staff status by retaining the differentials accorded to them such as shorter working hours, longer holidays, better pensions and improved sick pay arrangements. Finally, those on management grades seek to maintain their own status and differentials. In carrying out wage negotiations the various and sometimes conflicting demands of the different groups need to be resolved. Needless to say the exercise is difficult and the results will never please all of the people all of the time. Single-union agreements (*see* Section 6.1.3) contain a single-status clause, whereby all employees are employed on identical conditions, which overcomes many of these problems.

- **Pay rounds** It is normal practice for wage negotiations to be carried out once a year and an agreement reached by the settlement date. There is no uniformity on settlement dates and wage agreements are constantly being made. As successive agreements are made a new pay round is entered. The figures which emerge from one pay deal are then used by negotiators as a basis for their claim. Pay

rounds can also cause problems within an industry, particularly in large, multi-union environments. If each group or union has a separate settlement date an organisation can find itself in continuous negotiations. This is a very time-consuming business but also produces the effect called leap-frogging. Each successive group's claim seeks to exceed the last settlement and, rather in the manner of national agreements being improved at local level, use the last settlement as a base for their claim. It is then difficult to break this spiral. A solution to the problem of the pay round is for the firm to impose a standard settlement date for all groups, or implement single-table bargaining (*see* Section 6.1.3).

- **Comparability** A factor in most pay claims is the comparison of like job with like job to thereby claim a similar level of pay. If someone feels they are carrying out a similar job to another who is paid more, they are justified in their claim for an increase in pay. In some pay negotiations this can be a major factor with comparisons made between local firms employing similar grades of personnel, comparisons made between different groups of personnel within the same organisation or comparisons made between similar jobs in different sectors of employment. One method of evaluating the worth of a job is to use the process of job evaluation. There are many schemes of job evaluation which all seek to measure the worth of a job, usually by awarding points to the component factors of a job, e.g., skill, knowledge, experience, education and responsibility. Jobs scoring similar points on evaluation should be paid a similar wage, on the basis that the jobs are worth the same. Job evaluation schemes within firms often lead to a system of grading which rationalises the pay structure. Job evaluation across different sectors of employment is a difficult exercise as finding the common factors on which to base the analysis is difficult. If no such analysis is carried out then comparability is left to opinion which is even more inaccurate.

- **Low pay**   A number of jobs are notably low paid and workers in those jobs are constantly seeking to raise their levels of pay. Often these jobs are in sectors where collective bargaining is not well developed or where those concerned find it difficult to take collective action in pursuance of a claim. For example, nurses claim that they are on low pay for the job they do but are unlikely to resort to the normal forms of industrial action in order to press home their claim. Indeed the Royal College of Nursing has a no-strike rule. Farm workers are also in the low pay bracket but through geographical difficulties find collective action difficult to organise. In other industries the question of low pay relates to an extent to the lack of collective bargaining machinery. Wages councils (previously trade boards) were set up to rectify this problem by setting minimum wages and making attempts to develop collective bargaining machinery. The Labour party manifesto in 1990 contained a pledge to create a legal minimum wage.
- **Equal pay**   In many sectors of employment there is a history of differing pay rates for men and women. The Equal Pay Act 1970 (and its amendments) imposes legal requirements that are designed to eliminate the excesses of discrimination. There can be few firms today which would publish a list of pay grades; one for men and a separate, lower set for women. There are still many variations and anomalies that require attention. As these are attended to they will create an upward pressure on wage costs. The current position on equal pay is given in Section 10.4.3.

7.4.1 Wage agreements

The process of negotiating a wage agreement is based on exchanging information relating to each side's claim. The trade union side may commence by making its statement of claim, in which it specifies what changes it is looking for in the current round of negotiations. This will often be specific on detail and amounts and will seek to justify the claim. Such justification can be based on comparability (mentioned in Section 7.4 above), cost of living increases, the profitability of the firm and other factors.

When the claim has been laid before the negotiating body, the employer's side will reply. They may initially seek clarification of the points raised to ensure that there has been no misunderstanding. The central part of the reply will be to state how much the organisation is prepared to afford. This may be specific amounts, say on wage rates, or a global sum available for wage increases which can then be apportioned as the parties see fit.

The negotiations then move to a period of trying to find where movement can be made towards a settlement, given that there is a gap between claim and reply. Management may indicate that it is prepared to do more about one area of the claim than another. It may prefer a lower increase on basic wage rates but be prepared to pay more on output-related bonuses. This stage is often marked by buying and selling points in which one side offers a concession on a point in exchange for agreement on another. Management may make more money available for wages if there is agreement on greater flexibility among the workforce. Eventually, the parties will move towards a point where both sides are prepared to settle. Sticking points will have been resolved and general agreement reached on the major points.

There are some variations to the standard format of wage negotiations which may include the following:

- **Index linking**   In periods of high inflation, employees are concerned that any wage increase is not eroded before the next set of pay negotiations. To do this they may press for some kind of index linking or inflation proofing, so that as the rate of inflation changes, wages are altered in line with the Retail Prices Index or a similar measure of inflation. Such deals are uncommon as they add to unit costs and are inflationary. They were common during the early 1970s when pay policies allowed for index linking.
- **Bonus schemes**   A common method of increasing pay at local level is to negotiate a

bonus scheme usually related to output. Payment by results systems are not new but they flourished in the periods of pay restraint and pay policies as a means of circumventing the policy. The detail of the various bonus schemes available is too great to deal with here because of the plethora of schemes that can be used. They all seek to relate increase in pay to increase in output. This is quite easy to achieve in manufacturing industry but much more difficult in the public sector.

- **Guaranteed overtime** Most agreements will contain a clause relating to overtime and the rates to be paid for specific hours of overtime. Normally overtime is discretionary and is offered when demand dictates. In many sectors, however, a certain amount of overtime has become structural and worked permanently. This suits the employees as it boosts earnings and it suits the employer because it avoids employing extra staff and overtime can be cancelled easily. Trade unions generally oppose permanent overtime on the grounds that it deprives others of employment. A further step can be to insert a clause for guaranteed overtime whereby everyone is given a specified number of hours overtime per week. This will be paid for, at premium rate, regardless of whether it is worked or not. Employees are available and must work if required. In some instances this may suit the employer. If the organisation offers a round-the-clock service, this can be organised by having staff available on overtime at any time. Frequently, guaranteed overtime will not be a popular option as it adds much to costs and is always expensive as overtime attracts premium rates.

- **Open-ended settlement** One in which the agreement can be renegotiated at any time in the future. Alternatively there may be an escape clause which allows for the agreement to be renegotiated before the normal settlement date. Normally agreements are made for one year, with some exceptionally being made for longer periods. Attempts to have wages constantly under negotiation is a recipe for chaos, especially for the organisation. Not knowing what wage costs are in the months ahead can make commercial decision making very difficult, e.g., fixing prices.

- **End-loaded agreements** A device where the total wage award is staged over the period of the agreement, rather than the full amount at the beginning. This compromise is useful for employers in that it keeps down the cash wage bill for the current year. It is useful for trade unions in that it provides a higher starting point on which to base the pay claim in the next round of pay negotiations. For example, an end-loaded agreement may pay 5% on the settlement date and a further 2% ten months later.

- **Consolidation** For the purposes of calculating certain payments the basic wage is used. Holiday pay, sick pay and overtime premiums are based on the base rate. Consolidation is the process of including payments previously classified as additional payments into the basic wage, which becomes the basis for making these other payments. A wage claim may ask for a bonus to be consolidated into base rates. This merely reclassifies the bonus as part of the basic wage but creates an increase in the other payments such as holiday pay. As more items are consolidated into base rates this makes the other items of pay more expensive. It also means that the payments once considered as additional are now an integral, permanent part of base rates.

- **Packaging** A strategy that is sometimes employed in pay bargaining whereby management makes a comprehensive set of proposals which are to be accepted as a whole or rejected. There can be no negotiation on the content as the package stands as a complete entity. The union is then put in the position of accepting the package or rejecting it. Such a tactic reduces the time-consuming trading in normal negotiations. The formulation of a package needs to include a careful blend of attractive points and some less attractive points that the union may be persuaded to accept if the former are attractive enough. The offer of a package will often be presented

on the terms that, in the event of rejection, pay talks will revert to a lower opening position.
- **Productivity bargaining** *See* Section 6.1.4.

7.5 Example agreements

In Section 7.3 we examined the various types of procedural agreements. The general content of procedures and the specific clauses that appear in particular agreements were stated. It is not possible to provide model agreements that are universally applicable. The variety of arrangements for collective bargaining, reflecting the requirements in the different sectors of employment, preclude any one standard or model agreement. An agreement that would work in one situation would not work in another. This section aims to give example agreements to show the typical structure of an agreement. They do not purport to be examples that should be used but are included here to demonstrate the content and structure of an agreement.

7.5.1 Negotiating agreement

An agreement made on _____ between Tubebend Ltd and the Amalgamated Engineering Workers' Union, setting down the negotiating arrangements between the parties.

1 *Preamble*

1.1 Matters will be dealt with as quickly as possible taking into account the practicability of meetings and the complexity of the topics.
1.2 No industrial action will be taken by either side until this procedure has been exhausted.
1.3 This procedure shall be used to deal with matters of substance between the parties and for negotiating agreements on procedure.

2 *Negotiating committee*

2.1 The company and union agree to set up a Negotiating Committee to provide the means for negotiating the terms and conditions of staff covered by this agreement, as defined in the recognition agreement.

2.2 The company and union will each nominate five people to make up the management and union sides.
2.3 Each side will appoint a joint secretary who together will be responsible for calling meetings, preparing agenda and agreeing the record of proceedings.
2.4 Management shall take the Chair.
2.5 The Negotiating Committee shall meet regularly at intervals not exceeding three months.
2.6 All decisions of the Negotiating Committee shall be by the mutual agreement of both sides.

3 *Failures to agree*

3.1 Where there is a failure to agree at a meeting of the Committee, the Committee shall reconvene not more than ten working days later to continue discussions on the outstanding matter.
3.2 When the Committee decides it cannot resolve an issue the Chairperson shall resolve to refer the matter to a joint committee of the Engineers' Association and the union's full-time officers. The Chief Executive (or nominee) and the Senior Steward (nominated by the union) will meet with the joint committee. An equal number of officials from the Association and the union shall sit on the committee. The decision of this committee shall be binding on both parties.

4 *Variation or termination*

4.1 Variations to this agreement may be made by agreement between the company and the union. Any suggested amendments must be made in writing to the Joint Secretaries two weeks prior to a meeting of the Negotiating Committee. The Joint Secretaries will circulate members with the suggested wording of the amendment with the agenda.
4.2 This agreement will come into force on . . . and shall continue in force until terminated by the company or union giving not less than six months' notice.

7.5.2 Disputes procedure

An agreement made on _____ between Tubebend Ltd and the Amalgamated

Engineering Workers' Union, to be used to resolve questions and matters raised by individuals or the union on behalf of a group.

1 Preamble

1.1 Matters should initially be dealt with informally between the employee and their immediate supervisor or manager.
1.2 Matters will be dealt with as quickly as possible.
1.3 No industrial action will be taken by either side until this procedure has been exhausted.
1.4 A written record of each formal stage will be made by the company's representative and a copy sent to the union representative.

2 Procedure

2.1 *Stage 1* If the matter has not been successfully resolved by the employee's immediate supervisor or manager, the matter should be raised by the employee's union representative with the supervisor concerned. There should be a response within 24 hours and a proposal made to settle the matter within five working days.
If there is a failure at Stage 1 the next Stage shall be proceeded to within five working days, unless both parties agree otherwise.
2.2 *Stage 2* A meeting will be held between the departmental head and the shop steward. Either side can be accompanied by one other person plus the originator of the grievance.
If there is a failure to agree at Stage 2 the next Stage shall be proceeded to within five working days, unless both parties agree otherwise.
2.3 *Stage 3* A meeting will be held between the functional Director and the Union's Regional Officer.
If there is a failure to agree at Stage 3 the matter will be referred to ACAS for advice and conciliation.

7.5.3   Disciplinary procedure

An agreement made on _____ between Tubebend Ltd and the Amalgamated Engineering Workers' Union, to be used for all disciplinary matters arising with individual employees.

1 Preamble

1.1 The purpose of this agreement is to provide for standards of discipline and for the fairness and equality of the treament of individuals.
1.2 At every Stage the employee under discipline has the right to be accompanied by his/her trade union representative or another person.
1.3 After every Stage an employee has the right to appeal against a decision to the next level of the organisation. Such appeals should be lodged, in writing, within three working days.
1.4 Each Stage will be recorded in writing and a copy sent to the employee and his/her union representative.

2 Procedure

2.1 *Stage 1* If after being interviewed by the employee's supervisor, it is established there has been a breach of discipline, a verbal warning will be recorded against that employee. A verbal warning will remain on file for three months and then be removed.
2.2 *Stage 2* If there has been a further alleged breach of discipline, or a more serious breach of discipline, the employee will be interviewed by his/her departmental head or manager. If the breach is established, a written warning will be recorded against that employee. A written warning will remain on file for six months and then be removed.
2.3 *Stage 3* If there has been a further alleged breach of discipline, or a serious breach of discipline not warranting dismissal, the employee will be interviewed by his/her functional Director. If the breach is established, a final written warning will be recorded against that employee. A final written warning will remain on file for 12 months and then be removed.
2.4 *Stage 4* If there has been a further, alleged breach of discipline or an alleged case of gross misconduct, the employee will be interviewed by the Chief Executive. If the breach is established, the employee may be dismissed, with or without notice.

3 Appeals

3.1 Appeals against disciplinary action should be lodged within three working days of the interview.

3.2 The appeal will be heard within five working days, unless agreed otherwise, by the manager of the person issuing the warning.
3.3 Appeals against dismissal will be heard by another Board Director than the Chief Executive.

Agreed notes:
1 Misconduct includes any of the following

_____

2 Gross misconduct includes any of the following _____
3 An employee who appeals against dismissal will be suspended, with pay, during the period of the appeal.
4 Alternatives to dismissal include suspension without pay, loss of holiday entitlement and demotion.

7.5.4 Union representative credentials

1 *Preamble*

1.1 The objective of this agreement is to set out the rights and obligations of the union representatives who are recognised by the company.
1.2 The agreement states the credentials of such union officials.
1.3 The parties agree to observe the guidance set out in the ACAS Code of Practice Time Off for Trade Union Duties and Activities.

2 *Period in office*

The elected member will be the accredited representative until the next election.
Appointment will cease if the representative:
i leaves the company's employ
ii ceases to be a member of the union
iii transfers from the designated area of representation
iv resigns
v is required to stand down under union rules

3 *Roles*

The representative has two roles:
3.1 As an employee conforming to the same working conditions as other employees.
3.2 As a union representative subject to the rules and regulations of the union.

4 *Responsibilities*

4.1 As an employee to carry out the duties of the job held by the representative and on the understanding that reasonable time off will be allowed for the conduct of industrial relations.
4.2 As a union representative:
i to understand and abide by the agreements between company and union.
ii to use every endeavour to ensure that all members represented understand and abide by the agreements.

5 *Rights*

5.1 Reasonable amount of time off work to conduct company/union industrial relations business.
5.2 Representation by a union full-time officer when raising a grievance on his/her own behalf.
5.3 The use of the following:
i Company notice boards to make union announcements
ii typing facilities via personnel department
iii copying facilities
iv telephones for internal and local calls
v a room affording confidentiality

6 *Company undertaking*

The company undertakes that action taken by the representative in good faith and in pursuance of the representative's duties will in no way affect the representative's employment or prospects and terms and conditions within the company.

7.5.5 Redundancy agreement

An agreement made on _____
between Tubebend Ltd and the Amalgamated Engineering Workers' Union, setting down the negotiating arrangements between the parties.

1 *Preamble*

1.1 This agreement is made between the company and the union and covers employees in the bargaining unit as described in the recognition agreement.
1.2 The company recognises the union's responsibility for representing its members' interests. The company also recognises its

responsibilities to consult closely with the union in these situations.

1.3 The union recognises the company's responsibilities to plan the use of its staff required by the operating needs and profitability of the company.

1.4 Both parties agree to observe the legal requirements in force at the time regarding redundancies.

2 *Object*

2.1 to set up a procedure for dealing with a surplus staff situation when it arises and to state the main entitlements of the employee.

3 *Consultation*

3.1 Whenever a surplus staff situation arises and redundancy, reallocation or transfer of staff may need to be contemplated, discussions will be held as early as possible with the union to review the courses of action which might avoid redundancies.

3.2 When the company considers a surplus staff situation to be unavoidable it will write to the union following which either side may call a meeting of the Negotiating Committee within three working days. A Joint Working Group will be set up to deal with the business.

3.3 The Joint Working Party will be made up of an equal number of company and union representatives, to a maximum of six. The committee will be chaired by the senior management representative. The committee will meet as often as required and either side can request a meeting of the committee. The recommendations of the committee will be accepted by the Negotiating Committee.

4 *Procedure*

4.1 To resolve a surplus staff situation the following will be considered:

i   a restriction on recruitment into the categories affected and also where transfers may occur
ii an examination of opportunities for redeployment and to arrange transfers
iii termination of employment of those past retirement age
iv consider early retirement
v   volunteers for redundancy. Operational requirements take precedence and all those applying for redundancy may not be given it.
vi areas of work where staff could be transferred with retraining
vii temporary transfer on existing conditions

5 *Redundancy*

5.1 Should redundancies be necessary the following criteria will be used, in the order stated:

i   operational and job requirements
ii proficiency
iii preferences stated
iv suitability for retraining
v   length of service
vi personal circumstances

5.2 Systematic overtime will cease except where necessary.

5.3 The Joint Working Group will review individual staff cases to ensure the rules are applied correctly.

6 *Notice and termination*

6.1 Subject to legal requirements notice periods will be as defined in the contract of employment.

6.2 The scale of redundancy pay is set out in Appendix 1.

7 *Industrial action*

7.1 Both parties have entered into this agreement to avoid enforced redundancy. Any matter which cannot be resolved within this agreement will lead to an immediate meeting of the Joint Negotiating Committee.

8 *Period of agreement*

8.1 The agreement will come into force on the date of signature. It will not be retrospective. The agreement can be cancelled by either party giving six months' notice.

8.2 Amendment will be by joint agreement but no such changes shall be operative with reference to any current staff surplus situation.

Further reading

J Muir, *Industrial Relations Procedures and Agreements*

Mini-questions

7.1   Define a procedural agreement.
7.2   Define a substantive agreement.
7.3   Explain the legal position of a collective agreement.
7.4   Describe the relationship between a collective agreement and an individual's contract of employment.
7.5   Distinguish between a local and a national agreement.
7.6   State the arguments for formal, written agreements, as opposed to informal, unwritten agreements.
7.7   Specify the important features of a good procedural agreement.
7.8   List the different types of agreement that might exist in a large firm.
7.9   State the arguments for a single, fixed wage settlement date.
7.10 List the clauses that might exist in a typical wages agreement.

Exercises

7.1   Design a procedural agreement that can be used as a disputes procedure. Exchange your proposals with someone else and perform a critical appraisal of the proposed agreement.
7.2   As 7.1 but for a disciplinary procedure.
7.3   Describe the advantages and disadvantages of a fixed-term wage agreement.

Case studies

(1) The annual wage negotiations, page 300.
(2) Growing pains, page 307.
(3) Defective procedures are harmful, page 314.
(4) Sorry, you're redundant, page 319.
(5) Going to arbitration, page 322.
(6) Technology agreement, page 326.
(7) Negotiating a disciplinary procedure, page 328.

8

Historical aspects

8.1 Origins and growth

8.1.1 Early developments

The emergence of organisations that we would recognise today as trade unions has been a gradual one. The development into the large, complex organisations of today has taken place over the last 150 years or more. It is difficult to specify exactly when trade unions came into existence or to trace their origins. Before the Industrial Revolution there existed organisations that had some of the characteristics of modern trade unions. Trade societies (or guilds) existed from around the fourteenth century. These organisations were for the craftsmen of the day and had the aim of protecting and improving the lot of their members, as unions aim to do today. They operated an apprenticeship scheme and provided sickness and unemployment benefits. They consisted of self-employed artisans and journeymen and as such did not bargain nor did they have any central organisation. After the passing of the Combination Acts in 1800 (*see* Section 8.2.1) these organisations were made illegal and went out of existence.

Some trades had minimum wages under a variety of Acts of Parliament such as the Ordinance of Labourers 1349 and the Statute of Artificers 1563 which were legally enforced by local magistrates. The prevalent philosophy of the pre-Industrial Revolution era was the idea of fairness and justice as determined by the legal process. The artificers and journeymen looked to the courts for them to adjudicate on the question of a fair wage for their work. This thinking pre-dates the economic and market forces thinking that came to prevail by the end of the eighteenth century. The change in legal philosophy, to that based on the freedom of contract, changed the role of the courts so that we would not expect the courts of today to determine wage levels. The Acts referred to above were repealed in 1813.

The Industrial Revolution gained momentum in the last decades of the eighteenth century and continued to change society during the nineteenth century. From an industrial relations viewpoint the Industrial Revolution brought about a number of changes which created the environment within which trade unions would emerge and grow. The major, fundamental change was the movement to the factory system. With the advent of the technologies associated with steam power, the use of outworkers (people working in their own homes using their own tools) declined and factories expanded. The employer provided the premises, machinery and the means of production and the workers supplied only their labour. The former needed capital to acquire these assets hence the emergence of the new class in society, the capitalist/owning class.

This change to the factory system produced many changes, some of which are as follows:

- **Loss of independence** Workers were subjected to the employer's rules on hours of work, breaks and holidays and had in addition to work under supervision and works rules. The pace of work was determined by the machines and due to the long hours was fatiguing. People also lost their hand craft skills and became purely wage earners.

- **Employment of children** Children were used to supplement family income. This became an immediate problem in the early nineteenth century as some employers were accused of exploiting child labour and causing them to be put in great danger.

- **Poor working conditions** Buildings were often insanitary, badly lit and unventilated, and with little attention paid to health and safety, machinery was dangerous. This was exacerbated by employee fatigue caused by long hours of work. Many industries had their own particular hazards such as heat, humidity, dust, dirt, fumes, noise and cramped conditions. Legislation appeared very early in the nineteenth century in an attempt to make factories safer places of work.

These changes were catalytic in prompting intervention by the State. Concurrent with these economic changes was a change in outlook and philosophy. The new capitalist's ideals embraced the doctrine of *laissez-faire*. This led to the following:

- **The policy of freedom of contract** This is the legal theory whereby the parties to a contract, e.g., of employment or trade, are able to make their own terms free from third party intervention. This was a pervasive policy and extended to opposing intervention, by the government and trade unions, in the way in which employers ran their businesses. As a result there was opposition to the introduction of health and safety legislation on the grounds that this was an interference in how the owners ran their businesses. Trade unions met similar opposition when they emerged as organisations wishing to represent the employees, again on the grounds that they were interfering with the contract of employment.

  This latter interference also ran counter to the legal doctrine of restraint of trade. Basically this states (and still exists today) that any act in restraint of trade is unlawful. The courts will then seek to remove the hindrance to open, free trade. Trade unions were held to be acting in restraint of trade if they sought to influence a member's terms and conditions of employment. They could then be sued for acting in restraint of trade or prosecuted for conspiracy.

- **The operation of market forces** The prevalent economic theory was that all economic matters should be left to regulate themselves without interference. The forces of supply and demand operate in the market-place and determine the price at which the parties will strike their bargain. This can be applied to the labour market. If labour is in high supply and the demand is low then the wages offered are likely to be low. Any attempt to interfere in this by the law (compare the idea of a 'just wage' in Elizabethan times), by government or trade unions is to be resisted. Under this policy wages rise and fall in line with supply and demand, so that a fall in wages (or a rise in hours) is justified, as is a rise in wages, if conditions dictate.

- **The pursuit of self-interest** What this alleged, natural law espoused was that the interests of everyone (employer, employee, consumer, nation) are best served by letting everyone act in their own best interests. Self-interest would motivate people to become traders, merchants, employers, owners or whatever, and this would generate wealth for the community through the provision of goods and services and the provision of employment. Any interference by the State in this would hinder the process to everyone's detriment.

The doctrine of *laissez-faire* is closely identified with the name of Adam Smith. His famous book *The Wealth of Nations*, published in 1776, set down these ideas and was most influential. In addition to the economic ideas stated above, he also expounded the now familiar concept in labour economics of the division of labour. This idea was introduced into the early factories and was influential in the development of mass production systems in this century. It is still prevalent today. The division of labour is based on the idea that the most efficient way of organising a job is to break the total work done into small tasks. Individual workers then learn to be proficient in performing one small task rather than the whole job, and by combining the tasks of a number of workers the total job will be completed. The classic evidence of the economic benefits of this method was in Adam Smith's pin factory experiment. In this Smith compared the output of the traditional method of pin manufacture with a new method based on the division of labour. Traditionally the 18 stages of pin manufacture (such as cropping the wire, sharpening, forming the head, etc.) were all carried out by one person. Smith's idea was that one person should become proficient in performing one of these stages and carry out that task exclusively. There was a resultant increase in output due to the tasks being divided. Average output rose from 20 pins per worker per day to as high as 4,800.

The idea of the division of labour is important in understanding the nature of some of the problems associated with organisations. One of the reasons why people find their work so unsatisfactory and unmotivating is that the job performed, being one small task in a very large job, is inherently boring and lacking in interest. A further corollary to this breakdown into tasks is the mechanisation and eventual automation of these tasks. By breaking a job down into its elemental tasks, technology can be applied to these tasks (but not to the whole job). This concept was very influential in job design in the newly emerging factory system during the Industrial Revolution.

In the early part of the nineteenth century there is evidence to show the existence of some local societies of workmen that provided benefits to their members. Due to the Combination Acts these were largely secret and were of little significance to the industries of the day. There is evidence of a Millwrights' Union in London in 1789 and a Friendly Iron Moulders' Society formed in Bolton in 1809. The influence of unions as a bargaining agent, and the emergence

of industrial relations, was to happen later in the century. Strikes at this time were illegal and a striker could be taken to court on a criminal charge. In 1824 a Select Committee in Parliament was set up to look into the effects of the Combination Acts. The chairman, Hume, believed the Acts were repressive and ensured that evidence was given to show their ill-effects. An Act was passed in 1824 repealing the Combination Acts and allowing for the combination of workers (into unions) and employers. There followed a year of great activity and incidents of striking. A further Act of 1825 modified the 1824 Act so as to allow associations of workmen to improve wages and conditions, and gave a limited right to strike. Subsequent to these Acts being passed there emerged a number of unions among workmen. They tended to be among the skilled workers (wheelwrights, mill-wrights, masons, carpenters, etc.) and were local in nature and gave great emphasis to benefits. The Amalgamated Engineering Union traces its origins to organisations such as the Mechanics Friendly Union (1822) and the Steam Engine Makers' Society (1824) in existence at this time. The system of collective bargaining had not yet begun and there is little evidence of organisation in the factories or the mines. Many of the organisations that emerged were short-lived and none survived long enough to grow into a national organisation.

It was during this period that the State took its first steps of intervention in the new factories. The first Act passed dealt with the excesses of some employers with regard to child labour. The Health and Morals of Apprentices Act 1802 set down a maximum 12-hour day for apprentices in the cotton mills. Generally mill owners opposed the legislation because it was seen as an interference and because it would reduce profits and competitiveness. The movement supporting State intervention, on the other hand, included radical politicians, some enlightened manufacturers, medical practitioners and some religious groups. Gradually they won the battle for support in Parliament but the first legislation was limited and difficult to enforce. The 1819 Factories Act prohibited children under nine from working in cotton mills and children under 16 from working more than 12 hours a day. The 1833 Factories Act extended these rules to all mills, restricted the hours of work of children aged nine to 13 to nine hours a day, made two hours per day of schooling compulsory and, importantly, allowed for the appointment of four inspectors to enforce these laws. The 1842 Mines Act prohibited women and children under ten from working underground and the 1847/1850 Factories Acts restricted the hours of work for women and children to ten hours per day between 6 am and 6 pm. Further Acts were passed throughout the rest of the century, expanding the rules and extending them to other industries.

The first attempt to form a national union was made by John Doherty in 1829 with the General Union of Operative Spinners in Great Britain. The union faced its first test in 1830 when some Lancashire employers imposed a wage reduction. Due to lack of support for the ensuing strike, the action failed and the union disbanded. A sister organisation, the National Association for the Protection of Labour had a central, general committee comprised of delegates from local unions and a central strike fund to be used if members were on strike because of a reduction in wages.

Robert Owen was a man with some very novel ideas. In his twenties he ran the New Lanark Mills on cooperative lines and experimented with many new ideas. In 1834 he attempted to form the Grand National Consolidated Trade Union which was to be a nationwide union of workers in all industries. The union grew (some say phenomenally) but soon died down and ceased to exist. The Grand National Consolidated Trade Union failed for a number of reasons, the main ones being poor communications, illiteracy, low funds and employer opposition. These were the very reasons why trade unions generally found it difficult to establish themselves at this time.

During this period unions were also formed in the pottery and building industries but there was still a resistance to their existence. One practice used by employers was the 'document'.

A prospective employee had to sign a document to say that they would not join or take part in the activities of a union. In 1834 there was the incident of the 'Tolpuddle Martyrs'. These were six farm labourers from near Dorchester who were prosecuted under the Illegal Oaths Act 1797 (passed to prevent mutinies and not repealed until 1981). They were found guilty of secretly swearing themselves to an organisation and were sentenced to transportation to Australia for seven years. Although the sentences were commuted two years later, the case had the effect of dampening the spread of trade unionism. The decline of the economy in the late 1830s and early 1840s slowed down the growth of unionism, although there is evidence of unions forming, some for the first time, in the cotton industry, engineering and mining.

The period up to the 1850s was characterised early on by a total resistance by governments and by employers. After 1825 there were several unions formed in many industries. These tended to be local, lacking in leadership and placing great emphasis on benefits. However, striking was a feature of this time. Collective bargaining with employers had not yet begun and employers did not recognise unions in the workplace.

8.1.2 'New Unionism' and growth

The unions that formed in the period starting in the 1850s displayed certain new characteristics. It was these new characteristics that made them similar to present-day unions and for this reason they are called the 'new unions'. These unions were mostly craft unions some of which were formed much earlier but had changed over time. The Amalgamated Society of Engineers formed in 1851 was composed of engineers, machinists, smiths, millwrights and pattern makers. This union is held to be the first big union to display these new characteristics and is sometimes called a 'model' union. It had a centralised organisation with national headquarters and leaders. At national level there was a national executive council to control the union's activities with a regional/district structure between local and national level. It employed full-time officers to organise in the various areas. The union had a high level of contributions and a correspondingly high level of benefits for sickness, unemployment, death, funeral expenses and widows' benefits. Other characteristics, which prevail today in the craft unions, are the use of an apprenticeship system to restrict the supply of labour and an emphasis on the closed shop. These unions also had a democratic rather than bureaucratic structure with elected members holding office, attending delegate meetings and the use of ballots. During the period 1850–60 many unions emerged for craftsmen like tinplatemen, builders, carpenters, stonemasons and others. For example, in 1863 the North of England Ironworkers' Union was formed and has existed since then, being the Iron and Steel Trades Confederation of today. The United Plumbers' Association was set up in 1865 (now part of the EETPU) and the Electricians' Trade Union formed in 1869. The improvement of communications and travel helped very much in enabling the unions to function on a national basis. Many unions had their headquarters in London with branches throughout the country.

It was during this period that collective bargaining emerged with agreements between employers and unions on specific issues. These 'new unions' placed great emphasis on orderly collective bargaining and often had the policy of avoiding strikes wherever possible. Some unions only allowed strikes (officially) that were called at national level, with the local officers having no power to call strikes. The craft unions were particularly concerned to restrict the supply of labour to their craft to ensure a high demand for the skill and hence to demand high wages. Another issue that was often raised was that of a shorter working week and a reduction in overtime. As there was no national scheme for sickness and unemployment benefit these unions paid out high levels of benefits to their members, which attracted workmen to the union.

As a result of these unions having a central organisation, the national leaders met and formulated joint policies and plans. This led to the involvement of trade union leaders in politics and their agitation for reforms of various sorts.

In 1860 a trades council was formed in London which coordinated the activities of the unions. This form of joint action grew and led to the creation of the first TUC by the Manchester and Salford Trades Council in 1868, followed by a permanent body in 1870. During this period there was concern for some outbreaks of violence. The worst of these were the Sheffield outrages in 1866 which had been going on for some time and culminated in the blowing up of a house. These union-inspired attacks were designed to enforce union discipline and membership. A Royal Commission was formed in 1867 on which trade union leaders demanded seats. In the event they nominated a member and gave evidence. The Commission's findings led to the Trade Union Act 1871 (see Section 8.2.1). This led to a further growth of trade unionism. In the 1870s unions were formed for the railway workers, dockers, gas workers and agricultural workers, but still mainly in the skilled crafts sector of the workforce.

The spread of unionism to the unskilled workers did not come until some years after the craft unions had established themselves. Those trained in a craft, having a skill to offer, were in a much stronger bargaining position and more likely to become organised. In the late 1880s, after a series of successful strikes among the unskilled, a number of general unions emerged. These unions filled the gap left by the craft unions. In 1888 there was a strike of match girls against working conditions (the phosphorus in match heads caused 'phossy jaw') which led to the formation of a union. In 1889 the gas workers of London were organised into a union that fought for, and won, a reduction in daily working hours from 12 to eight. Following this in 1889 the London dockers (then still mainly non-unionised) formulated a demand for 'a tanner an hour' and time-and-a-quarter for overtime. A long strike followed, with all the dockers joining in. Finally the employers gave into their demand. Following the strike, a union was formed for dockers, which eventually became the TGWU. From this time on unions grew fast, especially the new general unions which relied for strength on numbers rather than on marketable skill. These unions were broadly similar to the craft unions but placed less emphasis on high dues and benefits. They were more inclined to striking as a tactic, especially as they had the power to call out large numbers at once.

8.1.3 The pattern this century

The growth of trade unionism in the last decade of the nineteenth centry continued into the twentieth century. After the setback of Taff Vale and the subsequent Trade Disputes Act 1906 (*see* Sections 8.2.1 and 8.2.2) the unions continued to grow. Trade unions were active and the incidence of striking very high, especially in 1910 and 1911 when the number of days lost through strikes was so great that it has not been equalled in recent times (nearly 41 million days lost). During the First World War, trade unionism was strengthened in many ways, both at national and local level. The need for intensive production for the war effort caused the government to involve union leaders in planning for this. One outcome was the Treasury agreements which were negotiated mainly by the craft union leaders. In exchange for dropping certain restrictive practices, allowing 'dilutees' (i.e., unapprenticed employees performing skilled employees' work), agreeing to compulsory arbitration and with no striking permitted, the government put a limit on company profit increases. The operation of these agreements necessitated close surveillance at shop floor level. This prompted the emergence of shop stewards to ensure that the new agreements were not abused, and the unions themselves encouraged this. However, in some areas this led to an extreme form of shop steward power. On the Clyde a shop stewards' movement formed which became very strong in controlling labour in the Clydeside dockyards which were vital to shipbuilding. The 'no-strike' clause was challenged in South Wales when 200,000 miners came out on strike. A government order to enforce the no-strike clause was useless (how do you arrest so many people!) so the government had to settle the dispute rather than break it.

An important development during the First World War was the changes made as a result of the Whitley Committees. In 1916 a Committee on Relations between Employers and Employed was set up under the chairmanship of J H Whitley, a Deputy Speaker. The Committee issued five reports and made a series of recommendations, many of which were adopted. The main thrust of the reports was to make recommendations which would improve relations between employers and employees. Probably the most important recommendation was that in those sectors having well-organised employers and trade unions there should be a three-tier system of joint cooperation. At national level there would be a joint industrial council, a middle level district joint council and a factory level works committee. The precise remit for each level was not given, save a proviso that there should be a clear distinction between the functions to be performed at each level. The JIC's were collective bargaining and negotiating bodies where national agreements were to be made between employers and trade unions. The DJCs would deal with matters of interpretation and detail, and the works committees were joint consultative committees to deal with specific matters at factory level. The number of JICs expanded rapidly with 73 set up by 1921 plus 33 interim bodies.

In some industries, such as engineering, JICs were not set up due to opposition to the idea. This opposition came from some trade unions in industries with a strong organisation and from some employers who clung to the idea of non-interference (*see* Section 8.1.1 above). However, they were popular in the government sector (local and central) and the utilities, where DJCs were set up and run. In other sectors DJCs were not formed even though JICs were. As a result of these developments there was a growth and shift to national collective bargaining and this in turn provoked the growth of national trade unions through mergers and amalgamations. The number of JICs fell during the 1920s to 47 by 1924, and the number remained the same through to the 1940s.

Two other developments to arise from the Whitley Committee recommendations have already been mentioned. Where employer and trade union organisation was weak it was recommended that the system of trade boards (introduced by the Trade Board Act 1909) should be extended. Trade boards were set up by the Minister of Labour if he felt there was no machinery for wage regulation in a trade. Also it was the intention that these boards would find a way of introducing and expanding collective bargaining into that trade. The number of trade boards expanded after the passing of the Trade Boards Act in 1918. The function of these is now carried out by wages councils of which there are 24. The industries covered include clothing manufacturers, licensed establishments and sack and bag makers! Those employed in agriculture have a separate system that covers wider terms and conditions of employment. The second development was the recommendation of one report on conciliation and arbitration. The recommendations led to the passing of the Industrial Courts Act 1919 which introduced a system of voluntary arbitration. The influence of Whitley is still very strong today in the UK industrial relations system, particularly in the public sector where the system of JICs and DJCs still operates.

After the war ended, the unions still maintained their growth and retained the power they had gained during the war. Soon the Depression of the 1920s had an effect. In many cases employers lowered the wages of their employees which naturally gave rise to unrest. In the early 1920s many unions merged and some of the large unions of today were formed: the AEU in 1921, the TGWU in 1922 and the GMBATU (now the GMB) in 1923. The main event of the 1920s was the 1926 General Strike. This originated in the mining industry, where employers wanted to extend working hours and cut pay. The miners struck when a temporary government subsidy finished and the employers were going to implement the findings of a Royal Commission to lower wages. The TUC had rallied support from its affiliated unions and on 4 May the General Strike began. Not all workers struck (the textile workers and Post Office did not) but sufficient did to cause major problems, especially

in transport. After some days of talking to the government, the TUC leaders negotiated a settlement and the strike ended on 12 May. For the miners, however, it was ultimately a defeat as they lost both claims for 'not a penny off the pay, not a second on the day'.

Following the General Strike union membership fell dramatically, partly due to the effects of the strike on morale and due to the effect of the Depression. Union membership fell for the next seven years and numerically did not recover for over ten years. The Second World War had the same effect on trade unionism as the First World War. In an effort to boost production for the war the unions were closely involved at both national and local level. Again dilution was brought in for the skilled trades and there were restrictions on the movement of labour. At this time there was a growth in union membership which continued into the 1940s. The current position on trade unions and membership is given in Chapter 2.

8.1.4 Postwar developments

The 1960s saw an increasing involvement of government in the economic affairs of the country, importantly from an industrial relations point of view, with the use of pay and prices policies. While the postwar boom was still leading to increased standards of living, a number of problems were emerging. As a result of the increase in the number of industrial disputes and, in particular, the large proportion of unofficial stoppages, pressure mounted for action to be taken.

In 1965 a Royal Commission was set up by the then Labour Prime Minister, Harold Wilson, under the chairmanship of Lord Donovan, an ex-Labour MP, who was an Appeal Court judge. The full title of the Commission was the Royal Commission on Trade Unions and Employers' Associations. Its terms of reference were 'to consider relations between managements and employees and the role of trade union and employers' associations in promoting the interests of their members in accelerating the social and economic advance of the nation with particular reference to the law affecting these bodies and to report'.

The report was a very comprehensive survey of the British industrial relations system and was supported by much original research. The main findings of the report were based on the observation that collective bargaining was based on two systems – a formal system and an informal system. The formal system was based on national collective bargaining which ostensibly provided industry-wide agreements. It involved very clear procedures and comprehensive agreements which were negotiated by national officials of the trade unions and employers and employers' associations. On the other hand the informal system operated at plant, factory or establishment level and was conducted by supervisors, managers and shop stewards. The commission did not argue that the dual nature of the system was inherently defective, but that the two systems should be integrated and made complementary to each other.

National agreements were being undermined by local agreements made between managers and shop stewards. The symptoms of this were observed in wage drift (see Section 7.4), restrictive labour practices, low productivity and the fact that disputes procedures were not restraining unofficial action. These were caused by a major defect in the system which manifested itself in the disorder at factory level. The conflict between the formal and informal systems also prompted this disorder. There was a need to develop orderly collective bargaining at factory level. It was observed that collective bargaining at factory level was informal, disorganised, arbitrary and incapable of bringing order to industrial relations. Agreements were made on an impromptu basis, frequently verbally with no written record and there was no company policy on which decisions could be based. The problem of strikes was also attributed to the disorder in factory level industrial relations. The suggested solutions of cooling off periods, conciliation pauses or compulsory ballots were rejected in favour of improving industrial relations at factory level. This would include developing explicit industrial relations policies and having procedural agreements that were formal, speedy, clear and effective. The high incidence of unofficial strikes was attributable mainly to the condition of industrial relations at the workplace.

The remedies suggested by the Commission included the following.

- **Control of incentives** Incentives were often used as a device to circumvent pay policy restrictions on basic rates and to supplement nationally agreed pay levels at local level. Indeed, incentives were encouraged as a means of improving productivity. Such increases are easier to implement in manufacturing industry where output can be measured easily. Often incentive schemes need to be properly negotiated in a substantive agreement and for the informal, subjective element to be eliminated.

- **Regulation of working hours** A notable feature of the British pattern of working is the existence of permanent overtime. Average working hours are always in excess of the basic working week. Overtime is used to supplement pay. For the employee overtime is welcome as it is paid at premium rate. For the employer it increases costs disproportionately, but is used to increase short-term capacity. Levels of overtime tended to be agreed informally between supervisor and shop steward and became available as of right rather than as demand dictated. In some extreme cases there were shop agreements whereby if overtime was worked by anyone, everyone in the department came in (regardless of work being available for everyone). Other instances included informal agreements that if a subcontractor worked weekends, then overtime would be made available to all the maintenance staff, again regardless of whether there was work for them to do.

- **Job evaluation** These are schemes which aim to determine the worth of a job. There are many schemes but the more sophisticated, quantitative schemes measure the worth of a job in terms of the qualifications and training needed, experience required, skills, responsibility for money, plant and people, working conditions, degree of autonomy or such other factors as are relevant to that group of workers. Points are awarded for the level required by the job for each factor. The total number of points awarded then determines the worth of the job in comparison to other jobs being evaluated. Job evaluation methods were devised and implemented to bring order and structure to grading and pay structures. The schemes are not a method for improving wages as they evaluate the job, not set levels of pay. They can, however, help solve the problems relating to anomalies, differentials, parity claims, leap-frogging and comparability studies. Again, job evaluation introduces order and formality into pay structures that frequently are in chaos and disarray.

- **Improvement in working practices** A much publicised aspect of the British way of working is the use of restrictive practices. These are mentioned in Section 6.1.4 and prevalent in many organisations. Frequently these practices evolved through informal agreements between supervisor and shop steward and gradually became accepted practice or, more insidiously, came about by supervisors and managers allowing certain practices to continue unchecked until the practice became the accepted way of operation. Such practices were introduced as a method of job protection but at the expense of inefficient operations. The rational restructuring of jobs is possible under productivity agreements (*see* Section 7.2.5) by gradually negotiating such practices away or by job evaluation. The elimination of unofficial working practices helps regularise job structures in organisations and makes for orderly management of the enterprise.

- **Facilities for shop stewards** In order to improve the standard of collective bargaining locally it was recognised that a key element in this was the shop steward. By improving the training of shop stewards and the facilities

available to them, this would help the process of collective bargaining. If it is necessary to formalise agreements at local level as recommended, shop stewards need to be prepared for this. An early Commission on Industrial Relations report on this stated the need to improve shop stewards' facilities and also highlighted the need to state formally the functions of the shop steward.

- **Development of management policies** A very strong recommendation was that organisations should, as a matter of urgency, develop and implement industrial relations policies. This would involve top management developing written policy statements on which the local system of collective bargaining could be based. With lack of direction from the top, the system is likely to be predominantly informal and lacking in direction and purpose. The Industrial Relations Code of Practice (*see* Section 11.1) emphasised this need for leadership by top management in the development of orderly collective bargaining.

- **Procedural reform** A notable feature of local bargaining arrangements was that they were informal and lacked the kind of procedural agreements that were capable of handling the various industrial relations issues likely to arise. The Donovan Commission commented that the changes should produce 'procedures which are clear where the present procedures are vague, comprehensive where present procedures are fragmentary, speedy where present procedures are protractive, and effective where present procedures are fruitless'. The existence of negotiating, disputes and grievance procedures are important (*see* Section 7.2) and would help reduce the problem of industrial disputes, particularly the unofficial strike. To encourage this procedure it was recommended that the Department of Employment keep a register of procedural agreements.

It is interesting to examine these recommendations to note how far-sighted the proposals were and the extent to which they have been implemented. Many of the suggestions are good industrial relations practice and as such are timeless. Certainly the structuring of industrial relations, including policy making and formal procedures, would help many firms today.

The Commission also suggested the registration of trade unions and that all the registered trade unions should be given legal immunity from legal action arising from inducing others to break their contract of employment. The setting up of a Commission on Industrial Relations was recommended to investigate cases and incidents reported to it. Such a Commission was set up in 1969 and it made several enquiries into various aspects of industrial relations. It did not last long, however, and was wound up in 1974 because its neutrality became untenable when, as a part of a government department, it had to implement controversial policies and handle politically sensitive tasks.

As a result of the Donovan Commission's findings and the persistent problems associated with unofficial strikes, the Labour government issued a White Paper entitled *In Place of Strife* in 1969. The Paper's introduction stated that it saw industrial relations as the means of directing conflict positively and there was a need for help to build an efficient, orderly, equitable system. The problems identified included the disparity of power between employer and employee and between groups of workers; the economic effect of strikes; poor consultation procedures; low trade union member involvement and the emergence of staff unions. There was a need to reform collective bargaining and provide new safeguards for the community and individuals. As in the Donovan Commission's recommendations, management should lead the changes by introducing sensible pay structures, procedural agreements for the effective solution of disputes and provide for references to arbitration. Finally the White Paper made the following suggestions:

- a conciliation pause of 28 days for unofficial disputes, serious strikes or if there had been inadequate joint discussion. This ran counter to the Donovan Commission's recommendations but was inserted to tackle the problem of the many short, unofficial stoppages that were a prominent feature at the time.

- the Secretary of State could impose a settlement of inter-union disputes. Particularly difficult disputes for management to resolve are those between trade unions themselves. Management often stands by helplessly as third party observers of a dispute that they are not party to but are directly affected by. There were no formal means of resolving such disputes so the government proposed providing the means themselves.

- the Secretary of State could order a strike ballot if it was felt to be justified. Again this was not a recommendation from the Donovan Commission but one to try to make industrial action official. Also, taking a ballot can introduce its own pause in a dispute and this allows tempers to cool. Employers could also then sue unofficial strike leaders.

- Unions would have to register with a Registrar and legal immunities for inducing breach of a contract of employment would be accorded to registered trade unions only. The process of registration would accord official status to a union and hence any industrial action taken by a nonregistered union could be identified as being actionable by the courts

- Introduction of the concept of unfair dismissal whereby an employee could not be dismissed except for a fair reason and in a reasonable manner.

In Place of Strife was rejected by the TUC, the Labour government had 53 of its own members vote against it and the Labour party's National Executive Committee rejected it. In spite of this the Labour government pressed ahead with draft legislation as it was felt the proposals had the support of the electorate. Labour MPs were prepared to revolt against the government in Parliament, particularly the trade union-sponsored MPs. At the very last moment there was agreement between the government and the TUC on an amended version of the TUC's *Programme for Action*. In this the TUC made a 'solemn and binding undertaking' to intervene in problem areas, especially in inter-union disputes. This led to the amendment of the TUC's Rules 11 and 12 (*see* Section 2.5.4). As a result of this the legislation was withdrawn at the last moment, and the Labour administration did not have further opportunity to introduce any other legislation as it fell at the next general election.

During this period the Conservative party developed its own policies for industrial relations. In 1968 it published a document entitled *A Fair Deal at Work*. Four problems were identified: industrial disputes; restrictive labour practices; excessive authority asserted by groups; and the misuse of power for sectional objectives. The proposals contained in the paper led to the Industrial Relations Act 1971. The Act was a very long and complicated one and was the first attempt to provide a comprehensive legal framework for industrial relations. The Act was based on four principles:

- collective bargaining freely conducted with due regard for the interests of the community
- the maintenance and development of orderly procedures for the peaceful settlement of disputes by negotiation, conciliation or arbitration with due regard for the general interests of the community
- the free association of workers in independent trade unions and of employers in employers' associations so organised as to be representative, responsible and effective bodies for regulating relations between employers and workers
- freedom and security for workers, protected by adequate safeguards against unfair industrial practices, whether on the part of employers or others

The Commission on Industrial Relations continued its existence as before and its purpose was to investigate situations and disputes and to issue reports.

The Act contained the following:

- the improvement of our voluntary system of industrial relations, principally through a Code of Industrial Relations Practice, which sets standards and gives guidance on the conduct of human relations in industry
- the establishment of new rights for the individual in relation to trade union membership and activity, protection against unfair dismissal, information about his or her employment and improved terms of notice
- the introduction of a new concept of unfair industrial practice
- the maintenance of these standards and rights through a new system of courts, comprising a national industrial relations court (industrial court) and industrial tribunals which will determine rights and liability and hear complaints of unfair industrial practice
- the establishment of a new system of registration for trade unions and employers' associations which confines privileges and general immunity from court actions arising out of industrial disputes to registered organisations – that is, those which have satisfied the Registrar that their rules meet certain minimum standards specified in the Act
- the introduction of new methods of settling disputes over the recognition of trade unions and their bargaining rights, and for improving procedures for handling industrial relations, notably with the help of the CIR
- new reserve powers for the protection of the community in serious emergency situations caused or likely to be caused by industrial action
- legal enforceability of agreements

In the event, the Industrial Relations Act caused widespread protest from the trade union movement. Unionists were opposed to much of the legislation because it shackled the unions and restricted their freedom of action. The policy of the TUC was to oppose totally the working of the Act and that any unions acting in defiance of this would be expelled. Some unions indeed were expelled for complying with some parts of the Act. For example, the National Union of Seamen, in order to retain its closed shop in the industry, registered under the Act, in defiance of TUC policy. The union was subsequently expelled under the TUC rules, ironically for seeking to maintain its position of strength within the industry. The TUC, and its affiliated unions, made the Act unworkable by not registering as a trade union with the Registrar of Trade Unions as required. This produced chaos because most of the legislation only operated if unions registered. Nonregistered unions were not recognised under the Act and so were denied the rights and privileges accorded to unions under the Act. There were some inevitable clashes in the courts leading to fines, and in two instances to imprisonment. One case against the TGWU led to them being fined £50,000 for contempt for not obeying a court order. In another case, five dock workers were gaoled for contempt in not obeying a court order not to refuse to work on vehicles using a certain cold storage depot. The Act never worked as intended and industrial unrest dominated the period of the Conservative administration. Eventually, under the threat of a second national miners' strike, Prime Minister Heath called a General Election in February 1974.

The incoming Labour government repealed the Industrial Relations Act in September 1974. After the second General Election of 1974 in October, the increased Labour majority meant that the government was able to pass a series of Acts relating to industrial relations. These Acts are listed in Section 8.2.3 and the details contained in Chapters 10 and 13–16.

8.1.5 Recent developments

The years of the Labour administration, led by Harold Wilson and, latterly, Jim Callaghan, were marked by a very close relationship between government and unions. While there was rarely total agreement on policies, often a consensus of opinion was reached. There were a series of agreements or undertakings made by the Labour government and the TUC. In essence these were bargains struck to secure union agreement on a range of economic issues in return for the government introducing and securing the passage of employment and trade union legislation favourable to the unions. Incomes policies (*see* Section 4.2.2) were a crucial element of the government's battle to reduce inflation. In order to implement these unpalatable policies the government had to secure agreement with the unions.

The passing of the Trade Union and Labour Relations Act in 1974 and its amendment in 1976, plus the Employment Protection Act 1975, were all part of this exercise. The Bullock Commission (*see* Section 16.2.2) was set up by Prime Minister Wilson in 1975, on the topic of industrial democracy. Its terms of reference were stated in such a way that made a presumption of trade union involvement in this process (*see* Section 16.2.2). This close involvement of the unions in government affairs came to an end in 1978. The Labour government, with a very low Commons majority, tried to secure a further round of incomes policy, but agreement was not secured and there were a series of damaging strikes, particularly in the public sector. This led to the so-called 'winter of discontent'. In the spring of 1979, Jim Callaghan called a general election which Margaret Thatcher won.

There was a complete change of policy and attitude when the Conservatives took office in 1979. They had pledged to amend much of the legislation passed by the previous administration, which they did. The aims of the legislation were twofold:

- to reduce trade union power in the workplace through restricting the power to call strikes and reduce the operation of the closed shop
- to reduce employment protection regulations. These, it was argued, were an interference in the marketplace and on a firm's freedom to operate. The government believed in deregulation.

The legislation, commencing with the Employment Act 1980 and continuing throughout the 1980s and into the 1990s, had a profound effect on the UK system of industrial relations. The Acts passed are listed in Section 8.2.3. Virtually every aspect of industrial relations was subject to amendment or abolition over the period:

- The closed shop was not banned but its continued existence was made subject to some very stringent requirements. Ballots were required to create or to continue with a closed shop. Those adversely affected by the operation of the closed shop were able to claim compensation, some being awarded large sums from a special government fund. The government objected to the closed shop on the grounds that it was an infringement of the freedom of the individual to choose to join an association or not. It was also seen as a means of reducing trade union membership because the closed shop forced people to join a trade union (*see also* Section 15.3).

- Picketing had never been tackled and was seen as important in reducing the blatant excesses of union power demonstrated in the 'winter of discontent'. Certainly there had been several incidents of violence mainly caused by large numbers of pickets. In the event the legislation and Code of Practice still allowed picketing but at reduced levels. Curbing the excesses seen previously proved difficult and the miners were able to use mass picketing in 1984 with the authorities powerless to ban it (*see also* Section 15.2).

- Political funds have always been a delicate matter as the Labour party derives such a large proportion of its income from the trade unions. The fall in trade union membership was damaging enough; to change the rules on political funds would have been disastrous. The 1984 Act made ballots essential if unions wished to create or maintain a political fund. The results of the ballots, it was hoped, would be against a political fund, thereby weakening the unions and the Labour party. The reverse turned out to be the case, with members voting in favour of political funds. The political objectives of unions were altered to restrict their political activities (*see also* Section 4.4.2).

- Trade unions require immunities from certain forms of legal action to enable them to authorise industrial action (without which they would be sued out of existence). The scope of the immunities was gradually restricted by the 1980, 1982 and 1984 Acts.

Immunity was only granted for strictly defined industrial action and only for disputes involving the union member's employer. The object of the legislation was to restrict the power of the unions in trades disputes and to strengthen the arm of the employer to take action against unions. In terms of reducing the number of strikes, the policy was very effective (*see also* Section 15.1).

- Wage determination is strictly a matter to be decided by the employer as determined by market forces. Wage councils, which had operated since 1909, were seen as a false means of determining wages. In 1992 legislation was passed to scrap the wage councils after their remits had previously been restricted. A major stumbling block for the government in Europe in 1991 was the proposal for a Directive on maximum working hours. Again the government argued that it is for the labour market to determine these matters, not for governments to dictate.

The whole question of regulation in the labour market became a major block to movement towards closer ties to Europe. The object of the Social Charter (*see* Section 17.2) was to create a more equal internal market and to aid the free movement of labour within the community. Finally the Conservative government was unable to agree to the concepts of the Social Charter and was excluded from the Social Charter of the Maastricht Treaty in 1992. Notably the UK was the only country to do so. The Social Charter was seen as a blatant attempt to regulate the labour market and to restrict the freedom of the employer to make decisions free from outside interference.

8.2 Legal developments

8.2.1 The recognition of trade unionism

The history of trade unionism is intrinsically bound up in the legal developments surrounding the legality or otherwise of trade union existence and activity. As mentioned in Section 8.1.1, the initial response to trade unionism, from a legal point of view, was one of total rejection. The Combination Acts of 1800 were passed to prevent any possible uprising similar to the one that led to the French Revolution in 1792. These Acts prohibited the combination of employers and workmen, all contracts to advance wages or working conditions and all meetings for such purposes. The Unlawful Societies Act 1799 and the Seditious Meetings Act 1819 had a similar effect. Trade unions (especially in the modern sense) were largely unknown and the Acts prevented their emergence. They also had the effect of destroying the craft guilds and, equally importantly, prevented employers from forming associations. At this time strikes were a criminal offence (although lockouts were not) as they were seen as a conspiracy 'in restraint of trade'. This last phrase is a common law legal doctrine that makes it illegal for a third party (e.g., a trade union) to interfere in a contract between two parties (e.g., a contract of employment).

The Combination Law Reform Act 1824, as its name suggests, repealed the Combination Acts so allowing the formation of trade unions. However, the legal right to strike was still suspect for the next 50 years. No significant new legislation was passed until 1871 when the Trade Union Act was passed. This Act was based on the recommendations of the Royal Commission that sat from 1867 to 1869. The Commission recommended the legalisation of trade unions and the protection of their funds. There was a divergence of opinion on the conditions that should be attached to the registering of a union. In the event the Trade Union Act 1871 followed the minority report and lifted legal restrictions from trade unions and protected their funds. The idea that unions acted 'in restraint of trade' was removed. A parallel Act, the Criminal Law Amendment Act 1871, introduced legal protection against the use of violence in picketing and striking. It created the offences of molestation and obstruction which would make certain areas of trade union activity illegal and leave offenders open to prosecution. At criminal law there were still several offences that could be committed under the Master and Servant Acts, including prosecution for striking, conspiracy to strike and intimidation. Hence the unions were at this time legally protected at civil law but trade unionists were still vulnerable under criminal law for certain of their activities.

There were two Acts passed in 1875 that altered the position at criminal law. The Conspiracy and Protection of Property Act repealed the Criminal Law Amendment Act 1871 and replaced it with a series of specific criminal acts such as using violence, persistently following, watching and besetting. More importantly, however, it stated that any act done by two or more people in contemplation or furtherance of a trades dispute is not indictable as a criminal offence (unless the alleged act is a crime). This freed workers from possible prosecution for a range of trade union activities. This Act also stated the position on picketing, which remains largely unaltered today (*see* Section 15.2). Another Act of 1875, the Employers and Workmen Act, repealed the criminal act of breach of contract, so that striking was no longer a criminal offence, and could be dealt with only at civil law. From this time trade unions were defined at law, their functions and funds protected and many of the criminal sanctions were removed. Trade union activities were largely protected within defined limits.

The law remained largely unaltered until the turn of the century and it was felt that the unions had gained recognition. However, this idea was dealt a blow by the Taff Vale case in 1901 (*see* Section 8.2.2). It had been presumed that unions and their officials could take industrial action (say strike) and not be liable at law. This view, confirmed by the House of Lords, was incorrect and the immunity given to unions was not as broad as had been assumed. Following this case, the Trade Disputes Act 1906 was passed to reverse the decision. The Act provided that any civil action in tort against a trade union, or its officers or members, could not be entertained in any court, if the activity was carried out in contemplation of furtherance of a trades dispute. The term 'trade dispute' was defined as a 'dispute between employer and workmen or workmen and workmen which is concerned with the employment . . . of persons'. This protection, in the form of an immunity, has stood virtually unchanged from then until the 1980s. This Act firmly established the trade unions legally and provided full protection for the unions, their officials and members and for their activities. That protection is now subject to a number of restrictions and regulations (*see* Section 10.2.2).

Soon after the Taff Vale case, a further case (involving the same union) caused a setback to the political side of a union's activities. Since 1871 a union's functions had been defined and its funds given protection. However, the increasing use of union funds for political purposes, mainly to support the Labour party, was challenged by a Liberal, Mr Osborne (*see* Section 8.2.2). The House of Lords decided that the use of a union's funds for political purposes was illegal as the definition of a union's purposes made no mention of political activities. As it was outside the powers (*ultra vires*) of the union to use its funds in this way, the union could no longer support sponsored MPs and the Labour party. Again a House of Lords decision was reversed by Parliament in the Trade Union Act 1913. This Act allowed the use of funds for political purposes providing the members agreed to this (in a ballot), that the funds were kept separate and the members were given a right to 'contract out' of the political levy if they wished.

The bulk of trade union law remained unaltered until after the General Strike in 1926. An Act was passed (the Trade Union Act) limiting the industrial action that unions could take and remain free from the threat of court action. The Act limited sympathetic action to that within the trade or industry and made illegal attempts to coerce the government either directly or by inflicting hardship on the community. It also made the political levy a 'contracting in' situation, so the presumption was that trade union members did not pay the levy unless they signed to do so. These restrictions were strongly opposed by the trade union movement and the Labour party but remained law until after the Second World War.

In recent times the legal position of trade unions was altered by the 1971 Industrial Relations Act. This complex Act altered much of the 1875 and 1906 Industrial Relations Act and introduced some new ideas on registration. The Act as a whole failed to work and was finally repealed by the incoming Labour administration in 1974. The Trade Union and Labour Relations Act returned the legal position of the unions to their pre-1971 positions. For the current position on this *see* Chapter 10.

8.2.2 Major cases

The previous section traced the development of statutory law. This section aims to trace the development of case law. The two are not entirely separable as often the court-made case law is an interpretation of statutory law. In the absence of statutory law the courts apply the common law (*see* Section 9.1). Over the years there have been many hundreds of court cases, now supplemented by thousands of tribunal cases. A few of the more important cases that illustrate the operation and development of English law on trade unionism will be discussed.

Hornby v. *Close* (1867)

This case illustrates the precarious nature of unions before the 1871 Act. The Boilermakers Society sued the treasurer of its Bradford branch for £24 that he owed the Society. The union presumed its funds were protected under the Friendly Societies Act 1855 under which unions had registered. However, the Appeal Court judges declared that the union was not protected by the Act as unions acted 'in restraint of trade' which made them illegal. Hence the union could not obtain its money back as it was not recognised at law.

R. v. *Druitt, Lawrence and Anderson* (1867)

A quote from the case shows how limited picketing had to be if it were to remain lawful: 'Even if the jury should be of the opinion that the picket did nothing more than his duty as a picket, and if that duty did not extend to abusive language and gestures . . . still, if that was calculated to have a deterring effect on the minds of ordinary persons, by exposing them to have their motions watched, and to encounter black looks, that would not be permitted by the law of the land'. It is unlikely that persuasion within this definition would have any effect.

J. Lyons and Sons v. Wilkins (1896)

This case related to picketing which, after 1875, was made a legal activity for peacefully obtaining or communicating information. In 1896 the Amalgamated Trade Society of Fancy Leather Workers struck against Lyons and picketed the place of work. There was no violence or threats but, on applying for an injunction against Wilkins, the secretary, Lyons was successful. The case was heard a second time and was appealed against but the courts held that the action was one of 'watching and besetting' which was still a criminal act. This illustrates that unions were still liable to have their activities restricted by the courts' interpretation of the law.

Taff Vale Railway Company v. Amalgamated Society of Railway Servants (1901)

This is probably the most famous of all union cases. From 1871 onwards unions had functioned more or less as they do today under the presumption that their activities (including striking) were legally protected. In August 1900 a signalman, who had led a movement for a wage rise, was moved to another district by the company. The men struck and were eventually backed by their union. The company tried to employ 'blackleg' labour but the men resisted this. Against legal advice, the company sued the union for damages for loss of profit during the strike. The company won its case but the union appealed and won its appeal. The company took its case to the House of Lords which decided that the union officials were capable of being sued for picketing action of this kind. The company was awarded £23,000 damages plus costs. This was a setback to trade unionism and the law was amended soon after by the Trade Disputes Act 1906.

Osborne v. Amalgamated Society of Railway Servants (1911)

The same union was involved in a further well-known case ten years after Taff Vale. This related to the use of union funds for political purposes which had become pertinent with the emergence of the Labour Party. The union contributed 1s 1d per year per member to the Labour Representation Committee (of the TUC) to support and secure representation in Parliament. Osborne, a Liberal, objected to this and argued that the union was *ultra vires* (outside its powers) in doing this. The case went to the House of Lords which decided that the objective of a union (as defined in the 1871 and 1876 Acts) did not provide for the supporting of a political party. Hence Osborne won his case and was given an injunction preventing the union from using its funds in this way. This caused a problem to Labour party finances and the situation was resolved when the Trade Union Act of 1913 was passed.

Bonsor v. Musicians' Union (1956)

This case raised two issues: one was whether a union could be sued and the other on the application of union rules. Bonsor was expelled from his union by the branch secretary. The secretary had acted according to the custom of many years standing but this was contrary to the union Rule Book. The House of Lords decided that while unions are not separate legal entities (as are companies or incorporated associations), they can be sued in their own name and damages awarded against them. Unions still are essentially collections of individuals. The union Rule Book should be followed and if not, the aggrieved member is entitled to damages. As a musician, Bonsor needed to be a union member (due to there being a closed shop) and he was awarded damages against the union for breach of contract.

Rookes v. Barnard (1964)

This case illustrates that well-established laws and practices may be challenged. Rookes was a draughtsman at BOAC and he resigned from the union DATA because he was disillusioned about its effectiveness. A closed shop operated, so Rookes' resignation destroyed the 100% membership. The shop steward and full-time official threatened a strike (in breach of a disputes procedure) if Rookes was not sacked. BOAC sacked Rookes and he then sued the steward and official for damages. Rookes won his case on the grounds that the wrong was the tort of intimidation which action was not covered by the Trades Disputes Act 1906. It demonstrated that the Act was not as comprehensive as had been imagined. A further Act in 1965 closed this loophole in the law.

Express Newspapers Ltd v. McShane (1979)

This case shows the interpretation a court put on an important section of an Act. In 1978 there was a dispute between journalists who were members of the NUJ and some provincial newspapers relating to pay. As there had been no settlement, the NUJ instructed its members at the Press Association to strike, so cutting off a supply of news to the provincial newspapers. This action affected the national newspapers, including *Express Newspapers* (the plaintiff in this case), as their journalists were instructed not to handle Press Association material. The newspaper sued the secretary of the NUJ and asked for an injunction to prevent the union calling a strike. In the Court of Appeal, the paper won as the court considered that 'an action done in contemplation or furtherance of a trades dispute' must be capable of achieving its objective. The House of Lords reversed the decision and said that if the union honestly believed that its actions would further or help the dispute, then the actions are legal and cannot be the subject of an injunction or damages. This interpretation of the law was very broad and has now been altered by the Employment Act 1980, which restricts the immunity to primary and secondary action. The kind of action in this case would now be covered under the 1980 Act.

Messenger Newspapers v. NGA (1984)

The Messenger Group of newspapers published a range of free newspapers in the Manchester area. The firm was owned and run by Eddie Shah, who became something of a celebrity at the time as a result of this case. A dispute arose between the company and NGA over the operation of the closed shop at two of the three printing plants owned by Shah. The company and the union failed to agree pay and conditions for NGA labour at one plant where a closed shop had been agreed. The company started to recruit nonunion labour in order to continue production, which was in breach of the closed shop agreement and entailed NGA labour handling nonunionists' work. Six NGA members took strike action and were dismissed. Industrial action then spread to the journalists working for the papers and to the other printing plants.

The company initially successfully applied for injunctions to have the industrial action and picketing stopped on the grounds that the secondary action was not legal. The unions disobeyed the court orders and the company applied for the sequestration of the union's funds, initially unsuccessfully. The NGA was fined £50,000. The action continued and a further court action brought a fine of £100,000 and sequestration of the NGA's assets. The union members' response was a one-day strike of the national newspapers.

Mass picketing was used, especially at the Warrington plant and the company issued further writs to prevent this action. This led to a further fine against the NGA of £525,000. The TUC intervened and initially backed the NGA but latterly withdrew its support.

The case illustrates the fact that the law ultimately dictates the outcome of a dispute but it still has difficulties controlling people's behaviour. The NGA was finally in a no-win situation but its members were able to take mass industrial action.

8.2.3   Major legislation

1349	Labourers Artificers, etc. Act	Introduced the idea of breach of contract. Allowed justices to set a fair wage.
1562	Statute of Artificers and Apprentices	Legal definition of apprentice laid down. Justices could fix wages. Penalties for breach of contract.
1800	Combination Acts	Made illegal any organisation of workers or employers as a conspiracy. Made illegal violence to persons or property or threats or intimidation.
1824	Combination Acts	Repealed.
1825	Combination of Workmen Act	The purpose of combinations restricted to questions of wages and hours. Introduced the offences of molesting and obstruction of persons at work.
1831/40	Truck Acts	Prevented the practice of employers paying in kind or requiring wages to be spent in company 'tommy' shops. Manual labourers to be paid in coins of the realm. Repealed 1986.
1859	Molestation of Workmen Act	Allowed peaceful picketing to be free from criminal prosecution.
1867	Masters and Servants Act	Reduced the criminal liability of employees for breach of contracts (e.g., strike) to those in 'aggravated' cases.
1871	Trade Union Act	Recognised and defined the legal status of trade unions. Removed the criminality of trade union activities. Recognised that trade unions acted in restraint of trade and attached no civil liability for this. Unions could register with Registrar of Friendly Societies. Agreements between unions and members not enforceable.
1875	Conspiracy and Protection of Property Act	Law on criminal conspiracy modified – agreements or combinations to commit criminal acts not actionable if done in contemplation or furtherance of a trade dispute. Made a criminal offence the wilful and malicious breach of contract that would have the effect of endangering life. An offence if someone uses violence or intimidates another/wife/children/property

or persistently follows or hides clothing or property, or watches or besets the place of work or residence to compel someone to do or stop doing something lawful.

1875	Employers and Workmen Act	Breach of contract a civil offence, not now actionable as a crime, e.g., striking.
1876	Trade Union Amendment Act	Laid down rules regarding the amalgamation of unions – required a 2/3 majority of those voting in each union.
1883	Payment of Wages in Public Houses Prohibition Act	Forbade the payment of wages in a public house, except for employees of a publican.
1887	Truck Act	Prohibited any condition of employment that stipulated where or with whom wages should be spent. Repealed 1986.
1896	Truck Act	Laid down the manner in which deductions could be made, e.g., fines and damaged goods. Repealed 1986.
1896	Conciliation Act	The Board of Trade could investigate trade disputes and provide conciliation and arbitration if the parties agreed.
1906	Trade Disputes Act	Gave trade unions immunity from actions in tort. Legalised peaceful picketing. Gave immunity to people acting in contemplation or furtherance of trade dispute.
1909	Trade Boards Act	Established trade boards to regulate wages in the 'sweated' trades.
1913	Trade Union Act	Restated the legal definition of a trade union. Introduced rules for the creation and maintenance of political funds. Fund needed voting for and limited use of the fund.
1917	Trade Union Amalgamations Act	Relaxed the rules on the majority needed to approve amalgamations to 50% of those entitled to vote and for a 20% excess of those in favour.
1918	Trades Boards Act	Empowered minister to set up trade boards in trades without adequate wage regulation machinery.
1919	Industrial Courts Act	Provided power for the Secretary of State to set up a court of inquiry into disputes. Extended the 1896 Act to include boards of arbitration. Established an industrial court for arbitration.

1920	Emergency Powers Act	A state of emergency could be declared if industrial action is depriving the community of the essentials of life, e.g., food, water, fuel, light or transport.
1927	Trade Union and Trade Disputes Act	Political strikes a criminal offence. Restrictions on picketing. Changed position to 'contracting in' for political dues. Civil servants to have their own unions. Public authorities could not compel trade union membership.
1946	Trade Union and Trade Disputes Act	Repealed.
1959	Terms and Conditions of Employment Act	An industrial court could order an employer to pay the terms and conditions of employment in an industry where there was an agreement to do so.
1959	Wages Councils Act	Consolidated previous trade board legislation. Changed name of trade boards to wages councils.
1960	Payment of Wages Act	Allowed for payment of wages by cheque if employee agrees.
1963	Contracts of Employment Act	Laid down minimum periods of notice. Required employer to provide a written statement of the terms and conditions of employment.
1964	Emergency Powers Act	Extended the powers of the 1920 Act and allowed for the use of the armed forces.
1964	Trade Union (Amalgamations) Act	Union mergers or amalgamations require a simple majority vote.
1965	Redundancy Payments Act	Introduced the idea of redundancy and an employee's right to be compensated.
1965	Trade Disputes Act	Created immunity from the tort of intimidation.
1968	Race Relations Act	Introduced the concept of making discriminatory practice unlawful in employment.
1970	Equal Pay Act	Provided for the right of equal pay for work of same or similar nature.
1971	Industrial Relations Act	Major Act reforming most previous industrial relations legislation. (*See* previous section.)
1972	Contracts of Employment Act	Extended the rules of the 1963 Act.

1973	Employment of Children Act	Stated the rules governing the employment of children below school leaving age.
1974	Trade Union and Labour Relations Act	Repealed the 1971 Act. Restored the pre-1971 position. Retained the unfair dismissal provisions.
1975	Employment Protection Act	Introduced a series of rights in employment – guaranteed payments, maternity rights, trade union membership, procedures for handling redundancies. Set up ACAS. Introduced rules on the recognition of trade unions and the disclosure of information.
1975	Sex Discrimination Act	Made it unlawful to discriminate against a person on the grounds of sex or marital status. Set up the Equal Opportunities Commission.
1976	Race Relations Act	Made it unlawful to discriminate against a person on the grounds of race.
1977	Criminal Law Act	Redefined the law on conspiracy. Agreements or combinations to commit acts not in themselves a crime, no longer a crime. If the acts were a minor criminal offence, and done in contemplation or furtherance of a trade dispute, the conspiracy not a crime.
1978	Employment Protection (Consolidation) Act	Brought together all previous legislation on rights in employment.
1979	Wages Councils Act	Consolidated previous Trade Boards Acts. Gave Secretary of State power to widen the scope of wages councils and to convert wages councils to statutory joint industrial councils. Repealed 1986.
1980	Employment Act	Restrictions on picketing at place of work. Made some secondary action unlawful. Changed the law on closed shops and unfair dismissal. Provided money for union secret ballots.
1982	Employment Act	Restricted the immunity of trade unions. Changed the definition of a trade dispute. Altered law on unfair dismissal in a closed shop.
1984	Trade Union Act	Introduced the need for ballots before industrial action and for trade union officials' elections. Changed the rules on balloting to set up a political fund and redefined the political objectives of a trade union.

1986	Wages Act	Repealed the Truck Acts, the Payment of Wages Act and the Wages Councils Act. Method of pay to be agreed between parties. Deductions from pay regulated.
1986	Sex Discrimination Act	Amended the rules on discrimination between men and women in relation to retirement.
1988	Employment Act	Allows union member to seek order against union; set up Commissioner for Rights of Trade Union Members, prohibits industrial action regarding closed shop; certain union ballots must be postal.
1989	Employment Act	Removes restrictions on employment of women and young people; amends SDA 1975 to remove other sources of discrimination; women can claim redundancy pay up to the age of 65.
1990	Employment Act	Removed immunities for all secondary action.
1992	Trade Union and Labour Relations (Consolidation) Act	Brought together various aspects of collective employment law; extends discrimination laws for nonunion membership to recruitment and selection.

Mini-questions

8.1 Describe the effect of the Combination Acts.

8.2 State what the GNCTU was.

8.3 Explain the offence the Tolpuddle Martyrs were charged with.

8.4 Explain what is meant by the term 'new unionism'.

8.5 State the year of the first TUC.

8.6 Explain the ways in which the First World War strengthened trade unionism.

8.7 Describe the basic cause of the 1926 General Strike.

8.8 Explain the term 'in restraint of trade' as applicable to a union's activities.

8.9 State why the Taff Vale case was so important.

8.10 Which Act did the Osborne case lead to?

8.11 Describe two court cases of importance in the history of trade unionism.

8.12 Differentiate between the 'contracting in' and 'contracting out' situations for political levy.

8.13 By referring to a suitable history book, briefly assess the impact of one of the following on trade unionism: (a) Tolpuddle Martyrs; (b) Robert Owen; (c) The Taff Vale case; (d) The General Strike.

8.14 Write short notes on the following topics: (a) the Combination Acts; (b) 'new unionism'; (c) the Treasury agreements.

8.15 List the similarities and differences between a craft guild and a trade union.

Further reading

Clegg, Fox and Thompson, *A History of British Trade Unions*, Clarendon Press, 1987, 0-19-828307-5

K Pelling, *A History of British Trade Unionism*, Macmillan, 1987, 0-333-44285-7

9

The legal system

The aim of this chapter is to give sufficient background information on the English legal system to enable the reader to understand the main aspects of the system. As much of our industrial relations system is governed by law, a basic grasp of the legal system is important. This chapter refers only to the English legal system. Scotland has a different system of law from the rest of the UK.

9.1 The law and the judiciary

9.1.1 Civil and criminal law

English law can be divided into two categories: civil law and criminal law. They are quite separate and distinct, having a different purpose and outcome. Civil law is the law relating to conduct between individuals or groups of individuals. If I am owed some money by someone I would make a civil claim for recovery of debt. A court would decide if I was owed the money and then, if I was, it would order it to be paid to me. The object of civil law is to resolve disputes between individuals and the sanctions imposed are court orders. The basic civil action is a claim for damages (money) by a plaintiff against a defendant. There is no element of a penalty being imposed on the guilty party, only a settlement that enforces a legal right.

Criminal law is the law governing the behaviour of individuals in relation to the State. If I steal something, I have broken a law of the State. I would be taken to court on a charge of theft and, if found guilty, I would be punished by the State, i.e., fined or imprisoned. The object of criminal law is to regulate the conduct of individuals and, in the event of someone not conforming, they are punished by the State. The criminal court action is a prosecution by the prosecutor (nominally the Queen) against the defendant. Criminal law does not attempt to settle disputes between parties. There can be an overlap between the two categories in that one act may lead to a civil case *and* a criminal case. For example, after an accident at work, the firm or a manager can be prosecuted under the Health and Safety at Work Act (and fined) and the firm can be sued for causing injury (and damages awarded) under civil law.

Most of the law relating to industrial relations is civil law. Unfair dismissal, redundancy, disputes, employment protection, contract and discrimination are all in the area of civil law, as there is a dispute between an individual and the employer. Some industrial relations activities are outside the scope of civil law. An important example of this is that of collective agreements, which are presumed not to be contracts and hence cannot be the subject of legal proceedings. Importantly, however, the content of the collective agreement is incorporated into the individual contracts of employment of those covered by the agreement. Other civil liabilities in industrial relations did exist, such as in the Taff Vale case where a union was successfully sued for loss of profit due to a strike. Much of this liability has now been removed by the immunities covering unions, their members, officials and activities (*see* Section 10.2).

There is some criminal law that applies in

industrial relations. The immunities mentioned above only cover civil wrongs (like tort and breach of contract), not criminal wrongs. Trade union officials and members have to observe the criminal law as do other organisations and individuals. There is an immunity against being prosecuted for conspiracy. At one time it could be a crime for two or more people to conspire to commit a civil wrong. Today, if there is a conspiracy to commit a civil wrong as part of trade union activity it is not actionable as a crime. Picketing is an activity that frequently breaks criminal law, and there is no immunity from this. There is an official Code of Practice which is relevant in a court case (*see* Section 11.6). Trade unionists can peacefully obtain and communicate information but in doing so should not break the criminal law, for example obstruct the highway. If they do, they can be prosecuted.

9.1.2 Sources of law

There is no single source of English law. You cannot go to any one set of books and read all the laws on a topic. There are, in fact, several sources of law:

Statutory law

Parliament has the supreme right to make whatever laws it wishes (except to bind itself for ever). The bulk of Acts of Parliament are introduced by the government, as bills, to put their policies into effect. A procedure is used and the bill has to pass through the House of Commons and the House of Lords before gaining its royal assent and becoming an Act. All laws remain in force until specifically repealed. The age of a law is irrelevant. Acts can create new laws, amend, repeal, codify or consolidate laws. The bulk of industrial relations law is statutory law contained in a number of Acts of Parliament. Such statutory law created legal immunities for trade unions (in the 1906 Trades Disputes Act). Amendments take place frequently, like the Trade Union and Labour Relations (Amendment) Act 1976 which amended the Trade Union and Labour Relations Act 1974. Repeals take place from time to time

such as when the Trade Union and Labour Relations Act 1974 repealed the Industrial Relations Act 1971. Sometimes the law in an area is put together (consolidated) in one statute, such as the Trade Union and Labour Relations (Consolidation) Act 1992.

Statutory instruments

Another type of statutory law is delegated legislation which has the same status and force as an Act itself. Statutory instruments are useful as they can be issued quickly and do not take up much parliamentary time. These instruments are issued by ministers under powers granted to them in an Act. The minister cannot make law (by issuing a statutory instrument) on any topic but only on the specific issues that Parliament allows under a specific Act. Instruments are subject to a check by Parliament. The minister has to present the instrument to Parliament for its approval before it is issued and becomes law. Instruments are also subject to scrutiny by a Joint Committee on Statutory Instruments. Several examples exist in industrial relations, like amending the limits for compensation for unfair dismissal and redundancy. The procedural rules of industrial tribunals are laid down in statutory instruments. Another form of delegated legislation is an order in council. This does not require parliamentary approval before being issued and can be issued during a parliamentary recess. Under the Emergency Powers Acts 1920 and 1964 an order can be issued to secure and maintain 'the supply and distribution of food, water, fuel, light . . . to ensure the public safety and the life of the community'. Such an order has been issued six times since 1945, most recently during the 1973–4 miners' dispute.

Common law

This is a very important source of law and probably the largest. This is the law that is based on the judicial decisions of previous court cases. This law derives from the decisions of judges in court that bind judges in similar cases, in the future, to come to the same conclusion. This process, which is called judicial precedent, is explained in Section 9.1.4. The bulk of English law is derived from common law although statutory law has taken over in some areas. Common law is a source of both criminal and civil law. Contract and tort are almost entirely common law with only a few Acts relating to those subjects. A lot of early industrial relations law derived from common law but has been altered by statute. Some examples of this were given in Chapter 8.

In order of importance, statutory law is a higher source of law than common law. Where common law and statute clash, the statute law must be followed. However, a court's interpretation of a statute cannot be interfered with by Parliament or ministers as the courts, being part of the judiciary, are independent of the legislature (Parliament) and the executive (government). If the courts do not interpret the law as Parliament intended, the Act has to be amended by Parliament. For example, the court's interpretation of 'in contemplation and furtherance of a trades dispute' in the McShane case (*see* Section 8.2.2) did not suit the government of the day so the legislation was amended in the Employment Act 1980 to restrict this court interpretation. The Act must now be followed, not the law in the McShane case.

EC law

As part of joining the Common Market in 1972, by signing the Treaty of Rome, the UK has to adopt EC law into its domestic system. Where domestic law and EC law clash, the rule is that EC law takes precedence. Hence community law is superior to UK law as are the judgements of the European Court of Justice. The implementation of EC law is achieved in two ways. The Commission can either issue a Regulation or a Directive.

- Regulations are EC legislation that are automatically applicable in all EC member states. For example, an EC Regulation requiring lead levels in petrol to be reduced to a specified level by a certain year is automatically law in the UK. It does not require the UK to pass legislation to implement the law.
- Directives are EC legislation that impose a requirement on member states to pass legislation to meet the requirements of the EC Directive. For example, a Directive regarding equal pay led to the 'work of equal value' amendment being passed in the UK. Currently the use of Directives has affected industrial relations in respect of equal opportunities, redundancy, transfer of undertaking and insolvency. Health and safety law has also been much affected in this way.

9.1.3 Codes of Practice

Codes of Practice are not strictly law and do not have the force of law in the same way as the sources in Section 9.1.2. However, Codes do have a semi-legal status in that they can be used in evidence to show that the law has not been complied with. In industrial relations there are nine Codes of Practice currently issued, which are examined in Chapter 11. Their use can be illustrated using an example from unfair dismissal. The manner of dismissal must be reasonable and this includes following the relevant Code. If the Code is not followed this can indicate that the manner of dismissal was not reasonable. It is not against the law to forbid a person to appeal against a dismissal but it is contrary to the Code. It is likely that if a dismissed person were not allowed to appeal against their dismissal, the dismissal would be unfair. Codes are useful in expanding the meaning of a point of law but without the necessity of being a complex legal document. Codes are written in fairly informal (nonlegal) language and are not interpreted as strictly as an Act. Often Codes have to be approved by Parliament before they can be issued as official Codes, as often a Code is issued under the authority of an Act of Parliament. This is the case with the nine Codes in industrial relations.

9.1.4 The role of the judges

An important aspect of our legal system is the role the judges have to play. As members of the judiciary their job is to enforce the law. As we saw in Section 9.1.2 regarding common law, the judges are involved in a major source of law. After hearing the evidence in a case, the judge sums up and, in doing so, weighs up the evidence in the case, discusses the legal aspects of the case and finally makes a decision (or puts it to the jury in a criminal trial). The important part of this process, as far as the legal system is concerned, is the statement of the legal reasons for the decision. This part is known as the precedent (*ratio decidendi*). The judges have a rule that they are bound by their own decisions. This is why the law relating to a topic is referenced as a case. This system is often referred to as case law, where the law is declared in cases. There is a hierarchy of courts (*see* Section 9.2.1) and a higher court's decision binds a lower court. The House of Lords is the highest court and no other court can overrule it, except now in respect of EC law where the European Court of Justice is the final arbiter. The lower courts (county and magistrates) and the tribunals do not create precedent but are bound by higher courts.

The judges have an important role in interpreting statute law. Parliament passes Acts that should operate in the manner it intended. It is then for the courts to interpret the wording of the Act as cases come before them. Parliament or government cannot interfere in this process. The detailed interpretation and meaning of the law is built on cases arising and the precise meaning of the law is given by the judges. The judges have their own rules of interpretation but must follow any rules set out in the Act itself or the rules of the Interpretation Act 1889 or the judges' own rules of interpretation. Again, the rules of precedence apply to this situation.

The judges of the Queen's Bench Division of the High Court also have a supervisory role. They can have court or tribunal cases referred to them under various prerogative orders. This provides a check, by the judges, to ensure that the courts and tribunals are acting judicially. If they are not, the High Court can issue orders to put the matter right. Industrial tribunals are subject to this scrutiny.

9.2 The administration of justice

9.2.1 Court structure

The courts are divided into two separate hierarchies: one to administer criminal law and the other to administer civil law. Figure 9.1 shows the courts' structure of England and Wales, in a simplified form. In practice there is some overlap, e.g., magistrates also deal with some civil matters relating to family and divorce.

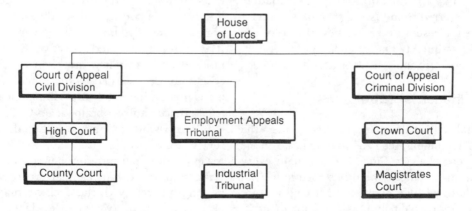

Fig 9.1 Court structure of England and Wales (simplified)

Tribunals, and industrial tribunals in particular, are separate from the main line of courts. The Employment Appeals Tribunal is part of the Supreme Court of Judicature, i.e., on a level with the High Court. Most civil matters specifically relating to industrial relations are referred to industrial tribunals. All criminal matters are dealt with by magistrates (for minor offences) or the Crown Court (for major offences).

9.2.2 The role of tribunals

During this century many statutes have been passed creating relations between individuals and the State (government departments or local authorities). Disputes that arise under such legislation are dealt with in tribunals rather than in the ordinary courts of law. Tribunals have the functions of a civil court to enforce the law but are not restricted by the rules and procedures of an ordinary court. The courts are overworked and cases take a long time to be heard. Costs are very high and the courts are slow and deliberate. Tribunals have the advantage of being quicker, cheaper, more informal, have greater discretionary power and can be staffed by experts in the field. Set against this, tribunals have disadvantages by being less precise than the ordinary courts. Tribunals only ever deal with civil law, never criminal law. In industrial relations many matters arising are referred to industrial tribunals. All employee rights like redundancy pay, discrimination, unfair dismissal, maternity leave and pay and time off for duties are matters that are referred to industrial tribunals. Often it is in the interests of both parties to resolve the situation as quickly and as cheaply as possible. To this end tribunals serve a useful purpose.

9.2.3 Industrial tribunals

Industrial tribunals were created under the Industrial Training Act 1964 to adjudicate on the training board levies. Since 1964 virtually every Act relating to employment has used industrial tribunals to resolve disputes of a civil nature. Currently industrial tribunals deal with about 40 separate references from unfair dismissal, redundancy and discrimination to time off work and maternity leave. In 1988 the tribunals heard 34,404 cases; 75% related to unfair dismissal and 14% related to redundancy. Of these applications, 4,815 were successful at a tribunal hearing.

An industrial tribunal is composed of a chairperson and two others: one from the employers (from a CBI list) and the other from the unions (from a TUC list). The chairperson has to be a lawyer of seven years' experience and some tribunals have a full-time chairperson, but the majority are part-time. The proceedings are directed by the chairperson but the other two members can contribute. The decision of the tribunal is based on each member having an equal say. Technically the chairperson can be overruled but generally decisions are unanimous. The hearings are in public. Parties can represent themselves or have others, including lawyers, appear for them. The procedure is fairly informal but follows a pattern of opening statements, evidence, calling witnesses, cross-examination and addressing the tribunal. Evidence is given under oath. Sometimes hearsay and unsworn statements are admissible as evidence.

The tribunal's decision is given at the end of the case after a recess. A written decision is given later by the chairperson. When this is lodged with the tribunal, the decision becomes binding. Industrial tribunal orders are not enforceable as ordinary court orders (through contempt laws). If an order is disobeyed the tribunal can award extra money. Money orders are enforceable as if they were a county court order. Costs are not normally awarded but certain expenses are paid. If a party had acted vexatiously (improper motive) or frivolously (no chance of success) costs may be awarded to the other side. Legal aid is not available for any tribunal hearing but legal advice can be obtained, up to £25 worth.

It is possible to have a tribunal's decision reviewed and to appeal against the decision. A review is only permitted under specific circumstances: if there is a clerical error, notice of hearing not received, the decision made in the absence of one party, or new evidence available that could not have been known at the hearing.

Decisions can be confirmed, amended or reversed on review. Appeal is open to either side against the decision of a tribunal, but only on a question of law. This means only where the decision of the tribunal may be in error in law can an appeal be made. If the tribunal has kept to the law but appears to have deduced the wrong facts from the evidence presented, there are no grounds for appeal. Such appeals on a question of law are made to the Employment Appeals Tribunal.

9.2.4 Employment Appeals Tribunal

The Employment Appeals Tribunal (EAT) is a full court of law that hears appeals on industrial relations law. The tribunal is part of the Supreme Court of Judicature. It is presided over by a High Court judge, its decisions are fully recorded (as a law report) and the decisions are legally binding precedents. The EAT is bound by decisions of the Court of Appeal and the House of Lords, where these are relevant. The judge sits with two or four lay members appointed from the employers (CBI) and unions (TUC).

The EAT hears appeals from industrial tribunals on questions of law on nearly all matters the tribunal deals with. The appeal can succeed on one of three points: the tribunal misdirected itself or misunderstood or misapplied the law; there was no evidence to support the tribunal's findings of fact; or no reasonable tribunal could have reached the decision it did. Fresh evidence is seldom allowed and the court uses the findings of fact given in the tribunal decision. Further appeals can be made to the Court of Appeal and again to the House of Lords on questions of law, if leave to appeal is given.

The EAT is also used as the appeal body from the Certification Officer. A union refused a certificate of independence can appeal to the EAT against the decision of the Certification Officer on a question of fact or law. Questions arising from the law relating to political funds and levies and trade union amalgamations are taken to the EAT. In 1989 the Employment Appeals Tribunal heard 646 appeal cases, of which 497 were under unfair dismissal legislation, 25 for redundancy pay, 49 on racial discrimination, 34 on sex discrimination, 9 on equal pay and 32 'other'.

Multiple-choice questions

9.1 Which of these may lead directly to a civil court action?
(a) speeding
(b) dismissal
(c) manslaughter

9.2 Which of these may lead to a criminal court action?
(a) redundancy
(b) discrimination
(c) picketing

9.3 List the sources of law in order of precedence.
(a) statutory law
(b) EC law
(c) common law

9.4 Who can reverse the decision of the High Court?
(a) the House of Lords
(b) a minister
(c) Parliament

9.5 Ministers can make law
(a) not at all
(b) under an Act of Parliament
(c) with Parliament's approval

9.6 Laws can lose their force
(a) only when repealed
(b) after 100 years
(c) never

9.7 Failure to observe a Code of Practice
(a) is not significant
(b) can be evidence of breaking the law
(c) can lead to prosecution

9.8 The highest court in the land is
(a) the Court of Appeal
(b) the Privy Council
(c) the House of Lords

9.9 Appeals from an industrial tribunal go to
(a) the High Court
(b) the County Court
(c) the Employment Appeals Tribunal

Mini-questions

9.1 Differentiate between civil and criminal law.

9.2 Explain how one act may lead to a civil and a criminal case.

9.3 Describe what a statute is and what a statutory instrument is.

9.4   Describe how joining the Common Market has affected the sources of English law.

9.5   Explain the status of a Code of Practice at law.

9.6   Explain the process of judicial precedence.

9.7   State the advantages of an industrial tribunal over an ordinary law court.

9.8   List six types of case that an industrial tribunal could hear.

9.9   Explain the financial considerations in taking a case to a tribunal.

9.10 Describe the role of the EAT.

10

Industrial relations law

10.1 The status of trade unions and employers' associations

In Chapter 2 we considered the characteristics of a trade union in terms of its purpose and function and took a similar look at employers' associations in Chapter 3. In this section we examine the legal status of these organisations. Characteristically there is some difficulty here. At law many organisations are recognised as separate entities. Organisations such as companies, local authorities, public bodies and nationalised industries are in themselves separate legal bodies set up by a process of law either under the Companies Act, a special Act of Parliament or Royal Charter. Just as individuals have a legal identity and can sue and be sued and prosecute and be prosecuted in their own name, then so can these organisations. The law calls these bodies incorporated associations. However, there is a category of bodies called unincorporated associations. Examples include local societies and clubs. It is generally held that such bodies are only a collection of individuals and do not exist apart from the members constituting the body. So if the local tennis club commits an offence it is a club member (usually an official) who is taken to court, not the club itself, as the law does not recognise it (the club) separately from the members.

Trade unions fall into this category of unincorporated associations, as do many employers' associations. Currently, under the Trade Union and Labour Relations (Consolidation) Act 1992, a trade union cannot be a corporate body (but employers' associations can) and so unions are

presumed to be an unincorporated association. Trade unions do have special features that distinguish them from the small local club. They have an often complex Rule Book, certain rights at law, power and a special status under the registration process and certification (*see* Section 2.3). Also their size makes them different. The courts have examined the legal status of trade unions from time to time. From 1871 (when registration was introduced) the unions presumed they, as a body, were free from court action, although they were able to make contracts, for example to employ people and buy goods and services in the name of the union. In the Taff Vale case the House of Lords decided a union could be sued in its own name, in that case the Amalgamated Society of Railway Servants, as opposed to a named individual. In the case of *Bonsor* v. *Musicians Union* in 1956 (*see* Section 8.2.2), Bonsor sued his ex-union for wrongful expulsion. The House of Lords was split in deciding if the union was a separate legal entity or not. The case did not clear up this point but left the trade union being, at law, a collection of individuals but with the possibility of being sued in its own name. Most legal actions against trade unions are taken out against named individuals (usually the General Secretary) rather than the union itself.

This state of confusion still exists today in that a trade union displays some of the characteristics of a corporate body but is fundamentally a collection of individuals, i.e., the members, with some being responsible as officials for the action taken on behalf of the union. The Trade Union and Labour Relations (Consolidation) Act 1992 states that a trade union cannot be a corporate body but it can sue and be sued in its own name and can be prosecuted in its own name and its funds can be used to pay damages and fines. Hence a union can employ people in its own name, and be sued if it fails in its obligations as an employer and be prosecuted if it breaks the criminal law.

10.2 Trade union immunities

10.2.1 The need for immunities

Many trade union activities would be illegal if the common law had not been altered. So far as the common law is concerned this illegality extends into several areas. The very existence of a trade union, to act on behalf of its members to maintain and improve their terms and conditions, was held in the early part of the nineteenth century to be illegal.

Restraint of trade

Under contract law, the two parties to an agreement (the contract between employer and employee) should be free to make whatever agreement they wish and not be restrained by a third party. A union, in seeking to impose certain terms and conditions on the contract of employment, is essentially a third party to the contract and is acting 'in restraint of trade'. If the common law relating to restraint of trade had not been altered, collective bargaining would not have evolved as we know it today.

Inducement to breach contract

A fundamentally important activity of any trade union is its ability to withdraw the labour of its members, or to threaten to do so. This again is a civil wrong at common law as it is inducing or committing a breach of contract. Picketing also falls into this category of inducing others to break their contracts of employment. A trade union official calling on members to work to rule, or go slow or strike is breaking the law on

a number of counts, such as inducement and interference with a contract of employment. Again, if the common law relating to inducement and interference had not been altered, trade unions and individuals would be acting illegally if they attempted to call a strike or go on strike.

The activities described above break both criminal and civil law and could lead to individuals, members and officials being either sued (under civil law) or prosecuted (under criminal law). Striking itself was a crime up until 1871, when the Trade Union Act abolished the crime. Other crimes were contained in the Conspiracy and Protection of Property Act 1875 which made violence illegal, also persistent following, hiding tools or other property and watching and besetting. Anyone committing these offences could be fined or imprisoned. Another crime that trade unionists potentially committed in organising workers was the crime of conspiracy. If two or more people agreed to combine to do anything that was unlawful (like being in restraint of trade or striking) they could be guilty of the crime of conspiracy, even if the planned act was not a crime.

Criminal law

The position today with respect to criminal law is that the offences specifically relating to legitimate trade union activities are no longer offences. The position on conspiracy is that if the planned act is not a crime and it is done in contemplation or furtherance of a trade dispute, then no offence has been committed. This enables, for example, a shop stewards' committee to organise a strike and not be guilty of conspiracy, which previously it would have been. However, if they plan to commit a crime, for example action involving criminal damage like breaking into a building, then they could be guilty of conspiracy. Striking is not a criminal offence. Picketing, which is examined in Chapter 15, usually verges on criminal activity and there is no immunity from being charged with a crime as a picket. The act of standing on the pavement is an offence of obstructing the highway (but is generally overlooked by the authorities). Trade unions and their members are required to observe the law as ordinary citizens and they are given no special treatment apart from that given by these immunities.

Civil law

At civil law, potentially there are several grounds for action against an individual, a trade union official and even a trade union for many activities. These include inducement, interference, intimidation and conspiracy. All these are listed under the general heading of tort. If anyone commits these torts they are liable to be sued for damages in the courts or be subject of a court order to restrain them from doing the action. This could lead to potentially enormous sums of money being claimed, even if the claim was limited to one for loss of profit. Some of our large companies make profits of several million pounds a day and if they were prevented from operating because of a strike they could claim loss of profit in damages. This leaves the trade unions vulnerable to claims that would bankrupt them. In order for a union and its members and officials to function effectively there needs to be a way in which they can carry out certain acts but be free from the threat of court action that could lead to a potentially destructive claim for damages. This is achieved through a series of immunities. These are statutory alterations to the law that prohibit a court action being taken out against an official or union that acts in certain specified circumstances. Providing the unions and individuals operate within the confines of the immunities defined by law, they can act free from possible legal action. The next section describes these immunities.

10.2.2 Protection for certain acts

The immunities for trade unions and individuals derive from the Trade Disputes Act 1906. This Act was the result of the Taff Vale case (*see* Section 8.2.2) in which a union had to pay heavy damages for calling a strike. These immunities have remained the basic protection up to the present time. There have been amendments: in 1927 (repealed in 1947), in 1971 (repealed in 1974), in 1976, in 1980 and 1982. This section will refer to the immunities that exist at present, laid down in the Trade Union and Labour Relations Act 1974 as amended by the Trade Union and Labour Relations (Amendment) Act 1976, the Employment Acts 1980, 1982 and 1988, and the Trade Union Act 1984. The legislation has now been brought together in the Trade Union and Labour Relations (Consolidation) Act 1992. The immunities are given in two parts, those to individuals and those to unions.

Immunities to individuals

There is an immunity set up to protect individuals against actions for inducing or threatening to break a contract. The contract in question is now limited to a contract of employment. There is a possibility of a court action where a commercial contract has been interfered with by some form of industrial action, for example interfering with a contract to supply goods or services. The immunity is limited to acts done by a person 'in contemplation or furtherance of a trade dispute' not being actionable in tort. The interpretation by the courts, of the phrase quoted, was very broad but is now limited by the Trade Union and Labour Relations (Consolidation) Act 1992. Only primary action is allowed, i.e., acts done in contemplation or furtherance of a trade dispute between employees and their employer. Any secondary action, i.e., action against any other employer than the employees' employer, is now no longer covered by the immunities granted at law. This means that if employees of another employer take industrial action to support other workers who have a legitimate trade dispute with their employer, they will not be covered by the legal immunities and can easily be sued. The immunity now only covers acts done to induce another to break a contract of employment or the right of someone to dispose of capital or labour as they please. The Employment Act 1982 (now the Trade Union and Labour Relations (Consolidation) Act 1992) makes a further restriction in that the immunity does not extend to include acts done for the purpose of compelling workers at another place of work to become members of a trade union. This restriction is to prevent the recruitment practice of a union that blockades goods going from and to nonunion labour workforces, in order to compel these workers to join the union.

The term 'trade dispute' is defined in the Trade Union and Labour Relations Act 1974 as amended by the Employment Acts 1980 and 1982. The current definition of a trade dispute is a dispute between workers and their employer and related wholly or mainly to:

- the terms and conditions of employment or the physical conditions of work
- engagement, nonengagement, termination or suspension of employees
- allocation of work between employees or groups of employees
- discipline
- membership or nonmembership of a trade union
- facilities for trade union officials
- the machinery for negotiation or consultation including trade union recognition.

Disputes between groups of workers, such as an inter-union dispute, are not covered by the definition. Hence any industrial action taken as the result of a dispute between groups of workers is not covered by the immunities and could lead to court action. The dispute must be 'wholly or mainly' related to the list of topics stated. The connection must be a primary and direct one and not just a loose connection. Any dispute that is primarily concerned with some other issue, e.g., a political campaign or protest, again would not be covered.

A further restriction is placed on the origins of the dispute. If the dispute concerns matters outside the UK then, unless workers in the UK are likely to be affected in respect of one of the matters stated above, the dispute is outside the legal definition of a trade dispute. For example, industrial action taken in support of sailors employed by a 'flag of convenience' country would not be granted immunity. The word 'worker' receives a similar restricted definition as being one who is, or was, employed by that employer. Hence sympathetic action by workers other than those employed by the employer with whom there is a dispute is not covered.

The immunity is not given where the industrial action being contemplated relates to establishing or maintaining a closed shop. This may occur where an employer has employed someone who is not a member of a union or a member of the particular union concerned, or where the employer is being pressurised into discriminating against someone for nonmembership. The Employment Act 1988 introduced this provision. Hence an employer could successfully seek an injunction in such circumstances to restrain someone from calling for industrial action or to order them to call off the action.

One point to note is that these immunities to the individual only apply to those who organise or act to commit these various unlawful acts. They are the protected ones. The employee who actually goes on strike, i.e., who commits the breach of contract rather than inducing it, is not covered. A striker is in breach of contract and can, theoretically, be sued for that. In practice this is never done. It is possible for an employer to consider that the breach is sufficient indication that the contract has come to an end and the striker has sacked himself. Furthermore, unfair dismissal cannot be claimed if this happens.

Immunities to trade unions

Trade unions, as a separate body, were once fully protected against any legal action by an immunity in the Trade Union and Labour Relations Act 1974. Now, as a result of the Employment Act 1982, they are given the same immunity as individuals (*see above*). Hence any action done in contemplation or furtherance of a trade dispute, by a trade union, is covered by the limited immunity. Action outside this definition (as described above) may be the subject of court action. This puts the union's funds in jeopardy and in the extreme may send a union out of existence. The damaging effect of a major strike could lead to court action for damages amounting to hundreds of thousands, or even millions, of pounds, plus legal costs.

Suing individuals for such large sums is not practicable as they will have only limited means with which they can pay any damages. In order to prevent catastrophic action against trade unions, the law limits the maximum amount of damages that can be awarded against a trade union. The maximum varies, depending on the size of union:

£10,000	less than 5,000 members
£50,000	more than 5,000, less than 25,000 members
£125,000	more than 25,000, less than 100,000 members
£250,000	more than 100,000 members

Additionally, damages cannot be paid from 'protected' property. This includes any private property belonging to the trustees or officers, the union's political fund or the union's provident fund.

For the purposes of deciding if a union is liable it is necessary to define if the action has been authorised by the union. A trade union is liable if the industrial action has been called in its name. The action must have been supported by a ballot (*see* next section) to qualify for immunity. Often the words 'official' and 'unofficial' action are used in this context. The usual meaning of these words is 'official' action has been called by a full-time union official and according to the rules of the union (and most unions only empower full-time officials to call a strike). 'Unofficial' action is action called by a lay official (shop steward or convenor) and often in breach of the union Rule Book. The law (now stated in the Trade Union and Labour Relations (Consolidation) Act 1992) states that a union is liable for any industrial action called by any trade union official or committee. Hence the national officials of a trade union cannot hide behind the argument that industrial action was called by a group of shop stewards and the union cannot be liable for their actions. Now they are liable unless they issue a repudiation. The repudiation, to be effective, has to be in writing to those who called the action and to

all those who are taking action. The repudiation has to point out that taking unofficial industrial action can lead to instant dismissal and there can be no claim for unfair dismissal in these circumstances. Indeed, any industrial action taken to support colleagues who have been dismissed for taking unofficial action is not within the definition of a trade dispute and leaves the union open to be sued (i.e., it has no immunity).

The current position on immunities is shown in Figure 10.1.

It is worth noting that an order of specific performance under contract law, whereby the court orders one party to fulfil its obligations under a contract, does not apply to a contract of employment. Hence courts cannot order employees back to work or to do certain work even if they are in breach of their contracts of employment.

As was noted for individuals, the immunity is not given where the industrial action being contemplated relates to establishing or maintaining a closed shop. This may occur where an employer has employed someone who is not a member of a union or member of the particular union concerned or where the employer is being pressurised into discriminating against someone for nonmembership. The Employment Act 1988 introduced this provision. Hence an employer could successfully seek an injunction in such circumstances to restrain a union from calling for industrial action or to order it to call off the action.

Ballots

The immunity of trade unions, as described above, is now subject to a further condition laid down in the Trade Union Act 1984 (now contained in the Trade Union and Labour Relations (Consolidation) Act 1992). This requires that a secret ballot must be held of those due to take part in the action and that they vote by a majority to say that they wish to take part in the action. If the detailed requirements of the law are not complied with then the union has no immunity at law against any legal action

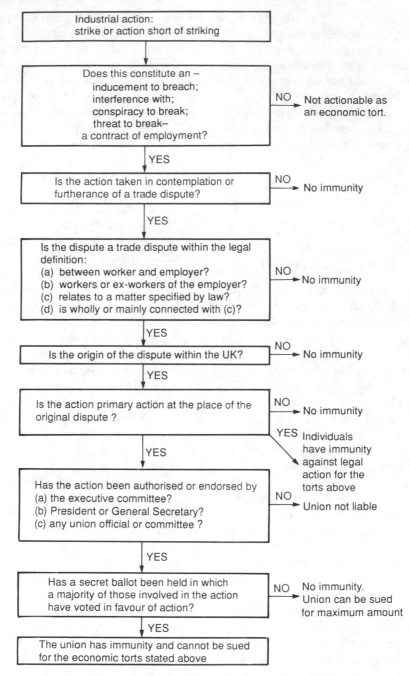

Fig 10.1 Immunities in trade disputes

regarding the industrial action. The court action can be taken by the employer, the employer's suppliers or customers (who are affected by the industrial action) or by a union member.

The dispute must have been approved in a ballot, held no more than four weeks before the action was endorsed or authorised. The following requirements apply:

- all members who are likely to be called to take part in the industrial action, and only they, must be given the opportunity to vote
- voters must be asked if they are prepared to take part in industrial action, either a strike or action short of a strike and they must be asked about both, if relevant
- that there is a majority reply 'yes' for the action to be approved
- ballot papers must contain the statement 'if you take part in a strike or other industrial action, you may be in breach of your contract of employment'
- all voters must be able to vote without interference, without incurring any cost, to vote in secret and for the votes to be fairly and accurately counted.

Separate ballots are required for each workplace unless there is a common factor connecting several places of work, e.g., they are all in the same occupational group and the union should inform all those entitled to vote of the outcome of the ballot.

Until 1993, government funds were available to assist trade unions to hold ballots prior to industrial action. The Certification Officer administered the system and in 1991 paid out £4.0m for all forms of trade union ballots. Now trade unions have to bear the cost of all ballots and must comply with the rules covering the use of ballots. Such ballots should be postal ballots, secret workplace ballots or ballots where the papers are handed out at work and returned by post. Trade unions and the TUC were vehemently against being forced to use ballots and the use of government funds for this purpose. Ironically there was a similar outcry when the government announced that it was withdrawing financial support for the scheme!

If the union does not comply with the requirements for a ballot before industrial action, a member of the union can complain to the Commissioner for the Rights of Trade Union Members (*see* Section 4.3.4). The Commissioner can assist in any legal action against the union such as seeking an injunction to stop the industrial action.

If the union is organising a workplace ballot, the employer can be requested to provide facilities for the ballot. These should not be unreasonably refused. A complaint can be made to an Industrial Tribunal if there is a refusal. A Code of Practice on Trade Union Ballots on Industrial Action has been issued (*see* Section 11.9). This Code makes many specific requirements which the union should comply with. Again (as with all Codes) it can be used as evidence in a court action. If an employer or union member or a supplier or customer (affected by the industrial action) were to take the union to court, the Code's requirements would be relevant in deciding if the law had been complied with.

10.2.3 Interlocutory injunctions

So far we have described the potential outcome of an industrial dispute in terms of an action for damages in the civil courts. More often than not an employer is concerned to prevent the action taking place in the first instance and rarely runs the risk of a damaging strike and then suing for damages. To prevent a potentially unlawful act occurring, the employer can seek an interlocutory injunction from the courts. This is a court order which restrains named people or a union from carrying out the alleged unlawful act until a full trial hearing. The object of an interlocutory injunction is to prevent the act occurring or continuing until a full trial can take place. In practice, a successful application for an injunction is very effective at halting industrial action. Clearly, swift action is needed in such circumstances, particularly when it may take up to a year or more for the full trial to commence. Injunctions can be granted in a matter of days. Before issuing an injunction a court has to decide if there is a serious issue to be heard and whether (in some circumstances) there is a possible legal defence to the action. Certain practical difficulties exist, as injunctions are only granted against named individuals or organisations. They are not issued as a blanket order. If the injunction does not name the organisers, the action may continue. An injunction against a union may not be effective if the organisers are not the known union officials.

Further court action may ensue where an interlocutory injunction has not been obeyed. This occurred particularly in the 1980s due to the trade union movement's political opposition to the Conservative administration's industrial relations legislation. As part of this protest, the unions and TUC have a policy of not cooperating in the workings of the legislation. On a matter of principle some unions refuse to recognise a court order issued as a result of the legislation. Should an injunction be disobeyed or ignored, the employer can then pursue the issue as a contempt of court. This can lead to a fine by the court to be paid by the individuals named in the injunction. Further disobedience, or refusal to pay the fine, can lead to further penalties including imprisonment. In the case of a union this can lead to the seizing of its assets, although 'protected property' cannot be seized. Unions, or their officials, can appeal against an injunction. This option may not be pursued if they object in principle to the legislation. Alternatively, the high costs involved may deter further legal proceedings. The court can also order the trade union to take steps to prevent the industrial action continuing. This can include the union taking disciplinary action against those who continue to take action or induce others to take action in contravention of the court order.

Apart from the complex, legal intricacies the other major, possibly more important, factor that needs to be considered is the effect of the proceedings on industrial relations. Prolonged legal action can exacerbate an already difficult situation. The long-term effects on industrial relations of going to court can deter some employers from bringing the force of law to bear on the situation. Also litigation is a drain on resources such as managerial time and money and always carries the risk of losing the case.

10.3 Employment protection

10.3.1 Trade union membership and activities

An important right is that of the freedom to join a trade union. Since the repeal of the Combination Acts in 1824 there has been no restriction on an employee joining a trade union or taking part in its activities, so far as the law is concerned. On the other hand, the law has not, until recently, given the positive right to join a union. The Industrial Relations Act 1971 introduced a protection against discrimination for registered unions and their members. The Trade Union and Labour Relations Act 1974 repealed this and a provision was put in the Employment Protection Act 1975 and reenacted in the Employment Protection (Consolidation) Act 1978. The present position includes some modifications under the Employment Act 1980 and is now contained in the Trade Union and Labour Relations (Consolidation) Act 1992. Basically there is protection for employees against employer discrimination not to have action taken against them, whether it be dismissal or action short of dismissal, to prevent or to deter them from being, or seeking to be, members of an independent trade union, or to take part in the activities of a trade union or to penalise them for having done so. Hence an employer cannot victimise anyone for their trade union membership (actual or intended) or for taking part in trade union activities. This victimisation could take the form of, say, not offering overtime work, not giving promotion or anything that treats a person less favourably than others. If a person is dismissed for trade union membership or activities, then they can claim unfair dismissal and such a reason is an automatically unfair reason (*see* Section 13.2.2) and compensation is awarded.

The right to take part in trade union activities is limited in two senses. One is that it has to be at the 'appropriate time'. This is defined as outside working hours or within working hours which the employer has agreed or consented to. Activities carried on outside of this definition do not give the employee the rights above. For example, if a union meeting is called in working hours and the employer either refuses permission or does not give consent, then the employees attending could be disciplined, for a minor breach of contract, with no claim under this section. Where there are arrangements for activities like consultations, meetings and ballots then the employees participating are covered. A second limitation is that the activities have to be part of ordinary trade union activity like attending meetings, voting and so on, but obviously exclude trade union action such as a go-slow, work-to-rule, overtime ban or strike. This is part of a trade dispute, not trade union activity.

A further right, under the Employment Act 1980, is that an employee has the right not to have action taken against them (whether it be dismissal or action short of dismissal) to compel them to be or become a trade union member. This is a right given to an employee to be free not to join a trade union if they so desire. This right did not exist where there was a closed shop unless the employee objected to joining a trade union on the grounds of conscience or other deeply held belief; or that the employee had not been, before or since the agreement, a trade union member; or that the agreement, made since August 1980, had not been approved by an 80% majority in a ballot. Under the Employment Act 1988, this right not to join a union, introduced in 1980, is made absolute. The law is now contained in the Trade Union and Labour Relations (Consolidation) Act 1992. The fact that there is a closed shop makes no difference. Indeed, if there is a closed shop and an employee is dismissed for not joining a union (or the specified union), the dismissal is automatically unfair. If a trade union puts pressure on the employer to dismiss, the union can be 'joined' in the tribunal action and made to contribute to, or pay the whole of, the compensation. Another rule is that the employer cannot force a non-trade union member to make an equivalent payment to a charity instead of paying the union subscription.

The Employment Act 1990 took this process a stage further and introduced a number of provisions covering recruitment and selection. Until 1990 there were no laws covering this part of employment. The 1990 Act makes it unlawful to refuse employment to anyone because they are a trade union member or they are not, or because they refuse to join or resign from a union. Where someone applies for a job which includes (explicitly or implicitly) union membership as a condition and is subsequently refused employment, there is an automatic presumption of discrimination. This means that the employer cannot use any other reason as a defence, even if the person was not suitable for the job. Refusal of employment includes not processing an application, causing the applicant to withdraw their application or refusing to make an offer of employment. This law applies to employment agencies as well as employers. This set of laws in effect bans the pre-entry closed shop (*see* Section 15.3.2) which is a feature of some industries.

A person discriminated against in this way can apply to an industrial tribunal. The tribunal can award up to £11,000 (in 1992) in compensation and the tribunal can apportion this between the employer and the trade union involved.

10.3.2 Time off work

With the extension of collective bargaining in this century it has become necessary for trade union officials to spend a proportion of their working hours on official union business. Should this time off not be granted by the employer, lay officials (shop stewards or convenors) would be unable to carry out many of their duties. Also if time off were granted but without pay, this would financially penalise the employees for being trade union representatives. Employees also, on occasions, need time off work to fulfil certain public duties like sitting as a magistrate or as a member of a local authority or public authority.

The Employment Protection Act 1975, now contained in the Trade Union and Labour Relations (Consolidation) Act 1992, created the legal right for an employee to take time off for these various trade union and public duties. Trade union officials of trade unions recognised by the employer have the right to a reasonable amount of paid time off work for their industrial relations duties and for training as officials. This right to paid time off is for those duties concerned with negotiations or other duties agreed with the employer. It does not cover internal union duties. The list of duties covers the same items as given in the definition of a trade dispute, listed in Section 10.2.2. The amount of time off is that which is reasonable in the circumstances. There is a relevant Code of Practice issued on this topic (*see* Section 11.4).

An employee has the right to be allowed time off, but not necessarily with pay, to take part in trade union activities, for example, taking part as a representative in official policy-making bodies such as the executive committee or representing the union on external bodies. The activities obviously do not extend to industrial action of any kind. The amount of time off is that which is reasonable in the circumstances. The Code of Practice referred to above is relevant to this right as well. An employee also has the right to be allowed time off, but not necessarily with pay, for a number of public duties. The list includes being a justice of the peace, a councillor, a member of a tribunal, health authority or water authority or a governor or manager of an educational establishment. Time off can be for attending meetings or carrying out the functions of that particular body. Again the amount of time off is that which is reasonable in the circumstances.

If an employer fails to give time off or sufficient time off or to pay, a complaint can be made to a tribunal. Where the employee wins their case the tribunal can order compensation to be paid and, in the case of trade union officials, the pay that is due to them.

10.3.3 Maternity benefits

There are a series of statutory rights that a pregnant woman can claim. These were introduced in the Employment Protection Act 1975, transferred to the Employment Protection (Consolidation) Act 1978 and the rights extended and modified by the Employment Act 1980. The law is now contained in the Trade Union and Labour Relations (Consolidation) Act 1992. There are four basic rights further explained below:

(a) not to be unreasonably refused paid time off for antenatal care;
(b) not to be dismissed by reason of pregnancy;
(c) to receive statutory maternity pay;
(d) to return to work after a period of absence.

(a) The Employment Act 1980 introduced this new right. If a woman has been advised to receive antenatal care, the employer should not unreasonably refuse her paid time off to keep her appointment. If the employer requests it, the woman should produce a certificate to show she is pregnant and show an appointment card. The rate of pay should be at the hourly rate calculated by dividing a week's pay by the normal or average number of hours per week for the period of time off. If the employer refuses to give time off, or pay, then the woman can complain to a tribunal. If the tribunal finds in favour of the woman, it can order compensation to be paid. If there is a refusal to give time off, the woman receives the pay for the period she should have been given off, even if she has been paid for this period. If there is a refusal to pay for time off, the tribunal can award the appropriate amount of pay for the time off taken.

(b) To dismiss a woman for the reason that she is pregnant is an automatically unfair reason. This right not to be unfairly dismissed is subject to some qualifications. The right arises only after two years' continuous employment (or full-time equivalent of working an average of 16 hours per week or an average of 8 hours per week after 5 years' service). A woman can be dismissed by reason of pregnancy where she is incapable of adequately doing her work or if it would be against the law to do that job while pregnant. However, if there is suitable, alternative employment the woman must be offered it and failure to do so renders the dismissal from her original job unfair. Any dismissal, fair or unfair, does not alter the right to receive maternity pay and the right to return to work. If a woman is dismissed by reason of pregnancy, she can take her case to an industrial tribunal in the manner discussed in Section 13.2.2, and may well receive compensation.

(c) Statutory Maternity Pay is payable to a woman who is pregnant, regardless of whether she intends to return to work or not. A woman is eligible if she pays National Insurance contributions, has worked for the employer for 26 weeks and is pregnant 11 weeks prior to the expected week of confinement. The woman can claim payment when she stops work because of her pregnancy and has given her employer notice of taking maternity absence.

The payments are treated as earnings and are payable for a period of up to 18 weeks, but she cannot receive them prior to the eleventh week before the expected confinement. Payment is made automatically for the six weeks prior to confinement, but cannot be received in addition to pay.

There are two rates of maternity pay:

- **Higher** 90% of average weekly earnings for the first six weeks. The other 12 weeks are paid at the lower rate. To be eligible for this higher rate, the woman must have been a full-time employee (or equivalent) for two years.
- **Lower** This is set at £47.95 per week (in 1993) and is paid for 18 weeks, unless the woman is eligible for the higher rate for six weeks.

Failure to pay can lead to a criminal prosecution. Any dispute arising regarding the payment is dealt with by a social security adjudication officer. The woman should use the firm's grievance procedure, where there is one. An appeal against the decision of the officer is made to a social security appeal tribunal.

(d) A woman is entitled to a period of absence from her job and to return to her former job after this absence. This is sometimes incorrectly described as maternity leave. Leave implies the benefits of a contract of employment continuing while away from work, say, like receiving pay. This is not the case for the statutory right of a pregnant woman, but this does not stop her employer paying her during the absence. This

right is given to a woman employed continuously for two years up to the eleventh week before the expected date of confinement, as a full-timer or equivalent, provided that she works up to the eleventh week prior to the expected date of confinement and that she produces a certificate, if requested, of the expected week of confinement. Also the woman has to inform her employer, at least 21 days before the period of absence, that she will be absent from work, that she intends to return to work, and state the expected week of confinement.

Before a woman, who has taken up the right to be absent, can return to work, two sets of correspondence may be required. The employer can write to the woman, not earlier than seven weeks after the notified date of confinement, asking if she still intends to return to work. To maintain her right, the woman must reply within 14 days, or as soon after as is reasonably practicable, that she intends to return to work. Later on the woman must inform her employer, in writing, of her intended date of return at least 21 days before the intended date of return. It is for the woman to decide the actual date of return. It must be within, or up to, 29 weeks after the actual week of confinement. This can be extended by a further four weeks if she is ill and provides medical certificates to show this.

A failure to allow a return to work is in effect dismissal. If her former job has been made redundant then the employer must offer suitable, alternative employment. If the employer does not, the dismissal will be unfair. If the employer cannot, the woman may be entitled to redundancy pay. An employer can claim that it is not reasonably practicable to offer the original job but can make an offer of suitable, alternative employment. If this is accepted, or unreasonably refused, the failure to allow a return to work is not a dismissal. The right to return does not apply to firms employing five or fewer employees, if it is not reasonably practicable to do so. It is for the employer to prove this. A woman who is refused the right to return to work can take her case to an industrial tribunal under a claim for unfair dismissal. Refer to Chapter 13 for details on this and what compensation may be awarded.

10.4   Discrimination in employment

During the 1960s and 1970s there were several Acts of Parliament passed that created the right of an individual not to be discriminated against by being treated differently from others because of that person's race or sex. These Acts had sections relating to employment, including seeking employment. There is also an Act that is specifically aimed at eliminating discrimination between men and women with respect to pay. A further type of discrimination has already been noted, that of the right not to be discriminated against because of trade union membership or nonmembership.

10.4.1   The Race Relations Acts and employment

The rights relating to racial discrimination in employment were created by the Race Relations Act 1968. The current law relating to this is in the Race Relations Act 1976. Discrimination consists of treating someone less favourably than would otherwise be the case. Racial discrimination is when this less favourable treatment is on the grounds of colour, race, nationality or ethnic or national origins. A second type of discrimination is also made unlawful. This is called indirect discrimination where a requirement or condition is applied equally to everyone that is not justifiable in terms of the job, that is to the detriment of someone of that racial group. This is to prevent someone attempting to circumvent the first, direct type of discrimination where underneath there is a motive to discriminate. The Act also specifies victimisation as an act of discrimination. If a person has made a complaint or allegation under the Race Relations Act or has given evidence against a discriminator or to a commission, then to treat less favourably because of that is discrimination.

A number of specified instances are listed which are discriminatory. In employment this can occur in advertising, recruitment or during employment. These include:

- to advertise with an indication of discrimination, even if it is lawful, except for genuine occupational qualifications and positive action
- the arrangements for deciding who will be offered the job
- the terms offered for a job
- the terms offered while in employment
- refusing or deliberately omitting access to, or the way the employer affords access to, opportunities for promotion, transfer, training or other benefits
- dismissal (*see* Chapter 13).

Discrimination, under the Act, can occur in other employment-related areas. These include discriminating against contract workers, in the selection of partners to a partnership, in the admission of membership to a trade union, employers' association, qualifying or professional body, or admittance by a training body or employment agency.

In certain instances it is possible to claim some exceptions from the general right not to be discriminated against. An important exception is if discrimination is necessary to fulfil the requirements of the job. This is called a genuine occupational qualification. There are instances given where this may occur but even then the employer may be challenged to show that the discrimination is necessary. These particular instances include dramatic performances or entertainment, acting as a model for a work of art, picture or film where authenticity is required. If the job involves working where food and drink is provided in a particular setting, a person of a particular racial group may be needed to provide authenticity. To advertise and select a waiter who is Indian for an Indian restaurant is not a discriminatory practice. Also, if a person is providing persons of a racial group with help for their welfare, that person can be of the same group. The exceptions under the heading of genuine occupational qualification apply to recruitment, selection and actions while in employment, in selecting contract workers or partners.

A further circumstance allows for some deviation from the general right not to be discriminated against. This is given in what the Act calls positive action. Discrimination can apply to everyone. It is just as much an offence to refuse a white man a job in order to appoint say an Asian or West Indian to correct a racial imbalance as it is to be discriminatory the other way. 'Reverse discrimination' as this is called, is not allowed under the Act. Everyone has to be given an equal chance, free from discrimination, but direct attempts to redress any racial imbalance in the structure of a workforce are not allowed. Positive action is allowed by certain bodies. Access to training by any body can be discriminatory. If there are no members of a particular racial group, or the proportion is small compared with the proportion in the population as a whole, these bodies can select or provide opportunities especially for that racial group. Employers can also take similar steps but only with respect to training. Discrimination in being selected for work is not allowed, in other words when people are selected for jobs there can be no discrimination as positive action. Trade unions, employers' associations and professional bodies can take steps to encourage members of all racial groups to be represented at all levels of the organisation. Again, these bodies can encourage and provide access to training, but at the point of selection there can be no discrimination.

There are a number of other unlawful discriminatory acts which include:

- **Discriminatory practice** It is unlawful to be involved in applying a discriminatory practice or to operate in such a way that involves such a practice.
- **Instructions to discriminate** It is unlawful to instruct someone to do an act that will break the law.
- **Pressure to discriminate** It is unlawful to induce someone, by giving rewards or issuing threats, to break the law.

The Act also makes it illegal for anyone to publish, or place an advertisement or notice which indicates, or might be taken to indicate, an intention to be discriminatory. Exceptions are given to cover adverts in the area of employment that indicate a genuine occupational qualification (as defined above) or to employment outside Great Britain, or the rules on birth, nationality, descent or residence applying to Crown jobs.

The enforcement of these provisions in all employment-related areas is by complaint to an industrial tribunal. Prior to deciding whether to take such action, the Act provides for a standard form of questions. The person against whom the allegation is made must answer the questions on the form. If the aggrieved person decides to go ahead with a tribunal case, the form can be used in evidence. When application is made to a tribunal, a conciliation officer from ACAS tries to promote a settlement. If there is no settlement, the case proceeds to a tribunal hearing. The applicant has to show there has been discrimination and it is then for the respondent to show that this was not so. If the applicant wins their case, the tribunal can make an order declaring the rights of the party; order compensation to be paid (up to a maximum of £11,000, i.e., the compensatory award under unfair dismissal); or to recommend a particular course of action. If the recommended course of action is not taken, compensation can be awarded. Alleged offences, by an employer, relating to discriminatory advertisements, discriminatory practices or instructions to or pressure to discriminate, can be made to the Commission for Racial Equality. If the Commission believes that there has been a contravention, it can issue a nondiscriminatory notice. This notice requires the person concerned to stop committing the act(s) complained of and to inform the Commission that the required changes have been made. The Commission can also require information to be supplied in relation to the notice.

Before issuing a notice, the Commission must inform the person concerned of its intention to serve such a notice, specifying the grounds, and giving that person the opportunity to make verbal or written representations within a period of not less than 28 days.

An appeal can be made to an industrial tribunal, within six weeks, or to a County Court if the matter is not within the remit of an Industrial Tribunal.

In 1989 there were 839 applications to an industrial tribunal under the Act's provisions. Of these 361 led to a hearing of which 270 had their complaints dismissed and 54 were awarded compensation. The balance of 316 were withdrawn without a hearing and 162 agreed a settlement at the conciliation stage. Of these, 49 cases went on appeal to the Employment Appeals Tribunal. The most frequently made award was in the range £300–£399, with 25 people being awarded compensation.

In addition to the legislation, the Commission for Racial Equality has issued a Code of Practice entitled 'Code of Practice for the Elimination of Racial Discrimination and the Promotion of Equality of Opportunity in Employment'. Extracts from this appear in Section 11.7.

10.4.2 The Sex Discrimination Act and employment

A very similar set of rights to those on racial discrimination are also given so that people are not discriminated against on the grounds of sex or marital status. The law relating to this is found in the Sex Discrimination Act 1975 and amended by the Sex Discrimination Act 1986 and the Employment Act 1989. The Act makes discrimination that favours either men or women unlawful, but the Act, and this section, refers to discrimination against women. The reverse is always true, except where favourable treatment is given to a woman because of pregnancy or childbirth. Discrimination occurs when a woman is treated less favourably than a man on grounds of her sex. This can be explicit or implicit. A second type of discrimination is also made unlawful. This is called indirect discrimination where a requirement or condition is applied equally to men and women that is not justifiable, say in terms of the job, that is to the detriment of the woman. This is to eliminate attempts to circumvent the direct discrimination but where there is an underlying motive to discriminate. In complaints of discrimination the woman has to compare herself to a man in similar circum-

stances. If the employer, or whoever, treats men and women the same, regardless of sex, there is no discrimination. The rules of discrimination also apply to married people, in that they have the right not to be discriminated against on the grounds that they are married. The Act also specifies that victimisation is also an act of discrimination. If a person has made a complaint or allegation under the Sex Discrimination Act or the Equal Pay Act, or has given evidence against a discriminator, then to treat that person less favourably is discrimination.

A number of specified instances are listed which are discriminatory. In employment this can occur in advertising, recruitment or during employment. These include:

- to advertise with an indication of discrimination, except for a genuine occupational qualification and positive action
- the arrangements for deciding who will be offered a job
- the terms offered for the job
- refusing or deliberately omitting to offer employment
- refusing or deliberately omitting to afford access to opportunities for promotion, training, transfer or other benefits, facilities or services
- dismissal (*see* Chapter 13).

Discrimination under the Act can occur in other employment-related areas. These include discriminating against contract workers, in the selection of partners to a partnership, in the admission of membership to a trade union, employers' association, qualifying or professional body or admittance by a training body or employment agency.

In certain circumstances it is possible to claim some exceptions from the general right not to be discriminated against. Certain occupations are exempt like midwifery, ministers of religion and the armed forces. The Act now applies to all firms, regardless of size and to private households, except if there is a genuine occupational qualification. Amendments to the Act are made for the police force and prison service. An important exception is claiming that discrimination is necessary because of the nature of the job. Where a person's sex is a 'genuine occupational qualificaton' for the job the employer can discriminate in giving access to the job or training for it. This occurs where:

- for reasons of physiology (not strength or stamina) or for reasons of authenticity, for example in dramatic performances or entertainment a person of a particular sex is required
- to preserve decency or privacy or where the job involves close physical contact and there might be a reasonable objection to a person of the opposite sex
- the job is in a private home and there could be reasonable objections based on close physical contact or knowing a person's intimate details, to a person of the opposite sex
- the job is in a location where the employer can only provide single sex accommodation
- the job is in a single sex prison or hospital
- there is a need for certain welfare or educational services to be provided by a particular sex
- the job involves duties outside the UK where the laws or customs preclude a person of a particular sex.

These exceptions do not apply to discrimination against married people or victimisation, but they do apply to the selection of contract workers or the selection of partners. There are two circumstances in which it is not unlawful for employers to discriminate. These are giving special treatment to women in connection with pregnancy and childbirth, and any provisions relating to death. The Sex Discrimination Act 1986 removed any discrimination in respect of retirement, so women are entitled to retire at the same age as men. The Employment Act 1989 provided that women can claim redundancy payment up to the age of 65, if that is the normal age of retirement.

A further circumstance allows for some deviation from the general right not to be discriminated against. This is given in what the Act refers to as positive action. 'Reverse discrimination' is not allowed, so that an employer cannot pursue a policy of employing more women to correct any imbalance in the workforce. Positive action is allowed by certain bodies. Access to training by any body can be discriminatory. Such bodies can also provide training for married women with a grown family to enable them to return to work. Employers can, where the number of persons of one sex is comparatively small, discriminate in providing training for the minority sex. However, discrimination in selecting for jobs is not allowed. Trade unions and employers' associations can take steps to encourage membership if the numbers of one sex are particularly low and to train such people for holding posts in the organisation. Reserved seats on committees or councils are not discriminatory.

There are a number of other unlawful discriminatory acts. These include:

- **Discriminatory practice**   It is unlawful to be involved in applying a discriminatory practice or to operate in such a way that involves such a practice.
- **Instructions to discriminate**   It is unlawful to instruct someone to do an act that will break the law.
- **Pressure to discriminate**   It is unlawful to induce someone, by giving rewards or issuing threats, to break the law.

Sexual harassment is not specifically mentioned but it could be classified as unlawful under the Act. Harassment is taken to mean behaviour intended to embarrass, humiliate or threaten a member of the opposite sex. It can include physical advances, verbal abuse or nonverbal gestures. The basis of the claim would be that a person of the opposite sex would not have been treated in that way in the same circumstances and that this treatment has led to some loss, such as disciplinary action, dismissal, transfer or failure to promote or train.

The Act also makes it unlawful for anyone to publish, or place an advertisement which indicates, or might be taken to indicate, discrimination. Exceptions are given to cover adverts, in the case of employment, that indicate a genuine occupational qualification. An advertisement that uses a description that indicates sex, is unlawful, for example, salesman indicates male, stewardess female. The advertisement should contain an indication to the contrary, by using the alternative form, for example, salesperson or by saying the job is open to both sexes. The Employment Act 1989 provides that it is not discriminatory to provide specified special treatment for lone parents. Otherwise this would be discriminatory against married couples.

The enforcement of these provisions in all employment-related areas is by complaint to an industrial tribunal. Prior to deciding whether or not to take such action, the Act provides a standard form of questions. The person against whom the allegation is made must answer the questions on the form. If the aggrieved person decides to go ahead with a tribunal case, the form can be used in evidence. When application is made to a tribunal, a conciliation officer from ACAS tries to promote a settlement. If a settlement is not possible, the case proceeds to a tribunal hearing. The applicant has to show that there has been discrimination and it is for the respondent to show that this was not so. If the applicant wins the case, the tribunal can make an order declaring the rights of the parties; an order for compensation to be paid (up to a maximum of £11,000, i.e., the compensatory award under unfair dismissal); or to recommend a particular course of action. If the recommended course of action is not taken, compensation can be awarded. Alleged offences by an employer relating to discriminatory advertisements, discriminatory practices or instructions to or pressure to discriminate, can be made to the Equal Opportunities Commission. If the Commission believes that there has been a contravention, it can issue a nondiscriminatory notice. This notice requires the person concerned to stop committing the act(s) complained of and to inform the Commission that the required changes have been made. The Commission can also require information to be supplied in relation to the notice. Before issuing a notice, the Commission must inform the person concerned of its intention to serve such a notice, specifying the grounds, and giving that person the opportunity to make verbal or written representations within a period of not less than 28 days. An appeal can be made to an industrial tribunal, within six weeks or to a County Court if the matter is not within the remit of an industrial tribunal.

In 1989 there were 935 applications to an industrial tribunal under the Act's provisions. Of these 300 led to a hearing of which 172 had their complaints dismissed and 78 were successful. A balance of 269 were withdrawn without a hearing and 366 agreed a settlement at the conciliation stage. In 42 cases compensation was awarded. The most frequently made award was in the range £200–£299. In 34 cases, the result was that they went on appeal to the Employment Appeals Tribunal.

In addition to the legislation, the Equal Opportunities Commission has issued a Code of Practice. This is entitled 'Code of practice, equal opportunity policies, procedures and practices in employment'. Extracts from this appear in Section 11.8.

10.4.3 Equal Pay Act

Prior to the Sex Discrimination Act 1975, there was an Act on the statute book relating to sex discrimination in matters relating to pay and other terms and conditions of employment. The Equal Pay Act 1970 (which did not come into force until late 1975) provided men and women with the right to equal pay and conditions where the work is the same or of a broadly similar nature. This has subsequently been amended by the Equal Pay (Amendment) Regulations 1983, the Sex Discrimination Act 1986 and the Wages Act 1986. While the title of the Act refers to 'pay', the object of the Act is to eliminate discrimination between men and women in the terms and conditions under which they are employed. Hence, differences in holiday entitlement between men and women could well be discriminatory under this Act and not merely items relating to remuneration.

The Act creates an implied term of equality which is included in every contract of employment. This states that where there is a term favourable to one sex, it shall apply equally to the other sex, or if there is a term that benefits a man on like work, or work rated as equivalent, the term shall apply to a woman.

The Act applies to all employees of all ages, full or part-time. The general rule now is that statutory requirements should not be discriminatory, and the Secretary of State for Employment has the power to remove such restrictions. Indeed, several have been removed, such as the restrictions under the Factories Acts relating to a woman's hours of work. One or two remain, such as the special treatment afforded to women in respect of pregnancy and childbirth. Notably, the original legislation allowed discrimination as regards 'retirement', i.e., women generally were required to retire at 60 and men at 65. In the case of *Marshall* v *South West Hampshire Area Health Authority* (1986), a nurse claimed the right to stay on at work after reaching the age of 60. The Authority claimed that 60 was the normal retirement age and they would not employ her beyond that age. Miss Marshall took her case to the European Court of Justice on a claim for equal treatment as laid down in an EC Directive on Equal Treatment. She won her case and subsequently UK legislation was amended. However, the law still only requires equal treatment in respect of retirement, i.e., a woman can retire at the same age as a man; there is no legal requirement to provide a pension to men and women at the same age. There must be equal treatment in terms of access to occupational pension schemes.

The basis of a claim is that a woman is being discriminated against, by her employer, in comparison with a male employee, employed by the same employer (or an associated employer). Usually this will mean employment at the same establishment unless there are common terms and conditions applying at different locations of the same employer. If a term exists for men only, then that term is automatically extended to women. If there is a term that is less favourable to women, then the more favourable term applying to men is automatically given to women, too. The only defence that an employer

can use is that the difference is justified on grounds other than sex.

The basis for comparison that can be used is:

- **Like work** This is where a woman is employed to do the same work as a man or it is of a broadly similar nature, i.e., the differences are not of any practical importance.
- **Work rated as equivalent** Where job evaluation techniques have been used, the results of this can be used as a basis for a claim of equality. If the study showed a material difference, then there would be no claim, unless the job evaluation exercise was, in itself, discriminatory. This is examined in Chapter 17. If the job evaluation exercise was discriminatory, the woman could make a claim for 'work of equal value' (*see below*).
- **Work of equal value** A woman can claim that her work is of equal value to a man's, even though it is not the same. In such cases a claim is made to an Industrial Tribunal which hears evidence from an independent expert to determine if the jobs being compared are equal in value. If they are, and the employer makes no acceptable counter-claim for a 'material difference', the Tribunal will uphold the claim. For example, a woman may be able to show that her job is of equal value to that of another job held by a higher-paid male colleague. The employer can claim that, because of recruitment difficulties, the job held by the man has to be paid at a higher rate. Where there is a claim for equal pay and the employer does not agree with it, the matter can be taken to an Industrial Tribunal. The claim can be made while the person is in their job or at any time afterwards. On application to a tribunal, the matter is referred to a conciliation officer of ACAS to see if a settlement can be promoted. If there is no conciliated settlement, the case is referred to a tribunal. If the claimant is successful, the tribunal can award two years' back pay and damages in compensation for non-cash benefits. In 1984, there were 70 applications to an Industrial Tribunal under

the Act's provisions. Of these, 24 led to a hearing of which 13 had their complaints dismissed and 11 were upheld. The balance of 31 were withdrawn without a hearing and 15 agreed a settlement at the conciliation stage. By contrast, in 1988, there were 1,043 applications. Of these 204 led to a hearing, of which 197 had their complaints dismissed and seven were upheld. The balance of 750 was withdrawn without a hearing and 89 agreed a settlement at the conciliation stage. Of these, 14 cases went on appeal to the Employment Appeals Tribunal.

10.5   Rights of a trade union member

Many pieces of employment law legislation have contained rights which are given specifically to members of a trade union. This is particularly true of the Employment Acts 1988 and 1989. The government believes there is a need to balance the power of trade union leaders, or provide a check to this power, by conferring legal rights on the individual member. The thrust of much of the 1980s legislation is to make unions more democratic in their operations and to be accountable to their members. A parallel development is to give the members the right to act in situations where the union is not implementing the legal requirements imposed on it. There are also safeguards given, to any member taking action against their own union, not to be victimised. The following rights are given to trade union members under various enactments:

- Not to have action taken against them by the employer, to prevent or deter them from becoming a trade union member.
- Not to have action taken against them, by the employer, to prevent or deter them from taking part in trade union activities.
- There is an implied term in the contract of trade union membership that the member has the right to terminate membership.
- In a closed shop situation there is a right not to be unreasonably expelled from a specific

trade union. The fact that the union has acted in accordance with its own rules does not necessarily make the action reasonable. A complaint can be made to an industrial tribunal (if the member has been readmitted) or to the Employment Appeals Tribunal (if the member has not been readmitted). The maximum compensation in an IT is £16,150 and in the EAT it is £26,810 (1993). The rule is to prevent union expulsion effectively causing someone to lose their job. An employee dismissed in this circumstance can claim unfair dismissal automatically. However, this may well change as there are proposals to virtually ban closed shops.
- Not to be unjustifiably disciplined by the trade union for specified action, like failing to support or take part in a strike or industrial action, or for alleging that a union representative has acted unlawfully. Discipline includes fines, expulsion or withholding benefits. This rule is designed to enable workers to act freely and in line with their conscience or wishes and not to be cajoled, pressurised or threatened by their union. A complaint can be made to an industrial tribunal (if the disciplinary measure has been reversed) or to the Employment Appeals Tribunal (if the disciplinary measure has not been reversed).
- The right to be balloted before industrial action. If the union authorises or endorses industrial action without holding a proper ballot (*see* Section 10.2.2) the member can seek a court order requiring the union to withdraw its order and to ensure members are not induced to take industrial action.
- A trade union member can apply to the Commissioner for the Rights of Trade Union Members for assistance to take legal action against a union in the previous item above or in relation to political fund ballots or the use of union funds or property (*see* Section 4.3.4).
- A member has the right to access their union's electoral roll, to ensure that it is accurate.
- A member has the right to inspect the union's accounting records and to be accompanied by an accountant.

- A member can take legal action against the union's trustees if they use or permit the use of union funds for an unlawful purpose, even if the direction by or to the trustees has been made under the union's rules.
- Time off work is allowed for trade union officials (*see* Section 10.3.2).
- To vote in the election of the members of the union's principal executive committee.

The rights of trade union members against the excesses of union officials has been brought into focus with the publication of the Lightman report in 1990 into the use of the National Union of Mineworkers' funds during the 1984 dispute.

Certain sums of money were collected at home and abroad to support the miners in their dispute. Complications arose because the union's official funds had been frozen by a court sequestration order and the officials did not have access to their normal accounts. However, the money collected abroad was kept in new bank accounts in various countries away from the authorities but which the NUM could access to support its members. The report cleared the officials of any serious misconduct (there had been accusations of personal gain and benefit) but there were criticisms that the union's executive committee were not kept informed and the members were oblivious of the actions of the officials. This is in contravention of the union's rules and is against the court rules of equity.

The officials concerned were issued with a writ, by NUM members, demanding the money (a total of £1.4m) kept in other accounts, with the International Miners' Organisation, that was collected from abroad for the dispute, be frozen until a court decides who should have the money.

The argument, of the NUM members, was that the money belongs to the NUM as it was collected to support their dispute. There is concern that all this was done without the knowledge or consent of the executive committee or members. This runs counter to the rules of accountability of trade union officials to their members. In the end there was an out-of-court agreement made so the case never reached the courts.

Mini-questions

10.1 Explain the difference between an incorporated association and an unincorporated association.

10.2 Describe what a legal immunity is.

10.3 State whether the legal immunities given cover employees who go on strike.

10.4 Explain the term 'in restraint of trade' with respect to a union's activities.

10.5 State three torts that a trade union official could commit in organising a strike.

10.6 Distinguish between primary and secondary industrial action.

10.7 State the meaning of the term 'official industrial action'.

10.8 List five areas of dispute that are covered by the term 'trade dispute'.

10.9 Distinguish between the functions for which *paid* time off work can be claimed and those for which time off can be claimed.

10.10 List the four rights given to a woman in respect of maternity benefits.

10.11 Calculate the maximum period a woman can be absent because of a pregnancy.

10.12 Define discrimination.

10.13 List four instances in employment where an act may be discriminatory.

10.14 Explain what a 'genuine occupational qualification' is. Illustrate your answer with two examples.

10.15 Define 'reverse discrimination' and state if this is legal or not.

10.16 Name three occupations exempt from the provisions of the Sex Discrimination Act 1975.

10.17 Define what 'positive action' is. Illustrate your answer with two examples.

10.18 Explain the principle underlying the Equal Pay Act 1970.

10.19 State if only women are given rights under the Equal Pay Act 1970.

10.20 What is the basis for a claim for equal pay under the Equal Pay Act 1970?

Exercises

10.1 Explain the likely state of affairs today if unions operated as they do now but were not given any legal immunities for their actions.

10.2 Describe how the common law doctrine of 'restraint of trade' affected trade unions in the nineteenth century. State the position regarding this today.

10.3 There are several limitations to the immunities given to individuals for their trade union activities. State the principal immunity and its limitations. What is the situation for acts committed outside this immunity?

10.4 Discuss the connections between unfair dismissal, dismissal by reason of pregnancy, the right to return to work and redundancy.

10.5 Explain the basic right of a person not to be discriminated against in employment on the grounds of race, instancing where this might occur. Discuss the exceptions that exist.

Further reading

K W Wedderburn, *The Worker and the Law*, Sweet and Maxwell, 1986, 0-421-37060-2

G Morris and T Archer, *Trade Unions, Employers and the Law*, Blackwell, 0-632-02966-8

M Winchup, *Modern Employment Law*, Butterworth, 1991, 0-7506-0335-6

B Titman and P Camp, *Individual Employment Law*, Sweet and Maxwell, 1989, 0-421-40660-7

N Selwyn, *Law of Employment*, Butterworth, 1991, 0-406-50455-5

11
Codes of Practice

While Codes of Practice are not strictly speaking law, they do have some legal force. They are official guidelines relating to a topic, often made under the authority of an Act of Parliament, that can be used in evidence in a court or tribunal to show that the law has not been complied with. Codes have the advantage that they are flexible and, being written in plain rather than legal English, are easy to understand. Codes are also helpful in giving practical meaning to words often used in legislation like 'reasonable', 'reasonably practicable' or 'unreasonable'. Currently there are eight official Codes in existence:

1   Code of Practice on Industrial Relations (withdrawn)
2   Code of Practice on Disciplinary Practice and Procedures in Employment
3   Code of Practice on the Disclosure of Information to Trade Unions for Collective Bargaining Purposes
4   Code of Practice on Time Off for Trade Union Duties and Activities
5   Code of Practice on Closed Shop Agreements and Arrangements
6   Code of Practice on Picketing
7   Code of Practice for the Elimination of Racial Discrimination and the Promotion of Equality of Opportunity in Employment
8   Code of Practice, Equal Opportunity Policies, Procedures and Practices in Employment
9   Code of Practice on Trade Union Ballots on Industrial Action.

The chapter gives a précis of these Codes but does not reproduce them in full. As with all official documents (including legislation) anyone requiring the exact wording should refer to the source document, not a possible plagiarisation or adaptation. Also, some of the Codes are quite long and would take up a disproportionate amount of room. The most important and relevant sections have been included, often in a condensed form. At appropriate points comments are included which are not part of the Codes.

11.1   Code of Practice on Industrial Relations

This Code was issued under the Industrial Relations Act 1971 but was maintained as an official Code when the Act was repealed in 1974. Some sections were superseded by the three Codes examined in Sections 11.2, 11.3 and 11.4. The Code was revoked in 1991 but is still pertinent and is retained in this chapter. The Code is quite extensive and covers most aspects of workplace industrial relations. This section is a précis of the main points and follows the sections of the Code.

Introduction

The Code gives practical guidance for promoting good industrial relations based on the principles of freely conducted collective bargaining, orderly procedures for settling disputes, free association of workers and employers and freedom and security for workers. The Code has two main themes, the vital role of collective bargaining and good human relations between employer and employee. Good industrial relations is a joint responsibility and needs the cooperation of all concerned.

Responsibilities

Management has the aim of conducting the business of an undertaking successfully. This includes industrial relations which should be given as much attention as other functions. The primary responsibility for the promotion of good industrial relations lies with management in taking the initiative to create and develop it. Where trade unions are recognised, management should maintain arrangements for negotiations, consultations and communications and for settling grievances and disputes; take steps to ensure that agreements are observed and procedures used; and make clear to employees that it welcomes their membership of a union and their participation in the union's activities. Effective organisation of work is an important factor in good industrial relations. Management should ensure that responsibility for each group of workers is clearly defined, each manager understands their responsibilities and has the authority and training necessary to do the job and employees and work groups know their objectives and priorities. All managers should receive training in the industrial relations implications of their job. The supervisor is a key post in the organisation and management should ensure that he or she is properly selected and trained, is in charge of a group of a size that can be supervised effectively, is fully briefed in advance of management's policies and that there is an effective link in the line of communications.

Trade unions have as their aim the promotion of their members' interests. They can only do this if the business prospers and they have an interest in the success of the undertaking. Trade unions should maintain arrangements for negotiations, consultations and communications and for settling grievances and disputes, take steps to ensure that their officials observe agreements and use procedures and maintain procedures for resolving inter-union disputes. Trade unions should encourage their officials to understand the policies and rules of the union, their powers and duties, and to be trained adequately.

Comment **The basis of good industrial relations is that management should manage the system. It is their prime responsibility and they should provide the requisite leadership. This involves the development of policies and the implementation of these. There is also a clear emphasis that adequate training be given.**

The role of trade unions is seen as working within the system and being cooperative. There is an emphasis on agreements and ensuring that these are used and adhered to.

Employment policies

Clear and comprehensive employment policies are essential. Management should initiate these policies in consultation with the employees' representatives. Human resource planning should look at existing staff resources, work out future needs and take steps to ensure that the needs are met. In operating its policies, management should avoid unnecessary fluctuations, cause as little disruption as possible and make arrangements for transfers. In recruitment and selection, management should decide on the qualifications and experience needed by candidates, consider transfer or promotion, base selection on suitability for the job and explain the main terms and conditions of employment and give relevant information regarding trade union arrangements before the applicant is engaged.

In the area of training, management should ensure that new employees are given induction training, any additional training necessary and ensure that young people are given broader initial training. Management should ensure that any further education and training is given when the content of the job changes and encourage employees to take advantage of relevant training and further education.

Responsibility for deciding the size of the workforce rests with management. Before taking the final decision to make substantial reductions, management should consult employees or their representatives. Redundancies should be avoided by restricting recruitment, retirement of those over retirement age, reduction of overtime, retraining or transfer and short-time working. If redundancy is necessary, management, in consultation with employees or their representatives, should give as much warning as possible, introduce schemes for voluntary redundancy, retirement and transfer, establish who is to be made redundant, give time off to find other work and decide when to make the facts public after telling the employees.

Comment This section provides more detail on the need for comprehensive policies to be laid down by management and it suggests several areas where these should be developed. Management should be proactive and lead. If there is no leadership from management, then the trade unions will fill that gap. There are many examples where industrial relations practice has developed on the basis of custom, with the power being exercised by the trade unions in the workplace. The Code, however, stresses the need for consultation. Decisions are made by management but the workforce, via the trade unions, should be consulted.

Communication and consultation

These are essential to promote efficiency and understanding. They are very important in times of change and major changes in working practices should not be made without prior discussion. There should be a two-way flow of information to and from employees. The most important method of communication is word of mouth but this should be supplemented by written information, training and meetings. Management should ensure that managers and supervisors regard it as their principal duty to explain management's policies and intentions and provide opportunities for employees to discuss matters affecting their jobs; managers must be kept informed of the views of employees.

Management should ensure that all employees receive a written statement of their terms and conditions of employment, especially to fulfil the legal requirements of the Employment Protection (Consolidation) Act 1978. Consultation is a process of jointly examining and discussing problems and seeking mutually acceptable solutions. Management should take the initiative in setting up and maintaining consultative arrangements but this should not be used to bypass or discourage trade unions. In setting up

arrangements, management should ensure that arrangements provide employees with the opportunity to express their views on proposed changes that affect them, that all the information required is given and there are effective means of reporting back to employees. Where committees are set up there should be agreement on the composition, objectives and functions of the committee, the arrangements for the nomination or election of representatives, the rules of procedure and the range of subjects to be discussed.

Comment The requirements for information for the purposes of collective bargaining has been subsequently expanded in a further Code of Practice (*see* Section 11.3). There is no stated position so far as industrial democracy is concerned, but the model on which the Code is based is one of joint consultation, using trade unions where they are present, but that it is management's right to decide. In other words, the Code falls short of suggesting joint decision making. There should be no change without discussion and consultation.

Collective bargaining

This establishes a framework between management and employees. It requires a reasonable and constructive approach in negotiation and a determination to abide by agreements from both sides. Where negotiations take place at more than one level, the matters to be bargained about at each level should be defined by agreement. Collective bargaining is conducted in relation to a defined group which can be covered by one negotiation process. These are called bargaining units and should cover as wide a group of employees as practicable. The interests of employees covered by a bargaining unit need not be identical but there should be a substantial degree of common interest.

A trade union may claim recognition for negotiating purposes. Management should take into account the extent of support for the claim among the employees and the effect of granting recognition on existing bargaining procedures. Management is entitled to know the number of employees who are members of the union making the claim. If the extent of the support cannot be agreed it should be determined by ballot. Responsibility for avoiding disputes between trade unions about recognition lies principally with the unions themselves. After recognition relations between management and trade unions which are recognised should be based on agreed procedures that provide clear rules and procedures. Managements should agree on the provision of reasonable facilities for unions to keep in touch with their members and to represent them effectively. Collective agreements deal with matters of procedure and substance. They should be in writing and there should be arrangements for checking that the procedures have not become out of date. Procedural provisions should lay down the matters to be bargained, arrangements for negotiating terms and conditions, the circumstances in which either party can give notice to renegotiate, facilities for trade union activities and the appointment, status and function of shop stewards, procedures for settling collective disputes and individual grievances and the constitution and scope of any consultative committees. Substantive provisions should cover wages, salaries, overtime rates, bonuses, piecework, hours of work, holiday entitlement and pay. Agreements may also cover techniques for determining levels of performance and job grading, procedures for handling redundancies and lay-offs, guaranteed pay, sick pay, pensions and the deduction of trade union contributions.

Comment The Code confirms the central position of collective bargaining in industrial relations and the role of negotiation in arriving at agreements which both sides will adhere to. Trade union recognition is not taken for granted and claims for recognition should be accompanied by substantial support from among the workforce – ballots being mentioned in this context.

The need for written agreements is underlined and the Code supports the idea of having procedural agreements and substantive agreements (*see* Chapter 7). It should be remembered that this Code was originally issued in the early 1970s, soon after the publication of the Donovan Report

which concluded that there was a great need for the development of clear, written agreements in British industrial relations.

Employee representatives at the workplace

Employees need representatives at the workplace to put forward their collective views to management. It is an advantage for management to deal with representatives who can speak for their fellow employees. This is widely done by accredited union representatives who act on behalf of union members – they are usually called shop stewards. The trade union should provide for their election, define the manner in which they can be removed from office and specify their powers and duties within the union. A shop steward's functions cover trade union matters like recruitment, maintaining membership and collecting contributions and industrial relations matters like handling members' grievances, negotiations and consultations. A shop steward should observe all agreements and take steps to ensure that those represented observe them. Trade unions and management should agree on the number of shop stewards and the groups they will represent. To encourage trade union members to vote in elections of shop stewards, management should offer the trade union the facilities to conduct these elections. Trade unions should notify management in writing when shop stewards are appointed and give their shop stewards written credentials that set out their powers, the period of office and the groups they represent. Where there are a number of shop stewards, they should consider electing a senior shop steward to coordinate their activities. Where there are a number of unions with a small membership, the unions should seek to elect one shop steward to represent all the unions.

Grievance and disputes procedures

All employees have the right to seek redress for any grievance, and they must be told how they can do so. Management should establish, with the trade unions, arrangements for raising grievances and having them settled fairly and promptly, preferably through a formal procedure. Individual grievance procedures should aim to settle the grievance fairly and as near as possible to the point of origin. Procedures should be simple and rapid in operation. Procedures should be in writing and provide that the grievance be discussed first between the employee and immediate superior, that the employee can be accompanied by a representative at the next stage and should be provided with the right of appeal.

Collective disputes procedures are two kinds: disputes of right relating to the application or interpretation of existing agreements or disputes of interest relating to claims by employees or proposals by management about terms and conditions of employment. The procedure should be in writing and state the level at which an issue should first be raised, lay down time limits for each stage and preclude any form of industrial action until all stages have been completed and a failure to agree recorded. Independent conciliation or arbitration can be used to settle all types of dispute.

Comment **An important aspect of any system of industrial relations is the need to provide for the resolution of grievances and disputes. There should be a procedural agreement which employees should know about. There is now a requirement for employees to be told about this in their statement of terms of employment (which employers are required to issue by law).**

The Code recognises two kinds of dispute: those of right and those of interest. Again agreements should provide for the resolution of both kinds of dispute. This categorisation of disputes is often recognised and can be useful in deciding if the dispute is one relating to existing agreements or is a new claim. Some systems do not delineate between the two.

The next three Codes were issued later than the code on Industrial Relations. They were issued under the Employment Protection Act 1975 and came into force during 1977. They elaborate on certain sections of the Code on Industrial Relations which the later Codes supersede, and the second and third Codes also expand on

certain rights given in the Employment Protection Act 1975.

11.2   Code of Practice on Disciplinary Practice and Procedures in Employment

This Code of Practice was issued in 1977 by ACAS under the authority given to it in the Employment Protection Act 1975 to issue Codes of Practice. This Code is relevant particularly to unfair dismissal claims made in industrial tribunals and it gives practical advice on disciplinary procedures. The Code is laid out in paragraphs under section headings. The following is a précis of the Code.

Why have disciplinary rules and procedures?

Disciplinary rules and procedures are necessary for promoting fairness and order in the treatment of individuals and the conduct of industrial relations. Rules set standards of conduct; procedures help ensure that the standards are adhered to and provide a fair method of dealing with alleged offences. It is important that employees know these rules and procedures and the Trade Union and Labour Relations (Consolidation) Act 1992 requires employers to provide written information regarding this. The rules and procedures are also important with respect to unfair dismissal.

Comment **The Code emphasises the need for explicit rules and a written agreement as the basis for good practice on discipline. Both are necessary. This links with the need for formal, written agreements in industrial relations. There is now a requirement for employees to be told about the disciplinary procedure in the statement of their terms of employment that they should receive from their employer (as a legal right).**

Formulating policy

Management is responsible for maintaining discipline and ensuring that there are adequate rules and procedures. The initiative for establishing these lies with management but if they are to be effective they need to be accepted as reasonable by those to whom they apply and those who operate them. Management should involve employees and all levels of management when formulating the rules and procedures. Trade union officials should be involved, particularly in agreeing procedural arrangements.

Comment **Again a Code emphasises the need for management leadership in this field. They should provide the rules and ensure that there is a procedure, although they should ensure that these should be acceptable to those affected by them. This Code uses the word 'involvement' but does not express an opinion on how this might be achieved. In some instances trade unions will say that it is for management to state the rules, but the procedural agreement should be negotiated between union *and* management.**

Rules

These will vary according to circumstances. Rules should be drawn up to specify those needed for efficient, safe working and for the maintenance of satisfactory relationships at the workplace. Rules should be readily available and management should make every effort to ensure that employees know and understand them. This may be best achieved by giving every employee a copy of the rules and should be part of the induction programme for new employees. Employees should be made aware of the likely consequences of breaking rules and especially of the conduct that may warrant summary dismissal.

Essential features of disciplinary procedures

Disciplinary procedures should not only be a means of imposing sanctions but should emphasise improvements of individual conduct. The procedure should be in writing, specify to whom it applies and provide for matters to be dealt with quickly. It should indicate the disciplinary actions that can be taken and the levels of management that have the authority to take the various forms of disciplinary action.

Individuals should be informed of the complaint against them, have an opportunity to state their case, and have the right to be accompanied by a trade union representative or fellow employee. The procedure should ensure that, except for gross misconduct, no employee is dismissed for a first breach of discipline, that action is not taken until the case has been investigated, that individuals are given an explanation for any penalty imposed and the procedure should provide a right of appeal.

The procedure in operation

When a disciplinary matter arises the supervisor or manager should establish the facts promptly. In serious cases consideration should be given to a brief period of suspension with pay while the matter is investigated. Before a decision is made, employees should be given the opportunity to state their case. Where disciplinary action is called for the procedure should be first to give a formal, oral warning, or for more serious offences a written warning. The next stage is a final written warning and the final stage disciplinary transfer, suspension without pay or dismissal, depending on the nature of the offence and the likely consequences of further offences. A right of appeal should be given at each stage and employees told how to make it and to whom. Special consideration should be given to employees on night shifts or in remote locations. Disciplinary action against trade union officials has to be handled carefully. Normal disciplinary standards apply to them as employees but the matter should be discussed with a senior trade union representative or full-time official. Criminal offences outside of employment should not be treated as automatic reasons for dismissal. The main consideration should be whether the offences make the employee unsuitable for that type of work.

Comment **This section and the previous one state the very vital practical aspects of a disciplinary procedure. Frequently in Industrial Tribunal cases relating to unfair dismissal, the employer has a fair reason for dismissal but the manner of the** dismissal is found to be defective (and the employee wins the case). If the sound practical advice of this section were followed, this would not occur so frequently.

A written procedure can often help, where all the parties concerned know what the procedure is and can adhere to it.

A further implication is that, if a case of discipline is badly handled, it has a deleterious effect on employee relations. If a fellow worker has been (in their eyes) badly treated, the group's morale will fall. Following the practical advice given here can avoid this pitfall.

Appeals

If the final decision within the organisation is contested, it might be appropriate to use the external stages of the grievance procedure and also when a disciplinary matter becomes a collective issue between union and management. Independent arbitration might be used as the means of resolving disciplinary issues.

Records

These should be kept, detailing the breach of rules, the action taken and reasons for it and whether an appeal was lodged and its outcome. Normally breaches of rules should be disregarded after a specified period of satisfactory conduct.

Further action

Rules and procedures should be reviewed periodically in the light of changes and revised to ensure continuing relevance and effectiveness. Any amendments and additional rules should be introduced only after reasonable notice to employees and their representatives.

11.3 Code of Practice on the Disclosure of Information to Trade Unions for Collective Bargaining Purposes

This Code was issued by ACAS in 1977. It gives practical guidance on the sections of the Employ-ment Protection Act 1975 (now contained in the Trade Union and Labour Relations (Consolidation) Act 1992) that give the legal right to independent trade unions to be given certain information in collective bargaining. The Act specified that employers may have a duty to disclose information that would be in accordance with good industrial relations practice. The provisions of the Code are relevant to this. The following is a précis of the Code.

Provisions of the Act

The Act places a duty on employers to disclose, at all stages of collective bargaining, information required by representatives of independent trade unions. The information requested has to be in the employer's possession and must relate to the employer's undertaking. The information that should be disclosed is that without which the trade union representatives would be impeded to a material extent in bargaining and which it would be in accordance with good industrial relations practice to disclose. No employer need disclose information that:

- would be against the national interest
- would be illegal to disclose
- was given in confidence
- relates to an individual
- that would cause substantial injury to the undertaking (except in its effect on industrial relations)
- was obtained for legal proceedings.

In providing the information, the employer is not required to compile or assemble information that would entail work out of all proportion to its value in bargaining. The union can require that the information be given or confirmed in writing. Failure to disclose can lead to a complaint to the Central Arbitration Committee. If the complaint is well-founded, the CAC can order disclosure. If this order is not obeyed, the CAC can make an award that has the effect of altering the terms and conditions of the contract of employment as the CAC considers appropriate.

Comment The need to provide more information, particularly during negotiations, has been contended for many years, particularly by trade unions. The argument from the unions is that they are in a position of disadvantage in bargaining as much of the information relating to a claim is held by management. If it does not disclose the information, or is selective, the unions cannot sensibly discuss the issues. Also, where information is not given, then suspicions are aroused and the element of trust, so vital to good negotiations, is lost.

In some companies, management also recognises that trade unions need adequate information to help the process of bargaining. To provide information builds up trust and cooperation and allows for informed, intelligent discussion. The usual proviso is that commercially sensitive information will not be disclosed.

By providing information, the process of collective bargaining will be strengthened because decision making will be more rational and the greater openness engendered by the disclosure of information will build up trust and confidence. To strengthen collective bargaining can only be good for industrial relations as the whole system is based on this process.

Providing information

The absence of relevant information may impede a trade union in collective bargaining, especially if the information would influence the formulation, presentation or pursuance of a claim. To determine what information will be relevant, negotiators should take into account the subject matter of the negotiations, the issues raised, the level of negotiations (department, plant, division or company) and the size of the company. Collective bargaining can range from negotiations on specific topics to those covering the terms and conditions of employment. The relevant information will vary according to the circumstances. These could include:

- **Pay** Structure of the payment system, job evaluation, earnings analysis, total pay bill, fringe benefits, and non-labour costs.
- **Conditions of service** Policies on recruitment, redeployment, redundancy, training, equal opportunity and promotion, appraisal systems, health, welfare and safety matters.

- **Staffing** Analysis of workforce, staffing standards, planned changes, investment plans.
- **Performance** Productivity and efficiency data, savings from increased productivity, return on capital, sales and state of the order book.
- **Financial cost** Structures, profits, sources of earnings, assets, liabilities, government assistance, transfer prices, loans and interest charges.

(These are examples, not a checklist or an exhaustive list.)

Restrictions on the duty to disclose

Some restrictions exist by law (*see* Provisions of the Act, *above*). Some examples of those that could cause substantial injury to an undertaking are cost information on individual products, detailed analysis of proposed investment, marketing or pricing policies, price quotas or tenders. These could cause injury such as lost customers or suppliers or prejudice the ability to raise loans. The employer has to establish that disclosure would cause substantial injury.

Trade union responsibilities

Trade unions should identify and request the information they require in advance of the negotiations. The request should state the information required and the reasons why it is considered relevant. Trade unions should inform employers of the names of the representatives authorised to carry out collective bargaining. Where there are two or more trade unions they should coordinate their requests. Trade unions should review existing or establish new training programmes to ensure negotiators are equipped to understand and use information effectively.

Employers' responsibilities

Employers should aim to be as open and helpful as possible in meeting trade union requests for information. Where a request is refused, the reasons should be explained. Information regarded as relevant should be made available as soon as possible once a request has been made. Employers should present the information in a form and style which recipients can be expected to understand.

Joint arrangements for disclosure of information

Employers and trade unions should endeavour to agree on how to implement the system of disclosure effectively. They should consider what may be required, what is available and what should be made available. Consideration should be given to the form in which the information will be presented, when it should be presented and to whom, and what information could be provided on a regular basis. Procedures for resolving possible disputes should be agreed and should normally be related to any existing arrangements.

11.4 Code of Practice on Time Off for Trade Union Duties and Activities

The original Code was issued by ACAS in 1977 but has been superseded by a Code issued in 1991 which incorporates the amendments made in the Employment Act 1989 which restricted the purposes for which time off work could be granted. Trade union officers have the right to reasonable time off work (sometimes paid, sometimes not) to carry out their duties. The Code gives practical guidance on what these rights mean in practice. The following is a précis of the Code.

General purpose of the Code

The general purpose of the Code is to aid and improve the effectiveness of relationships between employers and trade unions. Employers and unions have a joint responsibility to ensure that agreed arrangements seek to specify how reasonable time off for union duties and activities and for training can work to their mutual advantage.

Time off for trade union duties

The law is stated in Section 10.3.2. Basically the rights are given to trade union officials of independent trade unions who are recognised by the employer. They are entitled to reasonable time off for duties concerned with negotiations, or other duties where the employer agrees.

The Code gives illustrative examples under each of the headings which are included in 'trade union duties', i.e., those associated with collective agreements between the employer and the trade union:

- terms and conditions of employment, e.g.
  pay   hours of work
  holidays and   sick pay
     holiday pay   arrangement
  pensions   vocational training
  equal opportunities   notice periods
  working   utilisation of
     environment   machinery
- engagement or nonengagement, or termination or suspension of employment, e.g.
  recruitment and selection policies
  human resource planning
  redundancy and dismissal arrangements
- allocation of work or the duties of employment, e.g.
  job grading   job evaluation
  job descriptions   flexible working
             practices
- matters of discipline, e.g.
  disciplinary procedures
  arrangements for representing trade union members at internal interviews
  arrangements for appearing on behalf of union members before agreed outside bodies or industrial tribunals
- trade union membership or nonmembership, e.g.
  representational arrangements
  union involvement in induction

- facilities for officials, e.g.
  accommodation   equipment
  communicating the names of new
  workers to the union
- machinery for negotiation or consultation,
  e.g.
  collective bargaining grievance procedure
  joint consultation   communicating
                        with members
  communicating with other trade union
  officials

  Reasonable time off may be sought, for
  example, to:
  prepare for   inform members of
  negotiations   progress
  explain outcomes   prepare for
  to members   meetings with
                       the employer.

Training of officials in aspects of industrial relations

Training should be in aspects of industrial
relations relevant to the duties of the official.
There is no one recommended syllabus, as an
official's duties will vary according to:
  the collective arrangements at the place of
  work
  the structure of the union
  the role of the official.
The training should be approved by the TUC or
the union concerned. Union officials are likely
to be more effective if they possess the skills and
knowledge relevant to their duties. This could
include initial training on representational skills.
Reasonable time off could be considered where:
  the official has special responsibilities
  there are proposals to change the structure or
  topics of the negotiations or where significant
  changes in the organisation of work are being
  contemplated
  the law has changed.

Time off for trade union activities

To operate effectively and democratically, trade
unions need the active participation of members.
An employee, who is a member of an
independent trade union recognised by the
employer, is permitted to have time off work to
take part in union activity. The activities of a
trade union member could be:
  attending a workplace meeting to discuss and
  vote on the outcome of negotiations
  meeting full-time officials
  voting in ballots
  voting in union elections.
Where the member is a representative of the
union, activities can be:
  branch, area or regional meeting of the union
  meetings of official policy-making bodies
  meetings with full-time union officials.
There is no right to time off for union activities
which are industrial action. There is no
requirement to pay but employers may wish to
consider payment to ensure meetings are fully
representational.

The responsibilities of employer and trade unions

The amount and frequency of time off should be
reasonable in all the circumstances. Trade unions
should be aware of the difficulties and
operational requirements to be taken into
account when seeking or agreeing arrangements
for time off, e.g.
  the size of the organisation
  the production process
  the need to maintain a service
  the need for safety and security at all times.
Employers should bear in mind the difficulties
for trade union officials in effective representation and communication with:
  shift workers   part-time workers
  those employed at dispersed locations
  workers   with   particular   domestic
  commitments.
For the arrangements to work satisfactorily trade
unions should:
  ensure officials know their role, responsibilities
  and functions
  inform management in writing of the
  appointment or resignation of officials
  ensure officials receive written credentials
  promptly.

Employers should consider making facilities available to officials for them to perform their duties. Where resources permit, the facilities could include:

accommodation for meetings
access to a phone and other office equipment
use of a notice board
where justified, the use of dedicated office space.

Requesting time off

Trade union officials and members requesting time off should provide management with as much notice as possible and give details of:

the purpose of the time off request
the intended location
the timing and duration of the time off.
For training they should:
give a few weeks' notice to management of nominations
if asked, provide a copy of the syllabus or prospectus indicating the content of the course.
When deciding to grant requests for time off consideration should be given to the reasonableness of the request for example, to ensure adequate cover for safety or to safeguard the production process or the provision of service. Unions and managers should seek to agree on a mutually convenient time which minimises the disruptive effects.

Agreements on time off

There can be positive advantages for employers and unions in establishing agreements on time off which reflects their own situation. A formal agreement can help to:

provide clear guidelines
facilitate better planning
avoid misunderstandings
ensure fair and reasonable treatment

Agreements could specify:
the amount of time off permitted
the occasions when time off can be taken
when time off will be with pay

to whom time off will be paid
the procedure for requesting time off.
Agreements for time off and facilities should be consistent with other agreements, e.g., constituencies, number of representatives and the election of officials.

Industrial action

Employers and unions have a duty to use agreed procedures to settle problems. Time off is permitted for this purpose but there is no right to time off for union activities which themselves consist of industrial action.

Making a complaint

Where a grievance remains unresolved, a union official or union member has the right to complain to an industrial tribunal that their employer has failed to allow reasonable time off or has failed to pay for the time off (where appropriate).

11.5 Code of Practice on Closed Shop Agreements and Arrangements

This Code was issued by the Department of Employment in 1980. It provides guidance on matters arising out of the formulation and operation of a closed shop. The Code was issued after the 1980 Employment Act was passed. The main thrust of government policy has been to restrict the operation of the closed shop with a view to eliminating this practice. The basis for this policy is that the closed shop is claimed to be a restriction on the freedom of the individual to choose, i.e., to join or not to join, an organisation. The closed shop is also seen as a restriction on the operation of a free labour market. The restrictive practices that occur in some trades are seen as a source of inefficiency and should be eliminated. Also the trade unions gain considerable power through the closed shop and can, from this position, introduce restrictive practices which lower efficiency. The law on the closed shop and related matters has been altered since the Code was published and this must be taken into account (*see* Section 15.3). The following is a précis of the Code.

Introduction

The Code applies to all closed shops, whether written or informal agreements. The Code's general approach is that any agreement or practice on union membership should protect individual's rights, enjoy the overwhelming support of those affected and be flexibly and tolerantly applied.

Legal rights of individuals

This section is an explanation of the law relating to closed shops which is given in Section 15.3.

Closed shop agreements and arrangements

Before a closed shop is considered, employers and unions should think about the following:

- employers are under no obligation to agree to a closed shop
- they should expect a union to show a very high level of membership before agreeing to the introduction of a closed shop
- employers should have special regard to the staff who are members of a professional association having their own code of ethics or conduct (this might oblige the person not to engage in industrial action that could endanger health or safety and thence the person might reasonably object to joining a union)
- unions, before seeking a closed shop, should be recognised and have recruited voluntarily a very high proportion of the employees concerned
- a union should be sure that its members favour a closed shop and a high level of membership does not in itself indicate this
- negotiations should not start where another union has members in the same area before the matter has been resolved with the other union

- if proposals for a new closed shop agreement become a matter of dispute between employer and union, any agreed disputes procedure should be used.

Agreements should specify clearly their scope and content, in particular the class of employees to be covered and any exclusions. An agreement should indicate that the existing employees who are not members, but have a genuine objection on the grounds of conscience or other deeply held belief, will not be required to become members. They should specify a reasonable period within which employees should join the union. If an individual has been excluded or expelled by the union, no action should be taken against them until any appeal has been determined. An employee should not be expelled for refusing to take part in industrial action. The agreement should set out clearly how complaints or disputes arising are to be resolved, including giving the right for individuals to be heard and any questions about nonmembership of a union to be fairly tested. There should be provisions for periodic review and a procedure for termination.

Under the Employment Act 1980 a secret ballot should be held of those to be included in any proposed closed shop. Agreement should be reached on the terms of the proposed agreement and terms must be passed on to those affected by the agreement. The electorate should be all the members of the class of employee to be covered by the proposed closed shop including nonmembers. The ballot form should be clear and simple and the question asked limited to the single issue of whether or not membership of the union(s) should be a requirement for that class of employee. The ballot should ensure, so far as is reasonably practicable, all those entitled to vote have an opportunity of doing so and in secret, usually by way of a workplace or postal ballot. The administrative arrangements should be agreed in advance. The Employment Act 1982 lays down a minimum level of support, i.e., not less than 80% of those entitled to vote or not less than 85% of those who voted must vote in favour of the agreement. This gives the employer a defence against possible future unfair dismissal claims or complaints of action short of dismissal. While 80% (or 85%) is the legal minimum, this does not prevent an employer deciding that there should be a higher percentage in favour. Employers should agree with the union on the figure to be used before the ballot, and the figure should be made known.

In operation, a new or existing agreement should be applied flexibly and tolerantly with due regard to the interests of the individuals as well as those of the employer and the union. Before any potential new employee is recruited, they should be informed of any requirement to become a union member. The requirements of a closed shop should not be imposed on those not a party to the agreement, for example contractors, suppliers or customers.

All closed shop agreements should be subject to a periodic review. A review should take place every few years and more frequently if there is evidence that support for the closed shop has declined, where there has been a change in the parties to the agreement, if there is evidence that the agreement is not working satisfactorily or if the law changes. If in the course of the review the parties decide to continue the agreement, they should consider what changes should be renegotiated. If it is thought that the agreement is no longer needed, or there is insufficient support, the parties should agree that it lapse. Either party, having given notice, can terminate it. If the parties favour continuing the agreement they should ensure it has continued support. Where no secret ballot has been held, or one has not been held for a long time, it would be appropriate to use one to test opinion. Pre-entry closed shop agreements, that require people to be union members before they can be employed, should not be contemplated and, where they exist, the need for their continuance should be carefully reviewed.

Comment **The Code addresses several practical problems arising in a closed shop situation. There are a number of dilemmas confronting employer, employee and union which need resolving. Some have been addressed by legislation. The Code identifies a number of these:**

- those who are in a professional association that requires them not to take industrial action – this, as a matter of conscience, might prevent the individual from being a member of a union
- the formation of a closed shop should be based on the members being actively in favour of this, and high union membership is not sufficient evidence of this (the requirements of the Employment Act 1982, *see above*, are extreme, i.e., an 80% majority of those entitled to vote, voting in favour), also this support should be put to the test at regular intervals
- inter-union disputes can be very troublesome to employers as they are powerless to do much about them and there is the potential for rival unions in a workplace or section to be covered by a closed shop to fight over potential members – certainly, if the dominant union insists that all employees have to be members of their union (and no other), this could lead to a difficult dispute
- the vexed question of how to treat those employees who do not wish to become union members has gone through many changes, but the latest position, legislatively, is that a person has the right not to be a union member and should not be discriminated against or dismissed because of this, so the items in the Code relating to 'grounds of conscience' are no longer the legislative position.

Union treatment of members and applicants

Union decisions on exclusion or expulsion from membership in a closed shop should be taken only after making sure rules and procedures have been fully complied with. In handling admissions to membership, unions should adopt clear and fair rules covering who is qualified for membership, who has power to consider and decide upon applications, what reasons justify rejection on application, the appeals procedure and the power to admit applicants where an appeal is upheld. Unions should take account of factors such as whether the applicant has the appropriate qualifications for the type of work done by members of the union or section, whether the number of applications is so great as to pose a serious threat to undermining negotiated terms and conditions and whether the TUC's principles and procedures are relevant.

In handling membership discipline, unions should adopt clear and fair rules covering the offences for which the union can take disciplinary action and the penalties applicable, the procedures for hearing and determining complaints, a right of appeal, an appeals procedure and the right not to be expelled if an appeal is being pursued. Procedures should comply with the rules of natural justice including giving fair notice of the complaint, an opportunity to be heard, a fair hearing and an impartial decision. TUC guidance and appeals procedures should be borne in mind. A union should not consider taking action likely to lead to individuals losing their jobs until its own procedures have been exhausted and any industrial tribunal hearing relating to the case has been held. Disciplinary action should not be taken or threatened on the grounds of refusal to take part in industrial action called for by the union where the action would constitute a breach of law or a member's professional code of ethics or would constitute a serious risk to public safety, health or property or because the action was in breach of a procedural agreement or because the action had not been affirmed in a secret ballot. Also disciplinary action should not be taken against a member on the grounds that they crossed a picket line which the union had not authorised or which was not at the member's place of work.

Comment **The manner in which unions deal with applications for membership, discipline their members or expel them has a bearing on the closed shop. If an employee, or prospective employee, has difficulties gaining union membership, this could cause problems in a closed shop situation. If a member opposes the union on, say, industrial action and perhaps crosses a picket line, is the union entitled to discipline that member? The law now says that they cannot. Further, the member has the right to take the union to a tribunal and can, in some circumstances enlist the help of the Commissioner for the Rights of Trade Union Members.**

The closed shop and the freedom of the press

The freedom of the press to collect and publish information, comment and criticism is an essential part of our democratic society. All concerned have a duty to ensure that industrial relations are conducted so as not to infringe or jeopardise this principle. Journalists should enjoy the right to join trade unions and participate in their activities. However, the actions of unions must not be such as to conflict with the principle of press freedom. Any requirements on a journalist to join a union could create such a conflict. Individual journalists may genuinely feel that membership of a union is incompatible with their need to be free from the risk of interference. This should be respected by employers and unions. A journalist should not be disciplined by a trade union for anything they have written or researched for publication in accordance with generally accepted professional standards. Editors should be free to decide whether to become or remain a member of any trade union. Within the agreed basic policy of the publication, editors have final responsibility for the contents of their publications. An editor should not be subject to improper pressure, but should be free to decide whether to publish any material submitted from any source. This right should be exercised responsibly, with due regard for the interests of the readers of the publication and the employment, or opportunities for employment, of professional journalists.

Comment **The latest changes to the law in the Trade Union and Labour Relations (Consolidation) Act 1992 has introduced individual protection rights at the recruitment stage (for the first time in this area). These will make the pre-entry closed shop inoperable. The Code itself is in need of a revamp in the light of the many legislative changes since it was first issued.**

11.6 Code of Practice on Picketing

This Code was issued by the Department of Employment in 1980. It provides guidance on matters relating to picketing. Certain changes have been made to the law on picketing and shortly after the passing of the Employment Act 1980, this Code was issued. The following is a précis of the Code.

Introduction

The Code is intended to provide practical guidance on picketing in trade disputes for those who may be contemplating, organising or taking part in a picket and for those who may be affected by it. There is no legal 'right to picket' but peaceful picketing has long been recognised as being lawful. The law imposes certain limits on how and where lawful picketing can be undertaken so as to ensure that there is proper protection for those who may be affected by picketing. It is a civil wrong to persuade someone to break their contract of employment or to secure the breaking of a commercial contract. But the law exempts those acting in contemplation or furtherance of a trade dispute including picketing, providing they are picketing only at their own place of work. The criminal law applies to pickets as it applies to everyone else.

Picketing and civil law

This section is an explanation of the law relating to picketing which is examined in Section 15.2.

Picketing and criminal law

This section is also an explanation of the law relating to picketing which is examined in Section 15.2.

Role of the police

It is not the function of the police to take a view of the merits of a particular trade dispute. They have a general duty to uphold the law and keep the peace. The law gives the police discretion to take whatever measures may reasonably be considered necessary to ensure that picketing remains peaceful and orderly. The police have no responsibility for enforcing the civil law. The police cannot be required to help identify pickets, or help enforce a civil court order. The latter is the function of the court and its officers. As regards the criminal law, the police have considerable discretionary powers to limit the number of pickets where they have reasonable fear of a disorder. The law does not impose a specific limit on the number of pickets at one place, nor does this Code affect the discretion of the police to limit numbers. It is for the police to decide whether the number of pickets may lead to a breach of the peace. If a picket does not leave the picket line when asked, that person is liable to be arrested for obstruction of the highway or of a police officer.

Limiting the number of pickets

The main cause of violence and disorder on the picket line is excessive numbers. Wherever large numbers of people with strong feelings are involved there is a danger that the situation will get out of control and that those concerned will run the risk of arrest and prosecution. This is particularly so when people seek, by sheer weight of numbers, to stop others going to work or delivering or collecting goods. In such cases what is intended is not peaceful persuasion but obstruction, if not intimidation. This mass picketing is not picketing in its lawful sense of an attempt at peaceful persuasion but may result in a breach of the peace. Anyone seeking to support those in dispute should keep well away from any picket line so as not to create the risk of a breach of the peace. Large numbers on a picket line are also likely to give rise to fear and resentment among those seeking to cross that picket line. They exacerbate the situation and sour relations. Accordingly pickets and their organisers should ensure that, in general, the number of pickets does not exceed six at any one entrance to a workplace. Frequently a smaller number will be appropriate.

Comment **One of the uglier aspects of industrial relations that governments (of all persuasions) wish to eliminate is mass picketing. There have been several incidents where thousands of people** have picketed an establishment and this action has led to disorder and serious public order offences being committed. The right to picket was established over a century ago but there is always the need to balance this right with the freedom of the individual to live in peace. The Code seeks to do this by setting the boundaries of peaceful and lawful picketing. The number of pickets is an essential element in this.

However, the effect of the changes in the law and the issue of the Code still did not prevent mass picketing occurring during the miners' strike in 1984. Ultimately, legislation will not totally eliminate mass picketing, but it will constrain some from going to excess.

Organisation of picketing

The picket organiser, an experienced person, preferably a trade union official who represents those picketing, should always be in charge of the picket line. The organiser should have a letter of authority from the union which can be shown to the police and to people who want to cross the picket line. An organiser should maintain contact with the police. Advance consultation with the police is always in the best interests of those concerned. In particular, the organiser of pickets should seek advice from the police on the number of people who should be present on the picket line at any time and where they should stand to avoid obstructing the highway. The other main functions of the picket organiser should be to ensure that the pickets understand the law and the Code on picketing, to be responsible for distributing badges or armbands, which authorised pickets should wear, to ensure that employees from other places of work do not join the picket line and offers of support from outsiders are refused, to remain in close contact with the union office and to ensure that any special arrangements for essential supplies or maintenance are understood and observed.

Wherever several unions are involved they should consult each other about the organisation of picketing. It is important that they should agree how the picketing is to be carried out, how many pickets there should be from each union and who should have overall responsibility for

them. Everyone has the right to decide whether or not to cross the picket line. Disciplinary action should not be taken or threatened by a union against a member on the grounds that that person has crossed a picket line which it has not authorised or which was not at the member's place of work.

Comment Traditionally the organisation of picketing has been left to the union(s) concerned. This can be the branch or higher, depending on the nature of the dispute. In order to achieve some organisation in cases of, and responsibility for, picketing, the Code makes a number of suggestions. This does require the cooperation of the union officials concerned. At times of industrial dispute this may not be easy to secure.

A further technical problem has been that to serve a legal document on someone it has to be addressed to them. This then requires that the members of a picket line, which is subject to, say, a court order banning it, must be individually identified by name.

Essential supplies and services

Pickets should take great care to ensure that their actions do not cause distress, hardship or inconvenience to members of the public who are not involved in the dispute. Pickets should take particular care to ensure that the movement of essential goods and supplies, the carrying out of essential maintenance of plant and equipment and the provision of services essential to the life of the community are not impeded, still less prevented. Arrangements to ensure this should be agreed in advance between unions and employers concerned. The following list of essential supplies and services provides an illustration but is not comprehensive: supplies for the production, packaging, marketing and distribution of medical and pharmaceutical products, food and animal feed, and supplies essential to health and welfare institutions; heating fuel for schools, residential institutions and private residential accommodation; other supplies for which there is a crucial need during a crisis in the interests of public health and safety; supplies of goods and services necessary to the maintenance of plant and equipment; livestock; operation of essential services such as police, fire, ambulance, medical and nursing services, air safety, coast guards, and air-sea rescue; services provided by voluntary bodies and mortuary, burial and cremation services.

11.7 Code of Practice for the Elimination of Racial Discrimination and the Promotion of Equality of Opportunity in Employment

This Code was issued by the Commission on Racial Equality to give guidance to help implement the provisions of the Race Relations Act and to develop policies to eliminate racial discrimination and enhance equality of opportunity. This section is a précis of the main points in the Code.

Introduction

This reviews the legislation and states that employees of all racial groups have a right to equality of opportunity. Employers ought to develop programmes to give effect to measures for reaching such equality. The Code applies to all employers but recognises that small firms may have some difficulty in carrying out the Code's detailed recommendations. The Code shows what good employment practice is in recruitment, selection and training.

Responsibility of employers

It is the responsibility of employers to provide equal opportunities for all job applicants and employees. They should adopt, implement and monitor an equal opportunity policy. Employers should allocate responsibility for this to a member of senior management; discuss and agree the policy with the trade unions or employee representatives; ensure that the policy is known to everyone; provide training for all personnel; and examine, review and change the policy as necessary. Adverts should not be confined to publications which reduce the number of applicants from a particular racial group. Recruitment should not be confined to agencies that provide only or mainly applicants of a particular racial group. Similarly, recruitment should not be wholly or mainly through recommendation or through trade unions. Selection criteria and tests should not be discriminatory, e.g., require a standard of English higher than is necessary. The process of application, short-listing, interviewing and selection should not discriminate directly or indirectly. Similarly, transfers, training and appraisal should be made without discrimination. Disciplinary action should be checked for possible victimisation and for the effects of racial abuse or provocation, communication and comprehension difficulties and differences in cultural background or behaviour. Grounds for dismissal should be non-discriminatory. Communication training may be needed to avoid language difficulties endangering equal opportunities.

Employers should monitor the effects of selection decisions and personnel practices to assess whether equal opportunity is being achieved. This may include analysing the ethnic composition of the workforce by section and job category and analysing the selection decisions. The information should be carefully analysed in order to identify areas needing attention. This should include identifying if any individuals from a racial group are not applying for jobs, are not being recruited or promoted or are under-represented for training. Positive measures can be taken to balance under-representation, e.g., by encouraging job applications, use of agencies in areas where these groups live, encouragement to apply for promotion, transfer or training.

Individual employees

The attitude and activities of individuals are very important. Certain actions are unlawful such as discriminating in selection decisions, refusing to accept someone into a work group or victimising someone for complaining about racial discrimination. To assist, individual employees should cooperate in measures taken or press for their introduction, draw management's attention to suspected discriminatory acts or practices and refrain from harassment or intimidation. Individual employees from racial minorities should, where appropriate, seek means to improve their English, cooperate in industrial language training schemes and industrial relations training and take part in decisions to find solutions to any conflicts between cultural or religious needs and production needs.

Trade unions

They should ensure that their representatives or members do not discriminate in the admission or treatment of members. Trade unions should encourage and press for equal opportunities policies. Trade unions should not discriminate in their terms of membership or in the benefits, facilities or services provided. Unions can take positive action to provide training for members of racial groups which have been under-represented in membership or trade union posts. Unions should provide training for officers and members on their responsibilities for equal opportunities. Procedures and joint agreements should be examined to ensure that they do not contain indirectly discriminatory requirements or conditions. Trade unions should cooperate in the introduction and implementation of equal opportunities policies, the monitoring of the progress of these policies and the measures taken to eliminate discrimination.

Employment agencies

They should not discriminate in providing services to clients or publish discriminatory advertisements, nor act on directly or indirectly discriminatory instructions from employers. Their staff should be instructed not to ask for racial preferences, nor to draw attention to racial origins when recommending applicants, to report any discriminatory action and to treat job applicants without discrimination. Agencies should monitor the effectiveness of measures taken to ensure there is no unlawful discrimination.

11.8 Code of Practice, Equal Opportunity Policies, Procedures and Practices in Employment

This Code was issued by the Equal Opportunities Commission to give guidance for the purposes of eliminating discrimination in employment, to promote equality of opportunity and to help employers comply with the Sex Discrimination Act (the topic of equal opportunities is examined in more detail in Chapter 17 where many of the topics raised in the Code are discussed). This section is a précis of the main provisions in the Code. The advice is given to employers, trade unions and employment agencies on measures that can be taken to achieve equality. Individual employees at all levels have responsibilities too. Trade unions should give their full commitment to eliminating discrimination and to the successful operation of an equal opportunities policy. Much can be achieved through collective bargaining. Trade unions should cooperate in the introduction and implementation of equal opportunities policies or urge for their introduction. Trade unions have the responsibility that representatives and members do not discriminate on the grounds of sex or marriage in the administration or treatment of members. Employment agencies have a responsibility as suppliers of job applicants.

Role of good employment practices in eliminating sex and marriage discrimination

Organisations should establish and use consistent criteria for selection, training, promotion, redundancy and dismissal procedures which are known to all employees. On recruitment, any qualification or requirement applied to a job that restricts it to applicants of one sex or single people should be retained only if justified. Age limits should only be retained if necessary. If trade unions uphold such qualifications or requirements as policy they should amend the policy if it is potentially unlawful. Individuals should be assessed according to capability and should not assume that men only or women only will be able to perform certain kinds of work.

Genuine occupational qualifications can be claimed but not based on strength or stamina. Such qualifications should apply only to the minimum number of people necessary, not to all posts.

Advertising should encourage applications from suitable candidates from both sexes. Adverts should be placed in publications likely to reach both sexes. Stereotyping roles should be avoided. Vacancies to be filled by promotion or transfer should be published to all eligible employees. Employers notifying vacancies through careers services should ensure both boys' and girls' schools are approached. Tests should be checked for bias. Employees involved in selection should be trained in the provisions of the Sex Discrimination Act. Applicants from men and women should be identically processed. In assessing whether personal circumstances will affect performance of the job, this should be discussed objectively without detailed assumptions about marital status, children and domestic obligations. Questions about marriage plans or family intentions should not be asked.

On promotion, transfer and training any appraisal system should be examined for discrimination. Where a group of workers predominantly of one sex is excluded from applying they should have similar access to promotion transfer or training. Career development patterns should be examined to ensure that traditional qualifications are justifiable. Rules restricting or precluding transfer should be questioned. Policies and practices regarding selection for training, day release and personal development should be examined including age limits. Differences in treatment between men and women on the grounds of health and safety should be based on well-founded reasons. All terms of employment should be reviewed to ensure there is no discrimination. If part-time workers do not enjoy the pro-rata benefits, the arrangements should be reviewed.

Complaints of discrimination, victimisation and sexual harassment should be dealt with effectively and seriously. An employee who has taken action under the Sex Discrimination Act or Equal Pay Act should not be discriminated against. Care should be taken that members of one sex are not dismissed for performance or behaviour which would be overlooked in the other sex. Redundancy procedures should be reviewed to ensure that they would not have a disproportionate effect on a group of predominantly one sex. Access to voluntary redundancy benefit should be made available on equal terms to all employees. Downgrading or short-time working arrangements should not be discriminatory.

Role of good employment practices in promoting equality of opportunity

An equal opportunities policy should state that the employment policies, practices and procedures do not discriminate and provide genuine equality of opportunity. Trade unions have an important role to play in implementing and reviewing established procedures. The policy should be in writing and, where appropriate, included in the collective agreement. An effective policy needs the support of management and trade unions at the highest level. The Board of Directors should issue a statement setting out the commitment to equal opportunity, opposition to discrimination and determination to adopt proper procedures and practices to achieve these. Overall, responsibility for the policy should be assigned to a senior member of management, negotiating any action required with trade unions and ensuring the policy is known to all employees and job applicants. The policy should be monitored regularly. This may involve a joint management/trade union review committee. In large organisations a more formal analysis will be necessary.

Special training and encouragement can be given to those of a sex which has few or no members in particular work. This can include advertisements to encourage applicants, use of job agencies to encourage application, and giving encouragement to women to apply for management posts and skilled manual work. Help can be given to provide continuity of employment to working parents such as part-time or flexi-time, personal leave arrangements, child care facilities and enhancement of the statutory maternity provisions.

11.9 Code of Practice on Trade Union Ballots on Industrial Action

This Code was issued to give guidance to the various legislative requirements for unions to hold ballots to authorise or endorse industrial action. The matter is of importance to trade unions and trade union officials as their immunity to being sued or an injunction being issued against them as the result of calling industrial action is now dependent on a ballot being held to gain acceptance of their membership to such action being taken. This Code will be particularly pertinent in court cases, to determine if the requirements of the law have been fulfilled. Noncompliance with these laws could be extremely damaging financially to the union. The law is now contained in the Trade Union and Labour Relations (Consolidation) Act 1992. Additionally, a trade union member now has the right to challenge a union's call to take industrial action, on the grounds that a ballot has not been taken to authorise or endorse such a call, or the ballot is defective in some way. In determining if the ballot is defective a court will refer to this Code which sets out the standards required in considerable detail. The following is a précis of the Code.

Introduction

The purpose of the Code is to provide practical guidance to promote good industrial relations and to assist unions and their members involved in balloting. The Code is concerned with ballots which may protect a union from action in a court.

Whether an industrial action ballot is appropriate

A ballot should not take place until procedures have been exhausted, or where these do not exist, until reference has been made to a third party, e.g., ACAS. The union should only ballot for industrial action that is in itself lawful. The employer should be informed of the intention to hold a ballot. Where several unions are involved they should coordinate their arrangements.

Comment **This Code again reaffirms the basic rule in collective bargaining that industrial action should not be taken until procedures are exhausted. Procedures exist to resolve disputes, difficulties and problems, so they should be fully utilised.**

Preparing for an industrial action ballot

The individual(s) or body who would authorise or endorse industrial action (per the Rule Book) should establish the 'balloting constituency', i.e., ensure all those who will be called to take industrial action have the opportunity to vote. Votes should only be aggregated from different places of work where there is a 'common distinguishing factor'. Such a factor may be that the members are in a particular occupation or the members share a particular term or condition of employment.

The method of balloting is prescribed by law. It has to be a postal ballot or a workplace ballot (returned at the place of work or by post). It is also suggested that the employer provides facilities to enable this process. The union should ensure adequate arrangements for the scrutinising of the ballot. The questions on the voting paper should be simple and direct and elicit either a 'yes' or a 'no'. The question should not ask for opinion or whether the member is prepared to support action. Nor should the ballot paper suggest how the member should vote. Example voting papers are given in the Code. The printing and distribution of ballot papers should be scrutinised by an independent person. Care should be taken to avoid duplication, ensure security and be capable of being checked. The union should give background information to its members on the dispute and the issues arising, the action proposed, its timing, the majority required and the consequences of taking industrial action.

Comment It is essential to be seen to be democratic, that all those entitled to vote are given the opportunity to do so. The legal changes have tightened up against the often-criticised practices of show-of-hands voting at mass meetings. The aggregation of votes by unions is restricted in an attempt to contain industrial action to the minimum. Secondary action is now restricted (*see* Section 15.1.4) and the law has plugged the loophole of spreading industrial action legitimately by ballot by saying that the workers being balloted must have a common factor connecting them to the dispute. Merely saying it is sympathetic action is not an acceptable reason. The Code makes a number of suggestions to make ballots scrupulously fair. The ballot paper cannot have any bias in the way the statements are made or the questions are put. This eliminates the practice of a union trying to persuade its members of the correctness of its policy and that the ballot is merely seeking support for its policies. The requirements for the printing and distribution of ballot papers imposes requirements that should help to eliminate the problems caused in some unions where the system has been open to abuse. There have been numerous accusations of vote-rigging and bias in union elections and some unions have re-run ballots because of such difficulties. However, some unions have employed independent organisations, such as the Electoral Reform Society, to run their ballots.

Holding an industrial action ballot

The union should ensure that there is no interference with the balloting process. If a postal ballot, or return by post ballot, is used, the reply should be paid by the union. Every member entitled to vote should have the opportunity to vote. There should be adequate time allowed for the return of papers in a postal ballot. There should be a system of checking that ensures all those entitled to vote can do so and that no one votes who is not entitled to do so. Postal balloting should be provided for those entitled to vote but who cannot take part in a workplace ballot, with checks to avoid duplication. The issue of papers should not be carried out by a union official or anyone involved in the dispute. There should be adequate notice of the date, time and place of the ballot. The voting should be secret and anonymity should be preserved, including not being able to identify the voter in a postal ballot. A workplace ballot should be arranged to maintain the secrecy and security of the returned papers.

Comment The Code tries to ensure that the ballots are secret and fair, and of no cost to the voter. In some places of work, with shift work or remote locations, voting arrangements can be difficult. Nevertheless, everyone should be able to exercise their right to vote. The conduct of the ballot should be carefully administered to ensure no duplication, such as a person requesting a postal vote and then voting at work. It should not be possible to identify the voter and secrecy should be maintained at workplace ballots. If the voting is defective in any way, it could invalidate the ballot and then leave the union and its officials open to court action.

Following an industrial action ballot

After the ballot, unused papers should be destroyed. Papers arriving after the deadline should be rejected. Papers received by post should be kept secure until counted. Adjudication on spoilt papers should be done by someone not involved in the call for action. Papers once counted should be removed and stored securely. An independent scrutineer should be appointed to advise on suitable arrangements.

After the counting has finished, the results of the ballot should be made known as soon as is reasonably practicable. Industrial action should not be authorised or endorsed until the results of the ballot have been made known. Even if a ballot shows a majority in favour of industrial action, the union should try all other options rather than industrial action. Four weeks is allowed from the date of the ballot to when industrial action may be taken. After this time the original ballot is not valid. If the union decides to call for industrial action, it must inform its members of its decision and the reasons for doing so. It must also inform the employer and give the employer sufficient time to make arrangements to ensure there are no health and safety risks.

Mini-questions

11.1 Differentiate between a Code of Practice and a statute.

11.2 Explain the purpose of Codes of Practice in industrial relations.

11.3 Name three things management should do and three things that unions should do to promote good industrial relations.

11.4 State three provisions that should appear in a procedural agreement.

11.5 State three provisions that should appear in a substantive agreement.

11.6 State to which area of law the Code of Practice on Disciplinary Practice and Procedures is relevant and explain how it might be used in practice.

11.7 List five important features of a disciplinary procedure.

11.8 List five areas of information that should be disclosed to trade unions for collective bargaining.

11.9 Describe the time off that a trade union official can claim with pay.

11.10 Explain what training a trade union official might need.

11.11 Describe the conditions that need fulfilling if a new closed shop is to be introduced.

11.12 State the items that should appear in a closed shop agreement.

11.13 Describe the procedures unions should adopt in treating applications for membership.

11.14 Describe the Code of Practice's suggestions for the organisation of picket lines.

11.15 List five essential supplies or services pickets should ensure are not impeded.

Exercises

11.1 The Code of Practice on Industrial Relations suggests that management has certain important responsibilities for creating and developing good industrial relations. State what these are and discuss, with illustrations, what they mean in practice.

11.2 The Code of Practice on Industrial Relations states that clear and comprehensive employment policies are essential. Explain what these policies should include and how they can help industrial relations.

11.3 Explain the role of disciplinary rules and procedures and how they ought to be formulated and put into operation.

11.4 The Employment Protection Act 1975 imposes a duty on employers to disclose information. Explain how this can help industrial relations and describe the extent and limitations of this duty.

11.5 If a closed shop were being contemplated at a workplace, explain the considerations that management and unions ought to take into account.

11.6 One of the main problems associated with picketing is the numbers that are sometimes involved. Describe the Code of Practice's suggestions on this issue and examine how these proposals might work in practice.

11.7 Using the Code of Practice for the Elimination of Racial Discrimination, and any other relevant material, describe how recruitment and selection practices can be improved.

11.8 Suggest what items could be monitored as part of an Equal Opportunities policy. State what statistics you would use and how you would seek to make improvements in a number of the areas monitored.

Case studies

(3) Defective procedures are harmful, page 314.

(7) Negotiating a disciplinary procedure, page 328.

(11) Strangers at work, page 344.

12

The terms and conditions of employment

12.1 The contract of employment

12.1.1 Introduction

The contract of employment is central to the relationship that exists between employer and employee. The basis of the relationship is an agreement that exists between the two parties, and this agreement is legal in nature and it is legally enforceable as a contract. Almost all of the matters arising in employment are related to the contract of employment. The topics discussed in this book like unfair dismissal, redundancy, the closed shop, strikes and bargaining all relate to the contract of employment. For these reasons this chapter examines the contract of employment in some detail. There is a large body of law relating to contracts of one sort or another, and these legal rules apply to the contract of employment but with several modifications. There are rules regarding offer, acceptance, capacity, legality, consideration and termination which apply to the contract of employment. Generally contract law is derived from common law (*see* Section 9.1.2) but increasingly statute law has taken precedence, especially with respect to the contract of employment.

A contract can be defined as a legally binding agreement. The agreement of an employer to pay an employee in exchange for the employee working is one which is legally binding, so that if there is a dispute over the agreement the aggrieved party can go to the courts to seek redress. Once there is a contract, then all the rules regarding a contract apply. The essential features of a contract of employment are the two elements of pay and work. Without these two elements the contract cannot exist. It is worth noting that contract law does not decide on the amount of pay or work but only if the elements exist. Arguments relating to the amount of pay or quantity of work are not within the scope of contract law. If, at some point, either element ceases to exist, then the contract is broken or, in legal terms, breached. If an employee fails to be available for work through striking, the employer can consider the contract broken and at an end. In practice, of course, most strikers return to work and the contract continues.

The contract of employment has some special features. It is of a continuing nature. Most contracts are for a specific period, for example to supply some goods or perform a service, and often are completed quickly. The contract of employment is intended to run perpetually until some act terminates the contract like dismissal, redundancy, handing in notice or death. Another unique feature is that the courts cannot compel an employee to work by issuing a court order. The general rule is that if you have promised to do something as part of a contract this can be enforced by court order. The promise to work under a contract of employment cannot be enforced by court order, called specific performance. A final distinguishing feature is that a large number of the terms of the contract are implied. We shall examine this in Section 12.2.3.

12.1.2 Formation of the contract

Offer

Before a contract can exist there has to be an

offer followed by an acceptance of the offer. When you go into a shop you make an offer to buy goods which the shopkeeper accepts. The contract is made, you get the goods and the shopkeeper gets the money. The contract of employment also starts with an offer and acceptance. An employer may advertise a job. This technically is not an offer but an invitation for people to apply for the job advertised, or, in legal terminology, an 'invitation to treat'. There then follow applications, selection, interviews, shortlists, tests or whatever procedure is used. Finally the employer will offer someone the job. This can be done verbally or in writing. The person who is offered the job must accept the job as offered. Technically an acceptance that is conditional, for example if you accept saying 'I'll accept if you will offer me £500 a year more', is a counter offer and cancels the original offer.

Acceptance

Again an acceptance can be verbal, written or even implied by turning up for work on the start date. However, if the offer specifies the manner of acceptance, the acceptance must conform to this. For example, offers are usually made in writing and will ask the offeree to write back saying if they accept, in which case the acceptance must be in writing. Also a time limit on acceptance must be complied with. If the offer is open for a week, then the acceptance must be made within a week. Another rule of contract is that a written acceptance is made at the time the letter is posted, not the time the offeror receives the letter! A delay in the post will not lose you a job if the letter arrives after the final date, providing the letter was addressed properly and posted on time. Offers can be made subject to certain conditions like a medical examination or acceptable references. If after acceptance a person fails the medical or the references are not acceptable, the contract will no longer exist.

Once an offer has been accepted a contract exists. Its operation may not commence until some later date, as usually a period of notice has to be worked with the previous employer. For an employee who breaks their word there would probably be no legal consequences as a court would say the employer had suffered no loss and could find someone else to do the job. Alternatively, a cancellation by the future employer would not be actionable as the court would say that the employee can find another job. A failure to turn up on the start date may cancel the contract unless there is an acceptable reason, like illness, that prevented a start. The majority of contracts of employment are of a continuing nature although some are for a fixed term. A fixed-term contract is no different from any other except that the contract specifies that on some future date the contract will cease to exist. A few contracts of employment were for life, like those of university lecturers who had tenure of office for life. This guaranteed them a job until 65 or normal retirement age and only in extreme circumstances could the contract be terminated, for example for extreme misconduct. Redundancy was technically not possible but there could be voluntary severance.

The terms of a contract

In most areas of employment there is no written contract of employment. This must be contrasted with the legal requirement for a written statement of some of the terms of the contract. This aspect is dealt with in Section 12.2.4. A written statement of terms is not the contract itself but only evidence of some of the terms in it. Only in the case of a contract for apprenticeship or for a merchant sailor does a written contract have to be given. After the recruitment and selection procedure, not all the terms relating to the contract will be known to the employee. The major ones like pay, holidays and duties will have been discussed but the detail may not be known and other terms will not have been discussed at all. This does not alter the fact that all the terms and conditions relating to the contract apply even though they were not known at the time of acceptance or starting. It is presumed that the person accepting the job is satisfied and if not should have enquired further. It is no use saying about an unacceptable term, 'I didn't know that when I started' as it will still apply even though you do not like it. In fact, there are so many terms attached to a job, often very complex ones like pay structures, pension schemes and the like, that many employees of several years' service do not know about them in detail. Also putting them all down in one document would be very difficult. So the contract of employment is formed by offer and acceptance but the actual contract often does not physically exist but is made up of many terms that derive from several sources. All the terms form a part of the contract and are part of a legally binding agreement between employer and employee.

12.1.3 The features of the contract

Contracts for service and of service

As we have already stated, the fundamental element of a contract of employment is pay and service. There are two types of contract that come within this definition: a contract *for* service and a contract *of* service. We need to differentiate between the two because many of the statutory rights in employment apply only to a contract of service. A contract for service is an independent contractor or subcontractor relationship. A person employed under a contract of service is entitled to a written statement of terms, a minimum period of notice and can claim rights under unfair dismissal, redundancy, maternity pay and absence and union membership rights. A person employed under a contract for service is not entitled to these, nor are they covered by some health and safety legislation and the doctrine of vicarious liability (*see* Section 12.2.3).

A contract for service is akin to the position of independent contractor or subcontractor. Here the contract is to perform a particular task or service and once this is done the contract is at an end. If a firm wants its windows cleaned it will contact another firm that carries out this service, contract them to clean the windows and the relationship ends when the windows are cleaned. Such contracts are clearly for service: a specific and limited service. Other contracts are less easily categorised. To differentiate between

the two types, the courts have devised several tests. A common test is the control test. If a person is subject to the employer's instructions in what they do and how they do the work they are employed to do, then this would indicate a contract of service. This test was formulated in the nineteenth century when the law and judges spoke about the master/servant relationship. Today we would use the words employer and employee, but the idea still persists that the master or employer has control over their servants or employees. In some instances this test does not work. For highly specialised employees, like doctors or scientists, the employer might not have sufficient knowledge to say what should be done and how it should be done. To overcome this problem other tests have been devised like examining if the employer has the power to discipline, dismiss or promote and if deductions are made from pay and if a pension is paid. A recent test is one that says a feature of a contract of service is that the employee is employed as part of the business and the work is done as an integral part of the business, whereas under a contract for service the work is not integrated in the business only accessory to it, very much like the window cleaner example above. There is no overall test used by the courts. In some cases the control test will be the vital clue, in others the degree of integration in the business, while in others the fact that the contract is exclusive to that employer may be conclusive.

The context of the contract

Providing that it is established that the contract is one of service, and this is the case for the majority of workers, the contract of employment has several important features. The fundamental feature of pay and service was explained earlier. We have already mentioned the fact that the contract is usually on-going (as opposed to fixed term), that service cannot be enforced and the contract includes many implied terms. The termination of the contract of employment is subject to special rules. Two of the circumstances are dealt with in Chapter 13 (unfair dismissal) and Chapter 14 (redundancy). Notice can be given by either side to terminate the contract. An employee is entitled to do this for any or no reason, providing sufficient notice is given. Usually there is a term that specifies the notice required and, by law, the minimum is a week. The employer can give notice but the reason must be a fair one (*see* Chapter 13). The notice period is often specified but the minimum is a week for each year of service up to a maximum of 12 weeks.

An essential element of any contract is consideration. This is the concept of parties to the contract both giving and receiving something. In the contract of employment these are the essential features of pay (the employer gives pay, the employee receives pay) and service (the employee works, the employer receives service). The level of pay is a matter for the two parties to decide upon. Often it is determined by some collective agreement or standard scale. The Truck Acts stated that manual workers must be paid in coins of the realm, but this was to stop the nineteenth-century practice of paying in tokens redeemable at a company shop. The Truck Acts have now been repealed. Pay can be by cheque or direct credit if the employee agrees to it. The element of service is self-explanatory except that technically the employee must be available for work and the employer need not provide work.

Terms and conditions

Apart from the features already mentioned, the contract of employment contains a large number of terms and conditions. As jobs and organisations have become more complex then the terms and conditions of employment have become more wide ranging and complex. Below is a list of terms that could apply to a contract of employment, some of which will occur in all contracts.

- **Pay** Weekly rate, annual salary, bonuses, premiums, profit share, shares, commission, deductions, special payments, equal pay.
- **Holidays** Public holidays, service element, entitlement, when to be taken, pay for, leave for various purposes.

- **Sickness** Pay, service entitlement, sick notes, medical examination, medical suspension, medical transfer, maternity rights.
- **Pensions** Scheme, benefits, contributions, transferability, previous service entitlement.
- **Notice** By employer and employee, minimum length of, when to be given, retirement, redundancy, discipline.
- **Job title** Job description, main duties, flexibility, to whom responsible, authority and limits.
- **Procedures** For grievances, discipline, appeals and to whom, lay-offs, short time, closed shop, union membership.
- **Hours** Basic, overtime, compulsory overtime, flexi-time, call-out, standby, time off arrangements, compulsory stand-in, shift pattern.
- **Clothing** Protective, uniform, laundry facility, dress requirements.
- **Perks** Luncheon vouchers, meal tickets, expense account, subsidised travel, transport, suits, uniform, car, discount on goods, sabbaticals, low-interest loans, life insurance, medical insurance.
- **Welfare** Washing and changing facilities, lockers, rest rooms, canteen, toilets, convalescence.
- **Rules** Disciplinary, conduct, time-keeping, quality of work, health and safety, security.

Each job has its own set of terms and conditions. Often not all these are known as they may never operate for an individual, but if a disagreement or dispute arises the terms will apply. A rule of contract is that the parties are free to make whatever bargain they wish, providing there is agreement, however exceptional the terms. It is for the two parties to come to agreement but with the proviso that it does not break the law. If a contract is made that has a term below a minimum set by law, the legal minimum will apply. This rule of allowing the two parties the freedom to make whatever terms they wish gave rise to the problems caused by unions, as a third party, seeking to influence some of the terms of the contract of employment.

As we saw in Section 10.2, legal immunities were required to enable unions to negotiate the terms and conditions of their members' contracts of employment.

Full-time or part-time

The distinction between full-time and part-time work is important for a number of reasons. The main reason is that part time workers only acquire certain rights under employment legislation when they work more than a certain defined number of hours per week. The legislative position is that anyone who works 16 or more hours per week is the equivalent of a full-time worker, i.e., the rights under employment law apply to them. In addition anyone who works 8 or more hours a week for 5 years continuously acquires equivalent full-time status for the purposes of employment legislation.

12.2   Sources of terms

The very many different terms and conditions of the contract of employment are derived from a variety of sources. The sources of any individual contract will depend on the particular job and organisation. A shop floor worker in a heavily unionised, large, federated company will have most of his or her terms determined through collective bargaining and various agreements. A similar worker in a small partnership firm will have most of his or her terms determined by individual negotiation and agreement. One overriding fact is that where the law implies terms (*see* Section 12.2.3) these will automatically become part of the contract. It is possible to agree that some of these implied terms do not apply but this must be specifically stated and agreed. The presumption is that they apply and can be enforced by a tribunal or court. However, the law does not allow some implied terms to be excluded. Any term that states that a legal right is excluded when it cannot be, is struck out of the contract, i.e. the term is void.

12.2.1   Individual and collective agreement

The basis of a contract is that it is an agreement between the two parties. This agreement is reached usually at the interview and selection stage. When an applicant for a job accepts the job they automatically agree to the terms and conditions of the job. In most cases not all these terms will be known. For some jobs, especially completely new jobs or a top managerial job, the terms are discussed at length by the parties until agreement is reached. In the majority of instances, however, the terms and conditions applying to the job are already fixed. At the interview the employer makes the offer based on the set terms of pay, holidays, hours, etc., which the applicant either accepts or not. The room for maneouvre is limited and there is frequently no negotiation. This is necessary in an organisation to achieve uniformity among the workforce, otherwise the system would be chaotic and give rise to friction. Alongside the emergence of organisations was the growth of the trade union movement. A union's function is to negotiate to maintain and improve the terms and conditions of its members. This has led to a system of collective bargaining which we examined in Chapter 6. In many cases collective agreements cover many aspects of the contract of employment. The job, when offered to an applicant, consists of the terms agreed in negotiation with the union.

12.2.2   Rules and custom

Some of the terms and conditions of employment are derived from rules that the employer imposes on his or her employees. Often these are contained in a works Rule Book which the employer issues. The rules are often not negotiated but are unilaterally compiled by the employer. Such rules are applicable to employees providing they are communicated to them. This can be done by issuing a copy of the rules or by stating that certain rules apply and copies are available. Some rules might appear as notices. A notice saying that anyone clocking someone else in or out is liable to dismissal, is a rule. Other examples occur with safety notices requiring employees to wear protective clothing or equipment. These rules should be obeyed as part of the contract and, if they are not, the employee is liable to be disciplined. Most organisations have rules regarding conduct. These will state what is allowed or not allowed and the likely consequences if the rules are broken. They might include rules regarding theft, fraud, fighting, drunkenness, lateness, reporting sick or absent, clocking or signing in, dress and many others. Some jobs have rules regarding inventions and creative works where the patent or copyright becomes the property of the company. In the case of patents, the law allows this if the job is to invent, but in other cases, the inventor might be entitled to some of the monetary benefits of the invention. With some jobs there is sometimes a rule called a restrictive covenant that prevents that person going to work for a rival organisation within a specified area and within a specified length of time. These are legally acceptable (even though they are in a restraint of trade) if the term is reasonable in the circumstances.

Custom and practice can also play a part in determining some terms and conditions of employment. Some work practices, particularly among skilled employees, have led to what are called restrictive practices. In this situation there is a careful delineation of what jobs are done by which craftsperson. A fitter can only do certain jobs, or parts of them, and then an electrician may be required or a pipe fitter or an instrument mechanic. One person cannot do another person's work. This demarcation of jobs has derived from the custom and practice and has not been specifically agreed with the employer. In order to avoid industrial relations problems employers agree to the practice by implication (i.e., allowing it to go on). Any new employee is then subject to these restrictions which thus become part of the contract of employment. Another example of this is the closed shop whereby the practice grew that all employees in a certain grade were, or became, union members. Finally the practice was established, and became part of the contract of employment, that union

membership was a job requirement and new employees had to be, or become, union members. The situation has been modified by the law (*see* Section 15.3). A different example of custom occurred in a case of unfair dismissal where a man caught taking some of the company's product home, without permission, successfully claimed that the firm had allowed the practice to go on for such a long time that it was not a breach of his contract of employment. Custom had established the employee's right to this 'perk' and the tribunal said the dismissal was unfair. If the company wanted to stop the practice it should make a rule to that effect and enforce it.

12.2.3 The law

Both common law and statute law imply terms into the contract of employment. Both these are sources of implied terms. This means that all contracts contain these terms, even if either or both sides are unaware of them. The law says that they are terms and they can be enforced. In some cases the employer and employee can agree not to have these terms apply, but this must be stated and agreed. In other instances the law forbids this. Any implied terms are a minimum and can be improved upon by agreement between employer and employee. Legal sources of terms have become increasingly important in recent times, especially those from statute law.

Vicarious liability

The common law has implied a number of terms into the contract of employment for a long time. These are of less significance today as some are outmoded and others have been superseded by statute law. One very important implied term is that of the rule of vicarious liability. The rule, stated broadly, is that employers are legally responsible for the acts and omissions of their employees. If an employee does something wrong and injures someone, e.g., drives a fork lift truck recklessly and injures someone else, the injured person can (and would) sue the employer. This covers any act done in the course of employment, even if it is an act expressly forbidden. If there were a notice or instruction to fork lift truck drivers not to exceed five mph and a driver exceeded this limit and had an accident, the employer would still be liable even though the act of driving fast had been forbidden. Any act outside of 'the course of employment', e.g., a person driving a vehicle when it is not conceivably part of that person's job, is not covered by this. Such a person would personally be liable for any accident. The law refers to these acts as 'frolics' and they are not covered by the employer's vicarious liability. This implied term usually does not apply to contracts for service. If the disobedient fork lift truck driver above were employed as a subcontractor, the employer would not be liable for the accident.

Duties

There are several other terms implied by common law. These are usually in the form of duties from one party to the other. The duties of the employer include some terms relating to safety. There is a duty under a contract of employment for employers to take reasonable care of their employees. This term extends to the provision of safe working systems, adequate materials and effective supervision. However, the term is of little practical significance because if an employee is injured at work they would sue the employer under the law of tort rather than the law of contract. These duties are paralleled in the Health and Safety at Work Act 1974 which, in the event of a breach, may lead to a criminal action against the employer.

The duties of the employee include a term of obedience. This term has its roots in the times when judges referred to masters and servants. A wilful refusal to obey a lawful and reasonable order is a breach of contract. So actions like a walk-out, go-slow and work-to-rule can, and do, breach the contract. Rudeness and temper can have the same effect and can lead to discipline and eventually to dismissal. Refusal to carry out instructions based on a term of the contract can lead to dismissal. For example, there may be a term stating that employees have to be flexible

and be prepared to move job from time to time as demand dictates. An employee who refuses to move in such circumstances can be fairly dismissed. The law also implies a duty to be competent at the job the employee said they could do. An inability or incapacity to do the job can lead to discipline or dismissal. An employee also must take care not to cause damage or loss to the employer's property. The implied terms in this paragraph all have a bearing on unfair dismissal and, in particular, imply reasons for which a dismissal may be fair.

An important implied term is one that requires the employee to act in good faith. This includes several aspects such as not stealing, not selling secrets and not competing. Some employees in the course of their work get to know company and trade secrets. These can be in the form of pricing policy, formulations, customers, process details and so on. The employee has a duty not to use these secrets for personal gain. To use them for the advantage of a competitor or personal gain (e.g., an employee setting up their own business) is forbidden by the implied term of good faith and could lead to court proceedings. It is in order for an employer to include a restrictive covenant in a contract of employment to restrain ex-employees capitalising on their knowledge to the detriment of the ex-employer's business. Activities outside of work can affect the contract of employment. If misbehaviour is likely to be detrimental to the business, the employee can be dismissed. For example, an accountant found guilty of fraud outside of work would probably be unfit to continue in a position of trust.

Statutory law

A further set of implied terms in the contract of employment are derived from statute law. Many of these, often complex, terms are dealt with elsewhere in this book. Below is a list of these.

- **Unfair dismissal** The right not to be unfairly dismissed (*see* Chapter 13).
- **Redundancy** The right to claim redundancy pay if made redundant (*see* Chapter 14).

- **Maternity benefits**   The right to time off for antenatal care, maternity pay, maternity absence and to return to work (*see* Section 10.3.3).
- **Discrimination**   The right not to be discriminated against on the grounds of sex, marital status, race, trade union membership or activities (*see* Sections 10.3.1 and 10.4).
- **Time off**   The right to paid time off for trade union duties and time off for trade union activities and public duties (*see* Section 10.3.2).
- **Guaranteed pay**   The right to be paid five days' wages (maximum £14.10 per day (1993)) in any period of three months due to lay-off or short time. This is supplemented sometimes by temporary arrangements that pay considerably more, in an effort to forestall redundancies.
- **Hours**   Several industries are subject to statutory restrictions on hours. Shopworkers are subject to the Shop Act provisions relating to hours, half-days, mealtimes and overtime. The Transport Act also restricts the hours of drivers of public service vehicles, locomotives, goods vehicles and large motor vehicles.

The European Community have made proposals for a Directive on working time. This is part of the Maastricht Agreement but outside of the Social Chapter (*see* Section 17.2.1). The UK government disagrees strongly, in principle, with the direction of the EC but has to reach agreement on this and similar matters as they come under the head of health and safety. The UK approach is to let employers and employees settle these matters for themselves, free from government interference. The EC sees it as a matter of social regulation that workers should be entitled to certain minimum rights.

The Directive proposes minimum daily and weekly rest periods, a minimum annual holiday entitlement with pay, and limits on the hours of work and overtime for night workers. This became an issue in the UK where doctors were seeking to have their long hours of work reduced. The EC proposal was a maximum working week of 48 hours. This would cause considerable difficulty to hospitals where doctors work 80–90 hours a week.

- **Pay**   Orders issued by the Employment Appeals Tribunal (under the Equal Pay Act) apply. Also, fines can only be imposed if the terms and offences are specified, the fine is a reasonable amount and details of each fine are given. Finally, arrears of pay in a bankrupt company are treated as a priority debt. In the event of the debts not being paid, the Secretary of State can make payment from the Redundancy Fund. This includes amounts outstanding for an unfair dismissal award, guaranteed payment and paid time off. The employer can now pay new employees by cheque or directly into a bank account.
- **Pay statement**   Most employees have the right to be given a pay statement that shows the gross wage, the amount of fixed deductions, the amount of variable deductions and the net wage payable. The fixed deductions can be shown as a total and an annual statement given of what these deductions were.
- **Health and safety**   A wide range of duties are implied by statute law relating to health and safety. There are many industry-specific Acts, for example Factories, Mining and Quarrying, Offices, Shops and Railway Premises, that are beyond the scope of this book. Also, the Health and Safety at Work Act 1974 creates duties for the employer and employee but these are wholly criminal in nature and are not actionable at civil law. If, as the result of a statutory provision or a recommendation in a Code of Practice, a worker is suspended on medical grounds, the employer has to pay the employee full pay for up to 26 weeks. This applies only where the employee is capable of work and has not unreasonably refused suitable, alternative work.
- **Minimum periods of notice**   These are laid down by law and are:

  - for employer to employee, less than one month's service – none
    for continuous employment of less than two years, one week

for continuous employment of between 2 and 12 years – 1 week for each year of service

- for employee to employer, one week after one month's service.

Where the contract lays down longer periods, these apply. The following do not have this right: registered dock workers, merchant sailors, employees working abroad, Crown servants, members of the armed services and employees on fixed-term contracts. The periods of notice apply for redundancy and dismissal, unless an employee is summarily dismissed. Where specified in the works rules, or in some cases where there has been a breach of an implied duty, the employer can dismiss without notice. An employee is entitled to a normal week's pay (*see* Section 14.2.2 (b)) during the period of statutory notice (unless on strike or taking time off for which they are not entitled to be paid).

- **Equality** Under the Equal Pay Act 1970, an implied term of equality is included in all contracts of employment. This states that where there is a term favourable to one sex, it shall apply equally to the other or, if there is a term that benefits a person of one sex on like work (or work rated as equivalent or work of equal value) it shall benefit persons of the opposite sex.

12.2.4 Written statement

The original right for employees to be given a written statement of some of the terms of their contracts of employment was created by the Contracts of Employment Act 1963. This right was extended in 1972, 1974 and 1975 and the current provisions are stated in the Employment Protection (Consolidation) Act 1978. It is worth restating that these provisions do not mean that all employees have to receive a written contract of employment. The requirement is that the employer has to state, in writing, some of the main terms of the contract of employment. Often, as evidence that an employee has received

this statement, a signature is required. This should only be a signature to show that an employee has received the statement. In some circumstances, if the document purports to be a contract and is signed as such, that could be conclusive evidence that the document is the contract of employment. This could lead to difficulties, as a signed contract should contain all the elements of the contract of employment. Any claim to rights under a term not in the written contract could be rejected by a court or tribunal. The right under the legislation is to receive a written statement, which can be signed on receipt, stating the terms listed below. As we have noted in Section 12.1.3, the number of terms and conditions attached to a contract of employment can be numerous and most certainly more than the requirements under this section. The statement can be used in evidence to prove the existence of a particular term.

The written statement should be given to employees within 13 weeks of starting work. It applies to all full-time employees including those who average 16 hours per week or more, or those who average 8 hours a week after 5 years' service. Dockers, merchant sailors, Crown servants and employees working abroad are exempt, plus those who have a full written contract, like apprentices. The statement has to contain certain details plus a note on disciplinary and grievance procedures, but it can refer to documents where appropriate, providing these are accessible. The statement could contain the following information:

- the name of the employer and employee
- the start date of employment and if service with a previous employer counts as continuous employment
- the scale or rate of remuneration or the method of calculating it
- the interval of remuneration
- the normal hours of work and other conditions relating to hours
- holiday entitlement (including public holidays) and holiday pay
- sickness and injury pay
- pension and pension scheme

- notice required to terminate the contract on both sides or the dates of expiry of a fixed-term contract
- the job title

If there is no appropriate information under a heading, the statement must say so.

Additionally, the statement must have a note specifying any disciplinary rules that apply and to whom the employee can appeal against a disciplinary decision or to whom a grievance can be taken. This requirement does not apply to firms of 20 or fewer people. If there is a procedure for making an appeal, this should also be specified. Again, for the rules and procedures, documents can be referred to.

The documents referred to can be collective agreements, works Rule Books, booklets or orders. They must be kept accessible so that the employee has a reasonable opportunity of reading them in the course of employment. If changes are made to the terms, the employer has to inform the employee of the changes within a month of their introduction. Any documents referred to must be kept up to date but changes to the documents do not need communicating providing the employer undertakes, in writing, to keep the documents up to date. If there is a change of employer, a new written statement has to be given within 13 weeks. This is not required if there is a mere change of name. If the change of employer maintains continuity of employment the new employer only need state this and specify the date on which the employee's continuous period of employment began.

The European Community has made proposals for a Directive on this topic. They are very similar to the present laws in the UK. The EC proposals would cover all employees working 8 hours a week or more and the statement would have to be given within 2 months of starting work.

12.3   Pay

One of the vital elements in the employer/employee relationship is pay. Legally it is an essential term that the employer pays the employee in return for work. To work for no remuneration or reward does not constitute a contract. Collective bargaining is very much concerned with pay, particularly levels of pay. Collective bargaining has also been one of the key influencers on pay systems over the past century. More time is spent in negotiations over pay than any other item. Pay is also the single largest cause of strikes. This section examines some of the issues relating to pay and payment systems as there have been a number of significant changes in the 1980s to the traditional forms of payment system and remuneration packages.

Traditionally a contract of employment, particularly for the majority of employees, is that the employee is required to work a set number of hours per week for a specified wage. If extra hours are worked, extra money is paid, often at a premium. Where the contractual hours are not worked, pay is deducted and possibly, where the shortfall in hours is not for an acceptable reason, disciplinary action may be instituted. For others an annual salary is paid but this is often tied to a set number of hours of work per week with overtime payable.

There have been a number of minor changes over time. For example in the eighteenth century some employers paid their workers in tokens that could be redeemed at the company shop. This was subsequently prohibited by the Truck Acts. In this century the method of payment has changed from cash to direct debit arrangements. This did not take place without some problems associated with acceptance by employees used to receiving cash. A number of variations of payment system have been developed in various sectors. For example, in manufacturing industry there are many different schemes for payment by results and bonus schemes. Many of them developed from the turn of the century based on the work of F W Taylor (*see* Section 3.2.1). In the 1960s and 1970s such individual bonus schemes became unpopular as a result of severe industrial relations problems over the operation of the systems. Many became too complex and were open to abuse. Group based schemes were a favourite replacement as was measured day work. There has been little change in the 1980s though as an ACAS survey in 1988 showed few firms had given up individual incentive schemes or had plans to do so.

There have been a number of developments in the last decade which signal some fundamental changes to the traditional situation described above. The main reasons for firms wishing to introduce such changes is part of wider changes in the environment in which firms are operating and the culture of the organisation. The environment in which firms have to operate is much more competitive (for many firms this means globally) and market forces are the determining factor in the success or otherwise of a firm. The need to keep up with the competition, in order to survive and thrive, has put pressure on management to introduce changes, including those to payment systems. The culture of organisations has been changed by management to ensure success. This includes a sharp focus on efficiency of operations, improving quality, excellent customer service and need for all employees to contribute to the achievement of these aims. In working these through, managers have made demands on their employees to change. One vital aspect of this has been the need for flexibility within the workforce. Another important factor in creating pressure for change is the widespread use of technology in its various forms in most organisations. There has been, and will continue to be, a dramatic fall in the number of manual jobs and a blurring between blue and white collar jobs. Firms need increased flexibility to cope with the changes dictated by technology.

The traditional form of contract of employment straitjackets managers because of the rigidity of the system. Fixed hours of work on fixed pay schemes means that if managers wish to alter hours of work there would be a financial penalty through additional costs. For example, all firms have periods of high demand and low demand. If all employees are on fixed hours of work, overtime will need to be paid during periods of high demand and basic wages will still be paid even though there is not sufficient work (unless short time or lay offs are

declared). A further complication that has often caused industrial relations problems is that various sections of employees are treated differently. Manual workers tend to have poorer terms and conditions, staff workers better and top management the very best. The differentials are often substantial, not merely in terms of salary.

There have been a number of developments in payment systems that have addressed these problems.

Annual hours

Instead of specifying hours of work in terms of a set number of hours per day or week, the contract is to work a fixed number of hours each year. This can be achieved flexibly to suit the firm's needs. So employees can be required (under their contract) to cover for absent colleagues, extend the working day (or shorten it), cover for colleagues who are being trained, etc., without counting the hours worked and claiming the excess as overtime.

Standard conditions

Everyone is put on a standard contract. This can mean everyone, director to shop floor. The barriers and differentials are erased. No one clocks in or out, everyone has the same medical insurance, pension arrangements and so on. This also extends to everyone sharing the same facilities in the firm such as the canteen. The only remaining differential is the salary scale, where more senior employees are paid more. In fact, pay differentials have become a contentious issue in the late 1980s as top executives (notably in the newly privatised industries) have seen their salaries increase enormously in comparison to everyone else.

Pay structures

These have been rationalised to simplify what is frequently a complex situation. Grading structures still exist but with far fewer grades and a simple system to attach jobs to grades. This may still involve the use of a job evaluation system but there are problems associated with this as it requires the use of job descriptions which can be too restrictive and inflexible. Simplifying pay structures helps the process of flexibility as employees, if they are on the same grade, can be transferred to a different job without there being any arguments about a new rate for the job.

Performance-related bonuses

In line with improving business performance there has been an increase in the use of individual performance-related bonus schemes. Each individual is given a number of identifiable, measurable targets to achieve as part of their job. If the targets are achieved a bonus is paid. A similar system is merit bonuses. In some firms automatic annual pay increases have been scrapped and all pay increases are related to performance bonuses. In times of low inflation this might work, but if inflation were to rise, say to double figures, this scheme might be problematic.

Performance-related pay schemes have spread both to lower grades, e.g., white collar workers and to the public sector where PRP schemes have not been used as much to date. The industrial relations implications of this move are quite profound as the move is to individual contracts not collective agreements. Hence the nature of collective bargaining is set to change. This is also a reason why national agreements are in decline (*see* Section 7.1.2). An ACAS survey in 1988 found that about one third of firms had a performance-related bonus scheme but that these were limited mainly to white collar workers and larger firms.

Profit sharing

This method of rewarding employees is not new but there has been a revival of interest in it. The government has encouraged firms to implement such schemes by changing the tax rules. However, there has not been a substantial increase in the number of profit-sharing schemes. An ACAS survey in 1987 ascertained that one

quarter of firms surveyed had introduced such schemes in the last three years. The idea behind such schemes is that by sharing profits employees will be more committed to the organisation.

Mini-questions
12.1 Define what a contract is.
12.2 State the two parties to a contract of employment.
12.3 State the two essential elements in a contract of employment.
12.4 Briefly describe the two events that need to take place to form a contract.
12.5 Generally, does a contract of employment need to be in writing?
12.6 Define the 'control test' and state what it is used for.
12.7 State the legal minimum period of notice required by an employer and an employee.
12.8 List six of the important terms in a contract of employment.
12.9 List six sources of the terms of a contract of employment.
12.10 Explain what is meant by an implied term.
12.11 List five implied terms in a contract of employment.
12.12 Distinguish between a written statement and a written contract of employment.
12.13 State what a signature on a written statement should signify.
12.14 List six items that should appear in a written statement.
12.15 List two items that should appear as a note in the written statement.

Exercise
12.1 Discuss the relationship between an employer and employee. Explain its foundation in law and the implications of this.

Further reading

B A Hepple, *Labour Law and Industrial Relations*, Kluwer Law, 1992, 90-6544-641-9
K W Wedderburn, *The Worker and the Law*, Sweet and Maxwell, 1986, 0-421-37060-2
Work Research Unit, *Progressive Payment Systems*
ACAS, *Developments in Payment Systems*
N M Selwyn, *Law of Employment*, Butterworth, 1991, 0-406-50455-5

13
Dismissal

13.1 What is dismissal?

The whole basis of employment, is the contract of employment. This was studied in detail in Chapter 12. A characteristic of a contract of employment is that it is on-going (except for fixed-term contracts, which we will ignore). People at work expect to keep going to work and their employer expects them to turn up. However, there are ways in which the contract can end. The basic common law rule is that the parties are free to do what they wish within the terms of the contract. A contract of employment provides for notice to be given, either by the employee to the employer or vice versa. The contract will normally state the length of notice required, but it must comply with the Contracts of Employment Act 1963 requirements (now in the Employment Protection (Consolidation) Act 1978). Apart from notice requirements, either side could give notice and the contract would expire and, after the period of notice had run out, the employee would not have a job. Everything is fine if both sides mutually accept the situation. Thousands of people every year leave and get a new job, or have to retire or leave through ill-health or whatever.

The problem arises when the employee does not accept or agree to the termination of the contract. When the termination of the contract is not mutual and both sides are not in agreement on it ending, then a dismissal situation arises. This can happen when a person gets the sack for any of a host of reasons or is made redundant or even if the employer makes life so difficult the employee has to leave. Until 1971, the law

relating to dismissal (or the sack) was governed only by the common law rules. Basically these left the parties to their own devices. An employee could leave or the employer could give notice. There were no legal complications to this (there might be in terms of industrial relations trouble!) and the employer did not need to give reasons for the dismissal. In terms of redress in the courts and instituting civil proceedings, it was only possible to sue for wrongful dismissal. This action was based on a claim that the dismissal did not fulfil the requirements of the contract. Few cases were ever brought so the matter will not be pursued. You can still sue for wrongful dismissal today but it is rare.

In 1971 a new concept was introduced, in the Industrial Relations Act 1971. This was the concept of unfair dismissal. It is based on a dismissed person's employer showing that the dismissal was fair, or compensating the person for unfair dismissal. The idea is that the employee has a right to their job and, unless it is taken away fairly, compensation has to be paid for this loss. Under the legislation there have been many thousands of claims, some successful, leading to awards of compensation. The maximum compensation (in 1993) was £27,810, but it is highly unlikely that the circumstances will arise when this will be paid. Generally the amounts are a few hundred pounds. The details have changed since 1971, but the basic idea remains that a worker has the right to keep their job unless the dismissal by the employer is fair.

The Industrial Relations Act 1971 was repealed by the Trade Union and Labour Relations Act 1974. However, the provisions in the 1971 Act were transferred to the 1974 Act. This was amended by the Trade Union and Labour Relations (Amendment) Act 1976 and the Employment Protection Act 1975 and finally it was transferred to the Employment Protection (Consolidation) Act 1978, as a whole. There have been a few amendments under the Employment Act 1980 and Employment Act 1982.

There are two basic points to unfair dismissal:

- the dismissal must be for a fair reason
- the employer must have acted reasonably.

13.2 Reasons for dismissal

13.2.1 Fair reasons

The fair reasons laid down by law are as follows:

- related to capability or qualification
- related to conduct
- redundancy
- some other substantial reason
- if continued employment would result in a breach of the law

The employer has to show, to the satisfaction of the tribunal, that the reason was fair. If this is not done, the employee wins the case. If it is done, the tribunal moves to consider the next point of reasonableness. In practice the list above covers all manner of situations.

Capability is the ability of the employee to do the job. If they are incompetent or highly inefficient, they can be fairly dismissed, as can a worker producing poor quality work. If the employee becomes too ill or incapacitated (especially for physical work) the employer can fairly dismiss. A claim to possess a qualification that you have not got can lead to the sack. Conduct, including lateness, uncertified absence, fighting, drunkenness, indiscipline, lack of care, theft, fraud and breaking works rules, can lead to dismissal. Redundancy is dealt with in Chapter 14. Some other substantial reason ('sosr') is a category that is used where the tribunal thinks the reason was fair but it does

not slot into one of these three categories. For example, a member of a team of workers refusing to work overtime he had previously worked was sacked fairly not for conduct (a contract rarely makes overtime compulsory) but for sosr. The final reason is one which relates to the effect that, if an employee continued in employment, it would be in breach of the law. If a driver has their driving licence taken away, the employer can fairly dismiss in that circumstance as clearly the employee needs a licence to perform their duties.

The worker who has been sacked, or is under notice to quit, can ask the employer to supply a written statement of the reasons for dismissal. The employer must reply within 14 days, giving particulars of the reason for dismissal. This can be used in evidence at a tribunal. An employer refusing to do this or who, in the employee's opinion, gives an inadequate or untrue reason, can be taken to a tribunal. The tribunal can then make a declaration of what it finds to be the reason and award the employee two weeks' pay as compensation. This right is only given to employees with two years' service (full-time or equivalent).

13.2.2 Unfair reasons

There are two circumstances where the reason is not admissible to the tribunal and hence the dismissal is automatically unfair:

- Trade union membership or activities. If a person was, or proposed to become, a member of an independent trade union, or to take part in the activities of an independent trade union, and this was the reason for dismissal, this is unfair. 'Activities' does not mean industrial action activities like working to rule, overtime ban or striking, but means attending meetings, acting as a shop steward or convenor or any of the normal trade union activities. Often there are local rules regarding arrangements for this during working hours. Outside working hours people are free to do as they please.
- An employee who is dismissed for not being

a member of a trade union and refusing to be or become a member.

An employee who is dismissed on either of these grounds can apply to an industrial tribunal for interim relief. A tribunal can order reinstatement, re-engagement or the continuation of the contract of employment until a full hearing. Such an application has to be made within seven days of the date of termination.

There are two circumstances relating to pregnancy or maternity leave where dismissal is unfair.

- A woman who is sacked merely because she is pregnant, is unfairly dismissed. Only if the pregnancy makes the woman incapable of doing her job (or a law prohibits her doing it) can she be fairly dismissed. Further, if a woman is dismissed because of pregnancy and a suitable vacancy arises before she leaves and she is not offered it, then the dismissal is unfair.
- A woman is not allowed to return to work after a period of maternity leave. A woman has the right to return to work to her original job, or to one with terms and conditions no less favourable, within 29 weeks after the date of confinement. This does not apply to firms employing fewer than six people (*see also* Section 10.3.3(d).)

13.2.3 Closed shop and strikes

In a closed shop situation (*see* Section 15.3), there arises the problem of workers who are not trade union members, or who refuse to join the specified union, or are refused entry to the specified union, or object to joining any union. The basic rule was that the dismissal was fair if it was the practice for employees of that class to belong to a specified independent trade union, and the employee was not, or refused to become, a member of that union.

The Employment Act 1988 reversed this whole position so that, instead of allowing for the fair dismissal of a person because of the operation of a closed shop (given certain restrictions), a person cannot be dismissed in

such circumstances. Further, if a trade union organises or threatens industrial action to establish or maintain a closed shop, their immunity to being sued is removed (*see* Section 10.2.2). The Act specifically states that if the reason for action is because the employer is employing someone who is not a trade union member, or is to pressurise the employer into taking action against a person for non-trade union membership, the immunity is removed. This effectively prevents unions putting pressure on employers to dismiss non-trade union member employees. The law is now contained in the Trade Union and Labour Relations (Consolidation) Act 1992.

Strikes also pose a problem. A strike is a breach of a contract (*see* Section 15.1). Under ordinary circumstances the breach continues until there is a return to work, and then the contract continues. An employer is entitled to say that the breach of contract, because of the strike, has terminated the contract and those on strike can be sacked. This is a fair reason for dismissal (actually the law says the workers have sacked themselves).

If the employer cannot satisfy the tribunal that the reason was fair then the employee has succeeded in the case. If the tribunal is satisifed then the next question in Section 13.3 is considered.

13.2.4 Constructive dismissal

Under normal circumstances it is the employer who dismisses the employee who can then claim unfair dismissal. In certain circumstances an employee can serve notice to leave and then claim constructive dismissal. The grounds for doing this are that the employee was no longer able to continue working for the employer under the prevailing circumstances. This may be due to victimisation, harassment, being overlooked for promotion, the employer not fulfilling promises made, etc. If the employer's conduct shows that they no longer intend to be bound by an essential term in the contract, then the employee has grounds for giving notice, leaving and claiming unfair dismissal. The procedure followed is then the same as for a normal claim for unfair dismissal.

13.3   Acting reasonably

The question that next arises is whether the action of the employer was reasonable in dismissing the employee. The Employment Act 1980 amends the original wording to whether 'the employer in the circumstances (including the size and administrative resources of the employer's undertaking) acted reasonably in treating it as sufficient reason for dismissing the employee and that the question shall be determined in accordance with equity and the substantial merits of the case'. This typically laborious piece of legal wording means that the employer has to treat employees fairly and not sack them on the spot with no explanation or right to be heard. Often it is on this point that unfair dismissal cases are lost by employers, i.e., the reason is fair but the handling of it is not.

The circumstances of the dismissal are important. There is a Code of Practice on Industrial Relations (issued in 1972) and a Code of Practice for Disciplinary Procedures (*see* Chapter 11). These are not law but act as a yardstick against which the employer's conduct can be measured. If it falls below the standard required it may mean a lost case, but it is for the tribunal to decide finally. A general rule is that employees should not be sacked for a first offence, except in serious circumstances in which they know they would be sacked. For example, theft, fraud, clocking offences (if specified in the works rules) are all reasons for instant dismissal. Otherwise an employee should be warned about the behaviour and given the chance to improve. If, after repeated warnings, there is no improvement, then the dismissal would be fair. Certain guidelines exist and include the following:

- the right to be represented at a disciplinary meeting by a shop steward or colleague
- the right to explain their case before a decision is reached

- the right to appeal against a decision to a higher level of management
- a clear statement of the consequences of further breaches
- the right to be informed of the dismissal by a person having the power to dismiss

There have been cases where an employee has been in the wrong but still successfully claimed unfair dismissal. In one case an employee took money from a till, admitted the offence, but was considered unfairly dismissed because she was given no opportunity of explaining her action and was not sacked by someone having the authority to do so. Employees in higher positions may be treated more strictly, as much higher standards are required of them and they can be sacked without prior warning. The treatment of people who are ill requires special care. A person needs to be given the full opportunity to recover and return to work. Expert medical opinion should be taken and, if the employee cannot return to their old job, there should be a search for an alternative. Ill health is a fair reason for dismissal but needs treating with care in the circumstances. If an employee is being sacked for breaking works rules the employer should ensure everyone has the rules, and any amendments, brought to their attention. A plea of 'I didn't know the rules' might be sufficient to win the case. Some rules are obvious, like theft, but others vary from firm to firm.

If a disciplinary procedure exists (and there should be one) then it is important that it is followed. If the procedure has not been followed, it is not conclusive that the case is lost but it makes the case that much more difficult to prove.

13.4   Remedies

There are two remedies for unfair dismissal: re-employment and monetary compensation.

13.4.1   Reemployment

Tribunals must first look at the option of re-employment. A tribunal can make an order for reinstatement (same job back) or reengagement (similar job back). It first enquires if the applicant wants the job back. If not, the tribunal moves to see what compensation may be payable, but the applicant cannot refuse a reasonable offer of reemployment. If the applicant wishes to have a job back, the employer can claim that it is not practicable (the firm may have another full-time replacement). Also if the complainant caused or contributed to the dismissal, the tribunal could decide it would not be just to order the job back. A tribunal can make an order of reengagement or reinstatement which the employer should comply with. If not, the tribunal can make an award including an extra amount for noncompliance with the order. In practice there are few orders for reemployment. Less than 1% of tribunal cases involve an order of any sort.

13.4.2 Compensation

This is the remedy used in practice. Of all the unfair dismissal claims made, nearly half of them get compensation of some sort, about a third being conciliated settlements, the balance being determined by a tribunal. Compensation may consist of four parts:

- **Basic award** This is based on redundancy pay and is compensation for loss of the job:
  - for each year of service over 40 years of age 1½ weeks' pay
  - for each year of service aged 22 to 40 1 week's pay
  - for each year of service aged below 22 ½ week's pay
  (A week's pay is basic pay usually excluding bonus, overtime and shift allowances. There is a maximum claim of 20 years' service and ceiling on pay of £205 per week. So the maximum possible is £6,150, as of 1993.
- **Compensatory award** This is based on what the tribunal considers just and equitable in the circumstances for losses sustained. This claim needs itemising and can include loss of earnings, loss of pension, expenses involved, loss of perks, etc. Complainants must mini-

mise their losses, e.g., by trying to get another job. The maximum possible is £11,000 (1993).
- **Noncompliance award** If an order for re-engagement or reinstatement is made and the employer refuses to comply (unless it is not practicable to comply) there can be an additional award made, of between 13 and 26 weeks' pay. If the dismissal is on the ground of sex or race discrimination, this part of the compensation can be doubled, to between 26 and 52 weeks' pay. The maximum week's pay is £205, so the maximum claim possible is £10,660, as of 1993.
- **Special award** Where the reason for dismissal was trade union membership, non-membership or activities, a special award can be made. If the employee requested re-instatement or re-engagement but the tribunal did not make such an order, the award is one week's pay multiplied by 104 or £13,400, whichever is the greater, to a maximum of £26,800 in 1993. If the tribunal does make an order but the employer fails to comply with the order, the award is one week's pay multiplied by 156 or £20,100, whichever is the greater (no maximum).

In total this could amount to £27,810, but the circumstances would have to be extraordinary, for example, a long-serving employee (over 20 years' service) over the age of 60, being sacked for trade union activities and the employer refusing to have the person back after being ordered to do so. Claims under more than one head, e.g., for dismissal and sex discrimination, can only lead to one award, not two.

The tribunals have the power to reduce the award by the proportion the tribunal feels that the complainant had contributed to their own dismissal. This can run from a small percentage to 100%. Some cases may be technically unfair dismissal but the employee was so awkward, of bad character or had committed a serious offence, that the tribunal can take away some or all of the money. An award by a tribunal is enforceable in the ordinary courts (County Court or High Court) as if it were an ordinary court order. So, while a tribunal cannot force an order to be obeyed (because to disobey a tribunal order is not contempt of court like disobeying an ordinary court order), there can be enforcement of an award of money to compensate.

13.5 Procedure

Figure 13.1 shows the steps in the procedure for claiming unfair dismissal.

An important stage in the procedure for unfair dismissal is the use of an ACAS conciliation officer. The officer has to receive details of the case and has a duty to try to achieve a settlement. In two-thirds of the cases this occurs and a tribunal does not get involved.

The Employment Act 1980 allows an employer to 'join' a union or a union official in the proceedings for unfair dismissal. This can occur where an employee says the employer has taken action to compel the employee to become a member of a union, and the employer claims the union induced this action with threats of strikes (or other industrial action). This will be of importance in a closed shop situation where the union says it will no longer tolerate non-union labour and the employer, under threat of industrial action, has to pressurise the non-union member. A union or person 'joined' in an action can be ordered to pay some or all of the compensation awarded, as the tribunal sees fit.

13.5.1 Definitions

Continuous employment

In many cases compensation is based on receiving payment for each full year of continuous employment, i.e., the period of unbroken employment with the same employer. The calculation is in months and years and continuity is checked on a weekly basis. Periods of sickness, holiday, lay-off or absence through reason of pregnancy still count. If hours of work are temporarily reduced to less than 16 but more than eight for a period of less than 26 weeks,

there is still continuity of employment. If an employee is reinstated or re-engaged, the period between leaving and rejoining counts. Days or weeks on strike do not count towards continuous employment but do not cause a break in service. Hence when strikers return to work, they do not recommence their service from the start again but continue with a gap for the duration of the strike. However, a period of dismissal while on strike will cause a break of service unless the strikers are re-engaged. Days or weeks locked out by the employer do count towards service. If an employee is made redundant and re-engaged within four weeks there is no break in service and the period between counts as service. A period for which redundancy pay has been made does not count towards any future incidence of redundancy. The period of continuous employment includes any period of notice whether worked or not. This includes cases of instant dismissal where the statutory period of notice will be added to the date of termination.

Date of termination

This date is used to determine if the employee is entitled to claim unfair dismissal, i.e., has worked for more than the minimum period laid down (*see* Qualifying service, *below*). If the employer or employee gives notice, the date of termination is the date on which the period of notice expires. If an employee is given pay in lieu of notice, the date is the last date worked. In cases of summary dismissal the date is the date on which the employee was dismissed. If an employee resigns and claims constructive dismissal, the date of termination is that which it would have been if the employer had given notice.

Weekly pay

See Section 14.2.2(b).

Years of service

See Section 14.2.2(a).

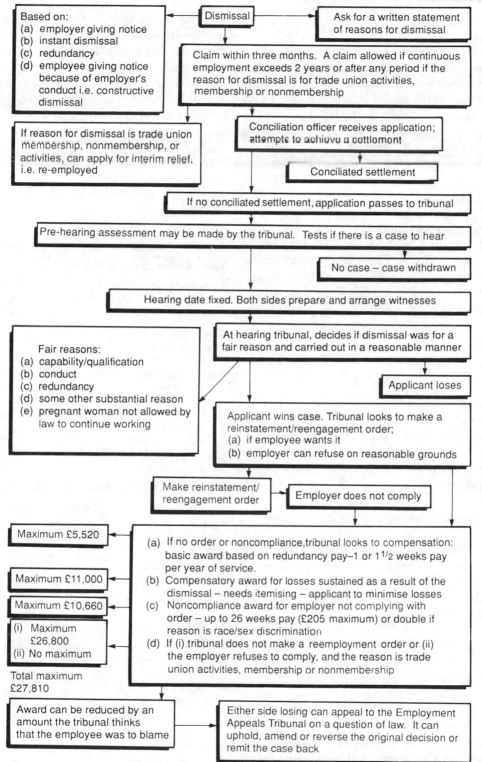

Based on:
(a) employer giving notice
(b) instant dismissal
(c) redundancy
(d) employee giving notice because of employer's conduct i.e. constructive dismissal

Dismissal

Ask for a written statement of reasons for dismissal

Claim within three months. A claim allowed if continuous employment exceeds 2 years or after any period if the reason for dismissal is for trade union activities, membership or nonmembership

If reason for dismissal is trade union membership, nonmembership, or activities, can apply for interim relief, i.e. re-employed

Conciliation officer receives application; attempts to achieve a settlement

Conciliated settlement

If no conciliated settlement, application passes to tribunal

Pre-hearing assessment may be made by the tribunal. Tests if there is a case to hear

No case – case withdrawn

Hearing date fixed. Both sides prepare and arrange witnesses

Fair reasons:
(a) capability/qualification
(b) conduct
(c) redundancy
(d) some other substantial reason
(e) pregnant woman not allowed by law to continue working

At hearing tribunal, decides if dismissal was for a fair reason and carried out in a reasonable manner

Applicant loses

Applicant wins case. Tribunal looks to make a reinstatement/reengagement order;
(a) if employee wants it
(b) employer can refuse on reasonable grounds

Make reinstatement/ reengagement order

Employer does not comply

Maximum £5,520

Maximum £11,000

Maximum £10,660

(i) Maximum £26,800
(ii) No maximum

Total maximum £27,810

(a) If no order or noncompliance, tribunal looks to compensation: basic award based on redundancy pay–1 or 1½ weeks pay per year of service.
(b) Compensatory award for losses sustained as a result of the dismissal – needs itemising – applicant to minimise losses
(c) Noncompliance award for employer not complying with order – up to 26 weeks pay (£205 maximum) or double if reason is race/sex discrimination
(d) If (i) tribunal does not make a reemployment order or (ii) the employer refuses to comply, and the reason is trade union activities, membership or nonmembership

Award can be reduced by an amount the tribunal thinks that the employee was to blame

Either side losing can appeal to the Employment Appeals Tribunal on a question of law. It can uphold, amend or reverse the original decision or remit the case back

Fig 13.1 Steps in the procedure for claiming unfair dismissal

Qualifying service

To claim unfair dismissal, an employee must have worked for the employer continuously for a minimum of two years at the date of termination (*see above*). This period falls to four weeks for dismissals on medical grounds because of health and safety requirements. There is no qualifying period of service for dismissals due to trade union membership, activities or nonmembership.

Exclusions

Some employees cannot claim unfair dismissal. These are: those without the qualifying period of service; part-time employees (*see* definition, *below*); anyone over 65 or those over normal retirement age; the police or members of the armed forces; employees working outside the UK; registered dock workers or share-catch fishers.

Time limits

A claim for unfair dismissal must be made to an industrial tribunal within three months of the date of termination. Application after that date will be heard only if it was not reasonably practicable for the claim to be made within the time limits.

Full-time worker

Anyone working under a contract of service and whose hours of work have exceeded 16 hours per week for two years or eight or more per week after five years' service, are entitled to claim unfair dismissal.

Transfer of undertaking

The Transfer of Undertakings (Protection of Employment) Regulations 1981 apply when a business is transferred to a new owner. The contracts of employment of existing employees are automatically transferred without any changes to the terms and conditions. Any fundamental change to the terms and conditions can lead to a claim for constructive dismissal, but not merely because there has been a transfer in ownership. An employer (old or new) can dismiss an employee if this is necessary for economic, technical or organisational reasons associated with the transfer. The dismissal would be unfair if the reason were purely because of the transfer.

13.5.2 Statistics

The following tables 13.1 and 13.2 give the figures for unfair dismissal applications and compensation.

Table 13.1 Unfair dismissal applications (1989)

Total number of cases: 17,870	
Cases not going to tribunal:	11,814 (66%)
conciliated settlement	6,935 (59%)
withdrawn	4,879 (41%)
Cases heard at tribunal:	5,786 (32%)
cases dismissed	3,620 (63%)
out of scope	927 (26%)
other reason	2,693 (74%)
cases upheld	2,166 (37%)
re-employment	58 (3%)
compensation	1,272 (59%)
no award made	39 (2%)
remedy by parties	797 (37%)

Source: Employment Gazette

Table 13.2 Unfair dismissal monetary awards (1989)

Amount	Number of cases	%
<£100	8	0.6
£100–£500	146	11.6
£500–£1,000	181	14.4
£1,000–£2,000	261	20.7
£2,000–£5,000	288	22.9
£5,000–£8,000	87	6.9
over £8,000	101	8.0
unspecified	190	15.1
Total	1,262	

Source: Employment Gazette

Multiple-choice questions

13.1 For which of these offences could you be sacked on the spot?
  (a) being late
  (b) off sick
  (c) stealing
  (d) producing bad work.

13.2 For which of the following offences could you eventually be fairly dismissed?
  (a) poor workmanship
  (b) absenteeism
  (c) fraud
  (d) not doing as requested.

13.3 You can refuse to join a trade union in a closed shop situation
  (a) if you wish to
  (b) if the union agrees
  (c) on grounds of religious faith
  (d) on grounds of conscience.

13.4 You can be fairly dismissed for being on strike
  (a) not at all
  (b) yes
  (c) if everyone is sacked
  (d) only if the strike is unofficial.

13.5 A pregnant woman can be fairly dismissed
  (a) if she cannot do her job
  (b) not at all
  (c) if she is too ill
  (d) for being pregnant.

13.6 Can a tribunal force an employer to take back a sacked person?
  (a) no
  (b) yes
  (c) if it makes an order
  (d) if the employee requests it.

13.7 A majority of people claiming unfair dismissal
  (a) go to a tribunal
  (b) are awarded compensation
  (c) withdraw or have the complaint dismissed
  (d) get their job back.

Exercises

13.1 Write an account outlining the main points of unfair dismissal in relation to the reason for dismissal and the handling of it.

13.2 Describe how it is possible for someone to have been unfairly dismissed even though they have committed a serious offence.

13.3 What remedies are available to an employee who has been unfairly dismissed?

13.4 Explain how it is possible to be awarded £27,810 for unfair dismissal.

Further reading

Anderman, *Law of Unfair Dismissal*, Butterworth, 1985, 0-406-10707-6
Hepple and O'Higgins, *Employment Law*.
N M Selwyn, *Law of Employment*, Butterworth, 1991, 0-406-50455-5
McMillan, *Workers' Guide to Employment Law*.

Case studies

(2) Growing pains, page 307.
(3) Defective procedures are harmful, page 314.
(7) Negotiating a disciplinary procedure, page 328.
(8) The mushrooming problem, page 331.
(10) Temper! Temper!, page 339.
(11) Strangers at work, page 344.

14

Redundancy

14.1 Defining redundancy

The concept of redundancy is based on the idea that a person has a form of property right to their job. Like any other piece of property owned by a person, if it is taken away by someone else that person must pay compensation. This idea came up in the last chapter, on unfair dismissal. In fact, redundancy is a fair reason for dismissal. Redundancy is a situation when the job an employee does is no longer required by the employer. Technically it is the job that is redundant or not needed, and the compensation is paid to the current holder of that job.

The Redundancy Payments Act 1965 put on the statute books the definition of redundancy. That is the employer has ceased, or will cease, to carry on the business for the purpose for which the employee was employed, either altogether or at that place. This covers the situation where the business closes altogether on that site or the branch is closed. As the firm no longer needs those employees, they are made redundant. A further situation in which redundancy occurs is when the requirements of that business for employees to carry out work of a particular kind (either at that place or altogether) have ceased or diminished. This covers the situation when, because of changes in method, product, technology or whatever, that particular kind of work no longer needs to be carried out. The Act was passed to provide compensation for individuals made redundant. In addition it was to encourage workers to leave one type of work (that was diminishing) for another job in an expanding sector. It was to discourage over-staffing and to minimise the industrial relations difficulties that can ensue when people are made redundant. In a judgement in 1969, Lord Denning said, 'The purpose of redundancy pay is to compensate a worker for loss of job, irrespective of whether that loss leads to unemployment. It is to compensate for loss of security, possible loss of earnings and fringe benefits, and the uncertainty and anxiety of a change of job. These may all be present even if a person gets a fresh job immediately.'

The provisions for redundancy were originally contained in the Redundancy Payments Act 1965, modified in 1969, and some new provisions brought in with the Employment Protection Act 1975. Now all the provisions are contained in the Employment Protection (Consolidation) Act 1978.

14.2 Redundancy payments

14.2.1 Eligibility

The redundancy payment is the compensation the employer pays to the employee for the loss of job sustained by reason of redundancy. It is a tax-free (if less than £25,000) lump sum paid to those eligible. The amount varies (*see* Section 14.2.2) depending on age and service. Those eligible are as follows:

- all those employees working under a contract of employment (including apprenticeships) who have worked for two years continuously from the age of 18

- all full-time equivalent workers, i.e., those who work on average 16 hours a week or more, or after 5 years' service, work on average 8 hours a week or more

There are some exclusions:

- those over normal retirement age
- dock workers, shore fishers, merchant sailors and civil servants. These may be covered by alternative schemes
- an unreasonable refusal of alternative employment (*see* Section 14.3.3)

Normally redundancy is declared by the employer, but it can be done by the employee because of lack of opportunity to work (*see* Section 14.2.3). Also the redundancies have to be handled in a prescribed way (*see* Section 14.3).

14.2.2 Calculation of payment

The formula for redundancy payment is based on years of service and age. The basic formula is:

For each year's service when aged 41–64
 1½ weeks' pay
For each year's service when aged 22–40
 1 week's pay
For each year's service when aged below 22
 ½ week's pay

The maximum number of years' service that can be claimed is 20 years, so giving a maximum entitlement of 30 weeks (20 years between 41 and 64). The maximum week's pay claimable is £205 (in 1993).

Total maximum redundancy pay is £6,150 (under the Act's provisions).

There are statutory definitions of the words used above:

(a) 'Years of service' is the number of whole years (52 weeks) that a person has been continuously employed by that employer. Changes of ownership (or nationalisation) do not affect continuity except if a different trade is followed. If a person is paid redundancy pay on a change of ownership then this obviously constitutes a break of service. Continuity is not broken for absence due to lay-offs, short time, sickness, pregnancy, holidays or injury. A temporary break in service occurs with strikes (but not lockouts) and military service in that the weeks out do not count towards total service but they do not cause a permanent break in the service. A person who has worked for a firm for exactly 10 years (520 weeks) but who was on strike at some time for 8 weeks will have a service entitlement of 9 years. The requirement of having exactly 52 weeks per year is relaxed by 14 days (up to 5 years' service) or 31 days (after 5 years' service).

(b) 'Week's pay' is the normal week's pay. For time workers on a fixed salary or wage, but including any regular bonus or allowance (except expenses), the pay for calculation purposes is the normal week's pay. Any casual overtime does not count. For workers on an output-based bonus, the week's pay is based on the pay received in the last 12 working weeks prior to leaving, divided by the actual number of hours worked, including overtime. Shift workers who work a variable number of hours in a week have their average number of hours calculated in the same 12 week period. Periods of strike, lockout, sickness or injury do not count towards the period.

Employees aged 64 are entitled to redundancy pay but have their payment reduced by one twelfth for every month after their last birthday. So that at their 65th birthday they are entitled to nothing.

The employer is required to give the employee a written statement indicating how the actual amount has been calculated. Failure to provide a written statement can lead to the employer being fined £200, or £1,000 if an employer fails to supply a statement after a request from an employee. A redundancy payment is free from income tax if less than £25,000.

14.2.3 Short time and lay-offs

A person who is on short time or is laid off can, in certain circumstances, claim redundancy and hence can make a claim for redundancy pay. Short time is where an employee is paid less than half a week's pay for that week (a week's pay having the same meaning as in Section 14.2.2(b)). A lay-off is where an employee gets no pay of any kind for that week; even though available for work, there is none to do.

An employee can claim redundancy if the employee has been laid off or put on short time (or a mixture of both) for either four consecutive weeks or any six out of 13. The employee can then make a written claim for redundancy pay. The employer can make a counter claim that normal working will resume within four weeks of the claim. If normal working does not occur, the employee can go ahead with a claim for redundancy. If normal working does occur, the employee will have to pursue a claim for redundancy in an industrial tribunal. After making a claim, the employee then has to serve notice and leave before being entitled to any payment. The person has to leave within four weeks of the claim or within three weeks of any counterclaim or tribunal award.

14.2.4 Leaving early

Employees under notice of redundancy who obtain another job, can hand their notice in (as required by the contract of employment) to leave early. If the employer agrees, the employees can leave early and this does not affect entitlement to redundancy pay. If the employer does not agree, the employees should stay to the end of the redundancy notice period if they are to receive redundancy pay. However, if the employees leave prior to this, the claim will have to be taken to an industrial tribunal. The tribunal looks at such cases in the light of the reason why the employer wanted the person to stay on and the reasons for the employee wanting to leave early. These provisions apply only during the period of legal notice entitlement under the contract of employment (*see* Section 12.2.3), not during any longer period under the individual contract. For example, an employee of five years' standing, who is entitled to 12 weeks' notice under their contract, can make a claim to leave

early only in the last five weeks of the 12, but not in the first seven weeks.

14.3 Handling redundancies

14.3.1 Consultations

The Employment Protection Act 1975 laid down provisions for the employer to consult trade unions regarding any proposed redundancies. The provisions apply (by law at any rate) to trade union members. Consultations must begin before the redundancies are declared with a view to discussing the plan to see if there are any ways of reducing the numbers involved or reducing the effects of the redundancies. The Act stipulates a minimum time period in which these consultations should take place. If between 10 and 99 are involved, it is 30 days and with over 99 it is 90 days. These minimum times can run concurrently with the periods of notice given to employees.

An employer is required to give a certain amount of information regarding the redundancies to enable the union to take part in any discussions constructively. The points of information to be given are as follows:

- the reasons for the proposal
- the numbers and description of employees involved
- the total number of employees of that description
- the proposed method of selection
- the proposed method of dismissing the employees and the period over which the dismissals will take place

Due regard will have to be taken of any local agreements. Often, in practice, the union and management have agreements relating to redundancies and these will obviously operate. The minimum they should contain are these statutory requirements plus others that have been jointly negotiated.

If the employer does not comply with these requirements, the union can take the employer to court. A notable instance occurred in 1992 when British Coal declared several thousand miners redundant (some with one week's notice). The NUM took British Coal to court and both the High Court and the Court of Appeal upheld the claim that the redundancies were invalid as the correct procedure had not been followed; neither the statutory requirements nor the domestic procedure. This embarrassed the government who had approved the announcement. British Coal were ordered to cancel the notices and go through the correct procedure.

The employer is required to reply to any representation the union makes on the matter of redundancy.

14.3.2 Protective awards

If an employer does not comply with the requirements of the law on consultations (as stated in Section 14.3.1), the union can apply to an industrial tribunal for a protective award. This has the effect of giving the employees who are under notice of redundancy, or who have been made redundant, a payment for a specified period. The length of the period does not exceed the number of days' notice required (as in Section 14.3.1). Where fewer than 10 employees are involved, the number of days is 28. The period runs from the date of application to the tribunal or the date of dismissal, whichever is the earlier. It is a defence for the employer to say that everything reasonably practicable was done or it was not reasonably practicable to comply with the requirements. A tribunal can enforce the payment of this award.

14.3.3 Alternative employment

If an employee is offered alternative employment (either in writing or verbally), the employee should not unreasonably refuse the offer. The renewal of the contract or reengagement has to take place before being dismissed or up to four weeks afterwards. The offer of employment can be in the same kind of job as before or in a new, but suitable job. If the employee unreasonably refuses the offer, there is loss of entitlement to redundancy pay. If the new job is on different

terms and conditions, there has to be a trial period. This is a minimum of four weeks but can be longer by written agreement. The offer can be with the same employer, a new employer (say after a take-over) or an associated employer. An associated employer is one that owns the original company or the two are owned by a third, like a group or combine.

If, during the trial period, the employee or employer terminates the new contract, the employee is treated as being dismissed under the old contract. This then raises the question of entitlement to redundancy pay. The employer can agree to pay. If not, the case can be taken to an industrial tribunal for it to decide if the employer or employee has acted reasonably. If the tribunal decides that the employee reasonably refused the new job after trying it, redundancy pay has to be made. It also has to be paid if the employer dismisses the employee as not being suitable in the new job. Dismissal for some other reason (e.g., misconduct) does not raise the question of redundancy pay. That would be an ordinary dismissal from the new job and is dealt with as unfair dismissal (*see* Chapter 13).

14.3.4 Time off for job hunting and training

An employee under notice of redundancy is entitled to time off work, which may be with pay, to look for a job or make arrangements for training. It is restricted to employees who have worked for two years continuously up to the date that the notice expires. This includes 'full-time equivalents', i.e., those who work 16 hours a week or more, or 8 hours a week after 5 years' service. The Act says the employer should give 'reasonable time off during the employee's working hours'. The employee is entitled to be paid at the hourly rate described in Section 14.2.2. An employee who is refused the right to time off or pay, can take the case to an industrial tribunal. The tribunal can make an award to the employee, if the case is proved, to a maximum of two fifths of a week's pay. This is a legal minimum and can be much greater if the contract of employment gives a greater entitlement.

14.3.5 Relationship to unfair dismissal

As explained in Section 14.1, redundancy is a special case of dismissal. Where everything goes according to the rules and procedures outlined in this chapter the dismissed employee has been fairly dismissed and is only entitled to redundancy pay. In some circumstances though, an employee can make a claim for unfair dismissal (which gives greater compensation). If the procedures for selecting the people for redundancy are not fair or the manner of implementing the redundancies is not fair, this can form the basis for a claim of unfair dismissal. Two reasons are specified as unfair:

(a) the reason for which the employee was selected for dismissal was an inadmissible one. (An inadmissible reason is one which is automatically unfair, as listed in Section 13.2.2.)

(b) the employee was selected for dismissal in contravention of a customary arrangement or agreed procedure and there was no special reason justifying a departure from that arrangement.

If an employee feels that the selection for redundancy was because of the reasons in (a), or the usual arrangements have not been followed, the case can be taken to an industrial tribunal on a claim for unfair dismissal. This can be done even though the employee has not been with the employer for two years. These events could occur where an employer wanted to get rid of some specific people and uses redundancy as an excuse. There are often customary rules for selecting people for redundancy. The most popular is last-in-first-out. If the traditional way is not used, the employer can be accused of victimisation and those so selected might be able to claim unfair dismissal successfully. The case will be the same as in Chapter 13.

An employee who successfully claims unfair dismissal is entitled to compensation under the provisions of unfair dismissal (*see* Section 13.4.2). This will be more than redundancy pay, as the basic award under unfair dismissal compensation is the same as redundancy pay. On top of that the person can claim a compensatory award. Alternatively there can be a claim for the job back by asking the tribunal for a reinstatement or re-engagement order.

An employee dismissed during the period of notice of redundancy may be fairly dismissed and lose entitlement to redundancy pay. The issue is one that is resolved by an action for unfair dismissal in a tribunal. The tribunal can decide if the dismissed employee is entitled to all or some or no redundancy pay. If the dismissal is unfair, the employee gets the normal unfair dismissal compensation.

Any employees who strike while under notice of redundancy can be sacked for being on strike but cannot lose their entitlement to redundancy pay. The period of striking does not count towards service entitlement (Section 14.2.2, *see under* 'Years of service') nor is it included in any pay calculations (*see* Section 14.2.2 'Week's pay'). The employer can require any employee who has been on strike to work beyond the leaving date by the amount of time the employee has been on strike.

In the leading case of *Polkey* v *A. E. Dayton Services Ltd* (1987) the House of Lords declared that failure to follow a fair procedure in making someone redundant makes the dismissal unfair, even if following a procedure would have made no difference to the outcome. Polkey had not been consulted about the potential redundancy and should have been, even though the job was clearly redundant. This should be followed for all employees, not just those who are trade union members to whom the legal provisions on consultation apply.

14.3.6 Local agreements

The details of redundancy and redundancy pay given in this chapter are the legal requirements laid down in the Employment Protection (Consolidation) Act 1978. These are a minimum that have to be complied with. If not the employee can take the issue to an industrial tribunal and, if the case is proven, the requirements will be enforced. Usually the employer has a redundancy agreement with the unions that is a considerable improvement on the legal minimum. As with all collective agreements, these agreements are not enforceable in the courts or in a tribunal, but only through the normal channels of industrial relations procedures. The benefits given in these agreements can be more than those specified in this chapter in terms of pay, notice given, time off for training and redeployment.

14.4 Redundancy arrangements

ACAS carried out a survey, in 1985, into the redundancy arrangements that existed in British companies and the results give a valuable insight into the topic and provide a substantial amount of data. Previous surveys revealed the emergence of certain practices such as the greater use of formal agreements, measures to minimise redundancy, redundancy selection criteria and extra-statutory payments, although the pattern across the several surveys was not even. The ACAS survey was based on 425 usable questionnaires returned from a range of companies, in different regions and in a variety of sectors. The questionnaire focused on the following aspects:

- **arrangements** whether the company had a policy, i.e., a formal statement by management or if it had a formal agreement with employee representatives or if it relied on 'practice', with no prior formal arrangements being made
- **measures to avoid or minimise job loss** e.g., natural wastage, reduction of overtime, retraining, redeployment, reduction in subcontracting
- **selection criteria** based on seniority, skills, experience, disciplinary and absence record
- **payments** whether the company made extra-statutory payments
- **consultation** whether the consultation procedures were more than the statutory minimum
- **additional measures** counselling, time off for job hunting or training, assistance with self-employment or help with job hunting

Extracts of the findings of the survey are now given, under the headings listed above.

Arrangements

The types of arrangements found were:

- redundancy agreement   48%
- redundancy policy   22%
- practice   30%

The survey showed a growth in the introduction of agreements in recent times although the *ad hoc* practice arrangement was introduced in several firms when they faced a sudden crisis, and this, they felt, was the best way to deal with the situation.

Measures to avoid or minimise job loss

Firms indicated which measures, from a list, they used. The results can be seen in Table 14.1.

Table 14.1

Measure	% used
Restriction on recruitment	74
Retraining/redeployment	61
Reduction in overtime	59
Early retirement	58
Termination of temporary staff	56
Short-time working	33
Reduction of subcontract work	24
Other	8

The average number of measures used was 3.9. Where the arrangements (above) were in the 'practice' category, there were fewer measures used. There was a wide variation in the number of measures used in different sectors, e.g., hotels and catering averaged 2.7 measures while motor vehicle manufacture was highest, using 4.6 measures. Notably, there was a strong correlation between the number of measures used and union membership density in the various sectors.

Selection criteria

Firms were asked which criteria were used and which was the most important and the results were as given in Table 14.2.

Data collected showed that the seniority/LIFO rule was less important in recent times than formerly, with the skills/experience criteria being

Table 14.2

Criteria	Criteria used (%)	Most important criteria (%)
Last-in-first-out	82	41
Skills/experience	69	39
Discipline/absence	32	3
Overall performance	30	12
Other	10	5

used more frequently than in the past. The LIFO rule is simple and seen to be fair, but firms find that reorganisation often requires the retention of certain skills and flexibility by personnel. Hence this criterion is used to retain the necessary skilled and experienced staff required for future operations. The majority (85%) of firms allowed for voluntary redundancy with those firms with an agreement arrangement more likely to allow this, while 6% of firms ruled out compulsory redundancy altogether. It was found that 65% paid above the statutory minimum and that, again, firms with an agreement were much more likely to pay more (72%) than those with a 'practice' arrangement (47%). Finally, the survey asked firms about the effects of their redundancy arrangements on industrial relations. See Table 14.3 for the findings.

Table 14.3

Effect	More likely (%)	Less likely (%)	No effect (%)
Cooperation with new working methods	44	3	47
Cooperation with introduction of new technology	29	4	55
Disagreements leading to industrial action	7	37	55

Increased cooperation was more likely in firms having agreements or a 'practice' arrangement as opposed to a policy arrangement. Those firms with an agreement reported that industrial action was much less likely (47% of firms) than those with a policy or practice arrangement (28% and 27% of firms, respectively). Where employees have been involved, there is likely to be increased harmony. Those firms with a policy, as opposed to an agreement, have probably tried to secure an agreement and failed, which would explain why they had a greater expectation of there being some kind of industrial action.

The conclusions of the report stated that not only are many firms now utilising much more sophisticated arrangements for redundancy, but that human resource planning is much better performed and this is avoiding the need for redundancies. Such measures are designed to create greater employment security with staffing flexibility.

Multiple-choice questions

14.1   Redundancy pay is
    (a)   to help until another job is found
    (b)   for loss of an old job
    (c)   in lieu of unemployment benefit

14.2   Claimants for redundancy pay include
    (a)   all full-time workers
    (b)   all full-time workers under retirement age
    (c)   all workers, full- and part-time

14.3   The maximum legal redundancy pay is
    (a)   £6,150
    (b)   £4,860
    (c)   £5,520

14.4   The following do not count towards service entitlement:
    (a)   military service
    (b)   holidays
    (c)   long-term sickness

14.5   Short-time working can lead to a claim for redundancy
    (a)   yes, under certain circumstances
    (b)   not at all
    (c)   if any short-time working occurs

14.6   An employee who finds another job
    (a)   has to stay till the end of the period of notice
    (b)   can leave and claim redundancy pay
    (c)   has the right to leave with redundancy pay

14.7   Consultations with unions about redundancies of more than ten people
    (a)   have to take place some time
    (b)   need not necessarily take place
    (c)   have to take place before declaring redundancies

14.8 An offer of alternative employment
(a) can be refused
(b) should not be unreasonably refused
(c) must be taken up

14.9 A person declared redundant
(a) cannot claim unfair dismissal
(b) can claim both redundancy and unfair dismissal
(c) can claim unfair dismissal under some circumstances

14.10 A person declared redundant who goes on strike
(a) loses redundancy pay
(b) can be sacked
(c) employee rights are not affected.

Exercises

14.1 Explain the meaning of redundancy, how it is defined, and some of the circumstances in which it may occur.

14.2 Describe the purpose of a redundancy payment and explain how it is calculated.

14.3 Explain the circumstances in which an employee can claim redundancy.

14.4 Why would an employee claim unfair dismissal even though they are being made redundant? What are the reasons for this?

Further reading

ACAS, Occasional paper No 37 *Redundancy arrangements*
Croners Guide Employment Law (Ed C Fisher), Croner, 1993, 1-85524-208-7
N M Selwyn, *Law of Employment*, Butterworth, 1991, 0-406-50455-5
McMillan, *Workers' Guide to Employment Law*
TUC, *Redundancy Arrangements*

Case studies

(3) Defective procedures are harmful, page 314.
(15) Redundancy at Toolcraft, page 357.

15

Industrial relations issues

15.1 Strikes and lockouts

15.1.1 Why strike?

One of the fundamental rights claimed by organised workers and their unions is that, in the event of total disagreement on a matter, employees can withdraw their labour. As was noted in Chapter 8 on the history of trade unions, this right has not always been granted or given legal immunity. Nowadays it is an accepted part of our industrial relations system that ultimately people can withdraw their labour and go on strike. In several situations union and management talk about and negotiate on issues, whether to do with disputes of right, disputes of interest, grievances, discipline or policy. Where there is a total failure to agree, the union may find the situation so unacceptable that the members will withdraw their labour and strike. This will continue until some solution is found to the problem. Also strikes can arise where management refuses to talk about a situation or policy. Strikes often occur during pay negotiations. At a certain point, if the management's latest (and often final) offer is not satisfactory to the unions, then the workforce will refuse to work again until an improved offer is made. This indicates to management the strength of the union's case in pressing for its claim. It does not mean that the union's claim has to be met in full, but that a compromise solution has yet to be found.

The bargaining power of unions is largely based on their ultimate sanction, the strike. A business cannot operate successfully without its full complement of employees. A withdrawal of labour by any section of an organisation will, sooner or later, affect the ability of the organisation to continue operating. The management will often wish to avoid a strike occurring and do everything to avoid this damaging situation arising. This has to be balanced with the cost of a settlement which would avoid the strike. In pay negotiations, a solution can be found by giving the unions virtually what they claim. But this may, in the management's mind, be too costly. Management then shows strength of feeling by resisting settlement on the union's terms. This then produces a deadlock that can only be resolved by further negotiations or arbitration. The unions believe that the organisation should pay the price for their members' labour. If the price is not right, there is no deal. If the employees did not have the right to strike, an employer could employ people on terms and conditions that the employer alone thought were right. An employee who did not agree would have little option but to accept or leave. The considerations management and unions apply in deciding what is acceptable for the terms and conditions of employment will necessarily differ. Management is primarily concerned with profits and business efficiency and the unions with the standards of living and work environment. However, a working compromise is reached in the majority of cases and without having to resort to sanctions like striking. In a minority of cases a compromise cannot be found and the employees withdraw their labour.

The decision to strike is not one taken lightly. Most of the topics on which unions and management have formal talks are the subject of an agreed procedure. Many firms have a disputes procedure which involves taking the matter through defined stages. The procedures are designed to avoid costly disputes (costly to worker and firm). No doubt countless potential strike situations are averted by the use of procedures. If the procedure is not adhered to, or the procedure is defective, the union side may see fit to use its ultimate sanction, like the strike, to try to push a quick settlement in their favour. The threat of a strike is a negotiating tactic used to convince the management of the strength of the union case. This may ultimately lead to a strike if the matter is not settled. Usually procedures contain a clause that sanctions may not be taken by either side until the procedure is exhausted. This may take some time or one side or the other may not adhere to the procedure, so that strike action is precipitated.

Official or unofficial

Strikes can be official or unofficial. An official strike is one that is called in accordance with union rules and has been authorised or endorsed by an officer or committee empowered to do so. Most union Rule Books have an internal procedure that must be operated before a strike is called. No union allows a shop steward to call a strike officially. A strike must be sanctioned by some full-time official, or more frequently by the national executive council (NEC). Some unions have to have a ballot of all members, others have to gain branch approval. However, once an official strike is called, i.e., the section of workers concerned are instructed to strike, the members are obliged to do so. If they do not, they are in breach of union rules and can be disciplined by the union for this.

The law now takes the position that any industrial action called by any trade union official, including shop stewards, is 'official' action and the union is liable for the consequences of that action. So that if a shop steward calls a strike and the workers take action without a ballot, the union will be liable at law for the action and could be taken to court. The

only way a union can avoid liability is by issuing a repudiation. This must be in writing to the officials calling the action and to all employees involved. Further, the law now allows employers to sack some or all of the striking workers who take 'unofficial' action and there is no right to claim unfair dismissal in this circumstance.

A predominant feature of the British strike scene is the very high proportion of unofficial strikes. Unofficial strikes are called outside the official union's backing, i.e., where the NEC has refused to sanction the strike or the internal procedures have not been used. Unofficial strikes are called by shop stewards, the branch or the members themselves. These unofficial, or wild-cat, strikes are often called at a moment's notice and are used, often in the heat of the moment, to give a show of strength of feeling on a matter. A union would find it difficult to officially sanction a strike when procedure had not been used or not exhausted. But going through procedure can cause frustration as often immediate answers are required, not ones taking several days or weeks. This impatience then leads to unofficial action. This type of action only lasts a short time, whereas official strikes tend to last a lot longer. Approximately 5% of strikes are official but they account for about 25% of days lost. Table 15.1 (given in Section 15.1.3 *below*) shows strike incidence in the UK and specifies the proportion of strikes that are official.

Lockouts

A lockout is where the employer prevents the employee from working. It is the reverse situation of a strike whereby the employer refuses to continue to employ those workers who are locked out, unless the situation is resolved. Lockouts occur less frequently than strikes, but it is a sanction that the employer can use. The employee can say that either the latest offer or solution to a dispute is accepted or the establishment closes until a settlement is reached. It can also be used to counter industrial action short of striking, like a work-to-rule. The employer may find the work-to-rule so damaging to the firm's operations that the employer says either there is a solution and a return to normal working or the establishment closes. The threat of a lockout is a tactic that can be employed to persuade the unions to settle the matter in question. In some instances it works, in others it can cause deadlock and a strike or actual lockout ensues.

Ballots

The need for ballots prior to industrial action (striking or action short of striking) has become part of industrial relations law. The Trade Union Act 1984 made it a requirement that if a union is to enjoy immunity from being sued for torts, in contemplation or furtherance of a trade dispute, it must hold a ballot of those taking part in the action. The law is now contained in the Trade Union and Labour Relations (Consolidation) Act 1992. Before a union officially authorises or endorses industrial action the Act's provisions must be complied with if the union is not to leave itself open to legal action. Authorisation involves an instruction to take industrial action; endorsement involves the union making unofficial action already taking place, official. A union is responsible for the instructions of its Executive Committee, General Secretary, President or any other person the Rule Book authorises to call industrial action. Additionally, the union is responsible for any committee's or official's instruction unless repudiated in writing to the officials calling the action.

Unofficial action (in the eyes of the law) remains as such until a ballot is held, even though it may have been endorsed as official by a committee or official. A further complication is that an interlocutory injunction (*see* Section 10.2.2) can be granted to an employer to have the industrial action stopped, if a ballot has not been held or the result was not in favour of the action. If official action has been approved in a ballot, the union has immunity and an application for an interlocutory injunction would fail (other legal factors being in order). The ballot has to be held within four weeks of the intended action but the action cannot become official by holding a retrospective ballot. The ballot must ask a question relating to the proposed industrial action which elicits a 'yes' or 'no' response. If a union wishes to have authority to call a strike or action short of a strike, it should ask a question on both issues. The question must point out that the action called for would involve a breach of contract. The voting must be by ballot paper and be free from interference. So far as is reasonably practicable this should be in secret, at work or by post, and at no cost to the member.

The requirement to hold a ballot prior to action being taken also provides extra time for the two sides to resolve the conflict. Often, in the heat of the moment, the situation gets out of hand and in the cool light of day the sides find a solution and resolve their differences. It is still the case that the largest number of strikes are of very short duration and anything that delays the short, sharp wildcat walk out will be beneficial.

15.1.2   Reasons for striking

Much has been written about why workers go on strike. Clearly there is no single reason and the actual reason depends on both the circumstances and the perspective taken. The right of workers to withdraw their labour has always been seen as the most important, fundamental right by trade unionists. As trade unions emerged in the mid-nineteenth century, one of the prime objectives of the early trade unionists' campaign was to secure the right to strike.

In Britain there has never been a positive right to strike. This is partially because the legal system is built on the principle that unlawful acts are an offence rather than stating that certain acts are positively allowed. As we saw in Chapter 10, striking poses a number of legal problems which were partially solved by the setting up of immunities. Having secured these, the trade union movement has enjoyed considerable freedom to strike.

The importance attached to the right to strike can be seen in the reaction to any proposals or enactments that reduce this right. In withdrawing their labour, a group of workers are able to take effective, collective action against their employer. To many trade unionists this balances industrial power as the employer is seen as possessing the greater power *vis-à-vis* the individual employee. The employer has the power to employ, dismiss (now curtailed by law), to order and to exact obedience and to fix the terms and conditions of employment. The employee has little power, except to accept what is offered and to obey. To demonstrate the unacceptability of some aspect of the employment relationship, the employee has to choose between continuing with the contract or breaking the contract. Clearly many workers collectively choose the latter when necessary.

Often simplistic statements are made relating to strike action. These usually are about labour economics and that strikes are about 'wanting more pay'. While it is true that the majority of strikes are nominally about pay and hours of work, it is not merely the immediate issue that induces a strike. In an environment where good industrial relations policies, practices and procedures exist, some very difficult negotiations can take place and no strike ensues. Conversely, in firms that have poor or no industrial relations policies, practices and procedures, a relatively trivial issue will precipitate strike action. The underlying cause of a strike may not be articulated or even known but the action is a means of demonstrating some deep dissatisfaction with the current state of affairs.

It has been observed in firms that have clamped down on union militancy and activities, leading to a lower frequency of strike action, that the incidence of other indicators of employee dissatisfaction increased. These include labour turnover, lateness and absenteeism. These indicators are a good measure of the level of satisfaction in a workforce but are statistically more difficult to analyse. Strike statistics are more readily available and are used to state an oversimplified case.

A further, important influence in the use of strikes as a measure of the state of industrial relations is the role the media play. Putting to one side the political aspects of media coverage (including the many accusations of bias), the use of strikes as a good story makes for wider public awareness of the situation surrounding a strike. As noted in the next section, the level of strikes in the UK may not be as economically damaging or as important as it might seem to be.

The explanation of strikes goes far deeper than a disagreement about pay or the exposure of certain people on the media. The paragraphs below suggest some of the possible reasons for striking.

The manifestation of conflict

A widely held view is that an inherent characteristic of organisations is the existence of conflict. (Some still cling to the unitary perspective (*see* Section 1.3) which does not recognise the existence of conflict.) This conflict, it is held, derives from the divergent objectives of the organisation and the individuals within it. The industrial relations system attempts to institutionalise this conflict by providing the means of resolving such conflict. Needless to say this does not always occur and when the system is unable to resolve the matter, the conflict spills over into industrial action. Industrial action is an expression of the divergent interests of the groups within the organisation and the organisation itself, or sometimes between the groups themselves. At some time, these interests are so far apart that the relationship breaks down.

The breakdown of consensus

This reason fits in particularly with the pluralist view of industrial relations. All the various groups in an organisation have differing viewpoints and objectives but manage to exist together. This is achieved by reaching a consensus with the various groups which produces a set of working relationships. By cooperating, a peaceful coexistence is reached. Sometimes this consensus cannot be achieved and cooperation breaks down. The result of this can lead to a withdrawal of labour until a formula is found on which a consensus can be built.

When a problem relating to a matter of fundamental importance to the relationship is not solved, there is a breakdown. Procedures exist to reach a consensus, hence the system's reliance on collective bargaining and negotiations.

Procedural inefficiency

A more pragmatic reason is that the procedures used to avoid conflict and reach a measure of agreement do not work fast enough. In the heat of the moment when problems arise or questions need answering, people become impatient for an answer. As was noted in Section 7.2.1, procedural agreements should provide for the speedy resolution of disputes, preferably by including time limits. In the absence of a quick settlement, or acceptable movement, those involved are then tempted to speed up the proceedings (or lack of them). Ultimately, this might involve going on strike as an act of impatience or frustration in order to achieve a quick settlement. The high proportion of unofficial strikes (*see* Section 15.1.3) is partially explained by the lack of procedures at workplace level. This was examined by the Donovan Commission which recommended the improvement of procedures for the settlement of disputes.

Negotiating tactics

The process of negotiating involves the use of argument to persuade the other side of the strength of your case. The object is to secure a movement, by the other side, to a point where settlement is possible. The tactics employed include the use of industrial power. This can involve the threat of industrial action. Management may then call the bluff of the union and see if the union will actually use this power. By refusing to yield to union demands, made under the threat of industrial action, the union may be forced to take action. Clearly the union will weigh up the risk of using such a tactic, as a strike is penalising to its members. However, the mandate of the negotiators may include the use of the strike weapon if a certain settlement is not reached. A further consideration is to assess the possible resistance to a strike by the employer. If the organisation is not trading very well and the order book is low, a strike may not be fully resisted by the employer. In good trading times, the employer will be prepared to pay the price of avoiding a strike.

Political

The Marxist view (*see* Section 1.3) is based on the premise that industrial conflict will exist as long as the current structure of society remains, because industrial conflict is only a reflection of the wider struggle in society. The power struggle is between the owners and capitalists and the providers of labour. Marx and Engels both saw that striking had a role to play but was not pivotal because it did not bring about the changes in society that were essential to improve the lot of the working person. Trade unions have a role to play in the battle between the classes and taking industrial action is part of that struggle.

There are others who see striking as a political activity (in the non-party political sense). Several writers, notably Blauner, have examined the alienation that can exist in organisations due to the nature of work. Workers can experience feelings of powerlessness, meaninglessness, isolation and self-estrangement. Workers who experience this will react in different ways such as daydreaming, leaving, absenteeism plus taking industrial action. In this way employees can express their dissatisfaction with their work and exercise some real power over their employer. It is an important managerial task to provide the right work environment that minimises these feelings of alienation. This includes devising methods of work, work organisation and employee involvement that moves the workers' experiences to control, purpose, social integration and self-improvement. This should lead to a reduction in workers' feelings of alienation and thence to less industrial action.

15.1.3 Number of strikes

The number of strikes and the number of working days lost through strikes over the years has fluctuated wildly. The broad pattern during this century has been an increase in the number of strikes and a decrease in the number of days lost. Taking into account the growth in the working population and the growth in organisations (particularly nationalised industries and public bodies) certainly the record is one of improvement. The trend has also been towards shorter, unofficial strikes where the situation, particularly in the period 1900–25, was one of a series of long, national, official stoppages. For example, from 1945 to 1972 there were no official strikes in the mining industry and in the period 1933 to 1953 there were no official national stoppages in any sector. The peaks in the strike statistics are caused by national stoppages. It does not require many days of striking in a large industry to produce a high figure of days lost. Prolonged national stoppages, such as the miners' strikes in 1973 and 1984, account for a very high proportion of days lost through striking.

The number of strikes tends to increase during periods of expansion. This is to be expected as labour tends to be in short supply and the trade unions possess more power to demand greater improvements in the terms and conditions of employment of their members. The severity of strikes tends to increase during periods of economic decline. During periods of restraint, when growth is low, less money is available to meet the demands of the employees. Often redundancies are associated with such periods. This leads to a complete breakdown of the employment relationship which is difficult to mend.

The number of days lost through strikes can be compared with the number of days lost through sickness or industrial accidents. These latter statistics tend to be more constant. It is virtually always the case that the number of days lost through strikes is less than those lost through industrial accidents. The overall economic effect of days lost through strikes is difficult to judge. The statistics are collected from organisations who suffer a strike. They supply the base figures on any stoppage of work that lasts for more than one working day. Some organisations may not be as fastidious in supplying the figures as some others, so the figures may not be correct from source. The days lost by organisations affected by a strike, e.g., through loss of supplies, cancelled orders, etc., are not included. This can be considerable where the strike is in the utilities, transport or communications industries. Stoppages in these sectors have a widespread effect and can cripple many organisations. The actual number of days lost may not reflect the actual loss of output. In many situations the work not done during the stoppage is compensated for on return to work by using overtime or by workers stepping up production to earn a larger bonus, to make up for the loss of earnings suffered during the strike. A further damaging effect is the psychological effect on customers. It is detrimental to the commercial interests of organisations, sectors or even nations to acquire a reputation for being strike-prone. However, this may be an impression that does not stand up to rigorous analysis. (As can be seen in Table 15.3, the UK's strike record is about average for an industrial economy and certainly is not the worst by far.)

A more detailed analysis of strike statistics shows that certain industries dominate in the figures. The dock, mining, motor vehicle, shipbuilding and iron and steel industries accounted for approximately 50% of strikes in the period 1966–70. These industries are highly organised by the trade unions many having a closed shop. They are also dominated by very large organisations. Also, the work carried out in these industries is often physically demanding, dangerous and repetitive. The environment lends itself to dissatisfaction among the workforce and this can be demonstrated in taking industrial action. At the opposite end of the scale, agriculture, gas, water, electricity, finance and distribution sectors accounted for a very low proportion of strikes.

Table 15.1 gives some figures for strike incidence in certain industries, based on the Standard Industrial Classification.

There is much evidence to show that there is a greater incidence of striking in large organisations compared to small ones. In the period

Table 15.1   Strike incidence in various industries (1991)

Industry (SIC)	Working days lost per 1,000 employees
Railways	10
Transport equipment	190
Public administration	96
Supporting transport services	1
Motor vehicles	19
Coal extraction	350
Other inland transport	101
Construction	15
Mechanical engineering	92
Paper, printing and publishing	4
Distribution, hotel and catering	2
Banking and finance	3
All industries and services	34
Energy and water	76
Manufacturing	46
Services	31

Source: Annual Abstract of Statistics

1971–3 99.9% of organisations employing up to 24 people were strike-free, 93.1% of organisations employing 200–500 people were strike-free while only 56% of organisations employing over 1,000 people were strike-free. The same survey demonstrated that 10% of the establishments affected by strikes accounted for 35% of stoppages and 79% of days lost.

Another factor affecting the level of strikes, particularly the number of strikes, is the effect of government policy and legislation. During periods of pay policy, especially where the policy has not been agreed with the trade union movement, there is a greater chance of strikes occurring. This transpired in 1979 when the Labour government pressed on with a pay policy without trade union support. Major strikes ensued in many public services such as the fire service and refuse collection. Legislation affects the propensity to strike. The 1971 Industrial Relations Act caused widespread discontent and led to a deterioration in relations with the government. The recent legislation in the Employment Acts of 1980 and 1982 and the Trade Union Act 1984 has curtailed the freedom to strike by amending the rules on immunities (*see* Section 10.2.2). Combined with the economic depression, high unemployment and falling trade union membership, the legislation

has caused a dramatic fall in the number of strikes and the number of days lost through strikes. However, the reduction in the UK's strike record during the 1980s cannot be attributed to the effect of legislation as other countries have seen a similar or larger fall in striking in the same period but without similar anti-strike laws.

The figures in Table 15.2 show the incidence of striking and the number of days lost in the respective years. The figures in Table 15.3 show the international comparisons for the incidence of striking. The UK is about half-way down the league. The figures in Table 15.4 show the duration of strikes.

Table 15.2   Strike incidence in the UK (1900–91)*

Year	No. of stoppages beginning in year	No. of workers involved in stoppages (000s)	Aggregate number of days lost in stoppages (000s)
1900	633	185	4,130
1910	521	514	9,867
1920	1,607	1,932	25,568
1930	422	307	4,399
1940	922	299	940
1950	1,339	302	1,389
1960	2,832	814	3,024
1970	3,906	1,793	10,908
1972	2,497	1,726	23,923
1974	2,922	1,622	14,845
1976	2,016	670	3,509
1978	2,471	1,003	9,391
1980	1,330	842	11,965
1982	1,538	2,103	5,313
1984	1,221	1,464	27,135
1985	885	737	6,372
1986	1,074	720	1,920
1987	1,016	887	3,546
1988	781	790	3,702
1989	701	727	4,128
1990	630	298	1,903
1991	369	176	761

*Data from *Annual Abstract of Statistics,* reproduced by permission of the Controller, Her Majesty's Stationery Office.

One problem that has always been apparent in British strike statistics is the high proportion of strikes of very short duration. Table 15.4 shows that 75% of strikes lasted less than five days. In addition, firms are not required to report

Table 15.3 Strike incidence – international comparison

	Days lost per 1,000 employed					Average 1974–8	Average 1982–91
	1974	1978	1982	1986	1990		
Italy	1,430	710	1,270	390	340	1,410	520
Canada	1,120	830	610	680	450	990	430
Australia	1,250	420	410	240	210	690	250
UK	650	410	250	90	80	380	270
Sweden	20	10	5	170	190	30	80
France	200	130	130	60	40	210	60
Denmark	100	60	50	40	40	90	140
Japan	270	40	10	10	–	130	10
Germany	50	200	5	–	10	60	30

Table 15.4 Length of strikes (1991)

Number of days	Number of strikes	%
<5	270	73.2
5<10	20	5.4
10<20	24	6.5
20<30	15	4.1
30<50	10	2.7
>50	30	8.1
Total	369	

Source: Annual Abstract of Statistics

stoppages that last less than 24 hours. Sudden walk-outs and returns do not show in these statistics. Frequently these short strikes are local, unofficial strikes caused by a row about an issue that suddenly flares up and dramatic action is taken in the heat of the moment.

There have been a number of proposals to alleviate this problem. The Donovan Report (1968) highlighted this and the Labour government in the late 1960s (when Barbara Castle was Secretary of State) made the proposal to introduce a 'cooling-off' period. This meant that there had to be a time lapse between the call for action and the industrial action being taken. The proposal was a cooling-off period of 28 days. That would clearly give plenty of time for tempers to cool! Indeed it might cause frustration! The same proposal was included in the 1971 Industrial Relations Act but was not included in the Trade Union and Labour Relations Act in 1974 (which repealed the former Act). The government's 1992 White Paper *People, Jobs and Opportunity* reintroduced the idea of a seven-day cooling-off period between a ballot result in favour of industrial action and the action being taken. It also suggests that the

union must inform the employer, in writing, of the details of the proposed action.

Current legislation focuses on the legal immunities (*see* Section 10.2) given to those who seek to organise or take industrial action. In doing this the government are trying to prevent stoppages by restricting the industrial action for which immunity is given. Where there is no immunity, the union, its officials and anyone who organises industrial action is liable to have court action taken against them. This could be an action for damages or for an injunction to be granted to prevent the action going ahead. Progressively, the legislation has narrowed the circumstances in which immunity is given or how the action is organised. From a union's point of view, to take industrial action without being covered by an immunity is very risky. It could jeopardise the continued existence of the union, as the fines and awards can be very high. The next section plots these developments through the 1980s.

15.1.4 Strikes and the law

The act of striking raises several legal problems. A strike is a breach of the contract of employment, as the employees are not fulfilling their side of the contract, i.e., are not working. Trade unions, if they called a strike, could possibly be sued for inducement, interference or intimidation. All these are civil offences, called economic torts. If the common law, expounded by judges in the courts, had been left to develop, unaltered by parliamentary legislation, the right to strike would have been severely restricted. As seen in Chapter 8, after the Taff Vale case, unions could be sued for the loss of profit resulting from the strike action. Given no immunity, and the size of present-day organisations, unions would soon be unable to continue any strike for very long. However, the legal situation relating to strikes is now fully covered by legislation in the form of immunities.

The legal immunities given to those who lead or organise a strike were defined in the Trade Disputes Act 1906. This was re-enacted (after its repeal in 1971) in the Trade Union and

Labour Relations Act 1974, amended in 1976, and has been modified by the Employment Act 1980, 1982 and 1988 and the Trade Union Act 1984. These enactments have now been consolidated into the Trade Union and Labour Relations (Consolidation) Act 1992. The position is that trade unions, officials, strike organisers and leaders are given immunity for 'acts in contemplation or furtherance of a trade dispute'. No court action can be taken for the civil offences described above. Note that the immunity does not cover criminal offences at all. The criminal law has to be obeyed by everyone.

The Employment Act 1980 modified the position in two ways:

- The immunity only extends to the contract of employment. If a commercial contract is interfered with, a person can be sued. If a contract to supply goods or a service is interfered with, say by a refusal to work on a particular job, a civil action could ensue.
- The immunity only extends to the firm at which the dispute arises. Secondary action (often called 'sympathetic industrial action') is industrial action taken by an employee against an employer who is not a party to the trade dispute. Such action is not covered by any immunity.

Sympathetic strikes by workers not directly associated with the original dispute are not covered by this immunity, and the strikers, the union or union officials can be sued.

The Employment Act 1982 made further changes to the law. The two important ones are these:

- A union's immunity is now subject to the same limitation that officials are, i.e., there is immunity for 'acts done in contemplation or furtherance of a trade dispute'. Previously unions could not be sued at all but now they can be if they act outside of the clause above.
- The definition of a trade dispute was narrowed to matters 'wholly or mainly related' to a dispute between 'workers and their employers'. This narrowly restricts the disputes covered by the immunity to those

employed by the employer and not those who work elsewhere. Inter-union disputes are not now covered.

The Trade Union Act 1984 introduced the requirement that, before the law would give immunity for any industrial action, a ballot had to be held of those being called to take the industrial action and the majority had to have voted 'yes'.

A survey indicated that up to 1987 there had been 80 court cases where an employer sought an injunction to lift industrial action. The majority of cases (43) were based on the lack of a ballot before strike action. A further 26 were based on the definition of primary action, which in 10 cases led to withdrawal of industrial action.

The Employment Act 1988 made it unlawful to take industrial action to enforce union membership. Thus, if an employer has, or is about to, employ a nonunion person in a closed shop situation, the union cannot take industrial action. If it does, there is no legal immunity for this action.

Certain groups in practice cannot strike. The Police Act 1919 forbids a police officer to join a trade union, except the Police Federation, and this body cannot, by law, organise a strike. Merchant sailors can only strike provided they give 48 hours' notice after berthing in the UK. Under the Emergency Powers Act 1964, an Order in Council can be made to send in troops to carry out services essential for public safety and the life of the community. This has been used seven times since 1945. Post Office workers should not endanger or retard the delivery of mail; to do so is a criminal offence, but strikers in the Post Office have so far not been prosecuted.

A strike has the effect of suspending the contract of employment. An employer can, in fact, regard a strike as a fundamental breach of contract that enables the employer to consider the contract terminated. Hence strikers can be fairly dismissed (*see* Chapter 13) for being on strike. This action is rare, though it may be threatened to try to secure a return to work. Usually, after a strike is over, the employees return to work and carry on as before. A strike does have the effect of causing a break in service. Certain entitlements, like redundancy pay and pensions, are calculated on 'years of continuous service'. A strike does not break the service such that the time starts afresh after the strike, but the period of the strike does not count in the total number of years worked. This can affect the final entitlement, if an employee has been on strike at any time during employment.

Strike-free deals

An often controversial new development in the 1980s revolved around the so-called strike-free deals which some unions entered into. The issue is complex from both an institutional, procedural and legal viewpoint.

- **Institutional** The trade union movement reacts strongly and emotionally when there is even a veiled threat that the right to strike is being eroded. The trade union movement was built on securing the right to strike and for the worker the strike weapon is the ultimate weapon against an employer. Strike-free deals are associated with agreements that contain a compulsory arbitration clause, often leading to pendulum arbitration (i.e., where the arbitrator has to choose between the employer's final offer or the union's final claim, *see* Section 6.4). The argument is that if the agreement is inexhaustible and contains a clause that industrial action cannot be taken until the procedure has been exhausted, then a union signing such an agreement is signing away its members' right to strike.

  For employers, it is clearly in their interests to secure industrial peace. The 1980s saw a major swing towards employers in the balance of power in industrial relations. Many employers capitalised on this changed environment to pursue changes in philosophy, style and organisation. Management exercised its right to manage and took a very positive, forthright position on industrial relations. This was not so much as to exclude trade unions but to change their role. The

'new' agreements are characterised by single staff status, employee participation, flexibility plus single-union recognition and a no-strike clause. This includes ensuring that industrial peace is secured by incorporating changes to agreements that will achieve this aim. The avoidance of strikes (and other forms of industrial action) is important to maintain efficiency, market share and long-term security. Unions can commit themselves to the future prosperity of the company by cooperating with management in achieving these aims.

- **Procedural** In practice there is less of a gap between conventional agreements and the 'new' agreements. Many conventional agreements contain clauses that limit the right to take industrial action until the procedure has been exhausted. This has not secured industrial peace in every instance. Unions have called industrial action whilst a matter is still in procedure, hence the large number of unofficial stoppages. However, this is made more difficult with the requirement to ballot the employees involved but is still not impossible. Also a union is now liable for all its officials (including shop stewards) who call for industrial action and if an unofficial stoppage occurs, perhaps as a tactic to press home the strength of the union case, the union could land up in court unless an official repudiates the action.

  It is possible, though not popular, to include a clause that industrial action is prohibited on economic issues for the term of the agreement (this is more common in America). Fords have such a clause as do Nissan. Another procedural possibility is to include a clause that states that industrial action is not allowed for the duration of the agreement. Others include penalty clauses against individuals who take any industrial action not allowed under the agreement, e.g., loss of bonuses.

  The so-called strike-free deals tend to include (though not universally) a compulsory binding arbitration clause and often it is this which causes the objections in principle from trade unions. Again, conventional agreements have a final stage which enables a matter to be referred to arbitration, but this will often be with the agreement of both parties, i.e., voluntary not compulsory. Also conventionally, arbitration awards may not be binding on the parties, although ACAS argue strongly that this should be the case and be agreed beforehand. Where compulsory binding arbitration clauses appear in an agreement it does eliminate the possibility of legitimate industrial action.

- **Legal**   Generally it is assumed that collective agreements are not legally binding, hence if either party does not adhere to the procedure the other side cannot take the matter to court. It is possible to make an agreement (including a 'peace' clause) enforceable by stating this explicitly in the agreement. The legal position for individuals is that if they strike they have in effect terminated their contract of employment, so a term in the contract not to take industrial action has little meaning anyway. Also to strike over a number of issues now, e.g., an inter-union dispute, is not covered by any legal immunity and leaves the union open to court action by the employer. Additionally, a union has to comply with a complex set of requirements regarding balloting members before industrial action can be taken. These requirements are set to change again to make a seven-day cooling-off period necessary plus written notification from the union to the employer of details of the intended action.

15.2   Picketing

15.2.1   The purpose of picketing

An activity closely associated with striking is that of picketing. Workers who have taken the decision to strike want their action to be both publicised and effective. By standing outside their place of work, they can demonstrate that they are in dispute and on strike. By telling their fellow workers and trade unionists, they hope to increase the effectiveness of the strike by spreading it to other sections. They also ask other non-employees of the firm to join them by refusing to cross the picket line. Commonly this is done to lorry drivers who are delivering or collecting goods. The pickets inform the driver of the strike and ask the driver to turn round in an act of support. If a strike is official, an official picket line will invariably be organised. In the past, any trade union members crossing a picket line of the union, or of a union supporting the strike, could be reported to their own union. This could lead to the members being disciplined by the union. This operated effectively with a union like the TGWU, where the majority of lorry drivers were in the union and often in a closed shop. If the driver crossed a picket line that driver would be reported and disciplinary action taken (e.g., a fine). This situation has been modified by the provisions of the Employment Act 1988. A union cannot unjustifiably discipline its own members, even for action taken within the rules of the union. The Act specifies that if a union disciplines a member for working during industrial action, this action is unjustifiable. The union member could then take the union to an industrial tribunal and claim compensation.

Picketing is also aimed at spreading the effectiveness of a strike by sending pickets to other sites of suppliers and customers. Pickets from the original place of dispute try to ensure that the strike has a maximum effect by spreading it into often unrelated areas. The miners' strike in both 1973–4 and 1984 saw pickets not just at pits but at coal depots, coke depots and power stations. Trade unionists believe in the principle of unity and solidarity and pickets are appealing to their fellow trade unionists to join them in their dispute by acting as a larger body of fellow unionists. The hoped-for effect is that extra pressure will be put on the employer at the original place of dispute to settle quickly and on terms nearer to the union's position.

15.2.2   The law and picketing

The legal position of picketing has always been vague and unsatisfactory. The act of picketing (like striking) would be a civil and often a criminal offence if there were no special law for this activity. The first main provision was given in the Trade Disputes Act 1906. It made it lawful for someone in contemplation or furtherance of a trades dispute to attend at, or near, a house or place of work if it is merely for the purpose of peacefully obtaining or communicating information or peacefully persuading anyone to work, or abstain from working. The Trade Union and Labour Relations Act 1974 re-enacted the same provisions, except it excluded picketing at a place where someone lives. This enabled anyone (associated with the original dispute or not) to picket virtually anywhere, except at someone's residence. The difficulty has always been what the limits of 'peaceful persuasion and communication' are. This is a question of interpretation and varies with the circumstances. There is the question of numbers: should there be 2, 10, 50 or what? Can someone be physically halted against their will? Can a lorry driver be forced to stop, having seen a picket line and decided to drive through? The police still have to ensure that there is no breach of the peace. If they reasonably anticipate a breach of the peace because of the picketing, they can move the pickets to avert this. Large numbers of pickets can cause obstruction.

The Employment Act 1980 further restricted picketing. This Act makes it lawful for a person in contemplation or furtherance of a trades dispute to attend at, or near, their own place of work. It allows a trade union official to picket with the members the official represents. A trade union official can only picket with the members the official was elected by. For example, a district official from Birmingham cannot picket in Manchester. A person sacked because of a dispute can picket at their previous place of work. Someone who has no fixed place of work like a lorry driver, can picket at the place where the work is administered from.

This Act severely restricts picketing. A person cannot picket anywhere, except the worker's place of work. This is a restriction that will defeat the effects of picketing seen in the 1970s, like the miners' strikes in 1973 and 1984,

Grunwick in 1978 and the steel strike of 1979. To be able to picket legally, the pickets have to be in dispute with their own employer and picket only their own place of work. They cannot picket a head office, nor an associated company, nor a customer or supplier, nor a company to which the striking employees' work has been transferred. It probably restricts picketing to the plant where the employees work. Where one company has several work units or plants on one site, picketing is restricted to the actual work unit of the striker.

Secondary action, i.e. industrial action taken by an employee against an employer who is not a party to the trade dispute, cannot be taken by picketers. If those on strike at once place of work attempt to spread the action by picketing other places of work, they (and their union) could be taken to court.

For example, if a department of machinists at one place go on strike, they can picket only their own place of work. If the company transfers the work to another of their works, the strikers cannot picket that second plant.

While this law is clear in its definition, there is much argument as to how it will be enforced. A picket line not covered by the Act is not committing a criminal offence in itself, so the police cannot be involved. If the picket line is breaking the criminal law, the police can obviously act. The use of civil remedies to restrict such picket lines not observing the Act involves the use of injunctions. To do this the people attending the picket line have to be identified. By whom? Then an injunction can be applied for, by which time the members of the picket line may have changed. If an injunction is granted, who is going to serve it on the pickets? Pickets can also be sued for damages for, say, loss of profit due to the activities of the pickets interfering with normal business.

The Employment Act enables the Secretary of State for Employment to issue Codes of Practice. One has been issued on picketing (see Section 11.6). The Code makes the following points:

- the number of pickets at an entrance to a workplace should be limited to what is reasonably needed (as a general rule, this should not exceed six)

- an experienced person, preferably a trade union official, should always be in charge of a picket line
- the organiser should organise the picket line, ensure that the picket is peaceful and lawful, distribute identification for authorised pickets, refuse outside support
- a trade union member who crosses an unofficial picket line should not be disciplined by the union
- pickets should ensure that the movement of essential goods and services is not impeded or prevented

15.3 The closed shop

15.3.1 Introduction

Closed shops are an important feature of our industrial relations system and became increasingly prevalent during the 1970s. They have been the subject of legislation since 1971. It is difficult to come to a definition of a closed shop that encompasses the wide range of practices that exist. W E J McCarthy used the definition, 'a situation in which employees come to realise that a particular job is only to be obtained or retained if they become and remain members of unions'. This is not appropriate to some closed shops as some closed-shop agreements allow some employees to be nonmembers. It is useful to distinguish between a 100% shop and a closed shop, as 100% membership is an objective of all unions, but it may not be the union policy to use the closed shop as a means to achieve this. More often, unions leave it to more informal procedures to obtain high membership, especially where specific agreements exist. There are instances where everyone in a section or department is in a union, not as the result of a closed-shop policy, but as the result of active trade union recruitment. The closed shop differs from this in that it attempts to ensure that all those in employment in a section or department will be members of a

union. Those entering employment will have to be, or become, trade union members.

Closed shops can exist either as formal union/management agreements called union membership agreements (uma) or as informal situations. The uma is a practice which was encouraged by the Trade Union and Labour Relations Act 1974. In the late 1970s new closed shops tended to emerge as the result of such agreements. These are formally negotiated agreements between union and management which both sides sign and recognise as an agreement. These are often compromises and overcome certain problems that often exist with the closed shop. However, it does regularise the situation, which is to the advantage of both sides. In traditional industries (shipbuilding, mining, railway, docks, steel), closed shops exist, not as the result of agreement, but as the result of custom and practice. Gradually a situation emerged whereby the practice was that all those entering employment had to be members of the union. This is particularly true of the pre-entry closed shop (*see* Section 15.3.2). In some instances, management acknowledges the situation and agree to work with it, especially with respect to recruitment. In other instances, management has not recognised the existence of the closed shop, but it operates none the less.

It is in the area of recruitment that problems can arise. If an employer interviews and recruits someone who is not, or will not become, a trade union member, then a difficult industrial relations problem will arise. In most closed-shop situations it would probably lead to a refusal to work with the person, which puts the employer and employee in a difficult position. This is overcome in some situations by the union supplying suitable applicants. In situations where the closed shop is recognised, the union steward or convenor may be involved in the recruitment by making clear membership requirements or by checking union cards. In any case the interviewer will make the union membership position clear. The legal position is entirely in favour of the individual. The Trade Union and Labour Relations (Consolidation) Act 1992 introduced the right for prospective employees not to be discriminated against in respect of trade union membership or nonmembership. Also employers cannot take any discriminatory action against employees in respect of union membership or nonmembership. This legislation is primarily aimed at reducing the effective operation of the closed shop.

The case for the closed shop from the unions' point of view is as follows:

- It strengthens their bargaining power because, by representing the whole of the workforce, the representatives speak for all the employees and the bargaining procedures are at their strongest.
- Unions, having negotiated improvements in the terms and conditions for their members, see nonmembers enjoying the benefits without contribution so they feel that the 'free-riders' should contribute, i.e. join the union, if they are going to benefit. Sometimes union members take industrial action, which costs the members in lost wages, and the union feel that this should be shared by all. Also, by having full membership, any action taken will be more effective, as any sanction taken will be comprehensive.
- Craft unions have used the closed shop to restrict the entry of prospective employees into a job by making a union card a prerequisite because, by doing this, they can control the supply of labour into that craft. Through ensuring that supply does not outstrip demand, the union can maintain a strong bargaining position.

The closed shop can also receive support from management:

- Fewer unions make collective bargaining and procedures easier to operate. Multi-union shops are potentially difficult to manage, as inter-union disputes can arise. An agreement for one union to represent the section eliminates the problem. Where closed shops exist, there are fewer unions to deal with. Annual wage negotiations become difficult where 'leap-frogging' can occur, i.e., where one union claim follows another and has to be better than the last.

- The situation that exists within the company may be acceptable to management as current practices may work well and there may be no desire to change, but equally, management has to weigh up the consequences of not recognising a closed shop in terms of possible industrial relations problems. Any attempts to change custom and practice are difficult unless there is some benefit to be derived.

The case against the closed shop is based mainly on the argument that it restricts the freedom of the individual to choose. An individual should have the right to join, or not to join, an association as the individual wishes. There should be no element of compulsion of membership in any sector of life, including employment. In extreme cases the closed shop can lead to loss of job. This can derive from the individual refusing to become a member, or the union expelling or refusing membership. Claims can be made for compensation (under unfair dismissal law, *see* Section 13.2.3). An employee who is sacked for not being a union member in a closed-shop situation, can claim unfair dismissal automatically.

The TUC has recognised this problem and has asked all unions to adopt into their rules an independent appeals procedure for applicants refused membership, or members who have been expelled. The TUC has set up an Independent Review Committee to examine such cases where problems still exist after internal union procedures have failed to resolve the situation. The recommendations of the Review Committee should be complied with, or the union concerned can be suspended or expelled from the TUC. Further to this, the TUC issued guidelines in 1979, one of which related to the closed shop. They recommend that unions in a closed-shop situation allow an employee the right not to join the union on specified grounds, like religious belief or conscience.

15.3.2 Types of closed shop

The closed shop can be broadly split into two categories: pre-entry and post-entry.

Pre-entry closed shop

A pre-entry closed shop is where union membership is a prerequisite to employment. This is achieved by insisting that the job applicant holds a card before being considered for employment. This is achieved in various ways as shown below in the following types of pre-entry closed shop:

- **Labour supply shop** Where a union office is the supplier of labour. This occurs in the supply of manual labour in the newspaper industry.
- **Labour pool shop** Employers recruit from a pool of labour created by the union. Once in the pool, a person can move from job to job without reference to the union. This occurs in the docks and with seafarers.
- **Promotion veto shop** Promotion to a higher grade of job is based on seniority of union membership. This occurs in the steel industry.
- **Craft qualification shop** Membership is restricted to those who have served an apprenticeship and the union controls the number of apprentices.

Skilled jobs are only to be obtained if the applicant has a union card. This occurs in printing. A system akin to this exists in the engineering industry, but it is not as rigid, as the unions do not control the number of apprentices. However, the situation does exist for some craft jobs, where the possession of a union card is a prerequisite to obtaining a job.

There is a further subdivision of the pre-entry closed shop into 'hard' and 'soft'. With the former, the prospective employee has to be a trade union member before being considered for the job. In the latter situation, the prospective employee has to be a trade union member prior to taking up the job. This classification is based on how the unions operate the pre-entry rules. As far as the employer is concerned, it is inconsequential and in many cases the employer may not know which situation pertains.

A survey carried out in February 1989 by the Department of Employment, found that, of the 1.3m employees in a pre-entry closed-shop situation, 800,000 were in a 'hard' entry shop. This total represents about 6% of the working population.

The latest legal changes are intended to ban the pre-entry closed shop. By giving applicants for a job and current employees the right not to be discriminated against because of nonmembership of a trade union, this will provide the means for employers and individuals to challenge the current system and operation of the pre-entry closed shop.

Post-entry closed shop

A post-entry closed shop exists where a job applicant needs to agree to join a union within a specified period of starting work if not a member already. In this situation the interviewer would make it clear to the applicant that this is a condition of employment. A greater proportion of these closed shops are covered by formal uma's and these often contain clauses allowing a person to be employed but not to join a union on certain specified grounds. Again, as the law stands now, if an applicant for a job is asked to become a union member and refuses, and is subsequently not appointed, there is an automatic assumption of discrimination against that person. This can lead to an industrial tribunal hearing where compensation can be awarded up to £11,000. The union involved can be joined in the action and the award may be payable by the union (in part or in whole).

The survey referred to above also indicated that 1.3m employees were in a post-entry closed-shop situation, which is about 6% of the working population.

15.3.3 Number of closed shops

The extent of the closed shop in Britain was ascertained in a study carried out in 1978. The sample covered 84% of an employee population of 22.2 million. It showed that at least 5.2 million employees were covered by some closed-shop arrangement, that is 23% of workers. This is a minimum figure as the balance of the population (16%) could well have contained closed shops. Table 15.5 shows typical figures for various industries.

A survey in 1964 indicated a 17% overall figure. The growth to 23% in 1978 conceals the true picture. Over this period the traditional industries, in which the closed shop is strong, have declined numerically, but the growth in other areas has more than compensated for this loss. Table 15.6 shows the changing pattern.

Table 15.5   Extent of the closed shop in some industries*

Industry	Number of workers (000s)	Minimum in closed shop (%)	Pre-entry closed shop (%)	Post-entry closed shop (%)
Mining and quarrying	341	87	0	87
Food and drink	696	38	1.7	36.5
Chemical	429	23	14.5	17.5
Mechanical engineering	925	45	8.5	39.8
Vehicles	764	48	8.5	39.8
Paper and printing	537	66	32.8	33.1
Gas, water, electricity	340	80	0	80.0
Transport	1,426	56	6.4	49.6
Distribution	2,683	15	0.7	14.1
Professional, scientific	3,575	3	0.1	3.4
Public administration	1,586	14	1.3	13.0

Table 15.6   Numbers covered by closed-shop arrangements*

Industry	Number covered by closed shop arrangements (000s)	
	1964	1978
Shipbuilding	150	99
Docks	68	30
Mining and quarrying	630	296
Paper and printing	295	394
Food and drink	35	266
Gas, water, electricity	30	273
Transport and communications	390	798

*Reproduced from *Employment Gazette*, January 1980, by permission of the Controller of Her Majesty's Stationery Office.

A recent survey, carried out by the Department of Employment in 1989, produced estimates for the closed shop based on a questionnaire survey. The results gave the trade union density figures listed in Table 15.7.

Table 15.7   Trade union density 1983–1989

	1983	1985	1987	1989
Union density among employees	49	47	46	39
Unions recognised at employees' workplace	66	63	62	57

Source: Employment Gazette, November 1989.

The results show the continuing decline of trade union membership, but the recent fall indicated could, according to the report's authors, be partly due to sampling error as the figures came from different surveys. However, there is a fall indicated not only in union membership, but also in unions being recognised in the workplace. This could partially be accounted for by the decline in the industries with traditionally high trade union densities and also by the increase in the number of small firms where both trade union membership and union recognition by employers are low. Alongside the fall in trade union membership and recognition, there is a natural expectation that there would be a proportional decline in the closed shop. This is not the case. The closed shop seems to be affected by different factors than those that affect union density. The figures given are estimates based on sampling and, as such, are subject to sampling error. Also the survey is based on a questionnaire. Employers may give a different answer from their employees because of their different perceptions. Employers will affirm the existence of a closed shop if there is a formal union-management agreement, whereas an employee may say a closed shop exists because everyone has to be in the union.

The closed shop is restricted to larger firms. Only 35% of workplaces with fewer than 25 employees had a closed shop and in firms with fewer than 25 employees there were no closed shops. This figure rises to 17% for workplaces with 25–99 employees and to 21% for workplaces with greater than 500 employees.

There is a wide variation in the extent of the closed shop in different industrial sectors. Table 15.8 shows some typical figures.

Table 15.8 The extent of the closed shop in some industrial sectors

Closed shop	Agri-culture	Energy/water	Metal engineering	Transport commun-ications	Financial services
Hard entry		18	7	9	
Soft entry		10	4	1	
Post-entry		3	11	12	
None	100	67	79	79	100

Source: Employment Gazette, November 1989.

15.3.4 Developments

The closed shop has always been a contentious issue both with employers, unions and politicians. In extreme cases the closed shop can be invidious. The industry greatly affected by the operation of a hard pre-entry closed shop was the national newspaper printing industry. The excesses were that all recruitment into the industry (permanent and casual labour) was controlled by the unions, usually SOGAT for the unskilled and the NGA for the skilled workers. It also gave the unions wide-ranging power in terms of staffing levels, job content, output levels, demarcation and even, in some instances, the content of the newspaper. Such excesses are rarely seen elsewhere, but the power attached to high trade union membership and control over recruitment into the industry is demonstrated in several other industries.

The union power in this situation rests in the local union officials and the membership, not with the National Executive of the national officials. This causes some industrial relations problems as the practices that build up are very often informal and outside negotiated agreements. Custom and practice established over time become the order of the day. With weak management, this leads to a strong, independent, local union, which is reinforced with the closed shop. Often union officials can do very little and management is left powerless. This is poor industrial relations, bad management and a recipe for disaster.

In such situations, the balance of power is in favour of the union. The shift in the 1980s has been for management's hand to be strengthened so that it is in control of the situation. One aspect

of this shift has been the attempts to reduce the extent of the working of the closed shop. The legislation passed by the Conservative administration, commencing with the Employment Act 1980, contained laws to reduce the impact of the closed shop. These are now contained in the Trade Union and Labour Relations (Consolidation) Act 1992. The current provisions include:

- Any employee who is discriminated against because of nonmembership of a trade union, or who is compelled to become a trade union member can take the matter to an industrial tribunal.
- A closed shop is only recognised as existing at law if the ballot requirements are fulfilled, which are that a ballot is held of all those affected by the closed shop and that 85% of those who voted and 80% of those entitled to vote agreed.
- Trade union immunity is not given for industrial action taken to introduce or support the continued existence of a closed shop, so any industrial action taken relating to a closed shop could lead to a court awarding damages against the union or an official.
- Any applicant for a job cannot be discriminated against because of nonmembership of a trade union. It is not lawful to make union membership a requirement for job application, selection or appointment. To do so could lead to an industrial tribunal hearing. Such action is presumed automatically discriminatory (regardless of any other reasons for not processing an application or offering a job).

The continued existence of the closed shop is seen by the Conservative administration, as a barrier to economic development. First, the closed shop is claimed to be in contradiction of the freedom of individuals to join or not to join an assocation of their choice. Such personal freedom should be given to all in employment. It is also seen as a barrier to employment, especially the pre-entry closed shop. There should be no artificial restrictions on entry to a job, e.g., trade union membership. They are also a restriction on free market forces operating in the labour market. By introducing regulations (via the trade unions) into the labour market, there is a fall in efficiency.

Further, the restrictive practices arising from the operation of the closed shop are seen as barriers to efficiency in industry. The need for a flexible workforce, capable of adapting to change is seen as paramount and the operation of a closed shop is a barrier to this. Also, the introduction of new technologies has been resisted or restricted due to the operation of such restrictive practices which characterise the closed shop, lending support to this view.

Overall, the direction of government policy in the 1980s and 1990s has been to restrict the operation of the closed shop, although (as seen in the previous section) there is little evidence of the success of these measures. There is little doubt that the Conservatives would ban the closed shop if that were possible. So far as the law is concerned, there is little support for the closed shop. Since the mid-1970s, the legislation has turned full circle, with little legal protection been given to support the closed shop. The answer now lies in whether employers and managers wish to see the decline of the closed shop by preventing its operation. Again, to date there is little evidence of such action and, where action has been taken, it has been against the excesses practised in industries such as the print industry. Indeed, the survey evidence is that employers are content to allow the present system to continue and are not inclined to wipe out the closed shop, which in some senses can be of benefit to employers if controlled and managed well by them.

15.4 Flexibility

An industrial relations issue that has been on the agenda for some time is the topic of flexibility. Attempts have been made to introduce greater flexibility through the normal processes of collective bargaining, i.e., negotiating change. More radical proposals have been introduced into the system, for example by using productivity agreements (*see* Section 6.1.4) to achieve major changes. The topic is even more pertinent today as firms are affected by a business culture that requires change to be a permanent feature of work life.

If firms are to embrace this idea and compete internationally, they need a flexible and responsive workforce that accepts change as a way of life. For organisations, one of the consequences of going through a constant process of change, is the need to have a workforce that is flexible, one which will adapt to new circumstances. Very little remains constant for very long and the dominant issue is the management of change. No longer are systems and products introduced to remain in place for a considerable period of time. They will have a limited life before being replaced by something else. The system of industrial relations is under pressure to adjust to this new situation. Those involved have had to address this topic.

Traditionally, employees are appointed permanently, full-time, to a specific job with a fixed job description. This may be so rigid that the job is to work on a limited range of tasks in one area or on one machine. There is little overlap and little room to change people around or re-specify their jobs. Employees are contracted for a set number of hours work each week which the employer is legally bound to. While this problem is not new, many more firms are now addressing this issue.

One example of this has been the demarcation between crafts in the manufacturing industry. A fitter had a strict job description, as did the electrician, the pipe fitter, the rigger, the trowel tradesperson, the carpenter, the instrument mechanic, etc. Strictly no other tradesperson could perform any task performed by another craft, and production personnel could not perform any of these tasks. There have been many disputes arising because of this, but this mitigates against flexibility and efficiency. Firms now require the fitter to carry out minor electrical repairs or machine operators to carry out simple adjustments to their machines.

This has required a major shift in thinking in

industrial relations. The unions defended their members' jobs and management found it difficult to find ways of changing the situation. Gradually, though, flexibility has been achieved as new agreements have allowed for this, with the necessary safeguards being built in. Often this has meant jobs being enlarged and enriched as a result of this, with many employees becoming competent in more than one sphere as training schemes to give them new skills have been introduced.

Technology has made a major impact here. Employees originally trained in electro-mechanical devices have had to gain an understanding of electronics, pneumatics and hydraulics as new machinery and equipment is employed utilising these control devices. In the administrative function, we have already noted the impact of computer-based technologies.

The key industrial relations issues here are:

- **Consultation** The way in which the changes are introduced, and three categories of policy can be identified:
  - autocratic/persuasive policy, with proposals for change being drawn up and the final plans presented by them as a finished article and management then seeking to implement them, possibly persuading employees of the merits of the scheme
  - consultative policy where management consults with its employees as the plans are developed to gauge reaction and canvas opinion
  - participative policy whereby all those affected contribute to the development of the plans.
- **Benefits** How the employees affected by the change benefit from the change in monetary terms and in terms of an improved working environment and an enriched job. Often pay negotiations will include this topic and the benefits of change can be distributed as part of the bargaining, but where a job evaluation scheme exists, the new jobs will need to be re-evaluated.
- **Training** This is necessary where the range of tasks required to be performed is altered

as there is a need to ensure that employees are adequately trained (under this head also comes the need to ensure the safety of employees and property).

Individual trade unions also have on their agenda the objective of sustaining or improving their level of membership. Often proposals can flounder where a particular union feels that its level of membership is under threat. Again the use of single-union agreements obviates this problem.

A survey carried out in 1989 by the Technical Change Centre reported on the changes that had taken place in 236 major manufacturing sites. This found that between 1981 and 1989 the majority of firms had shifted towards flexibility in, and between, maintenance and production. In 1981, 60% of firms identified that five separate functions were required in these two areas, while this was the case in 30% of firms in 1989. The shift occurred by combining some of the functions of the five occupations identified, i.e., fitter, fabricator, instrument mechanic, electrician and production operator. In 22% of firms there were only three categories operating and in a minority of cases there was interchangeability between several of these categories (which is the ultimate aim). However, in nine out of ten firms, there was still a clear delineation between production and maintenance.

A separate aspect of flexibility is the way in which firms employ people. There has been a change in personnel management thinking on this. There is talk now of firms having a number of 'core' workers who are functionally flexible, perform a range of essential operations and who are on permanent full-time contracts. Outside of this 'core' there are a number of options available to the firm:

- **subcontracting**, where the firm buys in expertise, which is economically attractive and efficient as the firm can buy in such help but does not have the problem of keeping expensive staff on permanent contract
- **temporary staff** who are employed to cover peak activities but whose contracts are terminated when demand falls which

introduces flexibility and can protect the core workers' jobs

- **part-time work** to cover fluctuations in activities (figures given in Section 17.1 show that the level of part-time work has expanded greatly – in some instances this is because it suits the employees, e.g., women with children at school)
- **job-sharing** is an option which suits some employees and can be beneficial to the employer because, instead of having a full-time job, dual expertise can be brought in with two people on a job share and, overall, the costs of employment are no higher than an equivalent single post
- **working from home** is a more recent option in several organisations by utilising computer-based technologies. In some instances, there are cost savings in travel and time, where an employee can use a remote terminal at home but still interact with those in the central office

Another aspect of flexibility is the move away from the traditional set standard working day. A common example of this is flexi-time where employees are required to work a certain number of core hours, so that everyone is present during some specified hours in the middle of the day, but start and finish times are flexible. There are variations on this theme, with some schemes allowing employees to accumulate 'extra' hours worked into their holiday entitlement.

Another idea is for the firm to vary the working hours of their employees depending on demand. Many firms are subject to periodic demand, e.g., monthly, seasonal. During periods of peak activity, longer hours are worked, with fewer hours being worked during a lull. In total, employees work a set number of hours per year.

A final idea to mention is the compressed working week. This is where the contractual hours are worked in 4 or 4½ days, giving a short day at the end of the week. There are clear attractions for the employees and it can give the employer certain advantages. For example, an engineering firm had a traditional 8 hour day, 5 days a week, with 4½ hours voluntary overtime on Saturdays (which had a 50% take-up rate), and maintenance was carried out on Sundays at double time. The new arrangements were 4 days 8.00 a.m. – 5.30 p.m., with a ½ hour break, plus Friday 8.00 a.m. – 11.00 a.m. Overtime was available for 5½ hours on Friday. This produced an 80% take-up rate. Maintenance was carried out on Saturday at time and a half. Also, technician staff were available to cover the Friday overtime as part of their normal time.

A notable feature of the 'new' collective agreements, especially single-union agreements, is that all employees are on contracts that require them to work a set number of hours per year. The actual number of hours worked per week will vary depending upon demand, absenteeism etc. Overtime is not necessarily paid when the number of hours worked per week exceeds the basic working week. Only when hours exceed a set maximum are overtime payments triggered or when hours exceed a certain total in a longer period, for example, over a three-month period. This is a clear example of the move to all employees being on staff-type contracts and the blurring of the distinction between manual workers, and blue and white collar staff.

An example of a 'new' type agreement is the agreement between Continental Can and TGWU. The package deal included the following points:

- no hourly rates of pay
- no clocking on or off
- flexibility
- multi-skilled work team

Any extra hours worked above the 2033 in the contract would be paid as a lump sum regardless of actual hours worked. Employees are expected to cover for absent colleagues, work extra hours in an emergency and work rest days on maintenance. Interestingly there is no record kept of hours worked or lateness. Employees work in teams and the system relies on the team leader and team members to put pressure on late or absent colleagues.

On flexibility the agreement states that

- there will be complete flexibility and mobility of employees . . .
- . . . efficient operations are dependent on fixed manning levels and absences will not be automatically covered
- . . . to remain competitive . . . changes in technology, etc. will be introduced and that such changes may affect both productivity and manning levels
- it is the company's intention to discuss fully such changes with the employees concerned
- to ensure complete flexibility of operations, employees will undertake training for all occupations as required by the company . . .

Clearly such an agreement constitutes a radical transformation of the traditional situation in very many firms. However, elements from such agreements are appearing in other contracts and agreements.

A model for the flexible firm was developed by the Institute of Manpower Studies in 1984. The proposals focused on the following categories:

- flexible personnel
- numerical flexibility
- functional flexibility

Flexible personnel

The total workforce of the firm was made up of three distinct groups:

- core workers who carried out the key activities. Their jobs were flexible, the terms and conditions were good and the firm invested in training them.
- peripheral workers who performed routine activities who are hired on contracts as demand dictates.
- external workers who were engaged on a subcontract basis.

Numerical flexibility

The use of more temporary workers, use of more part-timers, greater use of overtime and flexible working time, e.g., annual hours contracts.

Functional flexibility

- Maintenance jobs are expanded into related trades to give multi-skilled maintenance craftspeople.
- Process workers' jobs are expanded to provide greater mobility.
- Flexibility operates across job boundaries, e.g., process operators take on some routine maintenance or quality control.

Remuneration flexibility

- Moving to annual salary conditions for everyone rather than hourly rates
- Introducing flexibility on hours of work by scrapping the concept of the normal working week and requiring employees to work a set number of hours per year
- Removing the need to pay all 'extra' hours at overtime rates. By ensuring flexibility of hours to cover for absences, training, holidays and fluctuations in demand there is no need to pay overtime, at least not on an hourly basis.

ACAS carried out a survey in 1987 on labour flexibility in Britain. The survey confirmed that firms had a modicum of flexibility within its workforce but some of the more radical ideas (such as the Continental Can agreement) were not in evidence. The main findings were:

- Two-thirds of the organisations surveyed employed part-time workers, temporary workers and three-quarters used sub-contractors.
- The incidence of home workers and fixed-term contracts was low.
- The extent of annual hours contracts, job sharing and flexible working hours was low.
- One-quarter of firms had introduced one or more types of flexibility in crafts or skills in the last three years.
- 10% of firms had plans to harmonise one or more types of terms and conditions of employment.
- Organisations which recognised trade unions reported widespread introduction of flexibility.

15.5 Equal opportunities

The issue of equal opportunities has been on the industrial relations agenda for several years. The Equal Pay Act was on the statute book in 1970 and the debate had opened about the issue prior to this date. There have been several developments in recent times, with the law having been changed (*see* Section 10.4) and new Codes of Practice issued (*see* Sections 11.7 and 11.8).

The EC has been active in this area, having issued a number of Directives which are now enshrined in UK law. The Social Charter contains a number of proposals in this area (*see* Section 17.2) and there are further draft Directives emanating from the EC. However, the topic is still relevant today and there remains much to be done to achieve equality in practice.

Ultimately, though, the issuing of legislation, Codes and Directives is of little use unless it has the intended practical effect. Also, the issuing of rules and guidance must effect a change in attitudes. This is particularly true in this field, where prejudice can abound, attitudes, fears and beliefs can dominate and these dictate action.

The term 'equal opportunities' is now used to embrace all aspects of equality, not merely sex discrimination. Hence, it also includes discrimination because of race, marital status, age, disability, sexual orientation or any other situation where some people are treated less favourably than others. This makes the term comprehensive and enables firms to tackle this question as a totality rather than in a piecemeal manner, one topic at a time.

The extent of discrimination in the UK is well documented now, with evidence of bias in a number of areas. These are being tackled gradually with progress being made on several fronts. Tables 5.9 to 5.12 give some statistics which show the variations that occur in the fields of education and employment.

This list is not comprehensive, but the figures give a clear indication of the gender bias in some subject areas. Females still tend to study largely in areas traditionally seen as 'women's' subjects with very few opting for the traditionally 'male' subjects, which are mainly technology-related

Table 15.9 Subjects studied at university (1986)

Degree subject	Female (000s)	Male (000s)
Languages	18.3	7.7
Physical sciences	4.9	14.7
Mathematical sciences	4.3	10.1
Medical studies	4.2	1.9
Engineering and technology	2.7	24.3
All subjects	96.3	129.3

Source: DES University statistics.

and with a career aim towards industry. Also, there are proportionally more males than females going to university. In the relevant population cohort there are slightly more males than females, whereas the percentage of males taking degree courses is over 57% of the cohort.

The occupations that females enter also demonstrate a gender bias, as Table 15.10 shows for a selected number of occupations.

Table 15.10 Employment by occupation (1987)

Occupational group	Men 000s	%	Women 000s	%
Professional – management and administration	1,080	8	348	3
Professional – education, welfare and health	724	5	1,465	14
Professional – science, engineering and technology	966	7	107	1
Management	1,763	13	638	6
Clerical	945	7	3,129	30
Selling	654	5	1,012	10
Catering, cleaning and hairdressing	545	4	2,279	22
Production of metal and electrical goods	2,234	16	105	1
All employment	13,951		10,296	
Part-time	646	4.7	4,579	44.5

Source: Labour Force Survey 1987

The table gives some examples rather than the full list of all the categories. Where there is a bias, it is noteworthy that women are under-represented in several of the better paid occupations and they are in occupations that are dominated by poorer conditions of employment and where part-time work is commonplace (*see* Section 17.1 for more detail).

The numbers employed in the various sectors of employment also reveal a gender bias. Table 15.11 shows the relevant figures for a number of selected sectors.

Table 15.11   Employment by industrial sector (1987)

Sector	Female (000s) part-time	Female (000s) full-time	Male (000s) part-time	Male (000s) full-time
Agriculture	62	54	35	387
Metal goods manufacture	119	397	37	1,923
Other manufacture	242	632	59	1,379
Retail distribution	961	655	164	989
Hotel and catering	512	236	68	267
Banking and finance	350	795	81	1,162
All	4,969	5,275	1,036	12,818

Source: Department of Employment

These figures show the extent to which certain industries are dominated by males or females, and the varying extent of part-time work in the sectors, and who occupies these posts.

Finally, Table 15.12 shows the variations in earnings between males and females, despite the fact that the first piece of legislation passed to push for equality on pay was passed in 1970.

Table 15.12   Average earnings (1971–1987)

	1971 p per hr.	1981 p per hr.	1987 p per hr.
Women	47.2	241.2	386.2
Men	74.1	331.2	526.2
Differential	26.9	90.0	140.0
Womens' earnings as a percentage of mens'	63.7	72.8	73.4

Source: Department of Employment Gazette

While progress has been made over the period, there still remains a large differential between the earning power of the two sexes. The gap may narrow further as the 'work of equal value' basis for comparison of earnings (*see* Section 10.4.3) makes a wider impact. However, until there are equal numbers of both sexes in all occupations and in all industrial sectors there will not be equality of earnings.

15.5.1   Responsibility for equal opportunities

The primary responsibility for achieving equality lies with the management of organisations. It is they who must develop the policies and take action to ensure that equality becomes a reality. This in itself presents a problem as most senior management positions are held by white Englishmen. It is then argued that they, at best, are not in a position to manage this and at worst will perpetuate the old systems and ways, which will block any moves to equality. This is where positive action is required to ensure that minority voices have an influence on both policy and practice.

The first move is for an organisation to develop an equal opportunities policy. This will commit the organisation to achieving equality in various areas of its operations and should help secure the commitment of senior management to these ideals. An equal opportunities policy should contain the following:

- a definition of discrimination
- the organisation's commitment to equal opportunities
- specify the person responsible for the policy
- how the policy is to be implemented
- the employee's responsibilities in this area
- the procedure for dealing with complaints of discrimination
- examples of unlawful practice and how barriers will be eliminated
- the monitoring and review procedure.

A senior member of management should be made responsible for the policy and this should be someone at board level in the private sector. The Equal Opportunities Commission recommends that responsibility for implementing the policy should be given to a committee or working party. This body should be made up of management, employee and trade union representatives. The committee's terms of reference should include:

- analysing the information generated by the monitoring process
- assessing how the policy is working out in practice
- making recommendations for remedying any defects or failures
- assessing the success of the remedies

By involving employees in the process it will elicit their support for equality. Communication is also vital to ensure that all employees know the policy and how it is being implemented. For those who are involved in implementing the policy, at whatever level, they should receive training which will enable them to better understand what discrimination is, how it occurs and how it can be eliminated.

15.5.2 Equal opportunities in action

The following areas are potentially where discrimination can occur and there are also indications of what should be checked.

- **Recruitment** Check that programmes are equally directed at men and women, adverts reach all groups, not just a restricted number, the wording of adverts does not exclude any group, examples of drawings do not portray bias, jobs are open to all, not just a particular group and job descriptions are not biased.
- **Selection** Check that all applications are dealt with in the same manner, the criteria for shortlisting is fair and selection tests are related to the requirements of the job.
- **Training** Check that all groups are encouraged to undertake training, all groups receive comparable training, modes of attendance are not restrictive and the needs of all groups are catered for.
- **Promotion** Check that future requirements for senior posts are identified, paths for promotion do not contain any blocks for certain groups, the requirements for promotion are not restrictive and are genuine, access to promotion is open, the selection

procedure is free from bias, any appraisal system is based on objective standards and unsuccessful candidates are given reasons for their lack of success.
- **Terms and differentials of pay** Check that these are justified.
- **Conditions of employment** Check that pay structures have been reviewed, fringe benefits apply equally to all groups, part-timers receive pro-rata benefits, different working patterns could assist certain groups, special leave arrangements cater for the needs of all staff and job evaluation schemes do not contain hidden bias.
- **Grievances and disciplinary procedures** Check that the procedure deals sensitively and effectively with complaints of discrimination, victimisation or harassment, the procedure is applied fairly to all groups and there is not a disproportionate number of complaints arising from certain sections.
- **Leaving** Check the true reasons for people leaving, redundancy procedures do not adversely affect some groups and short-time working does not discriminate against some groups.

Mini-questions

15.1 Differentiate between an official strike and an unofficial strike.
15.2 What are 'wildcat' strikes?
15.3 Define a lockout.
15.4 What is 'continuous service'? Does a strike affect this?
15.5 What are the main reasons for picketing?
15.6 What does the law allow the picket to do?
15.7 Define a closed shop.
15.8 Explain the abbreviation uma.
15.9 Explain why management might argue in favour of a closed shop.
15.10 State the main objection to the closed shop.
15.11 Define a pre-entry closed shop and discuss the steps taken to stop this practice.
15.12 State if the number of closed shops increased or decreased in the last 10 years and explain why this is the case.

Further reading

P Blyton, *Changes in Working Time*,
R Hyman, *Strikes*, Macmillan, 1989,
0-333-47361-2
I Benson and J Lloyd, *New Technology and Industrial Change*, Kogan Page, 1983,
0-85038-284-X
W W Daniel, *Workplace Industrial Relations and Technical Change*, Pinter, 1987,
0-86187-941-4

TUC, *Equal Opportunities Policies and Procedures*
P Willman, *Technological Change, Collective Bargaining and Industrial Efficiency*, OUP, 1986, 0-19-827262-6

Case studies

(1)   The annual wage negotiations, page 300.
(8)   The mushrooming problem, page 331.
(11) Strangers at work, page 344.
(15) Redundancy at Toolcraft, page 357.

16

Industrial democracy

16.1 The concept of industrial democracy

16.1.1 Defining industrial democracy

So far we have looked at a variety of topics that describe and analyse the British system of industrial relations that pertains today. This chapter looks at the topic of industrial democracy which is just as pertinent as the other topics so far examined but which has made very little impact in practice on our system. Industrial democracy has no fixed definition and it is used to describe a variety of ideas to different people. It is generally accepted that industrial relations will move towards some form of industrial democracy as the next step in an ever-evolving system. What form it will take is not so certain. It will probably be a mixture of forms, depending on the industry or sector. It will also depend on unknown variables, like the political stance of the government of the day, especially if the changes are to have legislative backing. As we shall see in Section 16.2.3, as a country we are lagging behind most European countries in introducing some form of legislatively backed system of industrial democracy. This in itself gives rise to a pressure for change.

At this point it is necessary to try to define industrial democracy. Our current system of industrial relations is very much based on collective bargaining. A feature of collective bargaining is that it is a system in which each side defends its own interests against claims from the other side. Unions protect their members' interests and management protects the interests of the business and its shareholders. Collective bargaining is also based on the prerogative of management to make and implement policy, although it has to take into account the likely reaction of the workforce and unions. The distinctive feature of any form of industrial democracy, whether it be a participation scheme or worker control, is that the employees are involved in the decision-making process of the organisation. In practice this could be at work group level or at board level. The movement towards industrial democracy involves a change from a defensive, protective position to a more positive, direct involvement.

Collective bargaining has evolved over the years to include many topics (as we saw in Chapter 6) and has influenced management's decision making, in that often consultative stages have to be carried out before implementing a decision. For example, before redundancies are declared or working practices are changed, the workforce or unions have to be consulted, according to some negotiated procedure. This does not, however, take away management's right to make the decision in the first place and then to implement that decision. It may be in practice that resistance is so great that the decision is modified or eventually rescinded, but this is not due to a direct, positive involvement of workpeople in the process of decision making. The idea of industrial democracy is that employees are involved in making the decision being made on a particular matter. As we shall see later, this can involve a wide range of decisions like investment, planning, expansion, contraction, appointments, working practices, work allocation, organisation, technological change and many others.

The current responsibilities of directors in companies in the private sector are embodied in the consolidating Companies Act 1985. Their sole responsibility, at law, is to run the business in the best interests of the shareholders. This is often pointed out as a stumbling block to the idea of industrial democracy, because the involvement of employees in decision making will require decisions to be made with the employees' interests in mind also. It is argued that changes will have to be made in the law to accommodate any movement towards industrial democracy. If a decision is being made regarding an investment, any employees involved in that decision will want to evaluate the impact of it on their jobs and terms and conditions of employment. If the net result is unfavourable, they will doubtless argue against the proposal. Under current law, the directors' decision should be only that which is favourable to the shareholders. A law that required directors to make a decision that balances the interests of shareholders and workers will enable industrial democracy to work more effectively. In some situations there would be no clash of interest, so the issue would not arise.

An amendment to the Companies Act was made by the Employment Act 1982. This requires companies to make:

'statements describing the action that has been taken during the financial year to introduce, maintain or develop arrangements aimed at:

(i) providing employees systematically with information on matters concerning them as employees
(ii) consulting employees or their representatives on a regular basis so that the views of employees can be taken into account in making decisions which are likely to affect their interests
(iii) encouraging the involvement of employees in the company's performance through an employee share scheme or by some other means
(iv) achieving a common awareness on the part of all employees of the financial and economic factors affecting the performance of the company.'

Industrial democracy can therefore be seen as some form of co-determination between employer and employee, whereby both are involved and participate in the making of some, or all, of the decisions in an organisation. This contrasts with most current practices where there may be a consulting or informing stage but no participation. The exact form of this participation, and the reasons for doing it, vary widely but the characteristic is that of direct involvement by employees in some aspect of their life at work.

The process of decision making can be defined as making a choice between alternatives. This involves several stages and typically would include collecting the facts relating to the situation, formulating alternatives, assessing each alternative and finally making the choice of which alternative to implement. Schemes for participation operate at one or more of these stages. Some elementary schemes are little more than communication exercises and simply aim to give information relating to the situation under discussion. Other schemes involve employees in discussing the alternative forms of action that could be taken in a situation. Yet again, schemes can involve employees in assessing the alternatives and coming to some conclusion regarding the best course of action to take. Finally, though very rarely, employees may be involved in making the final decision. Usually this final stage in decision making is seen as a management prerogative and only the more radical schemes, such as worker cooperatives, achieve such a level of participation.

Some argue that the desire to participate derives from people's fear of the unknown or inexplicable. Not knowing what is happening or about to happen is frightening. People lose this fear if they know what is happening, even if the news is bad news. It is then argued that participation serves its purpose by informing people about the facts and creates an attitude of readiness to accept change. Systems may need reforming to carry this out effectively whereby workers are given a sense of involvement in the affairs of the organisation. This leads to improved motivation, increased efficiency and higher morale.

Decision making can also be examined in terms of the following.

- **Levels of decision making** The traditional, hierarchical organisation derives from the authority possessed by people, at the various levels in the organisation, to make decisions. Clearly supervisors are restricted in the decisions they can make as opposed to directors who are less constrained. Schemes for participation can be operated at different levels: briefing groups could operate at shop floor/workplace level, or there could be worker directors at board level.
- **Time span** This is the length of time between taking a decision and its achievement. At workplace level the time span is immediate. A supervisor makes a decision that has an immediate effect. A manager's decision to buy and install a new piece of machinery will take months. A board decision to diversify into new markets or introduce new products may take several years.
- **Breadth** This is the number of employees affected by the decision. Some decisions affect only the individual or group, while others affect the section or department, and yet others affect the whole factory or company. The decisions of autonomous work groups affect the immediate group; the decisions of a works council affect the whole organisation.

The choice of participation scheme will necessarily involve examining these aspects of decision making in organisations. Some argue that employees should participate at the level at which they work. A common argument is that at higher levels workplace representatives do not possess the expertise to make a valuable contribution. Participation is limited by the knowledge, skill and experience of employees. As a counter argument, training could be given and in time such representatives could make a valuable contribution. Schemes that produce immediate results and direct involvement, such

as group working practices, improve the individual's motivation and thereby raise efficiency and improve industrial relations. Participation at board level is said to be too remote and removed from the workplace to have very much effect. Certainly such indirect schemes do not involve many and in large organisations have little impact on the majority of employees.

16.1.2 Reasons for extending participation

There are a variety of reasons for extending worker participation. Many different and diverse bodies acknowledge that some form of industrial democracy is both desirable and necessary, but the objectives of these bodies, and hence their reasoning, can be quite different. The spectrum of opinion covers a broad range. The Institute of Workers' Control, whose arguments are based on a Marxist analysis, have the objective of worker control and ownership. At the other end of the spectrum are bodies like the CBI, who firmly believe in capitalism, but wish to see a movement towards industrial democracy to improve business efficiency. Listed below are some of the reasons often given to support the case for the extension of industrial democracy.

- **The development of the individual** If employees can gain more job satisfaction, then, as individuals, they can realise their full potential, to the benefit of both the individual and the organisation. It follows that organisations should change to bring about this realisation of potential. Various schemes have been tried to achieve this, like job enrichment and job rotation. By giving the individual greater involvement in the business, through participating in decisions, the individual will realise this potential more fully.

Schemes to involve the individual are called direct schemes. There have been many attempts to involve employees more fully in the success of their organisations. The widely reported ones involve the use of autonomous work groups (*see* Section 16.2.1). Clearly these schemes can and do improve the level of motivation of the individual. The criticism levelled at them is that they operate at a low level of decision making and do not have any influence on the decisions made at a higher level.

- **Worker protection** Many management decisions affect workers' jobs in some way. If there is no employee involvement in making these decisions this will create an atmosphere of insecurity. With the many changes that take place, like introducing new machinery, redundancies, mergers or rationalisation, the employee needs to be involved in such decisions. This will help to take out the element of insecurity and create an environment in which the employee can help make such changes successful.

  The effect of keeping individuals informed is a psychological one that removes the fear of the unknown. Some people are satisfied if they know what is going on. For example, the legal requirements for consultation before declaring redundancies exist for this reason. There is a movement towards extending such consultations to other topics, as seen earlier with the provisions of the 1982 Employment Act.

- **Government by consent**   Currently management imposes its decisions on employees, often with no prior notice or consultation. Without the consent of the employees, management cannot expect wholehearted commitment. If employees participated in making decisions, they would be more committed to the success of the enterprise.

  Under this heading comes the movement towards greater democratisation in our lives generally, and in our working lives in particular. As individual employees have invested their working lives and careers into the enterprise, the argument is that they should have an active say in the government of the enterprise. Certainly consent brings commitment but, some argue, a democratic decision may not always be the best decision.

- **Efficiency**   Employees have a great fund of knowledge and experience that they could bring to the enterprise. If they were allowed to join in management activity, they could use this knowledge and experience. The business would gain from joint analysis and the morale of the workforce would be raised.

- **Accountability** As there is greater government involvement in industry, and business has a greater impact on society generally, the accountability of firms should be increased. This should include a greater involvement of employees in determining what goes on at their own place of work.

- **Political** A radical argument for participation is that the system of capitalism (bosses and workers) stifles an individual's potential. There is a great need to change the system by which organisations are run. By such changes in ownership and control the injustices prevalent in the current system will be cured and then workers can realise their full potential. Schemes for worker cooperatives are based on these ideas.

16.2   Schemes for participation

16.2.1   The framework for industrial democracy

Any framework for industrial democracy needs to include the following dimensions:

- the degree of control over decision making with regard to the information channels and the influence on decision making, e.g., the upward flow of information, involvement in decision making
- the subject matter, that is, the issues over which control is exercised and whether it is departmental, local or company-wide – these can be represented as a spectrum (*see* Figure 16.1)
- the form of participation, whether this be direct, indirect, disclosure of information, profit-sharing, joint decision making, and, again this can be represented as a spectrum (*see* Table 16.1)

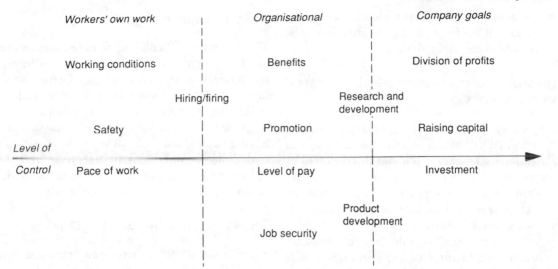

Fig. 16.1 Spectrum of topics covered by a scheme of industrial democracy

Table 16.1 Spectrum of types of schemes of industrial democracy

Worker control	Joint management	Cooperation	Consultation
Self-management; Worker autonomy; Worker superior to manager.	co-determination, e.g., 50/50 board.	employee can criticise; suggest; bring to management; adopt proposals.	prior notice given of changes; allowing comments; possibly reconsider decisions.

We will examine these points in greater detail here. The following detailed component set has been established based on empirical examination and current successful practice, proposing that all these should exist in some form for any scheme of industrial democracy to be successful. Again there is no precise formula for a scheme, but there are a number of conditions that should be met if a scheme is to succeed.

Participation in decision making

There should be an established flow of communication upwards from managed to manager. Employees should be able to contribute their knowledge to the decision making process. They should also be able to initiate discussion on a topic of their choosing – indeed, this last factor is held to be the threshold of industrial democracy. There should be face-to-face discussion and consultation and a means available for employees to meet the decision makers. The system should include feedback to employees on the reasons for the acceptance or rejection of ideas and proposals.

Feedback of economic results to all employees

There should be a monetary feedback to employees from the surplus they have helped to produce through a share in the profits or in productivity bonuses. This should:

- be related directly to what the worker has produced, so the employee can see a reward for their particular effort
- belong to the employee by right and not be subject to the discretion of some manager or committee
- be made to the entire group, to ensure social cohesion, otherwise, such payments could be divisive
- be separate from basic pay so that this element is separately identifiable

- be made to give regular feedback and, if greater effort is given, the rewards should be seen sooner rather than later

Full sharing of management level information with employees

Employees should have the information given to them to make decisions or against which they can judge decision making. Without this they will be suspicious and will be unable to evaluate decisions. Often the greatest fear is 'not knowing' and employees feel greater satisfaction in 'just knowing what is going on'.

Making information fully available presents a practical difficulty as some information is bound to be either confidential, commercially sensitive, secret or personal. There is also the alleged problem of untrained personnel being able to handle technical information. Nevertheless, there is much information that could be made available and which employees could intelligently handle.

Guaranteed individual rights

There is always a risk in being open and frank that there may be reprisals or that victimisation may occur. Employees could fear that by speaking up and criticising they will be 'marked people'. There should therefore be freedom of speech and of assembly to ensure that the process works. Secret ballots should be used where necessary to secure anonymity and there should be a right of appeal against certain management action, e.g., dismissal, transfer or demotion. Indeed, some propose that union officials should not be dismissed, transferred or demoted while in office to guard against victimisation.

Appeals procedure

There should be an independent board of appeal in the case of disputes. This could be by peer group, a joint peer group/managers group or an external board. This will militate against unilateral management decisions to manipulate the system that could otherwise go unchallenged.

Attitudes and values

This is a more difficult area to determine and set up, but everyone in the scheme should have a common, shared set of values. These should include flexibility, being receptive to new ideas, possessing an ability to fashion compromises, being open to being persuaded by discussion and having confidence in others. Without the underlying commitment by everyone and the attitudes required to run a scheme of industrial democracy, the scheme will not work.

The advantages and disadvantages

As with any system, there are advantages and disadvantages and schemes of industrial democracy are no exception. To radically reform an existing organisation on completely new lines is obviously a risk and the results may not be apparent for some time, perhaps several years. People take time to adjust to a new environment and many will be resistant, wishing to cling to the old out of a fear of the new. The table below gives a list of the advantages and disadvantages classified under five headings. Table 16.2 shows a list applicable to management and Table 16.3 a list applicable to employees.

Table 16.2   Advantages and disadvantages to management of industrial democracy

Factor	Advantage	Disadvantage
Ideological	Employee integration; union weakened and/or integrated into the enterprise	Criticism of, or challenge to, management authority
Economic	Improved employee efficiency	Cost, time and energy
Psychological	Improved motivation; reduction of stress	Tensions; frustration
Organisation	Reduction in bureaucracy; trained employees; negotiate change	Slowness; disorganisation
Sociological	Social regulation; social peace	Union opposition; middle management opposition

Table 16.3 Advantages and disadvantages to employees of industrial democracy

Factor	Advantages	Disadvantages
Ideological	Recognition of achievement	Manipulation
Economic	Profit-sharing or bonuses	Time and energy cost
Psychological	Job enrichment; lower stress	Loss of freedom; responsibility
Organisational	Decentralisation; delegation	
Sociological	Integration	Alienation

Clearly not all these will occur with any one scheme or, for any one organisation, but some will inevitably occur to some degree or other. Some may be short-lived and be part of the transition phase.

16.2.2 Industrial democracy in practice

There have been many different practical approaches to industrial democracy. Some are based on an evolutionary approach, others are revolutionary. Some say that any attempt at industrial democracy should start with the present system and modifications be made to it. The first step could be the issuing of more information and the extension of consultative processes. This has certainly been a feature of industrial relations practice in many workplaces where a greater amount of information is given by employers and, indeed, this is backed by legislation (*see* Section 10.3). Many establishments have joint consultative committees or works councils where information is received and given on a range of issues. Since 1978 firms have, where requested, set up safety committees on which safety representatives have the legal right to carry out certain functions and participate, to a large degree, in the health and safety aspects of the business (*see* Section 5.2.2). These are all a gradualist's approach to industrial democracy. Others would look to more rapid changes by radically altering the system quickly. Given a firm already in existence, it is difficult to effect such changes but new ventures can be made, for example into worker cooperatives.

Another classification of attempts at industrial democracy is based on direct and indirect schemes:

- direct participation is where an individual or group is involved in some management activity. Semi-autonomous work groups, as in the Swedish system, are an attempt to get the individual to participate more fully, and to influence what and how the work is done
- indirect participation is where a representative, say a union official, acts on behalf of the employees they represent. Worker directors are an example of this

From the late eighteenth century, there have been many ideas expounded and attempts made at forms of industrial democracy. They have included worker cooperatives, syndicalism, guild socialism, nationalisation, worker directors, works councils and semi-autonomous work groups. There have been other ideas for change, such as profit-sharing and bonus issues of shares and a further set of job-related ideas like job enrichment, job enlargement and job rotation. These ideas fall outside the definition of industrial democracy used in this book as they generally do not extend the participation of the employee in the policy-making and decision-making areas of the organisation. Below are brief descriptions of a few of the practical attempts that have been made at industrial democracy.

John Lewis Partnership

All the ordinary shares of JLP are held by the JLP Trust. The terms of the Trust only allow funds to be used for developing the business or for the benefit of employees. There is a Central Council which has the right to be consulted on all aspects of finance, has the full authority to administer a welfare fund and is the final court of appeal in disciplinary cases.

The Chairperson and Deputy hold the same positions in the trading organisation and three others are employee representatives. Four-fifths of the Council are elected by employees and the remainder by the Chairperson. The Chairperson can be voted out of office by a two-thirds majority of the Council.

Scott-Bader Commonwealth

The company is owned by its employees and was handed over to them by its founder, Ernest Bader. The Board of Directors is appointed by the Commonwealth and they are accountable to the Commonwealth.

The constitution states that 60% of profits are to be retained by the business and of the remaining 40%, half must go to charity or towards the development of other commonwealths. The members of the Commonwealth must agree to the maximum pay differential allowed in the company and the target is 7:1, highest to lowest.

British Steel

The British Steel Corporation set up an employee director scheme in 1967 along with a series of consultative committees as an extension of collective bargaining. The experiment ran for four years, after which the situation was reviewed. The scheme was revised in 1971.

The Corporation is divided into six divisional boards and there are three part-time worker directors on each board. They attend board meetings, are members of working parties, attend other meetings and maintain liaison with employees. The directors all hold trade union office (shop steward, convenor or works representative) and are nominated jointly by both union and management.

The scheme has been criticised mainly because the employee directors are distanced from the workers they represent and they tend to become management orientated. Also, the divisional boards do not make important policy decisions. This is the function of the main board on which there are no employee directors.

Post Office

A later experiment began in the Post Office in 1977. It was decided by a Joint Study Group that the main Post Office board and its regional boards on the postal and communications side, should have an equal number of management and union seats with a smaller number of independent directors. In the event, there was a 7:7:5 split of management, union and independent directors. The two main unions in the Post Office, the Communications Workers' Union and the Post Office Engineering Union, agreed on how to share their seven union seats. The employee directors are selected from among the employees and officers of the unions, and their names are submitted to the Secretary of State for Industry (who appoints the directors). At regional level, the boards were reconstituted on the same lines. At area level, new policy committees were set up to help ensure that local views were formulated and put to the boards at higher levels.

Work groups

Many of the early experiments at reorganising the workplace by direct employee participation were carried out in Sweden. Over 500 firms, with Volvo and Saab being the most famous, tried schemes of introducing semi-autonomous work groups. Under this system a group of workers who carry out a particular function, say wiring a car, are given all the equipment and material they need to do the job. They then decide, among themselves, how the job is to be organised, which tasks are carried out by whom, etc. Meetings are held regularly to iron out problems and discuss productivity. This scheme is now backed by law in Sweden.

Single-union agreements

A feature of some 'new' single union package deals is the creation of Advisory Boards. As part of creating a new atmosphere of cooperative industrial relations, companies are setting up management/employee advisory boards where all matters of company policy are discussed. This is part of the open style of management which characterises these deals. Employee representatives can be union or non-union employees.

Worker cooperatives

In recent times there have been several attempts at setting up worker cooperatives, although the idea dates back to the 1830s and 1840s. Under this scheme the workers themselves organise the business. They elect their own directors and managers and determine every aspect of the business.

This scheme was tried at the Triumph motor-cycle factory at Meriden and at Kirby Engineering in Liverpool. Both were companies that were on the brink of collapse and money was provided to set up the cooperatives. Neither has survived, largely because business was on the decline anyway. In Mondragon, in northern Spain, there are a series of successful worker cooperatives. These were set up in the early 1940s and the scheme is still expanding. It involves worker ownership (through buying shares), worker control and the provision of a whole range of facilities like banking, housing and amenities.

16.2.3 Proposals

Several bodies over the years, have drawn up proposals on industrial democracy. Below are brief descriptions of some of these proposals.

British Institute of Management

The Institute, as the professional body representing managers, has laid out its own set of proposals. It takes an evolutionary line but with a commitment to employee participation in decision making within an organisation. It believes that both management and employee have a common interest in the success of an undertaking and if employees can be more fully involved, the business will be more successful and the employees gain greater job satisfaction.

The Institute goes on to propose that participation agreements should be made between management and employees. Such agreements would provide the framework for participation within that company. Such agreements could include the appointment of employee directors and a structure of participation committees or councils.

Confederation of British Industries

The CBI position on industrial democracy is very similar to that of the BIM. It suggests that all companies employing over 2,000 people should have to negotiate a participation agreement, and this would be a statutory requirement. Firms not doing so within, say, four years, would have an agreement imposed on them by an independent, outside body. If employee directors were to be appointed, it suggests that these constitute no greater than one-third of the board. Again, the emphasis is on greater participation and information, especially at workplace level, and the CBI suggests a greater expansion of consultation and giving of information on a wider range of subjects. It suggests company councils could be created that would have to be consulted before decisions are made.

Trades Union Congress

The policy of the TUC is that industrial democracy should be extended. It takes a flexible approach, suggesting that every scheme should be designed to suit the particular needs of each organisation. Its main theme is that collective bargaining should be greatly extended to cover all the topics that affect employees, that a much greater amount of information should be given for the purposes of collective bargaining and that consultative and bargaining machinery should be merged. This means that decision making becomes a matter of negotiation between management and union. This is where the TUC and CBI proposals differ. The CBI wants to include all employees (union members or not) and to keep traditional negotiations outside of the consultative process.

The TUC suggests that worker directors be appointed, through trade union machinery, on a 50:50 basis with management. It recommends the adoption of the two-tier structure (like the German system) with a top, policy-making board and a management board responsible for the day-to-day running of the organisation. Changes to the law would be required to oblige companies to have regard to the interests of the employees as well as the shareholders, and also to extend the system into the public sector by having employee representatives on health boards and nationalised industry boards.

Bullock Committee of Enquiry

In 1975 a Royal Commission was set up to enquire into the subject of industrial democracy, with particular emphasis on the part trade unions could play in this. The terms of reference were criticised as being too narrow and the final report was constricted in what it could recommend because of the narrow terms of reference. The terms of reference were, 'Accepting the need for a radical extension of industrial democracy in the control of companies by means of representation on boards of directors and accepting the essential role of trade union organisations in this process, to consider how such an extension can be achieved taking into account the proposals of the TUC representatives on industrial democracy as well as experience in Britain, the EEC and other countries'.

The 12-man enquiry reported in 1977. The Committee recommended that, for companies employing 2,000 or over, there should be a right to have worker directors. The unitary board structure was kept with a formula of $2x + y$ for directorships, an equal number of shareholder and union appointed directors, x, and a smaller, odd number of independent directors, y. These independent directors would be jointly agreed between the other directors. In the event of deadlock, an industrial democracy commission could arbitrate.

There would be no legal compulsion for companies to have employee directors, but the system would be that if a trade union requested it, a ballot should be held regarding the issue. A secret ballot would have to be held of all employees and the requirement for the resolution to be passed would be a majority vote in favour, and that the majority consist of a minimum of one-third of the total number of employees. If passed, the unions would then select, from among their number, representatives to act as directors. It was suggested that a joint representatives committee be set up to represent all the unions in an establishment, who could then agree on a list of representatives to act as directors. All directors would have the same legal responsibilities but would make decisions in the interests of shareholders and employees. Also certain decisions currently made at the request of shareholders, like alterations to the company's memorandum of association or the recommendation of dividend, would be for the board only to raise at the annual general meeting.

A minority report, of the employer representatives on the Committee, dissented from most of the majority recommendations and came up with its own proposals. The publication of the Bullock Committee findings gave rise to much debate, not least because of its radical approach. In the event, the recommendations were never acted on by the government.

White paper on industrial democracy

About 15 months after the publication of the Bullock Committee findings, the Labour government drafted and published a white paper on industrial democracy, to cover both the public and the private sector. The paper recommended the extension of industrial democracy, but not by the imposition of a standard system. If voluntary agreement between management and employees proved impossible, there would be certain fall-back statutory rights. The proposed law would require all companies employing more than 500 people to discuss all major proposals that affect employees before a decision is made. This would include investment plans, mergers, take-overs, expansion or contraction and major organisational changes. A Code of Practice would be used to give extra guidance on this.

The paper agreed with the Bullock suggestion of joint representative committees, and suggested that these be set up and used as a channel for discussion. Also the fall-back statutory rights would be given to the joint committee. Any refusal to observe the legal requirements would lead to a reference being made to an industrial democracy commission (or maybe ACAS) who could report on the matter and maybe have powers of enforcement.

Employee representation at board level is seen in the paper as a natural progression from consultations on policy. If employees wished it, they should have the right to have representatives on their board. A two-tier structure is recommended, similar to the TUC proposals (*see above*). The proposals would be backed by statutory rights for employees in companies employing more than 2,000 people. The proportion of employee directors is left open but a one-third representation is suggested as a first stage. The policy board's functions would include the appointment of the management board, the setting of company objectives and approving strategic plans, monitoring the management board, supervising the company's financial affairs and making recommendations to shareholders at the annual general meeting.

The EC Fifth Directive

This Directive of the EC was first drafted in 1972. The proposal applies to nearly all private companies of over 500 employees. The proposals are for a two-tier structure with a supervisory board and a management board. The supervisory board would contain worker directors, who would either be elected and constitute one-third of the board, or would be co-opted to create a balance of representation. This top board would be responsible for policy making and be accountable to a general meeting of shareholders. The management board would consist of management, executive directors who would implement the policy of the supervisory board and be accountable to it for the day-to-day running of the company.

The Directive, in its original form, was never adopted. A fresh attempt was made in 1983 in a move to harmonise company law in the EC. The original proposals were retained and a further two added. The first allowed for an employee representative body at company level; the second for participation through collective

bargaining agreement procedures. The latter was inserted to appease the UK government who were opposed to any regulatory process, from the EC, imposing a scheme on the UK. In other words, the present arrangements in the UK would fulfil the requirements of the Directive.

The Vredeling-Davignon proposals

These were drafted in 1980 with the very cumbersome title of 'Procedures for informing and consulting employees of undertakings with complex structures, in particular trans-national firms'. The proposal required consultation in firms with over 1,000 employees, by requiring information to be given on all major decisions that could have serious consequences for the employees. Topics included the closure of production, restrictions/modifications to productive capacity, changes in work organisation, mergers or cessation of cooperation with other companies and measures affecting health and safety.

International Labour Organisation

This produced a set of recommendations on industrial democracy that were adopted in 1952. The basis was that, 'consultation and co-operation between employer and employee in the enterprise should be furthered in order to discuss matters of common interest which are not covered by collective bargaining and which are not part of regular employment conditions'.

These recommendations were added to in 1967, giving recommendations relating to the flow of information and again in 1971, which added the topics of the protection of worker representatives and facilities for such representatives.

The UK is a signatory to the ILO and should implement the ILO standards. This is not the case in practice and there are several instances where the UK has not implemented ILO standards.

16.2.4 European practice

The European experience in changing organisational structures and introducing some form of industrial democracy is far ahead of anyone else's.

Most European countries have some form of employee participation and often this is backed by a statutory requirement. For these reasons and, because being members of the EC makes European legal requirements compulsory (when the Eurocompany Statutes are passed), it is likely that some form of industrial democracy will be imposed in this country sooner rather than later. Below are some brief facts relating to several European countries' practices on industrial democracy.

Germany

There has been legislation relating to industrial democracy since 1951, when all companies in the iron, steel and coal sector employing more than 1,000 had to have worker directors. The system used is the two-tier supervisory board and management board structure. The top board has five shareholder directors and five employee directors plus one, jointly agreed, independent director. Employee directors are elected by the employees, but not through trade union machinery, and there is a compulsory allocation of seats for white collar workers and managerial levels.

Currently, the system has been extended to all firms employing more than 2,000. They must have employee directors on their supervisory boards, with half the seats allocated to them. The board, when constituted, elects its own chairperson and vice-chairperson. All firms (except family firms with fewer than 500 employees) must have employee directors on their supervisory boards. In this case they have one-third of the seats allocated to them. Also, each firm has to have a labour director on its management board. The director is a union representative and is responsible for social and personnel policy on that board.

In addition to board representation, there is a compulsory system of works councils for all companies. The function of the council is to receive information about the company and it can require explanations of company policy. The role of the council is advisory, but it can take the employer to the labour court if council's advice is ignored. The areas the works council can look at include hours of work, start and finish times, holidays, human resource planning and training. Companies over 1,000 strong must have an economic committee to discuss mergers, organisational changes and any matters likely to adversely affect employees' interests. Again, appointment is by election through a ballot of all employees. The works council nominates the employee directors on the supervisory board.

France

Since 1945, works councils have been a feature of the French system. French companies of more than 50 employees must have a works council, which is advisory in nature. It can look at works rules, hours, holidays, human resource planning and it must be informed of any planned redundancies involving 90 employees within a 30-day period. The representatives are elected by all employees, with designated seats for supervisory, professional and executive staff. The council is chaired by the head of the company. Only since 1958 can a union have a branch within an organisation and any recognised union can send a representative to the works council, but the representative has no voting powers.

Companies employing more than 50 people have to allow two delegates from the works council to meet with the board of directors. In 1975, a report suggested that worker participation should be extended but this has only gone as far as allowing employee representatives to have a supervisory role on the boards of companies employing over 2,000 people.

Holland

Works councils are also a statutory requirement in Holland and have been since 1950. Firms employing more than 25 must set up a council which has a consultative role. The council has the right to be kept informed on all aspects of the company's affairs. More recent legislation has given the council the power of veto over certain matters like transfer of ownership, total or partial closure, training, recruitment and welfare. The council can also participate in decisions on pensions, hours, holidays and health and safety.

Employee representatives are elected from among the employees with separate seats for manual and white collar workers. Union backed candidates are allowed to stand. Council representatives have the right to nominate and veto members of the supervisory board, although they cannot nominate current employees or full-time union officials who negotiate with the company.

Scandinavia

These countries have a long history of employee participation, mainly on a voluntary basis. Denmark, Norway and Sweden now all have a requirement to set up works councils, which are consultative in nature. There is a voluntary agreement in Denmark that every firm has a cooperative committee which has a 50:50 management:employee representation. The committee looks at conditions of employment, working conditions, safety and personnel matters. The law also gives employees the right to elect two members to the board of directors. There is a similar right in Sweden, except the process is compulsory, whereas the Danish one is at the request of employees through a ballot. In Norway, legislation passed in 1970 required firms employing more than 200 people to set up a 'joint assembly', which resembles a supervisory board. Employees can elect, through trade union machinery, representatives to one-third of the seats on the board. This assembly appoints the management and it can overrule the board of management and the shareholders' general meeting.

Belgium

Works Councils were established in 1948 and all firms of more than 100 employees are required to have a Works Council.

The size of the Council varies, but, in all cases, the management representatives cannot outnumber the worker representatives. Young employees have the right to be represented and the worker representatives are elected by the employees.

The Council has the right to information on finances and welfare provisions, to be consulted on work organisation, training and personnel policy and has decision-making powers on works rules, setting the criteria for dismissal, holidays and the management of welfare facilities. There is also the requirement to have a safety, hygiene and workplace improvement committee.

Luxembourg

There are two elements to Luxembourg's industrial democracy, which were introduced in 1919. The two are personnel representatives and joint committees. All establishments of over 100 employees have to have personnel representatives. These sit on committees for manual workers and for employees and are elected by secret ballot. There is a minimum of three worker representatives, but the maximum varies with the size of organisation.

The committee looks at personnel matters, helping settle disputes, has to be consulted on the administration of social welfare, assists in the prevention of accidents and diseases and encourages the rehabilitation of the disabled.

Joint committees have an equal number of employer and employee representatives. The numbers on the committee vary with the size of the firm, firms with between 150 and 500 employees having 6 members; 500 and 1,000 having 8; 1,000 and 1,500 having 12; 1,500 and 5,000 having 14 and over 5,000 having 16. The worker representatives are elected by secret ballot from candidates who represent, proportionally, the categories of employees. There is a separate franchise for blue collar and white collar workers.

The committee meets once every three months, although a quarter of the members can request an extra meeting. Decisions are made by voting and the Board of Directors must comment if they dissent from the decision of the committee. The terms of reference for the committee is that it can make decisions on technological change, health and safety, recruitment, selection, promotion, training, transfer and dismissal, appraisal and bonuses and has to be consulted about investment, changes in working methods, staff training, financial decisions affecting the structure of the company and receive a report on the financial state of the company twice a year.

16.2.5 Survey information

In order to gauge the level of interest in a subject surveys are used to elicit objective information. This section contains the summary of the findings of two surveys. The first was carried out by ACAS in 1990. The information was gathered by ACAS officers in the course of their work. It included information from 576 organisations, 72% being in the manufacturing sector and 53% recognised a trade union. The questions used related to consultation, rather than industrial democracy, but the survey does give an indication of the changes taking place. In firms where trade unions are recognised, managers consult on a wider range of issues, as do firms that are foreign owned. 45% of firms said that the range of issues consulted on had increased in the last three years. The number of topics covered in consultation was greater than the number covered in negotiations. With safety, welfare and the introduction of new equipment, consultation was the most common approach.

Joint consultative committees were used in about 40% of establishments and were more common in manufacturing and in large organisations. The median size of committee was 9, with a wide variation either side. Management representatives always outnumbered employee representatives. In most cases (85%) employee representatives were selected by election or some other means. In the other 15% of firms, management chose the employee representatives. The most popular topic of discussion was working conditions, followed by quality, new equipment and output. Half of the committees met monthly, with a quarter meeting bi-monthly. 19% of multi-establishment enterprises had a committee to discuss matters affecting more than one establishment.

Quality circles are a specific method of joint decision making on matters relating to quality. 40% of foreign owned plants operated quality circles as opposed to 23% of British owned plants. However, 25% of firms reported that they had set up quality circles in the last three years but no longer operated them. Joint working parties are sometimes set up as a joint problem-solving exercise for a specific topic. 40% of firms reported they had set up such committees during the last three years. They were more popular in large, unionised environments and foreign owned firms.

The second survey was conducted by the Department of Employment and involved 377 companies. The survey focused on the extent to which firms reported employee involvement under the following headings (as required by the Employment Act 1982).

- **Information/communication** Providing systematic information to employees
- **Consultation** Consulting employees or their representatives on a regular basis
- **Financial participation** Involvement of employees in the company's performance through share schemes, etc.
- **Economic awareness** Achieving a common awareness by employees of the financial factors affecting company performance.

Tables 16.4 to 16.6 show the findings of the survey.

Table 16.4 Categories of employee involvement, by company size. Percentage of companies.

Number of employees	Number in survey	0	1	2	3	4
250–1,000	267	6.0	9.4	13.1	33.7	37.8
1,001–5,000	88	0	18.2	11.4	26.1	44.3
Over 5,000	21	0	0	0	57.1	42.9
Total	377	4.5	10.9	11.9	33.2	39.5

Source: Department of Employment 1991

Table 16.5 Employee involvement practices, by company size. Percentage of companies.

Interactive practices	Size of firm			
	251–1,000	1,001–5,000	Over 5,000	Total
Briefing group	22.5	29.5	27.3	24.4
Consultative council	43.1	43.2	50.0	43.5
Quality circle/ suggestion scheme	14.6	21.6	9.1	15.9
Financial participation	75.7	79.5	81.8	76.9

Source: Department of Employment 1991

Table 16.6 Categories of employee involvement reported, by company size. Percentage of companies.

Number of employees	Number in survey	Information/ communication	Consultation	Financial participation	Economic awareness
250–1,000	267	80.9	66.3	75.7	69.3
1,001–5,000	88	80.7	65.9	79.5	73.9
Over 5,000	21	100	76.2	76.9	81.0
Total	377	81.7	66.6	76.9	70.8

Source: Department of Employment 1991

Mini-questions

16.1 State a definition of industrial democracy.

16.2 List five forms that industrial democracy might take.

16.3 State the basic responsibility of a director under present company law.

16.4 Differentiate between direct and indirect participation.

16.5 Briefly describe the Post Office experiment in industrial democracy.

16.6 Describe what a semi-autonomous work group is.

16.7 Explain the constitution of a board of directors as recommended in the Bullock Committee report.

16.8 Briefly describe the two-tier system of company boards.

16.9 Briefly describe the general role of a continental-style works council.

16.10 State the basic proposals in the EC Fifth Directive.

Exercises

16.1 Explain the idea behind industrial democracy and describe why you think that the extension of industrial democracy will help, or otherwise, in making businesses more successful and giving individuals more satisfaction in their jobs.

16.2 Differentiate between a traditional collective bargaining system and a system of industrial democracy. Describe some of the common features and the essential differences. Do you think that the two could be combined in some way by extending collective bargaining into the area of industrial democracy, as suggested by the TUC?

16.3 If you were speaking in a debate on a motion to extend industrial democracy, what reasons would you give to support your case for an extension?

16.4 State the main proposals of the CBI and the TUC on industrial democracy. Describe the common ground between the two bodies and their differences. Suggest how the two positions might be reconciled.

16.5 Evaluate the recommendations of the Bullock Committee with regard to industrial democracy, worker directors, their election and their functions. State if you think the proposals are workable or not, giving your reasons for this opinion.

16.6 If a German-type system of industrial democracy were to be adopted in the UK, state, with reasons, if you think the system would work and if it would improve the efficiency of companies. Include in your analysis the role of the two-tier board and works council.

Further reading

M Poole, *Towards a New Industrial Democracy*, Routledge, 0-7102-0916-9

Crisp, *Industrial Democracy in Western Europe*, McGraw-Hill, 0-07-082700-1

P Barns and M Doyle, *Democracy at Work*

J Elliott, *Conflict or Cooperation: The Growth of Industrial Democracy*, Kogan Page, 1993, 0-85038-758-2

B C Roberts, *Industrial Relations in Europe, Third Report from European Committee, House of Lords*, HMSO

C Crouch, *Industrial Relations and European State Traditions*, Clarendon Press, 1993, 0-19-827720-2

W Daubler, *Trade Unions in the European Community*, Lawrence and Wishart, 1992, 0-85315-766-9

17

Future developments

This final chapter takes a look at two topics in industrial relations that are fundamental to any discussion on the future system of industrial relations in the UK. They are not the only ones that are influencing the system. Several have already been mentioned. The move to single-union agreements, the use of binding arbitration, the shift to local bargaining, flexibility and multi-skilling and equal opportunities, plus legislative changes and government policy are all items that will shape the future. There will be an enduring debate on what the best system of industrial relations might be, how improvements can be made, developing and applying new solutions to problems, with different perspectives becoming dominant and unexpected occurrences all contributing to this. It is difficult to predict how things might develop and some of this chapter is necessarily crystal ball gazing. However, there are a number of dominant issues that will continue to be with us for the foreseeable future.

17.1 Occupational structure

An important factor affecting industrial relations now and in the future is the major, significant and permanent changes that are taking place in the industrial structure of the economy and the occupational structure of firms. This section looks at these changes in some detail and analyses some of the implications.

The changes can be grouped into:

- the decline in the primary (extractive) and secondary (manufacturing) industries and the growth of the service sector

- a change in the occupations of people employed in the various sectors
- demographic changes
- the size of firms

Let us look at these in detail.

Industrial change

The decline in the primary and secondary industries has been caused by two main factors. The first is the effects of international competition. Whereas the UK was one of the largest producers in the world of steel, machine tools, cotton and woollen goods and ships (to give a few examples) we have now slipped down the league to the extent that, in some industries, for example shipbuilding, we are no longer a force to be reckoned with. The factors causing this decline are several, but comparatively high wage costs and a lack of investment in new technologies are two of the reasons frequently cited.

In some cases, industrial relations have been a contributory factor. Unions and management have become trapped all too often in wars of attrition while the opposition from abroad moved into the markets and captured them. The traditional craft unions, bargaining from a position of strength, sought to maintain their status through the operation of demarcation between the crafts, which left little room for flexibility when this was required. When new technologies became available, they were not adopted or, if they were, there were costly strings attached which militated against the firm (and its employees) gaining the full benefits from the technology. Also, the strike record of some of these industries meant that efficiency was lower as a result of the days lost from disputes and the delivery performance of the firm was impaired. As the level of wage settlements increased, without parallel improvements in productivity, unit costs rose and products became uncompetitive. It should be pointed out that the fault for this should not be laid wholly at the door of the unions. Industrial relations management in many cases was poor, with a lack of imagination and radical ideas to overcome problems and to turn threats into opportunities. Managements became trapped in systems of their own making and lacked the courage to solve the crises. For many, it seems that the lesson could only be learnt (by employers and employees) through the effects of the recession that hit the UK economy in the late 1970s and 1980s. Table 17.1 shows the changes in the broad industrial categories and a few selected industries which demonstrate the extent of the change.

Table 17.1 Sector employment, by Standard Industrial Classification, 1982 and 1990

SIC class*	Numbers employed 1982 (000s)	Numbers employed 1990 (000s)	% change
0–9 All industries and services	20,896	22,854	+9.4
2–4 Manufacturing	5,761	5,150	–10.6
1–5 Production and construction	7,470	6,688	–10.5
6–9 Service	13,078	15,868	+21.3

*For the precise definition of the areas covered by the SIC classes, see the Annual or Monthly Abstract of Statistics for the list.
Source: Annual Abstract of Statistics.

The second factor causing this trend away from manufacturing industries is the effects of technology on these industries. Even if the manufacturing industries had survived the competition from abroad, they would not be employing people in the numbers they did, nor in the occupations in which they were previously employed. In every sector, technology (not just microelectronics) has had a major impact. Synthetic fibres took over from natural materials, plastics from metals, manually operated machines were automated, new tooling materials gave higher machining speeds, new processes were introduced, materials handling was speeded up, direct links between design and production were made and so on. All these changes have led to far fewer numbers of people being employed in these industrial sectors. One of the effects of technology is to substitute unskilled labour with technological devices, hence the lower labour requirements of the sectors that traditionally employed large numbers of unskilled workers. This trend is set to continue as firms strive to continually achieve greater competitiveness. There are still many jobs in manufacturing that can be automated. Another sector that is achieving greater productivity with far less labour, is agriculture. The combined effects of labour-saving machinery, the use of agro-chemicals and crop developments have led to a remarkable drop in the numbers employed on the land (which is set to continue) alongside record outputs.

Table 17.2 shows the long-term trend for the past three decades for the manufacturing and service sectors.

Table 17.2 Percentage of workforce employed in manufacturing and the service sector

Year	% of workforce in manufacturing	% of workforce in service sector
1961	38	25
1971	36	29
1981	29	61
1988	23	68
1990	22	69

Source: Department of Employment.

Table 17.3 shows the figures for the recent employment trends in several industrial sectors, using the Standard Industrial Classification (SIC) categories.

The forecasts for the future are for this trend to continue, with jobs being lost in the primary and secondary sectors and jobs gained in the services sector, as Table 17.4 demonstrates.

Table 17.3 Occupational trends 1985–1990

Sector	Annual % change	Numbers employed 1990 (000s)
Agriculture	−1.9	598
Energy and water	−2.6	526
Process industries	−1.5	728
Metal goods	−3.0	330
Mechanical engineering	−1.9	710
Electrical engineering	−1.5	775
Motor vehicle	−2.8	490
Food, drink and tobacco	−1.3	564
Textile	−1.7	475
Paper, printing and publishing	−2.1	440
Construction	−0.8	1,350
employed	−2.2	840
self-employed	+2.0	510
Distribution	+0.8	4,080
Finance and business services	+2.4	2,405
Transport	−1.2	1,293
employed	−1.5	1,180
self-employed	+2.5	113
Leisure	+2.4	2,953
self-employed	+4.4	560
Public administration	−0.9	1,460
Education	−1.2	1,450
Medical, health	+0.5	1,350
Welfare	+2.2	700

Table 17.4 Employment trends 1988–2000

Sector	Numbers employed 1988 (000s)	Numbers employed 2000 (000s)	% change
Primary and utilities	1,058	890	−15.9
Manufacturing	5,497	4,978	−9.4
Construction	1,626	1,857	+14.2
Distribution and transport	7,112	7,773	+9.3
Business and services	5,176	6,871	+32.7
TOTAL	20,469	22,369	+9.3
Whole economy	25,880	28,115	+8.6

The trade unions are well aware of these trends. Their membership levels have declined dramatically in the 1980s, and not just as a result of government policy and union unpopularity. The job losses indicated in the figures above are in the industries which have traditionally high union densities. Many unions are now targeting the newer areas of employment for recruitment drives, as many of these sectors have a low union density. It also means that the industrial relations practices in these firms will not be governed by tradition or custom and practice. The agreements reached in these firms incorporate flexibility, are often single-union agreements, multi-skilling is agreed upon and procedures contain binding dispute resolution.

A further effect of these changes impinging directly on industrial relations, is the way in which the benefits of these changes are shared out. Within the firm, unions have sought to ensure that their members share in the benefits of change by making claims for improvements in the terms and conditions of employment. This has led to a much shorter working week, higher wages, improved benefits (e.g., sick pay schemes), longer holidays and better pension arrangements. However, these have not been gained easily and sometimes not without bitter disputes. Collective bargaining seeks to balance the claims and counterclaims in these situations. Often arguments are based on the benefits of the change and the way in which these are to be shared out. After a firm has introduced new high productivity machinery, the employees feel justified in claiming a share in the benefits derived. The firm has to balance such claims against the need to lower unit costs, increase productivity and gain a return on the investment.

Occupational change

Alongside the changes described above, there is a similar set of changes taking place in the occupations people are employed in. One reason for this is the shift already talked about above.

The shift from primary and secondary sectors will inevitably lead to people being employed in different occupations. This change alone has not been very easy as people have, possibly in mid-career, had to change from one occupation to another and from one industry to another. In some cases employees have been made redundant and, after a period of retraining, taken up a new job. The number of unskilled jobs in the workforce, labourers and machine operators, has declined enormously.

As firms sought to shed labour that was no longer required, this led to some inevitable industrial relations problems. The number of redundancies in the early 1980s rose to a peak of 532,000 in 1981, falling to 227,000 in 1985 (Chapter 14 examines this topic in detail). This did lead to a number of lessons being learned about human resource planning in firms, improved redundancy agreements and the need to ensure that proper training is carried out to facilitate the process of change. Also, the process was often difficult and painful and there were many disputes arising in these situations. Some firms' personnel policies were more sympathetic than others. Some firms offered their employees, under notice of redundancy, a package that softened the blow of losing their job. For example, they provided retraining, help with setting up a business, counselling, courses, extra-statutory payments, long periods of notice, etc.

A further set of intrinsic changes that is taking place in all firms (regardless of the industrial sector) is in the kinds of jobs that people are required to do. The prime factor in this is the effect of technology. This has affected, and continues to affect, both the way in which jobs are done and the types of jobs that are carried out. One of the earliest effects of industrial technology was in the mechanisation, and later the automation, of tasks. This has led, over the years, to a lower requirement for manual, general and unskilled labour and to a greater demand for trained, skilled people.

The obvious modern example to give here is the impact of the microelectronic-based technologies. This has invaded virtually every organisation and has made a major impact everywhere. One area to feel this impact has been the administrative and clerical occupations. Traditionally this area has been a low capital, highly labour-intensive area. Many tasks were carried out by hand or with simple mechanical devices, but now, the computer and its related technologies have revolutionised the office. The word processor, facsimile machine, the photocopier, modem, telephone and other items have produced a capital-intensive, high productivity area. This has in turn caused fundamental changes to the kinds of jobs and content of the jobs carried out in the office. There are countless other examples that illustrate the fundamental nature of these changes. It has led to a greater need for people in managerial occupations and technical areas. The shift is on a large scale, as the figures in Table 17.5 show.

Table 17.5   Forecast changes in occupations 1987–1995

Managers	+300,000
Professional	+1,000,000
Clerical and secretarial	+<250,000
Sales and professional services	+250,000
Craft and skilled	+260,000
Operatives/labourers	−>300,000

Source: Social Trends

As firms undergo these processes of change, it is necessary to manage the situation to ensure an efficient and smooth transition. In general terms, there is a growing school of management thinking which says that in a modern industrial society, it is management's prime task to manage change. There is so much changing so rapidly that this is necessary. This contrasts sharply with the view that once systems are in place they are there to stay. Now systems are constantly in a state of flux.

This applies to industrial relations. So often, the resistance to change comes from the inability of the system to deal with change. There is a prevalent, traditional idea that agreements are sacrosanct. While it is a principle of collective bargaining that agreements should be honoured, it does not mean that they should not be changed. A stoppage in the mid-1980s by British Rail workers was a dispute about the introduction of flexible working patterns for drivers. This would have meant drivers working no more hours in total but perhaps working six hours one day and ten another. The union claimed that an agreement of 1919, guaranteeing an eight-hour day meant that this could not be put into operation!

In many firms there are procedural agreements in place for introducing change. This provides a means of introducing change into the workplace with the involvement of employees. Such agreements, sometimes called technology agreements, ensure that the potential industrial relations problems are addressed and resolved before a dispute arises.

In the late 1980s there has been a net growth in the labour market. Firms normally recruit school leavers to fill these vacancies, but, because of the demographic decline (*see below*), they have sought to recruit women who have left the labour force to have children, for instance. There has also been a rise in the number of part-time jobs. Table 17.6 below shows the growth in part-time work:

Table 17.6 Growth in part-time work (1983–1992)

Year	Number of part-time workers (m)
1983	4.29
1985	4.78
1987	5.16
1988	5.32
1992	5.78

Source: Training Agency

The union density among part-time workers is very low and trade unions are aiming their recruitment at this group.

Alongside this growth in part-time work (often taken up by women with children or older women), there has been a rapid expansion in the self-employed category and this very much in the service sector. This is a result of government policy to aid the recovery of the economy after the recession in the early to mid-1980s. Assistance was provided to encourage the growth of the small business sector to replace the jobs lost in the large, mainly manufacturing firms. Table 17.7 below shows these changes and Table 17.8 shows the growth in self-employment.

In 1988, 9% of self-employment was in manufacturing and 63% was in the service sector. Firms employing fewer than 20 people showed an aggregate net job growth of 290,000, while large firms had a growth of 20,000.

Table 17.7 Employment changes 1983–1988

Full-time male employees	decrease 150,000
Full-time female employees	increase 400,000
Part-time female employees	increase 600,000
Full-time males self-employed	increase 420,000
Full-time females self-employed	increase 120,000

Source: Social Trends

Table 17.8 The growth of smaller firms between 1978 and 1988

Year	Number of self-employed (000s)	% change
1978	1,907	
1980	2,013	5.6
1982	2,170	7.8
1984	2,496	15.0
1986	2,627	5.2
1988	2,986	13.7

Source: Department of Employment
% increase 1978 to 1988 is 56.6%

Demographic change

A very notable feature of the age profile of the population in the 1980s, and continuing into the 1990s, is the decline in the number of people in the late teenage and early twenties age group. In the late 1980s this has brought about a radical change in recruitment patterns in firms. As unemployment became less of a problem in the late 1980s and there was a recovery in the UK economy, firms who were looking for labour found it difficult to recruit school leavers in the numbers they required. This has led to firms looking to recruit from other sectors of the population, particularly in trying to attract women to return to work.

The effects of this were noted above, where the figures showed a record number of women to be in employment, albeit predominantly in part-time jobs. People in these jobs tend not to be trade union members and often they have limited employment protection rights as several of these rights only apply to people working 16 hours a week or more (or 8 hours after 5 years' service).

Table 17.9 shows the population figures for the UK and the trend of the figures in the age categories given.

Table 17.9 UK population statistics 1971–2001 (000s)

Age	1971	1981	1988	1991	2001
0–14	13,470	11,602	10,760	11,054	12,041
15–24	8,144	9,019	8,978	8,203	7,198
25–44	13,482	14,784	16,239	16,849	16,932
49–64	13,423	12,475	12,204	12,390	13,844
over 64	7,409	8,472	8,883	9,038	9,187
total	55,928	56,352	57,065	57,533	59,201

Source: Annual Abstract of Statistics

17.2 The European dimension

One of the most widely and hotly debated issues of recent times is the impact of the European Community on member states, the direction being taken and the goals being set by the EC. The speed of economic and social integration and the future vision for Europe have been talked about by all sections of society. Doubtless it is the one single issue that will most shape the future of the UK. It is particularly the social dimension that will affect industrial relations in the long term, although, of course, there are several economic dimensions which will also have an effect. There are several differing viewpoints, with their own visions, of where Europe should be heading.

On the one hand there are those who see the EC as a loose federation of countries with many links and common policies but essentially each country retaining its own sovereignty. Those who hold this view say that the British parliament, government and courts should remain supreme and should not be subordinated to any other body or 'super state'. This extends to restricting the interference of the EC to matters which it rightly can concern itself with, but these should be kept to a minimum. There is resistance to a single common currency or a unified legislative system as they feel that each country should be able to operate as its own demo-cratically elected governments determine. This would mean that the UK industrial relations system would remain within the control of the current UK agencies and that any regulation of the system by the EC should be resisted.

The other view is that, ultimately, Europe will become one large state with a common currency, one central bank, a unified legislative system, including courts structure, a powerful European parliament with the Commission taking the lead in all Euro activities. This will lead to the Europeanisation of all things and would have a profound effect on everyday life in the Community. One argument to support this view is that the trend world-wide is towards large economic units and that the single countries making up the EC cannot survive alone, only together. The advocates of this view in Britain are concerned that if the UK does not join in this movement, it will be left behind and cannot survive on its own. Such a view has many implications for industrial relations. One of the means of achieving a single European system is through regulation from the centre. This would ensure harmonisation in all EC countries by legislation. Hence, labour law could be har-monised by such a method.

Doubtless the way forward will be some middle road that achieves consensus and agreement from all concerned. The majority opinion is that there will be a strong movement to a closer knit European Community and long-term harmonisation will be achieved.

The exact nature of a pan-European industrial relations system is not clear to see, but certainly moves have already been made along this route in areas where it is easier to achieve this. An obvious example is, again, labour law. Some of the foundations of the UK industrial relations system are identical to the ideas emanating from Europe now (see below), so there may not be any need for radical change. What will happen is that our system will become closer to that of the other EC countries' systems. This is inevitable if one of the founding principles of the EC is to be achieved, i.e., the free movement of people. This again is examined in detail below.

Clearly there are many other considerations on this topic relating to economics, foreign affairs, security and politics that are beyond the scope of this book and many viewpoints between the two extremes stated above.

There have been two topics that have brought this debate into focus. The first is the target of completing the Single European Market by 1992. This has entailed many changes, some large scale and fundamental, to achieve a free movement of goods in the EC by the end of 1992. This has mainly affected the economies of the EC partners but firms, in adapting to the opening up of the European markets, are learning about the operations of their EC counterparts. This inevitably has had the effect of importing European practices into UK firms. Often in order to compete effectively, it is necessary to import some of the good practices employed by competitors. Also many EC firms are setting up operations in other European countries in anticipation of the SEM. Again this has the effect of spreading various EC countries' practices to other member states.

The second item that has brought out the arguments on the way forward in Europe was the publication in 1989 of the Social Charter. This in particular has a direct bearing on industrial relations and is examined in detail in the next section.

17.2.1 The EC Social Charter

The Treaty of Rome, signed in 1957 (the UK became a member in 1972), which established the European Economic Community, contained a number of Articles which bear on industrial relations. The exact nature of these is being worked out now and in particular the Social Charter elaborates on the detailed proposals. There are also a number of initiatives being pursued to extend industrial relations to Community level (as opposed to local or national level).

The objective of the Community is to achieve genuine economic and social union in member states, entailing the free movement of people, goods and capital by removing national barriers and the establishment of common policies in key areas designed to ensure equal opportunities, economic and social progress and the constant improvement of living and working conditions.

The social objectives of the EC are job creation, social consensus, improvements in living and working conditions, greater freedom of movement, social protection, more education and training, equal opportunities and respect for the rights of third world workers.

The Treaty of Rome contains a number of Articles on Social Provisions, some of which relate to industrial relations. Indeed some have already affected the UK in that EC directives have been translated into UK legislation, for example on redundancies, transfer of undertakings and equal pay. The section below is a précis of the Articles relevant to industrial relations.

Article 117 'the need to promote improved working conditions . . . so as to make possible their harmonisation whilst improvements are being made.'

Article 118 'promote close cooperation . . . in matters relating to:
employment
labour law and working conditions
basic and advanced vocational training
social security
prevention of occupational accidents and diseases
occupational hygiene
the right of association, and collective bargaining between employers and workers.'

Article 119 the principle that men and women should receive equal pay for equal work.

The Social Charter was published in 1989 and contained 19 Articles which covered a wide range of social rights. The matter was debated at the Strasbourg summit in December 1989. The UK found itself isolated, with the other 11 member states all prepared to sign the Treaty. The UK government was very unpopular with its EC colleagues but the objections were in principle and no amount of fine tuning would have enabled the UK to sign the Treaty. Mrs Thatcher was implacably opposed to any form of intrusion or interference by Europe in what she saw as the internal affairs of the UK. Also any such regulation by the EC was fettering the operation of free markets. In the end the UK was exempt from the provisions of the Social Charter.

The matter came up again at the Maastricht summit in 1992. The UK held the Presidency of the EC (held on a rotational basis) and the whole subject of the Social Charter became an embarrassment for the government. The Conservative party had by this time changed leader, to Mr Major, and had won a general election. There was no change of mind on the Social Charter and the UK once again was exempted from the whole of the provisions. There had been a softening of the government's line on Europe, in particular the UK had joined the European Exchange Rate Mechanism (ERM). Mrs Thatcher had been opposed to this move and in the end it was one of the political issues that brought her down when Mr Major replaced her as Prime Minister. The Labour party are still very strongly in favour of signing the Social Charter and would have done so had they won the general election in 1991.

It is difficult to measure the effect of being outside the Social Charter but in the long term it may well prove to be detrimental to the UK as all our partners in Europe move closer together and the UK stands isolated. In some areas the UK already has employment laws similar to the Social Charter provisions. In other areas, the EC is proposing changes to introduce Directives where the UK has repealed laws, e.g., the regulation of hours of young people. There is a complication in that the UK government, if it ratifies the Maastricht Treaty, is bound by the health and safety provisions of the Treaty (these are not contained in the Social Charter but in the main text). By a convoluted piece of logic, certain items that are arguably employment law have been put under the heading of health and safety. A further complication is that health and safety proposals in the Council of Ministers are subject only to majority voting not unanimity. Hence the UK can and will be forced to accept some changes to employment laws that it sees as regulatory and is opposed to as an interference in the labour market and it cannot veto these proposals as it can other matters.

Article 1 The right to work
- full employment
- the right of the worker to earn a living in an occupation freely entered upon

- free employment services
- vocational guidance, training and rehabilitation

This is a statement of intent and aspiration. Clearly the achievement of full employment is aided by industrial relations but is achieved as the result of economic policy. The third and fourth points are very sensible aids to ensuring a better guided and trained workforce, and are elaborated on in Articles 9 and 10.

Article 2 The right to just conditions of work
- reasonable daily and weekly working hours
- public holidays with pay
- annual holiday with pay
- reduced working hours or additional holidays for workers in dangerous or unhealthy occupations
- weekly rest period

The suggestion has already been made that 40 hours should be set as the normal working week and paid holidays are a feature of many contracts of employment, but not yet for everyone. The suggestion from the Commission is for four weeks paid leave.

The fourth suggestion is a novel one and is not much practised in the UK. The only current example is where workers have been over-exposed to radiation or poisons (such as lead) and they have the right to be transferred to work which does not expose the worker to the risk until medically advised that it is safe to return to the original job.

Article 3 The right to safe and healthy working conditions
- issue of health and safety regulations
- provision for the enforcement of health and safety regulations by measures of supervision
- consultation with employers' and workers' organisations on questions of safety and health

In the UK there is a well-established system for issuing and enforcing health and safety regulations. The system was given a major overhaul in 1974 as a result of the Robens Commission report, although the system relies heavily on self-regulation by management underpinned by some statutory requirements.

The UK enforcement agency is the Health and Safety Commission, plus officers from local authorities and water boards who have similar supervisory authority.

A number of Regulations were issued in the 1980s such as the Control of Substances Hazardous to Health (COSHH), Noise at Work Regulations, Construction Safety Helmets Regulations and the Electricity at Work Regulations. Some of these are designed to bring a common standard throughout Europe.

The Safety Representatives Regulations provide for consultation on health and safety matters in the workplace and the Health and Safety Commission has a tripartite board with representatives from both sides of industry.

There has been much progress in achieving the harmonisation of technical standards and one effect of this is to incorporate common standards of safety. Also, regulation and cooperation has ensured that there is an EC-wide common system for the transport of hazardous substances. The Hazchem warning signs on heavy vehicles enable authorities throughout the EC to recognise substances instantly in an emergency.

Article 4 The right to fair remuneration
- adequate remuneration
- payment for overtime
- nondiscrimination between men and women workers with respect to remuneration
- reasonable notice of termination of employment
- limitation of deductions from wages

The question of adequacy of remuneration is a difficult one to resolve. In a system of free collective bargaining it is for the prevailing market forces to decide what is 'adequate'. The EC is concerned to prevent some countries from using lower wage rates (cheap labour) to gain a competitive advantage and thereby deprive its workers of achieving a better standard of living.

There has been active legislation on equal pay since 1975 and this has been amended to bring it into line with EC recommendations (*see* Section 10.4.3). Notice that the requirements for a contract of employment are also a legal requirement (*see* Section 12.2.3).

Article 5 The right to organise
This has been the bedrock of the trade union movement since its inception. There is a right to organise workers in the UK, although the legal basis of this has evolved over time and has been subject to amendment. The changes to the law in the 1980s have been seen as an erosion of the freedom to organise and act collectively. The argument was made very strongly that the government was fundamentally wrong to ban unions from the Government Communications Headquarters on the grounds of national security.

Article 6 The right to bargain collectively
- joint consultation
- promotion of machinery for voluntary negotiation
- conciliation and arbitration
- the right to collective action

The right to joint consultation has never been laid down as a comprehensive right in the UK. We are behind all our EC partners in this respect, where they all have a legislatively backed scheme for consultation and/or participation. The topic was much debated in the 1970s but has faded away in the 1980s. There are no serious proposals being pursued at the moment, but specific rights exist in the matters of health and safety, redundancy and takeovers.

The machinery for promoting collective bargaining was put into place in 1909 (*see* Section 8.1.3) and the idea was that the Trade Boards (latterly Wage Councils) would evolve into a sectoral collective bargaining system. This has not been achieved in many sectors. In fact, Wage Councils were abolished in 1993.

The provision of a conciliation and arbitration service was established in 1945 and a system of state-backed arbitration goes back to 1896. ACAS provides this service at present (*see* Section 4.3.2).

The right to collective action has been given in UK law for over 100 years. However, the development of this right has been patchy (*see* Sections 8.2 and 10.2). In the 1980s restrictions have been introduced on the right to take collective action. This includes the requirement to ballot members before industrial action, the narrowing of the definition of 'dispute' and restrictions on the immunities provided to unions and officers who call industrial action.

Article 7 The right of children and young persons to protection

- minimum working age
- higher minimum age in certain occupations
- full benefit of compulsory education
- respect for the development of young people under 16 years and their vocational training
- fair remuneration for young workers and apprentices
- treatment of the time spent in vocational training as forming part of the working day
- annual holiday for young persons under 18
- prohibition of night work for persons under 18 years of age
- regular medical examination of workers under 18
- special protection for children and adolescents against physical and moral dangers

The minimum working age recommended is 15; in the UK it is 16.

Ironically, the Employment Act 1989 abolished the rules which restricted the hours of work of young people (previously in the Factories Acts). There have never been any rights to vocational training, although the YT scheme promised such training to any young person requesting it.

Article 8 The right of employed women to protection

- maternity leave
- illegality of dismissal during maternity leave
- time off for nursing mothers
- regulation of night work and prohibition of dangerous, unhealthy and arduous work for women workers

Statutory maternity rights were laid down in 1975 (*see* Section 10.3.3) and were amended in 1980. The regulations on the hours and type of work women could undertake have been repealed in the Employment Act 1989, which is a retrograde step in achieving these provisions of the Charter.

Article 9 The right to vocational guidance

There is no right to vocational guidance, although there is a service provided by local authorities in their careers service. This service was restricted in the past to young people up to 18 years old and this is still the dominant part of their work.

Article 10 The right to vocational training

- promotion of technical and vocational training and the granting of facilities for access to higher and further education
- promotion of apprenticeships
- vocational training and retraining of adults
- encouragement for the full utilisation of available facilities

This issue has been brought to the fore in recent times. There is a recognised need to train and retrain our workforce, but international and EC comparisons make bleak reading for the UK. The proportion of our workforce with any vocational qualification is almost the lowest among our EC partners.

One move in the right direction has come from the CBI and government. A CBI report in 1990 set a target of all 18-year-olds achieving a Level 2 National Vocational Qualification (NVQ) and 50% achieving a Level 3 NVQ. This has been accepted by the government as attainable and the newly formed Training Enterprise Councils are charged with achieving these aims.

Generally, though, training has been given very little attention. Retraining is not systematically carried out, although the need for it is well recognised. Management has not been trained to manage, but this should hopefully change now that management training has had the spotlight put on it with the publication of the Management Charter. Apprenticeships, in the traditional sense, have had a bad press in the last decade, with problems over restrictive entry (both age and gender) and the unions using them as a means of keeping numbers down in a trade to maintain wage levels. Also, there were problems over the traditional approaches to trade apprenticeships which perpetuated the restrictive practices in industry. This is the British interpretation of the term 'apprentice', but in other EC countries, the word is used to describe a trainee who is undergoing a period of planned training to enter a certain occupation. For example, it would be used for someone training in banking in Europe; the word would not apply to such a situation in the UK.

Article 11 The right to the protection of health
- removal of causes of ill health
- advisory and educational facilities
- prevention of diseases

In the UK there is an Employment Medical Advisory Service which provides an information and advisory service. It also has certain powers to require the medical examination of workers who are at risk from their work. There are specific provisions for young people under the age of 18.

Article 12 The right to social security
- establishment or maintenance of a social security system, to International Labour Office standards
- progressive improvements
- equal treatment of other nationals

Article 13 The right to social and medical assistance
- social and medical assistance for those in need
- nondiscrimination
- advice and assistance
- equal treatment of other nationals

Article 14 The right to benefit from social welfare facilities
- promotion of provision of social welfare facilities
- public participation in the establishment and maintenance of social welfare facilities

Articles 12, 13 and 14 are of importance for the free movement of labour, as someone moving to another country to work needs to have the security of knowing that such facilities are available to them.

Article 15 The right of physically and mentally disabled persons to vocational training, rehabilitation and social resettlement
- vocational training arrangements for the disabled

- placement arrangements for the disabled

The Disabled Persons (Employment) Act 1944 and 1958 set a quota of 3% of registered disabled people who should be employed by firms of more than 20 people (some firms are exempt). Company reports should also contain a statement relating to the disabled and there is a voluntary Code of Practice on the Employment of Disabled People. However, most firms do not comply with this and little is done to enforce this minimal requirement. Noticeably the European Social Fund has the unemployed disabled as a priority axis for funding, to develop schemes to encourage disabled people into stable employment.

Article 16 The right of the family to social, legal and economic protection

Article 17 The right of mothers and children to social and economic protection

Article 18 The right to engage in gainful occupation in the territory of other contracting parties
- liberal application of regulations
- simplification of existing formalities and reduction of chancery dues and taxes
- liberalisation of regulations
- the rights of nationals to emigrate

Article 19 The right of migrant workers and their families to protection and assistance
- free assistance and information
- measures to facilitate departure, travel and reception
- cooperation between social services
- no less favourable treatment of migrant workers
- family reunion
- security against expulsion
- transfer of earnings and savings

The outcome of the publication and debate on the Social Charter is that the Commission issued an 'action programme' to implement it. A total of 47 measures have been proposed and these will be activated as Directives or Regulations where appropriate (working hours, health and safety, equal treatment, worker participation) with others being dealt with some other way, e.g., wages and collective bargaining.

Maastricht Treaty

The Maastricht Treaty (1992) did not contain any more detailed proposals but made a general statement followed by some detailed Articles. Below is a précis of the Treaty's Social Policy:

Article 1 The Community shall have as their objectives the promotion of employment, improved living and working conditions, proper social protection, dialogue between management and labour, the development of human resources with a view to lasting employment and the combating of exclusion.

Article 2.1 The Community shall support:
- improvement of the working environment to protect workers' health and safety
- working conditions
- the information and consultation of workers
- equality between men and women with regard to labour market opportunities and treatment at work

Article 2.2 The Council may adopt, by means of Directives, minimum requirements for gradual implementation.

Article 2.3 The Council shall act unanimously on a proposal from the Commission on:
- social security and social protection
- protection of workers where their employment contract is terminated
- representation and collective defence of the interests of worker and employers

Article 3.1 The Commission shall have the task of promoting the consultation of management and labour at Community level.

Article 3.2 The Commission shall consult management and labour before making any proposals on social policy.

Article 4 Should management and labour so desire, the dialogue between them at Community level may lead to contractual relations, including agreements.

Article 5 The Commission shall encourage cooperation between member states and facilitate the coordination of their action.

Article 6 Each member state shall ensure the principle of equal pay for male and female workers for equal work is applied.

The one area where there has been considerable progress, and an area fully supported by the UK government, is in health and safety. In the UK, six new regulations came into force in 1993. These six, listed below, will be a major force for change and improvement in workplace health and safety:
- Management of Health and Safety at Work Regulations
- Display Screen Equipment Regulations
- Personal Protective Equipment Regulations
- Provision and Use of Work Equipment Regulations
- Workplace Regulations
- Manual Handling Regulations

17.2.2 The European dimension

One aspect of the social dimension of the internal market that has been recognised as significant by the European Commission, is the organisation of industrial relations at European level. One of the factors that it is necessary to consider in achieving a completed internal market is the full exercise of the freedom of people to move. This will, of course, include the ability to move jobs within the EC. In order to do this there needs to be compatibility within member states so that the person wishing to move is not inhibited by material differences, e.g., working conditions, hours of work, holiday entitlement, social protection, pension rights, union membership and health and safety. There are also opportunities and difficulties to be recognised and the reaction, fears and misgivings expressed by interest groups in the industrial relations arena.

The EC recognises 'the two sides of industry', i.e., unions and management, and sees these two actors as having the key roles to play in achieving any success in this area. Negotiation and consensus are seen as the key processes that will achieve results.

One key debate relates to the means of achieving the objectives of the internal market. There are two extreme views, with others lying somewhere between the two.

- **The normative approach** This calls for a single harmonising legal framework that is applicable throughout the EC and is achieved by means of Directives or Regulations (this has already been used in some areas such as health and safety, equal treatment and redundancies). However, as a means of achieving harmonisation on all topics relating to industrial relations, this is seen as too interventionist and states should be left to find their own way to achieve these objectives. It also militates against flexibility and adaptability in periods of change, because it leaves little room for innovation. Also, it takes away the autonomy of the two sides in industrial relations to make agreements. The concept of free collective bargaining includes the idea of freedom from governmental interference, including the EC.

- **The decentralised approach** This says that there is no need for regulation, it is for competition between social rules to decide what happens in the industrial relations arena. Free collective bargaining should operate, unfettered by any hindrance. This will allow for flexible management, innovation, freedom and autonomy. This is a very fragmented approach and is unlikely to achieve harmonisation and coherence across the Community. The approach is local and short-term as these are the determining factors. Rejection of some standardisation can hinder progress, e.g., in the realm of health and safety.

The approach suggested by the Commission is a 'middle ground' approach. It suggests three areas for action.

- **Harmonisation using instruments** In some areas this is advantageous, such as health and safety. It is also proposed that the setting of labour standards could help competitiveness. The view held is that genuine competitiveness is based not on lower wage costs but on quality, reliability and technological progress.

- **Convergence** This can be achieved through discussions by the Commission and through inter-Community exchanges. The topics that could be covered in this way are social protection and vocational training.

- **Innovation** Innovation and experimentation should be encouraged. This would mean providing the environment for doing this, analysing the results and then disseminating the conclusions. The community should provide for the free movement of ideas and establishing contacts.

The Community emphasises the role of the two sides of industry to enter into dialogue and reach agreement on these matters. At the moment there is little or no European dimension to collective bargaining, nor is there a European level in industrial relations. However, it is argued that there should be. This level should deal with matters that cannot be dealt with at a lower level, i.e., national, regional or local. The European levels should not be seen as an extra level in conflict resolution. Multinational companies can help this process as they will be directly affected by the internal market and will probably need to address a number of issues relating to this as a matter of some urgency. For example, the arguments of parity for workers doing the same work need not be argued merely at national level; why not at European level? The Commission also proposes a forum in which the problems raised by the opening of the internal market can be discussed and resolved.

Finally, the Commission has made a number of practical proposals.

- Study the practical conditions necessary for organising European level industrial relations. This includes:
  - identifying the obstacles which exist
  - studying the interrelationship between the European level and other levels
  - an institutional forum for discussing the problems arising

- catalogue the scope and limits on industrial relations in European multinationals
- deepen social dialogue by:
  - setting up sectorial level social dialogue arrangements
  - include topics relating to the internal market such as the free movement of people, e.g., equal treatment and vocational qualifications
- consultations with the two sides of industry and national authorities on the minimum social legislation required above the existing levels

The proposal was made in 1987, during the Belgian Presidency, that there should be a core of fundamental worker rights with a stable and common foundation for bargaining. The present suggestions for this are:

- the right to be covered by a collective agreement
- the possibility of all workers being able to join a social security scheme and to be covered by insurance
- prior information and consultation of workers in the event of major technological innovations or changes to their firms
- the definition of flexible employment contracts
- a standard employment contract
- a decision on continuing training

All these discussions have been wide-ranging and have gone into the issues in some depth and the whole process has pointed out a number of issues of fundamental, indeed, vital importance to the development of industrial relations over the next decade. Much of it is peering into the unknown and saying this is what *should* happen, but what will *actually* be achieved will depend on many factors, such as the will of the actors to participate, the perceived need for some of the points raised to be addressed and the reaction of politicians and governments. Whatever happens, it will certainly be very interesting watching the evolution of industrial relations in the near future.

Mini-questions

17.1 State two sectors that have increased in size and two that have decreased in size in the last 10 years.
17.2 List the occupational categories where there is a forecast of an increase in numbers employed and list those where there is a forecast decrease.
17.3 State whether, in the last decade, there has been an increase or decrease in
    (i) male full-time employment
    (ii) female full-time employment
    (iii) female part-time employment
    (iv) self-employment.
17.4 Briefly describe the age profile of the UK population and the trend over the next 20 years.
17.5 List five topics covered by the Articles in the EC Social Charter.

Exercises

17.1 Describe the fundamental changes to industrial sectors in the UK that have occurred in the last 20 years. Explain how this has affected industrial relations.
17.2 Describe the changes that have occurred in occupational categories in the UK economy in the last 20 years. Explain how this has affected industrial relations and the trade unions.
17.3 Discuss the statement 'the EC Social Charter will have a long-term detrimental effect on the UK economy'.
17.4 Explain the reasoning behind the EC Social Charter and, using examples, describe what effect some of it will have on industrial relations in the UK.

Further reading

W W Daniel, *Workplace Industrial Relations and Technical Change*, Pinter, 1987, 0-86187-941-4
I Benson and J Lloyd, *New Technology and Industrial Change*, Kogan Page, 1983, 0-85038-284-X
M Poole, *Toward a New Industrial Democracy*, Routledge, 0-7102-0916-9
P Blyton, *Changes in Working Time*
A Ferner, R Hyman, *Industrial Relations in the New Europe*, Blackwell, 1992, 0-631-185925

Assignments

These assignments have been designed as either class, seminar or individual exercises to test a number of learning objectives. Often they are set on the material in a particular chapter, but not exclusively so. The chapters are not identified as there might be a tendency to restrict the answers to the content of that chapter. Assignments 24 and 26 have factual or definitive answers and these are given on page 366.

Assignment 1

The group you work with is currently not unionised. A number of you feel that a trade union would be helpful and propose to set one up. Draw up a set of objectives for a trade union to cover the group. Use your own work group or a hypothetical one as an example. This exercise could be carried out as an individual or syndicate exercise.

Assignment 2

This is a class exercise; the class should be divided into three equal groups. Each group should then draw up a set of objectives for a union for covering:

(a) skilled workers
(b) operatives
(c) managers

Afterwards, regroup and compare the objectives drawn up by the three groups. Discuss the implications of any differences that arise.

Assignment 3

The firm you work for is undergoing a modernisation programme, both in the factory and in the offices. The production facilities are currently operated by skilled employees and will be fully automated. The office procedures at present involve a lot of form filling and manual processing and these will be redesigned around an integrated computer system. Management has evaluated the staffing levels as shown in Table A1.

Table A1

	Current	Future	Union
Production			
skilled	30	20	Craft
semi-skilled	15	20	General
unskilled	15	10	General
Administration			
clerical officer	15	7	Staff (1)
clerical assistant	25	10	Staff (2)
Programmer/operator	0	8	

The class should be split into five groups (not necessarily equal), one for each of the unions: craft, general, staff (1) and staff (2), and one group for management. In your groups decide how you are going to approach the impending changes and make proposals to overcome any difficulties you may foresee.

As a second stage, enact a meeting between management and the unions combined to try to negotiate an agreement on the changes.

Assignment 4

Carry out an investigation into the industrial relations role of a manager in your own workplace or at a local organisation. Initially, prepare a questionnaire that could be used to determine the degree and level of involvement in industrial relations of the person you hope to contact. Also, find out if the organisation is a member of an employers' association and, if so, what role this plays in industrial relations within the organisation.

When the questionnaire has been prepared, use it, preferably in an interview situation, rather than as a postal questionnaire. From the results, write a report on the industrial relations activity of the manager. This should be a factual report, not a critical or assessment report.

Assignment 5

A recently formed company had to hold back on pay increases whilst it became established. Now the employees feel that the company is on its feet and profits are substantial. They are making a wage claim this year of 10%. Suddenly, a government pay policy, with a maximum of 2%, is imposed. Suggest ways in which the employer and employees can act in this situation. What difficulties can you foresee and what possible solutions are there?

Assignment 6

A productivity agreement that is operating at a company has led to difficulties. These arise from the interpretation of an overtime clause that states: 'it is expected that employees will work a reasonable amount of overtime as requested by management to suit operational requirements'. The disputes procedure has been exhausted with no agreement. Conciliation has been suggested by one side and arbitration by the other. Which would you suggest, and why? How might these processes help? Write the terms of reference for the conciliator or arbitrator.

Assignment 7

As an industrial relations or personnel officer in a company, prepare a briefing paper for the Personnel Director on how the various services offered by ACAS can be of value to the organisation. If necessary, obtain some booklets from ACAS to help you.

Assignment 8

Mr B is a machine operator and shop steward employed in a small engineering company. He is a semi-skilled worker and has been employed for 4½ years.

In June 1990, as a result of an accident, Mr B is away from work. He is due to return to work on Monday 16 June. On Saturday 14 June he receives notice of dismissal.

The dismissal notice causes a two-day strike at the establishment. The result is that Mr B is suspended on full pay pending arbitration.

At the arbitration hearing, the company claims the following points:

(a) Mr B's sickness leave over the 4½ years has not been satisfactory – 1986, 4 days; 1987, 6 days; 1988, 2 days; 1989, 5 days; 1990, 2 days (separate days in all cases) – without a certificate.

(b) He has been late for work on a similar number of occasions over the 4½ years.

(c) He is accident-prone – eight accidents in four years. The insurers have written to the company stating that in their view he is a liability; he may suffer a serious accident and is not suitable for that job.

(d) He has been rude to his manager on more than one occasion.

(e) Taking work record, accident-proneness and behaviour into account, together these constitute reasonable grounds for dismissal.

The trade union states:

(a) On accident-proneness they say, Mr B is a conscientious shop steward who obeys the rules and reports all accidents, however minor. Many minor accidents are not reported, thus Mr B's record is not as bad as would appear. Only one accident has resulted in a claim, and only two accidents had caused absence from work.

(b) The rudeness incident was a minor one and been blown up out of all proportion.

(c) Mr B had complained about lack of safety precautions on a number of occasions.

(d) There was a personality clash between Mr B and the Managing Director, and the company was really trying to get rid of him because he was a shop steward.

(e) His attendance record was no worse than that of other people – why pick on Mr B?

As an arbitrator:

(a) What questions would you ask of both parties?

(b) What award would you make? The terms of reference are: 'Is the dismissal fair or unfair, taking all the circumstances into account?'

(c) Assuming you make a decision, is this final? If not, what is the next step?

(d) How important is the Code of Practice in this case?

Assignment 9

You have been elected to act as the shop steward for your group, either your work group or the class. A feature of this group is its low union membership. Prepare a statement that could be made into a pamphlet, trying to persuade the nonmembers to join the union. Give the reasons why you (as a steward) think people should join a union, and what the benefits of membership are.

Assignment 10

In your own place of work, the employees are currently not trade union members. There has been a feeling for some time that the employees should join a union. Some of the work group have made enquiries to a union about recruiting within the group. You wish to approach management about this issue and find out the reaction to the proposal.

(a) As a spokesperson for the group, write a memorandum to your manager, setting out why you think the group should be unionised, and what you feel the benefits would be to both parties.

(b) After you have written this memo, 'send' it to someone in your group.

(c) On the basis of the memo you receive, draft a reply, finally stating if you are prepared to accept unionisation of the group or not. Base your reply on the arguments and points raised in the memo, not on any preconceived ideas you have.

Assignment 11

You have been asked by a colleague at work, and you have accepted, to be nominated as a candidate in the election for a shop steward. The election will be contested by a number of candidates. Prepare a manifesto for your campaign to become shop steward, setting out your views on trade unionism, why you are a prime candidate and what you would do as a shop steward if elected. Assume any details about the group you are seeking to represent.

Assignment 12

For those of you who have jobs, answer the following questions yourself; for those of you who do not, ask someone who has a job, the following.

(a) Is there a national agreement covering that job?

(b) If there is, what particulars of the job does it cover?

(c) What collective bargaining takes place at local level? Are agreements made at local level?

(d) Which terms and conditions in the contract of employment are covered by agreements?

(e) Do any procedural agreements exist? If so, what do they cover?

(f) In the event of a grievance, what procedure does that person use?

Assignment 13

Carry out a survey of jobs advertised in national newspapers, local papers, journals and magazines. Make a note of the terms of the job that appear to be fixed and those that are open to negotiation.

Assignment 14

If you were being interviewed for a job and had to negotiate your own terms, how would you do it and what arguments would you use? This exercise could be carried out as a role play, with students acting as interviewer and interviewee.

Assignment 15

Draw up a table showing, in chronological order, the legal developments surrounding trade unionism. Give dates, Acts or cases and the main point(s) of the development.

Assignment 16

A friend, who has had a job for the last three years, comes to you for advice on how her pregnancy affects her job. Give a concise statement of:

(a) her rights

(b) what she needs to do to secure these rights.

Assignment 17

Select some job adverts from a local newspaper, national newspaper and some journals. Draw up a checklist of what is allowed and what is not allowed by law. Examine the adverts in the light of the Sex Discrimination Act and the Race Relations Act. Suggest any improvements that could be made.

Assignment 18

You have just been elected a shop steward. Not being sure of your rights as a shop steward investigate what you are entitled to by law and under any relevant Code of Practice.

(a) Make a list of what these are.

(b) Make a written submission to your manager to claim some (or all) of these rights, explaining what you are entitled to and justifying these claims.

Assignment 19

As a union member of a negotiating panel you are about to commence the annual wage negotiations. Set out a list of information that you might require management to give to you that would be of help in the negotiations. Take into account the relevant law and Code of Practice. Explain how you think each piece of information would help. Prepare a memorandum making a request to management for this information

Assignment 20

The work group you are a member of currently has a fairly high level of union membership. Recent branch meetings have considered the possibility of trying to make the area into a closed shop. You have been asked to draw up a checklist of what action needs to be taken and to note the points that have to be considered to comply with present legislation on this issue. Also note any requirements of the relevant Code of Practice.

Assignment 21

This is a role playing exercise for an employment interview.

(a) Draw up a brief job specification for a typical job, for example a clerk typist, shorthand/typist, telephonist or whatever.

(b) 'Send' this specification to another

member of the class who should then apply for the job, as specified, by writing a letter of application and sending it to the person who drew up the specification.

(c) Carry out an interview for the job between the two people concerned. Everyone will act as an interviewer and as an interviewee.

(d) In groups, or as a class, analyse what you found out about the person you interviewed and what you found out about the job on offer.

Assignment 22

This is an exercise to discover the terms and conditions of a particular job. Investigate either your own job or that of a parent, relative, friend or teacher. First draw up a checklist of terms that could exist in a contract of employment (avoiding confidential questions like actual pay). Discover how much the person knows about their contract by going through the checklist.

Assignment 23

Design a model written statement of the terms and conditions of employment that are required to be given by law. Draw it up with blanks for details to be entered in.

Assignment 24

Below are several case studies, drawn from actual tribunal cases. Look up the relevant law (as stated) and apply this to the facts given. This can be carried out as an individual or group exercise. After studying the cases and making relevant comments, compare findings.

(a) B was recruited by the Post Office under a scheme agreed between the PO and the union whereby permanent positions could be gained by employees on passing a test within three attempts. B failed the test for the third time and was dimissed.
Reference: Employment Protection (Consolidation) Act 1978, section 57(1) and (2) and section 57(4)(b).

(b) Following T's promotion in 1972 from sales manager to branch assistant manager, marital problems arose and T's work became unsatisfactory. T's wife frequently pestered one of the employer's directors, W, concerning the problems. In April 1973 W wrote to T emphasising the intolerability of the situation and reverting T to the position of sales manager. T refused this position and was dismissed. Evidence was given to the tribunal regarding bad timekeeping, absence without explanation and unsatisfactory commercial performance.
Reference: EP(C)A 1978, section 57(2)(b) and (3).

(c) D was dismissed for bad bookkeeping. Subsequent investigation disclosed irregularities which led to a criminal prosecution, although later D was acquitted.
Reference: EP(C)A 1978, section 57(1)(b).

(d) A redundancy situation arose while S was absent with back trouble. S was told he could either transfer to another mill or be made redundant. S was transferred while still absent. Shortly afterwards, work picked up and the whole workforce was needed. It was not P's policy to increase the workforce above the level it had been reduced to after the redundancies. S's services were therefore needed. Upon being informed by S's doctor that he would be fit for work in six to eight weeks, P dismissed S, stating that he could not hold the job open for that long.
Reference: EP(C)A 1978, section 57(2)(a).

(e) F was promoted to a post previously held by an efficient and skilled person. F proved incapable of carrying out his allotted tasks and, after being warned that he must improve his standards within six months, he was dimissed more than six months later, by K. The tribunal found that F had done his incompetent best and his dismissal was unfair, but the award was reduced by 50% for his contribution. K appealed.

Reference: EP(C)A 1978, section 57(2)(a).

(f) Nineteen employees walked out in mid-shift, leaving a high-pressure steam system switched on, following the dismissal of their shift manager. They did not say whether they would return and when they did so the next day they found the entrance locked and they were told there would be no work for them that day. The next day they were told that they had lost their jobs.

Reference: EP(C)A 1978, section 62(1).

(g) H, a night service fitter, described as a 'key worker', contracted industrial dermatitis after 6 years' employment with M and was absent for 21 months, during which time he sent in medical certificates. M employed a permanent replacement when H had been absent for five months but gave no notice to dismiss H. When H presented himself for work, he was told there was no work for him and was given his P45 and dismissed. There was no formal written contract of employment or other express provisions for dismissal through illness. M considered the contract at an end because of frustration.

Reference: EP(C)A 1978, section 57(3).

(h) In October an employer C, anticipating a cash flow problem, warned his small workforce that he might be laying them off. On 28 November the employees were laid off without further notice and no pay. One of them J, having taken advice, notified C that he regarded himself as having been dismissed and without notice or justifiable reason.

Reference: EP(C)A 1978, section 49(1) and Schedule 3 paragraph 2(1).

(i) A long-term employee, somewhat prone to fits of temper, told his employer after an altercation, 'I am leaving, I want my cards'. His wish was granted but, subsequently, he complained of unfair dismissal. A tribunal decided that the dismissal was unfair as words spoken in anger should not have been taken as resignation. The employer appealed.

Assignment 25

Over a period of six months an employee, Mr B, was late on 36 occasions and absent without explanation on 10. He received a number of private warnings. Finally he was told that if he were ever absent in an unauthorised manner or late again he would be given a warning in the presence of his shop steward in accordance with the factory procedure.

This was followed by at least one further absence, which was not dealt with. Later he went home at lunchtime one day without telling anybody. The manager sent for him and, in the presence of two shop stewards, he was dismissed.

Factory procedure:

(a) verbal warning
(b) written warning
(c) written warning and suspension of up to three days
(d) final warning in writing that dismissal may follow.

Mr B is 31 years of age, earning £200 per week and has been employed by the company for four years.

Divide the class into three groups.

Syndicate A: present the case for the employer.
Syndicate B: present the case for the employee.
Syndicate C: as a tribunal member
– what questions would you ask?
– what award would you make, if any?

Assignment 26

Calculate the redundancy payment entitlement in the following cases.

(a) A 45-year-old person who has been at the firm 15 years, and currently earns an average of £200 per week.

(b) A 25-year-old person who has been at the firm since he was 16 and currently earns £140 per week.

(c) A 62-year-old woman who has been at the firm for 23 years and currently earns £180 per week.

(d) A 62-year-old man who has been at the firm for 26 years and currently earns £200 per week.

(e) A 50-year-old person who started work exactly 7 years ago but who was on strike for 8 weeks during this period, earning £175 a week.

(f) A 45-year-old person who started work with the firm 20 years ago but spent 5 years of this time in the Army and was recently off ill for 18 months. He currently earns £150 per week.

(g) A 26-year-old woman who started work at 16 but has had two periods of 28 weeks maternity leave. She currently earns £150 per week.

(h) A 58-year-old person who started with the firm 25 years ago but left, briefly, for 6 months in his tenth year with the company. He currently earns £150 per week.

(i) A 46-year-old manager who started with the firm 18 months ago who currently earns £12,000 per year.

(j) A 45-year-old executive who has been with the firm 6 years and currently earns £18,000 per year.

Assignment 27

Following rumours of redundancies, your organisation has announced that 50 people are to be made redundant. No names have been given yet. An emergency branch meeting is called. You are requested by the branch to investigate the current rules relating to redundancy. Do not go into too much detail (say on calculation of payments) but set out the rights of the members in this situation as clearly and concisely as possible.

The exercise could be extended by each member of the class (or a spokesperson of a syndicate) giving a short talk on the various aspects of redundancy and taking questions from the rest of the class.

Assignment 28

The case study concerns an engineering factory, labour force about 250, nonfederated but heavily unionised.

The company had suffered only one short strike in its long history. In December, however, after discontent over pay, there was talk of industrial action: management warned all employees, via the works notice boards, that 'anyone causing a stoppage of work will be dismissed for industrial misconduct'.

On 22 January, management told a welder (with about 15 months' service) that he was being made redundant due to shortage of welding work. He would receive two weeks' pay in lieu of notice and finish that day at five o'clock.

After a rather stormy lunch-time meeting of fabrication shop workers, the steward asked the departmental foreman for permission to use the telephone to contact the union's full-time official, but this was refused. Then, at 2.00 p.m. all 90 fabrication men walked out on strike in protest.

Management immediately dismissed the steward for 'industrial misconduct in taking the workers out on strike following the earlier warning that such behaviour would lead to dismissal'.

The strike continued and two days later, the full-time official met management, who eventually proposed a compromise:

(a) the steward's dismissal to be suspended so he could resume work while talks took place.

(b) the redundant welder to stay sacked, as there was no work for him.

The men subsequently rejected this offer at a mass meeting, insisting that the welder must also be reinstated.

The strike continues.

Questions for syndicates:

(a) Do you agree with all management's

actions? If not, how would you have handled the immediate situation?

(b) What long-term measures, if any, would you propose to remedy the underlying causes of the dispute and improve industrial relations in the plant?

Assignment 29

Using the Department of Employment Gazette and the Annual Abstract of Statistics, extract the information required to fulfil the following tasks:

(a) plot a graph of the number of stoppages of work over a period of time

(b) plot a graph of the number of days lost over a period of time

(c) account for some of the peaks that occur

(d) compare the stoppages in a number of industries using a graph or a bar chart

(e) list the most strike-prone industries in rank order.

Case Studies

Introduction

This section is written as source material for those studying industrial relations, to apply what they know about industrial relations to novel situations, to gain further insights into the subject and to practise essential skills. By doing, we learn, and this is particularly true in using case studies, especially in a subject that is so practical.

The additional virtue of case studies is that they provide a realistic means of practising and improving skills. Industrial relations is a subject that requires a balance of knowledge and skills. The more that these can be tried and tested in a training situation, the more the student will develop before applying what has been learnt in a real situation at work.

This section provides fifteen cases of varying length and type. They cover a range of situations in a diversity of sectors to give variety. The subjects covered include all the main areas of industrial relations and Table C1 shows the range of topics covered; this can be used to choose a relevant case for a particular purpose. The cases all include an introduction to the topics covered and a guide is given on what previous learning activities the student should have undertaken. The possession of such previous knowledge and skills is not essential but the topics listed provide an indication of what is helpful in dealing with the case.

The cases are written in a range of styles, some descriptive, others containing narrative. Some focus on a particular issue, others cover a broader spectrum of the organisation. The majority of the cases are based on some real, live situation.

All the cases end with a range of exercises.

These are designed to focus on a range of activities that can be used by students and tutors. Clearly, these can be amended or new ones included to suit the needs of a particular group of students. The exercises include some for the individual student who is working alone (e.g. on a distance/open learning based course) or is given the exercise at the end of a class activity. Several exercises are group-based activities. The nature of industrial relations lends itself to this type of activity. These are vital for the development of the skills required of industrial relations practitioners. The development of skills is also in tune with current developments in education and training where much emphasis is being laid on the acquisition, development and assessment of skills.

Defining a case study

There are a number of definitions of what a case study is. The following is a useful working definition: 'a teaching device that utilises real life situations by placing students in a realistic position, presents them with actual conditions, forces them to think analytically and constructively, makes them consider alternatives, and forces them to arrive at a decision they can substantiate'. The primary purpose of a case study is to apply knowledge, skills, techniques, concepts and principles to situations that accord with reality. They require active student participation which is based on the sound educational principle that students are more likely to learn when they are involved and not

Table C1:   Topics covered

Topics	Case	Case	Case	Case	Case	Case
Agreements	1	3	4	5	9	
Arbitration	5	7	9			
pendulum	5					
Change	2	4	6	8	9	
Closed shop	11	15				
Code of Practice	3	7	11	13		
Competence	10	14				
Conciliation	8					
Consultations	2	4	5	8	15	
Credentials	12					
Custom and practice	9	12	13			
Disciplinary action	3	7	8	10	11	
Disciplinary agreement	3	7				
Disclosure of information	1	4	6			
Discrimination racial	11					
sex	2	13				
Dismissal	3	8	10			
Dispute	8	9	13	15		
Employment law	3	4	7	13		
Equal opportunities	13					
Health and safety	3	6				
Job grading	6	13				
Negotiation	1	2	3	4	6	7
	9	12	13			
Organisation	2	3	8	10		
Pay claim	1					
Policy	2	13	15			
Procedures	2	3	5	6	7	14
	15					
Recognition	2	12				
Redundancy	4	6	15			
Rules	7					
Sanctions	1					
Shop steward	8	12				
Strikes	8	9	15			
Technology	6	15				
Terms and conditions	1	2				
Union membership	2	11	12			
Working practices	8					

merely passive observers. Hence the moves in vocational education to student-centred learning.

A further basic point about a case study is that it is integrative in nature. Again, this accords with reality as the practice of management utilises a range of topics in dealing with live situations, not separating out the compartmen-talised subjects of traditional business education courses. Educational practice has followed this by providing courses that are integrated. Case studies provide an ideal means of delivering courses of this nature.

Cases can take several different forms. These can be:

1 situational – the information in the case is analysed and the problem is to be solved.
2 case history – a description of past events requiring analysis.
3 sequential – a case that unfolds in stages. As one situation is analysed another is issued.
4 live – information about an actual organis-ation (often doctored) is given for analysis.

They should all give a description of a situation and be capable of analysis. Cases should lead to different routes being taken to generate many alternatives with several solutions being given as possible answers. This contrasts with an exercise, where there is one ideal solution. This aspect of case studies often confuses students as they expect that there is one correct answer to a situation or problem and they search for this in vain. At the presentation stage students should be told that there is no one correct answer and it is for them to come to a justifiable conclusion.

Guidelines for tutors

Case studies can be used for both learning and assessment/examination purposes. Overall, case studies should improve students' ability to make good decisions and improve their judgemental abilities. The process of running a case often involves the students having to defend their statements and opinions and such challenges are useful, if sometimes harrowing experiences, from which they should learn much. This will involve character building and provide a sound base when they meet similar situations in their work.

As a teaching method case studies should develop the student's skills in the following areas:

1 analytical – the ability to classify, organise and evaluate information.

2 application – of knowledge, concepts, principles, techniques, etc.
3 creativity – generating alternative solutions and new ways of looking at situations.
4 communication – presentational, discussion, leading, supporting, arguing, reporting, synthesising, etc.
5 social – group working, listening, supporting, guiding, controlling, conflict resolution, etc.
6 self-analysis – building up belief systems, having them challenged, defending beliefs.
7 problem solving – the ability to define and solve problems.

The role of the tutor changes in running case studies. In traditional, didactic teaching, the tutor is dominant and active and the student subordinate and passive. With case studies the roles are reversed to a certain extent where the tutor is there as a facilitator, counsellor, helper, prodder, supervisor but has lost overall control by letting the students get on with the exercise. Cases always need justifying in terms of how they meet course objectives. They should never be used as an extra or be put in 'for a change'. Cases should make sense and fit into the scheme or a learning programme.

Prior to a case being run:

1 Tutors should be familiar with the case and the exercises and have a clear idea of the kind of outcomes they are looking for.
2 The purpose of the case should then be made explicit to the students. To issue a case and say 'get on with it' is poor educational practice and potentially disastrous.
3 After reading through the case the students should be given the opportunity to clarify any points on the case, without the tutor giving too many hints on the exercise itself.
4 At the end of the session the tutor should bring the case to an end by reviewing the outcome of the case (perhaps the students having made a presentation on this) and explicitly extracting the main learning points of the exercise. While there may be no set answer the students should have a clear idea about the learning outcomes.

The cases in this book have a number of exercises attached to them. It is not anticipated that all of them will be used together but tutors will choose from the exercises the ones that are appropriate. Clearly the exercises can be amended to suit particular needs. Having given a range of possible exercises this will provide a useful basis for learning activities or stimulate tutors to generate their own exercises. Some cases have two stages to the exercises to enable them to be developed a stage further. Tutors may wish to go straight to the second stage or carry out only the first stage. The tutor must select according to purposes he/she has set for the exercise overall.

It would be useful, where a case requires some definite, factual knowledge, such as legal requirements or points from an official Code of Practice, that students are given the opportunity of acquiring this before the case commences. It is wasteful to spend time arguing about facts that could have been established beforehand; this would aid the smooth running of a case if the information were made available beforehand, in the form of a handout or booklet, to enable students to make use of it as reference material during the case.

Selecting a case study

1 It should be relevant to what is being taught. It should be an integral part of the course, not a mere adjunct.
2 The case should contribute to the aims of the course. It should have some identifiable aim or cover some learning objectives of the course or unit.
3 The timing of running the case should be planned. It should come at an appropriate point in the course where it can be used to maximum benefit.
4 The length of the case needs consideration. The time taken should not be disproportionate to the learning achieved.
5 The chosen case should be appropriate for the students in terms of their level of ability and the skills to be utilised. It should seek to use their knowledge and experience and be rigorous but not beyond the capabilities of the students.

6 The learning outcomes of the case should be specified so that the tutor can identify to the students what they should get out of it. The students may be required to make an individual presentation or a group presentation or the outcome may be a piece of written work.

Guidelines for students

1 **Organise the information**   A case contains a large amount of information and this needs to be digested initially. A case should be skip-read first, to absorb the main themes then re-read in detail to collect all the finer details. A further re-read may be necessary when the tasks or exercises have been given. Clarification may be necessary at this stage to ensure that any ambiguities are cleared up. It may be useful to put the headings in order, or to restructure the information to give some coherence to the case. A summary of the main points can be helpful, but care must be taken not to extract a summary and then never refer to the text again. Finally at this stage, differentiate between what is substantiated fact and mere opinion. Opinions can be challenged later on, especially in the light of facts.

2 **Specify the problem areas**   The problems that appear in the case, and there are often several, should be written down. Some may need clarifying, others may be very difficult to find. Once written down the problems should be classified. This can be in rank order of importance. Problems of fundamental importance should appear at the top and the least significant at the bottom. Doubtless many of the problems will be linked and this can be shown. There are various techniques available to show linkages, e.g. a tree diagram which goes from the 'root' to the 'branches'. At this stage thought should be given to sorting out symptoms and causes. Several minor problems may all stem from one cause. Classifying problems into these two categories, symptomatic and causal, is very helpful.

3 **Generate alternative solutions**   At this stage the emphasis is on looking for all the possible solutions to each of the problems specified in Stage 2. Nothing should be excluded at this stage, even though it sounds unworkable as a practical solution. There are techniques for this from the formal questioning techniques associated with method study (applying the question why? to the who, where, when, what and how of the situation) to brainstorming and lateral thinking sessions. Creativity is a key skill that should be exercised. It may also be useful to employ any techniques that have been learnt, e.g. analytical or quantitative techniques. Several solutions may be linked and one solution may solve several problems. The solutions can be classified from the general through to the specific.

4 **Predict and evaluate outcomes**   This is the 'what if' stage. The question to apply to the alternatives generated is 'what if this alternative were implemented?' The basis for selecting a particular alternative solution is whether it provides the best solution to the problem. Some alternatives may create other problems, some just don't solve the problem, others are not practicable, etc. Where data are used, each alternative can be evaluated, e.g. costing out various alternatives, say, in a pay claim. The listing of outcomes will then form the basis for selecting the solutions required to solve the problems. There should also be an estimate of the likelihood of that particular outcome occurring. Not all outcomes will occur with the same degree of certainty.

5 **Choose the final solution**   The pros and cons of each preferred alternative are listed. The solutions that overall are adjudged the best or most beneficial are the solutions that will be implemented. This stage involves comparing the alternatives with each other to allow the final choice to be made.

6 **Communicate your choice to the people concerned**   After the choice has been made the solutions have to be communicated to those who have to put them into operation and to those who are affected. This stage is crucial in practice. Often managers may well have made a good decision but they fail to communicate it properly. Frequently in industrial relations, disputes arise

not because of the decision but the manner in which it is communicated (or not). Several of the cases in this book illustrate this. The processes of consultation, meetings, information bulletins, etc. are necessary for the successful completion of an exercise. Several exercises require the student to communicate the results orally or in writing. Such skills are essential to successful management.

Summary

1 Organise the information.
2 Specify the problem areas.
3 Generate alternative solutions.
4 Predict and evaluate outcomes.
5 Choose the final solution.
6 Communicate your choice to the people concerned.

Case 1
The annual wage negotiations

Analysis

One of the fundamental elements in our system of collective bargaining is the annual wage negotiations. They determine a large proportion of the terms and conditions of an individual's contract of employment, so that, depending on the outcome of the negotiations, this alone will meet the aspirations of the employees or not. The organisation is also greatly affected by the outcome of the negotiations. The level of pay award and the conditions of employment will determine the charge the organisation has to make for its product or services.

Pay negotiations are a difficult time within organisations with one or other side trying to maintain the upper hand and score points over the other side. Both sides are trying to signal – often a considerable period of time in advance of the negotiation date – what they are looking for in the deal. Added to this, pay negotiations are complex, with the topics under consideration not merely restricted to pay but encompassing hours of work, holidays, holiday pay, sick pay, overtime rates, unsocial hours allowances and many other local items.

This case examines the lead up to the annual pay negotiations of a typical company. It looks at local negotiations at workplace level, which is where most employees feel involved. Practice varies but most organisations have some element of locally negotiated terms.

Introduction

The annual pay negotiations were due to take place at the Eastern Clothing Co. The pay settlement date for the conclusion of the negotiations was 1 March. Traditionally talks start well in advance of this date and they have

Background knowledge

Before starting this case you should have some prior knowledge of:

1 the nature of collective bargaining;
2 the basis of pay/wage negotiations;
3 the information used/needed by both sides;
4 the arguments utilised in pay bargaining;
5 the process of and tactics employed in negotiations;
6 the sanctions available to management and trade unions to secure a bargain.

always been concluded prior to this date. The company is unionised, with a membership of around 60 per cent of the workforce. The range of topics within the remit of the negotiations has expanded over the years and now covers virtually all the terms and conditions of employment for the members.

Negotiations are conducted locally between the personnel manager, production executive, works director and three union representatives. The firm is a member of an employers' association though not a particularly active one. The district officials of the union are not involved in the negotiations. Usually exploratory talks are held in January, soon after the Christmas break. These are then followed by more formal talks held over the next month to six weeks. The timetable for the negotiations is agreed at the time.

Pay awards over the last few years have been about average for the industry but have not been excessive compared with other industrial groups. The workforce believes that it is soon due for a bumper increase to make up for the lost ground of recent years. For the production department, average earnings, including bonus, are £180 gross. The standard working week is 39 hours, with 18 days holiday a year (plus statutory holidays) which increases to 20 after 5 years' service. Holidays are paid at base rate. The company has not made anyone redundant in recent times, which is good for the industry. The numbers employed have remained constant for the last few years.

Commercially the company is reasonably successful and has maintained its share of a fiercely competitive market. The company produces mainly for the home market and concentrates on fashion wear. This means that it has to follow the trends in the market place and there have been a number of precarious times when the firm has awaited the outcome of the latest launch of fashion wear. Profits are again average for the industry but productivity has been declining in recent times and the firm is examining ways of increasing efficiency. This will mean the introduction of more sophisticated machinery that gives greater adaptability and more output per employee.

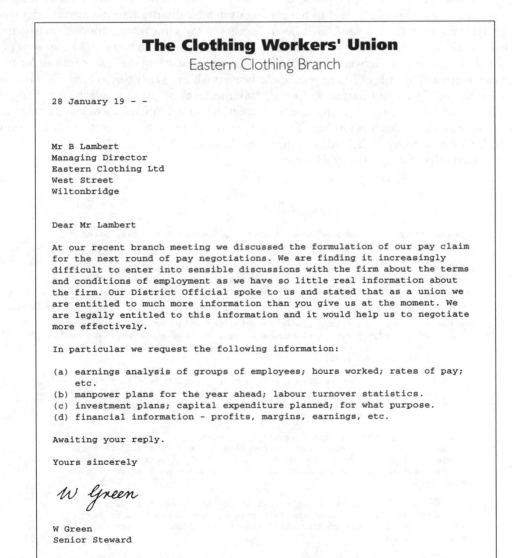

The Clothing Workers' Union
Eastern Clothing Branch

28 January 19 - -

Mr B Lambert
Managing Director
Eastern Clothing Ltd
West Street
Wiltonbridge

Dear Mr Lambert

At our recent branch meeting we discussed the formulation of our pay claim for the next round of pay negotiations. We are finding it increasingly difficult to enter into sensible discussions with the firm about the terms and conditions of employment as we have so little real information about the firm. Our District Official spoke to us and stated that as a union we are entitled to much more information than you give us at the moment. We are legally entitled to this information and it would help us to negotiate more effectively.

In particular we request the following information:

(a) earnings analysis of groups of employees; hours worked; rates of pay; etc.
(b) manpower plans for the year ahead; labour turnover statistics.
(c) investment plans; capital expenditure planned; for what purpose.
(d) financial information - profits, margins, earnings, etc.

Awaiting your reply.

Yours sincerely

W Green

W Green
Senior Steward

Pre-negotiation manoeuvres

The opening shots of this year's campaign were fired by the employers. They reported that the Christmas sales of their products had been disappointingly low and that there would have to be a period of restraint. With the firm being in the fashion market such fluctuations in the fortunes of the firm are common. This time the company has said that the underlying trend is towards a downturn in business and the future is looking rather gloomy. The managers have taken great pains to ensure that everyone knows about the situation and they all seem to have a very similar tale to tell. Overtime has been cancelled for all but a few of the very urgent, outstanding orders and employees have been warned that there will be little overtime available in the near future. Any extra output will have to be achieved within normal working hours.

The union response to this was low key. There is a great deal of seasonality to the trade and they are used to such tales of despondency. However, one or two members at a recent branch meeting said they felt that the management seemed especially convinced that things were not so good, thus this might not be a bluff. The same meeting went on to consider proposals from the stewards relating to the information made available to them by the management. The senior shop steward, who chairs the branch meetings, had received a document from the district officer which explained the type of information a trade union could request from management for the purposes of collective bargaining. He felt that in the past the union had been negotiating at a considerable disadvantage because it did not have access to the same information as management. Frequently the union had to take the word of the managers regarding the state of the order book, being unable to verify this as fact. The same went for the level of profit made by the firm. The meeting agreed to send a letter to the Managing Director to request that certain information be made available (see p. 301).

```
Extract from the February edition of Clothing News, the Managing Director's
article entitled 'Tightening our belts'

I always wish to be open with the employees at Eastern Clothing and give
them the facts relating to the current situation facing the firm. The
present picture is, I say with great sadness, not a very rosy one.

We did not do very well in the run up to Christmas, traditionally one of
our better times, and things are not looking too well for the Spring season
either. We are facing very stiff competition from home and abroad and the
contracts that we are securing are at such a low price that there is very
little profit in them at all.

... If we are going to move into a period of prosperity as a firm then I
have to say to you that we all need to pull together. This may well mean
in the near future all the things we may want may have to be delayed
until we see better times ahead.

... Another fact that is affecting all firms is the new, high technology
equipment that is now being used by some firms. These machines are very
efficient but also very costly. We may have to look at introducing some
of these machines at Eastern Clothing if we are going to keep up with the
competition.

... Finally, I wish to record my thanks to the employees that have
contributed to the success of the firm over the years but have to say
that these efforts, and greater, will have to be given if we are to
remain in business.
```

Gathering information

There was no reply to this letter. The union guessed that the request, never having been made before, had caused a stir amongst the managers. The union continued its usual lines of enquiry, through its trade union colleagues at local firms, to ascertain the level of pay settlements locally. It also collected some information on the indicators of the cost of living, such as the Retail Price Index.

The company in the meantime had lost no time in preparing itself for the pay talks. It also contacted local firms and tried to gain some information on local pay settlements and also collected the official figures on the Retail Price Index.

The company has a staff newsletter which is published every two months. The February edition, as with other editions, contained information on the company's fortunes and plans (see page 302).

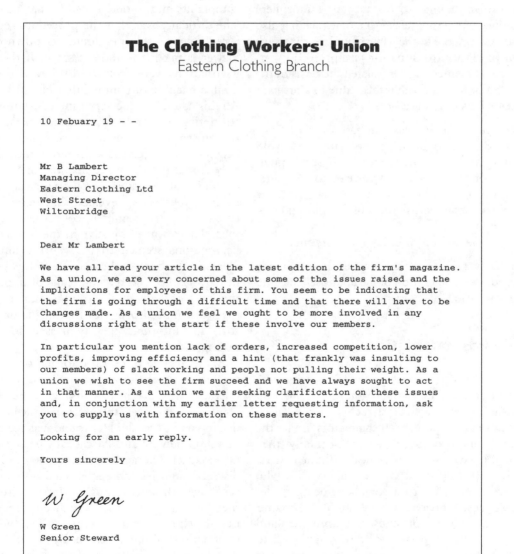

The Clothing Workers' Union
Eastern Clothing Branch

10 Febuary 19 - -

Mr B Lambert
Managing Director
Eastern Clothing Ltd
West Street
Wiltonbridge

Dear Mr Lambert

We have all read your article in the latest edition of the firm's magazine. As a union, we are very concerned about some of the issues raised and the implications for employees of this firm. You seem to be indicating that the firm is going through a difficult time and that there will have to be changes made. As a union we feel we ought to be more involved in any discussions right at the start if these involve our members.

In particular you mention lack of orders, increased competition, lower profits, improving efficiency and a hint (that frankly was insulting to our members) of slack working and people not pulling their weight. As a union we wish to see the firm succeed and we have always sought to act in that manner. As a union we are seeking clarification on these issues and, in conjunction with my earlier letter requesting information, ask you to supply us with information on these matters.

Looking for an early reply.

Yours sincerely

W Green

W Green
Senior Steward

The edition was received very coolly by everyone and created an air of gloom and despondency. Casual enquiries for further information made to the managers elicited a polite but unspecific response.

Pay claim formulated

A joint shop stewards meeting discussed the issue and concluded that the article might be an attempt to plant information prior to the annual pay talks trying to create an atmosphere conducive to a low settlement. The meeting also resolved to write to the Managing Director to ask him to clarify the situation (see p. 303).

The same meeting formulated the basis of the pay claim for the formal talks, due to start next week. This was based on:

1 an all round increase on base rates of 5%;
2 a reduction in the normal working week to 38 hours and a commitment to subsequent reductions over the next two years to 36 hours;
3 a consolidation of bonuses into base rates for the purposes of calculating holiday pay and sick pay; and
4 20 days' annual holiday for everyone.

There were also some smaller points made regarding the operation of the bonus scheme and the allocation of overtime.

Towards negotiations

As a result of the article in the house magazine and in the build up to the negotiations, the shop stewards were particularly active. They raised various matters as official complaints, under the complaints procedure, where normally they would have let supervision deal with the matter. This was confirmed by the supervisors who noticed that prior to a complaint being made, employees, who could have raised the matter with their supervisor, chose to ignore them and to go to the shop steward direct. This led to aggravation, as the complaints procedure requires that originators take the matter to their supervisor initially and, that if nothing happens, they can then take it to management through their shop steward. The kind of topics raised included many concerns over safety in the departments followed by the issuing of veiled threats about what might happen if nothing was done.

The reaction of management was one of stalling and playing for time. They accepted this as part of the campaign and privately wished that the MD had never written the offending article. They were careful to listen politely to the complaints and to take note of what was said. The difficulty was that the procedure required a reply within the time limits set down or the matter is taken to the next stage. If the wage negotiations were protracted this would create a huge backlog of complaints to be processed. All this could become very time-consuming and frustrating. The problem, which all the managers recognised, is that one of the complaints might become the subject of a dispute which would only jeopardise the wage negotiations.

Unofficial soundings taken on the shop floor, by the supervisors, revealed that many of the employees were genuinely concerned for their jobs. Their prime objective in the forthcoming negotiations seemed to be securing improvements in the bonus scheme. The bonus scheme has always been seen as a means of improving the level of individual earnings and much of the work indeed provides the means of doing so. This information was passed to senior management.

Another piece of useful information came to the attention of the senior steward. The telex operator was overheard talking to her friend about a series of telex messages that she had been dealing with recently. Her friend was the cousin of a shop steward and she casually passed on the information. The steward then made a few more discreet enquiries and encouraged his cousin to speak with the operator again. It transpired that the firm was in the advanced stages of negotiating a very large order with a multinational shopping chain. By dint of fortune this information was confirmed in separate reports coming from the sales office.

Talks begin

On Monday of the first week in February the negotiating committee met for the first time. The meeting started with the union making an opening statement which contained the claims mentioned above. They also stated that the current figures available for the Retail Price Index showed that inflation was currently running at 3½%. They also declared that their intelligence from local firms showed that wage settlements were running at 8% and moreover this was in firms that had a higher base rate figure to start with. Some firms had a base wage of £190 a week for operatives (on a 38 hour week) and they also enjoyed 20 days' holiday a year (on average earnings). The senior steward noted the great concern that the firm had found it fit to start a campaign based on fear of job loss and had not replied to the letter requesting information. He also said that even though they were not privy to the state of the order book, they had it on good authority that there was a lucrative order in the offing. The union side said that they were unable to negotiate sensibly in the absence of the facts and figures. Such facts as were divulged at the negotiations were selective and likely only to be those that supported the management's case. They needed the full range of facts on which to make a balanced decision.

The management reply to the opening statement by the union was to reaffirm the position outlined in the house magazine. There was a definite downturn in orders and this looked likely to be the case for the foreseeable future. Where the union had got its reliable (quote) information from, the management could not see. Much as they would like this to be the case, it was not. In reply to the statements about the rate of inflation, the personnel manager said that the figure quoted was the rate for the previous year but the official forecast for the coming year was a much lower rate of inflation, more like 2%. She also said that their information on local pay settlements was at variance with the union's information. While one firm had settled at 8%, it was because it had just recovered from a severe decline in business and

was allowing for an element of catching up. The clothing trade had never been able to pay high rates as the business was so competitive and open to foreign imports. The best the firm could do would be to hold on to what it had and have a year in which everyone consolidated their positions.

The final statement to the meeting by the senior steward was that if the management were not able to make a very definite offer which could be considered to be an improvement then he would have to report to the union meeting on the next day that management were not negotiating seriously. It would be very difficult for him to contain the reactions of the members and he could not be responsible for the problems that might ensue. It was agreed that another meeting would be held on Friday morning. The production executive said that, as a final statement from the management side for that meeting, he would like to end on a positive note by saying that there was a need to improve productivity. This meant there was room for increasing output related bonuses if the union was prepared to negotiate improved working practices. However, this did not mean that there was any room for manoeuvre on base rates or anything that added to overall costs with no related increase in output.

After the talks

The subsequent union meeting was indeed the stormy affair that the senior steward had predicted. A number of the employees wanted the negotiating committee to tackle the problem of base rates and holiday pay as a priority. Some of the more vociferous members asked for a commitment from the meeting that, in the event of no movement on base rates, the members should institute some form of industrial action. This was never put as a motion and was not taken as anything other than a few members letting off steam. Nevertheless they had some support. The meeting broke up with the stewards instructed to pursue the claim on base rates as a priority.

Shortly after the union meeting the supervisors heard stories about the real possibility of industrial action. This information was passed on to the senior managers. A further complication for management was that the large order that the union had got wind of had now been finalised. The exact terms of the deal were only known to two senior people in the sales department and the Managing Director. The order would provide work for the production unit for some considerable time. It was not due to start for six weeks but then would be steady work.

Exercises

Stage 1

1 The personnel manager is concerned that the negotiations are not going at all well. She contacts you, as a fellow personnel officer and member of the IPM. The request is that you act as an unofficial industrial relations consultant to the firm. Prepare a report, as the consultant, on how you think the firm should conduct the negotiations from now on. In addition, make recommendations on how the firm should conduct its industrial relations which would improve wage negotiations.

2 The senior steward contacts his district official to report on the proceedings and subsequent union meeting. The official decides to call on the firm the next day. As senior steward, make notes on the important features of the situation, as you see it, and list the options open to the union for the next stage of the negotiations.

3 As the district official after being briefed by the senior steward, make detailed notes on how the union ought to proceed in the next stage of the negotiations. Utilise the information raised in Exercise 2.

4 The Managing Director contacts the local employers' association to ask for their advice. He is concerned that the pay negotiations are entering a difficult phase. Draft the letter to the Association and draft a reply from them to the Director. If you are in a group 'send' the letter to another member of the group for a reply.

5 In groups, enact the next meeting of the negotiating committee. Prior to this, meet in separate union/management groups to decide your strategy. Select the roles each will play, based on a formal negotiation committee, i.e. chairperson, secretary, spokespersons etc. If possible video the proceedings. Prepare an agreed statement at the end of the official proceedings, including the next stage of the negotiations, if agreement is not reached.

6 As a member of a small group of trade union members, examine the possible forms of industrial action that the union could take. List these and evaluate them in terms of effectiveness, acceptability to the members and costs to both sides.

Stage 2

The next meeting of the negotiations committee makes some progress but there is a final failure to agree. There has been agreement on the following:
1 across the board 4 per cent pay increase;
2 consolidation of average bonus earnings (but not average overtime) for holiday pay only;
3 19 days' annual leave, rising to 22 days after 5 years of service.

The sticking point has been the claim for a shorter working week. The firm is adamant that it cannot afford to reduce the working week any more. It points out that the additional cost is too great and that the employees would only make it up in overtime anyway. The average working week within the firm is about 44 hours. When the basic working week came down from 40 to 39, the average working week did not change. The union counter claim that all the local firms in the area are now committed to a reduction in the working week with most on 38 in the current year and agreement to reduce to 36 or 37 hours in stages over the next few years.

1 At a meeting of the management side of the negotiating committee, formulate your strategy for the next stage of the negotiations. Decide how far you are prepared to go in sticking to your point or whether there is any room for bargaining.

2 The branch meeting held following the breakdown of negotiations has given its backing to the union negotiators to secure a reduction in the working week. The meeting did not decide on any specific sanctions that might be taken but gave a remit to the negotiators to take what action they felt was right. Meet as the union representatives and formulate your strategy for the next stage in the negotiations. Decide how far you are prepared to go to secure your stated aim, what you may be prepared to bargain on and what sanctions you might envisage threatening or using.

3 Convene a meeting of the negotiating committee to thrash out the remaining issues. Take it that both sides have said that this is the very last meeting on the issue and agreement must be reached or it is deadlock. Again run the meeting formally with people nominated to specific roles. Prepare an agreed statement at the end of the meeting.

Case 2
Growing pains

Analysis

As organisations expand there are always growing pains involved. One way in which this manifests itself is the need for structure and formality in staff relations. With a small number of people the managers can deal with individuals on a one-to-one basis and there is a great deal of flexibility. The structure of the organisation is undefined and adapts to suit the moment. There is little need to define roles or to have rules to define conduct within the organisation. Wages can be decided as between employer and employee.

As an organisation employs more people the need for a more formal structure becomes apparent. Rules are needed to deal with all employees in a fair and consistent manner. Difficulties arise particularly when a hierarchy emerges and each manager is required to treat their employees in similar manner. To remain without a structure for long when the organisation is growing, can lead to problems, which if they are not solved will lead to difficulties. The following case illustrates the sort of problems that can ensue in what is otherwise a flourishing firm.

Background knowledge

In this case you are required to examine an organisation during a period of growth and to analyse the problems that emerge.

Before starting this case you should have some prior knowledge of:

1 organisational structures;
2 the role and function of management, particularly policy making;
3 communication structures, consultations and negotiations;
4 human relations and motivation;
5 trade union recognition, recruitment and membership.

Starting up

Fifteen years ago Peter Robinson and his long-time friend Jim Lyons, decided to leave their employment with a national insurance firm and set up their own business. Having spent ten years of their working lives in the industry they felt the time was ripe to go out alone. They live in a relatively prosperous area in Cambridgeshire and were convinced that given a lot of hard work, they could establish a prosperous business. They set up an office in a small, rural town to sell car, household and life insurances along with personal investment schemes. Their respective experiences in insurance were complementary as were their characters. At first they employed part-time secretarial help as needs arose.

Through hard work and determination the business prospered, albeit with the occasional hitch. After three years they set up a second branch in a town nearby. They were then employing a number of secretarial staff and recruited young people to train up with the business. The pattern of work established in the branches was a reflection of Peter and Jim. They expected their staff to work hard and to high standards, impressing on staff that the continued existence of the firm, and its future growth, depended on building up a satisfied clientèle. If they were working beyond what is considered to be normal working hours they would expect staff to do so until the work was finished. Any staff not doing so were soon given a clear message that they were not the type of employee wanted in the firm. Peter in particular could be very direct and not a few staff had felt the sharp end of his tongue. In return those staff that did a good job were rewarded with pay rises and promotion.

Personnel

The idea that staff should be flexible was positively encouraged. If help was needed in a particular area then staff were expected to move in to help. A typist would act as receptionist, a receptionist would do some filing, a clerk would answer the phone. This was taken as normal practice and staff in general liked this as it gave them the opportunity to move around the office and carry out a range of tasks. Holidays had to be taken to suit the business and Saturday morning working was normal.

Over the next few years a number of other branches were opened and Peter and Jim took in junior partners to act as branch managers. As the network extended Peter and Jim spent more time away from the branches, working on the bigger deals with local firms for their insurance needs and building up a specialist investment service. This meant that more of the day-to-day

decisions of running the business were delegated to the branch managers. Gradually they were allowed to recruit staff and run the branches as they saw fit. Certain decisions had to be referred to Peter or Jim where certain expenditure was involved or where there were difficult technical problems. The branch managers were very much in the mould of Peter and Jim, demanding high standards and dedication. This led to tensions within the branches as the staff, particularly the newer ones who did not know Peter or Jim very well, looked on the job as a regular one with normal, fixed hours of work. The labour turnover was higher than could be expected even allowing for the relatively young age structure of the staff. Grumbles were frequent but there was no formal channel for these to be vented.

Organisation

The structure of the firm was rather chaotic with no formal staff grading or wages structure. After ten years of business the firm employed 45 people but Peter and Jim found a large proportion of their time was spent on developing the network of branches and diversifying the services of the firm. This meant that little attention was paid to internal affairs, but providing this did not interfere with their plans, then they saw little need to do so. Neither partner thought there was anything wrong with the business as it continued to expand and produce a handsome level of profits. The younger, ambitious staff, who were being trained in the insurance business, tended to stay with the firm as they saw the prospects with a smaller, expanding agency as a better prospect than working for the big insurance companies. Any conversation with them would not have revealed any problems, as they did not have the same perceptions as the clerical and secretarial staff. It appeared to all the staff that Peter and Jim were doing very well out of the business. They both had expensive cars, had purchased large houses and were able to holiday abroad.

The practice had always been for staff to be transferred between the various branches. This was part of the flexible approach the firm encouraged and was useful to staff, as it gave them a wider experience of other branches and to the firm, as it gave them a pool of staff to draw on. Transfers occurred during holiday periods or when there was a long-term absence. The system worked tolerably well but was not liked by those with local commitments after working hours. Travel on public transport in the area was difficult; the firm did not contribute to any increased travelling costs incurred. Transfers also gave staff the opportunity of exchanging information on the conditions of work at other branches and it soon became apparent that a wage policy did not exist. Also practice seemed to vary from branch to branch. Anyone transferred for any length of time soon had a grievance if they suffered any inconvenience as a result of the transfer.

Incidents

One young man from one of the branches was asked to go to another branch some distance away the next week. He said that he would find that difficult as he did not have transport and he already had a long journey into work. The manager insisted on him going and the young man, being rather timid, reluctantly agreed to try to get there. On the Monday following he did not arrive until 10.30 (instead of 9.00) and was reprimanded by the manager. The young man

---

10 October 19--

Mr P Robinson
East Anglian Insurance Co
North Street
Fenbridge

Dear Mr Robinson

I am writing to you to make a formal request for union recognition. In particular, it is for you to recognise the Insurance Staff's union as representing the staff of East Anglian Insurance. Currently about 20 of your staff are members of this union and it would make sense if these employees had their membership officially recognised to enable the union to perform its function properly.

The reason for the request is that it is now clear that the firm needs a union that can represent the views of the staff to management. Many of the aspects of industrial relations would improve if there were a union that could speak on behalf of its members. It would also provide a means of taking up matters with management and entering into some collective agreements on things like pay and conditions of work. The object of the exercise is not to create a division in the firm but to make for smoother running within the firm.

I would ask you to consider this request. I would welcome the opportunity to discuss this matter with you.

Looking forward to your reply.

Yours sincerely

P Marks

P Marks

was not given any opportunity to explain the situation to the manager who was new to the area. It happened that Peter was at that branch that day and being under pressure told the man that if he ever behaved in that way again he would be sacked.

Another incident concerned a young woman, a secretary at a branch, who was pregnant. Unfortunately the pregnancy was a difficult one and she had to have days off frequently or had to go to see the doctor. She carried on with the firm but was advised by her doctor to leave

THE EAST ANGLIAN INSURANCE COMPANY
Fenbridge

19 October 19--

Mr P Marks
C/o North Street Branch
Fenbridge

Dear Mr Marks

Thank you for your letter of 10th October.

We have considered your request for union recognition at East Anglian Insurance. Our initial response to this request is a firm no. We consider there is no place for a union within East Anglian Insurance. The management of this company is well able to conduct its industrial relations and employee relations without the need for a trade union. It is our experience that trade unions do not help and in many ways hinder. Our managers can be consulted at branch level and they can consult with us on matters they are not able to deal with.

We are somewhat disturbed that you (or others) have been recruiting staff into a trade union. This has been done behind our backs and we feel insulted that we have not been informed about this until now. We would remind you that we are the owners and managers of this organisation and before any changes are made authorisation should be obtained before action is taken. We are requesting that you inform us of those that have joined the union.

However, as you have highlighted an area where we recognise that potentially improvements could be made, we will employ a personnel consultant, part-time, to investigate the firm's policies and to make recommendations.

This investigation would be open-ended and the consultant would have a free hand in what he/she recommended.

Finally, a decision on the request to form a union in the firm would be left until the report has been received.

Your sincerely

P Robinson
Director

employment and have a protracted period of rest. The baby was due in about 15 weeks time. On informing her manager she requested that her job be left open for her, as there was the possibility, especially in this case, that there might be complications. The manager replied that the firm did not have a policy of keeping jobs open because they needed to be certain of where they stood with staffing. After thinking the matter through the woman resigned under protest. Later she lodged a claim for constructive dismissal which was turned down because she had not been with the firm for two years.

The new trainee

About two years ago Phillip was appointed a trainee at one of the branches. He had worked for a large insurance company and was felt to be an asset to the firm because of the training he had received with his previous firm. Unknown to the manager who appointed him, Phillip was a strong trade unionist and had been an organiser for the Insurance Staff's Union at his previous place of work. While not a militant, he stood up for people's rights and would air grievances on behalf of others. It was soon apparent that he would stand up to the manager and Peter where he felt there was a genuine grievance. His work was fine but clearly he had gained a reputation of being a bit of a stirrer. Secretly he went around other members of staff soliciting their support for the information of a union within the firm. This was helped by the fact that his job required him to travel around the branches. Gradually a number joined the union

---

12 January 19--

Mr P Robinson
East Anglian Insurance Co
North Street
Fenbridge

Dear Mr Robinson

Thank you for your letter of 19th October. I have also seen the consultant's report. It seems largely inconclusive and does not address itself to the central question originally raised, ie, trade union recognition at East Anglian Insurance.

I have talked to many of my colleagues and have been asked to re-submit a request for union recognition of the Insurance Staffs' Union at East Anglian Insurance. Currently 45 per cent of full-time staff and 30 per cent of part-time staff are now members of the union.

I do not accept your criticism of going behind your backs in recruiting members. This is a decision for the individuals concerned and employees have the right to join a union if they so wish. Clearly many of the employees have decided they wish to join and they have not been coerced into this. It seems to reflect the existence of a problem which you cannot sweep away.

I am requesting a meeting with you as a matter of urgency to discuss the recognition of the union at East Anglian Insurance.

Yours sincerely

P Marks

P Marks

but all this was unknown to any of the managers.

About 20 staff had already become members of the union. Phillip then took the step of making a formal claim for recognition of the union by the firm (see p. 309).

The reply received by Phillip from Peter is shown on p. 310.

Exercises

Stage 1

1 You have been appointed the personnel consultant by Peter and Jim. Prepare the report referred to. The terms of reference are to investigate the situation in the firm with particular reference to the need or otherwise for a trade union and to make recommendations on the means of improving industrial relations within the firm. Within the report note the methods you would use to carry out such an exercise.

2 You (or a colleague) are Phillip. State what you would do in the circumstances. Given that you will cooperate with the investigation, what evidence and suggestions would you give to the consultant? Submit this in the form of a memorandum.

3 The consultant asks to meet Peter and Jim to ask them questions about the development of the firm and their personnel policies. Prior to the meeting Peter and Jim meet to discuss their approach. Write notes that they would make in preparation for meeting the consultant. You are free to make whatever assumptions you wish on what stance they may make with regard to the issue of trade union recognition.

4 As part of the exercise the consultant wishes to ascertain the feelings and attitudes of the staff on a number of issues. He/she has made an appointment to come to your branch tomorrow. You have been asked to be the spokesperson for your branch, having been with the firm for some time and being respected by your colleagues. Write some brief notes on the

THE EAST ANGLIAN INSURANCE COMPANY
Fenbridge

16 January 19--

Mr P Marks
C/o North Street Branch
Fenbridge

Dear Mr Marks

Thank you for your letter of 12th January.

Clearly this is not a matter that is going to be resolved through correspondence. A meeting has been set up for a week on Wednesday at 10.00 am in my office to discuss industrial relations within the firm.

This should not be taken as an indication of our intention to allow trade union recognition at East Anglian Insurance.

Look forward to seeing you at our meeting.

Yours sincerely

P Robinson
Director

situation from the employees' point of view and what you would recommend should be done.

5 Acting as Jim Lyons, you have been told of the two incidents (referred to on pp. 309–11). Having elicited the facts of the two cases you analyse the situation with a view to making some conclusions regarding the running of the firm. Draw up such a short report.

Stage 2

The consultant's report has been published. It does not state whether a union should be recognised or not but suggests that the firm should institute systems that would allow this type of decision to be made. The report recommends that the firm should institute some kind of consultative system where the employees, at the branches, can become more involved in the business. The consultant mentions Briefing Groups as a possible system, providing the managers use them as a means of two-way communication to feed information back up the line.

Peter and Jim are relieved that the report does not directly recommend the introduction of a trade union and they see the way forward as instituting a consultative structure merely as a sop to the kinds of criticism levelled at them.

Some staff, especially the more vociferous ones, see the report as something of a 'whitewash' which comes to no specific conclusions. They are determined to press ahead for radical changes. They argue that the firm has been criticised and the only way forward is to introduce a trade union in each branch. Phillip is persuaded to make a formal request to Peter and Jim to form a branch of the Insurance Staff's Union at East Anglian Insurance (see p. 311). The reply received by Phillip from Peter is shown on page 312.

1 Role play the meeting between Peter, Jim and other senior partners (keep the numbers down to a total of, say, five) and Phillip, an Insurance Staff's Union official and other employee representatives (again keeping the total to five). The agenda for the meeting should be drawn up by the 'management' side prior to the meeting and 'sent' to the 'employee' side. Put a reasonable time limit on the meeting, allowing sufficient time for the participants to reach a conclusion. At the end of the meeting prepare agreed notes based on the meeting and state the conclusions arrived at.

2 The 'management' group should convene separately and consider the outcome of the meeting. Prepare a plan based on what needs to be done to put into effect the conclusions arrived at in the joint meeting. Pass this to the 'employee' group when you have this ready.

3 The 'employee' group should convene separately and consider the outcome of the meeting. Discuss the next stage in the plan to accomplish your objectives as a group of employees. Consider any communication received from the 'management' group.

4 Finally, reconvene the joint meeting to arrive at a final action plan based on the two groups' considerations of the previous meeting and any subsequent communication. At the end of a time-constrained discussion prepare agreed notes on the conclusion of the meeting (even if it is a final failure to agree).

5 As a branch manager, having read the consultant's report, write an appraisal of his suggestions. Include a further section on how these, or similar suggestions of your own, should be implemented at East Anglian Insurance to improve industrial/employee relations. Work out the practical details of your recommendations.

Case 3

Defective procedures are harmful

Analysis

One of the fundamental aspects of a good industrial relations system is the existence of workable agreements. The process of collective bargaining leads to agreements and it is these which provide the framework within which the cogs of the industrial relations machinery work. The need for agreements is manifold and includes the need to treat everyone with equality and fairness; agreements also provide the procedures that will be used in particular circumstances.

However, the mere existence of agreements does not necessarily mean that all will be well. The agreements themselves will need to be constructed so as to achieve their purpose. Poorly worded or defective agreements can be worse than having no agreements at all. This case examines a situation in which a disciplinary agreement exists but because it is a poor agreement it leads to a number of problems.

Another Monday morning

It was an ordinary Monday morning when Alf Ramsbottom arrived at his lorry depot in Felixstowe. He was feeling pleased with life as he surveyed his fleet of new Volvo lorries and the brand new BMW he had indulged in last month. He reflected that life had not always been like this. His father, who had set up the business, had not known such good times but would have been proud to have seen his son succeed in this way. The haulage firm was established in 1932 as a local contractor to deliver goods and farm produce in the area around Ipswich. It had, like all such businesses,

Background knowledge

In this case you are required to examine a number of practical incidents, usually relating to discipline, where things would have gone much better if the agreement that existed had been workable and had been used.

Before starting this case you should have some prior knowledge of:

1 managerial authority and responsibility;
2 the construction and working of procedures;
3 problem solving;
4 handling disciplinary action and dismissal.

had its ups and downs, and tended to follow the fortunes of the economy. The one factor that had caused FleetHaul to enter the big-time league of road hauliers was the expansion of the docks at Felixstowe. Alf had many connections locally and had timed his moves to perfection. Just when it was obvious that the future in road transport lay in containerised transport, Alf invested in lorries to take on this business. Through a lot of hard work and much support from his workforce, the firm had grown. They picked up a few, large contracts from the shipping firms and demonstrated their ability to operate throughout the country. The firm had not really looked back since the mid-60s and all the workforce had enjoyed the fruits of prosperity.

Problems, problems

This feeling of self-contentment did not last long though. Before Alf could enter his office on the

Monday morning for a meeting with his managers, he was approached by the yard foreman. Bob was a long serving and loyal employee of the firm but was lately finding the going hard and Alf suspected that Bob was not performing as well as he had in the past. As they met, Alf knew there was a problem; Bob both looked and felt angry. He opened up the conversation, not with his usual pleasantry, but dived straight in. 'It's now two weeks since I asked you to look into this question of men arriving late on weekends. I can't be here all the time to make sure they behave themselves. You know that if we are not at the docks on time, we are in lumber. And I tell you, we had a right load of trouble on Saturday. Same set of drivers, turning up when they think fit, not when we want them in. You said you'd have them on the carpet straight away and tell them that there's no weekend driving for those that can't get here on time'.

This rather threw Alf for a moment, as he could not remember what Bob was talking about. Then he recalled that Bob had said something to him last week about the lateness of the weekend drivers but did not recall having promised to do anything about it. Anyway, he felt that it was for the supervisors and managers of the firm to deal with those kind of day-to-day problems; he was there to secure orders and deal with the customers. 'OK Bob, I can see that this is bothering you, I haven't the time to look into these matters myself and you know that as supervisor you can deal with such incidents as a matter of discipline, after all we have got a procedure for that kind of thing. We have to use it or the union will have our guts for garters.' Bob replied: 'But you know that the procedure is not worth the paper it's written on. When did we last issue a warning and make it stick? We either get soft and let them off or we get the union coming down like a ton of bricks and you, and the others in there, back down. No use us doing anything if you lot won't back us'. Alf was not a born diplomat and had survived in a notoriously rough trade, but he was usually courteous to his senior staff and expected them to be the same. In particular he found Bob's

attack out of character. 'I will raise the issue at our weekly meeting which I am late for now, and we will decide what needs to be done. I'll let you know soon', and Alf strode off to the office.

His reaction was one of mild irritation. These small, fiddly problems always seem to get in the way and detract from the important business. He hoped that perhaps the meeting of his managers would help put this behind him. It was all right casting him in the role of big boss but he thought he had sorted the organisation out sufficiently well to see that problems of that nature were dealt with without reference to him. The firm was unionised and they had seen to it that there was an agreement on things like discipline (*see* Appendix on p. 318). Why couldn't people just get on with things!

Safety standards

His mood was to slip into one of greater irritability at the managers' meeting when the same topic was brought up. The garage manager, Chris, said that it was time to air a few internal grievances from the managers. He said that he, and a number of the other managers and supervisors, had all noted that the standard of discipline in the firm was slipping and this was having a detrimental effect on the firm as a whole. He related a situation regarding health and safety rules in the garage that was becoming almost impossible to deal with. Certain jobs in the workshop were dangerous and there were procedures which should be followed and protective equipment which should be worn. Recently there had been a lowering of standards and in spite of constant vigilance by the supervisors, it seemed the situation was still declining.

Chris said 'Last week I had a welder in my office and gave him a stern private warning that if he was found welding without wearing the correct goggles he would be disciplined and that could lead to him being taken off welding work, which is, as you know, well paid, and I'd put him on a lower grade job. The only reply I got from him was that the procedure did not allow for safety to be a matter of discipline. Blow me down, if later that day the steward didn't come in and tell me that if I tried disciplining his members on the grounds of health and safety, he'd take out an official complaint against me!'

The problem recognised

The meeting then spent a little time discussing the situation generally, with the consensus being that things were indeed getting worse but some merely commenting that it was all a sign of the times.

A final piece of 'any other business' came from the Office Manager, Sally. She said that she was of the opinion that the firm was in difficulties all round with discipline. Sally had been with the firm only one year and couldn't comment on the decline but came upon a number of incidents that she had found hard to deal with because there seemed to be no uniform system of handling discipline. Her item related to the fact that she had had to withdraw a disciplinary warning against a member of staff, for persistent lateness, because Sally had not invited her friend in with her when Sally had issued the warning. Sally said she knew of no such requirement, especially as the offices were not unionised, and felt that her authority had been undermined early on in her job at FleetHaul. The procedure made no reference to being accompanied by a friend or shop steward at a disciplinary interview.

The sacked criminal

Later that week the Transport Manager had an official appointment with the shop steward of the drivers' union. The firm was a virtual closed shop on the driving side of the business. The steward was a driver himself and had been with the firm for several years. He always drove a hard bargain but was also fair and would always seek a solution to a problem. Previous meetings, which were held quite regularly, had been fractious and sometimes heated, but the men respected each other.

The steward opened the meeting by saying that he was most alarmed about the difficulties that seemed to be arising in recent times. One case he wished to raise as an official complaint was related to the dismissal of a driver the previous week. The case was a very sad one and concerned a driver who had been found handling stolen goods; he had then been committed to a Crown Court for trial. There was no evidence that the goods had been stolen from FleetHaul. The driver's name was revealed in a court report and the Transport Manager had interviewed the driver the following day. The driver obviously had little to say about the offence but the Manager explained that the firm could not employ anyone who had acted suspiciously as customers would be reluctant to have anyone deliver their goods who was a suspected criminal. At the end of the rather tense meeting the Manager had dismissed the driver and given him four weeks' pay in lieu of notice. The case had aroused strong feelings amongst the drivers and had the yard not been so busy and the drivers occupied on long-distance deliveries, the incident could have led to a serious dispute.

Fortunately the temperature had dropped but the steward was still talking in terms of reinstatement for the man, pending the outcome of his trial. There were veiled threats that if the firm was not prepared to reconsider then there might well be a dispute arising and possibly union action. The Transport Manager had heard similar talk before but had the difficult job of deciding how much was bluff and how much was serious. The steward went on to state, in detail, that at the recent union branch meeting there was a great deal of resentment that the driver had been sacked. The steward ascertained that the driver had been told as soon as he walked in to the disciplinary interview that the case was open and shut and little could be said except to go through the motions of saying why he was being sacked. The Manager did not dissent from this account. Asked why the driver still had not received written confirmation of the dismissal nor a statement of the reasons for the dismissal, the Manager said that there seemed little point now but he would get round to it if the steward insisted. The meeting resolved nothing on the question of the sacking and the steward decided to see if anything happened as a result of the meeting and, if nothing did, to pursue it further and vigorously.

Persistently late

The steward decided to rub salt into the vexed question of discipline. He then raised the case of Tom. This was not as serious as the one of the sacked driver but was another example of management's ineptitude and blundering. Tom was a yard assistant who had previously worked for the firm as a driver but for the last six years had been in the yard on general duties. He had one weakness in life; his love of beer. This had caused a number of problems to him over the years, not least a difficulty in getting up in the morning after a session on the beer. There had been no known incident where his drinking had affected his driving, because he just never turned up the next day. Tom had been given a verbal warning for lateness 15 months ago during one of the firm's clamp-downs on timekeeping and absenteeism. The yard supervisor, who kept records of lateness and absenteeism, had called Tom into his office last week and issued Tom a final written warning (see below).

The steward observed that if the lateness and absenteeism had been persistent over the last 15 months, it seemed a little late in the day to issue another warning. Also, a 15-month gap between warnings meant that the first warning had now been wiped off the record and Tom would be starting with a clean sheet. Anyway, the firm had tolerated Tom for 24 years and he was part of the culture of FleetHaul. While not everyone could act like Tom it seemed harsh to expect a

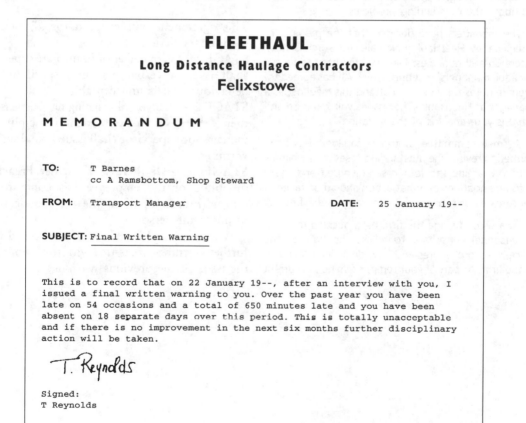

man of 63 to give up suddenly the habits of a lifetime.

The Transport Manager reported all this to Alf when they next met. They both expressed concern that the business was beginning to get bogged down with a number of niggling incidents and that one might lead to a major problem one day.

Exercises

1 Analyse the incidents in the case and prepare a report for Alf Ramsbottom stating what your analysis of the problems is and prepare a list of specific recommendations for action by him and his managers.

2 The steward reports the outcome of the meeting with the Fleet Manager to his District Official. As the District Official, reply to the steward recommending what the steward ought to look for in the new procedure. Also give advice on what the steward should do about the outstanding problems.

3 The managers have decided that the problem of discipline at FleetHaul now calls for some serious attention and remedies. The first step has been a call for a full managers' meeting, which Alf has agreed to. Prepare notes for when you attend this meeting, as a manager at FleetHaul. What issues will you raise and what is your analysis of the situation?

4 A small committee of three managers has been formed to review the outstanding cases of disciplinary action. Examine the four cases recorded and make recommendations on what action should be taken in those cases or similar ones occurring in the future.

5 At a second stage the firm have decided to retain a personnel consultant to advise the firm on the disciplinary procedures and how discipline is handled in the firm. As part of your remit, examine the current procedure in use at FleetHaul and state in what respects it is defective and what problems it is likely to give rise to. Prepare a consultant's report with recommendations.

6 Draw up a disciplinary procedure for use at FleetHaul. Apply the procedure to the incidents that arise in the case and state what the outcome would have been if a good procedure had been used properly.

7 As a training adviser to FleetHaul, draw up a training programme that you think the managers and supervisors should undertake to implement the new procedure. Concentrate on the topics that should be covered rather than the methods of delivery. Using the incidents recorded in the case as illustrative material, construct a 'compare and contrast' exercise for the members of the training programme.

Appendix

FleetHaul Ltd
Disciplinary Procedure

This agreement will be used for all cases of disciplinary action.

STAGE 1 – A manager or immediate supervisor shall issue a verbal warning, specifying the behaviour that is unacceptable.

STAGE 2 – If a verbal warning has been issued, then if there is a further breach of discipline the manager or supervisor shall issue a final written warning.

STAGE 3 – If there is a further breach of discipline or the employee has committed a serious breach of discipline the manager can dismiss that person.

Warnings shall be taken off the record if no further warnings are issued within 12 months of the issue of the previous warning.

Case 4

Sorry, you're redundant

Analysis

One of the problems that many organisations have had to face in recent times is that of how to reduce the number of employees in a firm. The occupational structure in the country has changed much in the postwar period, with the traditional industries declining – such as cotton, wool, railways, mining and shipbuilding – because of changes in technology and competition. Other industries have been radically affected by technological change where highly productive machinery and equipment has displaced slower, inefficient labour-intensive methods. Finally, economic factors have prevailed which have necessitated firms having to employ fewer people because of the downturn in demand.

Whatever the cause, the situation is not an easy one for any organisation to face. It causes morale to slump and individuals have to face a very difficult situation. How organisations approach the question of redundancy and how they process them, is an area that needs a great deal of attention and skill. This case examines a redundancy situation in detail and raises a number of questions relating to the subject.

The firm

It was a normal Friday afternoon at Sheetmet Co. The personnel in the Production Department were cleaning up the area after the day's work and sorting out paperwork. Everyone was looking forward to the weekend, especially as there was a social club fishing trip the next day. The operators, supervisors and managers got on well with each other and many of them saw each other outside work. The pace was slowing down, as it tended to on a Friday afternoon, as there

Background knowledge

In this case you are required to analyse a redundancy situation and to suggest how the case should have been handled. Times of redundancy are always difficult periods in any firm and they need handling in a very sensitive way. Before starting this case you should have some prior knowledge of:

1 the grounds on which employees can be made redundant;
2 the consultation procedures that should be utilised;
3 how redundancies should be declared;
4 what help employees should be given;
5 the law relating to redundancies;
6 the role of a trade union in this situation.

was no point in starting any work before Monday and the machines were always in need of a good clean.

Sheetmet was a firm of specialist sheet metal workers who made prototype work for a variety of industries and also carried out small batch work. They prided themselves on their skill. If it could be made of sheet metal, Sheetmet could do it. The firm employed 80 people but even at this size was friendly, with everyone, from directors downwards, on first name terms. The firm was clearly not in an expanding market with the competition coming from nonmetallic substitute materials, which were easier to fabricate than metal and altogether more attractive to designers. Nevertheless, it had maintained a healthy order book for most of the past ten years. However, recently those leaving, mainly through retirement, had not been replaced and it had become noticeable that there was an ageing workforce with few young people entering the trade to provide succession.

The declaration

Without anyone being particularly aware a notice appeared on the notice board. The board was full of posters, notices, minutes and informal notices but the new, clean sheet was conspicuous (see p. below).

There was a stunned silence as the word went round the department and everyone gathered round the notice board. People found it difficult to know what to say, especially to those affected by the redundancy notice. The supervisor was called over and he denied any prior knowledge of the notice. He could see the reaction of the group and went off to see his boss. He ascertained that the production manager and all the other managers were at a meeting, but no one knew where. Not one for giving up, he went to the directors' offices, only to find the doors firmly locked.

The selected few

Of the ten listed on the notice board, seven were under the age of 30 and had been with the firm less than two years. They had all received training within the firm and were considered to be skilled operators. It was commented that within the department there were six men who were within three years of retirement. They had casually commented that, had they been asked, they would cheerfully have volunteered for redundancy.

The same evasiveness persisted on Monday. Meetings seemed to be held everywhere and no one could be contacted. The ten men listed on the notice reported to the wages office where they were given their money. The situation did not improve when it was learnt that only two people were being made redundant from the offices, one of them being a part-timer. Eventually a

---

SHEETMET CO

M E M O R A N D U M

TO: All Staff

FROM: Peter Thompson, Managing Director   **DATE:**   6 November 19--

The Board have examined the future position of the company and regretfully announce that, due to the disappointing performance in the current financial year and the poor state of the order book, there is a need to reduce the workforce of the firm.

We have considered how best to implement this decision and have concluded that in the production department the last ten people joining the workforce are to be made redundant. These are ....

Arrangements will be made on Monday morning for these people to be paid in lieu of notice.

Peter Thompson

PJT/skl

deputation from the Production Department met the Managing Director. He went over the matter again in more detail and while fully sympathetic, said that there was nothing to be done. He was clearly agitated by the severe criticism of his handling of the situation. It was not the first time that he had had difficulty in dealing with problems that might lead to confrontation. That incident had occurred four years ago and had remained firmly in the memories of all.

The current position

The company continued to maintain a reasonable level of activity and the workforce was down to 60, other losses occurring through natural wastage. However, the recession was biting hard. Technical changes had meant less sheet metal work was needed and the future was looking gloomy. At the end of the financial year the firm was in the red and the projection for the next year was poor. Unless remedial action was taken, the firm, the accountant advised, was in danger. As 60 per cent of the direct costs were labour costs, it seemed inevitable that a reduction in human resources would be necessary. On this occasion the shop floor had become aware of the impending decision. Requests were made for information but the replies were evasive and vague. One lunchtime the employees organized an informal meeting in the canteen. At the meeting it was decided that the management should be approached officially.

Exercises

1 As the unofficial representative for the group you were very much involved in the redundancy incident four years ago. You reflect on this experience to formulate some ideas for the immediate situation. Write a short, analytical report on the original redundancy incident and draw up a 'lessons to be learnt' set of recommendations.

2 Management have agreed to meet a delegation of employee representatives in two days' time. Meet as a group of employees and draw up an agenda for that meeting with management. Specify the information that you will be seeking from management.

3 You will be involved in the meeting with the employees in two days' time as a manager. The Managing Director has tasked you with finding out the legal requirements relating to redundancy and to send a memo to him on this, in lay language.

4 You have also sought the advice of a personnel specialist on how a potential redundancy situation should be handled. Write a set of notes on the main points of what would constitute good working practice in this situation. You are particularly concerned about minimising the impact of reductions in human resources. Explore the range of possibilities available to the firm and list them.

5 Write a procedure for dealing with a redundancy situation, including the means of communication, notice to be given, consultations and the level of compensation to be offered.

6 Use this scenario as the basis for a joint negotiation exercise. Each side, employer and employees, should prepare their case first, then negotiate an agreement to cover:
   (a) consultation procedures;
   (b) the methods to be employed to minimise the effects of redundancy;
   (c) the basis of selecting people for redundancy;
   (d) the mechanism for processing redundancies.

7 Use the agreement from Exercise 6 to deal with the situation that currently exists with regard to the necessity of reducing human resources to maintain the firm's viability.

Case 5
Going to arbitration

Analysis

While the majority of matters arising within firms are dealt with and disposed of either unofficially or by using agreed procedures, there always are a few issues that are ultimately difficult to resolve. Even with the best procedures some very difficult problems might remain unresolved. When procedures have been exhausted and there is nowhere else to go, the dispute can continue and cause immeasurable harm to the organisation. Often it is at this stage that the dispute spills over into industrial action. To provide a way out of this impasse many procedures allow for arbitration or some other means of third party intervention to resolve the dispute. This case examines this process in detail by looking at the issues that are raised when referring cases to arbitration. While it is unlikely that all the points that are raised in the case would occur in any one firm, it provides a realistic scenario in which to examine these issues.

Going to arbitration – Introduction

Brandwells is an old established grocery firm that has survived the massive changes that have taken place in the retail trade and has become a successful firm. The company own 40 branches in the South-East, employing 200 full-time staff and 400 part-time staff. The firm has a very professional personnel function that has encouraged trade union membership within its branches and has consultation procedures to involve staff as much as possible in the firm. The recognition of trade unions has led to a number of collective agreements on various topics. There is a dispute and grievance procedure as well as a negotiating procedure. These have all worked

Background knowledge

In this case you will be examining the detail of referring disputes, grievances and unresolved questions raised in negotiations to arbitration. It will raise some issues of principle and also the practical points on how such references would work in practice and be incorporated into existing agreements. You will be required to look at the topic from several viewpoints.

Before starting this case you should have some prior knowledge of:

1 collective agreements; their structure and content;
2 the methods available for third party intervention to resolve disputes and outstanding questions;
3 the detail and possible variations in arbitration clauses;
4 pendulum arbitration; its use and possible benefits;
5 the similarities and differences of approach to arbitration by various groups, within an organisation.

well and industrial relations are considered to be very healthy.

The need has now arisen for these agreements to be improved. Recently there have been one or two incidents that have not been resolved by the procedures and have only been finally resolved with a great deal of hard work. The suggestion has been made that the agreements need a final stage adding that allows for third party intervention. Both management and unions have agreed on the principle of the need to incorporate such a change and in particular that some form of arbitration should be used. The next stage is to work out the exact means of achieving this. The current state of play is that both sides have gone away to think out their respective positions on the proposal. On this page and page 324 are the suggestions that have been formulated, but none of the groups that are being consulted have put their proposals up for discussion yet.

SHOP WORKERS' UNION

South-East District Office

4th February 19--

Mr P Brandwell
Brandwell Grocery Co
High Street
ROCHESTER

Dear Sir

Please find below our suggestions for a scheme of arbitration that could be included in the agreements we have with you.

1 Arbitration can be triggered off at any time when it is apparent that no further progress can be made, ie, a failure to agree has been registered.

2 Any settlement is entirely voluntary. The arbitrator's recommendations can be accepted, amended or rejected.

3 There can be an application for arbitration by either side where it appears to that side that no progress is being made.

4 The choice of arbitrator is to be agreed jointly.

5 The statements of case are to be submitted to the arbitrator first and then exchanged when he/she has received both statements.

6 There is to be a maximum time limit of three weeks between a reference to arbitration and the receipt of the arbitrator's report.

7 No legal representation is allowed by either side and only one advisor per side. Those entitled to attend are those who represented the sides at the last stage prior to the reference to arbitration.

8 The arbitrator's report can be published to all interested parties.

9 Both sides are bound to co-operate with the arbitrator, to meet him/her, make submissions and to be questioned.

Your faithfully

M Porter
Shop Steward

Shop Workers' Union

1 Arbitration can be triggered off at any time when it is apparent that no further progress can be made, i.e., a failure to agree has been registered.

2 Any settlement is entirely voluntary. The arbitrator's recommendations can be accepted, amended or rejected.

3 There can be an application for arbitration by either side where it appears to that side that no progress is being made.

4 The choice of arbitrator is to be agreed jointly.

5 The statements of case are to be submitted to the arbitrator first and then exchanged when he/she has received both statements.

6 There is to be a maximum time limit of three weeks between a reference to arbitration and the receipt of the arbitrator's report.

7 No legal representation is allowed by either side and only one adviser per side. Those entitled to attend are those who represented the sides at the last stage prior to the reference to arbitration.

8 The arbitrator's report can be published to all interested parties.

9 Both sides are bound to cooperate with the arbitrator, to meet him/her, make submissions and to be questioned.

Supervisors and Store Managers

1 A reference to arbitration should be the last stage in the procedure, when all other stages are exhausted.

2 Any settlement is to be agreed by both sides, based on the recommendations made by the arbitrator.

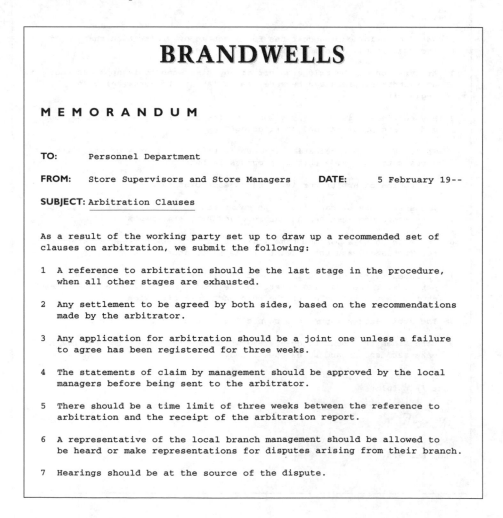

BRANDWELLS

MEMORANDUM

TO: Personnel Department

FROM: Store Supervisors and Store Managers   **DATE:**   5 February 19--

SUBJECT: Arbitration Clauses

As a result of the working party set up to draw up a recommended set of clauses on arbitration, we submit the following:

1 A reference to arbitration should be the last stage in the procedure, when all other stages are exhausted.

2 Any settlement to be agreed by both sides, based on the recommendations made by the arbitrator.

3 Any application for arbitration should be a joint one unless a failure to agree has been registered for three weeks.

4 The statements of claim by management should be approved by the local managers before being sent to the arbitrator.

5 There should be a time limit of three weeks between the reference to arbitration and the receipt of the arbitration report.

6 A representative of the local branch management should be allowed to be heard or make representations for disputes arising from their branch.

7 Hearings should be at the source of the dispute.

3 Any application for arbitration should be a joint one unless a failure to agree has been registered for three weeks.

4 The statements of claim by management should be approved by the local managers before being sent to the arbitrator.

5 There should be a time limit of three weeks between the reference to arbitration and the receipt of the arbitration report.

6 A representative of the local branch management should be allowed to be heard or make representations for disputes arising from the branch involved.

7 Hearings should be at the source of the dispute.

Head Office Management/Personnel Department

1 The reference to arbitration should be made only when all the stages of the relevant procedure have been exhausted, and a final failure to agree has been registered.

2 The award of the arbitrator is fully binding on both sides, without amendment.

3 Applications for arbitration shall be made jointly.

4 The arbitrator shall be chosen from a list supplied by the Institute of Arbitrators and that person be approached to act.

5 Statements of case to be exchanged before submission to the arbitrator.

6 There is always a need for flexibility and no time limits will be imposed unless jointly agreed between both sides.

7 Either side is entitled to be represented by whom they wish at the hearing.

8 The final award will not be published to anyone except those directly concerned.

9 Attached to the clause on reference to arbitration is a clause that no industrial action will be taken while the matter is still under consideration. Any such action will cease while the matter is under reference.

10 The hearing shall be held at Head Office.

Personnel Adviser's Suggestion

An internal report from a personnel specialist has recommended that agreement be sought on the following points:

1 when arbitration should be used and at what stage;

2 whether the settlement is binding or not; and if the recommendations can be the subject of further negotiation;

3 who can make application for arbitration;

4 how the arbitrator will be chosen;

5 if statements of claim are to be exchanged and when;

6 any time limits;

7 the right of representation;

8 the publication of the arbitrator's report and its circulation.

In addition the adviser had also suggested that the sides might wish to consider the use of pendulum arbitration. (This is where there is a normal reference to arbitration but the statements of claim are the basis of the recommendation by the arbitrator. The function of the arbitrator is to choose between the two statements but without amendment. Hence the award will be to accept the statement of either one or other side.)

Individual exercise

The three sets of proposals have been sent to you at the Institute of Arbitrators. As an industrial relations adviser, critically appraise the proposals and send a report to all three parties on the form and content that the arbitration clause/agreement should take. Provide the reasoning behind your recommendations. Provide an alternative report on the use of pendulum arbitration.

Group exercises

1 In three separate groups examine the three sets of proposals. Amend the proposals, as the group sees fit, to provide an acceptable set of proposals for that section in the company.

2 After the period of preparation in 1, form a negotiating committee and attempt to reach agreement on the arbitration clauses that could be used

in this situation. As you reach agreement on a clause, make a written record of it. Ensure there is agreement on the written clause.

3 Consider, in detail, the proposal for pendulum arbitration. Draw up a separate arbitration agreement based on pendulum arbitration. Again this can be a negotiation exercise, as in **2**, with each side preparing their case beforehand.

4 Use the arbitration agreement you have drawn up to resolve the disputes in Cases 11, 8, 9 or 15. Use the facts of the case:
  (a) to draw up agreed terms of reference;
  (b) for each side to make a statement of claim;
  (c) to make any representations allowed under the agreement.
Finally acting as arbitrator, issue findings on the case.

Case 6
Technology agreement

Analysis

With the rapid changes that are taking place in most organisations there is a need for a framework within which change can take place. One of the effects of technological change is that job content and methods are altered, often radically. There is always the fear that old skills will be displaced and with this the people that possess them. In order to ensure a smooth transition during a period of change an agreement will help resolve the problems by providing a framework within which they can be solved. This case introduces a procedural agreement whereby the decision to implement technological change is made subject to negotiation and joint agreement.

Introduction

From a set of proposals you will be required to negotiate a technology agreement. It takes the form of a procedural agreement which can be used in the future when any such changes are proposed. It is not expected that the detailed implications of a particular change are worked out but the agreement will provide a framework within which this can happen.

Background knowledge

In this case you will be negotiating an agreement that can be used when change is taking place within an organisation due to an application of technology.

Before starting this case you should have some prior knowledge of:

1 preparing for negotiations and taking part in them;
2 the effects and implications of technological change within an organisation, including job security, job design, organisation, health and safety and training;
3 the management of change;
4 the various views held by different parties on the last two issues;
5 policies and procedures on consultations, disclosure of information and decision making.

Management proposals

Aim

The company and union recognise that to ensure the efficiency and prosperity of the industry the most effective systems and equipment should be used with the aim of securing the future of the organisation and its employees.

Procedure

1 The company will use this procedure while new equipment is being introduced to achieve a smooth transition.
2 The company agrees to discuss matters relevant to the introduction of new systems and equipment, including working methods, staff levels and training.
3 The company will supply such information as appears necessary to keep employees informed of the systems and equipment to be installed.
4 The company will appraise the unions of changes at the regular meetings that are currently held.

Issues

1 *Job security* as far as possible the company will ensure that overall no job loss will ensue as a result of technological change.
2 *Redeployment* as far as possible employees will be offered redeployment elsewhere in the company if their current job is no longer required as a result of technological change.
3 *Redundancy* the company will offer voluntary redundancy to those who cannot be redeployed or to those who request redundancy.
4 *Job descriptions* all new jobs will be evaluated and the new terms and conditions will apply to the employees employed in the new positions. Any changes to existing job descriptions will be discussed with the individuals concerned.
5 *Health and safety* the health and safety aspects can be made the subject of a joint management/safety representative inspection when the equipment has been installed (as allowed for in the Safety Representatives and Safety Committees Regulations).
6 *Training* such training as is necessary will be provided by the company.
7 *Rewards* the pay of those operating the new systems and equipment will be reviewed in accordance with the current wage review system.

Union proposals

Aim

The company and union recognise that to ensure the efficiency and prosperity of the industry the most effective systems and equipment should be used with the aim of providing job opportunities, higher rewards and improved terms and conditions.

Procedure

1 The company will not introduce any new systems or equipment without first having exhausted this procedure.
2 The company will negotiate all relevant matters prior to the introduction of new systems and equipment including workloads, working methods, human resources levels, staffing arrangements, training, career progression and development, redeployment, changes in the terms and conditions of employment and compensation for any changes resulting.
3 Full information should be given by management to the union, prior to any decision to buy being made, to enable the union to fully appraise the situation. Information to comply with the requirements of Section 17 of the Employment Protection Act 1975 and the Code of Practice on the Disclosure of Information.
4 A joint union/management committee is to be set up to deal with the implications of all specific changes in systems and equipment to fully evaluate such changes in detail.

Issues

1 *Job security* there will be no overall loss of jobs as a result of technological change.
2 *Redeployment* any employee whose job is no longer required as a result of technological change shall be offered redeployment in the company with no loss of status and shall be given retraining where necessary.
3 *Redundancy* there must be a minimum of redundancies. Any that occur must be entirely voluntary with payments in excess of the statutory minimum.

4 *Job descriptions*   all new jobs must be jointly evaluated between union and management (*see* Clause 4 of the procedure). Any changes to existing jobs to be re-evaluated with no loss of status to the individual performing that job.

5 *Health and safety*   all aspects of health and safety to be fully discussed at the safety committee prior to any changes (as noted in the Safety Representatives Regulations and the Code of Practice).

6 *Training*   a training programme will be agreed between union and management. All those on training will suffer no loss of earnings during training or retraining.

7 *Rewards*   the benefits arising from the use of new systems and equipment will be shared between the company and employees. There should be a planned movement towards a shorter working week, longer holidays and a lower retirement age.

Exercises

1 Initially the union side and management side should meet separately to study their briefs. The proposals given can be added to, deleted or amended. At the preparation stage the arguments in favour of and against the proposals should be thought out.

2 After a suitable period of preparation the two sides should meet to discuss the proposals with a view to reaching an agreement. Preferably treat these negotiations more as a discussion on common ground rather than it being a conflict situation. As you progress agree on the wording of each clause, which should be recorded. In conclusion draft a final agreement based on the clauses recorded.

3 Use your final agreement as a basis for solving Case 15, Redundancy at Toolcraft.

Case 7

Negotiating a disciplinary procedure

Analysis

One aspect of day-to-day industrial relations that is of great importance is the need to deal with people fairly and consistently in matters of discipline. Many disputes are caused because disciplinary action has been taken against someone that is seen as unfair, discriminatory or victimising. The lack of a procedure leads to arbitrary decision making and inconsistency. In order to handle discipline in an orderly manner it is good practice to utilise a procedure agreed to and known by everyone. This eliminates possible arguments about the consequences of certain behaviour and the way in which employees are disciplined. On the other hand, procedures should not be so rigid that they do not allow some discretion. If the rules are written as 'musts' then they have to be applied no matter what the circumstances are and that can also lead to problems.

Union proposals

Preamble

This agreement is to be used in all cases where

Background knowledge

As disciplinary action may lead to dismissal then such action is linked inextricably to the law relating to unfair dismissal. The basic law is quite simple and straightforward. Disciplinary action is an everyday matter of industrial relations and all cases need handling with care, not least because a badly handled case might lead to a dispute and legal proceedings.

Before starting this case you should have some prior knowledge of:

1 the process of negotiating an agreement;
2 the preparatory stages prior to negotiations commencing;
3 the use of procedural agreements;
4 the law relating to unfair dismissal;
5 the Code of Practice on Disciplinary Practice and Procedures in Employment.

disciplinary action is to be taken against employees. The object of the agreement is to provide a fair and uniform procedure for dealing with all disciplinary matters.

Procedure

It is agreed that:
1 the issue will be resolved at the lowest possible level;
2 each stage will be completed as soon as possible, compatible with thorough investigation;
3 an employee has the right to be accompanied by a shop steward at all times;
4 at all stages an employee, against whom disciplinary action is being taken, has the right to appeal against that action. During the period of the appeal the action will be suspended. The appeal will be heard by a senior manager not previously involved;
5 a written record of each stage will be made, but only signed by an employee where it is an agreed record;
6 the union reserves the right to take whatever industrial action it considers appropriate at any time;

7 the union reserves the right to suspend this agreement at any time or to amend it by giving one month's notice.

Stages

Stage 1

If the employee has committed a proven minor offence, the employee's immediate superior will issue a verbal warning, but only after the employee has stated his/her case.

Stage 2

If an employee has received a verbal warning within the last month and has committed a further, proven minor offence, the departmental manager will issue a written warning.

Stage 3

If an employee has received a written warning within the last month and has committed a further, proven minor offence, the director responsible will issue a final warning.

Stage 4

If an employee has committed an act of gross misconduct or has received a final written warning within the last month and has committed a further, proven minor offence, the Chief Executive may, in extreme circumstances, dismiss or suspend the employee.

Management proposals

Preamble

This agreement is to be used in all cases where disciplinary action is to be taken against an employee. The object of the agreement is to provide a fair and uniform procedure for dealing with all disciplinary matters.

Procedure

It is agreed that:

1 the issue is to be resolved at the lowest possible level;

2 the issue is to be resolved within three working days;

3 an employee can be accompanied by a person of their choice, if they so wish;

4 at all stages an employee, against whom disciplinary action is to be taken, can appeal against that action;

5 a written record of each stage will be made by management and a copy sent to the employee. A signature will be required signifying they have received the warning;

6 while the matter is still within procedure no industrial action will be taken by either side;

7 this agreement can only be suspended by management giving six months' notice or amended by giving three months' notice.

Stages

Stage 1

If the incident is a minor offence and the employee has no previous warnings, the employee's immediate superior will interview him/her. The superior will then issue a verbal warning.

Stage 2

If the employee commits a further minor offence and has already received a verbal warning, the employee will be interviewed by their departmental manager. The manager will issue a written warning.

Stage 3

If an employee commits a minor offence and has already received a written warning, the employee will be interviewed by their director. The director will then issue a final warning.

Stage 4

For incidents of gross misconduct or where an employee commits a minor offence and has already had a final written warning issued against them, the employee will be interviewed by the Chief Executive. The employee will then be summarily dismissed.

Agreed notes

Offences

Gross misconduct	Minor offences
drunkenness	persistent lateness
fighting	poor attendance
theft	unacceptable quality
fraud	of work
sexual impropriety	incompetence
clocking in another	insubordination
person	unsafe working
	practices

For all alleged incidents of gross misconduct an employee will be suspended until the offence has been investigated and Stage 4 of the procedure can be organised.

Exercises

1 In two separate groups examine the proposals as either management or union representatives. The proposals can be amended, added to or deleted as the groups see fit. Prior to negotiation work out your strategy, the arguments you will employ, the points you wish to secure and the ones you are prepared to trade. Look for possible compromises that may be necessary.

2 After a period of preparation the teams should meet for negotiation. Each side should present their case and then discussion should be opened on the points raised. You should assign roles, such as spokesperson and secretary. As progress is made, agree the exact wording of the clauses and make a precise record. As a final stage agree the final wording of the whole agreement.

3 The procedure that you have finally negotiated can be used to resolve the disciplinary or dismissal situations in Cases 3 and 10.

Case 8
The mushrooming problem

Analysis

Frequently disputes are not straightforward, especially where the dispute is not confined only to one issue. More often the source of a dispute is a mixture of different issues and there is one final incident that precipitates the dispute. The difficulty in resolving these situations is knowing which of the many issues needs solving to restore normal relations. Indeed the major issue may change during the course of the dispute and the original cause may be forgotten altogether! The important lesson to be learnt from these situations is to deal with the issues quickly and decisively as they occur and to invoke procedures as soon as possible to solve them rather than leave the issues to fester. Inevitably problems that are left unattended become bigger rather than smaller and the minor soon becomes major. The following case relates to a situation in which this has happened and finding a solution may not be easy.

The Hertford Chemical Co

In its 12-year history the Hertford Chemical Co has built up a reputation as a supplier of chemicals to a range of manufacturers, mainly synthetic resins and bases for other chemical products. This reputation has been built on technical expertise and the ability to supply highly complex chemicals in large quantities. Out of the 120 employees ten are employed purely on development work with others involved in pilot plant work and transferring new formulations to the plant. On the main manufacturing plant there are 32 operatives split between four shifts, each headed by a shift supervisor. The plant works seven days a week, 48 weeks a year. The shifts of eight operatives

are split between two buildings with each group of four being headed by a section leader. The plant consists of a number of reaction vessels and mixing tanks with a complex of pipes, pumps, filters, by-passes, meters and other items of a typical chemical plant. Not all the vessels and tanks are used all the time as many of them are

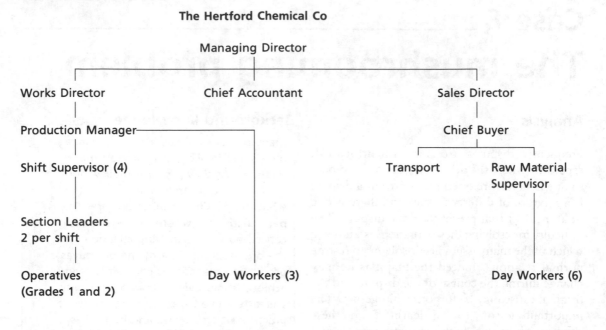

The Hertford Chemical Co

Managing Director

Works Director   Chief Accountant   Sales Director

Production Manager   Chief Buyer

Shift Supervisor (4)   Transport   Raw Material
                                                               Supervisor

Section Leaders
2 per shift

Operatives   Day Workers (3)   Day Workers (6)
(Grades 1 and 2)

suited only to the production of particular products.

Organisation

The organisation of the plant has grown in rather a haphazard manner with changes being made to suit the prevailing circumstances. The current situation is that the operatives have been trained (in the loose sense of the word) on certain items of plant and they stick to these, almost possessively. The operators and section leaders in the two buildings tend to be separate and, although they are next door to each other, there is little or no transfer of labour between the two. There is some logic to this in that the products are specific to the various items of plant and each operator builds up some expertise in the products made and in the operation of the plant.

For the ancillary operations on the plant, such as raw material delivery, product removal, cleaning and similar duties, there is a day team of six workers who carry out these functions during normal working hours (7.30 am to 4.30 pm) with a considerable amount of overtime worked to keep the plant serviced and to supplement income. The removal of solid products is wholly performed by a team of three men. They work normal day hours and much overtime during the week and at weekends. With the unpredictable nature of timing the completion of batches, planning their activities is very difficult. Between off-loading finished product from the plant they help with other ancillary duties.

Collective bargaining

The plant is unionised and while there is not a closed shop some 95 per cent of operatives are in the union. The supervisors are in a separate, staff union. Formal procedures are evolving but generally industrial relations are conducted 'by the seat of the pants' with each situation taken as it arises. Annual pay negotiations take place between the union officials and management but little else is negotiated formally. Generally, relations are quite good considering the industry and while the company has been expanding there have been few traumatic experiences.

Pay

The basic pay rates are quite low but earnings

are boosted with shift premiums and overtime. With the nature of the shifts everyone does some overtime as the basic working week is 39 hours and the average working week is 42 hours. The day workers' rates are also low but again they boost their earnings with regular overtime, both mid-week and at weekends. Overtime rates are time and one-third during the week, time and a half Saturday and double time Sunday and statutory holidays.

Conditions

The work itself is dirty and smelly and can involve some hard physical labour, especially when things go wrong. There is also an element of danger as most of the chemicals used are dangerous (some highly poisonous) and the reactions in the vessels are performed at high temperatures and can be violent. At other times it can be boring, for example when a batch of material is mixing, and this may go on for several hours with relatively little to do. The work also involves some technical knowledge in testing the product during manufacture which is carried out by the operatives.

Secret plans

Unknown to the shop floor or their union representatives, the Works Manager had instituted a drive to improve productivity. This included an improvement in labour productivity which he saw as being low due to a number of factors.

Primarily he was looking to change the patterns of working so that there was a greater degree of flexibility as between the operatives on the shifts, especially between the two buildings, and between the day workers and the shift workers. His fear was that if the present work arrangements became too entrenched it would become increasingly difficult to change the patterns of working. He believed the time was right as the firm was going through a not unfamiliar dip in the order book and, while there

was no threat to jobs, things needed tightening up to lower unit costs.

The prime target for reducing the wage bill was to reduce overtime payments. The total bill for overtime was very high, added to which it was causing productivity to fall because the marginal cost was high, especially with weekend working.

The Works Manager intended to achieve this through a steady, gradual process of minor changes rather than go for an all-out blitz on working practices. Currently he was not revealing his hand to the supervisors, although he would have to work through them. He had spoken about his plans to the Managing Director and to the Production Manager. The first step he had taken was to send a message to the supervisors asking them to ensure that if there was not sufficient work in one building to occupy all the operatives normally employed there, then they must transfer one (or more) operatives into the other building and put them under the charge of the section leader of that building. He asked the supervisors to monitor this by checking the signatures on the work sheets, as these would reveal whether any personnel had been transferred. In the event there were two occasions in the first week when a supervisor did effect a transfer, although notably it was the same supervisor and person on both occasions.

Further edicts

A further step was taken two weeks later. This time the Works Manager asked that where there was spare labour (either because there was no work for that vessel or it was on a long processing time) the operative should be given other duties. These might include loading solid, finished product (normally carried out exclusively by the day workers), loading raw material for another operative who needs some help or other duties that the supervisor might specify. Nothing much happened at first and monitoring this stage was more of a problem, as the supervisors had still not been informed of the reasons behind the moves, nor their cooperation sought. The Works Manager was reluctant to do this as the supervisors still identified themselves with the workforce rather than the management.

Alongside the exercise being carried out in the production unit, the day workers' manager had also been instructed to reduce the levels of overtime worked, both weekdays and weekends. The idea was to reduce the level of planned overtime and to slowly transfer this extra work to the shift workers. As the shift workers were being paid anyway, and there was no case for their numbers to be reduced, this seemed to be an efficient way of increasing productivity. Added to this there had always been more than a suspicion that 'while the cats were away the mice did play'. Supervising these workers outside the normal hours of the day managers had always been a problem. The shift supervisors maintained that their job was to supervise the plant and its operatives, not anyone else. For example, it was suspected that those booked on overtime would leave early and someone else would clock them out or, alternatively, they would be clocked in early on weekend mornings. Also the rate at which these people worked after normal hours was always commented upon as being exceptionally slow.

Something's afoot

Six weeks after the start of the campaign it was obvious to all that something was happening although no one knew quite what, or they kept it quiet. This created a feeling of unease and the union at its recent, unusually well-attended branch meeting, felt that vigilance was required to prevent the terms and conditions of the workforce being worsened by stealth. The shop steward went to see the Works Manager after the meeting but was given the rather bland reply that he was merely doing the job that he had always done and there was nothing to worry about. This did nothing to reassure the workers and the union policy adopted was to look out for any changes to current practice and to resist these, even if this meant a refusal to operate a new practice. The union promised to back anyone subject to disciplinary action as a result of this.

The new employee

Labour turnover at the Hertford Chemical Co is relatively high. The nature of the work and the unsocial hours combine to prompt people to leave for more convivial jobs. As a result of this, recruitment occurs quite frequently and often at very short notice. This has led to a quick hire policy; if they breathe, take them on! Such hasty decisions have seen some people recruited that, on reflection, should not have been taken on.

One person in this category was Stan Jessop. He quickly made his mark on the shift by becoming the loud mouth who made a nuisance of himself to everyone. The supervisors noted this after the first shift and had their suspicions confirmed time and again. The moment the position of shop steward fell vacant he virtually elected himself to it. In the event no one else stood for election, so he was elected unopposed. Secretly the managers were wishing they could fire him but he never quite gave them sufficient grounds to do so, although his standard of work was poor and Stan had high disregard for his supervisor or anyone in authority. He had had a verbal warning against him for persistent lateness but played a canny game and waited until the warning was about to be extinguished before reverting to his former bad habits.

The present weekend had been a busy one. Everything that could go wrong, had virtually happened. The supervisors had been frantically trying to keep the production programme together and a mixture of absences, breakdowns, lack of raw materials and technical difficulties had all combined to make it one of the worst weekends possible. The final problem arose on the Sunday night shift. As a result of the problems encountered over the weekend, the production programme had been revamped because certain equipment was no longer available until Monday morning when the engineers came in. This meant that operators had to be moved around to work on the equipment that was running. The shift supervisor, after taking over from his colleague at 10.00 pm, decided, in consultation with his section leaders, on the allocation of work.

This entailed Stan Jessop being moved from his normal duties to the next building to help them. There was plenty to do and it was agreed that it was best to keep Stan occupied. The supervisor approached Stan tactfully and explained the reasons for the request. This was met with a tirade of abuse and invective, the like of which the supervisor had never heard before (and he had a good command of the English language). It was clear that Stan would not carry out the request! The supervisor then reiterated his instruction and said that, in the event of Stan not doing as requested, the matter would be reported to the Works Manager and would almost certainly lead to disciplinary action. That argument only served to make Stan even more angry and to hurl accusations at the supervisor and management of victimisation. The supervisor walked away and left Stan to calm down and hopefully, after a time of reflection, go to his work. Unfortunately this did not occur. Stan made a round of the other operators and told them about the occurrence. He then returned to the supervisor and requested an emergency union meeting, which was refused.

The supervisor contacted the Production Manager and asked his advice on what to do. The advice was that in the event of Stan refusing to do the work as instructed he should be sent home, suspended on full pay, and told to report to the Works Manager the following morning. In the meantime, the supervisor should write a report on the incident for the Manager to collect in the morning. After receiving this advice the supervisor observed that Stan was still wandering round the plant speaking to anyone who would listen and even to those who did not want to listen. He had a cup of tea with him. This was against company rules, as it is illegal (on a chemical plant). He would not leave the plant when requested and he was trying to induce others to drink tea on the plant by bringing cups out to them. The supervisor spoke to him firmly and demanded he leave the plant and report back in the morning. Stan said he couldn't do that as he had been given a lift in by a colleague. The supervisor said that he would have to stay off the plant all night and could remain in the canteen.

Eventually Stan made his way to the canteen and fell asleep. He left at 6.00 am after the supervisor reminded him to report in later that morning.

The meeting

Stan eventually came in to see the Works Manager at 2.00 pm. By this time the Manager had been able to ascertain most of the facts relating to the previous night's incident and was ready for Stan. The meeting was very curt and bad tempered. When both men had calmed down there was some discussion on the issues after which the Works Manager said that Stan would be suspended on full pay pending a proper disciplinary hearing. Stan said that it would not be necessary. He could represent himself and wanted the present meeting to resolve the issue one way or the other. The meeting carried on and clearly no headway was being made. Stan stuck to the argument that the supervisor had no right to instruct him to do a job he had not been trained for, and it would be a safety risk if nothing else. The Manager said that the supervisor's order was legitimate and Stan should have done as asked. There were frequent asides into the incidents of shouting, abuse, tea drinking, lateness, attitudes and so on but this got neither side anywhere. Finally, at 4.30, the Manager said that if Stan was not prepared to consider another meeting to resolve the issue then the only course of action open to him was to dismiss Stan. At that Stan leapt up, stormed out of the room and was away down to the works. As he was unable to persuade the current shift at work to support him he left the site soon after.

The walk out

At 6.00 the next morning, when Stan's shift returned, Stan was in extra early to see all his colleagues. They were asked, by Stan, to come to a brief meeting in the canteen. The supervisor said they were not to have such a meeting in work time. This was ignored. The outcome of the brief meeting was that the workers said they would walk out in support of Stan and also to protest against the changes that were being made. The Works Manager had come on site extra early, in case there was any trouble, and immediately went in to see the workers before they dispersed. After a tense, short meeting the workers reaffirmed that they would walk out. The Manager said that obviously he could not forcibly make them stay but pointed out the possible consequences of their actions. This again had no effect. Finally the Manager stated that before walking out the workers should go onto the plant to make it safe and to ensure that any reactors currently in-process were not likely to cause a major incident if left unattended (this could well be the case when processing some products). The workers did not heed this request and promptly left the site. The supervisor contacted the Production Manager and others who were available to come in and assist in closing down the plant.

Fortunately the plant was in a condition whereby it could be closed down with little damage being done. At 1.00 pm the Security Officer of the firm who shared the site with Hertford Chemicals reported a small group of workers standing at the bottom of the drive. The Works Manager went to the gatehouse and soon determined that they were the striking workers. He walked down to see them and told them that they could reconsider their decision to strike but if they continued to stay out on strike they were not to remain on company property, particularly if they intended to picket the next shift, due on soon. They were told to leave. However, they did not leave as the entrance to the works was on a main road and clearly picketing was not possible there.

Exercises

1 What action should the firm take:
(a) to stop the picketing;
(b) to avert the industrial action spreading to the other shifts?

2 Convene a meeting between the Works Manager, the Production Manager, the union District Official and a shop steward from another shift. The meeting should consider how the dispute can be resolved.

An addition to this exercise could be that the Managing Director has set as a precondition to a discussion on the issues, that there is an immediate return to work. This is not negotiable.

3 Prepare a brief for the management side on the strengths and weaknesses of their case. Also present the options open to them, the possible outcomes and the points to which they should stick and those on which they should be flexible.

4 Prepare a similar brief for the union side.

5 Act as the conciliator to whom Stan Jessop's claim for unfair dismissal has been sent.

Prepare to meet the two sides and attempt to conciliate a settlement. Have members of your group take on the role of the other actors in this case. They should present their case to you, as conciliator, and you can decide whether to hold a joint meeting or separate meetings of the two sides. Keep in mind that the conciliator is only investigating the dismissal of Stan Jessop. Prepare a brief report on the outcome of the conciliation.

6 At the request of the Managing Director write a confidential report on the state of industrial relations in the firm. In particular he wishes you to analyse the various incidents of the case.

7 Act as an Industrial Tribunal to hear the case of Stan Jessop. (Assume that Stan was finally dismissed.) Role play the actors – Chairperson, employer panel representative, employee panel representative, employer (Hertford Chemical Co manager or solicitor), union official (or solicitor), Stan, his ex-shift supervisor, and anyone else needed as a witness. Arrive at a decision and write the promulgation for the case.

8 The Hertford Chemical Co has never employed a personnel officer until now. Partially as a result of this episode, the firm have employed you as their Personnel Officer. Review the existing industrial relations policies and practices, write a report on your findings and make recommendations.

9 After the dispute was resolved the Managing Director set up a small committee including the Works Manager, the Production Manager and the Personnel Officer to investigate and report on the means of achieving changes in working practices at Hertford Chemical Co. Produce a report that analyses the situation and recommends improvements to the system of management.

Case 9

Custom and practice

Analysis

In industrial relations it is often the small issues that become major which lead to a dispute that is difficult to resolve. To an outsider it seems senseless and pointless that the two sides can fail to agree on what appears to be a matter of insignificant detail. However, the parties to the dispute see it as a matter of principle or it is the small issue that finally 'breaks the camel's back' and merely represents a manifestation of the underlying poor state of industrial relations at a firm. This case is not unique in that it deals with the delicate issue of an alleged entitlement (i.e., extended tea breaks) by a group of employees built up over a period of time, and a manager's determination to alter this traditional custom and practice.

Introduction

The Romiley Manufacturing Co is an old established firm, the major part of whose production is exported. For some time they have been experiencing difficulty in keeping delivery dates. As a result orders have fallen off despite the advantages of a favourable exchange rate. In an effort to improve matters Tony Roberts, an outsider with a reputation for efficiency, was engaged six months ago as Works Manager.

Too long tea breaks

Roberts quickly began to tighten up on systems and practices. New systems of production control and quality control were introduced which, coupled with other changes, began to produce results. One aspect to cause Roberts concern was the length of the morning and afternoon tea breaks. These had been agreed in

Background knowledge

In this case you are required to examine the situation in a small firm where a manager is charged with making radical improvements in the firm's performance. In doing so he challenges some of the practices which the union argue have been established over time and which he counterclaims are in breach of existing agreements. The manner in which the manager tackles the issue helps precipitate a stoppage of work.

Before starting this case you should have some prior knowledge of:

1 the status and application of collective agreements;
2 the effects of custom and practice on these agreements;
3 the management and negotiation of change;
4 the benefits of consultation and agreement.

a signed union/management agreement, twelve years ago, at ten minutes, but had gradually increased to twenty. He was not only concerned about the loss of output this represented, and the effect on the firm's major problem of keeping delivery dates, but also because he saw it as a clear indication that supervision was far too easy going. Roberts firmly believed that supervisors should supervise and that agreements should be kept to the letter.

One day all members of supervision were called to a meeting where Roberts informed them of his intentions to have the tea-break agreement observed. He made it clear that supervisors would be held responsible for bringing their own departments into line as quickly as possible.

Having done his job properly, as he saw it, by first putting supervision in the picture, Roberts

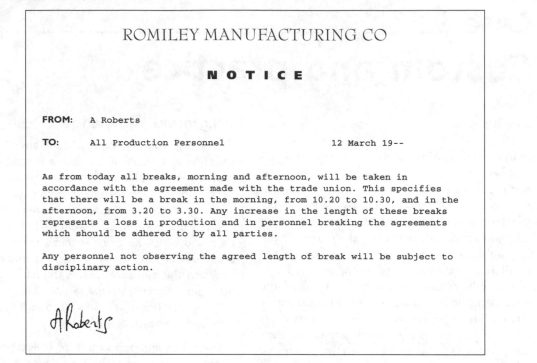

ROMILEY MANUFACTURING CO

N O T I C E

FROM: A Roberts

TO: All Production Personnel   12 March 19--

As from today all breaks, morning and afternoon, will be taken in
accordance with the agreement made with the trade union. This specifies
that there will be a break in the morning, from 10.20 to 10.30, and in the
afternoon, from 3.20 to 3.30. Any increase in the length of these breaks
represents a loss in production and in personnel breaking the agreements
which should be adhered to by all parties.

Any personnel not observing the agreed length of break will be subject to
disciplinary action.

A Roberts

sent for the Works Convenor, Charlie Wilson and informed him of his intentions. Wilson protested that the tea-break facilities were inadequate, and warned that there would probably be trouble. Roberts replied that the shop stewards had never complained or even mentioned the tea-break facilities to him since he joined the firm. He added that if there were aspects of facilities that needed improvement he would be prepared to discuss them, but only after the workers had made every attempt to observe the agreement on the ten minutes.

Simultaneously, at the time of this meeting, notices were posted in the factory informing employees that the agreed ten minutes must be observed and warning that, if necessary, disciplinary action would be taken against offenders (see above).

Shop floor reaction to this notice was immediate. The Works Convenor informed Roberts that unless the notice was withdrawn, there would be a strike. Roberts replied that he was acting within his rights in seeking to apply the agreement and while he hoped it would not be necessary to use disciplinary measures, any action taken would be subject to the agreed

disciplinary procedure. He would not however be party to allowing people to violate agreements, nor be blackmailed into paying them for not working. The strike took place.

Exercises

1 Having gathered the information relating to this incident, as Tony Roberts' immediate superior, carry out an appraisal on Roberts' handling of the affair. Prepare this as a statement to give to Roberts. At the end ask Roberts to see you regarding the matter.

2 As Tony Roberts, you have been summoned to your immediate superior. Prepare some notes on the incident, giving your explanation of what you have done and state how you are prepared to see the dispute settled.

3 Role play the meeting between Roberts and his superior.

4 The union have convened a meeting prior to the negotiating committee meeting. As Charlie Wilson state what you see as the important issues in the dispute and explain your approach to the meeting.

5 In a group, act as a negotiating committee convened to resolve the dispute. Each side should prepare their case in advance and the committee should proceed by:

(a) each side making an opening statement;
(b) identifying the main issues;
(c) making proposals that should lead to a settlement.

6 As a variation, the management side can make a precondition to the negotiations that there is a return to work. Introduce this to the negotiations in **5**.

7 Assuming that the dispute is not resolved by internal negotiation, either individually or in groups, set out the statements of claim to be submitted to an arbitrator by the union side and the management side.

8 Acting as an arbitrator study the statements of claim from each side. Set out the questions you would ask each side and put forward your proposals for a settlement.

9 Alternatively, the groups in **5** can act as union and management respectively and role play the process of conciliation, with one of the group nominated as conciliator.

10 As a personnel consultant, submit a report on how the firm should handle similar change situations and how it should proceed with any further changes it wishes to make.

Case 10
Temper! Temper!

Analysis

One of the functions of management is to employ competent staff that can cope adequately with the job they are employed to perform. Problems arise when it is clear than an employee is not competent and the work of the organisation is suffering as a result. Such people are often held in derision and they lack any authority or credibility. Management then has to decide what to do. Ultimately incompetence is a fair reason for dismissal but the situation has to be handled fairly. The employee needs to be made aware of his/her weaknesses and be told where improvement is necessary. The employee must be given time to improve and the support and help that may be required. The situation is even trickier when the person concerned is a member of management. This case, based on a tribunal case, illustrates this point.

Introduction

Every Thursday morning the managers at the headquarters of Auto Silencer Services meet to discuss various routine matters. The meeting is

Background knowledge

This case deals with a common problem facing many organisations of how to get the best performance from employees and what to do if their performance is not acceptable. The case is not merely about discipline, although that is part of the exercise. It is about how to handle people and how to get the best out of employees. Organisations have a duty to support their employees and encourage them. This is all the more crucial when the employee concerned is a member of management.

Before starting this case you should have some prior knowledge of:

1 recognising and identifying problems relating to the ability of staff performing their jobs to an acceptable standard and acting to effect an improvement;
2 handling these situations and giving the necessary support;
3 disciplinary procedures and action;
4 human relations; individual and group behaviour;
5 unfair dismissal and constructive dismissal.

quite formal and a secretary takes minutes and subsequently issues a report of the meeting, noting agreed action, etc. About 15 managers meet, including at least one director.

Explosion

The meeting planned for the Thursday in question was a routine one, with no unusual items likely to arise. Stephanie King, manager of the Administrative Support Unit was in attendance as usual. The meeting followed its normal path and was about to finish at 11.00 am when the Company Secretary, Alan Carter, interjected with an item. He immediately plunged into what could only be described as a tirade of criticism aimed personally at Ms King. He stated that the administrative staff were poorly managed and that he was deeply concerned that the company could no longer carry on without a radical change within the Unit. The blame, he said, lay wholly and completely with Ms King and if she could not cope with the job of Unit Manager then the company would have to think about her future with the firm. Mr Carter gave one or two examples of blunders that had occurred and spelt out the consequences of these in graphic terms. Finally, he said that he had to bring this up at the meeting because that morning two of the staff from Ms King's Unit had been to see him. The gist of their complaint was that they were no longer able to work in the Unit because of the bad feeling, backbiting, bickering and lack of discipline in the Unit. When pressed by Alan Carter to elucidate the two said that there had been a vote of no confidence in Ms King and it was a matter of 'she goes or we go'.

This attack on Ms King was entirely without precedent and out of character for the meeting to even raise such questions. The meeting was stunned into silence and nobody tried to stop Alan Carter. Eventually Ms King, desperately trying to maintain her composure, left the room. After the incident there were murmurings that it was not before time and that someone was bound to have said something sooner or later.

---

20 March 19--

Company Secretary
Auto Silencer Services
Broad Street
Darston

Dear Mr Carter

After the meeting this morning at which you carried out a most pernicious attack on me personally, I am writing to resign my position at Auto Silencer with effect from today. You have made it clear that you no longer consider me competent and have no faith in my performing the job adequately. Needless to say, I am most upset at the occurrence, what was said and the way you handled the situation. I would have thought that after 18 years of loyal service I was due better treatment.

I would be grateful if you would calculate the earnings due to me and forward them to me.

Your sincerely

S King

S King

Aftermath

Later that day Ms King delivered a short, rather pungent note to the Company Secretary. She did not turn up for work the next day but sent a curt message that she felt ill and would be away (see p. 340).

That same Friday Alan Carter had a meeting with the Personnel Director. They discussed the situation relating to Ms King. They decided that the attack on Ms King had been somewhat unwarranted and the matter had not been handled as it should have been. There was some friction between the two because there had been no prior consultation on what ought to be done about the situation. Ms King was regarded as an expert on the new office technology and finding a replacement would be difficult. Clearly her problems were staff management ones but not technical.

The outcome was that a letter was written to Ms King (see p. 341).

Return to work

The following Monday, after receiving the letter, Ms King returned to work and tried to carry on as normal. Nothing was said to her directly but the atmosphere was strained and unnatural. Things gradually returned to their previous position and the department settled down. Ms

AUTO SILENCER SERVICES
Broad Street, Darston

```
25 March 19--


Ms S King
20 Pintail Avenue
Darston


Dear Ms King

We are in receipt of your letter of 20 March and we have discussed the
situation regarding your continued employment with us. We accept that
in part we are to blame for the difficulties and we are not prepared
to accept your resignation.

However, we believe that there are some matters which we need to discuss
with you regarding your performance in the job. Overall, we are satisfied
with the work you produce. The main criticism made related to your handling
of staff and we will be looking for an improvement in this area. If there
is any way in which we can help we will be most willing to provide this.
We wish to monitor your progress in this area in the future, and will
review the situation after six weeks.

Would you please contact us at your earliest opportunity so you can start
back with us as soon as possible. Look forward to seeing you soon.

Yours sincerely

A. Carter

A Carter
Company Secretary
```

King resolved to try much harder with her relationships within the department and was cautious not to be seen to be victimising anyone whom she suspected had caused the trouble. After the six-week period mentioned in the letter she tried to book an appointment with Alan Carter and was told by his secretary that she would try to get a meeting arranged but that Mr Carter was very busy at that time as it was the financial year end. Ms King contacted the personnel department to arrange an appointment to see the Personnel Director. She was told that he was away on a course for the next month.

On the Thursday of that week Ms King was unable to attend the weekly meeting and sent a deputy in her place. Alan Carter took the opportunity to quiz the deputy on how things were in the Administrative Support Unit. He was told that things had not improved and if anything matters were getting worse. Several staff felt that they would be unable to continue to work in the Unit if Ms King remained in the post. She was still verbally insulting to staff, short-tempered if things went wrong, unable to explain the technicalities of the equipment to others and generally made life unbearable. The members of the meeting murmured that Ms King was clearly unable to supervise and there was an air of resignation that things were unlikely to improve. No decision was taken as the meeting did not handle such matters.

Head office was always a busy place but was currently under extreme pressure due to the need to produce the annual report. The Administrative Services Unit supplied much of the information for the report and hence felt the pressure. Ms King in particular set very high standards and felt that she had to produce the necessary information accurately and quickly. If this did not happen she tended to berate her staff and often lost her temper. The next Monday morning proved to be the final straw. An office junior, who had been with the company for only a short time, was processing some information on a word processor and pressed the wrong key. This cleared all the information from the computer which was needed urgently for another document. It was impossible for the staff to cover for this mistake even by rallying round and doing the work before Ms King found out.

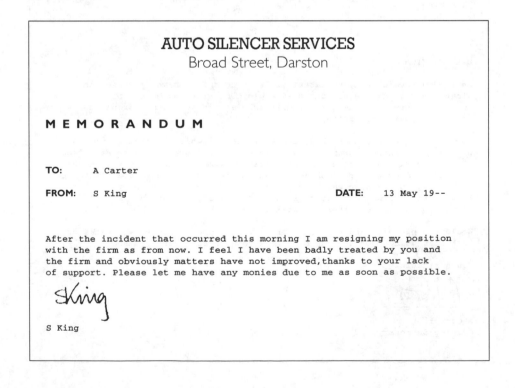

AUTO SILENCER SERVICES
Broad Street, Darston

MEMORANDUM

TO: A Carter

FROM: S King   DATE: 13 May 19--

After the incident that occurred this morning I am resigning my position with the firm as from now. I feel I have been badly treated by you and the firm and obviously matters have not improved, thanks to your lack of support. Please let me have any monies due to me as soon as possible.

SKing

S King

Frayed tempers

When Ms King found out she lost her temper. The young office worker was rounded on for being incompetent and for having wasted so much time. Before long the girl burst into tears but this did not stop the tirade from Ms King. One of the older ladies in the office approached Ms King and exhorted her to stop shouting and allow the girl to leave and recover. This had the effect of making Ms King more angry and the older lady was told to get out of the office and stop interfering. Within one minute the whole office was empty and a delegation went to see Alan Carter. The rest of the employees from the Administrative Section went to the canteen.

Having realised that she had gone too far and there was no way she could continue with the firm, Ms King swiftly wrote a letter of resignation and left it in the internal mail tray (see p. 342). She then left by a rear exit and went home.

When the letter of resignation reached the Company Secretary he immediately wrote to Ms King to accept her resignation and to say that her entitlements would be calculated and sent directly to her bank. This placated the still-angry employees from the Unit and they returned to work.

One week later the Managing Director received a formal letter from Ms King outlining that she had taken legal advice and was claiming constructive dismissal (see below).

Exercises

1 Write a letter from the Managing Director in reply to Ms King's letter.

2 As Ms King's legal adviser, set out what she will have

```
20 May 19--


Company Secretary
Auto Silencer Services
Broad Street
Darston


Dear Sir

Subsequent to my note of resignation and your reply accepting my
resignation, I am writing to inform you that I have taken legal
advice and have been advised that I have a case to claim constructive
dismissal. You will be receiving a formal notification from the
Industrial Tribunals.

The basis of my claim is that the firm did not give me sufficient
support in my duties and whilst certain problems had been highlighted,
nothing was done to help me. I was promised support but none was
forthcoming and even the review that was promised did not take place
because everyone was too busy. This made the situation completely
untenable and I felt I had to leave.

I am still awaiting the monies due to me and would ask that these are
forwarded immediately.

Yours faithfully

S King

S King
```

to do next to pursue her claim, given that the firm is not prepared to settle out of court. Assess the strength of her case and what evidence would be needed to prove her case.

3 Assuming that the claim is being taken to a tribunal hearing, as Personnel Director prepare the case on behalf of the firm. What would be the grounds for defence? What evidence would you collect and use?

4 Acting as the tribunal chairperson, using the information from Exercises **2** and **3**, or by providing your

own, decide the case. Write a promulgation for the case, giving the reasons for your decision.

5 As a Personnel Officer you have been tasked with producing a report on the incident for the next management meeting. Analyse the possible mistakes that the firm made in handling this situation. Suggest what the firm should have done to prevent the situation developing as it did. What changes would you recommend that the firm make to their systems to improve the situation, with particular reference to personnel policies?

Case 11
Strangers at work

Analysis

A problem that has always existed with the operation of the closed shop is that of the person or group who, because of their beliefs, refuse to join a union. The problem can become intractable because each side sticks to a point of principle. The union believes in the principle of unity and solidarity and the objectors in the principle of their (frequently religious) beliefs and individual freedom. This case examines the situation where there is a racial group which, because of its beliefs, objects to joining a union. Added to this there is the difficulty that arises in a multi-racial workforce where the cultural differences which exist between groups can lead to problems. It also raises the question of the role of management in these delicate situations, where they are not a party to the grievance but are affected by it.

The company

The Metal Fastener Group is a West Midlands based firm that manufactures a range of fasteners

such as specialist nuts, bolts, rivets, washers and screws. It is a typical firm for the area, employing 150 people of various ethnic origins. The firm has been very open in its recruitment of these groups and has enjoyed good relations with the ethnic communities both in the firm and outside. There has been little trouble in the firm as a result of employing quite a large number of Asians. The Personnel Officer has made particular efforts to ensure that this has been the case. As is often the case, communications have been given especial attention to the extent that some company documents are available to the Asians in their mother tongue. On the face of it, relations between work groups have been reasonable but the Asian workers have preferred to stay with each other rather than integrate. This has meant that the work groups are often all-Asian or all-white. This has not offended anyone and operations have not been affected.

The company's trading position is quite healthy but there is little potential for expansion. The industry is not expanding and the firm has to work on retaining its customers in the face of growing competition. So far there have not been

Background knowledge

This case examines two areas of industrial relations that are fraught with danger and difficulty – the closed shop and racial discrimination. These two areas touch on the fundamental aspects of relations in the workplace both in terms of the individual and the group. Because of the nature of these topics any problems that arise are frequently very difficult to resolve as both sides have very strong views on them, often backed by strong principles. Nevertheless, with careful handling such situations can be successfully resolved to everyone's satisfaction.

Before starting this case you should have some prior knowledge of:

1 the formation and operation of a closed shop;
2 the legal aspects of the closed shop and its relationship to unfair dismissal;
3 racial discrimination at work (direct and indirect);
4 the procedures to deal with claims for a closed shop;
5 the skills necessary to handle sensitive situations;
6 the Code of Practice for the Elimination of Racial Discrimination.

any redundancies but some positions have been left vacant and some natural wastage has occurred. In order to maintain its competitiveness the firm has instituted a number of cost cutting exercises. This has included an examination of labour costs. One way in which the firm has kept these costs down is by employing immigrant workers at wage rates that are considered to be low for the area, though not for the trade. Other local firms, especially in other trades, are able to offer higher wages and some skilled labour has been lost because of this.

Trade union membership

As with most metal fabrication organisations, trade unionism in the firm is strong. The Engineering Union has traditionally recruited in the firm and the level of union membership has been around 60 per cent on the shop floor. In recent times there has been a slight fall in this proportion. Recently, in moves to expand union membership, the union centrally has instituted a campaign for closed shops or 100 per cent membership. The union committee at Metal Fasteners is currently strong and wishes to respond positively to the policy statements of the union. Being aware of the possibility of the need for union protection in what may be difficult times ahead, the union officers within the firm have started a recruitment drive. This has yielded results and the level of membership has risen. Having seen the results of this, a recent branch meeting passed a motion to seek a closed shop agreement for the production departments.

The Asian workers have been approached and, after a discussion on the meaning of a closed shop, the group as a whole have refused to join the union. This had led to a number of informal discussions with the Asians but no headway has been made. The Asians have taken the matter up with their leaders in the community and they have been advised that it would be against their religion to join a union. At the present time the subject has become a source of friction and neither side is openly discussing the issue.

In order to maintain the momentum of the recruitment drive, and in spite of the Asians' refusal to join, the union have had a meeting with management at which they have officially requested a closed shop. Management asked if the union officials knew what the position of the Asian workers was with respect to joining a trade union. They said that the Asians had been approached and there had been a refusal but this did not in any way constitute a block to the union's proposal being made and implemented. The union said that the Asians were a part of the workforce and there was no objection to their presence but the union wished to pursue a policy of 100 per cent membership through the closed shop. However, both sides admitted that the refusal of the Asians to join a union was a problem that needed to be solved. The overall response of the management to the proposal of a closed shop was lukewarm as they did not see the necessity of a formal union membership agreement when the level of union membership was already very high. The firm has always actively encouraged union membership and has given the union a free hand in its recruitment activities. The union's closing statement was that they intended to pursue the matter of the closed shop with vigour and were not prepared to renege on the principles involved, namely full union membership.

The problem grows

The managers in the production departments took some informal soundings amongst the Asian groups. The story they were told was somewhat different to the one they had heard at the meeting. The Asians related stories of harassment and pressure, especially upon the younger Asians. They were concerned that they were being pressurised and had come to the conclusion that the closed shop was a means that the 'white' workers were employing to get rid of the Asian workers and to replace them with non-Asians. This seemed to be the case now that unemployment was a problem in the area. When challenged on why they had not raised this with the managers or supervision, the Asians said they did not think they would be given a fair hearing from the managers who were all white.

At the next union/management meeting the issue of the closed shop was raised and the managers gave evidence of the undue pressure they felt was being put on the Asians. There was concern that the good relations that the firm had had with the Asian community were being harmed and that they could not afford to lose 24 trained workers just for the sake of a closed shop. The union replied that they had not officially sanctioned or even suggested any action against the Asians. They wished that the matter be resolved through the channels of negotiation. However, they were not prepared to retract their claim for a closed shop and wished to press the claim.

The District Officer of the union had been contacted and he supported their claim for a closed shop. He was concerned though that the issue of the Asians refusing to join did not become a matter for media attention as this would lead to bad publicity for the union. The reports of the pressure, particularly the harassment, was not helpful to the union's cause and could lead to the closed shop issue being lost.

The problem finally explodes

The matter was never to be resolved in an orderly manner. The day after the union/management meeting an Asian was told by one of the protagonists for the closed shop (but not a union official) to go to the stores for a 'long weight'. The Asian, after being told by the storekeeper to await the item, returned to the shop floor after one hour. His supervisor, not knowing what was going on, reprimanded the Asian and warned him that to leave the shop floor for such a long time without permission could lead to disciplinary action. The Asian immediately saw this as yet another act to get rid of his people from the firm. The irate Asian went up to the person who had sent him to the stores and started to row with him. The consequence was that there was a brawl in which blows were exchanged. The fight was broken up and both men were taken to the Works Manager's office.

Exercises

1 What action should the Works Manager take against the two men who had been fighting?

2 As the Works Manager, make a report to the Managing Director on your recommendations on the outstanding issue of the closed shop, giving the reasons for your recommendations.

3 If you were the Personnel Officer referred to, what would your recommendations be in terms of:
  (a) the closed shop request;
  (b) restoring and improving race relations within the firm;
  (c) the disciplinary action against the two men.

4 The District Officer is informed of the incident and

that one of his members is to be disciplined as a result. What advice would you give to the local union officials at the Metal Fastener Group:

(a) regarding the claim for a closed shop;
(b) to improve relations between the union and the Asians;
(c) regarding the disciplinary action.

5 Discuss the manner in which the firm handled the situation, particularly with respect to race relations. What are the good points, the areas in which improvements could be made and the means that could have been employed to have avoided the incident? Do you have any recommendations for a practicable compromise to resolve the problems at the firm?

6 Assuming the role of a Community Relations/Race Relations Officer, specify the steps that should be taken at the firm, after the incident, to improve race relations. How would you recommend the closed shop issue be resolved?

7 As the leader of the local Asian community, whose advice was previously sought, what advice would you give to:

(a) the Asians at the firm;
(b) the Asian involved in the fight;

(c) what recommendations would you give to restore relations at Metal Fasteners?

8 Role play the disciplinary meeting between the white worker, the Works Manager, the Personnel Officer, the shop steward and the union District Official.

9 Role play the disciplinary meeting between the Asian, the Works Manager, the Personnel Officer and the Asian's community leader.

10 Role play the next union/management meeting convened to discuss the issue of the closed shop. You could include someone role playing the leader of the Asian workers.

11 As a race relations adviser, compile a report on the extent to which both the firm and the union have complied with the detailed requirements of the Code of Practice for the Elimination of Racial Discrimination and the Promotion of Equality of Opportunity in Employment. Where you find bad practice, make recommendations for improving or eliminating it.

Also examine the question of whether the requirement for union membership in a closed shop might, in this situation, be indirect racial discrimination.

Case 12
The unsuitable shop steward

Analysis

One of the features of collective bargaining is that a group of employees are represented by a person of their choice who will act on their behalf in discussions and negotiations with management. That person is variously called shop steward, father/mother of the chapel, corresponding member, work's representative or staff representative. Their function is the same; to be in contact with their members, to represent their members' views and to secure the best deal for

them. The manner in which the shop steward is appointed is a matter exclusively for the union. The rules are laid down in the union rule book or in the branch rule book. Providing these are observed then usually the person so appointed is the representative. The usual procedure is that after the person has been appointed a note is sent to the relevant manager for recognition by the organisation. In some firms this will involve issuing credentials, which lay down the basic rights and duties of the shop steward. It is rare for the management of a firm to refuse to issue

Background knowledge

In this case you will be examining the background and run-up to the election of a shop steward and the circumstances under which the management of a firm see fit to challenge the appointment of the steward. The whole situation is a very delicate one which requires industrial relations skills of a high order.

Before starting this case you should have some prior knowledge of:

1 the selection, election and notification of union officials;
2 the independence of trade unions;
3 a typical set of union rules regarding the appointment of lay officials;
4 the recognition and issuing of credentials to a union official;
5 the possible grounds for refusing recognition of a union official;
6 recruitment and selection procedures.

such credentials or refuse to recognise a duly elected official. When it does refuse, it has to be for an extremely good reason otherwise there will almost certainly be a dispute. Such action is seen as interfering in the internal affairs of the union. This case illustrates a situation in which a shop steward's appointment was not accepted.

The candidate

Bill Johnson had been a union man all his life. This was not surprising as his father had been a London docker and active in the union in the docks. There was a tradition in the Johnson family to 'get involved' in both trade unions and local politics. Bill had followed his father into the docks but this did not last long due to the decline in the industry. After he left the docks, Bill had a number of jobs in industry as a machine operator. He left the London area when work was getting hard to find and decided to live in one of the London overspill towns that were built in the 1960s. He never stayed long in a firm but always became involved in the union

activities and quite often held union office. It was not unusual for him to become a union official, as in many firms, finding someone willing to take on a union job was not easy, particularly amongst the local people, as they did not have a tradition of trade unionism.

Four months ago Bill started a job at Kingston Plastics as a machine operator. He immediately joined the shop floor union, the General Workers' Union, and started to attend union meetings, where he was vocal from the start. Being familiar with union procedures he impressed his colleagues with his enthusiasm and energy. Two months after Bill joined Kingston Plastics the shop steward elections were due. The current steward for Bill's group had stood reluctantly the year before and had always said that he would only stay on in the post until there was a more willing volunteer. The current steward made the point at a recent branch committee meeting about the impending elections that there appeared to be a more able and willing person than himself available for the post and he would stand down at the end of his term.

Subsequently, when nominations were requested, Bill's name was put forward. He was the only candidate for the section he worked in. Subsequently he was appointed as shop steward for the group; elected unopposed. The branch secretary then sent the list of the duly elected union officials to the Production Director in the usual way. The next step usually was that the Director replied officially, stating that the company recognised the named individuals as the union representatives for the particular groups.

The unacceptable nomination

The union were not anticipating anything different in this instance. The reply was not always received by return but the first indication of a problem this time was that a reply was taking longer than usual. After an undue delay a note arrived from the Director saying that 'the following were recognised by the company as the recognised union representatives . . .'

Notably the name of Bill Johnson was missing.

The reason for the delay in reply was not because the Director had been dilatory. Quite the reverse. Having received the note from the branch secretary, which contained Bill Johnson's name, he decided that Bill's situation would have to be investigated. Since his appointment there had been concern about him. Initially this was not based on any of his union activities, as management were always careful not to interfere in their business. Soon after Bill's appointment the shift supervisor commented to his manager that he 'had picked a right one this time'. Bill was an extrovert and not slow to make his presence known. A few days after starting he was criticising the firm, its bad management, the poor industrial relations and making comments that he would soon 'sort all that out'.

The recruitment procedure at Kingston Plastics was through advertisement in the local press, application form and interview by the Production Manager. Rarely were references taken up as there was always pressure to get people started as soon as possible and taking up references was always time-consuming. In Bill Johnson's case there was no reason, on the face of the application form or interview, to take up any references as everything appeared normal and in order.

Past history revealed

When Bill's name appeared on the union officials' list, his application form was taken out of the file. It revealed no inconsistency but the Production Director requested the Personnel Officer to seek references from Bill's previous employers, but to do this sensitively as suspicions might be aroused. The replies confirmed suspicions. He had a very different track record than the one on the application form. One firm had sacked him almost straight away but Bill had put them down as employing him for two years. The job titles he gave were also erroneous. Seeking further clarification, and hoping to elicit information that Bill's previous employers would not put on paper, the Production Director made

contact with them by telephone. Again, the firms that were prepared to talk confirmed the stories and they expanded on Bill's activities, particularly his union activities. The fact that other firms felt they could not give any further information indicated that they had had a problem on their hands but were reluctant to elucidate.

The senior managers decided that, until the position became clearer, they must oppose the appointment of Bill Johnson as shop steward. They could foresee disruption and that was the last thing they wanted. The difficulty was finding a way of doing this without raising accusations of victimisation. The possible grounds for not accepting his appointment were first that it did not comply with the union's rules and second it did not comply with previous custom and practice in the firm. They felt that both arguments were a possibility and they would pursue both lines to try and make a watertight case.

On the question of noncompliance with the union rules, the firm needed to tread very warily, as any investigation of this aspect might arouse suspicions and precipitate an early dispute. The appointment's procedure itself was not against union rules. There was the question of Bill's eligibility, whether he had been a bona-fide member of the union for the requisite period. The union Rule Book stated that for a person to be nominated as a union official they should have been a fully paid up member of the relevant section of the union for a minimum of one year. The managers did not know which union Bill had been a member of at his last place of work although they had ascertained that there had been a gap of two months in his employment between his last job and his appointment at Kingston Plastics.

On the second question, of custom and practice, they felt they could make a case that it was highly improbable that a person that had only been with the firm two months at the time of the nomination could know sufficient about the firm, its employees and its procedures to make a sensible contribution and act as a representative. Normally they would look to a nominee having been with the firm for two years.

Looking back at the records the managers found that no one had been appointed to a union post with less than two years' service. This seemed to strengthen their hand in this argument.

Trouble brewing

The pace started to hot up as soon as the note from the Production Director was received by the union secretary. The District Official was contacted and he met the branch chairperson and secretary the same day, but the information was not disclosed to anyone else. The District Official immediately took the line that the firm could not interfere with the appointment of an official and they would have to accept Bill Johnson's appointment without question. The firm were informed of the appointments and it was not for them to dictate whether a person was fit for office or not. If the person had been nominated by the group, they obviously were happy to have him as their representative, and if the branch had duly appointed him in accordance with their rules, then the firm could not object or refuse to recognise anyone. The three union officials decided that there would need to be a meeting with management immediately.

A meeting was convened between the three union officials and the Production Manager and Director and the Personnel Officer the next day. The meeting was a formal affair, where the union registered an official complaint and stated that if the firm did not recognise Bill Johnson as a union official immediately then there would be an official dispute. Not wishing to preempt a branch decision, the union side said that it was almost certain there would be an immediate stoppage of work. Management stated that they were unhappy with the appointment of Bill Johnson on the grounds that customarily nominees had been with the firm for a reasonable length of time and that two months was far too short. They hinted that they suspected the appointment did not comply with the union's rules. This merely elicited a stern rebuke from the District Official not to meddle in the union's internal affairs. The Personnel Manager tried to ascertain the facts regarding the length of Bill Johnson's membership with the General Workers' Union. This only served to antagonise the union officials. The meeting ended with management stating they would consider their position but were not prepared to give any undertaking on recognising Bill Johnson as shop steward.

Intelligence gathering

The supervisor from Bill Johnson's department was having a quiet pint in his local pub when he remembered that one of the members of the pub's darts team worked for a firm that Bill Johnson had previously worked for. He went over to the man and entered into conversation with him. He skilfully turned the conversation round to unions and casually enquired which union organised the shop floor at their firm. He was surprised to hear that it was the Plastics Industry Workers' Union. He then made a mental note of this interesting fact. The supervisor passed on the intelligence he had gathered the previous night to the Production Manager who in turn passed it on to the Personnel Officer and the Production Director.

The culminating act

The union, for their part, had called an urgent branch committee meeting. All the newly appointed officials were called, including Bill Johnson. While the District Official knew that the subject would be a delicate one to handle, he decided to go ahead with the meeting. The meeting decided that they would be solidly behind the decision to insist on the acceptance of Bill Johnson as a union official, although one or two did not see eye to eye with Bill. They did not pass a motion to call a full branch meeting nor to recommend industrial action at that stage. The District Official opposed any action that was rushed and ill-considered. When pressed he declined to state specific reasons and the meeting gained the impression that he knew more than he was prepared to make public. After the meeting he took the branch secretary on one side and admitted that Bill Johnson did not fulfil the union's requirements on length of membership. When Bill Johnson had joined Kingston Plastics he had put in an application for union membership directly to the district office. He had asked that his previous period of membership with the Plastics Industry Workers' Union be added to his membership of the General Workers' Union. Although a strange request, the District Official had agreed to it as Bill had offered to pay back-dated subscriptions.

After the branch committee meeting had disbanded, Bill Johnson returned to work. Later that shift Bill was approached by another worker with a complaint about the safety device on his machine which was not working properly. Always keen to take up problems, Bill went to see the shift supervisor. The supervisor asked why Bill was taking up the matter. Bill said he was the shop steward and was entitled to take up complaints. The supervisor replied that to his knowledge Bill was not a shop steward and he was to return to work. Bill replied that he was the duly elected union official and if the supervisor insisted in refusing to recognise his position he would report that to his members. Bill left the supervisor's office and was seen talking animatedly to several of the department's operators. The foreman contacted the Production Manager immediately and told him of the position.

Exercises

1 As Production Manager, what would you do in the immediate situation?

2 The branch secretary is informed of the incident. He arrives on the scene as Bill is still talking to the operators. As branch secretary what advice would you give your members?

3 List the possible outcomes that might arise from this incident. Which do you think to be the most likely? Describe the factors that will influence the possible outcomes.

4 Role play a meeting convened between the Production Director, Production Manager, Personnel Officer, District Official, branch secretary and branch chairperson. Negotiate to resolve the dispute. Prior to the meeting both sides should prepare notes on how they are going to approach the negotiations, the points they wish to secure and the ones they are prepared to discuss.

5 As an industrial relations consultant engaged by the firm, what detailed changes would you recommend that the firm make to their industrial relations and associated personnel policies to rectify the situation? Also what steps should be taken to restore normal relations between the firm and the union?

6 As the District Official, prepare a report on the incident to your Regional office. State what you believe to be the causes of the dispute and what action should be taken by the union to prevent problems like this happening again.

7 The Managing Director, on his return from a sales trip abroad several days after the events above, has been briefed on the situation. He has recommended that Bill be dismissed for dishonesty (the false statements made on his application form) and that should preempt any further discussion on the matter of Bill being a shop steward. The dismissal is to be nonnegotiable and Bill should be summarily dismissed immediately.

As Production Director, prepare a paper for the Managing Director on your reactions to this instruction.

Case 13

The shop floor worker

Analysis

Since the Sex Discrimination Act 1975 and the Equal Pay Act 1970 came into force employers have been forced to pay attention to the differentials that often exist in workplaces between the jobs men and women perform and the pay they receive. The application of the detailed requirements of the Equal Pay Act in workplaces has raised a number of difficult problems. Very often there are differences of interpretation and the lack of explicit job definitions, for example in the form of job descriptions, makes the situation even more difficult. Sometimes job titles are different but the jobs are, except for minor details, the same and any pay differentials are discriminatory. In other instances men and women are ostensibly performing the same job, with the same title, but men receive a higher rate of pay because they perform some tasks that the women do not. This case illustrates a problem of this kind where there is equality but not entirely!

The company

The Waterhead Mouldings Company was established in a small rural location 22 years ago. It has a workforce of 150, many of whom live locally. This has led to a stable workforce with exception of the younger women who tend to leave school and work for the firm for a few years until they marry and have a family. Even then they often return after a period of time and the firm considers applications from ex-employees favourably. The firm does not pay highly but for the area gives average pay and alternative employment is difficult to find. The firm is rather paternalistic but the atmosphere within it is very friendly, with many people knowing each other or being related.

Background knowledge

In this case you are required to examine a situation and highlight the inequalities that exist in a firm. Some may be deliberate, others purely innocent.

Before starting this case you should have some prior knowledge of:

1 organisational structures, hierarchies and promotions policies;
2 personnel and remuneration policies;
3 equal opportunities practices and policies;
4 the law, and its interpretation, on equal opportunities and especially equal pay (Equal Pay Act 1970);
5 the Code of Practice, Equal Opportunities Policies, Procedures and Practices in Employment (issued by the Equal Opportunities Commission).

The firm makes moulds and moulding machinery for the plastics and rubber moulding industry. There is a manufacturing department, which employs skilled tool makers. Supporting this is a stores area which houses all the raw materials including the steel, fasteners, fabrications, seals and so on. The stores personnel, of whom there are ten, are unskilled. They act as the goods inwards department, the stores issue to production and a store for part-finished goods and various pieces of production equipment. Most of the administration is performed by two clerks in the stores. There is a great deal of flexibility amongst the staff with the stores personnel performing most of the jobs as and when required and this suits everyone. However, as is the case in other parts of the firm, jobs have evolved piecemeal to suit the circumstances of the time rather than according to any plan.

Unionisation

The firm is unionised with the toolmakers in a craft union and the rest of the firm, including the stores area, in a general union. There have been few disagreements which have upset the settled atmosphere at Waterhead Moulding and the union officials have rarely had much to do. Usually any matters arising are dealt with in an unofficial and friendly way. This is true for the stores area as well. One of the stores personnel is the shop steward but the job is something of a sinecure. Where changes are made the manager informs the steward. There are also annual pay negotiations to deal with. Apart from this there is little call on the steward to do very much.

Equal opportunities investigated

About two years ago the union's regional office sent out some literature on the workings of the Sex Discrimination Act and the Equal Pay Act and said they were instigating a drive to enforce the letter and the intent of the law. Waterhead Mouldings was targeted by the union as one place where there might be some work to be done to bring the firm's practices into line. The unofficial senior steward went to see Jim Bolton, the Personnel Officer to raise the issue of equality. After some discussion the two agreed that a small committee should be set up to investigate this area of the firm's operations. Both agreed that neither knew much about the subject or how well the firm was implementing the law. They also agreed that the committee would have to include some women. Subsequently the committee was formally constituted. It included the Personnel Officer, as chairperson, a female representative from the office (albeit not a union official, as the office union representative was currently a man), a female representative from the production department (again not the official union representative) and the office manager. It was agreed that in the event of a tie the committee would vote for a change in favour of female members of staff.

The committee met quite frequently initially,

then less often as they seemed to lose momentum. They found a number of instances of discrimination in the firm and also it was noted that the senior positions in the firm were all occupied by men. For the latter it was decided to positively assist women in the junior positions to take training courses and for them to be given the opportunity to perform jobs that would enhance their potential for promotion. In the manufacturing department this solution could not work as all the operatives were men. The firm said they would consider employing women in such positions but there had never been any applications from women for such jobs. Ironically it was the unions who were held to blame for the male domination of the toolmaking trade with their recruitment policies for apprenticeships.

The stores area

It was in the stores that there were found to be considerable problems. There were three grades of storeperson (except that all the documentation referred to them as storemen). These were:

- **Senior storeman** A position of section leader/leading hand, where the person would be responsible for all the work in the stores. Currently there is a man in this position and he arrived at the position based on the usual internal rule of seniority. He is responsible for incoming stores and internal stores.
- **Storeman** A senior grade in the stores covering all the tasks in the stores. This would typically include accepting delivery notes, checking documentation, arranging off-loading, signing notes, assigning locations for stock and issuing stock. There is currently a man and a woman in this position. Again this position is achieved by seniority from the lowest grade in the stores.
- **Picker/packer** A position where the person handles stores and stock from locations within the stores area to the production department, helps off-load incoming goods and puts them in their correct location. They have to check that the documentation is

correct for part numbers, locations, quantities and for putting the documents out to the correct departments. There are five people in this position; all but one are women.

The committee was concerned that this area in particular needed to be investigated thoroughly as there were a number of discriminatory situations. A further complication that came to light, after enquiries into pay rates, was that the male storemen had a slightly higher rate of pay than the women. This had arisen historically as the result of a claim that men had to do all the lifting work and had to climb up steep ladders onto a mezzanine floor that the women would not go up to. The differential amounted to 2.2p per hour.

Exercises

Stage 1

1 Role play the committee as it investigates the situation in the firm and in particular the stores. The remit for the committee is 'to investigate the situation and to make recommendations to achieve equality of opportunity for all employees, with special reference to the stores area'.

2 Prior to the investigation prepare a file of notes on the case and collect material for:
  (a) the personnel manager, and
  (b) the trade union officials.

3 As an independent observer/consultant give your advice to the firm on what they need to do to bring practices into line with the law and the Code of Practice issued by the Equal Opportunities Commission.
  Include specific recommendations on a system that the firm could set up to monitor equal opportunities within the firm, the way the situation should be reviewed and the measures that need to be taken to rectify areas of discrimination.

4 As for **3**, but acting for the union.

5 Prepare a report emanating from the committee of investigation, with emphasis on practical recommendations.

Stage 2

The outcome of the investigation is that all the stores personnel are to be treated equally, the pay differentials are to be ended and the rules on promotion are to be amended.

A few days after the publication of the report there was an incident in the stores. The one woman on the middle grade was performing her duties as normal when the senior storeperson requested that she go onto the mezzanine floor to carry out a stock check. She immediately refused, saying that she was not going up the ladder and walking round the narrow flooring. The other man on the same grade heard of this and also refused to carry out the job on the grounds that everyone was equal and that included doing an identical job. The senior storeperson reported this to the production manager.

1 As the Production Manager, what action would you take? List the factors to take into account, the principles you would employ and make a plan of action. Who would you consult? What would you do immediately and in the near future?

2 As the stores shop steward, what advice would you give to the woman in the incident? As the men are also in the union, how will this affect the situation? The production manager is taking this as a refusal to obey a legitimate instruction and as such it is serious. Under the disciplinary procedure, it could lead to suspension.

3 The personnel officer has been informed of the incident. Prepare a memo from him giving advice to the production manager on what he ought to do.

4 Convene a special meeting of the equal opportunities subcommittee to examine this latest incident. Make recommendations to solve the problem.

5 The matter later becomes a matter of dispute. Convene a disputes committee and negotiate a settlement. Include the production manager, the personnel manager, the shop steward, a district union official and a member of the employers' association on the committee.

Case 14

The competent drunk

Analysis

When dealing with matters of discipline one of the important principles to be applied is the need to be seen to be fair and consistent. This is one of the arguments for having a disciplinary procedure. If people are treated fairly and consistently then there is often little ground for complaint. It is notable that frequently in the tribunal cases that lead to an award for unfair dismissal, the case is won or lost because the employer did not treat the employee fairly or as prescribed by a procedure not because the employer had no grounds for dismissal. The case which follows illustrates this.

Introduction

The PrintaPosta Co is a small printing firm specialising in printing posters. Its work is varied and the firm has built up a reputation, in the face of fierce competition, for its artwork and ability to produce high quality colour work. The firm employs 28 people in the design, production and despatch departments. The atmosphere is friendly but it often gives the impression of frenzied activity as the firm endeavours to achieve delivery dates. On occasions it takes on too much work but would rather overstretch itself than lose orders.

The competent drunk

The production section employs 15 people and is headed by a print worker of 24 years' experience. Jack Hall knows his trade well but has found life more than a little difficult in recent years because of the changes in technology. Jack has been with the firm since it began 15 years ago and the firm is very loyal to him for his hard

Background knowledge

When disciplining employees there is always a need to be seen to be fair and consistent. We all have an acute sense of justice and justice must be seen to be done. Procedures can help this process as they should be applied to everyone in the same manner. This is not to suggest that some discretion should not be applied. A good procedure should allow for this. The rigid application of firm rules can be seen as unjust as the opposite. The behaviour of supervisors and managers towards their colleagues must be consistent with that shown towards subordinates otherwise there is a cry of 'a law for them and a law for us'.

Before starting this case you should have some prior knowledge of:

1 the principles and practice of discipline and disciplinary action;
2 the role of the supervisor and manager in applying standards of behaviour at work;
3 the problems caused by an inconsistent approach to handling discipline.

work and dedication. Jack helped the firm through the first, difficult years and often he put in many more hours than he was paid for, just to see the work completed. The founder of the firm is aware of Jack's shortcomings but relies on him to run the production side of the enterprise while he concentrates on the design side. Jack is a good manager and can get the best out of people.

As a result of the added complexity of printing work and the need to keep up with the technological developments in the field, PrintaPosta created the post of Technical Supervisor last year. They recruited Phil Coggins, a young, recently qualified print technician to take on the technical side of the production section's work. This left Jack to concentrate on managing the department. Phil settled into the job relatively quickly and proved to be very good at his job. The firm is happy with the appointment and many of the technical problems that the firm had have now been solved.

However, there is one grave difficulty that has arisen. Phil has a drink problem. He has taken to going out at lunch times to meet his drinking partner and often comes back incapable of doing much work. On many occasions Jack has had to take Phil home in his car to ensure that Phil does not cause a disturbance or get into any danger. This has been noticed by the operatives in the section but the matter had not been brought to the attention of anyone else. Jack feels rather protective of Phil because he relies on him so much for the technical support he provides. If anything, Jack has covered up for Phil and tries to be very discreet in dealing with a situation he finds rather embarrassing.

Lately the situation has deteriorated so much that Phil has taken to having Monday mornings off quite frequently to recover from his heavy weekend drinking sessions. To cover himself when he returns he certifies himself sick as suffering from something other than a bad hangover. Jack tries to support Phil by making excuses for his absences but finds it more difficult on the occasions he returns to work drunk. Nothing has been said to Jack by any of the production department workers but he detects some unease about the situation and is lost to know what to do. He has spoken to Phil about the situation and Phil recognises that he needs to moderate his drinking but then, after a period of time off, falls back into his bad habits again.

One morning Pam, an operative on one of the new, recently installed machines, comes to see Jack. She tells Jack that she has had a lifelong friend staying with her from Canada and the friend is due to return to Canada that day. Pam asks if she can finish two hours early that day so that she can go to the airport with her friend. Jack, being under considerable pressure to finish a number of jobs that day, including the one on Pam's machine, says he cannot allow her the time

off. He says that he had intended to ask her to work over that night to finish the work. Pam becomes very irate and says 'You can let that lazy, drunken technician of yours have days off to go drinking but not an hour off for someone who never has any time off. We've noticed you taking him home after lunch because he's had too much booze. But you wouldn't take me to the airport in your car. I've had enough of this two-faced lot here'. At which she storms out the office, slamming the door.

Pam returns to her machine but is unable to concentrate on her work. At break time she tells all her colleagues about the incident. They support Pam and say they are prepared to back her. Still feeling incensed she changes and leaves the works without saying anything to Jack. She tells her friends they can tell Jack that she's in the pub waiting to stop Phil having too much to drink at lunch time.

Pam turns up for work the next day.

Exercises

1 What would you do if you were Jack:
  (a) when you found out that Pam had left the works;
  (b) when Pam returned the next day?

2 Give your written recommendations to the owner on what action the firm ought to take with regard to:
  (a) Phil's situation;
  (b) disciplinary action against Phil;
  (c) disciplinary action against Pam;
  (d) Jack's managerial performance.

3 As Jack, on reflection, what should you have done from the outset with regard to Phil? Detail the mistakes that you think you made and how you could have avoided them.

4 As the owner of PrintaPosta, state what systems you would institute to avoid the kinds of problems, highlighted in this case, occurring again. State what principles you would use as a guide for good managerial practice.

5 Role play a meeting between Pam, Jack and the owner called to discuss the incident of Pam leaving.

6 The owner has decided that Jack must deal with Phil and that the two must meet to resolve the situation.

(a) State the guidelines you would issue to Jack for the meeting.
(b) As Jack, prepare some notes for the meeting with Phil.
(c) Role play the meeting between Jack and Phil.

7 Write the documents that arise out of this incident. As Jack has dealt with these, write a letter/memo from Jack to:
(a) Pam, based on the outcome of Exercise 5;
(b) Phil, based on the outcome of Exercise 6.

Case 15
Redundancy at Toolcraft

Analysis

One of the consequences of technological change is that often there has to be a reduction in the workforce. The financial justification for the capital investment is that savings must be made on labour costs. While there is some inevitability about the march of technology, the consequences for the individual firm have to be worked out most carefully. When the numbers employed at a firm need to be reduced the means of achieving this needs to be worked out jointly, preferably using some agreed procedure. Where agreement is not secured the outcome may be disastrous. This case takes place in a small firm where these questions are raised but not satisfactorily answered.

The firm

Toolcraft is a light engineering firm that produces small components for the car industry on a subcontract basis. Its strength lies in its craft workers' skills to produce very high quality work to exacting standards. Although tied to the motor trade it has maintained a reasonably healthy order book overall but with some minor hiccups from time to time, which reflects the fortunes of the industry. It is a small firm, employing 55 people. Toolcraft is located in the

Background knowledge

In this case you will be examining a situation where a firm is introducing some new machinery, to improve methods and cut labour costs, and the consequent need to reduce the workforce. Initially this was not planned as a redundancy situation but subsequently became one.

Before starting this case you should have some prior knowledge of:

1 the justification and implications of a shift to capital intensive manufacture;
2 the means of achieving the reduction in human resources required as a result of 1;
3 the skills in handling such a situation;
4 group behaviour and dynamics;
5 the need for, and form of, consultations and communication in a firm;
6 the definition of redundancy and the procedures for handling redundancy.

Midlands, and it has a high level of union membership amongst its employees as a result of recruiting people from the engineering industry.

Industrial relations are fair, with an uneasy peace existing between the workers and management. This situation is partially a result of the firm always having to seek new orders to keep going. It rarely gets an order that keeps all the workforce occupied for more than a few weeks. This leads to a rather piecemeal approach to long-term planning because of the uncertainty of future orders. Another consequence is that rumours are often rife that the firm is going through a bad patch and that jobs are under threat. Again this is often fuelled by management refusing to talk about issues, due to this uncertainty, and by them often saying that if certain demands are made then that would jeopardise future business. Costs necessarily need to be pared to the bone in order to successfully tender for contracts.

The tool room

The production department is where industrial relations can be the most difficult. The majority of the workforce works in the two main departments and they are virtually closed shops. There have been one or two minor stoppages in recent times but nothing too devastating. The tool room however is not in the same category. Although all the men are highly trained engineers and are considered the elitist group amongst engineering staff, at Toolcraft they have an exemplary record. They are all in the union and have a great deal of loyalty to the union but are independently minded enough to decide for themselves what they will do rather than just follow the shop floor on an issue. Hence they did not follow the shop floor out during a recent stoppage. The tool room has a good record of efficiency and an enviable record on quality. As they are located away from the shop floor they keep themselves to themselves. As a group they are very cohesive and get on well with each other.

The dominant personality within the group is Chris Savage. He was the shop steward until recently and still remains the group's unofficial spokesman. While the group has a shop steward they nearly always defer to Chris for his advice. He is an excellent craftsman and is respected by everyone. The supervisor of the tool room is Geoff Bostock who is also a very good craftsman, having served his time in the trade and still reckoned to be one of the best. He knows his

men well and makes certain he keeps in touch. The record within the tool room is largely due to this atmosphere and Geoff often boasts about his enviable record to the other supervisors in the firm. The men, although particularly independently minded, always meet Geoff Bostock's requests and never have much cause to complain.

Due to the fluctuating level of orders, when orders are won they are always needed 'yesterday' and there is quite a lot of overtime worked when delivery dates are tight. This topic alone has caused more problems than any other within the production departments. The amount of overtime and its allocation always causes difficulty and unrest. It is almost impossible to plan it regularly but when it is needed it requires a flexible attitude by everyone. While the problem has been the subject of numerous discussions, there is still no workable solution. In the tool room the situation is different. They have a more flexible approach to moving round on the jobs they are currently working on. The amount of overtime is calculated by Geoff Bostock and then the detail on who comes in is worked out in conjunction with Chris Savage.

New machinery

In recent times the firm has been investigating new methods of manufacture in the tool room. Although the firm is able to produce the very highest quality product it is being beaten by the new methods that some of its competitors are employing. As a result of a number of orders being lost in recent times, the management have decided that the only way to remain in competition is to invest in some new equipment that will keep them in the market. A number of the older machines will have to be replaced and the level of automation on the new machines means that less labour will be required in the tool room. An estimation by management is that one person would have to leave the tool room. Geoff Bostock has been appraised of this and has had a private word with Chris Savage. The plan is that the last man in be transferred out of the tool room into the maintenance department where there is a requirement for a skilled man. This would mean a loss of earnings. The man selected, Bill Green, has been told about the position by Geoff Bostock.

The news was taken badly by everyone, and particularly by Bill Green. The men thought that the new equipment would need a period of commissioning and that the workload of the department would increase over time anyway. They had accepted Bill into their group and assessed him as a competent craftsman whom they did not want to lose. Bill refused the proposed move and made an official complaint to the shop steward. Discussions ensued and these did not get very far as management still considered that there would be a reduced work level in the tool room. They argued that the only economic basis for the investment in new equipment was to reduce labour costs. Both sides gradually got further entrenched in their respective positions and there was no obvious solution. The matter came to a head on a Friday, when Bill Green received his redundancy notice. The tool room staff walked out immediately.

Exercises

1 As production manager specify what you will do immediately you are aware of the walk-out. Prepare a brief for the Managing Director on the issues raised and the possible solutions for the immediate situation.

2 A meeting has been called between the production manager, Geoff Bostock, the union District Officer and Chris Savage. Role play the meeting to negotiate a settlement. Prior to the meeting both sides should meet separately to decide their strategy and tactics. Prepare notes specifying the main issues, what you are prepared to negotiate and what is nonnegotiable.

3 As a consultant to the firm, write a report suggesting what changes should be made within the firm. Base this on the object lessons of this incident.

4 You are a trainee in the offices and the Managing Director has asked you to help formulate some ideas on the issues raised. Draw up a list of the possible ways in which a firm can reduce its labour force, over time. Evaluate each policy and recommend a preferred range of policies and specify the ones you reject.

5 As a trainer with a local firm you have been asked to do some training for Toolcraft. Prepare some notes for a training session to be held for all the supervisors and managers at Toolcraft. The topic is 'the management of change'.

6 Geoff Bostock has come to you to ask for some advice. When there is a return to work (make some assumptions about the final outcome) he is worried how to carry on with the proposed programme of technological updating in the tool room. Advise him of the human relations aspects of how to deal with this problem. Use the report in Exercise 3 to help.

Answers to multiple-choice questions

Chapter 2		Chapter 9		Chapter 13		Chapter 14	
2.1	c	9.1	b	13.1	c	14.1	b
2.2	c	9.2	c	13.2	all	14.2	b
2.3	d	9.3	b, a, c	13.3	a	14.3	a
2.4	c	9.4	a	13.4	b	14.4	a
2.5	d	9.5	b	13.5	a	14.5	a
2.6	c	9.6	a	13.6	a	14.6	b
2.7	a	9.7	b	13.7	c	14.7	c
2.8	c	9.8	c			14.8	b
2.9	b, d, a, c	9.9	c			14.9	c
2.10	b, d, c, a					14.10	b

Answers to mini-questions

Chapter 2

2.1 To protect and improve the terms and conditions of their members.

2.2 Recruitment, settling disputes, provision of welfare, promotion of trade unionism, political objectives.

2.3 To negotiate, safeguard jobs, cooperation with employers.

2.4 Women, staff workers and some industries.

2.6 Covers those with a skill or trade, e.g., AEU, EETPU.

2.7 No restrictions on recruitment, generally for those with no skill, e.g., TGWU, GMB, USDAW.

2.8 Covers all those in a particular industry, e.g., NUM, UCW.

2.9 Covers nonmanual employment, e.g., MSF, GMB, BIFU.

2.10 A process whereby a union joins another body, e.g., unions joining TUC or Labour party.

2.11 Registration entitles union to tax-free status, certificate of independence given to union not under employer's control.

2.12 A process whereby unions join together to meet employers.

2.13 Trades Union Congress.

2.14 At Congress, each union has one card per 1,000 members which is used for voting.

2.15 Inter-union disputes.

Chapter 3

3.1 Sole trader, partnership company, nation-alised corporation, cooperative, local authority.

3.2 Public and private, limited by share.

3.4 Planning, coordination and control.

3.5 To run the organisation in the best interests of the shareholders.

3.6 An organisation of individual employers in an area or industry.

3.7 Negotiations, resolving disputes, giving advice.

3.8 National, national with branches, national plus local associations.

3.9 Confederation of British Industries.

3.10 Formulating policy for industry, encouraging efficiency of industry, developing industry's contributions to the economy.

Chapter 4

4.1 Legislature's role is to pass laws, the executive's role is to apply and administer the law and the judiciary's role is to enforce the law.

4.2 The legislature has had the role of creating law to control a trade union's function and it has given employees a number of rights in employment.

4.3 The executive administers law relating to redundancy payments, gives funds for industrial tribunals and funds for ACAS.

4.4 Unfair dismissal, redundancy, discrimination, maternity rights.

4.5 The Central Arbitration Committee is a committee of three that has cases for arbitration referred to it. A body set up under EPA 1975.

Chapter 5

5.1 Collecting dues, recruiting members, representing members, negotiating, communicating, resolving disputes.

5.2 Members, union structure, Rule Book, collective bargaining, branch.

5.3 The steward is used as the voice of the group represented; communicates to and from management; takes up grievances and disputes.

5.4 (i) Expansion of collective bargaining, number of issues negotiated has grown. (ii) Legislation. (iii) Organisational changes, large organisation, professional management, personnel function.

5.5 Collect dues, check cards, ensure rules are obeyed, attend meetings, recruitment.

5.6 Represent them, ensure they receive benefits, compliance with agreements, negotiation, communicating.

5.7 Desk or room, phone, access to typing and copying, information, meeting room.

5.8 Union rules, collective agreements, principles of trade unionism, management subjects, negotiating skills, law.

5.9 A senior steward elected from the shop stewards.

5.10 Investigate hazards, complaints, inspect, attend committee meetings, represent employees.

Chapter 6

6.1 An employer (or group of) and employee representatives negotiating the terms and conditions of employment for the group of employees.

6.2 Negotiating from strength of numbers; use of union research, backing of union and branch officials.

6.3 One set of negotiations covers many employees, can be orderly and controllable.

6.4 Union recognition and union organisation.

6.5 Balance of power between parties, determining the price of labour, government of industrial relations.

6.6 Free from outside or governmental influences.

6.7 For increasing productivity, employees receive improved terms and conditions.

6.8 Preparation, opening, argument, trading and closing.

6.9 Overtime ban, work-to-rule, boycotting, token strike, all-out strike, lockout, go-slow.

6.10 In conciliation, the parties reach agreement with help, a mediator suggests a solution, an arbitrator makes the decision.

6.11 It moderates the claims of both sides.

Chapter 7

7.1 An agreement that provides the rules or procedures to be used in a particular situation.

7.2 An agreement that provides the content and rules relating to the terms and conditions of employment.

7.3 Presumed not to be legally binding.

7.4 A major source of the terms and conditions of an individual's contract of employment.

7.5 A local agreement is made between the individual employer and the local union and a national agreement is made between employer representatives and national union officials, often involving confederations.

7.6 Uniformity and consistency, everyone knows, permanent, recorded, less ambiguous.

7.7 Written, allows for stages, gives time limits, specifies who is involved, can be amended with notice, moves to external resolution.

7.8 Negotiation agreement, disputes/ grievance, disciplinary, wages, union management agreement, redundancy, technology.

7.9 Prevents 'leap-frogging', more orderly,

cuts down on negotiations time, easier to plan for.

7.10   To whom the agreement applies, term of agreement, wage levels, overtime rate, special allowances, bonuses, sickness and holiday pay, renegotiation of agreement.

Chapter 8

8.1   To ban all organisations of workers and employers.

8.2   Grand National Consolidated Trade Union was an attempt by Robert Owen, in 1834, at forming a national trade union.

8.3   Secretly swearing themselves to an organisation, an offence under the Illegal Oaths Act.

8.4   The type of craftsman's union that emerged in the 1850s displaying the characteristics of a modern union.

8.5   1868.

8.6   Treasury agreements involved the unions, emergence of the shop steward, union cooperation needed for war effort.

8.7   The mine owners' attempts to lower wages and increase hours.

8.8   Unions interfere in the contract of employment between employer and employee.

8.9   It undermined the presumption that unions were then immune from legal action for striking.

8.10   Trade Union Act 1913.

8.12   'Contracting in' is where a union member has to sign to pay political levy. 'Contracting out' is where the member has to sign in order not to pay the levy.

Chapter 9

9.1   Civil law regulates behaviour between individuals; criminal law regulates behaviour between individuals and the State.

9.2   An accident can lead to a prosecution and a civil action for damages.

9.3   An Act of Parliament. A statutory instrument is a legal order issued by a minister under the authority of an Act.

9.4   Must adopt EC law into our system and where they clash, we must change our laws.

9.5   Not law but can be used in evidence to show that the law has not been complied with.

9.6   A judge's legal decision in a case that binds judges in similar cases in the future to come to the same direction.

9.7   Quicker, cheaper, informal, can use direction.

9.8   Unfair dismissal, redundancy, protective award, maternity leave, time off.

9.9   No legal aid (only advice), no costs awarded to winner. Public funds pay some expenses.

9.10   An appeal body from industrial tribunal on a question of law and from Certification Officer on question of fact or law on certificates of independence.

Chapter 10

10.1   Incorporated association is a separate legal body, an unincorporated association is not.

10.2   A legal process whereby an act is made legal when otherwise it would be illegal.

10.3   No, a striking employee is not covered by any immunity.

10.4   A union interferes in a contract of employment in being a third party involved in making the contract's terms.

10.5   Interference, inducement, conspiracy.

10.6   Primary action is that directed at the employer involved in the dispute. Secondary action involves another employer.

10.7   Action authorised by any official of a trade union.

10.8   Terms and conditions, engagement, dismissal, allocation of work, membership or trade union facilities.

10.9   Paid time off work for an official's trade union duties and training. Time off for trade union activities.

10.10 Paid time off for antenatal care, not to be dismissed, to receive maternity pay, to return to work.

10.11 11 weeks before confinement, 29 weeks after actual confinement plus four weeks' certified sickness.

10.12 Treating someone less favourably than another.

10.13 In recruitment, training opportunities, promotion, unequal pay.

10.14 Where the job calls for someone of a particular race or sex, e.g., a waiter or waitress in an ethnic restaurant or a residential warden at a male hostel.

10.15 By deliberate recruiting to redress a racial or sex imbalance in the workforce structure. It is illegal.

10.16 Midwifery, ministers of religion, underground mining and armed forces.

10.17 To encourage people of a particular race or sex into an occupation, e.g., special training courses and discriminatory recruitment on to these.

10.18 That in a contract of employment there is an equality term giving equal pay for the same or similar employment.

10.19 No. It applies equally to men.

10.20 Comparing the jobs in question.

Chapter 11

11.1 A statute has the full force of law. A Code of Practice can be used in evidence to show that the law has been broken.

11.2 To explain, expand and give practical meaning to legal provisions.

11.3 (a) Making arrangements for negotiations and consultations, observe agreements and welcome union membership.
(b) Arrangements for negotiations and consultations, observe agreements, understand rules and policies of union.

11.4 Matters to be negotiated, arrangements for negotiations, facilities, settling disputes.

11.5 Wages, overtime rates, bonuses, hours, holidays.

11.6 Dismissal. Relevant to the manner of the dismissal.

11.7 Establish facts, deal with matter promptly, allow to be accompanied, allow appeal.

11.8 Pay, conditions of service, staffing, performance, financial.

11.9 For trade union duties concerned with the employer, and for training for those activities.

11.10 Legislation, negotiating skills, communications.

11.11 A secret ballot to be held in which there is a minimum 80% majority of those entitled to vote and 85% of those who did vote.

11.12 People covered, exemption clauses, union application problems, disputes procedure.

11.13 Adoption of clear and fair rules, procedure for hearing complaints, appeals.

11.14 Have a trade union organiser who should have a letter of authority, contact police and ensure pickets know the rules of picketing.

11.15 Medical products, food and animal feed, heating fuel for schools and accommodation, goods and services for livestock and operating the emergency services.

Chapter 12

12.1 A legally binding agreement.

12.2 An employer (usually company) and employee.

12.3 Pay and service.

12.4 Offer and acceptance.

12.5 No.

12.6 The control test is a measure of whether the employer controls the work of an employee and the manner in which it is carried out. Used to differentiate between a contract *of* and *for* service.

12.7 One week employee to employer. One week per year of service (maximum of 12) employer to employee.

12.8 Pay, hours, holidays, pensions, sick pay, notice, procedures, rules.

12.9 Individual agreement, collective agreement, custom, works rules, common law, statutory law.

12.10 A term that is in the contract regardless of whether it is mentioned, or known, or not.

12.11 Common law rules, not be unfairly dismissed, claim redundancy pay, maternity rights, not to be discriminated against, time-off arrangements.

12.12 Written statement gives the main terms of the contract of employment, a contract of employment gives all the terms in the contract.

12.13 That the statement has been received.

12.14 Pay, holiday entitlement, sick and injury pay, pension arrangements, notice, job title, employer, start date.

12.15 Disciplinary rules, to whom appeals are to be made, any relevant procedures.

Chapter 15

15.1 Official strikes are called in accordance with union rules. Unofficial strikes are not.

15.2 Unofficial, often quick, stoppages.

15.3 An employer not allowing the employees to work.

15.4 Continuous service is an unbroken period of employment. Periods of striking do not count towards service but do not break continuity.

15.5 To spread the effects of a strike and to publicise it.

15.6 To communicate peacefully and persuade others to work or not to work.

15.7 Where a condition of employment is trade union membership.

15.8 Union membership agreement.

15.9 Reduces the number of unions, easier bargaining, present arrangements satisfactory.

15.10 Infringes the right of freedom of an individual to join or not to join an organisation.

15.11 Union membership is a requirement before being considered for a job. Employers cannot make union membership a requirement of recruitment or selection.

15.12 On the decrease.

Chapter 16

16.1 Where employees participate in decision making.

16.2 Semi-autonomous work groups, worker directors, cooperatives, nationalisation, works councils.

16.3 To run the company in the interests of the shareholders.

16.4 Direct participation is where the individuals are involved; indirect is through a representative.

16.5 An equal number of employee and management directors plus independents, on main and regional boards. Also use of policy committees.

16.6 Where a group of workers are given an overall task to do, and they decide how to do the work.

16.7 $2x + y$. Equal number of shareholder and employee directors (elected through the unions) plus a smaller, odd number of mutually acceptable independent directors.

16.8 A top, policy-making board, including worker directors, and a lower, management board to implement policy and carry out day-to-day running of the company.

16.9 To be given information, demand explanations and discuss company plans and policy.

16.10 All companies (over 500 employees) to have a two-tier board structure, with the top board containing worker directors.

Chapter 17

17.1 Increase – banking, insurance, finance; decrease – coal, shipbuilding, manufacture.

17.2 Decrease – operatives, labourers; increase – management, professional.

17.3 (i) Decrease; (ii) increase; (iii) increase; (iv) increase.

17.4 Fewer young people, gradually more people over retirement age.

17.5 Safety, conditions of work, fair remuneration, protection of young people and women, social welfare.

Answers to assignments

Assignment 24

(a) B's dismissal related to his capability and 'qualifications' to do the job. Failure to dismiss would have been a failure to honour an agreement with the union. Honouring such agreements would be 'some other substantial reason'.

(b) The tribunal should regard all the circumstances surrounding the case as relevant. In this case, the principal reason for the dismissal was T's unsatisfactory performance and conduct.

(c) D's acquittal did not prevent a finding of fair dismissal. The issue for the tribunal was whether the employers were justified in dismissing D, not whether, beyond all reasonable doubt, he had committed a criminal offence. D was fairly dismissed.

(d) Taking into account the nature of the ill health, the likely length of the absence and the need to have P to do the work, S was fairly dismissed. The basic question is whether, in the circumstances, the employer can be expected to wait any longer.

(e) An employer who gives an employee time to improve and then allows more time, is not to be criticised. He was fairly dismissed. The 50% reduction in the award was incorrect as F did not have any control over the conduct, especially if he was doing his best.

(f) G had been in fundamental breach of his contract of employment that amounted to a repudiation of the contract which had been accepted by the employer. There had been no dismissal when there was a lockout the following day. The men had dismissed themselves.

(g) The long-term absence had frustrated the contract and M were correct in assuming that the contract had come to an end. Failure to dismiss and to accept the medical notes were not conclusive evidence of the contract continuing.

(h) C could not, in the absence of an agreement to the contrary, lay off J without a week's notice or pay in lieu. The lay-off amounted to dismissal.

(i) In view of the fact that there was no ambiguity in the words used, the man had clearly dismissed himself and the employer had acted reasonably in accepting.

Assignment 26

(a) $5 \times 1\frac{1}{2} + 10 \times 1 = 17\frac{1}{2} \times £200 = £3,500.$

(b) $5 \times \frac{1}{2} + 4 \times 1 = 6\frac{1}{2} \times £140 = £910.$

(c) Maximum years $20 \times 1\frac{1}{2} = 30 \times £180 = £5,400.$

(d) Maximum years $20 \times 1\frac{1}{2} = 30 \times £200 = £6,000.$

(e) 6 years only count $\times 1\frac{1}{2} = 9 \times £175 = £1,575.$

(f) $5 \times 1\frac{1}{2} + 10 \times 1 = 17\frac{1}{2} \times £150 = £2,625.$

(g) $5 \times \frac{1}{2} + 5 \times 1 = 7\frac{1}{2} \times £150 = £1,125.$

(h) $14 \times 1\frac{1}{2} = 21 \times £135 = £2,835.$

(i) No entitlement, not having 2 years' service.

(j) $5 \times 1\frac{1}{2} + 1 \times 1 = 8\frac{1}{2} \times £205$ (max.) $= £1,742.$

Glossary

Affiliation A process whereby one organisation joins another organisation to have its views represented on that body.

Arbitration A process where a third party makes an independent decision to settle a dispute.

Associated employer Where one company is controlled directly or indirectly by the other, or if both are controlled by a third.

Boycotting A refusal to use a machine, operate a plant or work on a particular job.

Card vote A method of voting where delegates cast their votes in proportion to the number of members in that organisation or the number of members entitled to vote.

Check-off A system whereby the employer deducts union dues from wages.

Closed shop A situation in which trade union membership is necessary if a job is to be obtained or retained.

Code of Practice An officially issued document that gives guidance on a particular topic. It has semi-legal status in that it can be used in evidence in a tribunal to show that the law has not been complied with.

Conciliation A process where a third party assists the two parties in dispute to reach an agreement for themselves.

Confederation An organisation that is a collection of other organisations who join together for a particular purpose.

Contracting in/out The situation regarding the payment of a political levy whereby trade union members pay the levy unless they say they will not (contracting out) or where they do not pay the levy unless they say they will (contracting in).

Convenor A senior steward who is elected from among the shop stewards of a firm, who acts as the senior union representative on site. Technically convenors are not full-time officials as they are employees of their firm, not the union.

Demarcation A strict definition, usually by a union, of which worker or group does which task, with no one else being allowed to do that allotted task.

Differentials The difference in wage or earnings levels between groups of workers.

Dilutees The use of semi-skilled or unskilled labour to do a skilled job.

Flexi-time An arrangement regarding working hours whereby employees can start and finish at various times with a minimum number of core hours being set so that the total number of hours equals the normal working week.

Free-riders A term used to describe nonunion members in a union shop that benefit from union negotiations but have not contributed to the union.

Full-time equivalents A worker who is not on full-time hours but is considered as such, especially for statutory rights. At law this is defined as a person who works an average of 16 hours per week, or an average of 8 hours per week after 5 years' service.

Genuine occupational qualification In race and sex discrimination it is lawful to discriminate on the grounds of race or sex (but not against married people) if the job requires a person of a particular racial group or sex. It can occur in modelling, filming, dramatic performances, entertainment or, for sex discrimination, if it is necessary for reasons of decency or privacy.

Guaranteed payments A statutory payment that employers must make to workers laid off or on short time.

Immunities A legal process whereby the law allows certain acts to be carried out, free from possible legal consequences, where otherwise legal action could be taken.

Independent trade union A union not under the domination or control of an employer or employers' association and one which is not liable to interference by an employer (by providing finance or material support) that tends towards such control.

Joinder The right of an employer, in certain legal cases, to require a union or official to be a co-defendant in an industrial tribunal case.

Lay-off A temporary suspension of the contract of employment, usually because no work is available. It can be with pay, without pay or on part pay.

Leap-frogging A situation where each successive pay claim tries to achieve a settlement better than the previous one.

Mediation *See* Section 6.4.

Pay in lieu Receiving pay instead of working to the end of the required notice period after notice has been served.

Pendulum arbitration A form of arbitration where the arbitrator has to choose either the employer's case or the union's case, not the middle ground.

Picketing A situation where employees, or others, stand outside a place of work and try, peacefully, to persuade others to join or support the industrial action by not entering the premises.

Positive action In race or sex discrimination certain bodies can take steps to offer training to certain racial groups or a particular sex to encourage such persons to train for jobs.

Procedural agreement An agreement between management and unions on the procedure to be used to resolve disputes, grievances, disciplinary matters, redundancies or other matters.

Registration A process whereby a union or employers' association applies to the Certifi-cation Officer to be registered by him as a union or employers' association.

Restrictive covenant A term in a contract of employment restricting an employee, on leaving, from working for a competitor within a specified area within a specified length of time.

Reverse discrimination In race or sex discrimin-ation it is illegal to discriminate on the grounds of race or sex, in selecting people for jobs, to redress an imbalance in the workforce. Provid-ing opportunities for training can be given under positive action, but actual selection must be nondiscriminatory.

Secondary action Industrial action affecting an employer who is not a party to the original dispute.

Short time A temporary reduction in normal working hours, usually because no work is available. It can be on full pay or part pay.

Show of hands A method of voting whereby each member or delegate votes by raising a hand, with each delegate or member having one vote.

Single-union agreement An agreement between an employer and one union to represent all categories of employee.

Strike-free agreement An agreement which, in the event of a failure to agree, leads on to compulsory binding arbitration.

Token strike A restricted form of striking, usually a one-day strike or a series of one-day strikes.

Trade dispute At law this is defined as a dispute between workers and their employer that is wholly or mainly related to the terms and conditions of employment, engagement, non-engagement, termination or suspension of workers, allocation of work, discipline, mem-bership or nonmembership of a trade union, facilities for officials or the machinery for consultation, procedures and trade union recognition.

Trade union At law this is 'an organisation which consists wholly or mainly of workers of one or more descriptions and is an organisation whose principal purposes include the regulation of relations between workers of that description . . . and employers . . . or affiliated organisations . . . or representatives of affiliated organisations'.

Wildcat strike Unofficial strike, usually occurring on the spur of the moment.

Work-to-rule A form of industrial action where workers will carry out tasks only according to a strict interpretation of the rules of the job, refusing to do tasks that are strictly not part of their job.

Index

ACAS 64–6
  and arbitration 104, 144
  Certification Officer 30
  Codes of Practice 183, 185, 187
  and conciliation 103, 114
  and discrimination 171, 174, 175
  and dismissal 218
  functions 65
  survey on redundancy 227
  union recognition 87
  work of equal value 175
Accountability 40
Accreditation of officials 119
Advertisements
  racial discrimination 170, 195
  sex discrimination 172, 197
AEU
  benefits of 14
  craft union 25
  organisation 27–8
  origins 136
  single union agreements 111
Affiliation
  to Labour Party 68
  to TUC 15, 29
Agreements
  local and national 108–10
  nature of 106–8
  procedural 101
  productivity 118
  and shop stewards 75, 78
  substantive 101, 120
Alternative employment 225
Amalgamated Society of Engineers 15, 133
  Amalgamated Society of Railway Servants 145
APEX (now GMB) 26
Arbitration 65, 86, 104, 114
  pendulum 105
Association of Metropolitan Authorities 50, 53
ASTMS (now MSF) 11, 21, 26
Authority, definition of 40

Ballots
  and closed shop 119, 191
  Code of Practice 198
  and disputes 163, 198, 232, 238
  and political funds 71
  and trade union officials 28, 182
Bargaining power 85
Belgium, industrial democracy 267

Blauner 234
Bonsor v. Musicians' Union (1956) 145, 159
Bonuses 123, 210
Branches 27, 80
  and shop steward 78, 83
  of union 27–9, 80
Bridlington Agreement 16, 21, 118
British Coal 205
British Institute of Management and industrial
  democracy 263
British Steel and industrial democracy 262
Bullock Committee 141, 264
Burnham Committee 51
Businesses, types of 38

Callaghan, J 20, 141
CBI 52–4
  and Conservative Party 54
  and industrial democracy 263
Central Arbitration Committee 87, 104
  disclosure of information 185
  role of 66, 87
  Schedule 11 58, 66, 104
Certification Officer
  and ballots 28, 71, 165
  and Employers' Associations 50,52
  and independence 10, 23, 30
  and registration 10, 30
Chartism 67
Check-off system 76
Civil law 160
  courts of 155
  definition 152
  immunities 160
  injunctions 165–6
Closed shop 119, 142, 242–7
  Code of Practice 189–92
  definition 242
  and dismissal 167, 215
  joinder actions 167
  number of 244
  post-entry 244
  pre-entry 191, 244
Codes of Practice 179–200
  and ACAS 66
  ballots 165, 198
  closed shop 189–92
  disciplinary practice and procedure 183–4, 185–7
  industrial relations 107, 138, 216
  picketing 192, 241–2

racial discrimination 172, 195
sex discrimination 174, 196
status 154
time off for trade union duties 79, 187
Collective bargaining
  agreements and law 106–7
  basis of 85–7
  and contracts of employment 88, 295
  incomes policy 58–61
  and industrial relations Code 181
  and industrial relations policy 48
  reasons for 88
  and shop steward 78
  Social Charter 276
  state intervention 57–8
  units 89
Combination Act 1800 49, 86, 132, 143, 147
Combination Law Reform Act 1824 86, 132, 143
Commission for Racial Equality 171
  Code of Practice 195
Commissioner for Rights of Trade Union Members 66,
  71, 165, 176, 192
Commission on Industrial Relations 138, 139
Common law
  and contract of employment 160, 207, 213
  source of law 153
Communication 43, 181
Companies 38
Companies Act 1985 39, 256
Comparability 122
Compensation, dismissal 217
Conciliation 103, 114, 139, 171, 174
  collective 103
  process of 103
  role of ACAS 65
Conciliation Act 1886 63, 148
Conciliation Boards 102
Confederation of British Industries (see CBI)
Confederation, of unions 30–1
Conflict
  collective bargaining 121
  pluralist view 6–7
  and sanctions 97–102
  and strikes 233
Conflicts of interest 101, 121
Conflicts of right 101, 121
Conservative Party 60, 61
  and CBI 54, 69
Consolidation 124
Conspiracy 153, 160
Conspiracy and Protection of Property Act 1875 143,
  147, 160
Constitution 55
Constructive dismissal 215, 220
Consultation agreement 119
Consultations 181
  agreement 119
  and management 48
  and redundancy 117, 224
Contract of/for service 203
Contract of employment 201–12, 213
  and collective bargaining 85–6, 106
  formation of 201–3
  implied terms 206–9
  relation to dismissal 206
  and striking 161, 237
  terms and conditions 204

Contracting in/out 71–2
Contracts of Employment Act 1963 149, 209
Control, by management 42
Control test 203
Convenor 74
Coordination 42
Cooling-off period 139, 237
Core workers 248
Courts 155–7
Craft union
  characteristics 25
  and demarcation 92, 138, 247, 270
  emergence of 133–4
Credentials of shop steward 48
  example agreement 127
Criminal law 160, 193
  courts of 155
  definition of 152
  immunities 160
  and trade unions 134
CSEU 31, 80, 109
Custom, and contract of employment 205–6

Demarcation 92, 138, 247
Demographic change 274
Directives (EC) 154, 282
Directors
  as managers 38
  responsibilities of 256
Disciplinary procedure 115, 210
  example 126
Discipline
  Code of Practice 183–7
  notice of rules 215
Disclosure of information, Code of Practice 185–7
Discrimination see Racial discrimination; sex
  discrimination
Dismissal 213–21
  acting reasonably 216
  and closed shop 167, 215
  Code of Practice 183, 216
  compensation 217
  definition of 213
  fair reasons for 214
  for pregnancy 168, 215
  and redundancy 226
  remedies 216
  strikes 99, 215
  unfair 214–21
  wrongful 213
Disputes
  of interest 101, 121, 183
  of right 101, 121, 183
Disputes procedure 115, 183
  Code of Practice 182
  example of 125
Doherty, J 133
Donovan Commission 107, 109, 122, 136–8
Dunlop, J 7

EAT
  composition of 157
  and expulsion from union 176
  orders 208
  racial discrimination 172
  sex discrimination 174
  trade union recognition 30

unfair dismissal 219
work of equal value 176
EC
Fifth Directive 265
Maastricht 208
Social Charter 276–81
source of law 154
EETPU 14, 22, 25, 34, 81, 111, 134
structure of 29
Electrical Contractors' Association 51
Emergency Powers Act 1964 149, 153, 238
Employee participation *see* Industrial democracy
Employers' Associations
activities 50–2
origins 48–50, 86
status at law 159
types 50
Employment Act 1980 150
and closed shop 190
and dismissal 167, 216
and immunities 162
joinder actions 167, 218
and maternity rights 168
picketing 192, 241
strikes 238
Employment Act 1982 150
and closed shop 119, 181
and Companies Act 41, 156
and dismissal 214
and immunities 162, 167
and strikes 238
Employment Act 1988 151, 167, 176, 238, 240
and closed shop 119, 163, 167, 215, 238
and union discipline 176
Employment Act 1989 151, 173, 174, 187, 279
Employment Appeals Tribunal *see* EAT
Employment Protection Act 1975 141, 150
Code on Disciplinary Practice 183
Code on Disclosure of Information 185
and dismissal 214
and redundancy 117, 222
role of ACAS 64
Schedule 11 58, 104
time off for shop stewards 79, 167, 187
time off work 168
training shop stewards 79
and wages councils 57
Employment Protection (Consolidation) Act 1978 150
and dismissal 183, 214
maternity rights 168
and redundancy 222
time off work 168
trade union membership 167
writen statement 209
End loading 124
Engineering Employers' Federation 41, 51, 109
objectives 52
York Memorandum 51
Equal opportunities 251–3
Equal Opportunities Commission 174, 196, 252
Equal pay 123
and Treaty of Rome 276
Equal Pay Act 1970 123, 149, 174, 209
Equality term 209
ETUC 35
Europe/EC 275–6
Single European Market 276

Express Newspapers Ltd v. *McShane* (1979) 146
Expulsion from union 176, 191

Factories Acts 133
Factory system 130–2
Failure to agree 102, 114, 125
'Fair Deal at Work' 62, 140
Fair Wages Resolution 58
Father of the chapel 72, 77
Fawley agreement 50, 93
Final offer arbitration 105
Fixed term agreement 107
Flexi-time 227, 249
France, industrial democracy 243
Free riders 243
Full time, definition of 220

General Council (TUC) 33–4
General Strike 13, 75, 86, 136, 144
General unions 25, 134
Genuine occupational qualification
race 170
sex 172
Germany, industrial democracy 266
GMB 136
GNCTU 133
Go slow 101
Grievance procedure 115, 182, 210
Grunwick dispute 87
Guaranteed pay 208
Guilds 62, 130

Health and safety 81–3
and contract of employment 207, 208
Social charter 281
Holland, industrial democracy 266
Hornby v. *Close* (1867) 144
Hours of work 137, 207, 249
House of Commons 56, 61, 153
House of Lords 55, 155

ICFTU 35
ILO 35, 265, 280
Immunities 142, 144, 160–3
and closed shop 162, 215
and individuals 161–2
need for 160
to strike 161–3, 231, 237
for trade unions 162, 215
Implied terms 206–9
In Place of Strife 32, 62, 113, 139
Incomes policy 58–61
Incentives 123, 137
Independence of unions 30
Index linking 123
Indirect discrimination
racial 170
sex 172
Industrial action 26, 99–102
and ballots 139, 176, 198, 232
Industrial change 270
Industrial Courts Act (1919) 63, 136, 148
Industrial democracy 255–69
Industrial Relations Act (1971) 140, 149
collective agreements 106
registration 141
and TUC 157
and unfair dismissal 213

Industrial Relations in the 1990s 87, 106
Industrial revolution 37, 130
Industrial tribunals 156–7
  appeals from 157
  ballots 165
  maternity benefit 151, 168
  protective award 225
  racial discrimination 172
  reasons for dismissal 168, 214
  redundancy 225–6
  role and composition 156
  sex discrimination 174
  time off work 176
  trade union discipline 176
  trade union membership 167
  unfair dismissal 214, 217, 218
  work of equal value 175
Injunction 57, 241
  interlocutory 165, 232
Interim relief 215
Intervention by government 59
ISTC 134

Job evaluation 122, 137, 175
Job share 226
John Lewis Partnership 261
Joinder actions 167, 218
Joint Industrial Council 86, 121, 135
Joint Shop Stewards' Committee 80
Joseph, K 70
Jones, J 21
Judges 62, 155
Judiciary 55, 56–7, 155

Keynes, J M 59
Kinnock, N 69

Labour force survey 24
Labour Party
  affiliation to 68
  formation of 14, 67
  liaison committee 68
  and TUC 32, 33
  and unions 68
LACSAB 107
Laissez-faire 62, 131
Law
  civil/criminal 152
  legislature 54, 56
  sources 153
Lay-offs 99, 218, 223
Legislature 55
Leap-frogging 89, 122
Local agreement 89, 90, 108–10, 138, 226
Lockout 99, 218, 223, 231
Low pay 123
Luxembourg, industrial democracy 267
Lyon v *Wilkins* (1896) 145

Maastricht 208, 281
McGregor, D 45
Management
  functions 42–3
  of industrial relations 46–8, 138, 180
  role 40–1
Marshall v. *Hampshire Health Authority* (1986) 175
Marx, Karl 6, 67, 234

Maternity benefits 168
Maternity leave 169, 215
Mayo, E 44
Mediation 66, 103
Messenger Newspapers v. *NGA* (1984) 146
Mergers 21
Mother of the chapel 72, 77
MPs, sponsored 68
MSF 11, 21, 26
Munitions of War Act (1915) 63, 86

NACODS 26
National agreements 87, 90, 108–9, 137
National Arbitration Order (1940) 63
National Farmers' Union (NFU) 50, 51
National Union of Agricultural and Allied Workers 15, 50
NEC 27
Negotiating
  example agreement 125
  procedure 114
Negotiations 94–7, 234
  continuum 95
Neo-unitarists 5
New unionism 67, 86, 133
NGA (now GMPU) 25, 81, 101, 146, 246
Non-compliance award 217
No-strike clause 111
Notice
  minimum periods 208, 213
  and redundancy 224
  to terminate contract 203
NUJ 22, 146
NUM 26
  and Lightman Report 177

Objectives 40–1
Official action 163, 231
Organisation
  forms of 38
  objectives 40
Osborne v. *Amalgamated Society of Railway Servants* (1911) 71, 144, 145
Overtime ban 124, 137
Owen, R 133
Ownership 37–9, 220, 223

Packaging 124
Parliament 55, 56, 153
Part-time work 220
Pay Board 61
Pay and Incomes Board 249, 274
Pay comparability 91
Pay formula 91
Pay policies 58–61, 235
Pay review bodies 91
Pay rounds 122
Pay statement 208
Pay structures 211
Pendulum arbitration 105, 111, 239
Performance related bonus 212
Phillips effect 59
Picketing 142, 240–2
  Code of Practice 192
Planning, management function 42
Pluralist perspective 6, 233
Police Act (1919) 238

Policy
  industrial relations 46–8, 138, 180
Political action 71
Political aspects 67–70
Political funds of union 71, 142
Political objects of union 71
Polkey v. *Dayton* 226
Positive action
  racial 171
  sex 173
Post Office 238, 262
Post-entry closed shop 167, 244
Precedent, judicial 155
Pre-entry closed shop 191, 244
Pregnancy
  and dismissal 168, 215
  maternity benefits 168
Pre-hearing assessment 219
Procedural agreement 101, 108, 182
  content 112–14
  examples of 125–8
  industrial relations policy 48
  operation 234
Productivity agreement 118
Productivity bargaining 92–4
Profit sharing 212
Protected property, union 163
Protective award 225

Qualifying service 220

R v. *Druitt, Lawrence and Anderson* (1867) 144
Race Relations Act (1976) 149, 170, 195
Racial discrimination
  Code of Practice 172, 195
  Race Relations Act 149, 170
Recognition
  agreement 118
  of trade unions 47, 143, 181
Redundancy 222–8
  agreement 127
  alternative employment 225
  arrangements 227–8, 273
  consultations 117
  defining 222
  after maternity leave 169
  payments 223
  protective award 225
  weeks' pay 223
  years' service 223
Redundancy Payments Act (1965) 117, 222
Registration of unions 30, 139, 140
Regulations (EC) 154
Representatives
  credentials 48, 127
Responsibility 40, 180
Restraint of trade 131, 160, 206
Restrictive covenant 206, 207
Restrictive practice 92, 138, 206, 247
Reverse discrimination
  racial 171
  sex 173
Rookes v. *Barnard* (1964) 145
Royal College of Nursing 11, 113
Rule book, of union 12–13, 29, 74, 78, 115, 119
Rules 115, 205

Safety 81, 131, 207
  representatives 81–3
Safety Representatives Regulations (1977) 81–3
Sanctions 96–102, 113, 230
  by employees 100–1
  by employers 99–100
  reasons for 98–9
  use of 98
Scanlon, H 21
Scargill, A 20
Scientific management 43
Scott-Bader Foundation 262
Secondary action 161, 241, 238
Sequestration 57, 177
Sex discrimination 172, 197
Sex Discrimination Acts (1975) (1986) 150, 172, 196
  Code of Practice 196
Sheffield outrages 134
Shop stewards 73–80, 182
  Code of Practice 182
  disciplinary action 184
  emergence of 74, 135
  facilities 79, 138
  functions 75–7
  power 77–9
  unofficial action 231
Short time, and redundancy 223
Single union agreement 22, 81, 90, 110–12, 262
Sit-in 101
Smith, A 131
Social action theory 8
Social Charter (EC) 70, 142, 276
Social Contract 19, 61, 68
'Sosr' 214
Special award, unfair dismissal 217
Staff association 11
Staff unions 26
Stages, in agreement 113
State 55–72
  arbitration 64
  intervention of 57–8
  role of 55–7
Statutory Instruments 153
Statutory Maternity Pay 169
Strike-free deals 239
Strikes 231–40
  and continuous service 218, 223, 226
  and contract of employment 161, 237
  and dismissal 215
  number of 234–7
  official 163, 231
  reasons for 232
  and redundancy 223, 226
Subcontractor 203, 226, 249
Substantive agreements 101, 108, 120, 182
Sweden, work groups 262
Systems model 6

Taff Vale Railway Company v. *Amalgamated Society of Railway Servants* (1901) 63, 135, 143, 145, 159
Technology
  agreement 120, 274
  effects of 248, 271, 273
Terms of contract 89, 202
  sources of 205–9

TGWU 23
  formation of 134
  general union 26
  organisation 27
  rule book 12–13
Thatcher, M 69, 70, 141
Time limits
  agreements 113
  claims 220
Time off work 167
  for ante-natal care 168
  Code of Practice 187–9
  job seeking 225
  for public duties 167
  shop stewards' duties 79
Tolpuddle martyrs 133
Torts 160, 164, 237
Trade Boards 57, 136, 148
Trade dispute
  definition 143, 162, 238
Trade Disputes Act (1906) 135, 143, 148, 161, 237, 241
Trade Disputes and Trade Union Act (1927) 71, 148
Trade Union Act (1871) 134, 143, 147
Trade Union Act (1913) 71, 148
Trade Union Act (1984) 150, 163, 231
Trade Union (Amalgamation) Act (1964) 16, 149
Trade Union and Labour Relations Act (1974) 141, 150
  and dismissal 214
  immunities 162
  and picketing 241
  trade dispute, definition 162
Trade Union and Labour Relations (Consolidation) Act
    (1992) 10, 66, 71, 151, 159, 163, 167, 192, 215,
    238, 242, 246
Trade unions
  aims 12–13
  definition 10–11
  density 22–3
  discipline of members 176, 192, 240
  functions of 13–14
  joinder action 176 218
  members in 17
  members' rights 176, 191
  membership and activities of 176, 192
  membership and dismissal 214, 217
  mergers of 15–16, 21, 23
  numbers of 15
  recognition 47, 86–7, 143, 181
  recruitment 21
  registration 30, 139, 140
  rule book 12–13, 29, 74, 78, 115, 119, 159, 163
  status 159
  types of 25–6
Trades Councils 31, 134
Training
  for safety representatives 82
  of trade union officials 79
Transfer of Undertakings Regulations (1981) 220
Treasury Agreements 75, 135
Treaty of Rome 276
Tribunal
  in court's system 156
Truck Acts 147, 210

TUC
  affiliation to 11, 15, 29–30
  Bridlington Agreement 16, 21, 118
  and closed shop 192, 243
  formation of 31, 134
  industrial democracy 263
  and Industrial Relations Act (1971) 140
  and Labour Party 32, 68
  Labour Representational Committee 67
  parliamentary committee 67
  role of 31
  rules 32, 34
  and shop steward's facilities 79
  and Trades Councils 31

Unfair dismissal see Dismissal
Unincorporated associations 159
Unions see Trade unions
Union membership agreement 119, 242
Unitary perspective 4
Unofficial action 163, 231

Vicarious liability 206
Victimisation
  dismissal 215
  race 170
  sex 172
Vredling-Daignon proposals 265

Wage agreement 123–4
Wage bargaining 121–3
Wage determination 57, 142
Wage drift 90, 109, 121
Wage structure 122
Wages Act (1986) 151, 174
Wages Councils 57, 121, 123, 136, 142
Webb S and B 10
Week's pay 223
White collar union see staff union
Whitley committees 63, 86, 135–6
Wilson, H 21, 68, 141
Women
  equal opportunities 252
  maternity benefit 168
  seats on TUC 33
  union recruitment 21
Work groups 262
Work of equal value 175
Work to rule 100
Worker cooperatives 263
Worker control see Industrial democracy
Worker directors 261
Works rules 205, 216
Written statement
  for contract 107, 202, 209
  for dismissal 214
  for redundancy 223
Wrongful dismissal 213

Years of service 223
York Memorandum 51

Zero sum bargaining 92, 93, 98